BELIEF, LAW AND POLITICS

Cultural Diversity and Law in Association with RELIGARE

Series Editor: Prakash Shah, Queen Mary, University of London, UK

RELIGARE is a project on Religious Diversity and Secular Models in Europe funded by the European Commission under the Seventh Framework Programme. The project brings together an interdisciplinary team of high profile researchers and 13 academic institutions to collaborate on examining how existing policy and practice is suited to the demands of religious diversity within Europe and what legal models can be recommended to accommodate such diversity in future. More details on the project can be seen at its website: http://www.religareproject.eu/. 'Cultural Diversity and Law in Association with RELIGARE' provides an outlet for the results of specific research undertaken within the RELIGARE project.

Other titles in this series:

Family, Religion and Law
Cultural Encounters in Europe
Edited by Prakash Shah, Marie-Claire Foblets and Mathias Rohe

The Burqa Affair Across Europe
Between Public and Private Space
Edited by Alessandro Ferrari and Sabrina Pastorelli

Religion in Public Spaces
A European Perspective
Edited by Silvio Ferrari and Sabrina Pastorelli

A Test of Faith?
Religious Diversity and Accommodation in the European Workplace
Edited by Katayoun Alidadi, Marie-Claire Foblets and Jogchum Vrielink

Belief, Law and Politics

What Future for a Secular Europe?

Edited by

MARIE-CLAIRE FOBLETS
Max Planck Institute for Social Anthropology, Germany

KATAYOUN ALIDADI
Catholic University of Leuven, Belgium

JØRGEN S. NIELSEN
University of Copenhagen, Denmark

ZEYNEP YANASMAYAN
European University Viadrina, Germany

Routledge
Taylor & Francis Group
LONDON AND NEW YORK

First published 2014 by Ashgate Publishing

2 Park Square, Milton Park, Abingdon, Oxfordshire OX14 4RN
52 Vanderbilt Avenue, New York, NY 10017

Routledge is an imprint of the Taylor & Francis Group, an informa business

First issued in paperback 2020

British Library Cataloguing in Publication Data
A catalogue record for this book is available from the British Library

Library of Congress Cataloging-in-Publication Data
Belief, law and politics : what future for a secular Europe? / by Marie-Claire Foblets, Katayoun Alidadi, Jørgen S. Nielsen and Zeynep Yanasmayan.
pages cm.—(Cultural diversity and law in association with RELIGARE)
Includes bibliographical references and index.
ISBN 978-1-4724-5346-4 (hardback)
1. Summary report on the RELIGARE project. 2. Freedom of religion—European Union countries. 3. Religious minorities—Legal status, laws, etc.—European Union countries. 4. Religion in the workplace—Law and legislation—European Union countries. 5. Multiculturalism—Law and legislation—European Union countries. 6. Summary report on the RELIGARE project. I. Foblets, Marie-Claire, 1959– editor. II. Alidadi, Katayoun, editor. III. Yanasmayan, Zeynep. IV. Nielsen, Jørgen S, editor.
KJE5156.B45 2014
342.408'52—dc23

2014030046

ISBN 978-1-4724-5346-4 (hbk)
ISBN 978-0-367-60002-0 (pbk)

Contents

Notes on Contributors

Katayoun Alidadi is a legal scholar affiliated with the Leuven Institute for Human Rights and Critical Studies at KU Leuven, Belgium. She is co-editor, together with Marie-Claire Foblets and Jogchum Vrielink, of *A Test of Faith? Religious Diversity and Accommodation in the European Workplace* (2012) and was a project researcher in the FP7 RELIGARE project (2010–2013). Her research focuses on religious freedom, anti-discrimination law and reasonable accommodations in the workplace, in particular with regard to Europe and North America. She obtained her law degree from KU Leuven and holds an LLM in International Legal Studies from Harvard Law School (2005). She has worked as a corporate attorney at an international law firm in Brussels and as a public interest attorney at Public Counsel Law Center in Los Angeles. A member of the Bars of New York and California, she currently resides in the US.

Pasquale Annicchino is Research Fellow at the Robert Schuman Centre for Advanced Studies and is also a member of the EUI Ethics Committee. He has been Adjunct Professor of Law at Brigham Young University Law School (USA) and Visiting Professor at KU Leuven (Belgium).

He received his PhD in Law (2011) from the University of Siena. He studied as an Erasmus student at the School of Law of Charles IV University in Prague (Czech Republic) and at the European Academy of Legal Theory in Brussels (Belgium), where he obtained a double degree (LLM/DEA). He was Visiting Scholar at the Centre for Law and Religion of the Emory University Law School in Atlanta (USA) and specialised (LLM) in European Public Law at University College London (UK), where he also served as Editor in Chief of the UCL Human Rights Review.

He is the book review editor for *Religion & Human Rights: An International Journal*, and is a member of the editorial board of *Quaderni di diritto e politica ecclesiastica*, published by Il Mulino. His main interests include legal theory, law and religion, EU law, religion and politics.

Frédérique Ast, Doctor in European Human Rights Law, is Senior Legal Adviser within the French Defender of Rights. She investigates a wide range of discrimination cases, specialising in cases involving religion. As a Visiting Professor in the Faculty of Law at Lille (Catholic University), she also gives lectures on international and European non-discrimination and equality law.

Her publications relating to religion include *Les discriminations religieuses en Europe* ('Religious Discrimination in Europe') (with Bernadette Duarte, 2012), 'Tackling Double Victimization of Muslim Women in Europe: The Intersectional Response' (with Riem Spielhaus, *Mediterranean Journal of Human Rights*, 2012), 'Contribution of Secularism and Discrimination Law to Religious Pluralism: The French Experience' in *Yearbook on Human Rights and Humanitarian Action* (2011), *Equality Law in Practice – A Question of Faith: Religion and Belief in Europe* (2011) and 'Indirect Discrimination as a Means of Protecting Pluralism: Challenges and Limits' in *Institutional Accommodation and the Citizen: Legal and Political Interaction in a Pluralist Society* (*Trends in Social Cohesion* No. 21, 2009).

Juana M. Astigarraga Zulaica is a PhD candidate at the University of the Basque Country and researcher in the Department of Legal Theory, Constitutional and Administrative Law. Her PhD thesis deals with religious freedom in the European Union. She has been acting Director for Human Rights in the Provincial Government of Gipuskoa (Basque Country), and currently coordinates the Master's Programme on European Integration at the University of Basque Country's Department of Legal Theory.

Lori G. Beaman, PhD, is the Canada Research Chair in the Contextualisation of Religion in a Diverse Canada and Professor in the Department of Classics and Religious Studies at the University of Ottawa. Her publications include *Defining Harm: Religious Freedom and the Limits of the Law* (2008), *Varieties of Religious Establishment* (2013), *Religion in the Public Sphere: Canadian Case Studies* (2014), 'Is Religious

Freedom Impossible in Canada?' (*Law, Culture, and the Humanities*, 2010), '"It was All Slightly Unreal": What's Wrong with Tolerance and Accommodation in the Adjudication of Religious Freedom?' (*Canadian Journal of Women and Law*, 2011), 'Religious Freedom and Neoliberalism: From Harm to Cost-Benefit' in *Religion and Neoliberal Policy and Governance* (2012) and 'Battles over Symbols: The "Religion" of the Minority versus the "Culture" of the Majority' (*Journal of Law and Religion*, 2012/3). She is co-editor, with Peter Beyer, of *Religion and Diversity in Canada* (2008). She is Principal Investigator of a 37-member international research team whose focus is religion and diversity (religionanddiversity.ca).

Tom Bennett, BA LLB (Rhodes), PhD (University of Cape Town), Professor in the Department of Public Law, Fellow of the University of Cape Town and Alexander von Humboldt Foundation. His current research interests include customary law, traditional African religions, the implications of legal pluralism in a constitutional democracy and the emergence of an *ubuntu* jurisprudence.

Heiner Bielefeldt studied philosophy, Catholic theology and history and received his PhD and habilitation degrees in Philosophy (from the Universities of Tübingen and Bremen, respectively). Between 2003 and 2009 he served as Director of the German Institute for Human Rights, which is Germany's officially accredited national human rights institution. In October 2009 he took the newly established Chair for Human Rights and Human Rights Politics at the Friedrich-Alexander-Universität Erlangen-Nürnberg. In August 2010 he also assumed the position of UN Special Rapporteur on freedom of religion or belief.

In recent years, Bielefeldt has focused primarily on issues closely related to his UN mandate on freedom of religion or belief. His responsibilities as UN Rapporteur include diplomatic communication on individual cases, country-related reports and thematic work. In his thematic reports to the Human Rights Council and to the General Assembly he has dealt with freedom of religion or belief in the context of school education, the role of the State in facilitating interreligious communication, issues of State recognition of religious communities, conversion and missionary work, and religious minorities.

Eva Brems (LLM Harvard 1995, PhD KU Leuven 1999) is Professor of Human Rights Law at Ghent University. She has a broad range of research interests, with a particular emphasis on cross-cutting themes and diversity-related issues. She has been an activist in several human rights organisations, including serving as the Chair of Amnesty International Flanders (2006–2010), and has been a member of the Belgian Federal Parliament (2010–2014). She was the beneficiary of a European Research Council Starting Grant for the project Strengthening the ECHR: More Accountability through Better Legal Reasoning (2009–2014).

Peter Cumper is Professor of Law at the University of Leicester. He undertakes research in the field of law and religion, with particular reference to UK and European human rights law. He has published in a wide range of academic journals, and is the co-editor of *Minority Rights in the New Europe* (1999) and *Religion, Rights and Secular Society* (2012). At present he is the co-organiser of an Arts and Humanities Research Council (AHRC)-funded project on collective worship in UK schools.

Grace Davie is Professor Emeritus at the University of Exeter, UK and a senior adviser to the Impact of Religion Research Programme at Uppsala University. She is a past president of the American Association for the Sociology of Religion (2003) and of the Research Committee 22 (Sociology of Religion) of the International Sociological Association (2002–2006).

In 2000–2001 she was the Kerstin-Hesselgren Professor at Uppsala, where she returned for extended visits in 2006–2007, 2010 and 2012. In January 2008, she received an honorary degree from Uppsala. She has also held visiting appointments at the Ecole Pratique des Hautes Etudes (1996) and at the Ecole des Hautes Etudes en Sciences Sociales (1998 and 2003), both in Paris.

She is the author of *Religion in Britain since 1945* (1994), *Religion in Modern Europe* (2000), *Europe: The Exceptional Case* (2002) and *The Sociology of Religion* (2007/2013). She is the co-author of *Religious America, Secular Europe* (2008), *Predicting Religion* (2003) and *Welfare and Religion in 21st Century Europe* (2 vols) (2010 and 2011).

Marie-Claire Foblets, Lic. Iur., Lic. Phil., PhD Anthrop. (Belgium) is Professor of Law at the University of Leuven (Belgium) and since 2012 also Director of the Department of Law & Anthropology at the Max Planck Institute for Social Anthropology in Halle/Saale (Germany). She has held various visiting professorships both within and outside Europe. She has conducted extensive research and published widely on issues of migration law, including the elaboration of European migration law after the Treaty of Amsterdam, citizenship/nationality laws, compulsory integration, anti-racism and non-discrimination. In the field of the anthropology of law, her research focuses on cultural diversity and legal practice, with a particular interest in the application of Islamic family law in Europe, and more recently in the accommodation of cultural and religious diversity under State law.

Effie Fokas is a Research Fellow at the Hellenic Foundation for European and Foreign Policy (ELIAMEP), where she is Principal Investigator of the European Research Council-funded project Directions in Religious Pluralism in Europe: Examining Grassroots Mobilisations in Europe in the Shadow of European Court of Human Rights Religious Freedoms Jurisprudence (GRASSROOTSMOBILISE). Also at ELIAMEP she carried out a Marie Curie Fellowship studying Pluralism and Religious Freedom in Orthodox Countries in Europe (PLUREL). She was founding Director of the London School of Economics Forum on Religion (2008–2012) and is currently Research Associate of the LSE Hellenic Observatory. Her publications include *Islam in Europe: Diversity, Identity and Influence* (2007), *Religious America, Secular Europe? A Theme and Variations*, co-authored with Peter Berger and Grace Davie (2008), 'Islam in Europe: The Unexceptional Case' (*Nordic Journal of Religion and Society*, 2011) and '"Eastern" Orthodoxy and "Western" Secularisation in Contemporary Europe' (*Religion, State and Society*, 2012).

Michael Germann is Professor of Public Law, State and Church Law, and Ecclesiastical Law at Martin Luther University Halle-Wittenberg. He studied law in Tübingen, Geneva and Erlangen. He received his doctorate in 1999 with a thesis on law enforcement on the Internet. In 2001, he presented his habilitation thesis on the courts of the Protestant churches in Germany. Since 2002, he has been continuing research in Halle, mainly in the fields of Protestant ecclesiastical law and of religious freedom. His publications include an online commentary that portrays the constitutional articles of the German Basic Law protecting religious freedom as a system of inclusive State neutrality.

Kristin Henrard is Professor of Fundamental Rights and Minorities at the Erasmus School of Law (Erasmus University) in Rotterdam. She teaches courses on human rights and on minorities and fundamental rights, often with a multi-disciplinary dimension. From February 2005 to May 2010 she worked on her VIDI-project, funded by the Dutch Council for Scientific Research, regarding the implications for minority protection of the EU's Race Directive. During that time she was also a member of the Young Academy of the Dutch Academy of Sciences.

Her publications pertain to the areas of human rights and minorities and include an edited volume, *Synergies in Minority Protection* (2008), several articles in the *European Yearbook on Minority Issues*, an article titled 'Boosting Positive Action: The Asymmetrical Approach towards Non-Discrimination and Special Minority Rights' (*Heidelberg Journal of International Law*, 2011) and a Jean Monnet Working Paper on the CJEU's Feryn judgment.

Henrard is editor of the *Netherlands International Law Review*, the *Global Review of Ethnopolitics*, the *International Journal on Group and Minority Rights*, and of *European Autonomy and Diversity Papers*. She is a co-editor of the series *Group and Minority Rights*.

Christian Joppke holds the Chair in General Sociology at the University of Bern, Switzerland. He is also a recurrent Visiting Professor in the Nationalism Studies Program at Central European University, Budapest, and Honorary Professor in the Department of Political Science and Government, University of Aarhus, Denmark. He received a PhD in Sociology from the University of California, Berkeley in 1989. His recent books are *The Secular State under Siege: Religion and Politics in Europe and America* (forthcoming in 2015), *Legal Integration of Islam: A Transatlantic Comparison* (with John Torpey, 2013), *Citizenship and Immigration* (2010) and *Veil: Mirror of Identity* (2009).

Matthias Koenig is Professor of Sociology at the University of Göttingen and Max Planck Fellow at the Max Planck Institute for the Study of Religious and Ethnic Diversity (Göttingen). He has held visiting positions at the Ecole Pratique des Hautes Etudes in Paris, the University of Toronto and the University of Michigan in Ann Arbor. His research interests cover sociological theory, the comparative study of religion and secularism, human rights, and migration. He has authored two books as well as numerous articles in international journals such as *Acta Sociologica*, *Ethnic and Racial Studies*, *Journal of Ethnic and Migration Studies* and *International Sociology*. He is also co-editor of *Democracy and Human Rights in Multicultural Societies* (with Paul de Guchteneire, 2007) and *International Migration and the Governance of Religious Diversity* (with Paul Bramadat, 2009). His current work focuses on the constitutional and judicial politics of regulating cultural diversity.

Cécile Laborde is Professor of Political Theory at University College London. She has published extensively in the areas of republicanism and toleration, theories of law and the State, and global justice. Her latest book is *Critical Republicanism: The Hijab Controversy in Political Philosophy* (2008). She is the Director of UCL's Religion and Political Theory Centre. She is currently writing a book entitled *Freedom of Religion without Religion.*

Koen Lemmens (PhD, European University Institute, Florence, Italy) is Director of the Leuven Institute for Human Rights and Critical Studies (LIHRiCS). He is Associate Professor of Human Rights and Constitutional Law (KU Leuven), Associate Professor of Press Law (VU, Brussels) and an attorney at law, with a focus on proceedings before the European Court of Human Rights. He is National Director of the European Master in Human Rights and Democratisation (EUIC, Venice, Italy).

His research interests are constitutional law and European human rights, with a special interest in freedom of speech issues. Recent publications include 'Larvatus prodeo? Why Concealing the Face Can be Incompatible with a European Conception of Human Rights' (*European Law Review*, 2014), '(S)electing Judges for Strasbourg: A (Dis)appointing Process?' in *Selecting Europe's Judges: A Critical Review of Appointment Procedures to the European Courts* (forthcoming in 2015) and, together with Patricia Popelier, he is preparing *The Constitution of Belgium: A Contextual Analysis* (forthcoming in 2015).

Patrick Loobuyck studied religious studies at KU Leuven and ethics at Ghent University. He is currently Associate Professor of Religion and Worldviews at the Centre Pieter Gillis of the University of Antwerp and Guest Professor of Political Philosophy at Ghent University. His research focuses on liberalism, church–State regimes, religion in the public sphere, religious education, multiculturalism, Habermas and Rawls. He has published in several national and international journals, including *Islam and Christian–Muslim Relations*, *Religious Education*, *Political Quarterly*, *Journal of Church and State*, *Journal for the Scientific Study of Religion* and *Ethnicities*.

Jane Mair, LLB (Edinburgh), LLM (Cambridge), PhD (Edinburgh) is Senior Lecturer in the School of Law, University of Glasgow. Her research focuses on Scots and European family law, particularly the legal regulation of marriage, cohabitation and matrimonial property. Research in family law is complemented by her work in the context of employment and equality law. Much of her current work explores the influence of religion and belief in the development of family law, in shaping personal identity and as a source of values in family life. She is co-editor of a number of volumes published as part of the *European Family Law Series* (CEFL/Intersentia), including *The Place of Religion in Family Law: A Comparative Search* (2011) and *Juxtaposing Legal Systems and the Principles of European Family Law on Parental Responsibilities* (2010). Marriage is a particular interest, with its changing legal regulation, religious significance and social relevance highlighted in a recent contribution to an edited collection, *Marriage: A Lasting Legal Relationship* (2012).

Maleiha Malik is Professor of Law at King's College, University of London. She teaches Discrimination Law, European Law and Jurisprudence and Political Theory. Her relevant publications include *Discrimination Law* (2008), *Anti-Muslim Prejudice in the West* (2010) and *Minority Legal Orders in the UK: Minorities, Pluralism and Law* (2012).

Ronan McCrea (PhD, London School of Economics, 2009) is Senior Lecturer in the Faculty of Laws of University College London and a 2014–2015 Jean Monnet Fellow at the European University Institute in Florence. He is the author of *Religion and the Public Order of the European Union* (2010, paperback with new foreword, 2014) and *Religion et ordre juridique de l'Union européenne* (2013). He is a former *référendaire* (judicial clerk) in the Chambers of Advocate General Maduro at the Court of Justice of the European Union in Luxembourg, and is a member of the Bars of England and Wales (2003) and Ireland (2011). His recent publications include 'The Ban on the Veil and European Law' (*Human Rights Law Review*, 2013) and 'Religion in the Workplace: Eweida and Others v United Kingdom' (*Modern Law Review*, 2014). Since 2010 he has been Visiting Professor at Central European University in Budapest.

Jørgen S. Nielsen is Honorary Professor of Islamic Studies in the Faculties of Theology and Humanities, University of Copenhagen, and was previously at the University of Birmingham, UK. He has published extensively on Islam in Europe, including *Muslims in Western Europe* (2004), *Shari'a as Discourse* (co-editor, 2010) and *Religion, Ethnicity and Contested Nationhood in the Former Ottoman Space* (editor, 2012). He is Executive Editor of *Yearbook of Muslims in Europe* (since 2009) and the *Journal of Muslims in Europe*.

Saïla Ouald Chaib is a PhD candidate at the Human Rights Centre of Ghent University. She works on the ERC-funded project Strengthening the European Court of Human Rights: More Accountability through Better Legal Reasoning. In her research she aims at developing an inclusive approach to the freedom of religion case law of the European Court of Human Rights. Her publications include 'Doing Minority Justice through Procedural Fairness: Face Veil Bans in Europe' (with Eva Brems, *Journal of Muslims in Europe*, 2013) and 'Suku Phull v. France Rewritten from a Procedural Justice Perspective: Taking Religious Minorities Seriously' in *Diversity and European Human Rights: Rewriting Judgments of the ECtHR* (2012). Her research interests include the right to freedom of religion, minority rights, anti-discrimination law, accommodation of diversity, the position of Muslims in Europe and procedural justice. She is also co-founder and regular contributor to the blog www.strasbourgobservers.com, which provides commentaries on the case law of the European Court of Human Rights. She obtained her law degrees at the KU Leuven Kulak (Kandidaat in de Rechten) and at Ghent University (Master of Laws).

Eugenia Relaño Pastor (PhD, University of Granada, 2001) currently works as Legal Adviser in the Migration and Equal Treatment section of the Spanish Ombudsman. She holds a doctorate in Law and Bachelor's degrees in Political Science and Sociology. She is Assistant Professor in Complutense University (Madrid) and Professor in the Master's programme Islam in European Societies (Faculty of Anthropology, Complutense University). She has been a Fulbright Fellow in the Salzburg Seminar and visiting scholar in institutions such as the University of California at Berkeley, the Institute of Comparative and European Law at the University of Oxford, Harvard University and the University of Ottawa. She is a member of the Legal Working Group (LWG) of the European Group of National Human Rights Institutions (Council of Europe), the Platform on Migration Issues (the Council of Europe's Migration Coordination), the Minority Research Network and the Advisory Panel of Experts on Freedom of Religion and Belief, ODIHR-OSCE (2005–2012). Recent publications include 'Religious Pluralism in Liberal Democracies' in *Islam, Human Rights and Secular Values* (2012), 'Etudes de cas de discriminations religieuses en Espagne' in *Les discriminations religieuses en Europe: droit et pratiques* (2012) and 'Participation of Muslim Minorities in the Spanish Mainstream Society' in *The Interrelation between the Right to Identity of Minorities and their Socio-Economic Participation* (2013).

Lourdes Peroni has an LLM from Harvard Law School and a PhD in Law from Ghent University. She worked as a fellow at the Inter-American Commission on Human Rights and also as a fellow at Yale Law School. Her research focuses on religious freedom and on equality and non-discrimination at the intersection of gender, religion and culture. Her publications include 'Religion and Culture in the Discourse of the European Court of Human Rights: The Risks of Stereotyping and Naturalizing' (*International Journal of Law in Context*, 2014), 'Deconstructing "Legal" Religion in Strasbourg' (*Oxford Journal of Law and Religion*, 2013) and 'Vulnerable Groups: The Promise of an Emerging Concept in European Human Rights Convention Law' (with Alexandra Timmer, *International Journal of Constitutional Law I-CON*, 2013).

David Pollock (MA, Oxford, 1964) is a board member and past Chair of the British Humanist Association and of the Rationalist Association, publishers of *New Humanist* magazine. He was President of the European Humanist Federation from 2006 to 2012, chaired the Advisory Board (of NGOs) to the European Parliament Platform for Secularism in Politics, and set up the network of NGOs known as the Alliance for a Secular Europe. He currently represents the International Humanist and Ethical Union at the Council of Europe. He takes a special interest in public policy on the place of religion and belief in society in a context of human rights, equality and non-discrimination. He has written on various aspects of the subject (see www.thinkingabouthumanism.org), has spoken at EU, European Parliament, Council of Europe and OSCE conferences, and has given evidence to committees of both the United Kingdom Parliament and the Parliamentary Assembly of the Council of Europe. He was given the Distinguished Service to Humanism Award at the 2011 World Humanist Congress in Oslo.

Eric Roux is a French Scientologist who has occupied many positions in the Church of Scientology in France for more than 20 years, including lecturing on the Scientology religion at many levels. He is currently the President of the Union of the Churches of Scientology in France. He has worked on religious freedom and law and religion issues for many years at the national and international levels. He has written papers on these topics for many events, including at the OSCE, the Council of Europe, and the US Capitol, where he was an invited speaker. He also works on various interfaith platforms at the European level. He is a member of the Steering Committee of the European Interreligious Forum for Religious Freedom, the Advisory Board of the All Faith Network charity in the UK, and of the United Religions Initiative, the largest international interfaith platform.

Eduardo J. Ruiz-Vieytez is Director of the Human Rights Institute at the University of Deusto (Bilbao) and Associate Professor of Constitutional Law. He has been Legal Adviser of the Basque Ombudsman and the president of a Basque NGO working on the promotion of human rights of immigrants in Spain. He has also been a member of the Spanish Council for Integration of Migrants (the highest consultative body of the Spanish government on the matter), and participated in several missions of the Council of Europe concerning minorities. His fields of research are immigration and integration law and policies, national conflicts, minority rights and the relation between human rights and religious, linguistic and cultural diversity. Among other responsibilities, Ruiz-Vieytez is a member of the Board of Directors of the International Migration, Integration and Social Cohesion in Europe (IMISCOE) network and of the Board of the International Institute for the Sociology of Law.

Russell Sandberg is Senior Lecturer in Law at Cardiff University, where he conducts research at the Centre for Law and Religion. After graduating from Cardiff Law School in 2005, he received his doctorate at Cardiff University in 2010. He is author of *Law and Religion* (2011) and *Religion, Law and Society* (2014). He is co-author, with Norman Doe and Mark Hill QC, of *Religion and Law in the United Kingdom* (2nd edition, 2014), which forms part of the *International Encyclopaedia of Laws* series. He is co-editor, with Norman Doe, of *Law and Religion: New Horizons* (2010). He has also written over 40 book chapters and articles for a wide range of journals including *Public Law*, *Law Quarterly Review*, *Cambridge Law Journal*, the *Modern Law Review*, the *Oxford Journal of Legal Studies* and the *Ecclesiastical Law Journal*. He was a specialist Contributing Editor for *Jowitt's Dictionary of English Law* (2010). His recent research has included an empirical study of the operation of religious tribunals in Britain, funded by the Arts and Humanities Research Council (AHRC)/ Economic and Social Research Council (ESRC) Religion and Society Programme.

Adam B. Seligman is Professor of Religion at Boston University and Research Associate at its Institute for Culture, Religion and World Affairs. He lived for close to 20 years in Israel, where he was a member of Kibbutz Kerem Shalom in the early 1970s. He was a Fulbright Fellow in Hungary from 1990 to 1992. His books include *The Idea of Civil Society* (1992), *Inner-Worldly Individualism* (1993), *The Problem of Trust* (1997), *Market and Community* (with Mark Lichbach, 2000), *Modernity's Wager: Authority, the Self and Transcendence* (2002), *Modest Claims: Dialogues and Essays on Tolerance and Tradition* (2004), *Ritual and its Consequences: An Essay on the Limits of Sincerity* (with Robert Weller, Robert Puett and Robert Simon,

2008) and *Rethinking Pluralism: Ritual, Experience and Ambiguity* (with Robert Weller, 2012). He recently edited *Religious Education and the Challenge of Pluralism* (2014). He is Director of Communities Engaging with Difference and Religion (CEDAR), which leads workshops every year on contested aspects of religion, difference and the public square in different parts of the world.

Stephanos Stavros is the Executive Secretary to the European Commission against Racism and Intolerance (ECRI). He has spent most of his career in the Council of Europe (European Commission and Court of Human Rights, Legal Affairs and Administration), which he joined in 1994 after short spells in the Greek Ministry of Foreign Affairs and the Greek Council for Refugees. He studied law in Athens and London (LSE and QMC), where he obtained his PhD in 1989. He is the author of *Guarantees for Accused Persons under Article 6 of the European Convention on Human Rights* (1993) and several articles on the right to a fair trial, freedom of religion, national minorities and the international protection of migrants and prisoners. While working, he completed a distance-learning MBA (Henley Management College, 2004).

Andreas Stein is Head of Unit responsible for equal treatment legislation at the European Commission's Directorate-General for Justice. He is a German lawyer (Dr. iur., University of Hamburg) and has a postgraduate degree in International Relations (SAIS Bologna). After several years of practising as a judge at a labour tribunal, he joined the European Commission in 2001 and worked in the areas of private international law, gender equality law, competition law and European contract law before taking his current position.

Lucy Vickers is Professor of Law at Oxford Brookes School of Law. Her main research area is the protection of human rights within the workplace, with a focus on freedom of speech and religious freedom. She is the author of *Freedom of Speech and Employment* (2002), *Religious Freedom, Religious Discrimination and the Workplace* (2008), and a report for the European Commission, *Religion and Belief Discrimination in Employment: The EU Law* (2007).

Her recent work includes 'Religious Diversity in the European Workplace' in *A Test of Faith? Religious Diversity and Accommodation in the European Workplace* (2012), 'Promoting Equality or Fostering Resentment? The Public Sector Equality Duty and Religion and Belief' (*Legal Studies*, 2011) and 'Freedom of Religion and Belief and Employment in Faith Schools' (*Religion and Human Rights*, 2009).

Zeynep Yanasmayan is a researcher at the European University Viadrina, Germany. She received her PhD from the Faculty of Social Sciences at KU Leuven and previously worked as a postdoctoral research fellow at the Max Planck Institute for the Study of Religious and Ethnic Diversity (Göttingen) and as the Scientific Project Manager of the Religious Diversity and Secular Models in Europe – Innovative Approaches to Law and Policy (RELIGARE) project. Her research focuses on topics relating to migration and citizenship studies, Turkish minorities in Europe and the governance of ethnic and religious diversity. Her publications include 'Further Stay or Return? Insights from the Highly Educated Turkish Migrants in Amsterdam, Barcelona and London' in *Migrant Professionals in the City: Local Encounters, Identities, and Inequalities* (2014), 'Role of Turkish Islamic Organizations in Belgium: An Inquiry into the Strategies of TIFB and IFB' (*Insight Turkey*, 2010) and 'European Citizenship: A Tool for Integration?' in *Illiberal Liberal States: Immigration, Citizenship and Integration in the EU* (2009).

Lorenzo Zucca is Reader in Jurisprudence at the Dickson Poon School of Law of King's College, London. He holds the degrees of Maitrise from Paris 2 Assas, DEA from Paris 1 Sorbonne, MJur from the University of Oxford and a PhD from EUI, Florence. He is the author of *Constitutional Dilemmas: Conflicts of Fundamental Legal Rights in Europe and the USA* (2007) and *A Secular Europe: Law and Religion in the European Constitutional Landscape* (2012). He is currently working on a new project entitled *Secular Globe*, which focuses on global religious conflicts and transnational legal ways of dealing with them.

Foreword

Grace Davie

I am delighted to commend this important book to the widest possible readership. It contains the summary report of RELIGARE, a European project on religious diversity and secular models in Europe which focused on innovative approaches to law and democracy. It also contains a series of responses to the report from a wide variety of commentators, from within and beyond academia. Both the report itself and the commentaries on it merit sustained attention by a wide variety of audiences.

In order to appreciate this body of work to the full, however, it is necessary to place it in context – and in two ways. On the one hand it is important to grasp the complexity of the religious situation in Europe; it is this, after all, which has provoked the research and the subsequent reflections. On the other hand, it is important to note that RELIGARE was but one of several projects concerned with the implications of this situation for the maintenance of European societies as we know them. These projects should be seen in the round; taken together they indicate a step-change in research in this field, which has created a momentum of its own. Penetrating questions emerge which require an imaginative response.

First, then, the place of religion in twenty-first-century Europe. The crucial point in this connection is that several factors must be taken into account, which not only change and adapt over time, but push and pull in different directions.[1] The six factors are:

1. The role of the historic churches in forming European culture. This is incontrovertibly illustrated by the influence that the Christian tradition has had on time (calendars, seasons, festivals, holidays, weeks and weekends) and space (the parish system and the dominance of Christian buildings) in this part of the world. These attributes appear over and over again in the RELIGARE material.
2. An awareness that the historic churches still have a place at particular moments in the lives of modern Europeans, though they are no longer able to influence, let alone discipline, the beliefs and behaviour of the great majority of the population. Or to put this differently: despite their relative secularity, a significant number of European people are likely to return to their churches at moments of celebration or grief (whether individual or collective). In my own work, I have explored this state of affairs by means of two concepts: 'believing without belonging' and 'vicarious religion'.
3. At the same time, an observable change is taking place in the reduced, but still significant, churchgoing constituencies of the continent, which operate increasingly on a model of choice rather than on a model of obligation or duty. As a result, the membership of the historic churches – in line with almost all religious organisations – is changing in nature; it is chosen rather than inherited, though more so in some places than in others. In this sense the historic churches become one minority among many, albeit a privileged one.
4. This shift has coincided with the arrival in Europe of groups of people from many different parts of the world. This is primarily an economic movement, but the implications for religious life are immense. The growing presence of Christians from the global South alongside significant other faith communities has altered the religious profile of Europe. In addition, some of these communities are – simply by their presence – challenging some deeply held European assumptions, notably the notion

1 A more developed account of the argument presented here can be found in G Davie, 'Religion in Europe in the 21st Century: The Factors to Take into Account' (2006) 47 (2) *Archives Européennes de Sociologie/ European Journal of Sociology/ Europäisches Archiv für Soziologie* 271–96. The analysis is of particular relevance to (the former) Western Europe. The parts of Europe that were under Communist domination until 1989 have a rather different trajectory. They are less influenced by the relatively recent arrival of Islam and more by long-standing religious minorities – a presence very often brought about by historic border changes.

that religion should be considered a private matter. The existence of a sizeable Muslim population is of particular importance in this respect.

5. The growing ambiguity between the public and the private with respect to religion has provoked a further reaction. Europe's secular elites have been discomfited by this shift, largely because they did not anticipate a change of this nature. Increasingly they see it as their duty to question what is happening, sometimes aggressively, sometimes less so.
6. The final factor reveals a gradual, but growing, realisation that the patterns of religious life in modern Europe should be considered a 'distinctive case' – they are not a global prototype. In short, Europeans are beginning to appreciate that Europe is secular not because it is modern, but because it is European. It is equally true that some Europeans welcome this insight while others are disconcerted by it.

Although the great majority of media commentators fail to do so, it is important to consider these factors alongside one another in order to get a rounded picture of what is happening. The future is uncertain. Indeed, the current state of religion in Europe is paradoxical. On the one hand, religion has re-entered the public square and demands a response. On the other, a largely unchurched population has difficulty dealing with this situation in the sense that Europeans are rapidly losing the concepts, knowledge and vocabulary that are necessary to talk about religion – an inevitable result of persistent secularisation. How can we manage this situation more constructively? That is the challenge facing European societies today, to which RELIGARE offers a careful and considered response.

It is, however, but one of many responses – unsurprisingly given the paradox already described, which can be expanded thus. Religion (in all its diversity) is no longer invisible either to society as a whole or to the academic community. It is increasingly present in public debate, despite the fact that indices of religious activity are falling rather than rising. Immigration – the process by which the 'world' arrives on our doorstep – is a crucial element in this narrative, noting that the initial debate in this respect took place in terms of ethnicity rather than religion. This was so for an obvious reason: racial or ethnic differences were easier for social scientists to deal with within their existing paradigms than their religious equivalents. Bit by bit, however, the mismatch between the perceptions of Western scholars and the preferred identities of the incoming communities that were establishing themselves had to be acknowledged – a shift in which the presence of Islam was central. As a result religion and religious differences became increasingly relevant to the agendas of many European societies. Such issues, however, were more often than not constructed as a 'problem', an image exacerbated by the violence of events elsewhere.

What followed was essentially a delayed reaction. Denial that religion was a salient public matter gradually gave way to alarm, producing in a remarkably short space of time an impressive array of generously funded research programmes, a wide variety of government initiatives and an avalanche of publications. The details of this 'research mountain' can only be summarised here. They include renewed and well-organised attention to religion in the research communities of several European countries. The largest of these enterprises was the Religion and Society Programme in Britain, but similar undertakings can be found in the Netherlands, Switzerland, Denmark, Sweden and (to complete the list) Canada.[2] Simultaneously, the Sixth and Seventh Framework Programmes of the European Commission supported an extended series of projects relating to the growing diversity of Europe and its consequences for economic, political and social life.[3] RELIGARE was one of these. A noteworthy point in this connection was the strong emphasis on policy and policy recommendations underlined in the relevant research calls.

Indeed the subtext of all this activity – national as well as international – is unmistakable and revolves around the following question: Is the growing religious diversity present in this part of the world damaging to social cohesion, and if so, what is to be done? The multiple projects assembled in the initiatives listed

2 Full details of these programmes and their implications for the study of religion can be found in G Davie, 'Thinking Sociologically about Religion: A Step Change in the Debate', ARDA Guiding Paper Series 2011 (State College, PA: The Association of Religion Data Archives at The Pennsylvania State University 2011). Available at <www.thearda.com/rrh/papers/guidingpapers.asp> accessed 20 June 2014.

3 See <http://cordis.europa.eu/home_en.html> (accessed 20 June 2014) for more information about the European Commission's Framework Programmes.

above interrogate these questions in a wide variety of fields (politics, democracy, law, education, welfare), in which key values (tolerance, acceptance, respect, rights, responsibilities, inclusion, exclusion) are thoroughly explored. Unsurprisingly, much of this work foregrounds the presence and aspirations of minorities and the reactions of host societies to these groups. Identities can no longer be taken for granted in a continent where movement and migration are commonplace, including – it should be noted – the movement of populations from one part of Europe to another. Fluctuations in the economy are central to what is happening in terms of push and pull, and because they exacerbate the associated tensions.

A number of points emerge from this very rapid overview. First, it is important to differentiate between individual research projects and rather more organised forms of enquiry. The former have always existed, many of which have yielded significant data, not to mention new ways of thinking about religion. Since the millennium, however, something rather different has appeared: that is a series of initiatives or programmes which are designed to gather together a wide variety of projects and to ensure that these add up to more than the sum of their parts. It is the systematic approach to the study of religion which is new. This development, together with the strikingly generous funding that supports it, is growing in momentum. Second, the fact that so much research activity occurred at more or less the same time is not, I contend, a coincidence; it has been brought about by similar anxieties about the place of religion in modern European societies and is motivated by alarm rather than curiosity.

Whatever the motivations, the implications are far-reaching. The numbers of scholars involved in these activities, their individual and joint publications, the conferences that they both host and attend and the impact that their work will have outside as well as inside the academy have undoubtedly made a difference. New knowledge has been generated in abundance, a new generation of researchers has been trained, and new possibilities for collaboration are emerging all the time. As a result new fields of study are becoming apparent almost by the day. Among those in which I have been engaged are the growing significance of religion for law and law-making, the renewed attention to religion in connection with welfare, and fresh initiatives in healthcare and healing. All three, moreover, require the input of very different groups of scholars and in themselves have generated new forms of interdisciplinarity. The interactions of law and social science are particularly striking in this respect – all the more so because they are relatively new.

It is this context that I have had in mind when reading both the RELIGARE report and the reactions that it has provoked. The latter are many and varied and range from the enthusiastic to the sharply critical. Despite the variety, however, a repeating theme caught my eye: the need to balance attention to religion and thus the rights of religious people against those of other sections in the population, both small and large. In some cases, the logic demands that we keep in mind different minorities, thinking carefully how their relative claims can be dealt with fairly in a modern democracy. These minorities include the seriously religious themselves, who come in many shapes and sizes and who are sometimes opposed to each other; their alter-egos, the secularists; a varied, growing and increasingly confident LGBT community; those for whom 'freedom of speech' means pushing the boundaries regardless of the offence that might be given; and a group for whom other rights (for example those of children or animals) take precedence over religious stipulations. A number of the responses in this book can be read with this agenda in mind. Many of them address the notion of competing rights.

More searching, however, is the awareness that increasing attention to religion challenges not only other minorities, but the mainstream itself, that is, the conviction that modern societies will, necessarily, be secular societies. The link is particularly strong in Europe, where the connections between modernisation and secularisation have been assumed for centuries rather than decades. They are part of the air that we breathe. It follows that religion can continue to exist, but in the private sphere only; it will have no place in public life. Leaving aside the presumed accuracy of these statements, which is doubtful,[4] it is quite clear that the associated assumptions are no longer tenable – a statement that seriously discomfits those who have to deal with the practical consequences of this shift (politicians, policymakers, lawyers, civil servants, service providers, the media and so on). Examples of their work are examined in the RELIGARE report. They also

4 See for example the trenchant critiques in D Martin, *The Future of Christianity: Violence and Democracy, Secularization and Religion* (Ashgate 2011). Martin reminds us that religion has remained a significant element in public life even in Europe.

include those whose disciplines depend on a particular – and notably secular – reading of the European Enlightenment. Among them are the champions of social science.

Is it surprising, then, that the unpacking of these expectations, whether in practice or in theory, has provoked a lively debate, of which RELIGARE and the multiple projects referred to above are part? I have much enjoyed reading both the report itself and the expositions that follow, which reveal the different ways in which these questions can be tackled. I would like, however, to conclude with the issue that intrigues me the most. It can be articulated thus: supposing – against the run of much European thinking – that it is not only possible but 'normal' to be both fully modern and fully religious, how is European social science to accommodate this fact? And given that the disciplines in question rest to a considerable extent on an implicit elision between the modern, the secular and the rational, will this adjustment require a re-thinking of the philosophies of science that underpin their activities? Am I right, in other words, to argue that the serious study of religion cannot simply be 'added on' to the social sciences as we currently know them? If taken to its logical conclusions the turn to religion will not only penetrate the core of our disciplinary thinking, but will disturb – at times radically – the foundations on which much of this edifice rests.

Meeting this challenge is, in my view, the primary task for the new generation of scholars embarking in my own discipline (sociology), many of whom have cut their teeth as researchers in the accelerated programme of work outlined above. I hesitate to include other fields of study (including law) about which I know less, but whatever the case, our enquiries must be driven by empirical data and the critical analysis and examination of such data, not by the overly secular mindset that so often pervades the field. The RELIGARE report and the commentaries generated by its reading offer an excellent place to start.

Acknowledgements

A book such as this is by essence built on collaboration and is the result of joint efforts. As editors, we wish to warmly thank all those who contributed to its coming of age.

The starting point for this volume was the European interdisciplinary research project RELIGARE, a three-year programme (2010–2013) funded by the European Commission under its 7th Framework Programme. We are grateful to the Commission and, in particular, our Programme Officer Louisa Anastopoulou for the generous support provided.

We also wish to thank all the contributors, with whom we had the pleasure of working and exchanging ideas over the course of 2014. Without their enthusiasm for and commitment to this joint endeavour, the volume could simply not have come to life. Thanks are also due to members of the RELIGARE consortium.

We thank Dr Monica Sandor for helping get things started by collecting the papers and carefully following up with the authors. Dr Brian Donahoe picked up where she left off and saw the manuscript to completion, performing thorough editing and meticulous language review under an extremely tight deadline.

Ms Gesine Koch carefully formatted all the texts, and Ms Andrea Klein provided some much needed last-minute support with the finalising of the manuscript.

Finally, we would like to express our gratitude to Ms Alison Kirk at Ashgate Publishing, who was always patient, encouraging and available to answer the various queries along the way.

Acknowledgements

PART I
The RELIGARE Project and Final Report

Chapter 1
Introduction

Marie-Claire Foblets, Katayoun Alidadi, Jørgen S. Nielsen and Zeynep Yanasmayan

It is common in the field of business to talk of a 'disruptive' new technology or business model. Such disruption happens when some new method of production or organisation undermines and bypasses existing patterns in such a way that the new exposes the inefficiencies of the old or simply makes the old redundant. The motor car did this to the horse-drawn carriage, just as online retailing today threatens the local book shop and is replacing the travel agency in the high street.

In this sense, disruption can be applied as a metaphor to describe the changes which have taken place in recent years in the relationship between law, politics and belief in Europe. There are a number of interacting drivers of this disruption, some of which have acquired greater significance in the public mind than others. In her Foreword to this volume, Grace Davie points to some of those driving factors. Among them are the decline of the institutional power of traditional churches and their traditional links with political power, the weakening of their role as providers of ethical and social discipline to their followers, and with this weakening the growth of an open religious marketplace in which the individual is free to sample and choose among the many options on display. In the public mind and in the political debate, however, perhaps the single most important factor is the arrival of new religions in the European space.

Until the collapse of the Soviet system at the end of the 1980s one could argue that Europe east of the Iron Curtain had a radically different experience from the western half of the continent. Whether this image stands up to significant scrutiny is an open question, but what can be strongly suggested is that there has been a surprising degree of convergence since the change a quarter of a century ago. As the work of the various RELIGARE country teams shows (see the RELIGARE Report, this volume), the variations within Europe of the constructions of the law–politics–religion nexus do not easily succumb to a categorisation based on distinctions of East versus West, Catholic versus Protestant versus Orthodox or, for that matter, versus Muslim (in the case of Turkey). What is common across these countries is a resurgence of religion (although not necessarily in its traditional forms), the broadening of existing religious traditions, and a growing variety of religious experiences on display.

It is not only in Eastern Europe, where until the disappearance of the Iron Curtain there was an alliance of convenience between the atheist State and the official religious communities that gave the latter a privileged position, that traditional relations were broken. In the West as well, the legal and political arrangements that took place through the first half of the twentieth century confirmed a 'marriage of convenience' between religion and the State. But this convenient arrangement has been undermined by two apparently contradictory trends. On the one hand the continuing secularisation of society has diminished the moral authority of the churches, just as it has multiplied the number of spiritual, ethical and cultural reference points around which autonomous individuals can construct their own authority. At the same time we have experienced a resurgence of religion, but in the new environment it is one located outside the traditional churches. This most obviously applies to the 'new' (to Europe) religions of immigrant origin, first and foremost Islam, but also Sikhism, Hinduism, various forms of Buddhism, and others. While Islam in particular has attracted most of the public attention, other forms of Christian experience have also crept in, often of US origin. We are seeing varieties of Pentecostalism growing exponentially, alongside revivalist forms of Protestantism and post-Protestant phenomena. They often share a conservatism of family values which harmonises well with the 'immigrated' religions, while all are divided between political quietism and activism. In between, other beliefs and life stances have added their voices to the mix. And they have all found the margins and the weak points of the existing patterns of relations between religion, State and the public space, as the many cases which have appeared before the European Court of Human Rights bear witness.

The RELIGARE Project

The RELIGARE project[1] was the first and (thus far) only large-scale European Commission-funded project specifically geared towards researching the multifarious challenges raised by the increasing religious and philosophical diversity in Europe. As such, its very existence demonstrates the European Union's progression from an economic unit into a more complex political and social construction that regards issues related to social cohesion and human rights as part of its core activities.[2] On the other hand, other European organisations such as the Council of Europe and in particular the European Court of Human Rights (ECtHR) have engaged in debates for much longer, and recently a number of precedent-setting cases involving the accommodation of religious diversity have made their way to the forefront of public attention.[3] The RELIGARE project investigated not only EU law and ECtHR cases, but also the laws and policies of 10 representative States that were part of the investigation and the interaction between national-level and EU law, an area where history, local sensitivities and power struggles play a large role in setting laws and policies.

This book is the latest volume to come out of the RELIGARE project.[4] Part I of the book presents the text of RELIGARE's final report, which gathers together the principal findings of the three-year RELIGARE project. It sets out the main challenges posed by religious diversity in Europe and the need to accommodate certain aspects of this reality in law and policy. Specifically, it covers four spheres of public policy and legislation where the pressure to accommodate religious diversity has been most strongly felt in Europe: employment, family life, use of public space and State support mechanisms. The report, and this volume, however, not only identify some of the main challenges in these four spheres in national country contexts, but go a step further by engaging in efforts to come up with alternative solutions. In particular, policy recommendations – embracing a forward-looking approach – are formulated under the two yardsticks of 'inclusive neutrality' and 'justice as even-handedness' and directed towards governance units at the local, national and European levels regarding issues of religious pluralism and secularism.

In Part II, which makes up the greater part of the book, some 30 exceptional scholars, activists, legal practitioners and policymakers provide context and critique to the report. Some of the authors were involved in the RELIGARE project at various stages, others take a more outside perspective in formulating their considerations. The various responses focus on different areas of law and religion in Europe and beyond, and thus, we feel, make an invaluable contribution to the fractious debates that have started since the 'return of religion' to the public sphere.[5] What's more, the varied contributions more generally open an intellectual discussion on the topic of religion in Europe, which was the aim of soliciting responses following the closure of the RELIGARE project.

1 Religious Diversity and Secular Models in Europe (RELIGARE) (2010–2013), a collaborative research project funded through the European Commission's Seventh Framework Programme (FP7) and coordinated by the Catholic University of Leuven (KU Leuven); see <http://www.religareproject.eu/> accessed 30 June 2014.

2 As Herman Van Rompuy noted at the final RELIGARE conference (Leuven, 4 December 2012), 'Freedom and human rights … now belong to our core businesses'.

3 Examples of such precedent-setting cases include the *Eweida* case (*Eweida and Others v the United Kingdom*, App nos 48420/10, 59842/10, 51671/10 and 36516/10, 2013) and the two *Lautsi* cases in Italy (*Lautsi v Italy*, App no 30814/06, 2009 and *Lautsi v Italy*, App no 30814/06, 2011 ECtHR (GC), also referred to as *Lautsi I* and *Lautsi II*), to which several contributions in the volume refer. The *Fernández Martínez v Spain* case (App no 56030/07, 12 June 2014) offers another, more recent illustration of such a case.

4 The others are: S Ferrari and S Pastorelli (eds), *Religion in Public Spaces: A European Perspective* (2012); K Alidadi, M-C Foblets and J Vrielink (eds), *A Test of Faith? Religious Diversity and Accommodation in the European Workplace* (2012); S Ferrari and S Pastorelli (eds), *The Burqa Affair across Europe: Between Public and Private Space* (2013); S Ferrari and A Benzo (eds), *Between Cultural Diversity and Common Heritage: Legal and Religious Perspectives on the Sacred Places of the Mediterranean* (2014), all published in the Ashgate series *Cultural Diversity and Law in Association with RELIGARE.*

5 See, for example, G Kepel, *La Revanche de Dieu. Chrétiens, juifs et musulmans à la reconquête du monde* (Le Seuil 1991); published in English as *The Revenge of God: The Resurgence of Islam, Christianity and Judaism in the Modern World* (Polity Press 1994).

On Religious Freedom in Europe: Freedom versus Equality?

A number of the contributions could be recommended reading for any 'newcomers' to the debates, in particular as they both provide important background information and capture a certain *Zeitgeist* when it comes to religious freedom in the 'exceptional' European setting.[6] These contributions consider the ramifications of the secular context in which religious diversity, and in particular Islam, currently finds itself in Europe. This setting reflects a stressful unease with the presence of religion in the public sphere, and at times even bursts out in favour of a strong anti-religion antidote as remedy for so much religious visibility, confusion and convolution.[7] We include in this section contributions by **Heiner Bielefeldt**, **Ronan McCrea**, **Jane Mair** and **Russell Sandberg**. Heiner Bielefeldt's contribution on the topic of religious freedom in general, with a focus on the United Nations' approach to religious diversity, epitomises this approach. Bielefeldt, who is the UN Special Rapporteur on freedom of religion or belief, offers penetrating insights into some overarching debates and misconceptions in Europe regarding a human right – freedom of religion – which is considered 'less liberal' than the right to freedom of expression.

Ronan McCrea, for his part, sketches the challenges to the principles underlying the governance of religion in Europe introduced by new religious practices and gauges the extent to which accommodation for new practices should be granted. The author argues that the first feature of the 'European model', which is well entrenched in the case law of the ECtHR, is the individual autonomy approach to religion. This individualised view of religion is challenged by religious groups that pay more attention to the collective and ritualistic aspects of religion, which remain less protected under European law than individual choice and free expression in religious matters. Conceiving of the law as an imperfect tool to reflect social reality, McCrea argues that the unequal protection offered to forms of religiosity that are more difficult to translate into claims to private autonomy is legitimate given the liberal spirit of the European Convention on Human Rights. The second pillar he discusses is the separation of the realms of politics and religion, which becomes increasingly blurred with the return of religion to politics. McCrea argues that Europe should be firm about non-negotiable fundamental requirements of the democratic order such as gender equality and toleration of homosexuality, which can sometimes be religiously controversial. The third pillar that he addresses is the coexistence of the principle of separation and religiously flavoured cultural and institutional practices. This overlap of religious and cultural or national spheres is becoming problematic with the proliferation of diverse religious groups that cannot identify with such practices. McCrea recognises the pragmatic need to accept certain shared national cultural symbols that have religious origins but have acquired a post-religious meaning (such as the Swedish flag), but believes that the display of purely religious symbols (such as crucifixes) in the public sphere should be subjected to stricter scrutiny and greater regulation. 'The more religiously specific national symbols are', McCrea concludes, 'the harder it will be to achieve a common non-denominational national identity that wins the loyalty of religious minorities while maintaining links to an imagined shared past.'

A number of contributions engage with specific problems that come along with the protection of the right to freedom of thought, conscience and religion, while others consider the complementary framework of equality. The former include the contributions by **Stephanos Stavros**, **Matthias Koenig** and **Maleiha Malik**, while the latter is apparent in the contributions by **Michael Germann** and **Lucy Vickers**. Drawing a parallel between gender equality and religious equality, Vickers develops a nuanced argument based on the equality perspective. In doing so she provides additional support for the main arguments put forward in the RELIGARE report, most notably the assertion that the 'neutral' secular space is anything but truly 'neutral', and in fact advantages mainstream Christianity and disadvantages minority faith adherents. She also raises the question of what is gained by introducing the concepts of 'inclusive State neutrality' and 'justice as even-

6 As Berger, Davie and Fokas have noted, 'America is indeed "exceptional", but with regard to religion it is very much like the rest of the world – namely, very religious. The exception is Europe. (To be precise, western and central Europe)'; see P Berger, G Davie and E Fokas (eds), *Religious America, Secular Europe? A Theme and Variations* (Ashgate 2008) 9–10.

7 For instance, the RELIGARE report observes with regard to employment that 'discomfort with issues of religion, and especially minority religion, may indeed lead to avoidance of confrontation, either by employees staying away from the workplace or by decision makers diluting the ban on discrimination on the basis of religion or belief' (*Report*, 20–21).

handedness' in the final RELIGARE report. Her contribution, in support of the RELIGARE final report's call for improved protection of religious interest and a more inclusive State neutrality, concludes that approaches to gender equality can usefully inform the approach to religion:

> The creation of arrangements at work to enable women to balance private sphere concerns with their work roles has led to greater inclusion of women at work; similarly, allowing workplaces to adapt to the needs of religious minorities should lead to their greater inclusion in the public space of work. Encouraging some adaptation of workplace rules should not be seen, therefore, as an end to State neutrality, but instead as the development of a more inclusive and even-handed neutrality.

On the Reasonable Accommodation Debate

One of the core issues in the RELIGARE project, related to participation in employment of religious minorities, was that of reasonable accommodations. The final report makes a firm, and for some (too) audacious, recommendation to adopt an explicit duty of reasonable accommodation for religion and belief in Europe (*Report*, 19). This would fit with a substantive equality approach, complementing other legal tools such as indirect discrimination. A number of contributors comment on, criticise or, on the contrary, support this recommendation, including **Frédérique Ast**, **Peter Cumper**, **Cécile Laborde**, **Kristin Henrard** and **Andreas Stein**.[8] Andreas Stein, a policymaker at the European Commission, offers an interesting insider perspective on the RELIGARE report's recommendations regarding reasonable accommodation. He argues that the adoption of a duty of reasonable accommodation for religion or belief, on a par with disability, in the Employment Equality Directive would be unfeasible because 'the adoption of new EU anti-discrimination legislation, which has been immensely difficult in the recent past and is unlikely to fundamentally change in the near future', would require 'unanimity in the Council and can thus be effectively vetoed by any single Member State'. Stein furthermore posits that such legislation would add little new to what is already there in the form of protection against indirect discrimination.[9] What's more, Stein argues that

> the mere existence of a duty of reasonable accommodation does not per se imply a higher level of protection. The statutory obligation as construed by the US Supreme Court, which excludes the right to accommodation wherever any competing rights and interests of other employees are at play and whenever it would have more than a *de minimis* cost, would appear to at least possibly lag behind the current level of protection under EU law without such an express duty.

This conclusion, based on the situation in the United States, is open to debate, both because of uncertainty about the extent of the reasonable accommodation obligation in the United States and because of the costs of litigation in the United States (with contingency fees increasing the likelihood of a disgruntled employee wanting his or her day in court). Moreover, because of the generally positive attitude towards religion in US society, employers generally err on the side of caution and accommodate employees quite extensively despite the low *de minimis* standard. Nonetheless, this is an interesting debate which will be carried forward in Europe

---

8 Other contributions also address the reasonable accommodations debate, for example, Vickers, Malik and Loobuyck, but since that is not the main focus, they fit in better elsewhere. Vickers, for example, also addresses the issue of reasonable accommodations in the workplace. She sees the benefits, but sees a legal enshrinement as unnecessary considering existing protections under equality law. Her preference is for further development of protections against indirect discrimination by 'incorporating' the search for reasonable adaptations by the employer within the existing legal protections in the EU. Loobuyck, despite agreeing with a 'difference-sensitive' approach, is of the opinion that reasonable accommodations should be a matter of employers' goodwill rather than an enforceable right. He also holds that reasonable accommodation as an exception to the rule should only apply in extraordinary cases, most other cases leading either to rule change or to implementation for all.

9 Malik (summarily) and Vickers (more elaborately) likewise argue that existing provisions against indirect discrimination obviate the need for special reasonable accommodation legislation. Stein's argument, however, is the most sustained, utilising the functional equivalent argument.

in the coming years as the effectiveness of anti-discrimination norms in their application (and not just their implementation) will be subjected to closer scrutiny by the European Commission.

Cécile Laborde assesses the merits of the RELIGARE conceptual framework and the conceptualisation of religious accommodation from an egalitarian justice perspective. The author praises the capacity of 'inclusive even-handedness' to resolve inequalities between members of majority and minority religions, and particularly the principle's underlying intention to compensate for the costs that arise out of the interaction between the cultural norms of a given society and the exercise of basic religious rights by minorities. However, she criticises the egalitarian tenets of the framework. Taking substantive equality as the equality of outcome of different religious groups, she opposes it at two levels. On the one hand, she asserts that what needs to be equalised are the basic opportunities for social participation that should be available to all citizens, not 'religious opportunities'. On the other hand, it is these basic opportunities that need to be equal and not the *status* of religious groups. Therefore, she postulates, a ban on a minority religious practice or dress in the workplace should pose a problem at the level of the pursuit of these basic equal opportunities – that is, the right to work – rather than at the level of substantive religious equality. This view also requires a redefinition of basic opportunities in a culturally sensitive context. Laborde then goes on to define the limits of the concept of inclusive even-handedness. Internal limits include cases where accommodation would be undesirable because it would not offer a careful balance; she suggests that it would be better to create a law that is more equal for all, or repeal the measure completely. External limits, on the other hand, refer to situations where the framework of inclusive even-handedness does not offer sufficiently clear guidelines. Examples include cases where there is a clash between religious freedom (primarily but not exclusively of religious groups or faith-based organisations) and other principles and rights such as anti-discrimination and gender equality. Other contributions provide further examples and support for this argument.

Seeing Religious Diversity in Context

Considering the importance of the issues covered under religious freedom and equality in Europe today, the RELIGARE project should be seen as a vehicle for advancing socio-legal research in this field. Several authors in this volume, most notably **Lori Beaman** and **Effie Fokas**, place a great deal of emphasis on the importance of devoting particular attention to the concrete social, cultural and historical contexts in place in the various countries surveyed. This emphasis is also implicit in the contribution of **Eugenia Relaño Pastor**. This is an area where the asymmetry between the various traditions of religion and belief present in Europe most sharply challenges the worlds of politics and law. Many aspects of European public life have been historically determined by the dominant Christian traditions. Present generations tend to forget the often bloody conflict between State and religion, especially in the sixteenth and seventeenth centuries, which lie behind the twentieth-century legal settlements. Things like the timing of holidays, various daily expressions and social practices, and public rituals of State are taken for granted, as is, on the whole, the gradual withdrawal of the dominant churches from public life. The symbiotic link between a nation-State and a particular religion is taken for granted; it is part of the 'background noise' which no one pays much attention to. But to members of newly appearing religions, be they 'immigrated' like Islam or 'imported' like Pentecostalism, the 'background noise' can be deafening. The failure to acknowledge this problem can be perceived as exposing a double standard in a nominally applied principle of freedom of religion or belief. In the case of the 'immigrated' religions, the relationship between its followers and the nation-State is necessarily ambivalent. After all, for Muslims, Hindus and Sikhs, their historical memory of the European nation-State is one of being on the wrong end of an imperialism in which the freedoms of modern human rights were mostly ignored. If anything, the case is even stronger among people of African descent who live with the additional trauma of the history of slavery. Many of the 'imported' Christian revivalist movements have the United States as their main point of reference, with its very different history of religion–State relations, conscious of a heritage of their founders having to flee persecution at the hands of rulers and dominant churches for their beliefs and practices.

It is true that various initiatives during the lifespan of the RELIGARE project took on the question of the link between the constraints and characteristics of the various local settings, on the one hand, and what this may mean for critical and constructively forward-looking research on religious freedom in Europe on the other. For a project which aimed at providing concrete recommendations addressed to policymakers on different levels, this remains an important issue to consider. We can only hope that follow-up research will remain on the agenda for legal scholars as well as social scientists who are working *in situ* on religion, diversity and secularism in twenty-first-century Europe.

In this section of the volume we have included contributions from two other authors that express a similar view: **Adam Seligman**, who has been following the RELIGARE project from the very start, and **Tom Bennett**, who speaks from a South African context. Both make a very similar observation on the importance of putting the question of religious freedom in its historical and sociological context. These two contributions especially remind us of that other divide in Europe, the one between the civil code traditions of the European mainland and the common law tradition of the so-called Anglo-Saxon world. Tom Bennett's reflections in particular show how a multi-cultural approach in law to social, cultural and religious pluralism can be conceived of in ways that most of Europe would reject as unacceptable. Could such a focus on cultural rather than religious identity as an important dimension of personal law serve as a model of how to build flexibility into European legal systems? If so, how do we then prevent cultural identity from becoming a rigid and therefore fragile concept in European societies going through rapid and continuous transformation?

Religious and Philosophical Diversity and Secularism: Questioning Normativity

While all contributions engage with the RELIGARE findings, the contributions by **Christian Joppke**, **Koen Lemmens**, **Patrick Loobuyck**, **David Pollock** and **Lorenzo Zucca** do so in an unflaggingly focused way, either critically or approvingly so. They illustrate the diversity of responses among academics who have wide knowledge and expertise in these matters and thus serve to place the two suggested yardsticks as well as the final recommendations into perspective.

Christian Joppke, for instance, argues that we are witnessing a new turn of religious liberty rights. He admonishes the RELIGARE report for not being sufficiently clear about its stand on conflictual cases where the interpretation of religious liberty runs up against other principles such as antidiscrimination rights (for example gender equality) or, as Joppke puts it, against the 'social contract'. Is it alternative or complementary to antidiscrimination rights? In his view the conceptual framework chosen by the RELIGARE researchers is partly responsible for 'overshooting' religious demands and social contract considerations at large. He argues that the minority-sensitive nature of the conceptual framework allows for capturing these conflictual cases but ultimately draws a sombre picture of the social reality in Europe. An alternative perspective, he continues, would be to focus on the 'European model', which stresses the commonalities, particularly with regard to the principles of the protection of religious freedoms and the autonomy of religious communities. Joppke would like to have seen more critical engagement with the sustainability of the cooperation regimes and with a philosophical discussion of the limits that the concepts of secularism and liberalism can impose on the expression of not only minority religions but also majority religions.

Another critical view is expressed by Lorenzo Zucca, who is sceptical of the usefulness of embracing a normative framework that seeks neutrality, as he contends neutrality is part of the problem and not of the solution. Instead he proposes a genealogical approach, which deciphers the historical evolution of the stages of the conflict between the State and religion. He posits that, as the winner of the battle, the State is not a neutral umpire and it therefore needs to be 'corrected' by authorities at the European level. He thus conceives of both the European Union and the ECtHR as potential corrective powers that would assist in the creation of a free marketplace of religions, where the guiding principle would be pluralism. However, he also acknowledges that the main task of striking a balance between equality and freedom remains within the borders of the nation-States, which can only be achieved through fair and open collaboration. In this context, he also touches briefly upon the RELIGARE recommendation of establishing a permanent expert committee at the European level, judging it to be a thorny task.

Patrick Loobuyck and David Pollock, on the other hand, criticise the perceived pro-religion sympathy they see shining through in various aspects of the report. Their admonishments too are important to take into account. Loobuyck, in his contribution, zooms in on what he identifies as the 'pro-religion apriority of the RELIGARE project', and offers a critique that is rooted in political liberal philosophy. His remarks specifically touch upon the employment practices of faith-based organisations and schools and reasonable accommodations. Loobuyck makes a clear distinction between privately funded and partially or fully State-funded faith-based organisations and schools, leaving the former more room for autonomy and discriminatory and/or illiberal practices. He also distinguishes between jobs within these organisations that are directly related to religion or carry an ideological identity and those that do not necessarily require religious belonging or knowledge. Moreover, he ponders whether ideological neutrality could also be considered an acceptable justification for engaging in discriminatory hiring practices if, for example, a company were to claim ideological neutrality as a foundation and integral part of its corporate identity. He criticises RELIGARE for failing to be more explicit about these questions and the kind of boundaries it draws regarding these practices. Related to the point he makes about neutrality as an ideological identity, Loobuyck states that reasonable accommodation as a concept will gain more supporters if it can also expand to include other deeply held non-religious beliefs. This also relates to the more general argument he makes about the nature of religious freedom, which, in his view, should be interpreted more broadly so as to include non-religious practices and beliefs as well. Clearly, the phrase 'freedom of religion' in all cases stands as a shorthand for freedom of conscience, thought and religion, which is 'in its religious dimension, one of the most vital elements that go to make up the identity of believers and their conception of life, but it is also a precious asset for atheists, agnostics, sceptics and the unconcerned'.[10] To the extent that the concerns expressed by Loobuyck (and Pollock) are based on an assumption that the protections and inclusion argued for in the RELIGARE report do not apply to atheists, secularists or agnostics, that is a misreading. Without doubt, reasonable accommodation has important value for non-religious employees as well.[11]

Recent Developments

Finally, a number of contributions relate to issues that arose in the public debate at a later stage in the project, once the data gathering had been more or less finalised by the RELIGARE teams. We have placed these into a separate section not because they are any less important, but because they raise topics that were not explicitly addressed in the RELIGARE report, such as the development of a European foreign policy in the field of religious freedom and its protection. Considering the possible role of the European Union in the field of governance of religion, **Pasquale Annicchino** forcefully argues for coherence between the EU's external and internal actions. Similar to RELIGARE, Annicchino argues that remaining limited to the issue of competence would overlook the fact that EU policies already affect religious groups. Taking this as a departure point, he states that European policymakers will have to decide between the narrative of identity that underlies the status quo and the need to find a new paradigm with which to deal with the increasing pluralisation of European societies. He further argues that the EU should strike a good balance between its external and internal actions in the realm of religion in order to remain a credible and coherent international actor. In this vein, his contribution hints at the potential of the recently established *European Guidelines for the Protection and Promotion of Freedom of Religion or Belief*,[12] which is to be integrated into the EU's foreign policy and in its relationships with third countries.

The contribution by **Eva Brems**, **Saïla Ouald Chaib** and **Lourdes Peroni** addresses another hot topic when it comes to a minority religion (Islam) in the European setting and which was not covered extensively in the RELIGARE report, namely the issue of full-face veils in public settings.[13] Clearly the topic is of core

10 *Kokkinakis v Greece* (App no 14307/88, 25 May 1993), para 31.

11 In the US context, there have been various cases where accommodation is sought for non-believers/practitioners. For example, in the case *EEOC v Townley Engineering & Mfg.*, 859 F.2d 610 (9th Cir. 1988), an atheist employee requested exemption from having to attend devotional services in the workplace. It is true that such cases, considering the context and *Zeitgeist* sketched out above, are less pronounced in the European context, but this difference relates to the interplay between legal protection and the sociological reality, and does not detract from the principally inclusive nature of the concept of reasonable accommodations for both believers and non-believers alike.

12 See <www.eeas.europa.eu/human_rights/guidelines/index_en.htm> accessed 25 June 2014.

13 In this regard, we should note that one of the previous RELIGARE volumes focuses on this issue in particular (Ferrari and Pastorelli (n 4) 2013), while the work of Eva Brems and her team was presented at one of the RELIGARE conferences.

relevance to the aims of the project, which is why we invited the authors to submit this contribution. The authors present an argument against the adoption of so-called *burqa* bans in Europe, and in this way strengthen the recommendations against adopting general bans on the full-face veil in all public spaces as set out in the RELIGARE report under the two yardsticks of 'inclusive State neutrality' and 'justice as even-handedness'.[14]

A Truly Inclusive Europe Seen as a Collective Responsibility

We genuinely hope these contributors and others are able to utilise and build further on this collection of insights and arguments related to ongoing debates revolving around the sensitive and controversial issue of the accommodation of religion and religious diversity in Europe, even if not limited to the areas of employment, the public sphere, family law and State support systems. The rich and textured commentaries on the RELIGARE report provide a genuine barometer gauging the perspectives and debates on the ground in Europe regarding religion's undeniable role in society. We also hope policymakers find the responses useful and continue to engage with such debates, since in the end that is how academic findings and proposals can find their way into the more general sphere and effect change on the ground. And such change is much needed in Europe, although it is arguably more urgent in some areas and in some countries than in others. In the end, we hope that the final report and this collection of commentaries can add to the sometimes rich, sometimes meagre debate on certain impasses in Europe such as the *burqa* affairs, the reasonable accommodations debate, and the role of EU law in a number of controversial areas where religion is involved. Europe's diversity as reality is no longer a matter of debate, but how we can best engage *normatively* with the increasing heterogeneity which some constituents find unsettling or threatening will remain on the public agenda for some time to come. In the end, to use the apt words of American feminist and civil rights activist Audre Lorde, 'It is not our differences that divide us. It is our inability to recognize, accept, and celebrate those differences.' If anything, the RELIGARE findings illustrate that the realisation of a truly inclusive Europe remains an ongoing and elusive challenge, but that we all have considerable interest and responsibility in turning this aspiration into a reality.

Leuven/Halle/Birmingham, June 2014

14 'EU Member States should refrain from introducing a general ban on the full-face veil in all public spaces, in particular by recourse to criminal law provisions, and should assess the suitability of limiting the ban on wearing the full-face veil only to those places and situations where seeing the face of an individual is required for security purposes or where public or professional requirements demand that civil servants wear religiously neutral attire or that their faces can be seen' (*Report*, 33).

Chapter 2
The RELIGARE Report: Religion in the Context of the European Union: Engaging the Interplay between Religious Diversity and Secular Models

Marie-Claire Foblets and Katayoun Alidadi[1]

Executive Summary

In an increasingly globalised world, the EU today has to an unprecedented degree come to be composed of people of different ethnic, religious and national backgrounds. Legislatures and policymakers at various levels of the decision-making process are left with the question of how to respond effectively and appropriately to increasing social, cultural, religious and philosophical diversity in a democratic context. The RELIGARE project assessed in particular the issue of how to *strike a balance between the application of non-discrimination norms (and their further expansion) and the protection of the right to freedom of religion and belief.* The search for the right balance requires that controversies be addressed on both empirical and normative grounds: (1) continuing State discrimination in some cases against non-believers and new churches and confessional groups; (2) the contours of the right to freedom of religion or belief, individual as well as collective, in both the *forum internum* (conscience) and the *forum externum* (expression, practices); (3) unequal distribution of State support. The RELIGARE research covers 10 countries (Belgium, Bulgaria, Denmark, Germany, Great Britain, France, Italy, the Netherlands, Spain and Turkey), and focuses on four areas of participation in social life: (1) employment, (2) family life, (3) access to and the use of public space, and (4) State-supported activities.

The project's approach has been comparative and interdisciplinary, combining legal analysis with sociological data and qualitative interviews. It has yielded three types of research instrument:

- a database of case law for the 10 countries involved in the research;
- a series of thematic templates that summarise the relevant legislation, court cases and controversies in the various countries (these reflect, in a synthetic fashion, the arguments made both by the legislative branch and by the courts and tribunals, in order to address a number of particular situations);
- sociological reports, drawn up for the six countries where fieldwork was conducted (Bulgaria, Denmark, France, the Netherlands, Turkey and the UK).

These three instruments, each in its own right and in combination, allow for a systematic investigation of the existing legal frameworks within the different Member States combined with a sociological study. They make it possible to critically assess national practices and policies, their divergences and convergences, and to measure their impact on the key elements of EU policy for combating religious discrimination. The instruments, in combination, also show that there is no real consensus or clarity on what is or should be the

1 This report originally appeared on the RELIGARE website (see <www.religareproject.eu/content/final-summary-report-religare-project> accessed 29 June 2014) and is here reproduced with minor corrections. We would like to thank all the members of the RELIGARE research teams on whose work this report is based. The key findings comprise work by Katayoun Alidadi (Employment), Mathias Rohe (Family Issues), Silvio Ferrari (Public Space) and Francis Messner (State Support) and their teams. The sociological part of the research was coordinated by Veit Bader and Floris Vermeulen. We also wish to thank Lisbet Christoffersen, Jørgen Nielsen, Zeynep Yanasmayan, Sergio Carrera, Prakash Shah and Monica Sandor for all their assistance in the preparation of this report.

core of religion or belief. A number of paradigms inherited from the past and implicitly reflecting majority religions remain unquestioned in the case law; therefore, other perceptions of religion and its role in society, as identified in the sociological data and shown in the templates, are sidelined or ignored. While it is generally accepted that religion and belief are fairly well protected throughout the EU, the database as well as the templates indicate that religious discrimination is still a serious problem. Moreover, the variation among national policies also has an impact at the EU level: some national policies in the area of religion and belief impede the free movement of persons and services. It is to be expected that in the years to come not only the European Court of Human Rights (ECtHR) but also the European Court of Justice (ECJ) will be asked to play a greater role in the area of protection of the freedom of religion and belief by expanding the applicability of EU fundamental rights standards to certain types of action taken by the Member States, with a view to invalidating Member State action where it falls short of the level of protection afforded to fundamental rights under EU law. The sociological interviews, for their part, show where there is need for clearer and more explicit justification on the part of legislatures and why, in recent years, some actions in particular have given rise to critical comments.

Together, the data thus collected and presented schematically give a relatively complete and up-to-date image of what has already been done both at the EU level and by the Member States to combat religious discrimination. The findings also indicate where the priorities should be in the years to come – in which sector of social life in particular – in order to give religion and belief appropriate protection without adding to existing tensions that are clearly evident from the sociological investigations carried out.

The templates, database and sociological reports indicate the conditions under which taking a contextual approach indeed permits one to achieve (inclusive) neutrality. The RELIGARE research shows that *what guarantees appropriate protection is not so much justice in the sense of a 'hands-off' stance, but rather 'even-handedness' between competing interpretations of the freedom of religion.*[2] To have the law on one's side is not enough; people also seek justice.

Based on the main findings, the RELIGARE project advances a number of recommendations that are addressed both to the domestic authorities (Member States) and, in particular, to the EU institutions. The recommendations call for a more direct and active role for the EU institutions in developing a coherent policy framework that would strengthen the combat in Europe against discrimination on the basis of religion or belief in a way that is compatible with a democratic understanding of the functioning of pluralist democracies and can therefore help overcome divisions and segregations. This is especially crucial now that the EU has stepped up its efforts to protect the fundamental right to freedom of religion and belief in its external policies.

1. Summary Description of Project Context and Objectives

1.1 European Secular Models and their Interplay with Europe's Religious Heterogeneity

The RELIGARE research project took a thorough look at the complex interactions between two principles enshrined both in EU law and in the national constitutions of the Member States – freedom of religion and belief and non-discrimination – and aimed at *critically examining*, for the 10 aforementioned countries, the extent to which these principles are in tension with one another. Freedom of religion and belief is to be understood in a broad, generic sense: it refers not only to the protection, in law, of religion, but also extends, in line with the generally accepted meaning, to non-religious individuals and groups.

With a view to ordering the relationships between State institutions and religious groups and communities of conviction, the majority of national legislatures in Europe have made the historic decision to secularise

2 On the contextual approach as a solution to conflicts in a pluralist social context, see S Saharso and O Verhaar, 'Hoofddoeken in Holland. Een Verkenning van een Contextuele Benadering van een Multicultureel Conflict' ('Headscarves in Holland. An Exploration of a Contextual Approach to a Multicultural Conflict') (2002) 3 *Nederlands Tijdschrift voor Rechtsfilosofie en Rechtstheorie* 282–94; S Saharso and V Bader, 'Introduction: Contextualized Morality and Ethno-Religious Diversity' (2004) 7 (2) *Ethical Theory and Moral Practice* 107–15.

State law.[3] The hypothesis was that detaching the State and its institutions from religion would ultimately make society in democratic States more inclusive, providing a unitary legal and political framework within which religious and non-religious people can live together. In reality, however, the 'secular model' followed in various European States is both complex and varied. While most States officially commit themselves in one way or another to secularity, they also often maintain support for one or more religious organisations or communities of conviction. Moreover, in a rapidly globalising world, one can observe in Europe both a de-traditionalisation, in the form of the rise of the 'unchurched', and an emergence of new religious movements and alternative, non-institutionalised spiritualities. New religious (or confessional) pluralism is a fact, as is the dispersal of governance functions among various levels of decision-making bodies in matters that touch upon the relationships between the State and religions and beliefs (supra- and sub-national in addition to the national). In the face of these facts, what remains of the constitutional principle of the autonomy of the State from (organised) religion, and of religion from the State? Is the gap between an increasingly unchurched majority sentiment and the legal regulation of religion still in force evidence of hypocrisy, ethnocentrism, or perhaps just *bona fide* neglect of a developing trend? And what legitimate policy aims in this changing societal context still remain?

For analytical purposes, four different church–State models can be distinguished that are to varying degrees in place in European States.[4]

Models	**Examples**
States which proclaim a strict separation between State and religious groups	France, Turkey
States with established majority churches	England and Scotland, Denmark
States that have signed *concordats*/agreements with churches and religious communities	Italy, Spain, Germany
States with 'conditional pluralism'	Belgium, Bulgaria, the Netherlands

The first involves countries where there is, in principle, a strict separation between religious bodies and the State. In systems such as that in France (the *laïcité* model), State policy is required to be conducted by means of secular laws alone and is therefore kept strictly separate from religious beliefs. States following the French example relegate religion, in theory at least, to the private sphere and oppose an inclusion of religion in State law and administration. The Turkish system, on the other hand, combines this theoretical separation with the exercise of considerable support, control and influence over the workings of the majority religion – Sunni Islam. A second model, by contrast, accepts institutional links between State and religion, such as the arrangement in England between the Church of England and the State. The third model is the concordat model in place in Italy, Germany and Spain. In these countries, the State has signed an agreement with some religions, but this does not mean that public authorities ignore other religions: significant minorities may also be recognised and/or offered certain specific accommodations. A fourth model combines non-establishment with conditional (limited) legal, administrative and/or political pluralism. A State may support religions, but should it decide to do so, it must beware of favouring one religion over another. Countries like Belgium and the Netherlands fall into this last category, but there are differences: whereas Belgium has a system of funding in place benefitting the recognised religions, the

3 Regarding this choice, one that is quite recent in the history of democratic societies, see especially V Bader, *Secularism or Democracy? Associational Governance of Religious Diversity* (Amsterdam University Press 2007); A Dierkens and J-P Schreiber (eds), *Laïcité et sécularisation dans l'Union Européenne* ('Problèmes d'Histoire des Religions', tome XVI, ed. de l'Université de Bruxelles 2006); J-C Monod, *Sécularisation et laïcité* ('Philosophies', PUF 2007); L Zucca, *A Secular Europe: Law and Religion in the European Constitutional Landscape* (OUP 2012).

4 See esp. G Robbers (ed), *State and Church in the European Union* (Nomos 2005); European Consortium for Church–State Research, *Church and State in Europe. State Financial Support. Religion and the School* (Giuffrè 1992); S Knights, *Freedom of Religion, Minorities and the Law* (OUP 2007) 4.

Netherlands has no such official recognition. Moreover, in the Netherlands, the monarchy has been tied to the Protestant Church, though there is no State church (since 1815). Bulgaria is even more divergent, since its new constitution declares Eastern Orthodoxy to be the 'traditional' religion of the country (some have thus argued this is more in line with establishment). It is important to note that non-institutional links and engagements with religious communities (funding, support, dialogue) are the rule rather than the exception in most States.

1.2 Between EU Competence and EU Relevance

Before discussing the main findings of the RELIGARE project, it may be helpful to bear in mind the legislative framework put in place at the EU level, as well as a number of recent initiatives that were (or are being) taken by the EU authorities with regard to combating discrimination on the grounds of religion or belief.

The EU is addressing problems linked with discrimination on the grounds of religion and belief in at least three ways. First, there is the legislative framework put in place at the EU level to combat discrimination on the grounds of religion or belief in the area of employment and occupation. Article 10 of the Treaty on the Functioning of the European Union (TFEU) requires that the EU shall 'aim to combat discrimination' based on religion or belief (among other grounds) 'in defining and implementing its policies and activities'. Article 19 TFEU enables the Union to take appropriate action to combat discrimination based on religion or belief, among other grounds. One such action has been to approve and effectively apply the Framework Employment Directive,[5] which prohibits discrimination on the grounds of religion or belief in employment, occupation and vocational training. Another legislative action has been the directive (still pending) proposed by the European Commission known as the Horizontal Directive,[6] which aims to extend the scope of anti-discrimination to fields beyond the labour market. Following calls by the European Parliament and various civil society actors for the expansion of EU law protecting against discrimination, and after an elaborate consultation process,[7] the European Commission submitted the Proposal for the Directive on 2 July 2008.[8] Bearing in mind the political reality, and the fact that the Horizontal Directive may not – at least in the foreseeable future – be adopted, the RELIGARE research project has nonetheless taken a particular look at the text of the directive, in particular at the provisions regarding protected grounds which may affect the rights and duties of religious or philosophically motivated individuals and groups (for example, prohibition of discrimination on the basis of sexual orientation).[9] We will revisit this in section 3 below.

Second, among the action(s) and programmes to combat discrimination on the grounds of religion or belief, the following publications and resources have been produced (and also proven to be of particular relevance for the purposes of the RELIGARE research project):

1. In 2011, Equinet, the European network of equality bodies, published *Equality Law in Practice: A Question of Faith – Religion and Belief in Europe*.[10] This examines cases of religious discrimination and freedom of religion under Article 9 ECHR.

5 Council Directive 2000/78/EC of 27 November 2000 establishing a general framework for equal treatment in employment and occupation.

6 'Proposal for a Council Directive on Implementing Equal Treatment between Persons Irrespective of Religion or Belief, Disability, Age or Sexual Orientation', COM(2008) 426 final, Brussels, 2 July 2008.

7 Explanatory memorandum, COM(2008) 426 final, 3.

8 'Proposal for a Council Directive on Implementing Equal Treatment between Persons Irrespective of Religion or Belief, Disability, Age or Sexual Orientation' and explanatory memorandum, COM(2008) 426 final, 2 July 2008 <http://eur-lex.europa.eu/LexUriServ/LexUriServ.do?uri=COM:2008:0426:FIN:EN:PDF> accessed June 2014; see also Commission of the European Communities, 'Commission Staff Working Document accompanying the Proposal for a Council Directive on Implementing Equal Treatment between Persons Irrespective of Religion or Belief, Disability, Age or Sexual Orientation', SEC(2008) 2180, 2 July 2008 <http://register.consilium.europa.eu/pdf/en/08/st11/st11531-ad01.en08.pdf> accessed June 2014.

9 Even though the provision regarding disability accommodation or age discrimination could raise tensions, these will be not treated here, as they are not common or specific to the situation of religiously motivated entrepreneurs or companies with a religious ethos.

10 See <www.equineteurope.org/Equality-Law-in-Practice-Religion> accessed June 2014.

2. The overview prepared by the European Network of Legal Experts and published in 2011 in the *European Anti-Discrimination Law Review*.[11] The article reviews 10 years of case law on discrimination on the grounds of religion or belief and other grounds.
3. Also in 2011, the European Network Against Racism (ENAR) published a report entitled *Reasonable Accommodation of Cultural Diversity in the Workplace*.[12] The document defines reasonable accommodation as 'an adjustment made in a system to accommodate or make fair the same system for an individual, based on a proven need'.
4. The Network of Socio-Economic Experts in the Anti-Discrimination Field, funded by the European Commission, is currently preparing reports (at the Member State and European levels) on discrimination on the grounds of religion or belief. These reports will have a particular focus on employment and education.
5. Recently, the Directorate-General for Internal Policies (Department C: Citizens' Rights and Constitutional Affairs) issued a study entitled *Religious Practice and Observance in the EU Member States*. The study highlights 'present sources of conflict, … best practices and put[s] forward recommendations to promote both religious practice and observance and the respect of human rights'.[13]

This is just a selection, but what all these publications demonstrate is the growing interest on the part of various actors, including the EU, in understanding and combating discrimination on the grounds of religion and belief.

Third, one must not lose sight of Article 17 TFEU, which states:

> 1. The Union respects and does not prejudice the status under national law of churches and religious associations or communities in the Member States. 2. The Union equally respects the status under national law of philosophical and non-confessional organisations. 3. Recognising their identity and their specific contribution, the Union shall maintain an open, transparent and regular dialogue with these churches and organisations.

The third subsection of Article 17 TFEU requires specific action by the Union. In practice, this action is now in the hands of the President of the Commission, specifically his Bureau of European Policy Advisers (BEPA),[14] which acts under the President's authority.[15] The RELIGARE findings suggest that a number of the issues investigated may have an impact on all three subsections of Article 17. Religion and belief indeed involve, if not directly then indirectly, many fields of EU competence. They are listed below, in the section on the potential impact of the RELIGARE research project. Since the Commission can be expected to act as a monitor of the implementation of EU law, nothing prevents it from taking a more forward-thinking approach in its next Action Programme.[16]

1.3 Normative Framework: 'Inclusive State Neutrality' and 'Justice as Even-Handedness'

Two core principles are enshrined in the constitutions of the various States of Europe as well as in international human rights law: (1) freedom of thought, conscience and religion and (2) equality or the right to non-

11 *European Anti-Discrimination Law Review* (2011) 12 <http://ec.europa.eu/justice/discrimination/files/antidiscrimination_law_review_12_en.pdf> accessed June 2014.

12 See <http://cms.horus.be/files/99935/MediaArchive/publications/3rd%20Adhoc_report_FINAL.pdf> accessed June 2014.

13 The study is available online at <www.europarl.europa.eu/studies> accessed June 2014.

14 Established in 2004; see <http://ec.europa.eu/bepa/index_en.htm> accessed June 2014. The Bureau is the heir to the Group of Policy Advisers (GOPA) and before that the Forward Studies Unit (FSU), which together cover the period 1989–2004.

15 It has an Outreach team and an Analysis team that carry out BEPA's current Action Programme (2010–2014) <http://ec.europa.eu/bepa/pdf/about_pdf_see_also/action_programme.pdf> accessed June 2014. A special unit in Outreach is responsible for focusing on subsection 3 within the general context of European and global outreach.

16 In its 2006 Annual Activity Report (9), BEPA underscored the importance of an agenda that is future oriented: 'The BEPA privileges issues that have a strategic and/or structural cross-cutting nature, and concentrates on forward-looking analysis in the early stages of the policy planning cycle and on the development of policy options for consideration'; see <http://ec.europa.eu/atwork/synthesis/aar/aar2006/doc/bepa_aar.pdf> accessed 30 June 2014.

discrimination, including on grounds of religion or belief. The ideal that the EU itself stands for in this regard is formulated in Article 2 TFEU as follows:

> The Union is founded on the values of respect for human dignity, freedom, democracy, equality, the rule of law and respect for human rights, including the rights of persons belonging to minorities. These values are common to the Member States in a society in which pluralism, non-discrimination, tolerance, justice, solidarity and equality between women and men prevail.

Article 10 (ex Art. 13) TFEU further reinforces this principle: 'In defining and implementing its policies and activities, the Union shall aim to combat discrimination based on sex, racial or ethnic origin, religion or belief, disability, age or sexual orientation.'[17]

In assessing the various ways in which the 10 countries under scrutiny handle issues that relate to freedom of religion and belief and non-discrimination, the *RELIGARE researchers propose two yardsticks: 'inclusive State neutrality' and 'justice as even-handedness'.* 'Inclusive State neutrality' rejects a strict separation and 'strict neutrality' between the State and any religions or secular beliefs insofar as those positions could be interpreted as public hostility towards churches/religious communities and/or secular values. Experience shows that it is impossible to rigidly uphold a strict separation between the State and religion and a strict neutrality towards religion and belief. Experience also indicates that separation can be used to exclude, willingly or unintentionally, vulnerable minorities who are seen as 'outsiders'. Strict neutrality, when it takes on an ideological dimension, risks entering into competition with other ideas or systems – including religions – with claims on the public space. Inclusive State neutrality, on the other hand, offers an overarching framework for 'managing' competing claims on the public space, including those of religions and beliefs, in a way that recognises their roles and their right to make claims, while also refusing to favour one over another. The notion of inclusivity therefore serves as a guide to an equal opportunities policy, which within the framework of contemporary constitutional democracies includes equality of treatment of all individuals based on the principle of equal respect of human rights, civil liberties and social and economic rights. Inclusivity thereby challenges not only a strict State neutrality but also a strict equality and other strict standards that are in practice unachievable in the current state of affairs. For example, what is *strict equal treatment* of two religious communities, one with millions of followers and a well-established presence and the second counting mere hundreds of individuals, often newcomers, in a country?

Justice understood as 'even-handedness' further builds on this concept and recognises the legitimacy of active policies towards religion and belief, as long as they are applied in an *inclusive* way. The related idea of *equidistance* to be respected by the State towards different religions and beliefs under its jurisdiction connotes a certain hands-off attitude. From the perspective of inclusive even-handedness, diversity is an integral part of people's right to participation in society. Beliefs and practices are thus not seen as an obstacle, and neither are they seen as static. In fact, they may change over time depending on the circumstances (for example, mainstream or minority practices; conversion; revival of some traditions and interpretations, and so on). 'Inclusive State neutrality' and 'justice as even-handedness', taken together, mean that the State's policy should be fair to all in granting recognition to religions, beliefs and practices; the principle is respect, with any limits placed only by way of an exception, for example for the protection of the fundamental rights of others in accordance with the case law of the ECtHR.

The data collected within the framework of the RELIGARE research project offer various concrete illustrations of what these two yardsticks, in combination, can mean in practice: the purpose in using them is to develop a more substantive understanding of equality, one which improves inclusivity in practice. One might object that since, ultimately, 'inclusive State neutrality' and 'justice as even-handedness'[18] pertain primarily to the State–citizen relationship, it is therefore difficult to adapt them completely to 'horizontal relationships' between private persons. In private relationships, one relies on the prohibition against discrimination and

17 See also Article 21 EU Charter of Fundamental Rights.

18 Procedural even-handedness was also taken up by the Brighton ECHR Conference. See S Ouald Chaib and E Brems, 'Doing Minority Justice through Procedural Fairness: Face Veil Bans in Europe' (2013) 2 *Journal of Muslims in Europe* 1–26.

the protection of freedom of religion, which have become increasingly meaningful in recent years in the negotiation of such horizontal relationships. Yet in either case – State–citizen or private relationships – the underlying aim is inclusivity and, with it, the effort to render more transparent the grounds for the protection of freedom of religion and belief, taken in the broadest possible sense (that is, including secular beliefs) and to help fight discrimination and exclusion on these grounds as consistently as possible.

2. RELIGARE Key Findings

In this section, the main findings that have emerged from the RELIGARE research are briefly discussed. The presentation of each of the four areas of participation studied follows the same structure: after a summary of the key research findings, there follows a series of recommendations. The key insights and recommendations differ in various ways. These differences may be attributed to a number of factors, including the specificity of the challenges addressed in each of the areas, the existence of an EU legal framework and the prominence of the relevant challenges that emerged from the 155 sociological interviews conducted by the project team members. Underlying the entire project was the search for a balance between the protection of the freedom of religion and belief, on the one hand, and the principle of equal treatment and non-discrimination on the other, combined with an attempt to engage with the two yardsticks of 'inclusive State neutrality' and 'justice as even-handedness'.

2.1 Employment: Protecting the Freedom of Religion and Right to Equality of Employees and Employers in the Workplace

2.1.1 Religious diversity and the workplace – two clusters

The RELIGARE findings regarding the workplace can be divided into two clusters: the individual and the collective cluster. The individual cluster looks at a number of mechanisms that have been implemented in the workplace to protect and to various degrees accommodate (or not) religious or non-confessional beliefs, practices and identity. These mechanisms are mainly grounded in human rights reasoning and anti-discrimination legislation. They also include 'voluntary' good practices.

Under the *individual cluster*, the distinction was made between discrimination cases *sensu stricto* (dismissal because of religious affiliation[19]), and various accommodation cases involving private employees and civil servants:

1. conflicts or requests relating to religious dress (including the wearing of turbans and headscarves, not cutting hair, and so on) in both front-office and back-office positions;
2. requests motivated by a need to reconcile conflicting religious time and working time obligations;
3. requests for exemptions or alterations of particular job duties or circumstances, including socialising customs;
4. requests to use certain (often already existing) facilities or space, typically for prayer or meditation.[20]

Only some of these cases involve conflicts with other fundamental rights and can thus be regarded as 'hard cases'. 'Soft cases', where accommodations harm no compelling interests and are (nearly) cost free, have also been identified. Contrary to what one may think, even these 'soft cases' have not been unequivocally successful in court.[21]

19 One clear example of such discrimination is the so-called sect filter in place in Germany targeting Scientology cases.

20 For a more elaborate discussion and a list of illustrative cases from the RELIGARE templates, see K Alidadi, 'Reasonable Accommodations for Religion and Belief: Adding Value to Art. 9 ECHR and the European Union's Anti-Discrimination Approach to Employment?' (2012) 37 (6) *European Law Review* 693–715.

21 The recent *Eweida* case, as decided by British domestic courts, may be seen as such example where the request to wear a religious symbol in the workplace was denied even when there were no important conflicting interests. In this sense, *Eweida* differed from the three other British cases – *Chaplin*, *Ladele* and *McFarlane* – that also came before the European Court and were decided in the same decision: see *Eweida and Others v the United Kingdom* [2013], 37.

With regard to religious dress and symbols, the main issue is generally the Islamic headscarf (and to a lesser extent, the Sikh turban). Noticeably, most instances identified from the data relate to front-office workers (for example, cashiers, bus drivers and also – in the public sector – teachers). This points to the fact that the *visibility* of distinctive religious dress is regarded as problematic by many private sector employers (the same can be said for public sectors that regulate the dress of public school teachers). The case law, combined with the sociological country reports, confirm a pattern whereby religiously distinct workers are routed to the back office, a tendency that may be symptomatic of a European discomfort with public statements of religious commitment.

In conflicts between religious duties or observances and working time, objections to accommodation are often justified on the grounds that formal equal treatment is sufficient. Yet those who raise such objections tend to ignore the fact that, for example, the organisation of working time in Europe adheres to a calendar strongly inspired by the dominant religions, with only a few instances of structural accommodation for minority groups. In this context, maintaining a regime of formal (or strict) equal treatment under a non-neutral standard (in the sense of being inspired by a dominant religious tradition which it privileges) may turn out to be discriminatory.

The RELIGARE findings further point to a wide variety of issues such as workers refusing to perform certain job functions (registering same-sex partnerships, handling alcohol or pork), refusing to adhere to dominant socialising customs (for example shaking hands with people of the opposite sex), challenging the position of women in managerial positions in the workplace, and seeking to be excused from parties at work, among others. In the RELIGARE research the focus has been on 'hard cases' where religious freedom appears to conflict with gender equality, equal treatment of sexual minorities, and so on. In the sociological interviews, the overwhelming consensus among respondents (including, notably, secular respondents) was that in the workplace employers should try to accommodate the religious practices of employees, but not all agreed that a duty to do so should be enshrined in law.

Under the *collective cluster*, the following were addressed:

1. hiring and dismissal practices involving the 'religious ethos' exception (Article 4.2 Directive 2000/78/EC);
2. balancing job requirements with employees' privacy and family rights.

With regard to faith-based employers, there are two main issues to be mentioned. First, there are tensions between the claims of collective autonomy and the rights of individual workers. In this regard, 'more protection' for one translates into more restrictive rights for the other. In order to determine the appropriate response, one must therefore look at broader societal goals, for example greater leniency in the area of autonomy rights will limit access and inclusion.

Second, the current legal framework with a limited exemption for religious ethos companies has created misunderstandings and complexities of its own. This is an area where the legal framework could be fine-tuned and/or good practices in the national approaches could be helpful to other Member States struggling with similar issues.

2.1.2 Two relevant legal frameworks

Two legal frameworks are relevant when it comes to the protection of religion and belief in the workplace: the human rights framework and the non-discrimination framework. The first has been the purview of the European Convention on Human Rights and the European Court of Human Rights in Strasbourg, while the EU has taken the lead in formulating non-discrimination standards under a series of directives, in particular EU Directive 2000/78/EC, in the area of employment, occupation and vocational training. The interaction between these two frameworks is reciprocal and complex: they are sometimes complementary in their operations, at other times they find themselves in tension.[22]

---

22 L Vickers, 'Freedom of Religion and Belief, Article 9 and the EU Equality Directive: Living Together in Perfect Harmony' in F Dorssemont, K Lörcher and I Schömann (eds), *The European Convention on Human Rights and the Employment Relation* (Hart 2013) 1–25.

The RELIGARE data show that there are gaps in the existing legal protection that make it difficult adequately to address (even modest) claims for religious accommodation in Europe[23] and, in particular, that the tool of human rights 'allows for diversity only under certain limitations, thereby conditioning and at times even distorting these religious experiences based on interpretations that form, what some do not hesitate to call, the core of a (contentious) "Eurocentric approach". Freedom of religion derives its language and working categories from historical and dominant values.'[24] This is one of the reasons why the RELIGARE project makes a case for using the important additional tool of *legally enshrined reasonable accommodation on the basis of religion and belief in the workplace*. At the same time, it must be recognised that the two legal frameworks are not static but developing; thus the full potential of these instruments has arguably not been tapped. The proposal for a duty of reasonable accommodation, thus, should not be seen as a replacement of but rather a supplement to the protections in place.

With regard to the workplace, the RELIGARE data reveal various conceptions of 'equality', and the tensions between these conceptions and freedom and other values. More specifically, the idea of substantive equality may conflict with formal equal treatment: while under formal equality, the focus is on identical or similar treatment *irrespective* of particular personal characteristics, including religion, under substantive equality, the context-relevant religious or belief-based identities, beliefs and practices of employees sometimes *are* to be taken into account. This is a multifaceted exercise and entails:

- inclusiveness (full enjoyment of citizenship rights)
- redistribution (addressing the problematic socio-economic status of some ethno-religious communities)
- recognition (signal function)
- and symmetrical protection (procedural even-handedness applies to everyone, and is not conceptually limited to particular minorities)

Within this conception of equality there is a clear role for reasonable accommodation,[25] which questions the existing anti-discrimination paradigm. The idea behind reasonable accommodation is that 'by failing to accommodate, the characteristic can result in denying an individual equal employment opportunities'.[26] Therefore, 'Instead of requiring … people to conform to existing norms, the aim is to develop a concept of equality which requires (mutual) adaptation and change'.[27] In light of these normative choices, the mode of handling issues or conflicts (through judicial, legislative or regulatory means, or simply through the use of certain voluntary (good) practices) is not irrelevant. Soft measures should be complementary to more ambitious proposals for legislative change in a volatile environment.

2.1.3 Redefining the reasonable accommodation debate

The 200 national employment cases collected in this research point to the divergent approaches among Member States. For instance, the meaning of 'indirect discrimination' on the basis of religion or belief (and to what extent the prohibition against discrimination requires employers to offer reasonable adjustments) varies considerably despite the fact that all Member States must implement the Employment Equality Directive in an effective fashion. In the Dutch cases, the efforts of employers to look for alternative solutions to keep the employee on the job are taken into consideration. For instance, when the job application of a Muslim woman was refused by a call centre because the employer was of the opinion that the sound transition over the headset would be of lesser quality when worn over a headscarf (thus lowering the quality of the communication

23 Alidadi (n 20).

24 K Alidadi and M-C Foblets, 'Framing Multicultural Challenges in Freedom of Religion Terms: Limitations of Minimal Human Rights for Managing Religious Diversity in Europe' (2012) 39 (5) *Netherlands Quarterly of Human Rights* (*NQHR*) 388–416.

25 The concepts of reasonable accommodation and indirect discrimination may be seen as functional equivalents, but there are important differences.

26 L Waddington, 'Reasonable Accommodation' in D Schiek, L Waddington and M Bell (eds), *Cases, Materials and Text on National, Supranational and International Non-Discrimination Law* (Hart 2007) 629–756, 632.

27 S Fredman, 'Disability Equality: A Challenge to the Existing Anti-Discrimination Paradigm?' in A Lawson and C Gooding (eds), *Disability Rights in Europe: From Theory to Practice* (Hart 2005) 203.

between phone operator and customers), a cost-free alternative that would satisfy both employer and employee was available: the headset could be worn *under* the headscarf.[28] In contrast, in an employment dispute between a private employer and a saleswomen who sought to wear a headscarf on the job, a Belgian judge found it pointless to look into whether the parties considered a possible transfer to a 'back office position' since 'there exists no duty of reasonable accommodation'.[29] A recent German decision takes a similar approach to the Dutch cases. When a Muslim employee was dismissed from a supermarket because of his refusal to work with alcoholic drinks, the German Federal Labour Court held that the dismissal would be invalid if the employee could have been reassigned to other tasks (for example, transferred to the fresh food department).[30]

Labour issues related to the accommodation of religious practices in the workplace may also come up in the unemployment context. The Brussels Labour Court of Appeal in 2002 considered the case of a young Muslim teaching trainee who had started to work on a six-month internship contract. A few months into her contract she felt obliged to resign after the employer instituted the summer uniform earlier than expected. This uniform entailed wearing Bermuda shorts that revealed her calves, which the trainee felt would violate her Islamic duty of modesty in dress. And despite earlier verbal assurances that the winter uniform would be in place until her contract's end, the employer was not willing to make any adjustments for her. Her request for unemployment benefits was initially denied because she was considered to have voluntarily abandoned a suitable position without legitimate cause. The Court ruled in her favour, holding that she had a legitimate reason for resigning, as the position had become incompatible with her religious beliefs and thus unsuited to her.[31] The unemployment case reveals the consequences of exclusion from the workplace under a system which rejects any duty of reasonable accommodation to religious needs. Such refusal plays into the hands of employers who invoke grounds of cost considerations. However, our research shows that this approach not only pushes religious employees onto the unemployment line, but also fails to recognise that under this approach employees carry the burden disproportionately and that offering an existing employee some accommodation can also be to the employer's advantage (for example, someone familiar with and already trained in the company can remain a valued employee in an alternative position within the firm). In other words, it is not a zero-sum game.

To the extent that the debate on reasonable limits to accommodation is centred on the issue of 'cost' (economic or otherwise), either under the existing human rights and non-discrimination regimes or under a new form of protection, the RELIGARE team argues that the question needs to be redefined. One must also take into account the various (hard/soft) 'costs' to minorities and to the social welfare system. From the questions 'How much can it cost the employer?' and 'When is it (dis)proportionate for the distributive agent (employer) to carry the cost?', we should move to asking '*Who* should carry the various burdens?' and 'What is a fair distribution of burdens?', as well as 'Are there ways to reconcile various interests?' This approach provides an alternative way to consider the occurrence of religious 'claims'; in other words, we argue that the process of accommodation is always a two-way street and often the concessions made by the employees in question are not duly recognised.

There should be a genuine and meaningful right to freedom of religion, including for employees in the workplace.[32] It can further be argued that the collective aspect of freedom of religion requires a level of autonomy granted to churches and religiously oriented organisations, possibly justifying exemptions to general non-discriminatory hiring and dismissal practices. More questionable, however, are approaches to freedom of religion in the workplace that relegate religion to the private domain or hold that an employee can always resign from a 'voluntary position' in the event of a conflict between professional and religious commitments.

One particular challenge when it comes to the management of diversity in the workplace has to do with 'avoiding conflict' behaviour. Discomfort with issues of religion, and especially minority religion, may indeed lead to avoidance of confrontation, either by employees staying away from the workplace or by

28 ETC. no. 2006–215, 27 October 2006.

29 Labour Court of Appeal (4th chamber) no. 48.695, 15 January 2008.

30 Federal Labour Court of 24 February 2011, no. 2 AZR 636/09.

31 Brussels Labour Court of Appeal (7th Chamber) 17 October 2002.

32 In certain contexts, the freedom of conviction and belief is openly questioned and under threat (for example, debates in Belgium and in the Netherlands).

decision makers diluting the ban on discrimination on the basis of religion or belief. Pursuing protection often exposes contentious issues which in turn can lead to even more conflicts. The wish to avoid problems might then be a reason for upholding the status quo. The RELIGARE project argues that the idea of inclusiveness should not be seen as a way to 'contain' minorities and those who do not conform to the prevailing workplace standards. The idea is, rather, to give individuals adequate room to reconcile their various identities and commitments. Certainly a degree of adaptation to the workplace setting is necessary, but the integration of a widely diverse workforce in Europe should not require an *assimilative approach* to religion in the workplace, where 'passing' and coping (or even hiding) are routine requirements for employment participation. Sometimes, confrontations are not only inevitable but also necessary on the way to achieving sustainable long-term justice.

Similarly, there is a real danger that initial 'good practices' of accommodating religious diversity in the longer term may trigger restrictive responses in society and in the case law, and may even lead to restrictive legislation. To give an example, in Denmark, a Muslim trainee was turned down because she did not comply with the dress code prevailing in the Danish department store Magasin. The Eastern High Court of Denmark in 2000 found that the negative treatment of the trainee based on her religious garb constituted indirect discrimination. In particular, the court noted that Magasin did not have a clear dress code. The ruling in this case initially led many companies to change their employee clothing policies to accommodate religious dress. However, the first case prompted a chain of Danish supermarkets, including a group called Føtex, to adopt a restrictive dress code and strictly enforce it. When a case against Føtex involving the claim of a Muslim employee who had been fired for wearing a headscarf on the job came before the Danish Supreme Court in 2005, the employee's claim was rejected. The reasons were formalistic: unlike the Magasin trainee, this employee had been aware of company policy regarding clothing and had signed a document saying that she would adhere to these rules. The Føtex case thus established the right of employers to set requirements for employee clothing without a need to make room for dress mandated by employees' religions, as long as these requirements applied to all employees in the same position, that is, as long as there was formal equality or strictly equal treatment.

There are both economic arguments (cost–benefit) and rights-based perspectives for accommodating religion and belief in the workplace; at the EU level both arguments are relevant. There are arguments at an individual level: freedom and accommodation would allow the self-realisation of workers belonging to minority religions who live in a society based on traditional Christian values, where they are already disadvantaged in various ways. There are also (macro)economic arguments reflecting the 'business case for diversity' (for example, the fact that the ageing European workforce cannot afford to place certain groups and individuals on stand-by, but must give them meaningful opportunities to engage, build skills and succeed).

2.1.4 Policy recommendations with regard to employment issues

Three main topics have been identified as relevant for concrete recommendations for future policy initiatives, particularly at the EU level:

1. enforcement of *human rights and equality legislation*, in particular as it relates to religion (for example through human rights commissions and/or equality bodies dealing with religious inequalities);
2. exemptions from anti-discrimination laws and labour laws that may have to be granted to religious employers or organisations;
3. *reasonable accommodation* for religious observances in the workplace.

Recommendations addressed to EU policymakers

1. Track the legislative and judicial implementation of the Employment Equality Directive, in particular through available national case law applying the prohibition against discrimination on the basis of religion or belief. Develop a coherent and clear policy to address national decisions or developments that (often inadvertently) undermine the purposes of an anti-discrimination policy.
2. Include *religious* and *philosophical* diversity more clearly in the EU's discourse on the value of diversity.

3. Adopt explicit strategies accommodating EU employees from diverse religious backgrounds, promoting such strategies in other public and private workplaces through example.
4. Create or encourage platforms for exchange of 'good business' practices in respect of granting requests for religious accommodation, and promote these national or cross-national practices across EU Member States.
5. Amend the Employment Equality Directive to add a right for public and private employees to request reasonable accommodation on the basis of religious beliefs, practices and observances, unless such accommodation would result in a demonstrated disproportionate distribution of burden or cost.

Recommendations addressed to national governments

1. Establish an advisory service (helpline) for employers and other decision makers who have questions about religious accommodations in various work settings, possibly operated by an equality body.
2. Encourage the inclusion of workers from diverse religious backgrounds in the workplace through a variety of policy tools such as encouraging and incentivising company diversity plans (including *religious* diversity) and addressing the legitimacy of company 'neutrality policies'.
3. Adopt national legislation that gives employees a legal right to request reasonable accommodation for religious beliefs, practices and observances in public and private workplaces, unless doing so would impose a demonstrably disproportionate burden or cost on employers.

Recommendations addressed to local governments, trade unions, equality bodies and NGOs

1. Demystify the concept of indirect discrimination using information campaigns and informational resources directed at employers and employees.
2. Privilege and proffer as good examples and 'best practice' voluntary accommodations that help employees reconcile professional and religious duties and do not cause any organisational hardship.
3. Educate labour market stakeholders and the general public on common religious practices and observances of religious minorities in the country.
4. Emphasise the unacceptability of disadvantaging, treating negatively or discriminating against employees on the basis of their religion or belief, as well as on the basis of their religious or philosophical practices and observances.

2.2 Family Law: Religiously Inspired Family Laws and Private International Law Systems within the Territory of the EU

There is no direct EU competence for regulating substantive family law, and hence this area of the law continues to be a competence of the Member States. While the legal background of most States under study reveals the long-standing influence of religious laws based on Christianity (the exception being Turkey), secularisation has been a dominant trend across all the countries. Nevertheless, all of them also display considerable cultural and religious specificities in their legal ordering of the family. In recent years, family law issues – which touch on the most intimate sphere of life – have become increasingly relevant from an EU perspective, not least because the differential treatment among Member States of identical family situations has considerable impact on the effective implementation of the fundamental right of free movement within the EU.[33] A major issue in this context is the significant differences that continue to exist among Member States with regard to same-sex marriages and non-registered partnerships.[34] Under EU law, recourse to arguments which prevent recognition within the internal legal order of situations created abroad, and which thus present an obstacle to the free movement of people, can only be acceptable if they are justified, proportionate, and if they are applied in a non-discriminatory way. Decisions of the ECJ have thus far demonstrated that even

33 See Article 45 of the EU Charter of Fundamental Rights and of the Directive 2004/38/EC, the 'Citizens' Directive'.

34 See J Borg-Barthet, 'The Principled Imperative to Recognise Same-Sex Unions in the EU' (2012) 8 (2) *Journal of Private International Law* 359–88.

comparatively less sensitive issues – with no links to religion or belief – such as the family name, fall under EU-granted freedoms and basic rights.[35]

As things stand, it is unclear how the impact of cross-border family law restrictions will be judged by EU bodies in the foreseeable future, not to mention Article 9 of the EU Charter of Fundamental Rights, the implications of the EU's membership in the ECHR (particularly regarding Articles 8 (right to family and private life) and 12 (right to marry and found a family)), or the possible implementation of the proposed Horizontal Directive. It should also be noted that through the application of the new Rome III Regulation on divorce and legal separation[36] and other initiatives to unify conflict of law norms relating to the family (for example Regulation No 650/2012 on matters of succession), family law will gain ever more relevance at the EU level.

2.2.1 Private international law (PIL): the bulk of the case law on religiously inspired family laws in Europe

Many of the court decisions collected within the framework of the RELIGARE project reveal that the main legal conflicts revolving around issues of religious diversity and the family that have arisen in recent decades relate to private international law (PIL) issues. In practice, interactions with religious or religiously inspired family laws are of particular concern to people who have settled in Europe on a more or less permanent basis, but who nevertheless retain connections with their countries of origin, where religious family laws apply. They thus look for solutions that would allow them to harmonise their family lives with their international status, that is, to be able to enjoy equal recognition under civil law (in Europe) and, where applicable, religiously inspired law (in the country of origin). They operate in a 'transnational'[37] legal field where they seek to articulate their (personal) status in such a way that it can be effectively received in both legal orders involved: on the one hand, that of the country of emigration (that is, of origin), and on the other hand, that of their habitual residence.[38] Today it seems that it is primarily Muslims who – in various parts of Europe – are faced with the difficulty of combining respect for the laws enacted by the (secular) State in their country of residence with the laws that apply in their country of origin. The values of the latter are often endowed, in their view, with particular legitimacy.[39] Among the issues most frequently submitted to the courts are: the prerequisites for legally valid marriages and their recognition if concluded under religious (and State) laws abroad; some specific contents like *dower* payment obligations; and divorce issues, in particular the recognition of foreign divorces performed according to religious laws and the limits of the applicability of such laws under PIL provisions. In the latter case, the invocation of public policy appears to be the most recurrent argument: religious laws are criticised for treating sexes or religions/beliefs unequally. The case law differs significantly, however, from country to country.

---

35 See, for example, the ECJ judgment of 14 October 2008 in *Grunkin and Paul v Standesamt Niebüll*, Case C-356/06.

36 Regulation No 1259/2010; see esp. M Fallon, 'Le nouveau droit du divorce international selon le règlement Rome III: une évolution tranquille' (2012) 2 *Revue trimestrielle de droit familial* 291–317.

37 F von Benda-Beckmann, K von Benda-Beckmann and A Griffiths (eds), *Mobile People, Mobile Law: Expanding Legal Relations in a Contracting World* (Ashgate 2005).

38 See M-C Foblets and J-Y Carlier, *Le Code marocain de la famille. Incidences au regard du droit international privé en Europe* (Bruylant 2005).

39 However, one should not assume a one-to-one relationship between the law of the State of origin and the person's own legal consciousness, which may vary. Empirical studies show that many in the generation after the first do not necessarily think the same way as first-generation migrants. See especially N Asayyad and M Castells (eds), *Muslim Europe or Euro-Islam: Politics, Culture, and Citizenship in the Age of Globalization* (Lexington Books 2002); S Benhabib, I Shapiro and D Petranovic (eds), *Identities, Affiliations and Allegiances* (CUP 2007); J Cesari and S McLoughlin (eds), *European Muslims and the Secular State* (Ashgate 2005); H Coward, JR Hinnells and RB Williams (eds), *The South Asian Religious Diaspora in Great Britain, Canada and the United States* (State University of New York Press 2000); A Erdemir, H Rittersberger-Tiliç, A Ergun and H Kahveci (eds), *Rethinking Global Migration: Practices, Policies, and Discourses in the European Neighbourhood* (KORA 2008); M Howard Ross (ed), *Culture and Belonging in Divided Societies: Contestation and Symbolic Landscapes* (University of Pennsylvania Press 2009); GF Levey and T Modood (eds), *Secularism, Religion and Multicultural Citizenship* (CUP 2009); J Nielsen and S Allievi (eds), *Muslim Networks and Transnational Communities in and across Europe* (Brill 2002); Y Yazbeck Haddad (ed), *Muslims in the West: From Sojourners to Citizens* (OUP 2002).

2.2.2 Beyond private international law

The research on issues relating to family life carried out within the framework of the RELIGARE project also takes a more forward-looking approach, going beyond the boundaries of private international law. This approach is of a more *exploratory* nature: what other potential approaches might there be when it comes to the treatment, in secular civil law, of personal statuses that are religious in nature? The RELIGARE research looked at the following three possible solutions:

1. the incorporation into domestic (civil) law of religious rules, taking the example of the marriage contract in particular;
2. the development of alternative dispute resolution (ADR) mechanisms for certain types of family disputes;
3. recourse to European Community intervention (EU law) in (international) family matters.[40]

The reason for supplementing the repertory of private international law cases with a more future-oriented approach that explores the three aforementioned possible approaches is the following: over the years, the demographic profile of European communities of immigrant origin has undergone profound change. The presence of these groups and communities is not only linked to immigration, but now represents a permanent settlement in the countries of habitual residence in Europe. In many cases, these residents hold the nationality of the country of residence, while also retaining the nationality of their country of origin.[41] These developments are changing the status quo: matters of personal status become, in such cases, first and foremost matters governed by domestic substantive law. Account is generally taken of religion when some form of incorporation of religious law(s) in the domestic State legal order is allowed, such as the recognition granted to marriages contracted (and registered) before religious authorities. One possible alternative would be to encourage spouses to enter into (secular) contractual arrangements under civil law, thereby allowing such arrangements to accommodate religious requirements. Certainly the debate is a sensitive one, in particular when it comes to alternative solutions that raise the prospect of calling into question arrangements that have emerged from historical developments such as the monopoly of State law in family affairs. Prenuptial arrangements that govern relations between spouses are a well-established practice in the United States and seem perfectly reconcilable with the requirements of both religious (in particular, Islamic) and civil law. There is no reason to fear the introduction of similar practices in Europe; they would not threaten the exclusivity of State law in family matters.

The second avenue explored by the RELIGARE project is to accept that religious minorities be entitled to a certain extent to handle their family disputes in the informal sphere before bodies of their own choice, and in their own way. If such bodies are very carefully organised and create neither new forms of discrimination nor unjustified privileges for some groups only, their work may hold some helpful prospects. This may be the case, in particular, with individuals who have become full-fledged citizens of their country of residence and are thus bound by its legal system, yet nevertheless keep placing that system alongside religious norms that are reflected in practices and traditions. Admittedly, there is much contestation about the issue of religious ADR in particular.[42] However, it may be worth the effort to further assess the pros and cons of ADR in family matters, and while so doing to give particular attention to the experience of countries where ADR is increasingly accepted in religious contexts as well.[43]

40 On the pros and cons of this recourse, see, among others, J Meeusen, M Pertegas, G Straetmans and F Swennen (eds), *International Family Law for the European Union* (Intersentia 2007).

41 M Verwilghen, 'Conflits de nationalités. Plurinationalité et apatridie' (1999) 277 (II), *RCADI*. For an analysis of multiple nationality among persons from Islamic countries, see K El Geddawy, *Relations entre systèmes confessionnel et laïque en droit international privé* (Dalloz, Bibliothèque de droit international privé 1971); T Faist (ed), *Dual Citizenship in Europe: From Nationhood to Societal Integration* (Ashgate 2007).

42 On Canada, see AC Korteweg and JA Selby (eds), *Debating Sharia: Islam, Gender Politics and Family Law Arbitration* (University of Toronto Press 2012). For the UK, see the Arbitration and Mediation Services (Equality) Bill, which had its second reading in the House of Lords on 19 October 2012. That legislation seeks to secure that shariah bodies make decisions in compliance with, inter alia, the Equality Act 2010.

43 *AI v MT* [2013] EWHC 100 (Fam) concerning an award given by a New York *Beth Din* recognised by an English court. Canadian and British legislation already presupposes some kind of informal divorce process among Jews.

The third line of thought that calls for EU action is connected to the diverse forms of treatment that religious personal statuses receive in the different PIL systems of the Member States. The research conducted in the course of the RELIGARE project reveals important differences in the way traditions such as arranged marriages, polygamy and dissolution of marriage through repudiation are treated in the national legal orders of the Member States.[44] Institutions or traditions that run counter to individual autonomy and gender equality are in most cases refused any form of recognition, while in some cases mitigating circumstances may permit finding a viable solution. The disparate approaches to these issues constitute a true challenge from the point of view of EU law, since in practice this state of affairs can give rise to 'limping situations', whereby a situation lawful in one country is not recognised as such in another and thus presents a serious hindrance to the free movement of people within the Community. The aforementioned decision of the ECJ in the *Grunkin and Paul* case (n 35) may serve as an illustration here.

2.2.3 Policy recommendations with regard to family issues

Three observations form the basis for the recommendations below. First, the RELIGARE data show a widespread lack of sound legal information on the meaning and the role of religious family laws not only among minorities in Europe, but also among lawyers, judges and politicians. Second, the starting point for elaborating new approaches to religious family laws should preferably be the existing legal frameworks and their main characteristics. Third, there is no specific EU competence for regulating family law, thus the RELIGARE recommendations below include, to a great extent, *informal* initiatives and recommendations.

Recommendations with regard to PIL family issues

1. The Commission should assess the extent to which the intersection of religion and family law constitutes, in practice, barriers in the implementation of the Citizens' Directive (2004/38/EC), with a focus on the implications of these restrictions for the principle of non-discrimination, sufficient legal certainty and proportionality.
2. Courts and administrations often lack the means to thoroughly interpret foreign family laws and the way these laws are concretely interpreted and applied in the country of origin. Institutions for professional education and databases of case law and of foreign family laws (and their concrete application) should be established on an EU level, and better coordination of the different approaches is necessary.
3. The EU should encourage and develop further efforts towards mutual recognition of family law decisions by administrations and courts in all Member States. This can be achieved by either unifying PIL norms according to the Rome III model or by developing common standards regarding the scope and limits of the application of public policy against foreign norms. Unless further measures are taken at the EU level, even if only on an informal basis (for example, via information, cooperation or education), it is likely that the low level of legal coherence within the EU today will continue to prevent an increasing number of EU citizens from making use of their basic right to move freely within the EU. This situation clashes with the EU's international reputation for implementing human rights standards in an efficient and neutral way. In its negotiations with third countries, the EU's credibility when it comes to defending and advertising such standards is permanently at stake.
4. EU-wide uniform standards should be developed regarding the application of foreign religiously inspired norms or decisions delivered abroad under such norms. The traditional approach of examining only the result of the application of foreign norms – instead of (re)examining the norms themselves thoroughly – grants more stability (and also international harmony) in family relations and legal security for the parties irrespective of their actual residence. A careful contextual appreciation of each case involves three steps: first, the foreign institution must be evaluated on the basis of *reliable information*; second, it must be *compared to other institutions of the law of the land*

44 For an illustration, see M Fallon and J Erauw, *La nouvelle loi sur le droit international privé belge. La loi du 16 juillet 2004* (Kluwer 2004); J-Y Carlier, M Fallon and B Martin-Bosly, *Code de droit international privé* (Bruylant 2008); R Mehdi, W Menski and JS Nielsen (eds), *Interpreting Divorce Law in Islam* (DJØF 2012).

in its relevant elements, distributing rights and duties between the parties involved; third, it must be clarified whether and to what extent the parties are entitled to waive certain rights voluntarily (by using dispositive law) in the event of differences between the requirements of the legal systems involved, provided no mandatory State protection governed by mandatory legal rules, including *ordre public*, is at stake.

5. Awareness of the fact that European family law systems derive from a Christian background, despite the fact that they have been translated into secular forms, should be increased. Thus, specific needs of new religious minorities should be appropriately addressed, with the aim of helping to maintain the balance: whereas the application of the public policy exception in PIL is meant to meet the requirements of human rights and their high standards of protection, irrespective of the concrete situation of the parties involved, sustainable solutions – including for families with a religious minority background – should be given priority under the applicable law. This may mean, under certain conditions, recognition of decisions delivered in the countries of origin of couples or litigants from migrant or religious minority backgrounds. In particular, initiatives to further *coordinate* the recognition of divorces under foreign (religious) laws are recommended.
6. Initiatives to increase mutual cross-border recognition of State court (or administrative) decisions should be fostered, enabling parties to regulate their family relations in a harmonious way, including across borders if they wish to do so. In particular, the potential benefits to be drawn from *optio iuris* (choice of State law determined by contract) in family relations[45] (that is, by encouraging parties to make use of their autonomy, in particular with regard to marriage contracts) should be further assessed.
7. Legal practitioners (judges, State officials and lawyers in general) should be offered professional training in techniques of PIL and accommodation available within existing law, as well as on the contents of religiously inspired foreign legal institutions. Application of foreign religious laws should not be rejected automatically on the assumption that 'secular courts are not entitled to enter into religion'.[46] Foreign family laws, provided they are the formal or official law of a country, regardless of whether they are secular or religious, should indeed be treated according to the common principles of PIL.
8. Databases of case law and good practices for professional education on an EU level should be established; they should include information on foreign, religiously inspired laws, in particular those laws that conflict with domestic law, and on the way they are applied in the country of origin.[47]
9. The use of legal experts in courts should be extended where necessary (for example in arranging settlements).
10. Customers/litigants/disputants: individuals – in particular those with migrant backgrounds – should be appropriately informed of the existing legal procedures as well as of the contents and orientation of the law in the country of their habitual residence.
11. Cooperation with religious institutions: joint initiatives should be taken by State authorities and religious organisations or persons with a view to taking – to the extent possible – an unequivocal stand that some relevant aspects of religious (family) law(s) are in conflict with European family law, making it clear that in such cases the law of the country of residence has precedence in principle. Such a stand would necessitate greater outreach on the part of the State to these institutions without necessarily seeking to control them; 'dialogue' is the key word here.

45 cf F Swennen, 'Family (Self-)Governance at the Boundaries of a Privatized Family Law' (2011) 19 (2) *European Review of Private Law* 209–23.

46 This is a well-established but possibly misleading term. In some cases Western courts have wrongly refused to apply foreign law taken to be religious and thus not applicable by a secular institution, for example, concerning the Iranian law on divorce (Berlin Court of Appeals, *IPrax* 2000, 126; reversed by the German Federal Supreme Court, *FamRZ* (2004), 1952). It should be noted that any law regulating worldly affairs is secular 'law' when applied by State institutions, irrespective of possible religious impact.

47 If the agreement by the husband is not documented, a judicial divorce might be not recognised, for example, in Iran; thus, if the family is travelling to Iran, the husband could still claim to be married, preventing the (divorced) wife from leaving the country.

Recommendations with regard to domestic legal institutions and ADR According to contemporary European legal understanding, family law issues are perceived as private matters, but the State is entitled and even obliged to intervene in case of violation of the weaker party's interests (not restricted to domestic violence). Therefore:

1. ADR mechanisms should meet the standards of impartiality and professionalism. Access to State courts should remain open at all times. This condition is equally true for religious ADR mechanisms and institutions. All kinds of groups – including non-faith-based groups – should be entitled to set up their own ADR mechanisms within the limits set by the procedural laws of the State.
2. The main goal of allowing ADR mechanisms to operate in family matters should be to strengthen and improve acceptance of the principles of the legal order and access to its mechanisms. Free choice to regulate one's private matters has to be respected, and the State should not intervene there, as long as there is mutual respect for the rights of the persons involved and decisions are made professionally and free of undue pressure.
3. There are profoundly different convictions as to the acceptance of marriages registered by religious institutions but having civil legal effects. Some Member States maintain a well-established system of such registrations (for example, Denmark, Spain and the UK), whereas others, like France and Germany, would reject these for legal-historical reasons. Thus, any recommendations must take such differences into account. As already mentioned above, in all Member States, public information about the prerequisites for legally valid marriages should be increased. Norms simply prohibiting exclusively religious marriages do not appear to solve the whole problem of legally invalid religious marriages.
4. The legal prerequisites for entering into a legally valid marriage – whether civil or religious – should be much clearer. As a matter of fact, religious marriages as such have no legal effects under the family law rules of most Member States. There are countries (Italy and Spain, for example) where religious marriages can have civil effects provided they respect all the conditions required for performing a civil marriage. Yet where religious organisations are authorised to register marriages under the law of the State, as is the case for England and Wales, they must ensure that the couples they marry meet the necessary civil requirements so that they do not produce marriages that are invalid under civil law. Otherwise, parties who thought they were validly married may find themselves in the position of not being able to claim their rights in State courts and before the public authorities.[48] It is thus strongly recommended that the legal prerequisites for a valid marriage (civil and religious) be made clear in *all* EU Member States.
5. Legislatures in the Member States should be encouraged to draw clear legal lines between desirable and non-desirable forms of ADR. Insofar as Member States wish to keep the monopoly on family law issues with State courts and institutions, which is also justified, they should take the appropriate measures to guarantee access to these institutions to everyone efficiently. These involve:
   i. providing information about access to State institutions and their functions, including information about the compatibility of State law and religious convictions, for example in marriage issues;
   ii. providing effective legal aid for those in need;
   iii. increasing cultural sensitivity on the part of State institutions concerning the religious and cultural needs of minorities, which are less well known among the religious or cultural majority, and trying to find ways for reasonable accommodation within the framework of the existing law and its institutions;[49]
   iv. making available information about the formal and material legal prerequisites to enter into a legally valid marriage and about the consequences of marriages that are not contracted in the proper civil

48 See the RELIGARE working paper on ADR <www.religareproject.eu/content/alternative-dispute-resolution-europe-under-auspices-religious-norms> accessed June 2014.

49 These recommendations have already been accepted by a working group on ADR and 'parallel justice' established by the Bavarian Ministry of Justice in 2012 (chair: M Rohe). They are about to be published by the Ministry and to be discussed by the German conference of Ministries of Justice.

form and are thus considered legally invalid. In countries where the registration of legally valid marriages by religious institutions is permitted, the public authorities should ensure that religious institutions and the public are correctly informed of the legal prerequisites for such marriages. Cooperation with religious organisations can considerably increase the efficiency of such efforts.

2.3 Access to and Use of Public Spaces

2.3.1 Two thematic foci

The RELIGARE research on issues relating to the neutrality of the public space focused on two cases in particular: *religious dress codes* and *places of worship*. The empirical findings of the RELIGARE research with regard to public space issues show that the debates in the countries under scrutiny tend to revolve particularly around these two cases. These issues are prominent in the media and also in parliamentary debates, but it also appears that in the past few years a significant number of disputes have been settled through the courts.

2.3.1.1 Religious dress codes The RELIGARE data show that each of the 10 countries under scrutiny has to date followed a different route to regulating the question of religious dress codes.

Full-face veil Regarding the full-face veil, France[50] and Belgium[51] have adopted laws that prohibit appearing in public with one's face covered. In both cases the prohibition applies to the entire public space. At the opposite end of the spectrum is the UK, where the minister for immigration in 2010 dismissed any provision aimed at banning the *burqa* or *niqab* as 'unBritish'.[52] There are no legislative or administrative provisions forbidding the *burqa* or the *niqab* at the national or local level, nor are there any directives by professional organisations on this matter. A third route hinges on local law: the State abstains from outlawing the use of the full-face veil throughout its territory, but the ban may be introduced by mayors or other local authorities by means of administrative provisions. This is what happened in Spain[53] and, for a certain period, also in Italy.[54] A different approach is taken in Denmark, where, apart from a single piece of legislation prohibiting the wearing of religious or political symbols in court, there is no law forbidding the wearing of the full-face veil, nor are there any local administrative provisions outlawing its use. Instead, there is some case law and also a series of documents issued by professional bodies and government directives that supply guidelines for dealing with the most controversial cases. By these means, for example, it has been established that women wearing the *burqa* or *niqab* can ride public transport, but photo IDs require the identification of the bearer, and that schools and universities may (but are not obliged to) prohibit the full-face veil where it hinders non-verbal communication between students and teachers. In these and other cases a pragmatic and functional approach has been adopted. The full-face veil as such is not perceived as a garment that violates fundamental human rights, and thus the general attempt has been to find a solution that guarantees, as far as possible, women's right to wear the *burqa* or the *niqab*; only for functional reasons has the wearing of this garment been forbidden.

RELIGARE data indicate, however, that current debates on the full-face veil are frequently driven by an ideological approach that focuses on values and principles, claiming their general and undifferentiated application, but they fail to examine, case by case and within their own context, those situations where the

50 The Belgian Law of 1 June 2011 instituting a 'prohibition on wearing clothing that covers the face, or a large part of it' (*Loi visant à interdire le port de tout vêtement cachant totalement ou de manière principale le visage*) came into force on 13 July 2011. See E Brems, 'Doing Minority Justice through Procedural Fairness: Face Veil Bans in Europe' (2013) 2 *Journal of Muslims in Europe* 1–26.

51 *Handelingen* Vlaams Parlement 2011–2012, Commission C171, 20 March 2012, 48–55.

52 See <www.theguardian.com/uk/2010/jul/18/burqa-ban-unbritish-immigration-minister> accessed June 2014.

53 It must be noted that one of these local bans, issued by the municipality of Lleida, has been successfully appealed and was overturned by the Spanish Supreme Court (Tribunal Supremo decision of 6/2/2013, Recurso Casación 4118/2011, published on 28 February 2013, <www.ara.cat/societat/Sentencia-Uso-burka-Lleida_ARAFIL20130228_0001.pdf> accessed June 2014).

54 In the past, municipal acts have banned the wearing of the full-face veil in some municipalities, but the administrative courts and the Council of State declared them illegitimate. See S Pastorelli, 'Religious Dress Codes: The Italian Case' in S Ferrari and S Pastorelli (eds), *Religion in Public Spaces* (Ashgate 2012) 235–54.

full-face veil ban might clash with the principle of non-discriminatory access to and use of the common public space. The debate tends to be monopolised by, on the one hand, those who believe that the full-face veil – always and everywhere – offends women's dignity, public order, security and gender equality, and on the other hand, those who consider it a manifestation of faith, personal self-determination, freedom of expression and practice of religion that must be guaranteed without exception.

Based on the RELIGARE findings, which include the sociological reports, it appears that *the two yardsticks of 'inclusive State neutrality' and 'justice as even-handedness' would permit a less confrontational, more balanced way to tackle this issue*, namely by carefully assessing the different problems that the full-face veil can present to an orderly enjoyment of the common space. A general ban on wearing a full-face veil affects the accessibility of the common space, for women in particular. Yet it is a space where the right to move freely within the territory of a State is, in principle, granted to any person, and the scope for limitations is thus restricted (see, in this sense, the ECtHR decision in the *Ahmet Arslan v Turkey* case[55]). Evidently, there are situations where seeing the face of a person is necessary (when checking identity documents, for example), and there are also certain activities that can be hindered by a veil covering the whole face, such as when driving a car, and occasions when appearing with one's face covered can give rise to social alarm. In these and a limited number of other instances, it appears to be legitimate to prohibit the wearing of the full-face veil in common areas, based on a pragmatic rather than an ideological approach, that is, on the basis of a concrete examination of the situation that takes account of the rights of others to the enjoyment of the same common public space, and their right to free movement as well. In these cases it is not the symbolic meaning of the full-face veil (which varies from person to person and can never be ascertained with certainty) that is at stake, but rather the social difficulties it may cause. This functional approach allows for measures to be adopted that are proportionate to the practical problems raised by the wearing of the full-face veil and that also take account, as far as possible, of the individual's freedom of religion and expression. If there is evidence that wearing the full-face veil is not a matter of free choice but the consequence of, for example, an imposition by others, public authorities may be expected to prioritise the protection of individual freedom. Once this freedom is safeguarded, however, wearing clothes that are part of a religious practice or manifest a religious and cultural conviction cannot be limited in the public space as long as there is no evidence of infringement upon the right of others to freely move within that same space.

Religious symbols worn by teachers at school As far as religious symbols worn by teachers and students at school are concerned, a general prohibition is in force in French public schools.[56] In Belgium the trend is to follow the same approach. Some German federal states prohibit teachers from wearing religious symbols, but the prohibition does not apply to Christian symbols.[57]

Here again, an inclusive and even-handed approach would offer a more nuanced solution. A first step in the reasoning is to take it for granted that fostering tolerance and respect for pluralism is (or should be) one of the most important goals of the educational process in a context of pluralistic democracy. This goal can be reached only if teachers provide an education based on an impartial approach to the religious and philosophical convictions[58] of the students and their parents (see Article 2 of the First Protocol to ECHR), in order to prepare students to recognise the role played by religions and other beliefs and worldviews in individual and social life. At the same time, students should be shielded from any bias or false comparisons as well as from any ostentatious and/or imposed manifestation of religion or belief on the part of the teachers. In performing their work, teachers should be guaranteed the right to freedom of thought, conscience and

55 ECtHR, *Ahmet Arslan and Others v Turkey*, App no 41135/98 (23 February 2010).

56 'Loi 2004–28 du 15 mars 2004 encadrant, en application du principe de laïcité, le port des signes ou de tenues manifestant une appartenance religieuse dans les écoles, collèges et lycées publics' (15 March 2014) *Journal officiel de la République française*; 'Loi 2010–1192 du 11 octobre 2010 interdisant la dissimulation du visage dans l'espace public' (12 October 2010) *Journal officiel*.

57 Laws regarding the ban on religious dress for teachers are in force in a few of the German federal states; see S Fogel, 'Headscarves in German Public Schools: Religious Minorities are Welcome in Germany, Unless – God Forbid – they are Religious' (2006–2007) 51 *New York Law Review* 619–53.

58 'Religious and philosophical convictions' should be read in connection with the expression 'religion or belief' of Article 9 ECHR.

religion, and cannot be prevented from manifesting their religious or philosophical convictions unless these conflict with the school's secular character. However, these manifestations must respect the right of students and (depending on the students' age) of their parents not to be exposed to forms of indoctrination that violate their freedom of thought, conscience and religion.

Teachers can thus be prohibited from wearing religious symbols and clothing that, in a given context, might have an indoctrinating effect on students, provided that this prohibition is proportionate to the specific situation and is applied in a non-discriminatory manner. By way of a provisional conclusion and considering that each educational context has its own specificities, it appears sensible to adopt a case-by-case approach that refrains from applying the same rule to different situations. An even-handed approach offers more possibilities for taking into account the distinctive circumstances that have an impact on the delicate balancing of teachers' and students' rights. At the same time, such an approach requires some guidance to ensure that it offers the necessary legal certainty.

Religious symbols worn by students at school In the case of religious symbols worn by students at school, the reasoning is slightly different: manifesting one's religious or philosophical conviction through the wearing of symbols and religious items of clothing by students at school is an expression of the right to freedom of thought, conscience and religion granted by Article 9 ECHR. According to the ECtHR case law, such manifestations can be subjected only to the restrictions 'necessary in a democratic society in the interests of public safety, for the protection of public order, health or morals, or for the protection of the rights and freedoms of others' (Article 9 ECHR). As repeatedly affirmed by that Court, there is less potential for students to indoctrinate others than for teachers. The right to manifest one's religion or philosophical convictions through symbols and clothing should therefore be limited only when it represents a concrete danger to the principles of tolerance and mutual respect that are essential for any educational environment. Once again, each case has its own specificities that need careful (even-handed) consideration. Moreover, a general ban on religious symbols worn by students, though accepted by the ECtHR when the State's policy is to safeguard the secular character of its schools, may be problematic in light of another fundamental principle of the educational process, namely, pluralism. Justice understood as even-handedness requires that a general prohibition should be the last resort, to be used only in cases where other less restrictive means do not allow for an adequate solution. The arguments in favour of an inclusive case-by-case approach already mentioned in reference to teachers apply *a fortiori* in the case of students.

2.3.1.2 Places of worship Places of worship play a key role in the expression of any religion or belief. The RELIGARE research has addressed three sub-issues in particular: the construction and the opening of places of worship; the reassignment of former places of worship for other purposes; and the location as well as the rules and regulations that apply in the case of public and private burial grounds or cemeteries. The cross-country comparison indicates that although, in principle, all religious communities can expect to be treated equally (this applies explicitly to Belgium, Bulgaria, Italy, the Netherlands and Spain), in practice this is clearly not the case. In Turkey, for example, non-Sunni groups within Islam are not granted the treatment enjoyed by Sunni Muslims; in Italy, although the law is the same for all and does not distinguish between religions, in practice it is extremely difficult to open or build any type of religious monument that is not a Catholic church. In some cases formal procedural reasons are invoked to withhold administrative permission to build – protest by neighbours, sometimes accompanied by threats of violence (in Bulgaria, England and Wales), anticipation of excessive noise at night (Germany), and traffic congestion combined with a lack of parking space (France).

There are also important differences between national policies regarding the financing of places of worship. The Danish State supports the building of places of worship belonging to the State church (Lutheran). In Belgium, the government does not generally give financial support to the building of places of worship, but it does offer, to recognised religions, the right to such support for maintenance and renovations of their buildings. Bulgarian law allows the government to support the building of a place of worship, but when and how this is done is at the discretion of the local authorities. In France, the government may not in principle fund places of worship, but recent legislation allows local authorities to issue leases for places of worship, especially where the building in question is also used for other purposes (see also p. 37 below).

2.3.2 A key conceptual proposal: not one public space, but three kinds of public space

The data collected within the framework of the RELIGARE project on the different ways European States have opted to achieve the neutrality of the public space clearly indicate the intricacy of the question whether the public space can ever be neutral (from a religious or philosophical point of view).

The answer to this question depends on what one understands by 'neutral': if a neutral public space ought to be one that has no distinctive quality or characteristics, then the answer cannot be but negative. Public space, in all its various manifestations, has always had distinctive characteristics that derive from the history, culture and belief of the people who live in it. As religion is one of these characteristics, a public space cannot be expected to be entirely religiously neutral: even the most anti-religious States (for example Enver Hoxha's Albania) could not, in practice, build a public space totally devoid of religious characteristics. If, however, the term 'neutral' is used in the sense of 'having no preference', being even-handed, fair and impartial, the conclusion cannot be so clear-cut, and one needs to distinguish between the various possible meanings underlying the expression 'public space'; an understanding of all these meanings taken in combination allows for a more *accurate analysis of the comparative data.*

The RELIGARE team posit a new conceptual understanding that distinguishes between three different public spaces: common, political and institutional. These three types of public space need not necessarily be seen as physically or temporally separate; rather, they coexist and overlap to a considerable extent. A square, for example, is typically a public space that can be common, political and institutional at the same time, depending on the use made of it. The same applies to the school: it is a space that is common, political and institutional at the same time. With this consideration in mind, it is possible to differentiate some characteristics of these three dimensions of the public space.

1. Under this classification, the *common* space is understood as the physical space that people have to enter in order to meet their basic needs; in this sense, it is inescapable. This space is not accessed with the intention of participating in a political debate, but simply to get to and from work, for example, or to buy daily necessities. The communication process that takes place in this space is not primarily political. Of course, wearing a cross, a kippah or a turban may convey a message concerning the religious belief of an individual, even when that individual is doing his or her shopping. But the same kind of message can also be conveyed by his or her haircut, earring or tattoo, and there is no reason why religious symbols should be regulated more restrictively in such situations than other symbols. From a normative point of view, the *common* space must be kept as accessible as possible to avoid segregating in their homes people who feel bound to manifest their religion or belief in some way when entering the public space.
2. The *political* space in this schema can be understood as the space of debate and discussion where the public discourse takes shape. It should not be regarded only as a space of intellectual 'argumentation about the truth value of propositions', but more broadly as 'a realm of creativity and social imaginaries in which citizens give shared form to their lives together, a realm of exploration, experiment, and partial agreement';[59] it is the space where new 'normative worlds', as Robert Cover puts it, take shape.[60] It is frequently also a metaphorical space, although it can take the form of physical locations (Speaker's Corner in London, or a political rally in a square, for example). In order to perform its function of providing room for open and democratic debate, the political space should be free and pluralistic: the visible presence of different religions and beliefs in this area is indispensable to the pluralism on which a democratic society is based (as affirmed by the ECtHR's decision in *Metropolitan Church of Bessarabia v Moldova*, 2001).
3. Finally, the *institutional* public space can be understood as the place where binding deliberations that are compulsory for all are conducted (parliament, the law courts, public administration and so on). It is not only the space of debate and discussion, but the place of decisions that, once taken, have to be respected by everybody. A law court is not a TV talk show; a court delivers an enforceable judgment

59 C Calhoun, 'Afterword: Religion's Many Powers' in E Mendieta and J Vanantwerpen (eds), *The Power of Religion in the Public Sphere* (Columbia University Press 2011) 129.

60 R Cover, 'Violence and the World' (1985–1986) 95 *Yale LJ* 1601–29.

> that determines who is right and who is wrong. In order to gain the general respect and recognition that is required for the enforcement of such binding decisions, this space must not only be fair and impartial, it must also be perceived as such.

In the three public spaces identified above, individuals act in a different capacity according to the role they take or the task they are expected to perform in that space. A public school, for example, is attended by students and teachers. Once they have entered the school doors, students retain their private status, while teachers acquire a more public status. Consequently, when a student wears a headscarf she is manifesting her personal conviction or belonging; when the scarf is worn by a teacher, this private dimension cannot be dissociated from the public one. This role differentiation may help explain why the case law in most countries investigated within the framework of the RELIGARE project indicates greater willingness to accept a student's scarf than the scarf worn by a teacher. One speaks of the same space (the school), but seen through the lens of the various roles performed by the actors, one distinguishes two different groups of people who take different roles within that same space. Even-handedness implies that one takes a different position depending on the role and responsibility of the person(s) involved.

One can also look at the public space issue from an angle that is neither spatial nor personal, but *functional*. From this perspective, the notion of public service comes to the fore: the school or the hospital provides a public service, independently of whether it is a public or a private school or hospital. At present, the tide seems to be turning towards the expansion of public services rendered by private institutions (including in fields that were traditionally the reserve of the State, like security, management of prisons, and so on). From this functional point of view, new questions arise: are all public services, without distinction, to be provided in a 'neutral' way? When a religious or belief-oriented private institution provides a public service, is it obliged to give up its religious characteristics or beliefs?

The distinction between the three spaces, each with its own characteristics and uses, allows for the application of differentiated solutions to different situations. The typology also yields two yardsticks of equal treatment, through the combined tests of *inclusive State neutrality* and *justice as even-handedness*. By emphasising the diversity of spaces, the inclusivity test focuses not so much on the *substance* of religions or beliefs, but distinguishes instead between *modalities* of management of the public space, and it makes this management depend on the functions one particular space has within a particular context. By focusing on the various functions a particular space may have in a concrete situation, no actor in the public space is confined to a single identity. The aim is to include all parties (individuals) concerned through a careful examination of the characteristics of each situation placed in its own context. It is against this backdrop that a number of specific recommendations have emerged from the RELIGARE project.

2.3.3 Recommendations with regard to public spaces

2.3.3.1 Recommendations with regard to religious dress codes

1. *Combating discrimination.* Both the EU Commission and the Member States should assess whether the existing rules concerning the wearing of religious symbols or clothing by students and teachers in public schools respect the national provisions adopted pursuant to the proposed Horizontal Directive. While pursuing the discussions on the proposal for the Horizontal Directive, one relevant question to assess is whether the prohibition on wearing the full-face veil in public spaces and the provisions concerning the wearing of religious symbols by students in public schools that are in force in France and Belgium constitute a form of discrimination in light of Art. 2(2) of the proposed directive.[61]
2. *Providing guidance.* Drawing inspiration from best practices that have proven successful at national and local levels, the Commission should help disseminate information that can aid the public authorities of the EU Member States in addressing the issues of the full-face veil and of religious symbols worn by students and teachers at school in a way that is in compliance with ECHR norms and EU laws. EU Member States should also consider the possibility of establishing advisory bodies

---

61 See n 5.

at the local level, with the participation of different stakeholders, which would provide guidelines on the issue of religious symbols/clothing worn by students and teachers at school in a way that respects the specificities of each situation.

3. *Protecting women's freedom of choice.* EU Member States should assess the effectiveness of the existing legal frameworks aimed at protecting women against being forced to wear religious or special clothing and, where there may be such compulsion, increase the level of protection.
4. *Avoiding unnecessary prohibitions.* Legislatures should refrain from enacting a *general* prohibition preventing teachers from wearing religious symbols and clothing at school, provided it is possible to address the issue on a case-by-case (school-by-school) basis through the intervention of the school authorities. Authorities should limit the prohibition against students wearing symbols and clothing expressing their religious or philosophical convictions to situations where such restriction is strictly required to guarantee the carrying out of school activities and no reasonable accommodation of the religious needs of the student seems negotiable. In both cases, if the competent authorities deem that a general ban on religious symbols and clothing worn by teachers or students at school is required, this should be formulated in terms that are non-discriminatory and that place as few limits as possible on the freedom of thought, conscience and religion of students and teachers alike, as well as the right to education. Finally, EU Member States should refrain from introducing a general ban on the full-face veil in all public spaces, in particular by recourse to criminal law provisions, and should assess the suitability of limiting the ban on wearing the full-face veil only to those places and situations where seeing the face of an individual is required for security purposes or where public or professional requirements demand that civil servants wear religiously neutral attire or that their faces can be seen.

2.3.3.2 Recommendations with regard to places of worship

1. Government authorities should effectively apply the principle of equal treatment to the building and opening of places of worship. It is unacceptable that the discretionary powers of local authorities allow them to treat different religious groups differently when it comes to the acquisition or lease of a place of worship.
2. Religious communities are entitled to be treated even-handedly with respect to bell-ringing or calls to worship. Even-handedness also means that government authorities take into account all contextual factors, looking for a fair balance – preferably, through negotiation – between what is acceptable to impose on a neighbourhood and the requirements of the protection of religious freedom.
3. If a place of worship is no longer used for its initial purpose, it is recommended that the owner (most often the religious community concerned) be allowed to link the selling of the building to conditions governing its future use, and that these conditions be legally enforceable on the buyer and his or her successors.
4. Finally, it is recommended that legal steps be taken to ensure equal treatment of all religious groups as regards burial or cremation. Restrictions imposing serious constraints on the wishes of various religious communities concerning burial or cremation should be critically assessed: are they still justified in light of contemporary means of protecting public health?

2.4 State Support Mechanisms

The RELIGARE project has also investigated the issue of State support to religious and other communities of conviction, in particular the funding of clergy salaries and the financing of a number of core religious activities and institutions. Special attention has been paid to the funding of places of worship, the access to and funding of religious and philosophical broadcasting on public media channels, and the funding of training for religious leaders. Subsidies for charitable, educational or social activities under the guardianship or responsibility of religious or philosophical organisations have not been taken into account. Where religious institutions receive public subsidies for these activities, it is generally conceived of as remuneration for a public mission. Such 'secular' activities carried out by institutions or individuals sharing a common religious conviction therefore fall outside the scope of the RELIGARE research strictly speaking.

At first sight, the issue of public financing of religious and philosophical organisations seems remote from the competencies of the EU. Article 17(1) and (2) of the TFEU confirm this. Sociological and demographic changes in European societies mean, however, that the financing of religions and philosophical organisations poses a key challenge to constitutional arrangements and regulations of State support as they have been elaborated in the past in the internal legal order of the Member States. In order to assess the challenges that State support to religious groups (and occasionally also to secular organisations, as is the case for the humanist movement in Belgium and the Netherlands) actually poses to public policies, closer attention needs to be paid to the impact, in practice, of State support: who are these groups and is State support even-handedly distributed among them? Two recent developments that are characteristic of European societies appear of particular relevance here because they challenge policy and decision makers ever more pressingly in an increasingly diverse societal context: individualisation of lifestyles and personal convictions, and the steady increase of secularisation. They are reflected in policies of deregulation and privatisation which, in turn, result in the financing of religious groups being left to market forces and the private sphere.

The RELIGARE project undertook a comparative examination of the various regulations that apply in the countries under scrutiny. The method adopted has been an analysis in two steps. First, it distinguishes five models of State support to various religious groups,[62] paying special attention to certain injustices that are the consequence of a lack of adaptation (of the historical legislative framework in place) to recent socio-demographic developments in contemporary European societies. Secondly, the analysis looks towards the future: what models offer better alternatives, and is there a role for the EU in promoting such alternatives? In section 2.4.1 below, the focus is on the latter question: what alternatives to the existing models of State support could be developed and what role could the EU play in this? The comparative analysis of sociological data collected by the RELIGARE project shows increasing criticism of the historical models of State support. The criticism, however, targets not so much the principle underlying such support, but rather the way the existing mechanisms are being implemented: discriminatory biases and the lack of equivalent public support for sometimes long-established communities and newly arrived religions or beliefs. Adaptations have been made in some countries, but for the most part they are still based on the existing design, often with no assessment of the place of or the role played by religious and, more broadly, belief groups in State and society. It is not enough to extend support to other groups beyond the ones that have hitherto been the beneficiaries, since even then some groups will still be excluded or even discriminated against. Moreover, it does not suffice to draw inspiration from experiences and models from abroad, given how deeply each model is rooted in the history of a particular country and in certain equilibria that have not been easy to achieve.

2.4.1 A forward-looking approach: pragmatic steps in search of a more 'inclusive' and 'even-handed' way to determine State support

The comparative investigation of different models in force reveals that mechanisms of State support for religion, which were mostly designed in an era when traditional religions still formed the majority (and were hence much more important than they are in Europe today) and, moreover, could in some cases lay claim to compensation for the confiscation of their property, are now the subject of increasing criticism. The main criticism is that they fail to meet the conditions of equal treatment of religious and belief groups both old and new, with the numbers of the latter growing just about everywhere in Europe. These groups are not only linked with post-war migrations, but also with the free movement of persons within the territory of the EU and with the phenomenon of new individual religious choices. Moreover, non-religious people ask for respect for the freedom not to have a religion.

In subsections 2.4.1.1 and 2.4.1.2 below, a number of policies (possible alternatives to the present models) are sketched out. They draw on what has already been put in place in some countries, or adopt a more future-

62 (1) The State intervenes only using mechanisms provided for in common law: maintaining monuments, tax exemptions, and so on; (2) States provide direct State support to recognised religions; (3) taxpayers allocate a portion of their tax to a religious denomination or church; (4) religions are funded by their own members; (5) a general ban on or abolition of direct public subsidies for religion.

oriented view. At this stage, it may be useful to recall the position of the ECtHR on the principle of State support to religions. An examination of the case law of the ECtHR reveals that the Court does not exclude differential treatment, but it requires a balanced and explicit justification in an objective and reasonable manner. However, one significant trend in the ECtHR's interpretation of the Convention is the progressive strengthening of the requirements of non-discrimination. It entails that national legislatures are required, whenever necessary, to adjust existing mechanisms of support with a view to offering equivalent benefits to *all*, including non-majority and/or non-traditional groups. The requirement comes very close to the standards developed by the RELIGARE project: 'inclusive State neutrality' and 'justice as even-handedness'.

2.4.1.1 The fiscal route One way to support religions is indirect financial support of religious denominations (and other non-religious organisations) by means of tax benefits for their charitable, educational or social activities. This arrangement exists in all 10 countries analysed by the RELIGARE project. In some countries, this indirect form of support is also made available for religious activities. In practice, tax exemptions and tax deductibility arrangements for donations and bequests allocated to religious communities along with other non-profit organisations are a way to support funding of religions by members and followers; they can benefit from an extensive range of tax exemptions and deductions that are in some cases linked to activities and services (exemption from value-added tax (VAT) or VAT reduction for the supply of goods and services, exemption or reduced rate of business and corporation tax). Other types of exemption may also apply, such as exemption from inheritance tax, exemption from tax on donations and bequests, tax deductibility for donors, exemption from property tax for buildings mainly used for public worship, and so on.

If some activities of religious organisations are to be understood as serving economic purposes, they are generally subject to taxation rules that apply equally to other economic activities as well. In certain countries religious organisations are exempted from VAT on the acquisition and construction of real estate or on services and supplies of goods, provided their services are open to the public.[63] In most cases, a distinction is made between commercial and non-profit activities, as well as between religious or non-religious purposes. In the UK, for example, construction or acquisition of a building is zero-rated for VAT if it is wholly used for charitable purposes.[64] In practice, a *de minimis* non-charitable use of 5 per cent of the building's floor area is permitted. The rule sounds simple, but is not always easy to implement since it may not always be possible to distinguish between commercial and non-profit or religious activities carried out within the same building.

Similar exemptions apply to property tax, provided the buildings are used for public worship.[65] In case of mixed commercial and non-profit use of one and the same building, the exemption applies on the basis of evidence that the space is used mainly for public worship (at least 70 per cent in the Netherlands).[66] In other cases the exemption is strictly limited to the percentage of the property in which non-commercial activities take place (*Imposta municipale unica* [IMU] in Italy). In Spain, tax benefits are granted to the main denomination and to historical religious denominations (recognised, registered or having an agreement with the State). Therefore, tax exemption is available to the Catholic Church but also, albeit to a lesser extent, to religious denominations that have cooperation agreements with the State. Respondents interviewed on the issue were demanding an extension of the tax exemption to all registered religions (*Registro de entidades religiosas*), arguing that, if benefits are granted on the grounds of religious aims and public benefit, it does not make sense to limit them to denominations with cooperation agreements with the State. Alignment of religious organisations with other types of organisations should make it possible to extend the tax benefits to other denominations as well, provided they comply with minimum standards that apply equally to all.

The RELIGARE data regarding allocation of tax incentives exhibit a certain convergence across the different national legal systems; this applies to the requirement that the activity be non-profit in nature, as

63 Belgium: VAT Code, Art. 44, § 2, 11°; France: General Tax Code, Art. 261.

64 HM Revenue & Customs 2008.

65 Belgium: Income Tax Code, Art. 12; England and Wales: Places of Worship Registration Act 1855; France: General Tax Code, Art. 1382–4e and Art. 1407.

66 *Hoge Raad* (Supreme Court of the Netherlands), 4 December 1991.

well as to more specific admissibility conditions such as numeric size of the beneficiary groups, reference to promotion of human rights, presence or absence of an explicit reference to religious activities, financial transparency and so on. A presumption of public benefit for religions is included in some domestic legislation by explicitly including certain religious organisations among tax-exempt public benefit organisations (PBOs) (Bulgaria, Denmark, France, Italy, Spain) or treating 'advancement of religion' as a charitable purpose (Germany, UK).

A significant recent trend throughout Europe is the demand that minority groups be better supported financially. A recurrent claim is that tax benefits for groups or organisations should not depend on their legal status, but should instead be allocated on the basis of their public benefit purpose, a non-discriminatory criterion ensuring (inclusive) State neutrality, equality and transparency. Equal treatment should apply to groups and communities, irrespective of their doctrine, historical role or legal status. Public authorities (tax administration, State bodies, independent commissions and so on) should not be allowed to require more than the fulfilment of minimum conditions, in particular by checking an entity's compliance with public order, a criterion that applies indiscriminately to every type of organisation.

Tax exemptions and deductions may also serve another aim, namely to encourage taxpayers to make donations to groups and communities of their own choice. This type of funding therefore seems to be consistent with the principle of freedom of religion, as well as with the freedom not to identify with any religion: it is based on social consent and to a certain extent also on social utility.

At present, Member States retain a considerable margin of appreciation in granting tax exemptions. For the sake of 'inclusive State neutrality' and also of 'even-handed' distribution of the benefits, it should be a requirement that public authorities in each country disclose clear and reliable information on their assessment criteria when granting exemptions to groups and/or associations. The EU plays only the subsidiary role of tax coordination (and harmonisation for VAT). The European Commission checks that taxation (or non-taxation) does not create an obstacle to the free movement of goods (Art. 28 TFEU), free movement of capital (Art. 63 TFEU) and the free supply of services (Art. 56 TFEU) within the internal market. If the Commission detects a failure to comply with EU law, it may initiate an infringement procedure.

In the future, it would no doubt benefit minority groups in particular if the EU could provide the Member States – proactively – with a common set of assessment criteria that could ensure better coordination of the conditions placed on tax benefits and, by so doing, promote non-discriminatory tax treatment across all Member States.

2.4.1.2 Other methods: funding the training of community and group leaders; protection of cultural heritage The results of the RELIGARE project also show evidence of alternative models of public support to religions and beliefs. One notices in particular the growing importance of the technique of project financing. Funding the training of religious and philosophical leaders and programmes for the protection of cultural heritage are two such forms of project financing.

The training of religious leaders Religious leaders can be a driving force in helping minority groups or communities in particular strengthen their position in society and express their claims whenever they feel it necessary. As spokespersons for the community, they are usually also in contact with State officials and/or members of other communities and intermediary groups. However, RELIGARE data also suggest that leaders are often not (yet) sufficiently acquainted with the institutional landscape of the country, let alone with its legislation. It often happens that, for lack of adequate training, they cannot offer the appropriate support to their group or community.

In most European countries the training of religious leaders is well established itself as a historical feature of the status of religious denominations and, consequently, of their funding. In practice, ministers of religion from 'established' or 'recognised' religions (or mainstream, as is the case for Sunni Islam in Turkey) are either trained at public universities (Denmark, United Kingdom) and university seminaries (Turkey, Bulgaria) or at private universities and university seminaries (France, Belgium, Spain, Italy, Netherlands). Faculties of theology in public universities, for example, are funded at least partly by public authorities. Religious groups more recently established in Europe cannot offer equivalent training facilities for their religious leaders, with the exception of Germany, where Islamic theology has now become part of the university system and is funded by State authorities. In the Netherlands, a similar development appears to be in process.

Support from the Member States for setting up a suitable system of training for religious leaders, ensuring that minority groups are offered facilities equivalent to those offered to other religious and philosophical groups, would constitute a form of support that could be perfectly in harmony with the principles of 'inclusive State neutrality' and 'justice as even-handedness'.

State support for the protection of cultural and religious heritage Yet another form of project financing is the protection of religious and cultural heritage. Although public interest in heritage and its maintenance varies, it is considerable in all 10 countries under scrutiny and it has grown over the years. With some noticeable but very limited exceptions, one can observe many common points in the way European countries manage and preserve religious heritage. Among these commonalities figures the financial support given to religious groups and communities for the maintenance of historic buildings. This support is quite systematically and narrowly linked to the cost of such maintenance. The logic applies particularly to religious buildings, especially places of worship that are seen as counting among the most valuable parts of common cultural heritage. Whether located in the countryside or major cities, religious buildings play a central part in the debate over how best to preserve heritage.[67]

A challenge that should not be underestimated, however, has been the steady growth of mass tourism. This has given rise to new situations: religious heritage buildings are, in a growing number of cases, considered to be first and foremost cultural heritage, separated from their traditional function as places of worship. This gradual, but nonetheless radical, change in both the perceptions and the actual use of religious heritage buildings changes the situation: does the subsidy given for the upkeep of a building or place of worship benefit primarily the religious group that claims it, or the visitors who are interested mainly in the cultural significance of a place, whether or not this is linked to religion?

Generally speaking, the present situation is the following: religious heritage can benefit from direct State support, but only as a part of cultural heritage and not on religious grounds. The main criterion for allotting funds is the condition that the property be an open place of worship. It is the result of religious heritage now being conceived of as part of national history (Belgium, France, the Netherlands, some buildings in Germany, where churches are State-owned, and Italy – Fondo edifici di culto). In the Netherlands, the legislation accepts that although religious buildings are privately owned by religious groups, some of these buildings, as listed monuments, are entitled to benefit from regular direct public grants. The same is true in Bulgaria and Spain. In the case of Bulgaria, additional funds can be provided by the Council of Ministers of Religious Denominations Directorate.

2.4.1.3 State support to religion and belief in the media Another particular form of State support that deserves to be mentioned here is State support to religion and belief in the media. The State has a specific responsibility in plural(ising) societies. Its task 'is not to remove the cause of tension by eliminating pluralism, but to ensure that the competing groups tolerate each other',[68] where the position of minorities needs special attention.[69] Public media are an important instrument for the State to protect, advance and even guarantee this pluralism.

Generally speaking, the national broadcasting regimes in place in several Member States offer airtime to religious groups as well, in one way or another. This tradition goes back to the origins of the broadcasting regimes. Situations vary across Europe, but in general access to public broadcasting is made possible for a plurality of religions in the majority of the 10 countries researched. Such arrangements do not exist, however, in Bulgaria and Turkey. The outcome for the Muslim communities is very different in the two countries.

---

67 For the same reason, buildings of an alien religion seem to be offensive to the majority.

68 ECtHR, *L. Şahin v Turkey*, App no 44774/98 (10 November 2005), para 107.

69 As the ECtHR stresses: 'Democracy does not simply mean that the views of a majority must always prevail: a balance must be achieved which ensures the fair and proper treatment of people from minorities and avoids any abuse of a dominant position'; ibid, para 108.

Religious broadcasting on public channels (10 countries researched)

Type A	Type B	Type C	Type D
Only dominant religions receiving access; no real presence of other minority religions	**Religious broadcasting, but no *direct* access for religious groups;** strong predominance of the 'established' or dominant religion	**Plurality of religions receiving direct access**	**Plurality of religions *and* non-religious groups receiving direct access**
Turkey 1 (I) **Bulgaria** 1 (O)	**United Kingdom** Christianity dominant **Denmark** PL dominant (but also J, I, RC, P*dif*) **Italy** RC dominant (but also P)*	**France** 5 (RC, P, J, I, B) **Spain** 4 (RC, J, I, P) **Germany (federal)** 4 (RC, P*dif*, J, but also I)	**Belgium (federal)** *Flemish Community* 6 (RC, P, J, I, O, Hm) *French Community* 4 (RC, P, J, Hm) *Germanophone Community* 2 (RC, P) **The Netherlands** 7 (RC, P, J, I, B, H, Hm; system of State-supported religious broadcasting ends in 2016)

The information given refers to State-supported airtime on one or more public channels for the religions listed (data from 2012).
RC = Roman Catholic, PL = Protestant Lutheran, P = Protestant, P*dif* = different Protestant denominations, J = Judaism, O = Orthodox, I = Islam, B = Buddhism, H = Hinduism, Hm = Humanism / Freethinkers
* Incomplete information.

Guaranteeing access to radio and television channels does not, however, necessarily go hand in hand with full State funding of the programmes broadcast. As things stand, public channels have very limited resources for offering airtime to religious groups. In Belgium, for example, the national legislation provides for extremely poor airtime and budgets.[70] The Netherlands will soon change its policy on religious broadcasting by ending access and funding in 2016. This radical change has its origins in current policies of financial restraints.[71]

Strikingly, State support for religious broadcasting does not always correlate with the traditional systems of State support for religion: countries *without* regular church financing, such as France and the Netherlands, have nevertheless set up a generous policy of airtime for religious broadcasting. This may have to do with the fact that broadcasting is a technology that developed well after the establishment of the historically developed State–religion(s) regimes.

The growing variety of groups that claim access to airtime raises questions of selection of the groups eligible for a broadcasting licence. In their policies of distribution of airtime (that is, setting the criteria for access to and the different allocations of airtime), the State neutrality principle requires that authorities refrain from being partial to certain religions. The criteria developed for the allocation of airtime have raised questions on State neutrality in different countries (Belgium,[72] the Netherlands,[73] Germany[74]), as a consequence of the

70 Maximum 50 hours television per year for *all* religious and non-religious groups (Flemish Community). The Roman Catholic Sunday mass is, however, kept outside this maximum time budget.

71 Explanation of the new government policy (6 December 2012) in *Parliamentary Documents*, Tweede Kamer der Staten-Generaal 2011–12, no. 33400-VIII-29, pp. 4–5.

72 Conseil d'Etat, *Association protestante pour la radio et la télévision*, no. 11838 (26 May 1966).

73 Raad van State (*Commissariaat voor de Media, Humanistisch Verbond en Humanistische Omroep Stichting, st. Contactorgaan Moslims en Overheid, st. Verzorging Kerkelijke Zendtijd e.a.*) 10 January 2007. Rb. Amsterdam (*Humanistisch Verbond & Humanistische Omroep Stichting v Commissariaat voor de Media*), 5 July 2006. Rb. Amsterdam (*Nederlandse Moslim Raad, Humanistisch Verbond & Humanistische Omroep Stichting, Stichting Verzorging Kerkelijke Zendtijd v Commissariaat voor de Media*) 5 July 2006.

74 Case of the Bavarian *Bund für Geistesfreiheit Bayern*: Bayerischer Verwaltungsgerichtshof (7. Senat), no. 7 BV 06.764, 29 January 2007.

fact that the State tends to be more 'interventionist' when the number of competing candidates for airtime is increasing.[75]

The growing number of State-funded religious broadcasters also gives rise to problems of accountability and transparency (the Netherlands[76]). As a result of their internal diversity (and disunity), Dutch Muslims, for example, lost their share of Dutch radio and TV airtime in 2011,[77] and only got it back in 2013.[78] In Bulgaria, given the absence of regular Muslim religious broadcasting on Bulgarian public television channels, the Turkish Muslim minority watches the Turkish media.[79] Non-religious communities (especially the humanist movement) have entered the radio and television scene in Belgium (since 1932 for radio and 1951 for TV) and the Netherlands (since 1926 for radio and 1971 for TV). In other countries (France,[80] Germany,[81] UK[82]), non-religious organisations have not yet succeeded in gaining access to broadcasting time on a comparable basis on nationwide channels.[83]

The available data on the broadcasting regimes in the 10 countries under scrutiny show that, over time, the evolution of State policies follows the same pattern, starting with regimes that only accept the presence of a traditional majority (State) religion and ending with a more inclusive broadcasting regime, mirroring in some way the new religious and philosophical diversity in society. The research data for the 'Type A' countries show that minority religions attach considerable importance to being present in the mass media, not represented by others, but gaining access to public channels themselves (Bulgaria[84] and Turkey[85]). The media regulator in Bulgaria received complaints from non-registered religious minority communities with reference to the presentation of their activities in broadcasts by TV operators.[86] The research data for 'Type D' categories point to the growing organisational difficulties arising from an increasing religious 'external pluralism' on the public channels (the Netherlands).

---

75 M Stock, 'Islam im Rundfunk – wie eigentlich?' (2007) 226 *Arbeitspapiere des Instituts für Rundfunkökonomie an der Universität Köln* 30–31: 'Je mehr sich der multireligiöse Meinungsmarkt nun aber bevölkert … umso mehr nimmt auch der öffentliche Regulierungsbedarf zu. Wir werden dann eine kommunikations- und medienrechtliche "*Marktordnung*" brauchen' ('The more religions on the religious market, the greater the need for regulation. Then we will need a "market regulation" on the communication law and media law level').

76 Problems with the financial (mis-)management of funds were present in the small Buddhist, Hindu, Muslim and Jewish broadcasters.

77 Raad van State (*St. Moslimomroep v Commissariaat voor de Media*) 13 July 2011.

78 The candidate Muslim organisation gets 175 hours on radio and 58 hours on TV. Decision of the Commissariaat voor de Media (Dutch Media Authority), announced 11 April 2013. See <www.cvdm.nl/content.jsp?objectid=13985> accessed June 2014.

79 See E Krasteva-Blagoeva, 'Symbols of Muslim Identity in Bulgaria: Traditions and Innovations', 4 (paper, conference *Islam und Muslime in (Südost)Europa. Kontinuität und Wandel im Kontext von Transformation und EU-Erweiterung.* Berlin, Institut für Slawistik der Humboldt-Universität zu Berlin – Südosteuropa-Gesellschaft e.V. München, 7–8 November 2008).

80 Sénat 12ème législature, Question orale sans débat n° 1166S de M Gérard Delfau (Hérault – RDSE), *JO Sénat* 16 November 2006, p. 2851. Conseil d'Etat, 1 October 1980, *Union des Athées*, no. 17651. See A-M Oliva, 'Emissions religieuses et service public audiovisuel' (2006) 51 *Droit et Culture* 103–12, available at <http://droitcultures.revues.org/836> accessed 25 July 2014.

81 On the amount of airtime for the humanist organisation Bund für Geistesfreiheit Bayern, see Bayerischer Verwaltungsgerichtshof (7. Senat), no. 7 BV 06.764, 29 January 2007.

82 British Humanist Association, *BHA Briefing 2009: BBC and Humanist Broadcasting*, 2009, 5. National Secular Society, *Religious Broadcasting*, to the BBC Charter Review Committee of the House of Lords, 10 October 2005, 16, available at <www.secularism.org.uk> accessed June 2014.

83 On the *local level* the situation can be different. In Bavaria, for instance, a Freethinker organisation is participating on a regular basis in religious and life stance radio broadcasts on *Bayern2* (as is the case for Jehovah Witnesses and Seventh Day Adventists).

84 See ECtHR, *Glas Nadezhda EOOD and Elenkov v Bulgaria*, App no 14134/02 (11 October 2007).

85 The other representatives (that is, other than the representative of the Atatürk Thought Association (ADD)) and experts from different religious and belief backgrounds stated that 'there could be such broadcasting on State media but … there should be some criteria assuring equality between different religious and belief groups and preventing political misuse' and 'if there are programmes on religion and religious groups, these should be prepared by specialists of the respective faith, or at least under their consultancy'; *RELIGARE Report WP7 Turkey*, 2012, 47.

86 GEG-contribution for Bulgaria in *Good Practice Exchange Seminar on Public Policies on Combating Discrimination on the Ground of Religion or Belief*, Brussels 18 October 2012, GEG-contributions, 18.

2.4.2 Policy recommendations for State support to religion and belief

In assessing techniques for the public funding of religious (and exceptionally also secular groups, as is the case in Belgium and in the Netherlands), the RELIGARE project has focused on activities that are specifically religious or philosophical in nature; it left aside the funding of more peripheral forms of social action. One major finding resulting from this assessment is that, rather than call into question the principle of such funding itself, respondents emphasised the need for greater transparency and objectivity of public funding techniques. Applying inclusive even-handedness in a procedural approach would mean that all stakeholders take part in the discussion on whether and how State support should be provided and which participatory techniques are best adapted for facilitating the distribution of this support.

Given that the EU authorities lack competence in this area, over the short term substantial differences among the policies of the Member States will necessarily persist. A lack of competence at the EU level does not mean, however, that EU authorities have no responsibility for the possible effects of EU policies on the status of religious and philosophical groups (or their individual followers) in Member States. The EU authorities are not empty-handed: the Commission provided itself with an instrument that enables EU policymakers to evaluate the human rights aspects of proposed new legislation at an early stage: the 'impact assessment' (see section 3.1.2.3 below). Impact assessments, which also take into account the possible impact of policy proposals on human rights (the catalogue, formulated in the Charter), are relevant for the position of the freedom of religion or belief in its collective dimension too.

1. The EU Institutions should include religion not only in its individual but also in its collective dimension (the human rights position of religious and non-religious communities of conviction) systematically in the Integrated Impact Assessments as a structural component in the policymaking process.
2. Regarding tax policies, any policy that is being put in place should promote the alignment of churches, religions and belief groups with organisations acting for public benefit (PBOs), irrespective of their legal status within the State (recognised, registered and so on).
3. Tax deductions for donations, bequests and inheritance in favour of public benefit organisations (PBO), including religious organisations, may be a means to encourage the funding of religions by their members and followers by (a) increasing the rate of deductibility; (b) subtracting deductions from taxable income, rather than from actual tax due; (c) raising the limit of the deduction and (d) lowering the threshold for deductibility, in order to open up the tax facilities to lower income groups as well.
4. The EU promotes projects that benefit society at large. With regard to the status of PBOs and the European tax framework for PBOs, the EU could play a more pro-active role in determining a common concept of public benefit with a view to achieving a better coordination of the national systems in place.
5. Within its competence of tax coordination, the EU should further promote transparency and accountability of the groups receiving support as a way of combating any indirect discrimination resulting from further developing a common tax policy.
6. In the area of religious / cultural heritage, the EU could play a constructive role by supporting programmes that make it possible to critically assess the difficulties that come with the intermingling of religious and cultural heritage, and in particular in the case of reassigning religious heritage buildings for other uses.
7. More specific means that are to be taken into consideration if a system of State-supported religious broadcasting is maintained (external pluralism):
   - When public radio or television channels are operated by (or under the responsibility of) the State, an equitable and transparent procedure should be allowed for providing various religious or belief groups with access to these public channels.
   - The position of minorities should not be neglected, nor should the organisational specificities of some minority religions in particular (as is the case for Islam).
   - Even where religious communities or groups have no access to licences for their own radio or television on public channels, access to other radio and television programmes (for instance, news programmes and documentaries) should be made possible in order to reflect diversity of religions and beliefs in public dialogue on various subjects that matter in society, including 'religion' itself.

- Religious and belief groups should not be particularly disadvantaged from owning or operating radio or television facilities (on national or local level).[87] States upholding a ban on religious channels should reassess the necessity and effectiveness of a ban in the light of growing religious diversity.

3. Religion and EU Action

Introduction

The RELIGARE project focused on tensions between the application of non-discrimination norms and the fundamental right to freedom of religion and belief. It has shown that tensions arise in various areas of social life, which may in the end escalate into intricate legal conflicts. Some of these clashes have gained considerable public attention, such as the debate about the wearing of the Islamic headscarf in French public schools and in private workplaces, the discussions about the display of crucifixes in public schools in Italy and, more recently, the ritual circumcision debate in Germany. In cases of 'clashing rights', balances must inevitably be struck, however imperfect these may be, and any constraints must be justified. What role(s) should the EU institutions play in this area? In what matters can they be expected to take the initiative in the years to come?

This section advances a number of concrete recommendations to the European institutions for developing a coherent legal and policy framework that addresses issues of freedom of religion and belief. It identifies no less than three types of actions that would enable the EU to become more deeply engaged in the combat against religious discrimination and in the guarantee of religious freedoms broadly understood. The proposals are based mainly on the findings of the RELIGARE research project, but do not of course exclude the possibility that in the years to come, the EU would take yet other initiatives or become more closely involved in the struggle for equal treatment of all persons in Europe, taking account of religion or belief.

The *first* type of action consists of *legislative instruments*. The EU has already developed several such instruments – some more constraining than others – intended to render more effective the fight against certain forms of exclusion or discrimination on grounds relating to religion and/or belief. To date, Directive 2000/78/EC is one of the principal instruments adopted by the European Union to combat discrimination in the employment sector. The new Horizontal Directive has since been proposed. A *second* type of initiative involves the various *participatory procedures* (encounters, dialogues and reflection on the future) – whether already in place or yet to be set up – among the EU institutions and various groups and/or persons concerned directly or indirectly with discrimination on grounds of religion and/or belief and, more generally, with diversity policies. Article 17(3) TFEU reflects this sort of deliberative participation. Finally, a *third* type of action or initiative is the *involvement of experts*, either by commissioning reports on specific topics, as was the case with the RELIGARE project, or in the form of expert groups with a consultative role, that would be available to the EU institutions, when needed, to examine specific questions in greater depth.

> From a policy perspective, the three types of initiative are clearly different in nature and it is only those legislative instruments with direct effect that are binding on Member States. But taken together, they would enable the EU to make a greater investment in elaborating a policy that, on the one hand, takes into account the sovereignty of States in managing religious and philosophical diversity in the internal legal order (the principle of subsidiarity), while on the other hand ensuring that this management is respectful of minimum standards of protection (fundamental principles) that are applicable across the entire territory of the EU. All three types of action are necessary for setting up a policy that is inspired by the ideal of the greatest possible inclusivity, that is to say, where individuals are respected in their diversity, and that seeks to benefit from the active and committed participation of all its members, taking account of their religion or belief, if that is their wish. The fight against discrimination is not sufficient in and of itself; it must be accompanied by participatory procedures that are both open and democratic.

87 See *Guidelines for Review of Legislation Pertaining to Religion or Belief* (adopted by the Venice Commission, 18–19 June 2004), Warsaw, OSCE-ODIHR, 27 <www.osce.org/odihr/13993> accessed June 2014.

3.1 Three Types of Action at the EU Level

3.1.1 The legislative route: on the proposed Horizontal Directive

Building on the EU's existing framework of rights, and more particularly on Directive 2000/78/EC, the EU could decide to *extend* its non-discrimination (and integration) arsenal to issues pertaining to religion and belief *outside the scope of employment* by giving further support to the legislative procedure leading to the adoption of the proposed Council Directive on implementing equal treatment between persons irrespective of religion or belief, disability, age or sexual orientation.[88]

On the one hand, such an extension would align EU law with what has already been achieved in several Member States which, in their domestic anti-discrimination legislation, go further than Directive 2000/78/EC, albeit with some modifications. On the other hand, one must remain realistic: the text of the so-called Horizontal Directive has for several years now been the object of considerable political reticence; its adoption would not be a smooth path. Moreover, it is essential to study attentively the reasons given by those Member States that oppose the directive, in order to be able to take these into account without necessarily giving up the aim of having the debates reach a successful end and then seeing the adoption of a European legislative instrument that would considerably extend the scope of the struggle against unjustified exclusion. In its Green Paper accompanying the proposed Horizontal Directive, the European Commission has expressed its wish to 'complete' the European non-discrimination framework.[89]

Considering the above, and without in any way detracting from the advantages one might expect from an additional European legislative instrument that widens the scope of the fight against discrimination to include the entire field of services, it can be said that from the perspective of the principles of religious freedom and non-discrimination, the proposed Horizontal Directive is a missed opportunity. One may, for example, criticise the current version of the text for limiting the EU's reservation of reasonable accommodation to one particular vulnerable group (individuals with disabilities) and not extending it to reasons of religion or belief. This may block the avenue of reasonable accommodation for reasons of religion or belief in the foreseeable future by prioritising the protection of persons with disabilities. One wonders whether this normative choice is consistent with the EU's 'Europe 2020' strategy for 'smart, sustainable and inclusive growth': policies can add to sustainable and inclusive growth, and work towards an inclusive labour market that fully takes advantage of the skills and talents of its (ethno-religiously) diverse population, with due regard for fundamental rights in the workplace.

There are two possible attitudes in this regard. One either takes a pragmatic approach that consists of maintaining the text in its present version, without adding to the protections it currently contains, in the hope of thereby maximising the chances of success in the difficult negotiations among Member States concerning an instrument that does not enjoy unanimous support. Or one tries to be more ambitious and take advantage of the fact that the directive has been in the pipeline for a long time – the fate of the proposed Horizontal Directive at this time still remains unclear – to suggest amendments to the text that has been put forward.

Another possible criticism, based on a detailed analysis of the text of the proposed directive, is that religious-ethos organisations may feel their freedom and autonomy are restricted by standards of non-discrimination, while individual members of religious minorities facing hostility will obtain additional protection against discrimination in important public spheres. The proposed Horizontal Directive, by expanding the right to non-discrimination on the basis of sexual orientation and of religion or belief (two highly relevant grounds) to the broad societal areas of education[90] and goods and services, would indeed affect the position of commercial

88 COM(2008) 426 final (2 July 2008).

89 'Communication from the Commission to the European Parliament, the Council, the European Economic and Social Committee and the Committee of the Regions on Non-Discrimination and Equal Opportunities: A Renewed Commitment', COM(2008) 420 final, 4.

90 In the Commission's proposal the protection of individuals on the basis of religion or belief was watered down in the area of education, but religiously motivated organisations received a certain degree of leniency (at least the State would have the discretion to award such leniency). The European Parliament's proposed amendments have made the protection against discrimination in the education field more effective, but have also closed off avenues for the exercise of freedom of religion where that is seen to infringe on or endanger other important rights and values (access to education, equal treatment of sexual minorities). See European Parliament legislative resolution of 2 April 2009 on the 'Proposal for

operators with strongly held beliefs, religious schools and religious-ethos companies offering goods and services available to the public. The proposed directive would not only give certain rights and remedies to individuals, but also implies obligations on the part of faith-based organisations and religious individuals in certain circumstances (for example hotel owners). Tensions could arise where religious groups, particularly religious minority groups, were no longer allowed to define autonomously the specific services they (want to) offer to particular individuals or groups. There may indeed be justification for allowing direct distinctions to be made by religious-ethos organisations or individuals offering services from the perspective of a consistent religious ideology, in light of the legitimate aim of freedom of religion. Such an arrangement may be one way to ensure improved consideration of the fundamental right to freedom of religion in the balancing of rights and interests that is inherent in formulating norms regarding non-discrimination.

These few criticisms in no way detract, as pointed out above, from the merit of a European legislative instrument that would extend the fight against unjustified exclusions – including discrimination on grounds of religion and/or belief – to the vast area of services. But one should not miss out on the opportunity also – from the outset – to examine in greater detail the weaknesses of the existing text, or at least the undesirable and/or unforeseen effects that risk emerging, as well as the new tensions to which it might give rise. This is all the more urgent since the directive has not yet been given final approval.

> One of the highest priority recommendations put forward by the RELIGARE research partners is therefore the suggestion to undertake further study – on a comparative basis, taking into account the specificity of national situations (that is, in domestic law) – of the various potential effects of the entry into force of the Horizontal Directive, including any deleterious (that is, discriminatory) and/or unpredictable effects of such a legislative instrument.

Among the questions to be looked at in greater depth, there is the issue of what to do about ambivalent situations: what would be the implications of such an EU directive for cases that are on the borderline between religious and secular? If the Horizontal Directive comes into force, there will be stiff competition between autonomy of religion and the obligations that fall under the directive. Where will the boundary be drawn between the autonomy of faith-based organisations and the expectations of public State support in combating discrimination based on sex and gender? Will it be as broadly drawn as in the US (US Supreme Court case law)? Should the directive also apply to religious education, or only to all the other aspects of schooling? Religious discrimination within the context of religious education offered by confessional schools is probably difficult to address, but as far as sex discrimination is concerned there should be no exemption. If the directive is approved, faith-based organisations providing a public service, such as adoption agencies, would also be under pressure to comply with non-discrimination rules, even if they are not State funded. Only in the realm of their own directly religious or spiritual services could they continue to choose freely whom they appoint and to whom they offer services. And if they want to have charitable status, they will also have to comply with non-discrimination laws. All these issues, and many more, would need to be further investigated.

3.1.2 The consultative process

A second type of action that would enable the EU institutions to give more weight to a resolutely inclusive European policy is that of consultation. Three forms of this process can be identified: the participatory process as enshrined in Article 17(3) TFEU; internal consultation among EU services and administrations; and, finally, the obligation to undertake an 'impact assessment' before introducing any new legislative or judicial measure that directly or indirectly affects religion in the broadest sense. The impact assessment does indeed involve a form of consultative procedure. As indicated above, participatory procedures are all the more important given that they draw inspiration from a more constructive logic than anti-discriminatory measures. The struggle against discrimination does not suffice in and of itself – it must be accompanied by participatory procedures that are open and democratic.

a Council Directive on Implementing the Principle of Equal Treatment between Persons Irrespective of Religion or Belief, Disability, Age or Sexual Orientation', COM(2008) 426 – C6–0291/2008 – 2008/0140(CNS).

3.1.2.1 On Article 17 of the Treaty on the Functioning of the European Union (TFEU) According to Article 17(3) TFEU, the EU is bound to maintain an open, transparent and regular dialogue with churches, religious associations and communities, and philosophical and non-confessional organisations that are recognised as such at the national level in the Member States and adhere to European values. In principle, Article 17 is incumbent upon all EU institutions; in practice, however, it is the European Commission, and more particularly the Bureau of European Policy Advisers (BEPA), that is entrusted with maintaining such dialogue with interlocutors at various levels, whether in the form of written exchanges, meetings or specific events. In a recent decision the European Ombudsman, in response to a complaint in which mainly the Commission was targeted, attempted to clarify the meaning of the three adjectives 'open', 'transparent' and 'regular'.[91] What kind of dialogue should the EU institutions have with religious and civil society groups? The EU institutions have a certain margin of discretion in framing the dialogue with a view to the implementation of Article 17; in principle, however, they are bound to invite to the dialogue all churches, religious associations or communities, as well as philosophical and non-confessional organisations that are recognised or registered as such at a national level and adhere to European values. One of the principal aims of the consultation made obligatory by the procedural provision of Article 17 is to guarantee regular and direct contact – at various levels and in different ways – between the highest European political institutions and representatives of religious communities and various communities of conviction (including non-confessional ones) throughout Europe. In the long run, this makes Article 17(3) TFEU a potential tool for a truly participatory democracy at a very high level. In its own way, it reiterates the principle of participatory democracy contained in Article 11(2) TEU.

The future will determine what will be the impact of this principle, but its importance for issues that are related to religion and belief in particular should not be underestimated. On the one hand, the consultative process enables EU institutions – at this stage BEPA more specifically – to be kept informed of the situation and aspirations of various interlocutors on matters that are of particular relevance to them and exchange views with them. On the other, it enables EU institutions and the Commission in particular to take certain initiatives which, without infringing on the provisions of paragraphs 1 and 2 of Article 17 TFEU (which confirm the principle of sovereignty of the Member States in all areas concerning their relations with churches and non-confessional organisations under their jurisdiction), *would guarantee a more consistent implementation of EU law in areas that relate to the protection of the freedom of religion and belief taken in the broad sense.* In his decision, the European Ombudsman rightly recalled that the main objective of Article 17(3) TFEU is to allow the discussion of concrete legal questions and existing legislative provisions, and that doing so is perfectly compatible with the provisions of paragraphs (1) and (2) of the same article: 'Conducting a dialogue on an issue dealt with in existing legislation cannot but constitute constructive action.'[92] The European Commission embodies and upholds the general interests of the Union and should be the driving force in the Union's institutional system, including in matters that relate to religion and belief whenever relevant within the framework of administering and implementing Community policies and of enforcing Community law (jointly with the Court of Justice).

The RELIGARE project fully supports the Ombudsman's suggestion, articulated in the aforementioned decision, in which he 'urges the Commission … to develop the understanding of how Article 17 TFEU should be interpreted and applied … and, if necessary, to draw up guidelines in terms of how exactly it plans to implement Article 17 TFEU'.[93]

3.1.2.2 Consultation among various services (directorates-general) and administrations Without waiting for the Commission to align itself with the position of the European Ombudsman in its dialogue with civil society on questions relating to freedom of religion and belief, it may be useful here to stress the urgency of another type of consultative procedure that could be set up at the European level. The RELIGARE research partners have observed that there is a lack of coordination internally among the different services that, within

91 Decision of the European Ombudsman in his inquiry into complaint 2097/2011/RA against the European Commission.

92 ibid 48.

93 ibid 63.

the European institutions, are called upon to consider questions of religious discrimination.[94] A suggestion that thus emerges from the RELIGARE project after three years of research on EU policy in ensuring respect for freedom of religion and belief is that a permanent consultative mechanism be put in place among the services in order to enable the teams to listen to each other's views on certain priorities and, as far as possible, to undertake joint actions. One possibility would be to activate an inter-service group on religion and belief that would facilitate the systematic and regular exchange of information among directorates-general at the Commission level and coordinate the Commission services working in the area. This would make it possible to put into place a policy of internal consultation on religious questions and matters relating to the diversity of beliefs any time these require action on the part of the EU. We give a few examples of such situations below, based on the findings of the RELIGARE research, which in our view would merit being discussed internally and in a transversal fashion within the EU institutions so as to facilitate better-coordinated action.

The RELIGARE findings suggest that there are a number of issues which require forward thinking in terms of the current (and future) BEPA Action Programmes:

With regard to the *workplace*: the EU has competence to intervene in the way Member States, within their internal legal order, balance claims pertaining to the protection of the freedom of religion and belief and the requirement of non-discrimination, including the public acceptance of the expression of certain identities. A potential expansion of the equality principles contained in EU Directive 2000/78/EC (Employment Equality Directive) – that is, combating discrimination on the basis of religion or belief – to other fields of social life as well, for example the provision of services (the Horizontal Directive proposal), would necessarily enhance the scope for such intervention and therefore create the need for optimal coordination among various directorates-general.

With regard to *family life*: both historically and in the present, majority Christian traditions have had a considerable impact on family arrangements. The variations among the different legal practices of the EU Member States can adversely affect the freedom of movement and residence within the Union. Further coordination among the Member States is necessary to take account of this, but doing so is likely to put some pressure on interpretations of Article 17 (1) and (2) TFEU and so should be anticipated by the Commission.

With regard to the *public space*: two aspects in particular have a significant impact on areas of EU competence, directly or indirectly (through the application of the European Convention on Human Rights in EU law). *First*, recent (national) court decisions have driven Member States further apart in their views of the place of religious expression in the public space; this applies particularly to the bans on certain kinds of religiously motivated dress. *Second*, in a number of Member States the application of equal treatment requirements is being extended to faith-based organisations. These are two sources of evidence of the fact that, within the EU, the concept of 'public order' is given divergent meanings in the different Member States. Here again, expectations of equality and freedom of movement potentially clash with the protection of the freedom of religion and belief enjoyed by individuals and communities within Member States, and therefore put Article 17 (1) and (2) TFEU under pressure.

In sum, the RELIGARE project has identified a significant and growing tension between basic human rights, especially respect for private and family life (Article 8 ECHR; Article 7 EU Charter), freedom of religion and belief (Article 9 ECHR; Article 10 EU Charter), and prohibition against discrimination (Article 14 ECHR; Articles 20 and 21 EU Charter). These tensions intersect with tensions between the programmes of various EU Commission directorates, especially Education, Employment, and Home Affairs, and with the principles of reasonable accommodation in connection with religion.

> A mechanism of continuous and transversal reflection and mutual consultation at the level of the directorates-general would probably be the most suitable place for coordination to take place, in terms of the internal and external networking on which the current (and future) Action Programme focuses. This may require, in the longer term, that questions on the interaction between religion and belief, the wider secularity of the European space, and the programmes of the various relevant Commission directorates-general are addressed more firmly after consultation between these programmes and in line with the future work of the Bureau of European Policy Advisors (BEPA). Moreover, a more active role could be envisaged for the Fundamental Rights Agency regarding religious affairs.

94 In the same vein, on this lack of coordination, see M Hartlapp, J Metz and C Rauh, 'The Agenda Set by the EU Commission: The Result of Balanced or Biased Aggregation of Positions?' (April 2010) 21 *LSE Europe in Question Discussion Paper Series*.

3.1.2.3 Impact assessment and the compatibility with fundamental rights The third and last form of action drawing inspiration from the consultative process that we bring here into the discussion of European policy on religious matters – taken in the widest sense – is that of the impact assessment, and more particularly the stakeholder consultation.[95] Regular dialogue (Art. 17 TFEU) and stakeholder consultation (impact assessment) are interrelated issues, fitting in well with the tradition of the Commission's 'Culture of Consultation and Dialogue' (2002).[96]

In 2010 the European Commission developed its Charter Strategy outlining the way in which the Commission plans to implement the EU Charter of Fundamental Rights.[97] The 'Operational Guidance on Fundamental Rights' (2011),[98] one of the outcomes of the EC Charter Strategy, is a specific instrument for EC staff preparing *impact assessments*, providing guidance on how EU legislative proposals may have an impact on fundamental rights (and, when policy options raise fundamental rights issues, DG Justice staff will be invited to the Impact Assessment Steering Group).

Impact assessments are an important tool for demonstrating that in the development of new EU legislation, full account is taken of the human rights protected by the EU Charter. For this purpose a 'Fundamental Rights Check-List' has been introduced.[99] The EC decided that human rights issues should be addressed in the early-stage preparatory consultations.[100] According to the procedure, stakeholders should give their input during these consultations.[101] As a result, EU policy options that would violate fundamental rights should be discarded.[102] This also applies to the compatibility with respect for the protection of the freedom of religion and belief enshrined in Article 9 ECHR and in Article 10 of the EU Charter. Yet, the concern should also be that where EU institutions are acting within the confines of EU competencies, EU policymakers take account of existing domestic (national) arrangements for relations between the State and religion (ranging from regimes offering full direct State support to religious groups and communities of conviction to the regimes that provide very little or only indirect State support). EU policies (and legislation) cannot ignore the commitments and obligations which Member States historically have taken upon themselves with regard to the freedom of religion and belief, as well as the freedom of association and, when relevant, property rights.

95 On the Commission's use of the technique of the 'impact assessment', see <www.ec.europa.eu/governance/impact/index> accessed June 2014.

96 European Commission, 'Towards a Reinforced Culture of Consultation and Dialogue: General Principles and Minimum Standards for Consultation of Interested Parties by the Commission', COM(2002) 704 final.

97 European Commission, 'Strategy for the Effective Implementation of the Charter of Fundamental Rights by the European Union' COM(2010) 573 final.

98 European Commission, 'Operational Guidance on Taking Account of Fundamental Rights in Commission Impact Assessments' SEC(2011) 567 final.

99 The Check-List Questionnaire reads as follows:

(1) What fundamental rights are affected?

(2) Are the rights in question absolute rights (which may not be subject to limitations, examples being human dignity and the ban on torture)?

(3) What is the impact of the various policy options under consideration on fundamental rights? Is the impact beneficial (promotion of fundamental rights) or negative (limitation of fundamental rights)?

(4) Do the options have both a beneficial and a negative impact, depending on the fundamental rights concerned (for example, a negative impact on freedom of expression and beneficial one on intellectual property)?

(5) Would any limitation of fundamental rights be formulated in a clear and predictable manner?

(6) Would any limitation of fundamental rights: – be necessary to achieve an objective of general interest or to protect the rights and freedoms of others (which)? – be proportionate to the desired aim? – preserve the essence of the fundamental rights concerned?

100 SEC(2011) 567 final, 11.

101 SEC(2011) 567 final, 13.

102 The available sources do not explicitly mention the collective dimension of the fundamental rights of freedom of religion or belief, relevant for the legal (human rights) status of churches and religious associations or communities and non-confessional organisations. This collective dimension is, however, an integral part of the developing ECtHR case law on religious freedom (and related human rights guarantees). The right of freedom of religion and belief guaranteed in Art. 10(1) of the Charter 'corresponds to the right guaranteed in Article 9 of the ECHR and, in accordance with Article 52(3) of the Charter, has the same meaning and scope'. The collective aspects of this freedom are therefore part and parcel of the protection offered by Art. 10 of the Charter. At the EU treaty level, the fundamental value of this collective dimension is also stressed by Art. 17(1)(2) TFEU, an article that includes a dialogue obligation (17(3)).

> After three years of research on the commitments that come with the obligation both for Member States and the EU institutions to provide appropriate protection to individuals and communities claiming their freedom of religion and belief, the RELIGARE project suggests three impact assessment procedures: one with a view to involving stakeholders in EU policy preparation (consultation and advice) on topics that are relevant for religious and non-confessional communities of conviction; a second on the position of religion and belief in its collective dimension; and a third on EU law and its transposition/implementation by member States (EU guidelines for national governments).

Involving stakeholders in EU policy preparation (consultation and advice) on topics that are relevant to them This would require organising, at an early stage of the EU legislative process, transparent consultations with all relevant stakeholders,[103] including representatives of religious and philosophical organisations, with a view to informing them in a timely fashion of new legislative measures or instruments that are in the pipeline and, with their help, assessing the potential (un)intended consequences of such measures. Stakeholder consultation should include smaller and/or less well-known groups, and not just traditional churches and the humanist movement.[104] This will offer a more complete picture of the possible effects of new EU policy measures on groups of stakeholders – large and small. The right to equal treatment and the principle of non-discrimination (as well as the principle of justice as even-handedness) are at stake here.

Impact assessment for the position of religion and belief in its collective dimension Impact assessment is an instrument that is not completely new in the context of State legislation on religion. In 2004, the Venice Commission produced a series of concise general guidelines for national authorities engaging in new legislation affecting religion.[105] The Venice Commission is known for being a prominent external advisor to national authorities in matters of minority protection. In the same vein, integrated impact assessments, as a structural component in the EU political process, should also address matters related to freedom of religion and belief in its collective dimension (the human rights position of churches and non-confessional communities of conviction). It could help prevent unintended side effects of new EU policies or legislation, such as producing new or reinforcing existing tensions between groups and communities within the national context of some Member States in particular.

Impact assessment on EU law and its implementation/transposition by Member States – EU guidelines for national governments Member States are responsible for the implementation/transposition of EU legislative instruments into their internal legal order. To help Member States ensure that the freedom of individuals and communities defined by religion and belief is respected and complies with the European human rights requirements, the EU (more specifically, the EU Human Rights Agency) could develop guidelines suggesting the introduction of similar techniques (consultation, impact assessment) to the national authorities as far as the implementation of new EU legislation is concerned.

These guidelines could be: (1) general guidelines; (2) guidelines developed *case by case* (thus focusing on the subject concerned); or (3) guidelines that take into account the different existing types of constitutional models with regard to the relationships between the State and religions.

3.1.3 The use of expertise

Finally, a third type of action or initiative that would make it possible for the EU institutions to strengthen their policies regarding the various issues identified by the RELIGARE research is the use of expertise, whether in the form of studies commissioned on chosen subjects, as was the case with the RELIGARE project, or through

103 At the Member State level this type of consultation is sometimes well established (in Belgium, for instance, consultation of stakeholders is a structural phase in the legislative process of the Flemish Community); consultative bodies are present in other countries as well.

104 COMECE, CEC and IHF are strong, permanent and the most visible dialogue and consultation partners for the EU. They are represented (by their own 'diplomats') in Brussels. New minorities do not have equal means (and thus) equal access to participating in these types of consultations or dialogues.

105 *Guidelines for Review of Legislation Pertaining to Religion and Belief* (adopted by the Venice Commission, 18–19 June 2004), Warsaw, OSCE-ODIHR <www.osce.org/odihr/13993> accessed June 2014.

setting up expert groups at the service of the EU institutions to help examine particular questions in greater depth and which would in a sense have a consultative competence. The Directorate-General for Justice, for instance, invites experts who wish to provide their specific expertise on certain topics to the EU institutions. Such a *database of independent experts* allows the DG for Justice to make contracts with experts for occasional tasks (drafting brief reports, assistance with their events, and so on) when needed.[106] With regard, in particular, to issues of religious discrimination throughout the EU, the RELIGARE project recommends that the Commission set up *a permanent working group of experts*. Given the diversity of the issues involved and the complexity of the various commitments and obligations of Member States to guarantee that a due balance is struck between, on the one hand, the freedom of religion and belief of individuals and communities and, on the other, the rights of others to be free from discrimination, the involvement of several areas of expertise is required. Such a permanent body of experts may prove particularly useful, if not indispensable, over the medium term in order to move beyond the inadequacies of *ad hoc* policy and help the Commission work out adequate legislative instruments to strike a balance between freedom of religion or belief and other discrimination grounds.

3.2 The Wider Policy Implications of the RELIGARE Findings

The RELIGARE research has identified a number of similar themes in the different national orders and shown how both legislation and case law handle them, both in national and international courts. The latter is all the more relevant since all EU Member States are bound by the ECtHR and ECJ case law. The case law so far available, however, exhibits some inconsistencies. More than a decade after the adoption of Directive 2000/78/EC, the ECJ has not issued a single decision on discrimination on the grounds of religion or belief. 'The case law of the Strasbourg courts that has direct relevance to the current issue of religious pluralism is but fragmentary and casuistic', the Dutch human rights expert Titia Loenen wrote a few years ago.[107] The way in which the ECtHR has viewed the protection of religious freedom to date is indeed difficult to summarise in a few sentences, precisely because of its fragmentary nature. The RELIGARE findings give insight into how the domestic courts and public authorities in the Member States cope with this fragmentation. One trend that emerges from both national and ECtHR case law is the differentiation between two aspects of religious freedom: the so-called *forum internum* (internal forum), which refers to adherence to a religion or other belief system, and the *forum externum* (external forum), which refers to the various ways in which one can give expression to that conviction.[108] The difference is important for a good understanding of the scope of the protection that the law has thus far given to religious freedom. The data illustrate this clearly. Courts in general take a closer look when the *forum internum* risks coming under threat. Where, by contrast, it is a matter of the manifestations of a religious belief (*forum externum*), the ECtHR in particular is more inclined to trust the contracting States and to allow them to determine for themselves when and how their policy should impose concrete limitations on freedom of religion and belief, and how lenient they should be towards the protection of certain practices dictated by religious or other philosophical beliefs.[109] In the case law of the ECtHR regarding the wearing of the Islamic headscarf, this tendency is clearly present.[110] The ECtHR states in this regard: 'Where questions concerning the relationship between State and religions are at stake, on which

106 See <http://ec.europa.eu/justice/newsroom/contracts/2007_172522_en> accessed June 2014.

107 MLP Loenen, 'Het EHRM en de Grenzen van Religieus Pluralisme' ('The ECtHR and the Limits of Religious Pluralism') (2006) 252 *Nederlands Juristenblad* 304–10 (our translation).

108 On the difference between *forum internum* and *forum externum*, see esp. K Hanson, 'Artikel 9. Vrijheid van Gedachte, Geweten en Godsdienst' ('Article 9. Freedom of Thought, Conscience and Religion') in J Vande Lanotte and Y Haeck, *Handboek EVRM, Deel 2. Artikelsgewijze Commentaar* (ECHR Handbook, part 2. Article-by-Article Commentary), Volume I, 813ff.

109 In this regard see, among others, J Murdoch, *Protecting Right to Freedom of Thought, Conscience and Religion under the European Convention on Human Rights* (Strasbourg, Council of Europe 2012) 83.

110 ECtHR, *Dahlab v Switzerland*, App no 42393/98 (15 February 2001); ECtHR, *Leyla Şahin v Turkey* (29 June 2004); ECtHR, Grand Chamber, *Leyla Şahin v Turkey* (10 November 2005, para 78); ECtHR, *Köse and Others v Turkey*, App no 26625/02 (24 January 2006); ECtHR, *Kurtulmus v Turkey*, App no 65500/01 (24 January 2006); ECtHR, *Fatma Karaduman v Turkey*, App no 41296/04 (3 April 2007); ECtHR, *Çağlayan v Turkey*, App no 1638/04 (3 April 2007).

opinion in a democratic society may reasonably differ widely, the role of the national decision-making body must be given special importance.'[111]

On the scope of the margin of appreciation that the ECtHR allows to the States, one particular case recently has been the cause of vivid debate among legal scholars: the *Lautsi* case.[112] On 3 November 2009, a Chamber of the Second Section of the ECtHR ruled that Italy may no longer display crucifixes in public schools.[113] The fallout from this ruling was unprecedented.[114] As a reaction to the judgment, two fronts, so to speak, emerged. On the one hand, the critics: not only in Italy, but in the rest of Europe as well, the decision of the Court was subjected to sharp criticism.[115] On the other hand, a number of authors agreed with the judgment and saw it as a step in the right direction.[116] Italy went on to request – and obtained – a referral of the case to the Grand Chamber. In its second judgment, of 18 March 2011, the ECtHR ruled that Italy was justified in making it mandatory to display crucifixes in public school classrooms. This decision, too, elicited mixed reactions.[117] The judgment is based on the principle of the margin of appreciation.[118] It leaves the contracting States extensive freedom to determine how they wish to deal with religious and philosophical pluralism within their internal legal order,[119] given their own specific political, economic, social and cultural situation and in the light of the evaluation of the situations on the ground.[120]

The *Lautsi* case and, more recently, the *Eweida* case[121] are just two examples, but the RELIGARE data show that in various Member States similar issues are at stake, where the question is whether all the conditions have been met for an even-handed balancing in the event of a conflict played out between the majority group within society and a minority that opposes mainstream opinion. 'Local', context-oriented arguments also play a role in determining how (concretely) the principle of inclusive neutrality may be applied, and the demand of toleration requires that one take into consideration not only the interests of the majority but also the (justified) demands of *all* those concerned. If public authorities (including the courts) are reticent with regard to accurately balancing, in an even-handed way, the interests at stake, the weaker parties risk getting the short end of the stick. The right of minorities – whether religious or other – to religious freedom comes under pressure if the majority in a diverse society puts the imprint of its own conception of the 'good life'

111 ECtHR, Grand Chamber, *Leyla Şahin v Turkey* (10 November 2005), para 109.

112 ECtHR, Grand Chamber, *Lautsi and Others v Italy*, App no 30814/06 (18 March 2011).

113 ECtHR, *Lautsi v Italy*, App no 30814/06 (3 November 2009).

114 See, among others, D McGoldrick, 'Religion in the European Public Square and in European Public Life: Crucifixes in the Classroom?' (September 2011) 11 (3) *Hum Rts L Rev* 451–502.

115 See, among others, J Weiler, 'Lautsi: Crucifix in the Classroom Redux' *EJIL Talk!* <www.ejiltalk.org/lautsi-crucifix-in-the-classroom-redux/> accessed June 2014.

116 S Mancini, 'The Crucifix Rage: Supranational Constitutionalism and Counter-Majoritarian Difficulty' (2006) 6 *EuConst* 6–27; C Panara, '*Lautsi v Italy*: The Display of Religious Symbols by the State' (2011) 17 *European Public Law* 139–68; G Andreescu and L Andreescu, 'The European Court of Human Rights' *Lautsi* Decision: Context, Contents, Consequences' (2010) 9 (26) *Journal for the Study of Religions and Ideologies* 47–74 (Andreescu and Andreescu give arguments for and against, but were convinced at the time that the Grand Chamber would confirm the reasoning of the Second Chamber).

117 In this regard see, among others, P Annicchino, 'Winning the Battle by Losing the War: The Lautsi Case and the Holy Alliance between American Conservative Evangelicals, the Russian Orthodox Church and the Vatican to Reshape European Identity' (2011) 6 (3) *Religion and Human Rights* 213–19; K Lemmens, 'Kruisbeelden in Klassen Mogen toch Volgens EHRM' ('Crucifixes are Allowed in the Classroom after All') (6 April 2011) *De Juristenkrant* 3; L Zucca, 'A Comment on Lautsi' *EJIL: Talk!* <www.ejiltalk.org/a-comment-on-lautsi/> accessed June 2014; J Temperman (ed), *The Lautsi Papers: Multidisciplinary Reflections on Religious Symbols in the Public School Classroom* (Martinus Nijhoff 2012).

118 See in this regard the dissenting opinion of judges Malinverni and Kalaydjieva <http://hudoc.echr.coe.int/sites/eng/pages/search.aspx?i=001-104042> accessed June 2014.

119 See, among others, SC Prebersen, 'Evolutive Interpretation of the European Convention on Human Rights' in P Mahoney and R Rysdal (eds), *Protecting Human Rights: The European Perspective* (Heymans 2000) 1127–37; A Nieuwenhuis, 'European Court of Human Rights: State and Religion, Schools and Scarves. An Analysis of the Margin of Appreciation as Used in the Case of *Leyla Şahin v Turkey*' (2005) 1 (3) *Eur Const L Rev* 495–510; G Pitt, 'Religion or Belief: Aiming at the Right Target?' in H Meenan (ed), *Equality Law in an Enlarged European Union: Understanding the Article 13 Directives* (CUP 2007) 209ff.

120 We rely for this description on J Vande Lanotte and G Goedertier, *Handboek Belgisch Publiekrecht* (Handbook of Belgian Public Law) (Die Keure 2010), marginal number 252.

121 See n 21.

upon legislation. Freedom of religion and belief is also and should remain, if not primarily, a fundamental right of minorities.

It is the latter concern that brought the RELIGARE project to advance the two yardsticks of 'inclusive State neutrality' and 'justice as even-handedness' at this (still) early stage of EU policymaking in the search for the right balance between the requirements of non-discrimination and equal treatment and the protection of freedom of religion and belief taken in the broad sense. The standards set by 'inclusive State neutrality' and 'justice as even-handedness', in combination, confirm that the national margin of appreciation is not unlimited – it is mainly about due process and contextualised argumentation. It goes hand in hand with a European oversight both of the laws themselves and of their implementation. That is, when the ECtHR investigates whether a national measure is justified in principle, it also looks at whether the measure is proportionate to the objective sought.[122] In a sense, the two yardsticks of 'inclusive State neutrality' and 'justice as even-handedness' underscore the fact that national governments (legislatures as well as courts) have increased responsibility to ensure that, within the framework of their specific constitutional context, there is a careful and responsible weighing up of whether or not to allow and/or restrict specific forms of manifestation of religious or other beliefs. 'Inclusive State neutrality' and 'justice as even-handedness' do not stand in the way of the relationship between public authorities and religions and beliefs being seen from the perspective of subsidiarity. Furthermore, they do not necessarily mean that stricter demands as regards compliance with constitutional principles related to the freedom of thought and expression may not be imposed.

Legislatures should also systematically, as far as possible, take an approach that opts for inclusive even-handedness. Failing that, any restriction imposed by the law on freedom of religion is likely to be seen by some as discriminatory and conducive to negative feelings either towards public authorities or others groups and communities. What should not happen is that a significant number of persons in the EU see themselves as increasingly subject to restrictions that they consider unjustified and that, in their view, constitute discrimination against them. That would certainly not be a trustworthy blueprint on which to build when rethinking the interface of religion and secularism in the Europe of the future.

122 See, for instance, ECtHR, Grand Chamber, *Leyla Şahin v Turkey* (10 November 2005), para 110: 'The Court's task is to determine whether the measures taken at national level were justified in principle and proportionate.'

PART II
Responses to the RELIGARE Report

Section 1
Religious Freedom in Europe: The Intricacies of Equal Treatment Policies

Chapter 3
Freedom of Religion or Belief: Anachronistic in Europe?

Heiner Bielefeldt

Liberal Objections to a Liberal Right

From early on, freedom of religion or belief[1] met with resistance from religious traditionalists who frequently suspected that a human rights approach to handling faith issues would undermine religious values, communitarian loyalty and people's sense of sacredness. Such resistance continues to be vocal in many parts of the world. However, whereas in Europe traditionalist objections to freedom of religion or belief have become comparatively rare, we are currently witnessing the emergence of new types of scepticism towards this particular human right. What is new is that objections to freedom of religion in Europe more and more come from 'liberal' angles. Quite a number of people who understand themselves as 'liberals' in the broadest sense of the word and who generally support human rights display mixed feelings when it comes to discussing the implications of religious freedom for democratic European societies. It seems that freedom of religion or belief is the only classical liberal right which does not currently receive unanimous approval within the various liberal milieus in Europe.[2]

To give an example: in 2012 a German lower court judgment on ritual circumcision of underage boys triggered quite an emotional public debate that became, at times, aggressive.[3] When interviewed by the media about this complicated issue, I was repeatedly asked, 'What should have priority in your view, religious freedom or the human rights of small children?' Or in more general terms, 'Don't you think that human rights should prevail over freedom of religion?' Those asking questions of this sort obviously assumed that human rights on the one hand and freedom of religion or belief on the other are contradictory normative standards which somehow exclude each other. Any response to such questions required, first of all, a clarification that freedom of religion or belief itself has the status of an established human right. Since the Virginia Bill of Rights it has been enshrined in numerous human rights documents, including the Universal Declaration of Human Rights, the International Covenant on Civil and Political Rights, the European Convention on Human Rights and the Fundamental Rights Charter of the European Union.[4]

The chief problem underlying the juxtaposition of human rights and religious freedom, as expressed in the type of interview questions mentioned above, is not a lack of knowledge. One may suppose that those assuming such a juxtaposition know quite well that freedom of religion or belief, for whatever reasons, has factually become an element of various national, European and international human rights guarantees. The main problem, rather, is *a lack of acceptance* of that fact. It seems that freedom of religion or belief has meanwhile received the somewhat dubious reputation as a human right which allegedly is less human, less liberal, less egalitarian and less secular than other human rights.

Why is that so? Freedom of religion or belief obviously has to do with convictions and conviction-based practices, many of which claim a transcendent, 'transhuman' origin, while human rights are explicitly

1 I will generally use the formulation 'freedom of religion or belief', which is a shorthand representing the full title 'freedom of thought, conscience, religion or belief'. For stylistic purposes I will at times resort to alternative formulations such as 'religious freedom'.

2 In this article, I do not define the terms 'liberal' and 'liberalism'. Obviously, they can represent very different political currents and social milieus. In the course of the article, it will become clear that freedom of religion or belief can serve as a watershed between different understandings of 'liberal' and 'liberalism'.

3 In December 2012, the German Federal Parliament passed a law which clarified that the circumcision of boys, under certain conditions, remains permitted. The public discussion largely ebbed after the adoption of the new law.

4 See Article 18 of the UDHR, Article 18 of the ICCPR, Article 9 of the ECHR, Article 10 of the EU Fundamental Rights Charter.

conceptualised as 'human'. Some observers appear to presuppose that a general contradiction exists between the human and the transhuman. They may also point to long-lasting historic conflicts between the modern human rights movement and religious authorities in Europe and elsewhere. Moreover, although freedom of religion or belief carries 'freedom' in its title, this particular right has sometimes been invoked to limit other freedoms, in particular freedom of expression. Well-known examples include the UN debates on 'combating defamation of religions', in which respect for the religious feelings of conservative believers has been played off against frank, open and provocative discussions.[5] Hence, the impression has arisen that freedom of religion or belief often conceals anti-liberal interests. In addition, discussions about headscarves, turbans, halal or kosher food, prayer rooms at the workplace, religious holidays, exemptions from sports education and many other practical issues have led people to conclude that religious minorities typically invoke freedom of religion or belief in order to request some sort of special treatment. Whereas human rights in general display a strong egalitarian spirit, freedom of religion or belief *prima facie* points in the opposite direction, or so it is perceived. Does this right not pave the way to preserving old and creating new privileges, in violation of the principle of equality and at the expense of effective anti-discrimination agendas? Many people may feel that there is some truth in this allegation. On top of all of this, adherents of strict secularism may fear that, by admitting religious arguments and religious symbols to the public sphere, the right to freedom of religion or belief could become the entry point for religious policies which in the long run will endanger the secularity of the public political and legal order in Europe.

Assuming that human rights can be defined as secular rights of freedom and equality of all human beings, some observers doubt whether freedom of religion or belief fully shares the defining characteristics of a human right. At first glance, it may appear to be less human, less liberal, less egalitarian and less secular than other human rights. Critics may go a step further and allege that this right is even used for anti-human, anti-liberal, anti-egalitarian and anti-secular purposes.[6] Against such charges, this contribution demonstrates that freedom of religion or belief, when correctly understood, is fully in line with the human rights approach. Moreover, a comprehensive perspective on human rights would be inconceivable without appreciating the relevance of freedom of religion or belief for societies, including European societies.

The Human Rights Characteristics of Freedom of Religion or Belief

Human Beings as Right Holders

Unsurprisingly, freedom of religion or belief is often associated with the promotion of religion in society, since it is a right which obviously deals with religion and belief, as the title indicates. However, the decisive point is that this happens in an *indirect way*, that is, through claims put forward by human beings. To use a frequently cited short formula: freedom of religion or belief, strictly speaking, 'protects believers rather than beliefs'. One may rightly object that believers and beliefs are necessarily intertwined, since no one can earnestly speak about believers without considering their beliefs. And yet it remains true that human rights tackle that interrelatedness between believers and beliefs consistently *from the angle of the human being*. What in a purely academic context may appear as a trivial remark has political significance. Against the background of a widespread misperception that freedom of religion allegedly protects 'the interest of religion' as such, it cannot be emphasised enough that this right rather recognises human beings in their dignity, freedom and equality. In this sense, freedom of religion or belief is not less 'human' in its focus than freedom of expression, freedom of assembly, the right to food, the various rights of habeas corpus or any other human right. Rather than protecting religious truth claims, religious traditions or particular religious identities as such, it aims at empowering human beings.

One main reason (not the only reason) for the consistent focus on human beings as right holders is the reality of irreconcilable differences in worldviews and practices. Whereas some religions are based on holy books transmitted through divinely chosen prophets, other religions do not have the notions of prophethood,

5 For some details see the section 'A Comprehensive Right to Freedom' below.

6 See also H Bielefeldt, 'Misperceptions of Freedom of Religion or Belief' (2013) 35 *Human Rights Quarterly* 33.

scriptural revelation or even God. What is sacred for one community may remain opaque to another community, and the values that one group holds in high esteem may simply look strange and incomprehensible to others. Therefore legal recognition in the framework of human rights cannot immediately be accorded to the particular contents of religions or beliefs – their truth claims, holy persons, scriptures, practices and so on – but only to *human beings* as the responsible agents who hold, cherish, develop and try to live up to such convictions. In short, freedom of religion or belief does not protect religious traditions, but instead facilitates the *free search and development* of faith-related identities in the broadest sense of the word. And rather than promoting specific religious norms, its purpose is to ensure equal respect for *human beings as potential holders of profound convictions* and faith-based practices, whatever their specific contents may be.

Focusing on human beings as right holders does not imply the adoption of an anthropocentric worldview in which the human being figures as 'the measure of all things',[7] as conservative critics have often suspected. It also does not mean that one subscribes to Ludwig Feuerbach's position that God is a mere product of human imagination and the projection of unfulfilled mundane yearnings.[8] Freedom of religion or belief can well serve as a normative reference for positions which claim to originate from a divine – and in this sense 'transhuman' – source. It may cover voluntary acts of surrendering oneself to God, for instance by entering a monastic order. A person can even believe that personhood is a mere illusion which should be removed as an obstacle on the path to higher wisdom. The point is that even in such clear cases of transanthropocentric or 'transhuman' views, it always remains the human being who professes the respective view and will be held accountable for any practical acts that follow from such a conviction. Although the human being is not necessarily 'the measure of all things', it does function as 'the measure of all rights', so to speak. In that sense freedom of religion or belief, too, is a right only accorded to human beings.

Taking the human being as the systematic starting point for understanding freedom of religion or belief requires us to go beyond any predefined definition of classical religions. The term 'religion' in the title of this right serves as a proxy for existential, identity-shaping convictions and conviction-based practices in a much broader sense. The often used short formula 'religious freedom', therefore, does not fully cover the broad range of convictions and practices falling within the ambit of this human right, whose full title is 'freedom of thought, conscience, religion or belief'.[9] The UN Human Rights Committee, which is the expert body in charge of monitoring the implementation of the International Covenant on Civil and Political Rights, confirmed the necessity of keeping the understanding of this right open and inclusive. In its General Comment No. 22 on freedom of religion or belief (issued in 1993) the Committee pointed out: 'Article 18 protects theistic, non-theistic and atheistic beliefs, as well as the right not to profess any religion or belief. The terms "belief" and "religion" are to be broadly construed.'[10] This broad understanding ultimately follows from the focus on human beings, which, in the spirit of universalism, must include everybody in their various identity-shaping profound convictions and conviction-based practices.[11]

A Comprehensive Right to Freedom

Nothing has contributed more to the impression that freedom of religion is a 'less liberal' human right than its mistaken invocation in anti-blasphemy debates. While in this context freedom of expression typically figures as the epitome of a liberal right that backs all sorts of free speech, artistic experimentation, public criticism and non-violent provocation, freedom of religion or belief is often perceived (or used) as a counter-right, as it were, in that it allegedly puts limits on an allegedly 'overly extensive' expressive freedom. In short, whereas freedom of expression signals a green light for open debate, freedom of religion seems to function more like a stop sign.

7 This is the proverbial motto of the ancient sophist Protagoras.

8 See L Feuerbach, *Vorlesungen über das Wesen der Religion* (Verlag von Otto Wigand 1851) 241.

9 The component of 'belief' has, inter alia, the function of indicating the inclusion of profound convictions outside the realm of traditional religions. This also includes agnostics and atheists. The fact that many of them call themselves 'non-believers' is a source of major confusion in this regard. The French version ('liberté de religion et de conviction') may be less likely to create confusion.

10 Human Rights Committee, General Comment no. 22, UN Doc. A/48/40, vol I, annex VI, para 2.

11 See TJ Gunn, 'The Complexity of Religion and the Definition of "Religion" in International Law' (2003) 16 *Harvard Human Rights Journal* 189.

A much discussed example is the case *Otto-Preminger-Institut v Austria*, which the European Court of Human Rights decided in 1994. The Austrian administration had confiscated a film deemed offensive to the feelings of Christians because it placed central persons of the Christian tradition in a pornographic context. In its judgment the Strasbourg Court did not see a violation of the complainant's freedom of expression. The Court held that the issue 'involves weighing up the conflicting interests of the exercise of two fundamental freedoms guaranteed under the Convention, namely the right of the applicant association to impart to the public controversial views ..., on the one hand, and the right of other persons to proper respect for their freedom of thought, conscience and religion, on the other hand'.[12] This formulation displays an understanding of freedom of religion or belief and freedom of expression as two more or less contradictory rights. The majority decision (a four to three decision) was heavily criticised by the judges Palm, Pekkanen and Makarczyk, who argued that the assumed antagonism between freedom of religion or belief and freedom of expression does not exist. In their minority vote they sketched out a decisively liberal understanding of freedom of religion or belief: 'The Convention does not, in terms, guarantee a right to protection of religious feelings. More particularly, such a right cannot be derived from the right to freedom of religion, which in effect includes a right to express views critical of the religious opinions of others.'[13]

Much more politicised discussions on similar issues took place in forums of the United Nations. Between 1999 and 2010 the Organisation of Islamic Cooperation (OIC) regularly tabled a resolution titled 'combating defamation of religions'.[14] Apart from giving the impression that religions *per se* could receive legal protection of their reputation – which is an idea clearly at odds with the human rights approach – another major problem of the OIC resolutions on defamation was that they appeared to legitimise anti-liberal measures, possibly even including draconian blasphemy laws.[15] In Pakistan, one of the leading OIC countries, ill-defined blasphemy offences can lead to a death sentence.[16]

In discussions on the resolutions on combating defamation of religions, Asma Jahangir, the then UN Special Rapporteur on freedom of religion or belief (who incidentally also lives in Pakistan), pointed out that there can be no right of religious groups to be free from criticism or even ridicule.[17] Establishing such a right would ultimately amount to the end of a free society based on open public discourse. By rejecting the OIC approach on defamation of religions, Jahangir took a position similar to the minority vote in the Otto-Preminger case. She emphasised: 'Freedom of religion primarily confers a right to act in accordance with one's religion but does not bestow a right for believers to have their religion itself protected from all adverse comment.'[18]

In her criticism of the anti-defamation resolutions, Jahangir clarified that no abstract antagonism exists between freedom of expression and freedom of religion or belief. Rather, both freedoms presuppose and reinforce one another. Ample evidence demonstrates that anti-blasphemy laws, besides having a chilling effect on free speech, also threaten religious minorities, such as Christian minorities or the Ahmadiyyah community in Pakistan. Such restrictive legislation also has an intimidating effect on religious dissenters, critics, agnostics or atheists. Hence, overcoming anti-blasphemy legislation is ultimately in the interest of both freedom of expression and freedom of religion or belief. Rather than standing in opposition to one another, those two rights can and do mutually reinforce one another.

---

12 ECtHR, *Otto-Preminger-Institut v Austria*, App no 13470/87 (20 September 1994), s 55.

13 ibid, Joint Dissenting Opinion of the Judges Palm, Pekkanen and Makardzyk, s 6.

14 See Commission on Human Rights resolutions 1999/82, 2000/84, 2001/4, 2002/9, 2003/4, 2004/6 and 2005/3; General Assembly resolutions 60/150, 61/164, 62/154, 63/171, 64/156 and 65/224; Human Rights Council resolutions 4/9, 7/19, 10/22 and 13/16. For a critical assessment, see RC Blitt, 'The Bottom Up Journey of "Defamation of Religions" from Muslim States to the United Nations: A Case Study of the Migration of Anti-Constitutional Ideas' (2011) 56 *Studies in Law, Politics and Society* 121.

15 See J Temperman, 'Blasphemy, Defamation of Religions and Human Rights Law' (2008) 26 (4) *Netherlands Quarterly of Human Rights* 485.

16 See Freedom House, *Policing Belief: The Impact of Blasphemy Laws on Human Rights* (Freedom House 2010) 69–87 (on Pakistan).

17 See Report of the Special Rapporteur on freedom of religion or belief, A Jahangir, and the Special Rapporteur on contemporary forms of racism, racial discrimination, xenophobia and related intolerance, D Diène, Implementation of General Assembly Resolution 60/251 of 15 March 2006 entitled 'Human Rights Council', A/HRC/2/1, 10.

18 ibid para 37.

To assume that freedom of expression is somehow 'more liberal' than freedom of religion or belief is a systematic mistake. The relationship of the two rights is not an antagonistic one in the sense that the first gives a green light to free provocations, while the latter chiefly operates as a stop sign. Instead, the two rights share the general goal of safeguarding communicative freedom to the greatest degree possible. This common purpose literally renders them neighbouring rights, protected in Articles 18 and 19 of the Universal Declaration, Articles 18 and 19 of the International Covenant on Civil and Political Rights, Articles 9 and 10 of the European Convention on Human Rights and Articles 10 and 11 of the EU Fundamental Rights Charter.[19] While they are not identical in their precise contents, both rights largely move in the same direction.[20]

Freedom of religion or belief is not in any sense 'less liberal' than other rights of freedom, such as freedom of expression, freedom of association, freedom of assembly, and so on. Its purpose is to empower human beings to freely find their ways in the broad area of religious or non-religious convictions, conscience-based personal positions and communitarian practices, the development of religious or belief identities, the organisation of religious community life, and many other issues. People have the freedom to search for an ultimate meaning in life and to come to the most divergent results (or none whatsoever) in such endeavours; to communicate their convictions, beliefs or doubts openly; to live in accordance with the tenets of their faiths; to worship alone or together with others; to grow up and remain within their faith communities or to abandon their inherited beliefs; to establish appropriate infrastructures needed for the development of their communities; to defend old or create new religious organisations; to manifest religious or belief orientations visibly, including by obeying particular dress codes; to promote their convictions publicly and invite others to join their communities; to educate their children in conformity with their own religious or moral convictions and to organise community schools for this purpose. Needless to say, this list of sub-freedoms of freedom of religion or belief is non-exhaustive.[21]

Diversity-Friendly Equality

Freedom of religion or belief is not only an obvious right to freedom; it also has a strong equality dimension which it shares with other human rights. In practical terms, equality is chiefly operationalised in non-discrimination clauses which enlist the prohibition of discrimination based on religion or belief together with other grounds of specifically prohibited discrimination. In November 1981 the UN General Assembly furthermore passed a declaration specifically dedicated to combating discrimination on the grounds of religious or belief-related differences. Article 3 of the UN Declaration on the Elimination of All Forms of Intolerance and of Discrimination Based on Religion or Belief sends a strong message by underlining that 'discrimination between human beings on the grounds of religion or belief constitutes an affront to human dignity and a disavowal of the principles of the Charter of the United Nations'.

Nevertheless, freedom of religion or belief is sometimes perceived as blurring the egalitarian spirit of human rights or leading to a less strict understanding of equality. This impression may have originated from specific requests put forward by religious minorities concerning dress codes, dietary rules, prayer rooms, holidays, partial exemptions from school education and many other issues. In the face of such specific demands, some people wonder whether freedom of religion could become the entry point for requesting

---

19 The same 'neighbourhood' occurs in Articles 4 and 5 of the German Basic Law, Articles 13 and 14 of the Greek Constitution, Articles 6 and 7 of the Constitution of the Netherlands, Articles 29 and 30 of the Romanian Constitution, Articles 15 and 16 of the Swiss Federal Constitution, and so on.

20 See MD Evans, 'The Freedom of Religion or Belief and the Freedom of Expression' (2009) 4 *Religion and Human Rights* 197.

21 Of course, freedom of religion or belief is not without limits, but imposing limitations on the exercise of a right to freedom is always sensitive. On the one hand, it is a truism that a person's or group's freedom cannot be completely unlimited, since making use of one's own freedom might negatively affect the rights of other people or other important public interests. On the other hand, the general need for some limitations can easily become a pretext for imposing arbitrary, discriminatory or overly broad restrictions. The question of how to draw limits and how to prevent the frequent abuse of limitation clauses therefore requires caution and diligence. Article 18 of the Covenant entails some indispensable criteria in this regard, and the UN Human Rights Committee has devoted several paragraphs of its General Comment No. 22 to further clarifying this issue.

privileged treatment and exceptions from general rules which everyone else is expected to abide by. Does it in practice function as an anti-egalitarian right which more or less dilutes non-discrimination agendas?

To answer this question, we first of all should recall that in the context of human rights equality never means sameness. The principle of equality must always be seen in close conjunction with the principle of freedom, and vice versa. Without taking account of equality, rights of freedom would amount to privileges of the happy few. Likewise, without regard to freedom, the principle of equality could be mistaken for uniformity, a misunderstanding already manifested in Edmund Burke's polemics against the French Revolution.[22] By contrast, human rights empower human beings – on the basis of equal respect for everyone – to pursue their freely chosen life plans, to enjoy respect for their irreplaceable personal biographies, to express their diverse political opinions or to freely manifest their different faith-related convictions and practices. Instead of leading to homogeneous or uniform societies, working for the equal implementation of human rights for everyone makes societies more diverse and more pluralistic. The Council of Europe was well advised to launch a pro-diversity campaign under the motto 'all different, all equal'.[23]

In the framework of human rights, equality per definition is a diversity-friendly equality. In no area should this be more obvious than in the context of religion or belief. What makes the fight for equality and non-discrimination in this field particularly complicated is the experience that religious communities – Jews, Christians, Muslims, Mormons, Baha'is, Hindus, Buddhists, Taoists and others – have *very different* needs which they wish to see respected in practice. They follow different liturgical calendars, they prescribe different dietary practices, and they may believe in different forms of religious self-organisation. What does 'equality' mean in this regard? It certainly cannot be an equality of results. Allowing all religious communities to ring church bells, if they should choose to do so, would be an absurdity. Instead, the principle of equality must come into play at an earlier stage. Legislators should engage in intensive consultations with members of religious or belief minorities before issuing legislation that could adversely affect the religious convictions and practices of minorities. This is not an easy task, and it can only be tackled in a spirit of open communication and mutual trust.

Particularly complicated questions arise around issues of indirect discrimination. Apart from direct and straightforward forms of discrimination against religious minorities (which continues to be a reality in all European countries), discrimination can also occur in indirect forms. It is sometimes concealed under seemingly 'neutral' rules which, although on the surface apply to everyone equally, have disproportionately negative effects on members of minorities. For instance, public holidays usually reflect the dominant religious and cultural tradition in a country. While adherents of mainstream religions usually do not encounter problems in combining their job-related obligations with celebrating their religious holidays, the situation of religious or belief minorities can become quite complicated. For instance, huge problems may arise for people who feel religiously obliged not to work on specific holidays. Jews or Seventh-Day Adventists have even lost their jobs as a result of their refusal to work on Saturdays.[24] Another example of possible indirect discrimination related to seemingly neutral rules is dress code regulations in public institutions or private companies that prohibit public servants or employees from wearing religious garments. While on the surface affecting everyone equally, such regulations frequently impose disproportionate burdens on members of religious minorities.

The principle of 'reasonable accommodation' can lead to solutions in such circumstances. Its purpose is to overcome the indirectly discriminatory implications of those societal or legal norms which stem from the dominant religious traditions of a country and to create more suitable conditions for members of minorities, who should be able to live in accordance with their convictions. In some situations, this may justify exceptions from general rules if that is the only way to avoid conflict with deeply held normative convictions. At the same time, such measures of accommodation should remain within a 'reasonable' framework, that is, they must do justice to important interests of public order and in particular the human rights and basic freedoms of others.[25]

For all the difficulties that may arise in complicated cases, some forms of accommodation have already become standard practice in many public and private institutions in Europe. An example is respect for dietary

22 See E Burke, *Reflection on the Revolution in France* ([original 1790], Dent 1910).

23 See <http://www.coe.int/t/dg4/youth/coe_youth/adae_campaign_EN.asp> accessed 27 June 2014.

24 See (with reference particularly to US American experiences in this field) MC Nussbaum, *Liberty of Conscience: In Defense of America's Tradition of Religious Equality* (Basic Books 2008).

25 See J Maclure and C Taylor, *Laïcité et liberté de conscience* (Boréal 2010).

needs originating from religious prescripts or other conscience-based reasons. Many schools, universities and companies have found pragmatic ways of accommodating the diversity of religious holidays, and there are also successful examples of allowing people to perform their prayer rituals within such institutions. In short, provided there is good will on all sides, practical solutions can in most cases be found. It is important not to forget such overall positive experiences in discussions about accommodation of specific religious needs.

At the same time, complicated questions can emerge. How should the State respond to conscience-based demands for an exception from mandatory school attendance which in many countries has the status of a constitutional norm? Although in most cases the demands for accommodation merely relate to specific parts of school education, such as sports or biology classes, the question of where limits can or must be drawn worries legislators, courts and the general public. To give another example, how far can accommodation go if a Sikh boy insists on keeping his *kirpan* (a dagger with great symbolic meaning) in class, despite the school's clear anti-weapons regulations? In a much discussed case the Canadian Supreme Court decided in favour of a young Sikh, while at the same time demanding that his *kirpan* be safely sewn into his jacket.[26] Over the years, US courts have issued conflicting judgments on the question of whether adherents to indigenous religions should have the right to smoke peyote in a ritualistic setting despite the fact that the consumption of peyote generally collides with anti-drug laws.[27]

Policies and measures of reasonable accommodation often meet with scepticism among the general populace. One reason is fear that embarking on such policies could open the floodgates to an inflation of demands. It is here that the 'reasonableness' criteria must come into play. Reasonableness implies, inter alia, that those who request specific measures of accommodation can be required to demonstrate the seriousness of their claims. They have to present credible arguments that, without appropriate measures, they would suffer an existential conflict, that is, a dilemma of a serious nature. Deriving from freedom of thought, conscience, religion or belief, reasonable accommodation should not fall prey to mere trivial matters; the idea is not simply to become a reference norm for all kinds of personal tastes or preferences. Reasonableness in this context thus also means seriousness. In some cases it may be difficult to discern a serious religious or belief-related demand from more trivial interests. When confronted with such questions, those in charge need professional advice based on a clear understanding of freedom of religion or belief.

Another main objection reflects the widely held impression that reasonable accommodation privileges certain people at the expense of equality. If handled appropriately, however, the opposite is true. Instead of operating as an anti-egalitarian principle, reasonable accommodation translates the principle of equality into different societal contexts. And rather than diluting equality, reasonable accommodation contributes to an appropriately complex conceptualisation of equality based on equal respect and concern for all human beings, with their diverse biographies, convictions, identities and needs. In the words of Gabrielle Caceres, 'reasonable accommodation aims at relaxing generally applicable rules in order to guarantee a more substantive equality in which the specificities of everyone are taken into account'.[28] It does not privilege certain groups of people but finally contributes to a diverse society to the benefit of all. In this sense reasonable accommodation can and should be a positive part of any anti-discrimination agenda.

A few years ago, the European Court of Human Rights decided in favour of a Polish prisoner who for conscientious reasons insisted on receiving vegetarian food.[29] This successful case of accommodation, however, has thus far been exceptional in the Strasbourg jurisdiction. In general, European legislatures and courts have been very reluctant to accept reasonable accommodation as a legally binding principle.[30] The EU-funded RELIGARE research project comes to the conclusion that reasonable accommodation, in particular in

26 See *Multani v Commission Scolaire Marguerite-Bourgeoys and Attorney General of Quebec* [2006] Supreme Court of Canada, 1 SCR 256, 2006 SCC 6.

27 See WC Durham and BG Scharffs, *Law and Religion: National, International, and Comparative Perspectives* (Aspen 2010) 218ff.

28 G Caceres, 'Reasonable Accommodation as a Tool to Manage Religious Diversity in the Workplace: What about the "Transposability" of an American Concept in the French Secular Context?' in K Alidadi, M-C Foblets and J Vrielinek (eds), *A Test of Faith? Religious Diversity and Accommodation in the European Workplace* (Ashgate 2012) 284.

29 See ECtHR, *Jokobski v Poland*, App no 18429/06 (7 December 2010).

30 For a critical analysis (with a particular focus in the workplace), see S Ouald Chaib, 'Religious Accommodation in the Workplace: Improving the Legal Reasoning of the European Court of Human Rights' in Alidadi, Foblets and Vrielink

the workplace, is even denied in situations where respective measures would be nearly cost-free. According to the RELIGARE scholars, 'there are gaps in the existing legal protection that make it difficult adequately to address (even modest) claims for religious accommodation in Europe'. Hence, the project recommends 'the important additional tool of *legally enshrined* reasonable accommodation on the basis of religion and belief in the workplace' (*Report*, 19).

The call for an understanding of reasonable accommodation as a legally binding principle could furthermore be based on the 2006 UN Convention on the Rights of Persons with Disability (CRPD), which reflects the more advanced human rights discussion. Article 5, paragraph 3 of the CRPD states: 'In order to promote equality and eliminate discrimination, States Parties shall take all appropriate steps to ensure that reasonable accommodation is provided.' The CRPD is the first international human rights convention that enshrines reasonable accommodation as a legal principle. While it focuses exclusively on persons with disabilities, it seems only fair to conclude that the principle should also apply in other areas of non-discrimination work, including the elimination of discrimination based on religion or belief.

Justifying Inclusive Secularity

It is well known that the term 'secular' and its derivatives carry the heavy historical baggage of long-lasting conflicts over the role of religion in public life.[31] In particular, during the nineteenth century, a number of European countries were politically torn between religious and secular camps. Even today the adjectives 'secular' and 'religious' are often interpreted as reflecting irreconcilably antagonistic political interests. This perceived antagonism can spill over into discussions on freedom of religion or belief and cause anxiety that this particular right could become the entry point for religious interests into the public sphere, with possible detrimental effects on the secularity of the State. On a closer look, however, it turns out that this supposed antagonism does not exist. On the contrary, freedom of religion or belief can provide a justification for an inclusive concept of the secular State.

In order to be able to guarantee freedom of religion or belief for everyone, the State should develop an open constitutional framework in which religious and belief pluralism can unfold freely and without discrimination. The 'negative' implication of this positive task is the requirement that the State should not identify itself with one particular religion or belief (or one particular type of religions) at the expense of equal treatment of the followers of other faiths. This certainly presents a challenge to countries in which religions and State institutions are closely interwoven, in particular countries with the tradition of an official religion or State religion.

Official religions are a widespread phenomenon especially in the Islamic world, but official religions also continue to exist in parts of Europe (*Report*, 12f). The practical implications of having an official religion differ widely from country to country, ranging from a more or less symbolic superior rank of one religion to rigid measures aimed at protecting the predominant role of the State religion against any denominational competition. It should be noted, however, that restrictive policies do not merely exist in States that have formally embraced an official religion. In many supposedly religiously 'neutral' States, too, the constitution or other legal documents refer to the cultural heritage of the country, in which certain religious denominations have played predominant roles. Legal reference to the predominant historical role of one particular religion can easily become a pretext for discriminatory treatment of the adherents to other religions or beliefs. This danger increases if the invocation of a religious legacy is part of national identity politics.

What are the consequences of these observations? International human rights law does not prescribe one particular model according to which the relationship between State and religion should be organised. Different societies may follow different paths, provided they honour their human rights obligations. However, as the UN Human Rights Committee has pointed out, States have to ensure in any case that having an official religion – or making reference to the historical roles of a particular religion – does not lead to a *de jure* or *de facto* discrimination against members of other religions and beliefs. In its General Comment 22 the Committee insists that

(eds) (n 28) 33–58; L Loenen, 'Accommodation of Religion and Sex Equality in the Workplace under the EU Equality Directives: A Double Bind for the European Court of Justice' in ibid 103–20.

31 See H Lübbe, *Säkularisierung. Geschichte eines ideenpolitischen Begriffs* (Alber 1965).

> the fact that a religion is recognised as a State religion or that it is established as official or traditional or that its followers comprise the majority of the population, shall not result in any impairment of the enjoyment of any of the rights under the Covenant, including Articles 18 and 27, nor in any discrimination against adherents to other religions or non-believers.[32]

The burden of proof in this regard always falls on the State.

At the end of the day it seems difficult to conceive of an application of the concept of an official State religion that in practice does not have adverse effects on religious minorities. When the State officially announces a State religion in the constitution, the law mostly ceases to reflect the religious variety of the society, thereby possibly opening the floodgates to arbitrary action and religious discrimination. Hence there are good reasons to pursue policies of disentangling State and religion in order to create the space for religious and belief-related pluralism to unfold freely and without discrimination.

Freedom of religion or belief, understood as a human right for all without discrimination, can thus become a powerful argument for establishing secular constitutions. At the same time, freedom of religion or belief serves as a critical benchmark to distinguish between different versions of secularity, secularism, *laïcité* and similar concepts, all of which show a peculiar ambivalence: on the one hand, the secularity of the State can represent a formal commitment to accommodate religious pluralism in a spirit of respect for everyone's equal freedom of religion or belief; on the other hand, the term secularity (and the same holds true for the other concepts just mentioned) can also become a proxy for non-commitment, that is, a strict 'hands-off' policy in this entire area. Moreover, secularity can even become a pretext for imposing anti-religious or post-religious worldviews. Classical examples include George Holyoake's 'secular society', the German 'Monistenbund' headed by Darwin's ardent disciple Ernst Haeckel, and Auguste Comte's vision of a scientific 'religion de l'humanité'. Once such a secularist worldview gets directly entangled with State politics or State institutions, the effects are strikingly similar to those of traditional State religions. Indeed, claims of secularism can become ideological ingredients of authoritarian control politics, and they can back restrictive political agendas that aim at purging the public sphere of any visible or audible religious manifestations.

Given this ambivalence of the term 'secular', conceptual clarification is all the more necessary. Freedom of religion or belief has a lot to contribute in this regard. It provides the starting point for an 'inclusive' understanding of the secular State,[33] as opposed to 'exclusive' readings of State secularity. Any consistent implementation of freedom of religion or belief presupposes a policy of deliberate 'non-identification' of the State with any particular religion or worldview in order to be equally fair, open and inclusive to people of different faith orientations living under its jurisdiction. Neither should the government use (or rather abuse) a religion or worldview as a source of its own political legitimacy, nor should it privilege one particular tradition, perhaps with a view to promoting national cohesion or for any other political purposes. In order to make it clear that such deliberate non-identification, despite the *prima facie* negative formulation, has a positive significance, one could further qualify it as 'respectful non-identification'. After all, it is out of respect for everyone's equal freedom of religion or belief that the State should exercise and institutionalise such deliberate self-restraint. Respectful non-identification can be understood as the negative corollary of a positive task, which is creating space for the free unfolding of religious or belief diversity in a country. A secular constitution providing such space would thus be an example of an inclusive secularity, as opposed to exclusive readings which restrict the space for manifesting diversity.

Contributing to a Richer Understanding of Human Rights

The discussion of the various components which define freedom of religion or belief should have dispelled the misperception that this right is in any sense less human, less liberal, less egalitarian and less secular than other human rights. Being fully in line with the human rights approach in general,[34] freedom of religion or belief

32 See General Comment No. 22, para 9.

33 In a similar vein, Foblets and Alidadi (*Report*, 15ff) employ the term 'inclusive State neutrality'.

34 See H Bielefeldt, *Philosophie der Menschenrechte* (Wissenschaftliche Buchgesellschaft 1998).

consistently focuses on human beings as right holders; it includes a broad range of sub-freedoms in the area of thought, conscience, religion or belief; it aspires to overcome all forms of direct or indirect discrimination in the area of religious diversity; and it can become a powerful argument for establishing secular constitutions based on an inclusive rather than exclusive understanding of secularity.

Freedom of religion or belief should be seen as part of a broader human rights package. As underlined by the 1993 Vienna World Conference, the various human rights normatively belong together in that they mutually presuppose and reinforce one another. In the language of Vienna, all human rights are 'universal, indivisible and interrelated and interdependent'.[35] This holistic understanding does not deny the possibility, and indeed reality, of serious conflicts between different human rights concerns. Rather, the Vienna formula reminds us of the *practical task* to keep the broader human rights agenda intact against tendencies of fragmentation which in the long run would weaken or even destroy the entire system of human rights protection. For instance, without freedom of expression or without habeas corpus guarantees, human rights would not even be conceivable in theory; ignoring the right to education would undermine the preconditions for any consistent practical implementation of human rights; and without due account of the principle of gender equality, human rights would lose their credibility as universal standards. Freedom of religion or belief, too, has an indispensable role within the system of human rights in that it guarantees respect for people's profound conviction and conviction-based practices.

Dealing with freedom of religion or belief can furthermore sensitise us to the complexity of the human condition. Human beings have complex needs and aspirations, all of which deserve to be taken seriously in the sphere of rights. This necessarily includes people's deep convictions and commitments, many of which claim a transcendent origin. There is no contradiction between 'human' rights and an appreciation of those sources of identity which are conceived as 'transhuman' by believers. On the contrary, ignoring those dimensions of human life would likely cause serious shortcomings in the understanding of human beings in general.

Likewise, freedom is also a complex phenomenon. Taking freedom seriously, above all, requires respect for the broad diversity of freely chosen ways of life, including forms which do not fit the usual patterns of a liberal lifestyle. There is a real danger nowadays in Europe that liberalism may in the long run sink into mere 'lifestyle liberalism', that is, a complacent attitude which only recognises a certain urban, ironic and religiously dispassionate lifestyle while turning a deaf ear to the demands, wishes and needs of people outside specific 'liberal' milieus. In the late eighteenth century Moses Mendelssohn, the founding figure of Jewish liberalism, had already criticised the tendencies within the enlightenment philosophies of his day to breed new forms of hegemony and intolerance that particularly threatened religious minorities, including his own community.[36] His remarks continue to be topical in Europe today. Dealing with freedom of religion or belief can become an incentive for reflecting on the dialectics of the enlightenment and for recapturing liberalism's more demanding traditions, epitomised by philosophers such as Locke, Mendelssohn and Kant.[37]

As previously mentioned, freedom of religion or belief furthermore helps sharpen the awareness that, in the context of human rights, equality can never mean mere sameness or uniformity. Implementing freedom of religion or belief without discrimination presupposes an investigation into the ultimate source of normative equality, that is, the equal dignity of all human beings. It is noteworthy that the first sentence of the preamble of the 1948 Universal Declaration of Human Rights, that is, the first ever international human rights document, explicitly makes a connection between everyone's 'inherent dignity' and their 'equal and inalienable rights'. A dignity-based equality can only be a complex equality which takes into account the specific needs, demands and aspirations of each individual. In practice, this requires the elimination of all forms of discrimination based on religion or belief, including indirect discrimination, through policies of reasonable accommodation and other measures.

Finally, freedom of religion or belief provides a yardstick by which to distinguish between different understandings of the secular State. Today, most European States call themselves 'secular' or refer to concepts such as 'secularity' or '*laïcité*'. The precise meanings of these self-descriptions are often far from clear.

35 Vienna Declaration and Programme of Action, UN Doc. A/CONF.157/24 (Part I), ch III, Section I, para 5.

36 See M Mendelssohn, *Jerusalem, or, On Religious Power and Judaism* (A Arkush tr, with an introduction and comment by A Altmann, University Press of New England 1983).

37 See H Bielefeldt, *Symbolic Representation in Kant's Practical Philosophy* (CUP 2003).

Secularity can represent inclusive policies of accommodating religious or belief-related pluralism in an open constitutional framework, but the same term can also be used as a proxy for restrictive measures which aim at pushing religion and belief back into a mere private sphere. Dealing with freedom of religion or belief can lead to more normative and phenomenological clarity in this field. It is obvious that, from the standpoint of freedom of religion or belief, only an inclusive understanding of secularity can make sense.

To sum up, freedom of religion or belief is certainly more than a mere remainder of the past which, for whatever reasons, historically made it into human rights catalogues. It can trigger highly relevant debates about European politics, European values and European self-understandings. It may also add a fresh perspective to the perpetual discussions about the dialectics of enlightenment, modernity and, last but not least, liberalism. The strange observation made at the beginning of this chapter that European liberals – or at least some of them – increasingly voice scepticism towards this classical liberal right should indeed make us think more profoundly about which sort of liberalism we wish to promote for the twenty-first century.

Chapter 4
Proceeding from Combat to Concept in Religious Freedom and Equality Policies in Europe

Michael Germann

The question of 'how to respond effectively and appropriately to increasing social, cultural, religious and philosophical diversity' (*Report*, 11) has been crucial since the beginnings of the modern State. In the diverse histories of the European States, the different contexts have led to different answers. Nevertheless, they are all more or less converging on common legal standards based on religious freedom and equality. These standards involve both political programmes and constitutional rights, the implementation of which demands subtle legal concepts in order to manage and balance antagonistic interests. In their domestic legal orders the EU Member States have been developing and practising such legal concepts for a long time.

One of the merits of the RELIGARE project is that it has the potential to help EU policies move beyond mere political programmes and catch up with more elaborated legal concepts. Developing this potential requires going beyond comparing the different 'models' of institutional arrangements dealing with religious diversity that are already in place in the European States (*Report*, 13). Any reduction to 'models' risks overemphasising single features, for example by describing the German legal order as a 'concordat model' and underestimating its predominant constitutional arrangements. The RELIGARE findings propose a number of sophisticated legal concepts that should inspire both legal policy and further research in this field.

On the 'Combat' against Discrimination

The report identifies, as a key to managing diversity, 'the combat in Europe against discrimination' (*Report*, 12). Concerning the notion of 'discrimination', it is most convincing to look at the individual and his interest in enjoying equal opportunities to participate in social and cultural life, and consequently at religious communities and their respective interests in which individuals may wish to deploy themselves. Managing diversity in a liberal society will be concerned with these actual interests rather than abstract ideals of political order.

Concerning the strong emphasis on a 'combat' against discrimination, which is conspicuous throughout most of the report, it is worth asking who the combatants are. While the EU is presumed to be on the side of the good guys, the opponents remain unnamed. Discrimination seems to rage as an unattributable phenomenon, which the report observes to be 'still a serious problem' (*Report*, 12), like a plague to be fought, or a disinterested but devastating monster to be wrestled. In fact, it will always be the choices and the behaviours of human beings that are addressed as discrimination and 'fought'. Where discriminatory acts pursue no other interest than to harm their victims, combating discrimination legally simply means asserting the interests of the victims by suppressing such acts. More often, however, actions are driven by interests other than the desire to harm others, but entail treating someone or something unequally. Unless that interest is in and of itself unacceptable and thus to be considered unacceptable like the intention to merely do harm, combating discrimination presupposes that the interest to be treated equally prevails over the interest to act in a way that implies, in some respects, unequal treatment. This will often be the case, but it is sensible to be prepared for cases in which the interest implying unequal treatment prevails and which, consequently, must be exempt from the combat against, and the very notion of, discrimination. In other words, the 'combat' against discrimination is conditional on an accurate distinction between unjustified and justified unequal treatment, the term 'discrimination' being strictly confined to an unjustified one.

In view of the 'combatants', it seems necessary to consider that the most important arena of the 'combat' in question is supposed to be the legal relationship between public power and private persons. There, such 'combat' on the part of public power is legally defined, to a certain extent, in terms of criminal law. Where discrimination occurs in the shape of criminal violence or offence, it will be fought through criminal prosecution. Beyond the scope of criminal law (and even in its arrangement and application), the actions of private persons have to be handled, in the first instance, as a particular exercise of civil liberties. Civil liberties are not conditioned on complying with moral standards, not even with the essentially moral standards of equal treatment. Legal obligations to act in a non-discriminatory manner must therefore take into account the civil liberties at stake. Consequently, non-discrimination policy by means of legal obligation should be understood not as 'combat' or a 'fight', but as an ambiguous tool for balancing social interests in conflict.

Beyond the means of legislation and law enforcement, non-discrimination policy by public authority (and, more importantly, civil organisations) may comprise publicity campaigns promoting an attitude of tolerance and may be, in this sense, a form of 'fighting' against intolerant dispositions in societies.

Apart from that, and in the first place, the imperative of non-discrimination is addressed to the public authority itself. In this respect, public authority does not have to 'fight' against discrimination, but simply to refrain from engaging in it. In this same respect, furthermore, the demands of non-discrimination and those of religious freedom are not antagonistic, but essentially congruent. It is again the public authority that the RELIGARE report addresses when it expresses the concern that 'perceptions of religion and its role in society' that diverge from 'paradigms inherited from the past regarding (majority) religion' risk remaining 'sidelined or ignored' (*Report*, 12) in legal and legislative practice.

On Some Basic Premises of EU Non-Discrimination Policy

If the EU is to play 'a more direct and active role' in developing policies concerning religious freedom and equality (*Report*, 12), it seems important that this role be clearly defined in form and content. As regards form, the EU remains bound by the frame of its competencies. As regards content, the EU would be well advised to manage the issues of religious freedom and equality with the concepts that are outlined in the RELIGARE report.

Pursuant to Article 19, Section 1 of the Treaty on the Functioning of the European Union (TFEU) (referred to in *Report*, 14), the EU is required to 'combat discrimination' 'without prejudice to the other provisions of the Treaties and within the limits of the powers conferred by them upon the Union'. A measure like the proposed Horizontal Directive (*Report*, 14; 42–43) would have to be tied to a specific EU competency.

The RELIGARE report also asserts that 'EU policy options that would violate fundamental rights should be discarded' (*Report*, 46); even better, they *must* be discarded. Impact assessment is essential in this respect. The dialogue of the EU with religious communities under Article 17, Section 3 of the TFEU (*Report*, 44) requires the EU to recognise context-oriented arguments concerning religious interests.

On the Relationship between Non-Discrimination and Religious Freedom

The report sets non-discrimination and freedom of religion in opposition to one another (*Report*, 11; 12; 17). It finds that 'tensions between the application of non-discrimination norms and the fundamental right to freedom of religion and belief … arise in various areas of social life, which may in the end escalate into intricate legal conflicts', and acknowledges the possibility of 'clashing rights' (*Report*, 41). Where conflicts of this kind occur, the 'search for a balance' (*Report*, 17) is a crucial concern, and the concept of 'inclusive State neutrality' is the right instrument to manage those conflicts.

It seems worthy to note, however, that the two principles come into conflict only in cases where religion motivates discriminatory actions, or where non-discrimination requires interference with religious freedom. More often, religious freedom and non-discrimination do not conflict, but embrace an identical interest. 'Inclusive neutrality' is a demand that both have in common. A non-inclusive concept of neutrality would interfere with both religious freedom and non-discrimination no less than a bias towards or against a particular religious position would do. For this reason, the most important concern is not necessarily that 'expectations of equality and freedom of movement potentially clash with the *protection* of the freedom of religion and belief enjoyed by individuals and communities within Member States' (*Report*, 45, emphasis added). Rather, the concern is that they will clash with efforts to make society conform to a mainstream opposed to certain religions or to religion at all – in other words, they will clash with the *disregard* of freedom of religion and belief.

On 'Substantive Equality' and 'Reasonable Accommodation' in Conflicts

In practice, conflicts differ from one another depending on which realm of social life they engage. The RELIGARE report has focused on four areas where participation in social life is interwoven with religious interests: employment, family life, access to and the use of public space, and State-supported activities. With respect to the scope of some existing and future non-discrimination laws, one might add access to professional or commercial services offered to the public, which is, in its legal structure, presumably similar to access to employment.

In the area of employment, the report identifies convincing examples of conflicts that demand an accommodation. It is perfectly correct to state that 'a regime of formal (or strict) equal treatment under a non-neutral standard (in the sense of being inspired by a dominant religious tradition which it privileges) may turn out to be discriminatory' (*Report*, 18). Moreover, even under an apparently 'neutral' standard, formal equal treatment is discriminatory if it fails to accommodate specific religious needs. In this case, it reveals itself to be a form of 'indirect' discrimination, as defined by, for example, Directive 2000/78/EC in Article 2, Section 2 lit. (b): 'an apparently neutral provision, criterion or practice [that] would put persons having a particular religion or belief … at a particular disadvantage compared with other persons'.

In place of formal equality, the report justly recommends a 'substantive equality', which has proven to better enable religious freedom by entitling 'context-relevant religious or belief-based identities, beliefs and practices of employees' to 'reasonable accommodation' (*Report*, 19). A merely formal equality paradigm is unsuitable to cope with religious freedom. Consequently, an anti-discrimination paradigm which binds itself to formal equality irrespective of religious interests must be questioned (as the report does on p. 19) and replaced with a substantive concept of non-discrimination. 'Reasonable accommodation' is, in effect, a demand not only of religious freedom, but also of non-discrimination. In the area of employment, anti-discrimination law should oblige employers to provide for reasonable accommodation of working conditions to meet the specific religious interests of their employees.

Reasonable accommodation takes account equally of the employers' interests. They can include, on their part, non-discrimination concerns. One type of such concerns is a non-discrimination policy of the employer towards third parties, as in the case of the registry offices which must perform their task of registering same-sex partnerships irrespective of the personal convictions of the particular officers (*Report*, 18). Another type of relevant employers' interest that falls under the rubric of religious freedom and substantive equality comes into play when an employer with a religious profile wants to be able to assert that profile internally or externally, for example, in hiring practices (*Report*, 18). Protecting such interests is the function of autonomy granted to religious communities.

Regarding conflicts between the collective autonomy of a 'faith-based' employer and the individual autonomy of an employee, it is true that 'a greater leniency in the area of autonomy rights will limit access and inclusion' (*Report*, 18), at least in the sector concerned; but it is equally true that a non-lenient, assiduous 'combat' of the State against practices suspected of being discriminatory will limit the autonomy of religious communities, urge them to make the choice between their religious profile and their role as employers, and thereby limit their access to and inclusion in the market as employers. This is paradigmatic of the relationship between obligations imposed by anti-discrimination laws and religious autonomy (*Report*, 42–43).

The cases identified by the RELIGARE project show that the relationship between non-discrimination and the freedom of religion and belief is multi-faceted and demands a well-developed and subtle concept of non-discrimination. The concepts of reasonable accommodation and even-handedness are important tools for achieving this objective. In sum, I can say that the policy recommendations with regard to employment issues given in the report (pp. 21–22) are thoroughly convincing.

The area of family law is a good example of a context in which freedom of religion and belief and the principle of non-discrimination are both on the same side of a conflict. Whenever the application of a family law provision interferes with religious freedom, it can be perceived as unequal treatment if the religious concepts concerned do not comply with the concepts shaping the respective provision. The same is true in private international law when a court or public authority feels bound to refuse the applicability of a foreign family-law provision. Legislation can provide for 'reasonable accommodation' and substantive 'even-handedness' in this area by conceding a certain space for contractual clauses differing from the State family law model, and by respecting the findings of alternative dispute settlement procedures under due conditions (as suggested by the report, 22–28).

Non-discriminatory access to and use of public spaces will accompany freedom of religion and belief, too. Implementing non-discrimination and religious freedom allows pluralism to become visible. Banning religious plurality from the public space cannot be based on the concern for non-discrimination. If restrictions are imposed, they must be justified by other concerns. The concepts of 'inclusive State neutrality' and 'justice as even-handedness' (*Report*, 16) can help to strike the balance between religious freedom and those other concerns.

On 'Inclusive State Neutrality' and 'Justice as Even-Handedness' as Key Concepts for the Implementation of Religious Freedom and Equality

As these brief remarks on the connection between religious liberty and non-discrimination have shown, the essential legal concepts elaborated by the report are powerful tools for coping with religious pluralism. In fact, pluralism characterises not only the actual use of religious freedom and the concepts of 'what is or should be the core of religion or belief' (*Report*, 11–12), including non-religious positions (*Report*, 12), but also the concepts of what religious 'freedom' and 'discrimination' imply. When the application of international norms on religious freedom and discrimination allows for a 'margin of appreciation', it takes account of that pluralism to a certain extent, and it is not necessarily at the expense of religious freedom or non-discrimination. 'Inclusive State neutrality' and 'justice as even-handedness' define limits to the national margin of appreciation (*Report*, 50) also with regard to secularist ambitions promoting non-inclusive neutrality, that is, pseudo-neutrality.

The concepts of 'inclusive State neutrality' and 'justice as even-handedness' are not specific to the protection of minorities (as the report appears to assume on p. 50). Even if a descriptive approach may find that legislatures and courts tend to follow the mainstream, a normative approach has to abstract from how the relevant interests are distributed among the majority or minorities. If the courts try to countervail the apparent 'weakness' of a minority position, they risk missing 'even-handedness' no less than in the opposite case. Likewise, the concept of 'inclusive State neutrality' comprises both minorities and the majority. Protection of religious minorities does not depend on disadvantaging the majority religion. Freedom of religion and belief is primarily, if not essentially, a fundamental right of everyone and every group, regardless of whether they belong to the majority or to a minority.

The concepts of 'inclusive State neutrality' and 'justice as even-handedness' prove to be key concepts for the implementation of religious freedom and equality. They apply directly to the State–citizen relationship (*Report*, 16), and only indirectly to horizontal relationships between private persons. This is due to the fact that the State plays a specific role with respect to religious freedom and equality – a fact which too often is disregarded by non-discrimination policies. Further research on how to respond to religious diversity and how to shape the concept of a secular State in the context of EU policies should take the RELIGARE findings as a basis.

Chapter 5
The Right to Religious Freedom: A Modern Pattern of Differentiation and its Development[1]

Matthias Koenig

How States should respond to religious diversity has become a major issue of contestation throughout Europe, as the research findings of the RELIGARE project amply document. Against the background of their specific historical trajectories of State formation and nation building, different countries respond differently to the claims to recognition articulated by religious minorities in the public sphere. The RELIGARE report makes a strong and well-grounded normative argument regarding how to render such responses more inclusive and more balanced in providing for both religious freedom and non-discrimination by relying on the principles of 'inclusive State neutrality' and 'justice as even-handedness'. However, the report does not identify the societal conditions under which these normative ideas can actually be realised. In the following, I aim to provide some analytical tools for assessing such conditions by discussing causal mechanisms that historical sociologists have identified in the development of the right to religious freedom. By taking a decidedly historical and comparative perspective, I also aim to situate the RELIGARE findings in a broader context of ongoing scholarly debates about religious freedom.

Religious freedom has been regarded as a pattern of differentiation between State, nation and religion and has thus played an important role in the grand narrative of secularisation.[2] That narrative, however, has typically remained rather vague with respect to causal conditions and processes through which the separation of politics and religion is to be explained.[3] Moving forward therefore requires engaging more decidedly in identifying generalisable mechanisms of differentiation. Ideas certainly figure prominently as necessary conditions, but they cannot sufficiently explain critical breakthroughs in the differentiation of religion and politics. Interest constellations also figure prominently as sufficient conditions for such critical breakthroughs, but they cannot explain whether the breakthroughs will stabilise into routine practice. Only through the socio-legal dynamics of increasingly autonomous juridical fields, I argue, have patterns of differentiation become thoroughly institutionalised.

This chapter proceeds in three steps. First, I characterise the differentiation pattern enshrined in the right to religious freedom in ideal-typical fashion. Second, I show why ideas and interests are insufficient to explain the differentiation pattern in the case of the first instance in history of the emergence of the right to religious freedom – in the United States – and I highlight the importance of socio-legal dynamics. Third, I indicate how similar dynamics have played out in the European context, which is at the centre of interest of the RELIGARE project.

Religious Freedom and the Differentiation of State, Nation and Religion

To characterise the differentiation pattern contained in the right to religious freedom, it is useful to start by situating it within conceptions of toleration as distinguished by political philosopher Rainer Forst.[4]

1 This chapter is a slightly revised version of a paper originally published in German in K Gabriel, C Gärtner and D Pollack (eds), *Umstrittene Säkularisierung* (Berlin University Press 2012) 293–312.

2 Compare J Casanova, *Public Religions in the Modern World* (University of Chicago Press 1994) 4.

3 On this topic see Casanova's recent critical revision of his earlier writings, J Casanova, 'Public Religions Revisited' in H de Vries (ed), *Religion: Beyond the Concept* (Fordham 2008) 101–19.

4 See R Forst, *Toleranz im Konflikt. Geschichte, Gehalt und Gegenwart eines umstrittenen Begriffs* (Suhrkamp 2003) in particular 42–48.

First, religious freedom differs from a 'permission' concept of toleration. That concept refers to forms of cooperative partial legal autonomy enjoyed by (some) religious minorities in the decentralised power structures of vast empires,[5] and revocable privileges granted to (some) religious minorities in the centralised confessional States of the early modern period, such as in the French Edict of Nantes (1598, revoked in 1685) and the English Toleration Act (1689). Second, religious freedom differs from the 'coexistence' concept of tolerance, whereby, particularly in the Holy Roman Empire of the German Nation after the European Wars of Religion, existing religious conflicts were pacified and pragmatic coexistence was practised out of a collective interest in peace and order.[6] Rather, the right to religious freedom corresponds to a third type, namely the 'respect' conception of tolerance, whose normative meaning entails the mutual respect for the right of all citizens to enjoy equal liberties, whether they are members of the religious majority or a religious minority.[7]

The right to religious freedom thus has a dual differentiating function. On the one hand, it limits the political power of the sovereign State over the individual.[8] Ideal-typically speaking, it does so in multiple ways: by liberating religious belief and its practice from State power (individual freedom of conscience and the individual freedom to practise one's religion); by protecting the internal autonomy of religious communities from interventions by the State (corporative religious freedom); and by forbidding the State to favour one specific world view, whether of a religious or non-religious nature (neutrality and fundamental distance). The role of the citizen is thus differentiated from the role of religious membership.[9] On the other hand, religious freedom, understood as a right to which everyone is *equally* entitled, also frees the political community of equal citizens – that is, the nation – from any expectations of religious consensus. As Martha Nussbaum pointedly formulates it, '[l]iberty of conscience is worth nothing if it is not equal liberty'.[10]

Given these features, it is not surprising that genuine religious freedom has encountered strong structural resistance, and thus that its realisation is highly improbable. It encountered structural resistance not only in the form of the continued expansion of State authority starting in the early modern period in Europe,[11] but even more so in imaginations of political community that perpetuated expectations of homogeneity from the epoch of confessionalism through modern semantics of national identity.[12] This makes it all the more necessary to ask how we can explain this differentiation pattern of State, nation and religion: Under which conditions and through which causal mechanisms was the right to religious freedom institutionalised?

5 On patterns of differentiation in early modern empires, see the classic work of SN Eisenstadt, *The Political Systems of Empires* (Transaction Publishers 1963); on the Ottoman Empire, see the impressive work of K Barkey, *Empire of Difference: The Ottomans in Comparative Perspective* (CUP 2007); and on the modern colonial empires, see P van der Veer, *Imperial Encounters: Religion and Modernity in India and Britain* (Princeton University Press 2001).

6 A vivid depiction of the everyday forms of such coexistence concepts of tolerance can be found in BJ Kaplan, *Divided by Faith: Religious Conflict and the Practice of Toleration in Early Modern Europe* (Harvard University Press 2007).

7 Such equal liberties are initially justified as a *birthright* but in the end are also linked to the idea of democratic self-legislation; see Forst (n 4) 550 and 572.

8 From more recent literature, see A von Ungern-Sternberg, *Religionsfreiheit in Europa: Die Freiheit individueller Religionsausübung in Großbritannien, Frankreich und Deutschland – ein Vergleich* (Mohr Siebeck 2008); on the American context, see M Nussbaum, *Liberty of Conscience: In Defense of America's Tradition of Religious Equality* (Basic Books 2008). For a concise differentiation theoretical analysis, see H Tyrell, 'Katholische Weltkirche und Religionsfreiheit: Christentumsgeschichtliche und differenzierungstheoretische Überlegungen' in K Gabriel (ed), *Religionsfreiheit und Pluralismus: Entwicklungslinien eines katholischen Lernprozesses* (Schöningh 2010) 197–260, especially 241.

9 See T Parsons, *Das System moderner Gesellschaften* (Juventa 1972) 112; on the interpretation of basic rights as an institutional means of securing the modern pattern of differentiation, see also the early writings of N Luhmann, *Grundrechte als Institution. Ein Beitrag zur politischen Soziologie* (Duncker und Humblot 1965).

10 M Nussbaum (n 8) 2; on the equality principle significantly promoted by James Madison, see in particular 91.

11 See W Reinhard, *Geschichte der Staatsgewalt. Eine vergleichende Verfassungsgeschichte Europas von den Anfängen bis zur Gegenwart* (C.H. Beck Verlag 1999).

12 AW Marx, *Faith in Nation: Exclusionary Origins of Nationalism* (OUP 2003); A Smith, *Chosen Peoples* (OUP 2003); H-G Haupt and D Langewiesche (eds), *Nation und Religion in Europa. Mehrkonfessionelle Gesellschaften im 19. und 20. Jahrhundert* (Campus 2004).

Processes of Differentiation in the United States

Ideas of Religious Freedom

A first and venerable answer to this set questions focuses on the role of ideas. Indeed, it is difficult to deny that the ideas of the inaccessibility of conscience, the natural freedom and equality of people and the self-legitimation of political authority, as well as the entire 'immanent framework' so impressively reconstructed by Charles Taylor,[13] were necessary preconditions for conceiving religious freedom. Specific relevance has been attributed, since Georg Jellinek,[14] to radical Protestant justifications for tolerance. Thus, theological ideas of a free conscience, accountable to God alone and immune to any exercise of external force, were at the background of the passionate argument for a strictly universalistic concept of religious freedom as proposed by Roger Williams, who had himself experienced persecution. Or to use Jellinek's own words, 'the idea of legally establishing inalienable, sacred rights that the individual obtains at birth … does not have political but religious origins'.[15] Others have regarded such justifications for tolerance as mere 'transition theories', emphasising that the right to religious freedom requires a generalisable justification, free of any religious reference, and highlighting the importance of ideas formulated during the Enlightenment (or even later).[16] Whatever the accurate genealogy of the idea of religious freedom, the question remains why this idea, once formulated, was advanced by political actors – given the obstacles of expanding State authority and imaginations of national community.

That a genealogy of ideas of religious freedom provides at best a partial explanation is shown by a quick glance at American constitutional history, where the ideas of Roger Williams long fell on deaf ears. In fact, having fled from England and become a majority in parts of New England, the Puritans at first attempted to establish classical confessional polities in which Baptists and Quakers, Anglicans and Catholics were disadvantaged by virtue of church tax systems, exclusion from active voting rights, and later also by banishment, imprisonment or torture. Despite the importance that Williams and his justification for an absolute freedom of conscience later gained in the collective memory of the United States, his Rhode Island was *not* a representative case, but rather (along with Pennsylvania and New York) an exceptional outlier where minorities who were banned or had fled from Massachusetts, Connecticut, New Haven and Plymouth found refuge. In the southern colonies (such as Virginia), where the Anglican Church was dominant, the separation of church and State lay far in the future as well. In general, the idea that a political community required religious conformity remained dominant in the seventeenth century, and in those places where freedom of conscience was grudgingly granted (such as in Massachusetts in 1692), the communities followed the example of the British Tolerance Act, which meant that some minorities were tolerated while others – such as Catholics – were not.[17]

Interests in Deregulating the Religious Field

A second attempt to explain religious freedom therefore highlights material and ideal interests.[18] These interests are at the centre of a strong theoretical model recently formulated by political scientist Anthony

13 See C Taylor, *The Secular Age* (Harvard University Press 2007).

14 See G Jellinek, *Die Erklärung der Menschen- und Bürgerrechte. Ein Beitrag zur modernen Verfassungsgeschichte* (2nd expanded edn, Duncker & Humblot 1904).

15 ibid 46. Traces of this argument can be found in Weber's own scattered remarks on human rights; see M Koenig, *Menschenrechte* (Campus 2005) 111–17; H Joas, *Sakralität der Person – Eine Neue Genealogie der Menschenrechte* (Suhrkamp 2011) 54–59.

16 See Forst (n 4) 241, 243; Nussbaum (n 8, 43) claims that Roger Williams, his thoroughly religious motives notwithstanding, did not use religious but Stoic arguments to justify the right to religious freedom.

17 Of the more recent historical literature, see in particular P Hamburger, *Separation of Church and State* (Harvard University Press 2002); JH Hutson, *Church and State in America: The First Two Centuries* (CUP 2008).

18 As Jellinek (n 14, 35) himself wrote: 'The history of politics is still far too much literary history rather than a history of the institutions themselves' ('Die Geschichte der Politik ist heute noch viel zu viel Literaturgeschichte, viel zu wenig Geschichte der Institutionen selbst'). It is thus not without reason that recent historical research has moved political

Gill.[19] Gill starts with typical preferences for rulers (maintaining power), religious majorities (monopolising the religious field) and religious minorities (deregulating the religious field). He then identifies typical conditions under which the deregulation of the religious field through religious freedom becomes more likely. On the political side, this includes the prospect of stable power, in light of which the legitimacy gains of favouring religious majorities become negligible. On the religious side, it includes religious pluralisation, which increases the opportunity costs of discriminating against minorities. Under the assumptions of rational choice, these two conditions push political actors to advance religious freedom.

If we follow recent historiography, the American origins of religious freedom that form Gill's most thorough case study seem to confirm his model. It was trade interests that convinced the British crown – following the example of the growing economic power of the Netherlands – to adopt a tolerant religious policy towards the colonies, thereby setting in motion religious pluralisation.[20] Meanwhile, within the colonies, the economic need for immigration, trade and mobility made a restrictive religious policy unattractive, while religious minorities were no longer content with toleration, but asked for full equality. The War of Independence took care of the rest. With the famous Bill of Rights (1786), Virginia ended the discrimination against Baptists and Presbyterians in order to ensure their mobilisation in the war. New England loosened restrictions on the Catholic Church when alliances with Quebec and the French Crown became necessary, and the need to unite all States forced the newly independent federal State to commit to religious neutrality.[21] Article VI of the American constitution (1787) abolished religious tests as a prerequisite for public office, and the First Amendment obliged Congress 'to make no law respecting an establishment of religion prohibiting the free exercise thereof' (1791), thereby marking the climax of an attempt to differentiate between State, nation and religion that was anything but uncontroversial at the time.

Of course, Gill's model is subject to the objection that it underestimates that *some* religious or philosophical idea of religious freedom was necessary for religious minorities to demand full equality and for political actors to perceive new choices in regulating religion.[22] One could also cite increasing theological scepticism towards a faith-based State (such as in English Tractarianism or later in French Ultramontanism).[23] Yet the explanatory content of Gill's interest-based model retains considerable value. First, it defines a whole series of situation-based conditions for the political provision of religious freedom. It is precisely these definitions that enable the formulation of explanations for the different variations of religious freedom as a

---

motives into the foreground: see J Whaley, 'Religionsfreiheit' in F Jaeger (ed), *Enzyklopädie der Neuzeit* (Band 10, Metzler 2009) 1064–71, in particular 1065. In the general literature on fundamental rights, the shift from a history of ideas to social history is common as well; see in particular the works of W Schmale, *Archäologie der Grund- und Menschenrechte in der frühen Neuzeit: Ein deutsch-französisches Paradigma* (Oldenbourg Wissenschaftsverlag 1997) (on Jellinek 52–57); P Blickle, *Von der Leibeigenschaft zu den Menschenrechten. Eine Geschichte der Freiheit in Deutschland* (Beck 2003) (critique of Jellinek 251).

19 See A Gill, *The Political Origins of Religious Liberty* (CUP 2008); for an earlier statement of this argument, see R Finke, 'Religious Deregulation: Origins and Consequences' (1990) 32 *Journal of Church and State* 609–26.

20 Even Roger Williams could – much like William Penn and other contemporaries – employ utilitarian arguments: '[I]n not cutting off their many religions, it has pleased God not only not to be provoked, but to prosper the State of the United Provinces' (thus he wrote in *Bloudy Tenent of Persecution*, here quoted from Hutson (n 17) 25). The fact that Rhode Island came to enjoy such religious tolerance due to the charter of 1663 is the result of precisely such economic motives; see Hutson, ibid 27.

21 On Virginia, see J Ragosta, *Wellspring of Liberty: How Virginia's Religious Dissenters Helped Win the American Revolution and Secured Religious Liberty* (OUP 2010), in particular 166. On New England, see in particular CP Hanson, *Necessary Virtue: The Pragmatic Origins of Religious Liberty in New England* (University of Virginia Press 1998).

22 For a critique of Gill's work, see, for example, I Katznelson, 'Regarding Toleration and Liberalism: Considerations from the Anglo-Jewish Experience' in I Katznelson and G Stedman Jones (eds), *Religion and the Political Imagination* (CUP 2010) 46–69, here in particular 65; AT Kuru, *Secularism and State Policies toward Religion: The United States, France, and Turkey* (CUP 2009) 21.

23 On the nexus of interests and ideas in the political emancipation of the Jews in England, again see Katznelson (n 22) 65; on the Oxford Movement, see J Heim, 'The Demise of the Confessional State and the Rise of the Idea of a Legitimate Minority' in JW Chapman and A Wertheimer (eds), *Majorities and Minorities* (New York University Press 1990) 11–23, here in particular 15. On Ultramontanism, see E Perreau-Saussine, 'French Catholic Political Thought from the Deconfessionalisation of the State to the Recognition of Religious Freedom' in Katznelson and Stedman Jones (n 22) 150–70, here in particular 163.

modern pattern of differentiation in Europe. It is obvious that religious minorities had less power to negotiate and that religious freedom was therefore more closely tied to State interests in the religiously homogenous territorial States of continental Europe than in North America. Just think of France, where the idea of religious freedom – from the *Déclaration des Droits de l'Homme et du Citoyen* (1789), to the civic constitution of the clergy, to the organic articles under Napoleon all the way to the law regarding the separation of church and State (1905) – was permeated through and through with the Gallican tradition.[24] Second, Gill's model identifies a veritable causal mechanism of self-increasing differentiation. Once pluralisation, such as in the North American case, has reached a critical mass, it increases the opportunity costs of restrictive religious policies, resulting in the gradual deregulation of the religious field, which in turn enables further pluralisation, and so forth.

Institutionalising Religious Freedom in the Judicial Arena

But the actual problem of an explanatory model based on interest constellations is that it cannot explain the conditions under which religious freedom is not simply politically granted, but *institutionalised* as a legally enforceable right even in the face of opposing constellations of political and religious interests. The fact that constitutional history is only partially grasped by a history of constitutional documents becomes particularly clear in the American case. It took many decades until the 'political disestablishment' of the Revolutionary era led to religious freedom becoming a legally enforceable right. In part this was due to the fact that the Constitution and its Amendments at first only applied to the federal level; not until 1833 did the last state (namely Massachusetts) carry out political 'disestablishment', and even after that the Supreme Court declared itself incompetent to protect civil rights and liberties within the states. More important was the fact that the very few decisions on the First Amendment that the Supreme Court did hand down in the nineteenth century only partially recognised the demands made by religious minorities, if they did so at all.[25] In most cases, the opposite was true. Many decisions were based on the legal doctrine that 'Christianity is part of the common law', or were under the influence of an ideal of uniformity that had been taken from the confessional field and brought into the civic-religious arena. These decisions thus generally reflected the continuing hegemony of Protestant elites and their power to define national identity. Significantly, the Supreme Court case *Church of Holy Trinity v United States* (1892) resulted in a unanimous decision in which Judge David J. Brewer could declare: 'This is a Christian nation'.[26]

American constitutional history further underscores the fact that the symmetrical interpretation of an equal right to religious freedom encountered considerable resistance in times of forging national identities. The question thus arises: How was this resistance, which Gill neglects for the most part, overcome? I therefore argue that a full explanation of the institutionalisation of religious freedom must go beyond both ideas and interests and take into account socio-legal dynamics. Religious minorities can successfully obtain religious

24 For a comparison of the French and American versions of religious freedom, see M Gauchet, *La Révolution des droits de l'homme* (Gallimard 1989). Comparative analyses of the processes of emancipation of religious minorities within the formation of nation-States in the nineteenth century can be found in R Liedtke and S Wendehorst (eds), *The Emancipation of Catholics, Jews and Protestants: Minorities and the Nation-State in Nineteenth-Century Europe* (Manchester University Press 1999). For more recent varieties of religious freedom in post-authoritarian and post-socialist transformation societies, see J Anderson, *Religious Liberty in Transitional Societies: The Politics of Religion* (CUP 2003) (on Gill, critically, at 199).

25 This applies to Mormons in regard to polygamy (see *Reynolds v United States* (1879)), in part also to Jews in regard to the Sabbath (see *Soon Hing v Crowley* (1885)), and to Catholics in regard to the financing of parochial private schools (see *Board of Education v Minor* (1872)); on the nineteenth century, see in general L Fisher, *Religious Liberty in America: Political Safeguards* (University Press of Kansas 2002); RT Handy, 'Minority–Majority Confrontations, Church–State Patterns, and the U.S. Supreme Court' in JF Sarna (ed), *Minority Faiths and the American Protestant Mainstream* (University of Illinois Press 1998) 305–34; J Hitchcock, *The Supreme Court and Religion in American Life* (vol I, Princeton University Press 2004).

26 On the genesis of the 'Christian nation' discourse, in which the First Amendment is understood as a guarantee of State neutrality between Protestant denominations, see SK Green, *The Second Disestablishment: Church and State in Nineteenth-Century America* (OUP 2010) 91ff. Indeed, even 40 years later the same court stated in a decision, albeit no longer a unanimous one (5:4), 'We are a Christian people'; see *United States v Macintosh* (1931), quoted in Handy (n 25) 307f.

freedom even in the face of oppositional interest constellations when they find judicial opportunity structures, which are themselves the result of the increased autonomy of the judicial field.[27]

The fact that the Supreme Court became a powerful sanctioning authority in the United States in the middle of the twentieth century regarding the right to religious freedom has indeed been attributed in large part to the increase in the autonomy of the judicial field. This growth in autonomy can be seen most clearly in the professionalisation of the legal field that occurred at the end of the nineteenth century in response to the conflicts over autonomy between the law schools and the Protestant elites.[28] These conflicts resulted in a 'legal disestablishment' in which both the legal concept of Christianity as an element of the common law as well as the 'Christian nation' discourse lost plausibility.[29] In their place, objectivity, neutrality and, in Weber's sense, formal rationality became the models for legal interpretation and jurisprudence. This did not mean that limitations to religious freedom, drawn by an assumed religious, moral or civilising consensus, were entirely eliminated, but it did divest that consensus of its Protestant exclusivity. In the 1920s and 1930s, the dominant jurisprudence – in reaction to increasing State authority under Wilson – made the fundamental switch to a system based on subjective civil rights and liberties. The 'incorporation doctrine', through which the Fourteenth Amendment (1868) also binds the individual states to the Bill of Rights, was increasingly applied in 'free exercise' and 'non-establishment' cases, which in turn became more frequent due to religious pluralisation and strategic litigation by religious minorities. From this point on, the Supreme Court developed strict standards for the protection of an (equal) right to religious freedom and finally carried out the actual 'constitutional disestablishment' when, in the famous cases *Everson v Board of Education* (1947) and *McCollum v Board of Education*, it elevated the term 'wall of separation', originally taken from side remarks in a letter by Thomas Jefferson, to the level of constitutional law.[30]

In sum, the American case points to the importance of courts as independent sanctioning entities for the institutionalisation of the right to religious freedom; they protect the rights of religious minorities not only against State intervention, but also against normative expectations held by the religious majority.[31] However, this requires not only a formal separation of powers, but also, and most importantly, the social disembedding of a judicial field in which the individual logic of constitutional legal rationalisation can blaze a path. The causal mechanism of self-increasing differentiation can be summarised as follows: once constitutional courts have gained a critical threshold of autonomy, this creates opportunity structures for religious minorities in their battle for recognition, and the litigation by these groups in turn provides opportunities for the systematisation of basic rights, and so forth.

Human Rights and the Judicial Politics of Governing Religious Diversity in Contemporary Europe

We can also expect to find this mechanism outside America, due to the global scale of the constitutional revolution that occurred in the twentieth century. In post-totalitarian democracies (Japan, Italy, Germany), in post-communist transformation States (Poland, Hungary, Russia), and even in the British Commonwealth

27 Terminologically I loosely draw on Pierre Bourdieu's field theory, which has been receiving increasing attention within the sociology of law; see P Bourdieu, 'La force du droit. Elements pour une sociologie du champ juridique' (1986) 64 *Actes de la recherche en sciences sociales* 3–19.

28 See D Sikkink, 'From Christian Civilization to Individual Civil Liberties: Framing Religion in the Legal Field, 1880–1949' in C Smith (ed), *The Secular Revolution* (University of California Press 2003) 310–54.

29 On the long and arduous process of 'legal disestablishment', see in particular Green (n 26), specifically 205ff.

30 Jefferson's letter to the Danbury Baptists (1802), in which he refers to a 'wall of separation between Church & State', has been interpreted in different ways: some scholars argue that the Supreme Court violates the phrase's original sense, which referred to the (secular, not sacred) powers of the office of the president; see, for example, Hutson (n 17) 175ff; for a critical view of Hutson's text, see Ragosta (n 21) 148.

31 The fact that litigation by marginal religious groups more deeply anchors religious freedom in a society is demonstrated for the American case by F Way and B Burt, 'Religious Marginality and the Free Exercise Clause' (1983) 77 *American Political Science Review* 652–65. On the other hand, a more sceptical conclusion can be found in the analysis of jurisprudence since the 1980s by J Wybraniec and R Finke, 'Religious Regulation and the Courts: The Judiciary's Changing Role in Protecting Minority Religions from Majoritarian Rule' (2001) 40 *Journal for the Scientific Study of Religion* 427–44.

(Canada, New Zealand, even Great Britain), catalogues of basic rights gained greater significance while constitutional courts gained greater authority. Different opinions exist within the literature on the sociology of law regarding the origins of this global shift of power into the constitutional legal arena.[32] Everywhere this shift has occurred it has resulted in States being obligated to reduce governmental favouritism to religious majorities and to maintain equal distance from religions. According to the provocative thesis of Ran Hirschl, even in those States whose constitutions explicitly include a religious standardisation (such as in Israel, Malaysia, Pakistan), constitutional courts have led to a secular containment of religion due to the interests of the judicial profession and its alliance with political and economic elites.[33]

Crucially, the limitation of State sovereignty in regulating religion today has a strong international legal dimension. Even within the Westphalian system, States did not have unlimited sovereignty. Rather, starting in the seventeenth century, it was established practice for States to demand guarantees for the rights of 'their' religious minorities when concluding peace treaties with one another. Even during the nineteenth century, States legitimised military engagements in the Ottoman Empire by claiming the need to protect Christian minorities. By the time of the League of Nations, at the latest, the minority rights of others, particularly of the Jewish minorities in Europe, had become the subject of international treaties.[34] However, State sovereignty was not fundamentally limited until the Charter of the United Nations (1945) and the two major human rights pacts (1966), which marked the transition to a post-Westphalian system. While individual rights had only been enforceable qua citizenship until that point, they now were conceived and institutionalised as universal human rights.

Along with the rise of human rights, international judicial bodies were created with new sanctioning power, thus influencing the political treatment of religious minorities around the world.[35] Again, it is the causal conjunction of legal mobilisation by religious minorities and non-governmental organisations with the interests of the legal profession in an increasingly transnational judicial field that has filled formally codified human rights conventions with life.[36]

The European Court of Human Rights (ECtHR), which figures prominently in the RELIGARE project findings, provides an instructive example in this regard.[37] Initially, the right to religious freedom (Article 9 of the European Convention on Human Rights, 1950) stood in the shadow of the Catholic reinvention of a Christian Europe, and few politicians at the time had any intention of giving legal teeth to the Court.[38] In the 1990s, however, the ECtHR gained increasing institutional autonomy and became the focus of an exponentially

---

32 For an explanation that points to the increased sense of right and wrong and collective mobilisation as the origin for this shift, see C Epp, *The Rights Revolution: Lawyers, Activists and Supreme Courts in Comparative Perspective* (University of Chicago Press 1998); for a 'realistic' explanation that locates the origin in the interests of economic, political and judicial elites in maintaining their threatened (by democracy) hegemony, see R Hirschl, *Towards Juristocracy: The Origins and Consequences of the New Constitutionalism* (Harvard University Press 2004).

33 Hirschl lists various reasons why constitutional courts have a secularising effect even in constitutional theocracies, including an explanation based on Bourdieu's field theory; see Hirschl (n 32), in particular 72ff.

34 Regarding the long history of the protection of minorities in the system of sovereign States, see S Krasner and D Froats, 'Minority Rights and the Westphalian Model' in DA Lake and D Rothchild (eds), *The International Spread of Ethnic Conflict: Fear, Diffusion and Escalation* (Princeton University Press 1998) 227–50; and on minority protection in the League of Nations, see C Fink, *Defending the Rights of Others: The Great Powers, the Jews, and International Minority Protection, 1878–1938* (CUP 2004).

35 On this topic, see D Philpott, 'Religious Freedom and the Undoing of the Westphalian State' (2004) 25 *Michigan Journal of International Law* 981–98.

36 The influence of international legal treaties on local politics has been documented in many cases; on religious freedom, see B Simmons, *Mobilizing for Human Rights: International Law and Domestic Politics* (CUP 2009) 167ff; on the contribution by religious organisations, see AD Hertzke, *Freeing God's Children: The Unlikely Alliance for Global Human Rights* (Rowman & Littlefield 2004); GM Thomas, 'Constructing World Civil Society through Contentions over Religious Rights' (2004) 3 *Journal of Human Rights* 239–51.

37 For an extended discussion of this topic, see M Koenig, 'Human Rights, Judicial Politics, and Institutional Secularization: Contentions over Religious Diversity at the European Court of Human Rights' in W Kymlicka and J Bolden (eds), *International Approaches to the Governance of Ethnic Diversity* (forthcoming).

38 This according to the recent historiography of human rights, which points to the significance of Catholic personalism (as developed by, for example, Jacques Maritain and Pierre-Henri Teitgen) and the rejection of a 'mechanical principle of equality' (Gerhard Ritter) during the 1940s and 1950s; see S Moyn, 'Personalismus, Gemeinschaft und die

growing number of litigation cases. Hence, in its jurisprudence the Strasbourg Court has carefully but steadily protected the religious freedom of minorities in situations of entrenched relations between nation-States and religious majorities, first in the post-communist States of Eastern Europe, and most recently also in Western Europe. The Court has thus become a potential motor for the civic inclusion of religious minorities. At the UN level, similar trends can be observed. The Human Rights Committee, charged with monitoring compliance with the International Covenant for Civil and Political Rights (ICCPR), has become a focal arena of transnational religious minorities, such as Sikhs, in their struggle for recognition.

In sum, the expansion of a legal field composed of disembedded legal professionals and social movements provides a crucial condition for formally guaranteed rights to become regulative institutions that promote the civic inclusion of religious minorities.

Conclusion

I have argued that both ideas and interests have to be situated within wider institutional and field dynamics shaped by the interplay of legal professionals and social movements. To illustrate this general argument I sketched mechanisms through which religious freedom, one of the core components of human rights and one of the yet unsettled issues of civic inclusion in contemporary societies, has become institutionalised. In contrast to the partial autonomy granted by imperial authorities and the tolerance provided under an absolutist regime, and in contrast to pragmatically motivated coexistence, the right to religious freedom aims for a symmetrical recognition of religious minorities and majorities as equal citizens within a community. Its institutionalisation depends on a complex set of factors, including interactive sequences of jurisdictional claims of legal professionals and contentious politics of social movements. Scrutinising such factors helps the analyst go beyond linear conceptions of the differentiation of religion and politics and to rectify its oft-bemoaned explanatory deficit.

The RELIGARE report offers a nuanced account of complex legal regimes that govern the new religious diversity in Europe across various policy domains, and its recommendations clearly go beyond linear narratives of secularisation. The theoretical argument and historical panorama given in this chapter might help situate RELIGARE's arguments yet more explicitly within an analytical framework with explanatory ambitions. I would also hope that this contribution will stimulate critical reflection on the precise conditions – ideas, interests and institutional configurations – which may foster or inhibit the realisation of the ambitious normative principles and policy measures recommended in the report of the RELIGARE project.

Geschichte der Menschenrechte, 1945–1966' in S-L Hoffmann (ed), *Moralpolitik. Geschichte der Menschenrechte im 20. Jahrhundert* (Wallstein Verlag 2010) 63–91, in particular 84f.

Chapter 6
It's All about Relationships

Jane Mair

A Troubled Background

In recent years, religion has emerged as a significant problem in many European countries and for the European Union as a whole. Contemporary concern about religion in Europe was not sparked by a single event or by one particular religion but, rather, by a diverse range of developments and trends that have coincided under a common heading. The presence of religion has been seen in political unrest, democratic challenge, social unease and legal dispute. While the religion which has attracted most European opposition is Islam, there are concerns too about the presence of conservative Christian beliefs and unease about the apparent emergence of newer religious and spiritual groups. Although for some in Europe religion is a source of strength and guidance, for many its recent re-emergence presents a problem: it is seen as something to be resisted and constrained.

The perception of religion as a problem has been exacerbated by the fact that its presence was largely unanticipated. Put simply, for many, the role of religion in Europe belonged in the past: a force which had evidently lost its political position, its legal authority and, to a great extent, its personal significance. This settled landscape, however, in which religion was part of a shared history from which modern secular Europe had emerged, has changed. Religion, as a current and pressing social concern, has been revitalised. In recent years, the topic of religion has re-entered European consciousness with an unexpected force, and its impact has been distinctly unsettling. The social, political and legal challenges it brings have been highlighted and analysed extensively, and they continue to cause concern. This shift from religion as part of the past to religion as a pressing contemporary challenge has been seen in popular media, political and social debate and in legal courts throughout Europe. It has also been reflected in academic writing and intellectual commentary, with strong evidence of a 'quantum leap'[1] in European research into religion.

In the construction of much contemporary debate, there has been a tendency to set religion apart, hold it at a distance, to present it as 'the other'. This might be explained partly by the suddenness and unexpectedness of its reappearance. In legal analysis, it is also due to the familiar contexts and frameworks within which religion has been situated. The secularisation thesis, central to modern liberal understandings of European democracy and constitutional theory, requires and expects separation of church and State. Linked to this structural separation is the dominant dichotomy between public and private, with religion, personal adherence and belief belonging in the private.[2] Informed by these pre-existing paradigms of division and separation, responses to religious elements in contemporary Europe have been constrained. This is particularly evident in legal debate, where 'religion is often regarded … as a matter of private freedom, as though it occupies a space which is other to law, the State and our public sphere'.[3] Much debate about the proper place of religion in modern Western democracies has been dominated by reconsideration of the presumed distance between church and State and by attempts to rebuild boundaries and to develop strategies to return religion to its proper place.

Religion has been constructed as separate and it has further been presented in the language of individualism, epitomised by the concept of the protection of individual rights. Much of the controversy surrounding the

1 G Davie, 'Thinking Sociologically about Religion: Implications for Faith Communities' (2012) 54 (3) *Review of Religious Research* 273, 274.

2 See, for example, D Meyerson, 'Why Religion Belongs in the Private Sphere, not the Public Square' in P Cane, C Evans and Z Robinson (eds), *Law and Religion in Theoretical and Historical Context* (CUP 2011) 44–71.

3 M Davies, 'Pluralism in Law and Religion' in Cane, Evans and Robinson (n 2) 72–99, 72.

recent emergence of religion has been highlighted by individual claims for religious freedom and religious protection, claims which focus on the clash between competing individual legal rights and between conflicting interpretations of legal rights.[4] Although human rights are inclusive and universal in their foundation and their scope, in their application and enforcement they fix on the isolated individual. While individual rights are subject to limitations in terms of mutual respect and balanced by principles of accommodation, the principal focus of a rights-based framework remains the individual holder. Individual human rights, when placed in the context of diversity of belief, can reinforce the isolating and competing nature of religious rights. When the clashing rights of different individuals and the opposing views of diverse religions are placed at the centre of attention, it is inevitable that one side will always be, at best, disappointed.

The RELIGARE Report: Relationship Counselling

Against this background of separation, division and individual claims of right, the RELIGARE report, *Religion in the Context of the European Union*, sounds a very different tone. In method, structure, language and proposals, it signals clearly that its interests lie not in separate spheres and isolated personal space but instead in the encouragement of communication, engagement and interplay. While recognising and acknowledging the individual elements and characters that make up the contemporary story of religion in Europe, the focus is not on their distinctive separateness, but on their interaction and intersection: for RELIGARE, it is not about the individuals, their isolating interests and their competing claims; it is, rather, all about their relationships.

At the heart of the project is the legal relationship between 'two principles enshrined both in EU law and in the national constitutions of the Member States – freedom of religion and belief and non-discrimination' (*Report*, 12). EU equality law in its current form has expanded far beyond what was ever envisaged in the very limited beginnings of Article 119 of the Treaty of Rome. Through a range of principles, articles, directives, jurisprudence, soft law and policy, the scope of EU equality protection has undoubtedly been extended, but with that extension has come increased difficulty and uncertainty. Identifying, understanding and applying European legal norms is complex, all the more so when those norms are translated into the words of national regulatory provisions and when they interact with provisions and jurisprudence which have developed through the alternative route established by the European Convention on Human Rights. The language of legal protection for freedom of religion and against religious-based discrimination is relatively well known and well established, but the meaning and the practical implementation of these familiar legal words is much less understood.

It is not surprising that there is tension between these two principles. They emerge from different foundations and, while to some extent they retain links to the original economic origins and free market objectives of the Union, they have moved far beyond them into territory which is much less comfortable for lawyers and legal rules. The language of dignity, tolerance and solidarity is the language of relationships, but how is it to be given effect in terms of law? Using language, and implementing legal provisions, that signal tolerance and equality but without full understanding and effective implementation may result in unanticipated harm rather than intended benefits. What the RELIGARE report proposes is the use of 'two yardsticks' which offer 'an overarching framework for "managing" competing claims' (*Report*, 16). These 'yardsticks' are offered as a way of establishing a workable relationship between two complex principles, and in their language and intention – to be inclusive and even-handed – there is further resonance with what might be regarded as essential elements in the creation and maintenance of good relationships.

Speaking to Each Other

The emergence of religion as the object of contemporary academic analysis and research has been evident across a range of disciplines, with legal discourse sitting side by side with that of politics, philosophy

4 See, for example, J Martinez-Torron, 'The (Un)protection of Individual Religious Identity in the Strasbourg Case Law' (2012) 1 *Oxford Journal of Law and Religion* 363; N Cox, 'The Clash of Unprovable Universalisms: International Human Rights and Islamic Law' (2013) 2 *Oxford Journal of Law and Religion* 1.

and sociology. Initially, perhaps, the novelty of the emerging religious question was enough to occupy the attentions of each individual discipline; more recently, however, they have begun to turn to each other for enlightenment and support and, while such interaction can be difficult[5] and can expose a lack of shared language and understanding, the benefits of interdisciplinarity are worth pursuing. For law, an inward looking focus may rely on out of date paradigms and result in misleading conclusions.[6] Sociology can inform legal analysis through its identification and understanding of the different guises and influences of religion, and anthropology can help to situate and explain religion and religious practices within wider patterns of behaviour. An interdisciplinary approach, which seeks to build in particular on the relationships between law, anthropology and sociology, is central to the methodology of the RELIGARE project and informs the findings (see *Report*, 'Executive Summary'). An understanding of the mutual benefits of research relationships is evident in the carefully constructed and effective methodology, and it sets the tone for a report in which the need for nurtured relationships and the benefits of good communication are highlighted at many levels.

... in Conciliatory Language

In recent years, Europe has been 'torn between rigid secularism and selective ... support of religions';[7] it has been confronted by 'alien concepts'[8] and forced to decide between a 'clash of legal cultures'.[9] To look only at language and choice of words is to oversimplify, but language nonetheless has an important role to play both in the construction of debate and in promoting effective communication. From the outset, with a title centred on 'Engaging the interplay', the words of the RELIGARE report signal very clearly the underlying intentions of its authors.

European research into contemporary religion might be divided into phases: first, the identification and tracing of religious influence and issues; second, attempts to analyse, categorise and theorise; and third, acceptance and a need to move forward. The RELIGARE report fits into the third: 'having exhausted all the possible angles from which to highlight the problems ... there is a need to consider alternative ways to make sense of the relationship'.[10] The sociological surveys and database of cases make clear the existence and extent of religion in Europe and highlight the problems that are caused by the revitalisation of religion. The report, however, chooses not to dwell on these problems, but instead adopts a pragmatic and positive tone. The language is of conciliation and mediation but, more than that, it focuses firmly not on separation, individuals and rights, but on interaction, communities and relationships. While not everyone can have their own way all the time, we can all expect to be made welcome and to be treated with even-handedness. The tone is pragmatic, stressing the responsibilities and realities of engagement with others. The message, while neither underestimating the practical challenges nor diminishing the legal complexities, is one of common-sense fairness and relationship management: relationships thrive on openness and the ability to listen and adapt, and sometimes they require compromise.

... to Encourage Clear Communication

Throughout the RELIGARE report, the tone is of openness to the possibility of connections. Rather than looking for divergence, the focus is on convergence; rather than seeking separation, the focus is on engagement. This is particularly evident in the discussion of the increasingly complex and fragmented regulatory frameworks

5 G Davie, 'Law, Sociology and Religion: An Awkward Threesome' (2012) 1 *Oxford Journal of Law and Religion* 235.

6 See, for example, R Sandberg, 'Church–State Relations in Europe: From Legal Methods to an Interdisciplinary Approach' [2008] *Journal of Religion in Europe* 329.

7 S Ferrari, 'Law and Religion in a Secular World: A European Perspective' (2012) 14 *Ecclesiastical Law Journal* 355, 362.

8 A Buchler, *Islamic Law in Europe? Legal Pluralism and its Limits in European Family Law* (Ashgate 2011) vii.

9 W van Rossum, 'The Clash of Legal Cultures over the "Best Interests of the Child" Principle in Cases of International Child Abduction' (2010) 6 *Utrecht Law Review* 33.

10 E Wilson, 'Rethinking Religion and Politics in Postsecular Europe' in C Jedan (ed), *Constellations of Value: European Perspectives on the Intersections of Religion, Politics and Society* (LIT 2013) 121.

which operate in respect of religion. Indeed, the insight into connections extends beyond the project's specific focus on religion.

The European Community and Union project was always ambitious, but in recent times it has grown significantly. Territorially it has expanded, with the accession of new and diverse States which, in turn, may dilute the shared core of common history, experience and values. Legally its competence has expanded, as the Union moves into areas and activities with increasingly tenuous links to the original economic focus. Traditional structures and established understandings may no longer fit current needs. European regulatory mechanisms have developed far beyond the familiar and relatively easily understood measures of treaties, directives and decisions. Established normative frameworks have become fragmented and enmeshed within a much more extensive network of policy and dialogue. It can become very easy to lose sight of how different elements fit together, how principles interact, where old connections disappear and new ones align. Legal relationships – and those between individuals and organisations – require clear communication and good understanding in order to operate effectively. This is reflected particularly in the report's attention to clear and integrated proposals.

Regulating Relationships

As the RELIGARE report highlights (*Report*, § 2), the four substantive areas raise different issues and require a range of approaches, but through each of them runs a strong theme: the importance of making connections and building good relationships. In some areas, too much focus on individual rights in separate spheres has perhaps distracted attention from relevant relationships. While employer and employee, husband and wife, parent and child are, in daily life, all about relationships, in legal terms they have become characterised by individual rights. Motivated by equality, legal rights have historically been invoked to balance the highly unequal status of the parties involved but, in that process, less attention has been paid to the relationships themselves. For 'master and servant' to become 'employer and employee', there needed to be some equalising of their respective status. Similarly, within families, the historic power of the father had to be balanced by the increased rights of first the mother and then the child. Individual rights have an undeniable importance in facilitating the formation of relationships, but once individual rights have been established, how are they to be accommodated within the context of relationships? In other domains considered in the report, the significance of continuing or changing relationships between State and religion has become lost by focusing primarily on historical separations and divergence rather than looking for new points of connection. In each of the RELIGARE report's four areas where religion is a matter of current concern in Europe, there are relationship issues: some are old relationships suffering from neglect, some dysfunctional relationships which would benefit from counselling, some unruly ones which require ordering, and some are at a very early stage and are yet to be explored.

Employment: Workable Relationships

Modern European employment law is built on the framework of a universal floor of rights. Since the 1970s, when European social law came to life in the equal pay decisions of the ECJ in *Defrenne v Sabena*,[11] the EU has persisted in its attempts to develop a distinctive model for the European workplace. While there have been some measures aimed at strengthening collective employment regulation, it is in the area of individual rights, and in particular those which guarantee the right to equal treatment, that most success has been achieved. Individual equality rights for workers have brought undoubted benefits, but it might be argued that there is a danger of the rights developing a freestanding existence of their own and losing touch with the grounding relationship of employment. Pregnancy is a striking example, where protection of the fundamental right is guaranteed almost regardless of the needs of the employer and the traditional model of the employment relationship.[12] While such strong fundamental rights bring benefits for individuals, the fear is sometimes

11 Case 43/75 [1976] ECR 455.

12 See, for example, *Tele Danmark A/S v Handels-og Kontorfunktionaerernes Forbund I Danmark*, Case C-109/00 [2001] ECR I-6993.

raised that they do so at the risk of wider harm to female employment and to gender equality in terms of caring and domestic labour. Rather than providing an opportunity for employer and worker to engage in open communication about each other's needs, issues related to pregnancy and childcare have come to be regarded as 'out of bounds' for discussion.

While the approach which has developed in respect of pregnancy is undoubtedly strong in terms of individual legal protection, it may not be enough for the long-term benefit of working relationships: it may encourage resentment on one side and fear of disclosure on the other, and it does little to challenge the settled stereotype of female worker/carer. In assessing workplace issues around religious dress and religious duties, the focus of the RELIGARE report is firmly on the relationship between worker and employer. Borrowing from the disability discrimination model, a key proposal is the introduction of an 'additional tool of legally enshrined reasonable accommodation' (*Report*, § 2.1.2). Instead of focusing solely on individual rights and freedoms, which, when faced with other conflicting rights, are forced into a win or lose confrontation, the pragmatic proposal is 'to give individuals adequate room to reconcile their various identities and commitments' (*Report*, § 2.1.3). The cynical might say that, without clear legal force, irreconcilable differences will remain, but common sense suggests that a relationship model, designed to avoid some of the inherent stress of a head-to-head clash and to encourage each side to listen and adapt, is more likely to succeed. The intention is not merely superficial industrial harmony, maintained only by avoiding confrontation, but rather a good working relationship where both sides seek to understand the needs of the other, a relationship which accepts that compromise at times, on both sides, may be required.

Families: Sensitive Relationships

For a report which emphasises the value of relationships, family law is of course an obvious focus of attention. Family relationships are at the heart of many of the issues concerning religion identified in the course of the RELIGARE project. This is hardly surprising, as both family law and religion are concerned in 'the most intimate sphere of life' (*Report*, § 2.2). Marriage in particular is a contested relationship, currently caught between conservative and progressive values, religious traditionalists and secular modernisers. Unlike employment, however, where RELIGARE proposes the reworking of a relationship already well established within the sphere of EU law, in the context of family law, the focus is on developing new relationships. For many reasons, the debate around religion and family law within the EU 'is a sensitive one' (*Report*, § 2.2.2). Not only are strongly held and often opposing views of different groups involved, but it is sensitive too in terms of jurisdiction, as the EU has no current competence in respect of substantive family law and only recently developed competence in respect of private international law in family matters (*Report*, § 2.2).

The role of the EU within the context of private international law is at an early stage, and some of the wider tensions inherent in the relationship between European harmonisation and national sovereignty are highlighted from the perspective of religion and the way it is treated by different Member States. Looking beyond this limited current competence, the RELIGARE project explores future potential relationships between European and national law within the scope of regulation of family life. The key relationship to emerge in this context is between the country of origin and the country of residence of individuals living within Europe. The solution being sought is one which would allow such individuals 'to harmonise their family lives with their international status' (*Report*, § 2.2.1), in other words, to combine in their personal, family and community lives the elements of their origins and their current status which are essential to their human identity. The report encourages more sensitive understanding of the key relationships which lie behind the identities of Europe's citizens.

Public Space: Complicated Relationships

A key theme in much recent legal writing about religion has been the supposed division between public and private. The classic liberal solution to tension between the need for tolerance and the unlimited diversity of religious beliefs and values was to separate the public from the private, regulating the public according to shared civic values while leaving individuals to conduct their private lives according to their own religious – or other – beliefs. The effectiveness and reality of this division have been subject to challenge in recent debates, and some of the most notorious legal decisions in Europe have concerned the points where the private enters into the public.[13] These cases are reflected in the third substantive area considered by RELIGARE, which concerns religion in the context of public spaces, with a particular focus on religious dress codes and places of worship. Here again, a strong narrative of relationships can be discerned.

In European society, which purports to value diversity, and in modern life, where fashion is an important means of self-expression and strict codes of dress have all but disappeared, the consternation caused by headscarves and face veils has been remarkable. A wide divergence is noted in the national response of Member States to such garments, and interesting questions are raised about the relationship between individuals, their personal choices and the symbolic strength of clothing and accessories. While certain badges of membership are accepted as part of modern living, others provoke outrage and fear. The RELIGARE report begins to highlight some of these complexities and contradictions with a view to moving towards more nuanced regulation which pays greater attention to the personal relationship between wearer and veil and to the individual suitability of dress to function (*Report*, § 2.3.1.1).

Just as a veil might be a personal choice or a sign of lack of choice, buildings and public spaces cannot always be judged on their appearance alone. In the RELIGARE report, they are presented not as fixed and immoveable structures, but as spaces where people come together to interact in society. Public spaces can be flexible spaces, their nature shaped and changed by their use. A church can be not simply a religious building, but a multi-functional space with different meanings for worshippers, tourists and local communities.

Relationships are complicated, and that truism applies not only to interpersonal relationships but to the relationship between individuals, their outward appearance and their environment. To achieve equality and freedom in ways which promote inclusion and even-handedness, legal regulation must attempt to understand and reflect some of that complexity.

State Support Mechanisms: Neglected Relationships

The starting point for discussion of the role of religion in Europe is that 'the majority of national legislatures … have made the historic decision to secularise State law' (*Report*, § 1.1). A particular focus of much recent analysis of religion in contemporary Europe has been the detailed tracking and consideration of the complexity and diversity which lies behind this apparently clear and simple separation of church and State (*Report*, § 1.1).[14] While for most European countries, government is 'conducted by means of secular laws alone' (*Report*, § 1.1), what emerges from contemporary research is that there is considerable evidence of the variety of ongoing relations and continuing support for at least some religious organisations. Perhaps the neglect of these continuing relations was *bona fide*, resulting from the belief that there had indeed been a real break between church and State, or resulted from a lack of self-awareness of the 'hypocrisy' and 'ethnocentrism' that such continuing support could indicate, or from a failure to notice 'a developing trend' towards 'increasingly unchurched majority sentiment' (*Report*, § 1.1).

It is against this background of – until recently overlooked – relationships that the RELIGARE project identifies its final area of interaction: the operation of 'State support mechanisms' (*Report*, § 2.4). While 'the issue of public financing of religious and philosophical organisations seems remote from the competencies of the EU' (*Report*, § 2.4), more familiar European spheres of regulation such as taxation, training and broadcasting are employed to demonstrate the links between the EU, State support and religious groups. Comparative sociological data is also used to highlight the inequalities which have developed through failure to adapt to 'recent socio-demographic developments' (*Report*, § 2.4). This section of the report provides ample evidence of the relevance of the relationship metaphor to the RELIGARE project itself and to the proposals resulting from it: the interaction of different branches of EU regulation, the complementarity of direct support and tax exemptions, and the interplay of religion and culture. One relationship which is particularly highlighted is that between different religious organisations. While many Member States continue in a variety

13 See, for example, D McGoldrick, 'Religion in the European Public Square and in European Private Life: Crucifixes in the Classroom?' (2011) 11 *Human Rights Law Review* 451.

14 See, for example, N Doe, *Law and Religion in Europe: A Comparative Introduction* (OUP 2011).

of ways to provide support to religious bodies, there tends to be a hierarchy that favours established religions over those more recently arrived or formed.

Harmony Restored?

It is not only in Europe that religion represents a problem, but it is in the European context that the emergence of religion has posed a particular challenge because of its threat to the dominant discourse of harmonisation. The European social model was designed to be peopled by European citizens sharing common values and benefiting from common rights. Security in this shared vision has been shaken, both by the physical presence within Europe of non-European communities who live (at least partly) by other values and by the expression of religious beliefs and motivations by those who were presumed to be secular Europeans. The loud expression of their difference, at a time when Europe is stressing commonality, threatens the cultural coherence and harmonious values at the heart of the European democratic project.

Working with failing relationships, the RELIGARE report has explored past faults, mediated compromise settlements and counselled parties in preparation for future engagement. It emphasises throughout the values of openness, communication, engagement, mutual respect and trust at all levels of EU institutions, structure and society. The report can be read as a reordering of relationships, 'a trustworthy blueprint on which to build when rethinking the interface of religion and secularism in the Europe of the future' (*Report*, § 3.2). While positive about the future, it also acknowledges, particularly in its final section on EU action (*Report*, § 3), the possible need for further support. The RELIGARE report has returned relationships to the core of European democracy and highlighted their centrality to the project of cooperation and harmonisation. While its principal objective was to respond to the disruptive effect of religion, its insights and recommendations are likely to have a significance which reaches far beyond.

Chapter 7
Religious Freedom and Accommodation in the United Kingdom

Maleiha Malik

Demystification is especially important in the context of religious freedom. There is a commonly held assumption that religious belief is a 'pure' right and the crowning achievement of human rights in the secular modern world. Although it is true that religious freedom is an important human right and constitutional guarantee in liberal democracies, this assumption should not stop us from scrutinising it more closely. Methods from history and analytical approaches from the social sciences, especially from sociology or anthropology, are essential for a full understanding of the concept of religious freedom. I want to illustrate how religious freedom needs to be understood in a more complex way than is often assumed.

The common assumption is that religious freedom is a universal human right that is being undermined by irrational religious forces in the West and especially by Muslim societies that refuse to extend this right to non-Muslims. Yet, as recent historical and anthropological analysis reveals, religious freedom is not an essential universal concept that can be understood without taking into account historical, political, economic and cultural factors. For example, the modern Western concept of religious liberty that is the foundation of the right to religious freedom in the United Kingdom has a complex history. It emerges out of 'domestic' struggles between different Christian denominations, but it also has an international aspect. For the European missionaries of the nineteenth century, religious liberty was the crucial means of securing the right to proselytise freely among the people that they colonised, such as the Coptic Christian communities in Egypt and Hindus, Sikhs and Muslims in British Colonial India.[1] The European Union has recently followed the United States in introducing provisions that link its external foreign policy aims to the promotion of religious freedom.[2] There is, however, a need for vigilance to make sure that EU foreign policy relating to the promotion of religious freedom does not collapse into an excuse for bias, missionary activity and modern-style proselytising in non-Western countries.

Closer to home, one of the most startling legal developments of recent times is the increase in the volume of cases involving religious discrimination or the right to freedom of religion,[3] as the following recent cases in the UK attest.

Ladele v London Borough of Islington [2009] EWCA Civ 1357

A Christian registrar of marriages argued that a requirement to conduct a same-sex civil ceremony was a breach of her right to freedom of religion under Article 9 of the European Convention on Human Rights and constituted religious discrimination under the Employment Equality Directive/Employment Equality (Religion or Belief) Regulations 2003. She won in the first instance in the Industrial Tribunal. She lost in the Employment Appeals Tribunal and the Court of Appeal. She lost her case in the European Court of Human Rights.

---

1 S Mahmood, 'Religious Freedom, Minority Rights and Geopolitics', *The Immanent Frame* (5 March 2012).

2 P Annicchino, 'Freedom of Religion or Belief in the Foreign Policy of the European Union: Much Ado About Nothing?' in R Alvira and MA Glendon (eds), *Religion and Civil Society: The Changing Faces of Religion and Secularity* (Georg Olms 2014).

3 M Malik, 'Religious Freedom, Free Speech and Equality: Conflict or Cohesion?' (2011) 17 (1) *Res Publica* 21–40.

***Eweida v British Airways PLC* [2010] EWCA Civ 80**

A Christian employee of British Airways claimed that the dress code of BA (which required personal jewellery to be concealed by the uniform) discriminated against her as a Christian because it did not allow her to wear a cross in such a way that it was visible to the public. The Court of Appeal held that there was no indirect religious discrimination because there was an insufficient group aspect to indicate that others shared her religious conviction to *openly* display the cross. Lord Justice Sedley held that even if Ms Eweida could establish that there was indirect discrimination on the basis of her needs as a single individual, the BA dress code could be justified as a proportionate means of achieving a legitimate aim.

The *Ladele* and *Eweida* cases were decided by the European Court of Human Rights on 15 January 2013. Ms Ladele lost her case, but Ms Eweida won.[4] How should we understand these cases? I want to suggest that simply citing religious freedom or religious equality cannot, of itself, resolve these issues. The framing of situations such as the *Ladele* case as a problem of the right of religious individuals not to be discriminated against leads us to an impasse. The debate very soon collapses into a clash of rights or a clash of equalities – 'my right to religious equality versus your right to equality on the grounds of sexual orientation'. Moreover, framing the issue as a question of equality means that any expression of disagreement with equality legislation by religious people is treated as problematic even if they have not acted on those views to commit a discriminatory act. Of course, where speech becomes a course of conduct that constitutes harassment, it is regulated and prohibited. Moreover, the freedom to state one's beliefs is legitimately more limited in the workplace, where the interests of protecting employees may justify curtailing the free speech of religious people who do not believe in equality for women, gays or lesbians. Nevertheless, some speech in the workplace may fall short of constituting harassment and it may not be a threat to the working atmosphere for women, gays and lesbians. This means that religious people who simply (and politely) state their beliefs about equality on the grounds of gender or sexual orientation may be penalised in spheres such as the workplace. As Andrew Koppelman argues, there is a joint interest in allowing a dialogue between religious people and gays and lesbians so that both sides can understand, challenge and reconsider what seem to be entrenched viewpoints.[5]

An alternative way of framing the issue is as a matter of religious tolerance rather than equality. On this analysis, there is recognition that the viewpoints of some religious people towards women, gays and lesbians are not compatible with our contemporary commitments to equality. In such cases, the speech–conduct distinction becomes crucial: those with strong religious beliefs about women, gays and lesbians can hold that view; they may even appropriately express that view; but they cannot act on that view in a way that constitutes discriminatory harassment (through their speech) or discriminatory acts (through their conduct). So, for instance, Ms Ladele can hold the view that she does not agree with same-sex civil partnerships. However, she cannot act on those beliefs in certain spheres that we consider important areas in which gays and lesbians should be guaranteed equality, including the provision of public services such as the registration of marriage and the provision of goods and services in the private sector.

It is often argued that there should be 'accommodation' of the religious conscience of, in this case, Ms Ladele by allowing her to claim an exemption based on religion and belief. But we already grant significant exemptions that allow religious organisations (rather than religious individuals) to discriminate against gays and lesbians. We have, as a society and a political community, already reached the appropriate balance between the rights of the religious and equality for women, gays and lesbians that is enshrined in our equalities legislation. If the religious want to change this balance and equilibrium, then it is, of course, possible for them to organise and try to effect such changes through democratic processes. In fact, it is often argued that the exemptions that have already been granted to religion and belief in the UK's Equality Act 2010 are too wide and in breach of EU requirements. The requirement that exemptions should be 'proportionate' was removed after a defeat not in the House of Commons, but through a vote in the House of Lords in January 2010.

4 *Eweida and Others v the United Kingdom*, App nos 48420/10, 59842/10, 51671/10 and 36516/10 (decisions of 15 January 2013).

5 A Koppelman, 'You Can't Hurry Love: Why Antidiscrimination Protections for Gay People Should Have Religious Exemptions' (2006–2007) 72 *Brooklyn L Rev* 125; C Stychin, 'Faith in the Future: Sexuality, Religion and the Public Sphere' (2009) 29 *Oxford Journal of Legal Studies* 729–55.

In my view there is still a problem in these cases because the right to same-sex civil partnership and the right to equality on the grounds of sexual orientation are constitutional matters. Ms Ladele is, therefore, claiming an exemption from a constitutional provision of which Parliament has already decided the proper scope of exemptions. In other words, the issue has already been legislatively determined, and there should not be a judicial renegotiation of exemptions that compromise the constitutional right to equality on the grounds of sexual orientation. Moreover, even if there were other registrars willing to perform the ceremony, there are questions about how such an exchange of personnel would be administered as a matter of course.

Even if the accommodation of an individual such as Ms Ladele could be administered so that the couple received exactly the same service in practice, there is still a major problem, as summed up by the Court in a recent Saskatchewan case involving legislative exemptions for marriage registrars who do not want to perform same-sex ceremonies.[6] Although an identical service may be provided, there is still a detriment because gays and lesbians are being shunned by public officials entrusted to provide them with public services. The following passages from the Saskatchewan case are relevant:

> It would be a significant step backward if, having won the difficult fight for the right to same-sex civil marriages, gay and lesbian couples could be shunned by the very people charged by the Province with solemnizing such unions.[7]

> Negative effects of this sort would not be restricted to those gay and lesbian individuals who are directly denied marriage services. A more generalised version of it would obviously be felt by the gay and lesbian community at large and, indeed, there is no doubt it would ripple through friends and families of gay and lesbian persons and the public as a whole. Simply put, it is not just gay and lesbian couples themselves who would be hurt or offended by the notion that a governmental official can deny services to same-sex couples. Many members of the public would also be negatively affected by the idea.[8]

This analysis provides a framework for making sense of the recent decisions of the European Court of Human Rights in relation to religious freedom in the *Eweida* and *Ladele* cases. In situations such as *Eweida* (religious symbols, dress codes or religious holidays), reasonable accommodation of religion does not have any impact on constitutional rights, but it is subject to balancing with other interests. The European Court of Human Rights was correct in judging in favour of Ms Eweida, thereby allowing her to wear her cross along with her uniform at work. This decision confirms the RELIGARE report's conclusion that 'the integration of a widely diverse workforce in Europe should not require an *assimilative approach* to religion in the workplace' (*Report*, 21).

But the decision of the European Court of Human Rights in *Ladele* is also correct. The fact that Ms Ladele was already working as a marriage registrar in Islington before the introduction of the Civil Partnership Act 2004 made this a difficult case to adjudicate. In the Court of Appeal, Lord Neuberger, the Master of the Rolls, noted that Ms Ladele and her employers were faced with a dilemma. Nevertheless, the decision in *Ladele* is correct law and politics. There should be no accommodation for the religious where the exemption is from a key constitutional or human right such as the right to equality. Individuals cannot expect to directly influence public services so that they conform to their personal religious beliefs, especially where that accommodation constitutes a breach of the constitutional or human rights of another citizen.

In extremis, the religious tolerance that underpins religious freedom in the European Union can be enforced through constitutional, human rights and equality law. But it is also a political and ethical virtue and a matter of how we live our lives as citizens even where the law is not involved. Finally, then, although I have focused on law and legal cases, I want to end by emphasising the importance of using non-legal techniques of arbitration or mediation to resolve conflicts between religion and equality. Better training and management in the workplace should be supported to prevent disputes (for example, between religious conscience and sexual orientation equality) from becoming acrimonious. In some cases, the reallocation of work duties and rosters

6 *Marriage Commissioners Appointed under the Marriage Act (Re)*, 2011 SKCA 3.
7 ibid para 94.
8 ibid para 96.

can address the issue without the need for disciplinary proceedings or litigation. In the UK, for example, the main statutory workplace arbitration service (ACAS) has issued guidelines about how employers can reconcile their responsibilities under the Employment Equality (Religion or Belief) Regulations 2003 and the Employment Equality (Sexual Orientation) Regulations 2003.[9]

This approach is in keeping with policy recommendation 2.1.4 (c) of the RELIGARE report, which endorses 'reasonable accommodation for religious observance in the workplace' (*Report*, 21). All this is possible within the existing concept of indirect religious discrimination that is already a part of EU discrimination law without the need to introduce an additional duty of reasonable accommodation of religion and belief.

Conflicts such as the *Ladele* case require a range of responses. The institutional context is critical in all these cases. The debate about how to resolve conflicts and the resulting negotiations between groups need to be carried out within mainstream political and legal institutions. Civil society and the media are also important actors within this process. We must recognise diversity within groups, but also remain vigilant about the risk of harm to vulnerable individuals from oppression within groups. This procedure is likely to ensure the broadest range of participation in public debate and political negotiations. In this way the painful compromises that are an inherent part of the European Union's response to new conditions of religious diversity, as well as EU equality law and policy, are more likely to command the consent of all those involved. As the RELIGARE report observes, 'Sometimes, confrontations are not only inevitable but also necessary on the way to achieving sustainable long-term justice' (*Report*, 21).

Points of difference and friction between individuals and groups can often act as a catalyst towards a stable form of integration that avoids the worst injustices of forced assimilation. In some cases we must be satisfied with an outcome that is a patient and resigned *modus vivendi*. More optimistically, this technique also has some potential to generate a deeper and more meaningful identification with national and local institutions, in a joint enterprise, that creates social cohesion and sustains a coherent political community rather than a plethora of self-interested splinter groups. Discussions about competing interests and conflicts that are conducted in this spirit may be able to contribute to a sense of belonging on the part of all citizens, which can be effectively hammered out through debate and compromise carried out in the public sphere.

9 B Savage 'Sexual Orientation and Religion or Belief Discrimination in the Workplace' (ACAS 2007).

Chapter 8
Religion, Law and State in Contemporary Europe: Key Trends and Dilemmas

Ronan McCrea

RELIGARE has done significant work on the mapping of evolving methods of dealing and engaging with religion in contemporary Europe. A major focus of the work has been to identify when existing structures and norms may exclude or discriminate against minority faiths. Such structures exist in the legal and constitutional realm as much as in the workplace or social life. In this piece I would therefore like to examine patterns of dealing with religion in the legal and constitutional sphere and to assess the degree to which they require adaptation in Europe's changing religious environment. I will start by briefly identifying three pillars that undergird common European approaches to the relationship between religion, law and State. I then consider how diversity challenges each pillar and what kind of changes ought, or ought not, to be made in response to such challenges.

Common Features of European Approaches to Religion, Law and State: The Three Pillars

There is significant divergence in the approaches of European States to the relationship between religion, the law and the State. Some States have official State churches, some recognise a number of faiths, while others are officially secular. However, despite the diversity in symbolic and institutional terms, there is significant overlap between States, and a clear European template that is reinforced by pan-European institutions can be identified.

Pillar I: An Individualistic View of Religion

The European Court of Human Rights has repeatedly made clear that, insofar as fundamental rights law is concerned, religion is 'primarily a matter of individual thought and conscience'.[1] This is underlined in the text of Article 9 of the ECHR, which protects freedom of 'thought, conscience and religion', and is reflected in the case law of the Strasbourg Court, which has seen Article 9 as being primarily directed at protecting the right of individuals to choose their own beliefs. Institutional autonomy and collective aspects of religion can also be protected, but these are viewed by the Court as secondary elements whose protection is often linked to the need to make the commitment to individual religious freedom effective. This is a view which is not universally shared. For many, religion's communal and ritualistic elements are of primary importance; the law of some States views religious harmony as a value of greater importance than individual choice and free expression, while many Muslim States regard the prevention of apostasy as more important than individual choice in religious matters.

Pillar II: Separation of Religion from Law and Politics

Although religion and State are often entwined, the separation of religion on the one hand and law and politics on the other is a fundamental pillar of European approaches to religion in public life. As Mark Lilla points out, separating religion from politics is neither natural nor inevitable, but is a rather curious intellectual

---

1 This statement has been repeatedly made by the Court, most recently in *Eweida and Others v UK*, App nos 48420/10, 59842/10, 51671/10 and 36516/10 (judgment of 15 January 2013), paragraph 80.

exercise that came out of the specific circumstances of European history.[2] Furthermore, as Habermas has rightly noted,[3] de-linking one's political actions from one's religious beliefs is particularly difficult for believers in missionary faiths for whom the imperative of eternal salvation ought logically to take priority over the need to respect individual choice in matters of faith or the need to preserve interfaith harmony. Nevertheless, the intellectual exercise of separating religious beliefs from politics is strongly established in Europe. *Eurobarometer* surveys indicate that religion is a very weak influence on individuals' political views.[4] Indeed, the idea of separating the realms of religion and politics is so entrenched in Europe that it is often more of a socio-political expectation than a strict legal principle. Though strict institutional separation of church and State is relatively rare in Europe, legislation in European countries does not cite religious norms. Furthermore, the European Union has made it clear that 'democratic secularism' is a condition of accession, while the European Court of Human Rights has ruled that theocracy would breach the European Convention of Human Rights.[5]

Pillar III: Cultural Overlap

This separation of religion and politics exists alongside strong cultural and institutional links between European States and particular faiths. In almost all European States, the majority of the population adheres to one faith, which is reflected in both communal arrangements and the denomination-specific flavour of some national cultural symbols. Many flags, such as those of the Scandinavian countries, bear crosses; national holidays such as Saint Patrick's Day in Ireland are religiously linked; and in historically Christian countries, working arrangements such as weekends and holidays remain structured around the Christian Sabbath and Christian festivals such as Christmas and Easter. National cultural icons such as Notre Dame in Paris, the Book of Kells (an illuminated gospel from the ninth century) in Ireland and Michelangelo's *Pietà* in Italy are also clearly linked to particular religious traditions. Thus, a secular political order sits alongside cultural and communal symbols and arrangements that reflect the historical predominance and disproportionate cultural influence of particular faiths in particular countries.

Challenges to Existing Patterns

This curious mixture of an individualised approach to religion, a separation of religion and politics and cultural links to a particular faith is coming under increased strain in contemporary Europe. Greater religious diversity is raising complex issues in respect of each 'pillar' of established European patterns of dealing with the relationship between religion, politics, law and the State and is highlighting tensions between pillars, most notably the degree of tension between an individualised view of religion and a religious element to collective national identity. More diverse approaches to what constitutes the core features of religion challenge established patterns of protecting religious freedom. The growing presence of religious faiths with less tradition of separating religion from law and politics brings potential conflicts with political and legal norms that require limits on religious influence in these areas. Finally, the weakening link between nationality and a particular faith calls into greater question the status of religiously linked symbols and arrangements as representative of the State as a whole. I would like to deal with each of these challenges in turn.

Dilemma I: Religious Diversity and What is Protected by Religious Freedom

The individualised view of religious freedom discussed above is most consistent with a Protestant vision of religion as primarily a matter of the individual's belief and conscience. The rise in religious diversity in

2 M Lilla, *The Stillborn God* (Knopf Books 2007).

3 J Habermas, 'Intolerance and Discrimination' (2003) 1 (1) *International Journal of Constitutional Law* 2, 7.

4 *Eurobarometer* 69 (2008), available at <http://ec.europa.eu/public_opinion/archives/eb/eb69/eb69_values_en.pdf> accessed 27 June 2014.

5 See R McCrea, *Religion and the Public Order of the European Union* (OUP 2010) chapter 6.

Europe, and particularly the increased presence of forms of religion that place less emphasis than Western Protestantism on the individual conscience element of religion, has strengthened long-standing criticisms of Article 9 jurisprudence of the European Court of Human Rights that argue that the Court has failed to give sufficient protection to religion's collective aspects, to forms of religion that focus more on ritual, and to religion as a way of life rather than as a personal belief system.

It is certainly important to ensure that a lack of familiarity with a particular faith or simple ethnic chauvinism do not lead to a lesser degree of religious freedom being granted to adherents of minority religions than is accorded to adherents of culturally entrenched faiths. However, in verifying that such an inequity is not occurring, the question should not be whether the vision of religious freedom underpinning the Strasbourg Court's jurisprudence is capable of covering everything that can be described as religion. The European Convention on Human Rights is a liberal document that defends religious freedom not to protect religion itself (even when it has upheld restrictions on anti-religious speech, it has done so on the basis of the need to protect the feelings of believers, not to protect religion itself).[6] Rather, freedom of thought, conscience and religion is protected as part of a broader set of liberal freedoms that protect the individual's right to construct an identity that is meaningful and appropriate for herself.[7] The task of the Court is not to identify what, as a matter of sociology or theology, falls within the category of religion, but to identify what it is that is valuable about religious freedom and to ensure that the right to freedom of religion is protected.

Such an approach means that some of what is considered to be religious may fall outside the contours of Article 9. The law is an imperfect tool that is required to recast complex social and emotional realities in such a way that they can be transformed into general principles. Such a process can never hope to capture the full richness of the entities so reconstructed. The relationship of an employee to her employer often involves an intense emotional commitment to a career that is a vital part of the employee's identity, yet the law can only treat it as a form of exchange of labour for remuneration. Similarly the legal form of marriage hardly fully represents the emotional reality of a couple's life together. So it is with religion. The full significance and diversity of religious experience cannot be reflected in the law. Rather, the law must, as it does in many other areas, pare down a very broad and complex social and emotional phenomenon to the particularly important and valuable elements whose protection can be formulated into a general principle.

In the European context, the fact that religious freedom is guaranteed alongside a number of other individual autonomy rights such as the rights to privacy, freedom of expression, and freedom from torture and arbitrary detention, as well as the fact that the text of Article 9 covers freedom of thought and conscience as well as religion, indicates that the core element of what is to be protected is indeed the right to individual autonomy in matters of belief where religion is regarded as key. While a sense of religious community or the importance of religious ritual may be key elements of religion for many, it is only insofar as such elements of religion can be shown to relate to a liberal and autonomy-focused view of religious freedom that they are likely to be protected. This approach to the protection of religious freedom has been subject to criticism on the grounds that it is insufficiently protective of collective elements of religion or of forms of religion that cannot easily be linked to claims to individual or associational autonomy in matters of belief.

We should be vigilant to ensure that we do not dismiss a claim to religious freedom simply because the religion contains elements that are unfamiliar or exotic. As Laborde rightly argues, we must take care to verify that existing structures do not contain unjustifiable biases that are often somewhat hidden.[8] That does not mean, however, that a system for the protection of religious freedom must ensure that everything that falls within the category of religion is treated as having an equally pressing claim to protection. Religion is a vast and diverse category that covers a large spectrum of claims and behaviours, some very noble and morally compelling, others quite unworthy and trivial. No legal system could or should hope to grant equal weight to every aspect of the vast range of phenomena that make up religion. The key question is, therefore, whether there is a good case for treating as more deserving of protection the elements of religion that the European Court has identified as the core of the right protected by Article 9. The Court has so far adopted a view

6 *Otto Preminger Institut v Austria* (1994) 19 EHRR 34.

7 This is also the approach taken by the EU's *Guidelines on the Promotion and Protection of Religion or Belief*, Council of the European Union, Foreign Affairs Council Meeting, Luxembourg, 24 June 2013.

8 C Laborde, *Critical Republicanism: The Hijab Controversy and Political Philosophy* (OUP 2008).

that religion is primarily about individual conscience and autonomy. It has not done so merely because this reflects a Protestant view of religion (although cultural traditions, including a cultural affinity for individual autonomy, inevitably influence what individuals regard as important). Rather, it has done so because, as custodian of the interpretation of a charter of liberal individual rights, it rightly sees religious freedom as an element of a broader liberal commitment to securing individual autonomy in key matters of personal identity. Clearly, liberal theories of religious freedom underpin the views of religious freedom as expressed in a liberal fundamental rights charter. While such an approach will mean that forms of religiosity that are more difficult to translate into claims to private autonomy will receive less protection, that is the inevitable result of the fact that the ECHR is a text committed to the protection of liberal values and that signatory States are committed to being liberal societies that value liberal principles.

Collective religious liberty and communal rights can often have a very competitive relationship with individual autonomy rights (for example, the imposition of ethos-loyalty requirements on employees of religious schools and hospitals). Accordingly, religious traditions that place greater emphasis on communal ties than on individual choice in matters of faith may face greater difficulty in articulating claims in terms that are likely to fall within the scope of a liberal rights charter. While we must be careful not to disadvantage or discriminate against unfamiliar forms of religious belief and practice, we should not 'throw the baby out with the bathwater' and undermine the liberal and egalitarian orientation of the right to freedom of conscience and religion as it has been constructed in European law.

Dilemma II: Religion in Politics

The second challenge to established patterns of dealing with religion relates to the return of religion to the political sphere. Many culturally entrenched denominations did not easily or entirely accept the limitations on religious influence over law and politics. The Catholic Church only fully embraced liberal democracy and religious freedom after the Second Vatican Council, and many religions have continued to play an active role in debates on laws in relation to matters such as gay rights, marriage, abortion and the beginning and end of life. However, generally it has become accepted in Europe that religions ought not to be able to use the law to enforce compliance with their teachings and should not exercise a controlling influence over law and politics. This is not the case in many areas of the world from which many migrant communities in Europe originate. Religion plays a decisive political role in many countries, particularly in the Muslim world, while in many States in Africa and the Middle East (both Christian and Muslim), the law of the State is used to enforce compliance with religious teachings, most notably in relation to the prohibition of homosexuality.

Olivier Roy has noted that many in Europe have felt threatened 'by the emergence of new communities who do not feel bound by old compromises painfully worked out' between the religious and the secular.[9] The responses of European States and institutions to the new political prominence of religion have gone in both directions. On the one hand, political institutions have sought to bring religion into the political process through programmes of structured dialogue with religious bodies such as that operated by the European Union,[10] which was recognised in the Lisbon Treaty (this is occurring at the State level, too). On the other hand, States have increasingly been identifying acceptance of limits on religious influence over law and religiously controversial principles such as gender equality and toleration of homosexuality as fundamental requirements of the democratic order. This can be seen in the accession process to the European Union, which required Romania to defy pressure from the Orthodox Church and decriminalise homosexuality as a condition of joining the EU, and the European Commission's identification of 'democratic secularism' as an entry condition for future members.[11]

It can also be seen on an individual level with the proliferation of integration tests in a number of States that require immigrants to indicate awareness of, or in some cases, acceptance of principles such as gender equality and gay rights as conditions of naturalisation. This has been most notable in France, where the authorities refused citizenship to a woman on grounds of her 'radical practice' of her religion and

9 O Roy, *Secularism Confronts Islam* (G Holoch tr, Columbia University Press 2007) 6.

10 See Consolidated Treaty on the Functioning of the European Union, Article 17.

11 See McCrea (n 5).

rejection of gender equality,[12] and to a man who refused to let his wife speak or leave the house without his permission. In both cases refusal was justified on the basis of a failure to accept the fundamental values of the French Republic.[13]

In some countries (not including France), the tests have been applied in a deeply discriminatory way. It is not just that many, such as the National Front in France, have discovered a love for secularism that they did not have before it became a stick with which to beat immigrants. Some States have exempted immigrants from Western States but still subject the secular *bona fides* of those from Muslim-majority States to much more intense scrutiny.[14] Such a blatantly discriminatory approach is entirely unacceptable. However, if fairly applied, such tests can serve important goals. Theocracy and a desire to use the law to enforce religious teachings, as we see, for example, with the persecution of homosexuals in Uganda and Iran or the oppression of women in Saudi Arabia, are incompatible with liberal democracy. Migration law regularly allows States to favour those with ethnic or linguistic ties to a State or with desirable qualities such as higher levels of education, special skills, youth or good health. It is not unreasonable for States to similarly favour those potential immigrants and possible future citizens who are committed to tolerance and equality over those who cannot accept gender equality, the secular State or toleration of homosexuality.

Dilemma III: Diversity and Culture

The final challenge to Europe's established method of dealing with the relationship comes from the residual, denominationally specific flavour of cultural symbols and arrangements in the context of increasing religious diversity. As populations of European States have become more religiously diverse, the ability of a particular faith to act as part of a shared national identity has diminished. In part this is because there are many ethnic communities that do not share Christian cultural loyalties, but it is also because the numbers of self-declared atheists and agnostics are rising rapidly. The UK census of 2011 showed a surge in the percentage of people who said they had no religion, from 15 per cent at the time of the previous census in 2001 to 25 per cent in 2011.[15] Previously, many of those who are not particularly religious were content to describe themselves as Christian on cultural grounds: in Europe, the numbers of such nominal Christians have long exceeded those who profess belief in the core tenets of the Christian faith. But as religion and national identity have gradually begun to separate, religious identity becomes more a question of ideology and belief than of membership in a national community. This has encouraged those who are not true believers to move from a nominal Christian identity to a more clearly non-religious one.

Once nationality is no longer synonymous with a particular religious denomination, the symbols of that religion lose their ability to act as uncontroversial national cultural symbols. Where they might once have been shared, now such symbols become highly contested. For example, in Ireland in 2007, Ravinder Singh Oberoi, a Sikh, challenged the uniform rules of the Garda Reserve, the volunteer force within the Irish police, because he felt he should be allowed to wear a turban.[16] In San Marino in 1999, three incoming MPs went to the European Court over the traditional oath they were required to take on the basis that its reference to 'the holy Gospels' violated the rights of non-Christian deputies.[17] And in Italy in 2011, Soile Lautsi, an atheist mother, took her children's school to the European Court of Human Rights for displaying crucifixes in the classrooms. In the UK, the National Secular Society has taken legal action to challenge the practice of saying prayers before local council meetings and in State schools.

Yet these challenges to religious symbolism in public have not all been successful. The Irish police argued that the police force must be religiously neutral (even though the badge of that same force is based on imagery

12 Conseil d'Etat, Section du contentieux, 2ème et 7ème sous-sections réunies, Séance du 26 mai 2008 – Lecture du 27 juin 2008 N°286798 – Mme M.

13 See 'Algerian-Born Man Living in France is Refused French Nationality' (*The Guardian*, 9 June 2011) <www.theguardian.com/world/2011/jun/09/man-refused-french-nationality> accessed 27 June 2014.

14 See McCrea (n 5).

15 See, R McCrea, 'Is Migration Making Europe More Secular?' (*Aeon Magazine*, June 2013) <http://aeon.co/magazine/world-views/ronan-mccrea-secular-europe/> accessed 27 June 2014.

16 ibid.

17 *Buscarini v San Marino* (1999) 30 EHRR 208.

of Celtic Christian monastic art, which is seen as an important part of Irish national cultural heritage), and the High Court in Ireland rejected Mr Oberoi's claim.[18] Mrs Lautsi's initial victory in Strasbourg was reversed on appeal on the basis that the 'passive symbol' of the cross on a classroom wall was not sufficiently indoctrinating to trigger the intervention of the European Court.[19] And a victory in court for the National Secular Society in its challenge to council prayers[20] may be followed by political defeat as the UK government has promised to legislate to reverse that decision. Nevertheless, the proliferation of challenges to these residually Christian symbols in public life shows how, in a more diverse Europe, the Christian flavour of public institutions is becoming increasingly controversial.

There is no escaping the fact that the more religiously specific national symbols and arrangements are, the more difficult it will be to fully include members of religious minorities into society and to win the loyalty of all to a shared sense of citizenship and national identity. Furthermore, the weaker the sense of multi-faith citizenship is, the harder it is to gain acceptance for compromises on the part of religious individuals in the name of citizenship or the need to live together harmoniously.

Nevertheless, as Charles Taylor suggests, sustainable political communities are not made up of 'a scratch team of history with nothing more in common than the passenger list of some international flight'.[21] The 'imagined communities' that constitute nation-States require some degree of communal identity and communal events that come out of a particular history. Being a particular history, it will bear to a greater degree the marks of those faiths, identities and institutions that influenced that history. The particular historical circumstances of each national history will chime with the identity and beliefs of some more than others. British republicans, for instance, live in a State where monarchy has been a central feature of the country's history and what Churchill called 'the long continuity of our institutions'. It is therefore unavoidable that in Britain, many national communal events, if they are to have any historical resonance, are going to be linked to the monarchy. It would be nice if events could be based on something more egalitarian, but this is not year zero and culture cannot be created from scratch.

Communal occasions that are not linked into some longer historical tradition are generally failures at catching the popular imagination. No significant sense of togetherness has resulted, for example, from the promotion of 'Europe Day' by the EU. In Britain, therefore, the alternative to royal communal events is really no engaging communal events at all and fewer chances to feel connected to those around you, in short, a more atomised and lonely society.

In many countries such national events have a particular religious flavour. In Ireland, Saint Patrick's Day has become a celebration of national identity, culture and a way for citizens to feel connected through a shared commitment to society and its cultural traditions. The history of the day itself is a celebration of the coming of Christianity to Ireland, and the churches probably derive some boost from the association. Non-Christians however, by and large, have been happy to overlook religious bits they might not agree with in order to join in a celebration of national belonging.

There must, however, be limits to the degree to which a religiously diverse citizenry must be expected to accept the symbolic privileges of culturally entrenched faiths. Where a symbol with religious origins, such as the Swedish flag, has developed an independent post-religious meaning, it is reasonable to expect everyone to accept its presence in public contexts. One might even argue that explicitly religious symbols such as Michelangelo's *Pietà* could be seen as having artistic qualities that would make it reasonable to use as a cultural symbol of the Italian State, given that it can be seen as symbolising an artistic and cultural heritage of which Italians of all faiths, and those without religious beliefs, could be proud.

Symbols such as a crucifix on the wall of a State school are much more difficult to see in more inclusive non-sectarian terms. Even if such a symbol was not found to be sufficiently oppressive to trigger European intervention in *Lautsi*, the presence of such a symbol, which has neither the post-religious meaning of the

18 *Oberoi and Another v Commissioner of An Garda Síochána* 2013 [IEHC] 267.

19 *Lautsi v Italy*, App no 30814/06 [2009] ECHR 1901 (03 November 2009).

20 *National Secular Society & Anor, R (on the application of) v Bideford Town Council* [2012] EWHC 175 (Admin) (10 February 2012).

21 C Taylor, 'Liberal Politics and the Public Sphere', Discussion Paper 15 (The Centre for the Study of Global Governance, London School of Economics 1995) 19.

Swedish flag nor the artistic justification for its presence of the *Pietà*, can be seen as preserving and imposing a degree of religious specificity in public space that is inappropriate and unhelpful in a diversifying society.

A critical and open attitude to national culture is vital. National cultures must be open to the contributions of faiths and cultures whose large-scale presence is a recent phenomenon. National cultures can and should change over time to reflect the input of a more diverse citizenry. However, it is also necessary to ensure that such evolution will not involve a complete breach with the past and will allow citizens to maintain a feeling of connection with their fellow citizens and with future and past generations.

Conclusion

European approaches to the relationship between law, religion and State are the outcome of a very specific history. This history has been marked by Christianity's important historic role in the identity of most European States and the long struggle between mainly Christian religious influences and secular-humanist influences (while secularism may have grown out of elements of Christian theology, it has proved to be a rebellious 'child' which clashed repeatedly with its religious 'parent' in the course of European history). Migration and other factors have meant that there is increasing religious diversity in Europe. Along with this greater diversity comes more pronounced divergence of opinions regarding issues such as what is covered by the term religion, what the primary focus of religion is and what the appropriate role of religion in legal and political life ought to be. It is not surprising, then, that established patterns of dealing with religion have been increasingly questioned.

European States must be careful not to stick thoughtlessly to established patterns in the face of increasing diversity. It is all too easy to fail to see or to disregard the exclusionary potential of established patterns that do not pay attention to the needs of adherents to faiths whose large-scale presence in Europe is more recent. An open, critical and reflective attitude towards established means of regulating religion's relationship to law, society and State is needed.

On the other hand, in assessing whether existing structures need to be adapted or retained, the key question is not whether such structures are or are not compatible with the claims that any particular faith may make. After all, the claims made in the name of religion are many and varied. Some claims are harmless, even laudable, while others are much less laudable and potentially disruptive of political stability and threaten the freedom, privacy and equal status of others.

European societies will need to reassess the relationship between law, religion and State in the light of increased religious diversity. Such a process should reflect on the goals served by established structures. Laws and principles limiting religious influence over and involvement in law and politics serve to ensure the stability of societies that are permanently divided on ultimate matters of religious truth and to protect the interests of those (such as women, gays and lesbians) who suffer under laws influenced by dominant patriarchal interpretations of religions in many areas of the world. The mere fact that some religious traditions are unaccustomed to or resent principles that limit their ability to enforce religious teachings through law cannot be sufficient to require the abandonment of such important norms.

On the other hand, some loosening of traditional ties between particular faiths and particular national identities is inevitable. Continuity with a particular cultural tradition and links to a shared imagined past are necessary but, as previously mono-faith societies become more religiously diverse, there must be some recognition of this diversity and a consequent reduction in the religious specificity of national cultural and symbolic life. While symbols such as flags have achieved a degree of independent meaning separate from their religious origins, the role of purely religious symbols (such as crucifixes) in the public sphere must be reconsidered. The more religiously specific national symbols are, the harder it will be to achieve a common non-denominational national identity that wins the loyalty of religious minorities while maintaining links to an imagined shared past.

It is likely that, as cultural norms surrounding religion in Europe become more diverse, regulation of the relationship between religion, State and law by implicit cultural norms will become increasingly difficult. In the United Kingdom, for example, a tacit understanding that blasphemy laws would rarely if ever be used to stifle mockery of religion did not survive *The Satanic Verses* affair and the attempt by evangelical Christians to censor *Jerry Springer: The Opera*; in the end, the offence of blasphemy was abolished altogether in 2008. Cultural expectations of reticence regarding religious matters in public contexts have also been replaced by harder-edged legal norms restricting religious symbols in State contexts and even in social life in a number of European States.[22]

Drawing up explicit legal norms in such an area will be an immensely difficult task. What is needed is a process of thoughtful clarification that balances a critical approach to existing norms and openness to change, on the one hand, with an awareness of the elements of the existing arrangements that have served European States well, on the other. There may be non-negotiables in the process of adaptation. Feminism, secularism, some link to an imagined shared past, and an ethic of citizenship and commitment to religious coexistence are all worthy elements of the approach of many States, and should not be abandoned. Neither the assertion that a norm is discriminatory (in the sense of being difficult to obey for those of a particular religious tradition) nor an assertion that a particular norm is a national tradition should be enough to condemn or retain the norm in question. Rules that are difficult for intolerant or misogynistic belief systems to accept may be perceived as exclusionary, but they also bring great benefits in terms of a large degree of religious freedom, including freedom *from* religion. On the other hand, history is littered with traditions that have been questioned and rightly discarded as both exclusionary and useless. In short, in carrying out the delicate task of adapting to religious diversity, decision makers must bear in mind that not all that has been is good, but that some of what has been is there for very good reasons.

22 See, for example, the 2004 French law on ostentatious religious symbols in schools and bans on the full-face veil in public in France and Belgium in 2010.

Chapter 9
Religious Diversity and EU Action: The Overwhelming Impact of Subsidiarity on Legislative Instruments

Juana M. Astigarraga Zulaica and Eduardo J. Ruiz-Vieytez

Introduction

One of the main issues arising from the conclusions of the RELIGARE project concerns the role to be played by EU institutions in respect to religious diversity. This can be understood as the question of whether or not the EU and its institutions should play a more active role in ensuring that religious and philosophical diversity in Europe are an asset in the long term. From this perspective, the fact that religious freedom is a well-established fundamental right at the European level (and in all the domestic constitutional frameworks of EU Member States) opens a debate about the real involvement of the EU in the protection and promotion of this right. Our goal with this analysis is to point out the difficulties involved in one of the central pillars of the strategy suggested by the RELIGARE final report, that is, positive intervention by the EU through, among other measures, legislative action. The difficulty lies in the fact that too much weight is given in this area to the principle of subsidiarity as the expression of the sovereignty of the Member States in managing philosophical and religious diversity. The effects of the disproportionate weight attached to subsidiarity can be observed in the limited scope of action that European legislative measures devote to ensuring minimum standards of protection of freedom of religion.

Our hypothesis is that, of the three types of EU action discussed by the RELIGARE report – legislative instruments, participatory procedures and the involvement of experts – legislative instruments have thus far proven to be the least effective because their force is dramatically diminished by the substantial presence of subsidiarity. To provide some additional support for this idea, we will refer to Europe's constitutional treaties as well as those directives and regulations that expressly refer to religious aspects and in which the predominance of the subsidiarity principle can be easily observed.

The Disproportionate Weight of Subsidiarity in EU Legislative Action on Religious Freedom

Context

In his famous speech delivered in Washington DC on 30 April 1952, French economist Jean Monnet, one of the founding fathers of the European Union, said, 'We are not bringing together states, we are uniting men'.[1] At the heart of his words lay the idea that the European Community was not merely a union of States, but rather an entity whose purpose was to unite people. He thus placed human beings and their rights at the centre of the project of a European union.

But protecting fundamental rights was not a priority for the founding fathers of the European Community. This is not surprising in light of the fact that the Community was originally constituted for the purpose of achieving economic aims related to a single European market.[2] Safeguards to fundamental rights were put

1 *Nous ne coalisons pas les Etats, nous unissons les hommes*. Speech delivered by Jean Monnet on 30 April 1952 at the National Press Club, Washington DC. Available at the University of Pittsburgh's website in the Archive of European Integration (AIE) <http://aei.pitt.edu/14364/> accessed 29 June 2014.

2 In this regard, the most straightforward example is the inclusion of the principle of equal pay for male and female workers for equal work or work of equal value (Article 119–1 of the Treaty Establishing the European Community (TEEC),

in place in response to an economic need, not as a result of an explicit constitutional impulse, and rights protection in the European Union continues to bear the marks of this characteristic of the EU's origins.

However, the process of European integration itself, as well as the ever-growing scope of the EU's powers and their increasing influence on the lives of citizens, have led to a situation in which the EU must become more involved in protecting and managing fundamental rights, including freedom of religion, rights of religious minorities and respect for religious diversity, all of which are explicitly referenced in the treaties that form the constitutional basis of the EU.[3] And indeed, European society is increasingly diverse, and the issue of religion continues to be present in incidents of elevated social tension. Outward manifestations of religious freedom or the rights of religious minorities – issues that affect work obligations, the display of religious symbols and urban planning, among other aspects – pose the greatest challenges in terms of rights management. In light of these debates, and with Europe in the midst of a political and economic crisis and in great need of better integration, we must ask ourselves whether the EU might be able to intervene more effectively in order to ensure a minimum standard of rights protection. Of the three potential areas of intervention in Europe discussed in the RELIGARE report, the potential impact of the first – urging the implementation of legislation – is still significantly limited due to the disproportionate presence of the principle of subsidiarity in both primary law and secondary law. Furthermore, in addition to the incorporation of the principle of subsidiarity, the Member States have also reiterated a desire to maintain and build on the existing acquis.[4]

Primary Law

The importance of the principle of subsidiarity is quite clear in the treaties that form the basis of the EU. It expressly appears in Articles 5 and 12 of the Treaty on European Union (TEU), in Articles 69 and 352.2 of the Treaty on the Functioning of the European Union (TFEU) and in Article 51.1 of the Charter of Fundamental Rights of the European Union (ChFR). According to Article 5.3 of the TEU:

> Under the principle of subsidiarity, in areas which do not fall within its exclusive competence, the Union shall act only if and in so far as the objectives of the proposed action cannot be sufficiently achieved by the Member States, either at central level or at regional and local level, but can rather, by reason of the scale or effects of the proposed action, be better achieved at Union level.

The principle is also present, albeit not explicitly, in other articles of the constitutional treaties. For the purposes of our discussion, Article 17 of the TFEU is particularly relevant. It states that 'The Union respects and does not prejudice the status under national law of churches and religious associations or communities in the Member States'. Furthermore, the article continues, 'Recognising their identity and their specific contribution, the Union shall maintain an open, transparent and regular dialogue with these churches and organisations'. Nevertheless, the importance of the principle of subsidiarity does not mean that the EU has absolutely no influence in this field, as can be deduced indirectly from Article 17 of the TFEU.[5]

In respect to the protection of fundamental rights in the EU, Article 6 of the TEU establishes what is known as the 'multi-level' system of fundamental rights protection. Thus, in the EU, fundamental rights are

---

now Article 157 of the Treaty on the Functioning of the EU (TFEU)). This was not included for the purpose of guaranteeing gender equality, but rather as a response to pressure from France: because the country was obliged by its own constitution to obey this principle, it feared that it could face competition from countries in which gender-based pay discrimination was not prohibited. In addition, the founding States knew that they were already committed to fundamental rights, both because these rights were protected by their respective national constitutions, and because they were members of the Council of Europe, and most of them had already ratified the European Convention for the Protection of Human Rights and Fundamental Freedoms (ECHR) five months before the treaty establishing the European Coal and Steel Community (TECSC) was signed in Paris on 18 April 1951.

3 Article 2 of the Treaty on European Union (TEU) and Articles 10 and 22 of the Charter of Fundamental Rights of the European Union.

4 S O'Leary, 'Aspects of the Relationship between Community Law and National Law' in NA Neuwahl and A Rossas (eds), *The European Union and Human Rights* (Martinus Nijhoff 1995) 23–49, esp. 49.

5 F Allucino, 'Costituzionalismo e diritto europeo delle religioni' (CEDAM 2011) 135.

safeguarded through a triple system of protection consisting of the ChFR, the European Convention for the Protection of Human Rights and Fundamental Freedoms, and their counterparts in domestic legal systems. In the interplay between these three systems, the minimum standard for rights protection is set by the Council of Europe's system, and both constitutional law and Union law are subject to the former, as is stated in Article 52.3 of the ChFR. However, this does not preclude the possibility of EU legislation providing more extensive protection.

The meaning and scope of fundamental rights are thus established by the Convention, and subject to interpretation by the European Court of Human Rights (ECtHR). Therefore, although the Union has not delineated the rights contained in the Charter, in cases in which rights in the Charter correspond to rights guaranteed by the Convention, their meaning and scope are defined in accordance with the Convention. This is the case with the freedom of thought, conscience and religion, laid down in identical terms in Article 10.1 of the ChFR and Article 9.1 of the ECHR.

At the same time, Article 6 of the TEU clarifies that the provisions of the ChFR shall not extend in any way the competences of the Union as defined in the Treaties. Furthermore, paragraph 3 of the article states that fundamental rights as guaranteed by the ECHR and 'as they result from the constitutional traditions common to the Member States, shall constitute general principles of the Union's law'. Thus, domestic legal orders, following the principle of subsidiarity in religious matters, enjoy a broad margin of discretion in determining the meaning of freedom of religion.

As for the concrete position of religion in the ChFR, Article 10 recognises the right to freedom of thought, conscience and religion, Article 22 guarantees respect for religious diversity and Article 21 prohibits discrimination based on religious grounds. In this respect, Article 10 of the TFEU states that the Union shall aim to combat discrimination based on religion and Article 19 of the TFEU clarifies that the Council may take appropriate action to combat discrimination based on religion or belief. Finally, the right of parents to ensure the education and teaching of their children in conformity with their religious, philosophical and pedagogical convictions is recognised by Article 14, although in this particular case, the concept of subsidiarity is also present, as the Treaty pledges to guarantee this right 'in accordance with the national laws governing the exercise of such freedom and right'. Subsidiarity is likewise present, this time in a general sense, in Article 52.4 of the ChFR, which states that 'in so far as this Charter recognises fundamental rights as they result from the constitutional traditions common to the Member States, those rights shall be interpreted in harmony with those traditions'.

As we have seen, both the ChFR and the TEU refer to the constitutional traditions shared by the Member States, thus clearly granting subsidiarity a great deal of weight in this area. This is particularly worrisome in an area in which national traditions vary so widely, both in their treatment of different religious organisations and in their interpretation and regulation of abstract concepts such as public safety, public morality and need in a democratic society. It is difficult to identify common European constitutional traditions regarding freedom of religion, non-discrimination on the basis of religion and protection of religious minorities. Indeed, different constitutional traditions have very different ways of safeguarding freedom of religion; what's more, the reality of religion in Europe is veritably kaleidoscopic, a phenomenon which has intensified in recent years as a result of migration and developments in communications. In this sense, although the idea of the separation of church and State is a principle of the protection of religious freedom in the European Union,[6] the many – and sometimes very strong – ties between given churches and certain States are not considered an obstacle to the exercise of the freedom of religion as long as the principles of equality and non-discrimination are respected.[7]

6 Union law does not specifically mention 'secularism' or 'the separation of church and State', but it is implicitly present. We need look no further than the debates that surrounded the ratification of the European Constitution: some delegates called for the treaty to include an explicit reference to Christianity in its preamble, arguing that it is one of the hallmarks of EU identity. In the final version, the second paragraph of the preamble reads: 'Drawing inspiration from the cultural, religious and humanist inheritance of Europe, from which have developed the universal values of the inviolable and inalienable rights of the human person, freedom, democracy, equality and the rule of law ….' The preamble thus recognises the importance of Europe's religious heritage, but does not identify this heritage with a particular faith.

7 For a detailed analysis of the common constitutional traditions regarding freedom of religion, see E Relaño Pastor, 'La libertad religiosa en la Unión Europea: la Carta de Derechos Fundamentales y la futura Constitución Europea' (2004) 12

Such an ambiguous constitutional foundation makes it very difficult to encourage common legislative action that effectively negotiates the issue of subsidiarity. In addition, the lengthy delay in the introduction of an actual charter of fundamental rights in the EU led to the directives and regulations playing an important role in determining the meaning and scope of the right to freedom of religion within this framework. A complementary, panoramic analysis of the secondary law that makes reference to religious issues is therefore relevant to our discussion.

Secondary Law

A number of directives and regulations have been used to regulate various factors affecting religious freedom. This legislation explicitly refers to religious elements, and thus has indirectly come to define this fundamental right. The legislative measures that will be analysed in the following pages touch on different religious elements, showing some of the criteria by which the EU institutions have indirectly regulated this field. These legislative instruments are presented below in chronological order.

(1) Council Directive 93/7/EEC of 15 March 1993 on the return of cultural objects unlawfully removed from the territory of a Member State[8]

On 15 March 1993, the Council passed Directive 93/7/CEE, on national treasures of historical or artistic value, which protects ecclesiastical goods, among other objects. In the context of this Directive, they are granted protection because they are considered cultural objects, as defined in both Article 1[9] and item A.2 of the Annex.

The principle of subsidiarity is present in the contents of the Directive. Thus European Community legislation includes a special provision for ecclesiastical goods, specifically as regards the return of goods that have been unlawfully removed from a country. Article 7 establishes a special time limit on the return of these goods. In the case of ecclesiastical goods that are subject to special protection arrangements under national law, the time limit for their return is increased to 75 years, except in Member States in which proceedings are not subject to a time limit or in cases in which there are bilateral agreements between Member States that establish a period greater than 75 years.

(2) Directive 95/46/EC of the European Parliament and of the Council of 24 October 1995 on the protection of individuals with regard to the processing of personal data and on the free movement of such data[10]

In its treatment of the processing of individuals' personal data, this second Directive establishes special categories of data, including personal data relating to religion. Article 8, paragraph 1 states that 'Member States shall prohibit the processing of personal data revealing racial or ethnic origin, political opinions, religious or philosophical beliefs, trade-union membership, and the processing of data concerning health or sex life'.

The Directive also includes a series of exceptions to the aforementioned paragraph: it does not apply if the subject has given his or her consent; if processing is necessary to protect the vital interests of the subject or another person and the person is physically or legally incapable of giving his or her consent; if processing is carried out by a religious organisation in the course of its legitimate activities with appropriate guarantees and only under certain circumstances; if the data were previously made public by the subject; or if processing is required in order to make a medical diagnosis or provide care, as long as the processing is carried out by a health professional subject to the obligation of professional secrecy or by another person subject to an equivalent obligation of secrecy.

Revista Española de Derecho Europeo especially 585–87; A Fernández-Coronado, *El derecho de la libertad de conciencia en el marco de la Unión Europea: pluralismo y minorías* (Colex 2002), especially 129–34.

8 *OJEC* L 74, 27 March 1993.

9 Article 1 defines 'cultural object' as an object that belongs to or forms an integral part of, among other categories, 'the inventories of ecclesiastical institutions'. The Annex of the Directive further specifies the objects classified as 'national treasures', and includes: 'A. 2. Elements forming an integral part of artistic, historical or religious monuments which have been dismembered, more than 100 years old.'

10 *OJEC* L 281, 23 November 1995.

Directive 95/46/EC also grants a good deal of leeway to national legislation, reiterating this position frequently in Article 8.[11] Article 8, paragraph 4 is especially noteworthy in this regard: it grants Member States the possibility of establishing additional exceptions to the prohibition of data processing laid down in paragraph 1 for reasons of substantial public interest, provided that appropriate safeguards are put in place.

(3) Council Directive 2000/78/EC of 27 November 2000 establishing a general framework for equal treatment in employment and occupation[12]

As mentioned above, the protection of freedom of religion in the European Union has always been closely tied to the principle of non-discrimination. The first recital of this Directive reaffirms the Union's respect for fundamental rights by expressly referencing Article 6 of the TEU.[13] Furthermore, the purpose of Directive 2000/78, as laid out in Article 1, is to establish a general framework for combating discrimination on the grounds of religion or belief, among other types of discrimination, with a view to putting into effect the principle of equal treatment in Member States. To this effect, Article 2 defines the two types of discrimination – direct and indirect.

Article 4.1, however, is even more relevant to our discussion. It introduces an exception to the general principle of non-discrimination in the workplace by providing that a difference of treatment based on a characteristic related to the grounds in Article 1 does not constitute discrimination in cases in which 'by reason of the nature of the particular occupational activities concerned or of the context in which they are carried out, such a characteristic constitutes a genuine and determining occupational requirement, provided that the objective is legitimate and the requirement is proportionate'.

In addition, as regards the collective or institutional dimension of freedom of religion, Article 4(2) explicitly mentions churches and organisations whose ethos is based on religion or belief: in these cases, Member States are permitted to have provisions in their national legislation pursuant to which a difference of treatment based on a person's religion or belief does not constitute discrimination where,

> by reason of the nature of these activities or of the context in which they are carried out, a person's religion or belief constitute a genuine, legitimate and justified occupational requirement, having regard to the organisation's ethos. This difference of treatment shall be implemented taking account of Member States' constitutional provisions and principles, as well as the general principles of Community law, and should not justify discrimination on another ground.

This is a reiteration of the leeway granted to national legislation regarding the right of churches and other public or private organisations whose ethos is based on religion or belief to require people working for them to act in good faith and with loyalty to the organisation's ethos. Case law has established that the professional activities referred to here are those associated with relationships that develop within these organisations but which are not closely related to religious activities. They are subject to private State law, in contrast to activities that are closely associated with religious activities, which are subject to regulations established by the religion itself. But it is worth pointing out that this exception does not apply to all activities, but rather only to those in which, by reason of their nature, a person's religion constitutes a genuine, legitimate and justified occupational requirement.[14]

(4) Directive 2001/29/EC of the European Parliament and of the Council of 22 May 2001 on the harmonisation of certain aspects of copyright and related rights in the information society[15]

---

11 See Article 8, para 2, point (a) and also paras 5 and 7 of the same Article.

12 *OJEC* L 303, 2 December 2000.

13 This reference to Article 6 is deliberate. As the Charter of Fundamental Rights of the European Union was not in force at the time, by alluding to Article 6 of the TEU, the Directive invokes the ECHR in order to provide a basic definition of the right to freedom of religion for the purpose of safeguarding it against the violation of the principle of equality.

14 For a detailed analysis of this Directive, see MF Fernández López and FJ Calvo Gallego, 'La Directiva 78/2000/CE y la prohibición por razones ideológicas: una ampliación del marco material comunitario' (2001) 59 *Revista andaluza de trabajo y bienestar social* 125–63.

15 *OJEC* L 167, 22 June 2001.

The third paragraph of Article 5 of Directive 2001/29/EC permits Member States to establish a series of exceptions to the general rule regarding the reproduction, communication or making available of protected works for religious reasons. In any case, the decision regarding whether or not to adopt these exceptions is left to Member States. Thus, regulations regarding these rights are granted greater leeway and subject to fewer restrictions in the following cases:

> (c) reproduction by the press, communication to the public or making available of published articles on current economic, political or religious topics or of broadcast works or other subject-matter of the same character, in cases where such use is not expressly reserved, and as long as the source, including the author's name, is indicated, or use of works or other subject-matter in connection with the reporting of current events, to the extent justified by the informatory purpose and as long as the source, including the author's name, is indicated, unless this turns out to be impossible. …
>
> (g) use during religious celebrations or official celebrations organised by a public authority.

(5) Directive 2003/88/EC of the European Parliament and of the Council of 4 November 2003 concerning certain aspects of the organisation of working time[16]

Directive 2003/88 establishes minimum safety and health requirements for the organisation of working time as relates to periods of daily rest, breaks, weekly rest, maximum weekly working time, annual leave and aspects of night work, shift work and patterns of work. Article 17 gives religious institutions special consideration, as it permits Member States to establish exceptions to the general regulations[17] in the case of 'workers officiating at religious ceremonies in churches and religious communities'. Once again, the wide margin granted to Member States can create serious disparities in how religious diversity is treated in a given area.

(6) Council Regulation (EC) No 2201/2003 of 27 November 2003 concerning jurisdiction and the recognition and enforcement of judgments in matrimonial matters and matters of parental responsibility[18]

Regulation 2201/2003 indirectly recognises the legal validity of decisions handed down by ecclesiastical courts. This Regulation replaces Council Regulation (CE) No 1347/2000 of 29 May 2000, also on jurisdiction and the recognition and enforcement of judgments in matrimonial matters and in matters of parental responsibility for children of both spouses.[19] However, it retains Article 40 of the former Regulation, now Article 63,[20] which holds that decisions regarding canonical marriages handed down by ecclesiastical courts that have civil effects in Portugal, Italy and Spain will, by virtue of these States' respective treaties (concordats) with the Holy See, be recognised by the other Member States under the same conditions established for the decisions addressed in the Regulation. The article underwent another revision when Malta joined the European Union[21] in order to take into account Malta's agreements with the Holy See on the civil effects of the

---

16 *OJEU* L 299, 18 November 2003.

17 Specifically, Member States are permitted to derogate from Articles 3 to 6, 8 and 16 of the Directive. Articles 3 to 6 refer to daily rest, breaks, weekly rest and the maximum weekly working hours. Article 8 refers to the duration of periods of night work, and Article 16 deals with establishing reference periods.

18 *OJEU* L 338, 23 December 2003.

19 *OJEU* L 160, 30 June 2000.

20 Article 63. Treaties with the Holy See:
(1) This Regulation shall apply without prejudice to the International Treaty (Concordat) between the Holy See and Portugal, signed at the Vatican City on 7 May 1940.
(2) Any decision as to the invalidity of a marriage taken under the Treaty referred to in paragraph 1 shall be recognised in the Member States on the conditions laid down in Chapter III, Section 1.
(3) The provisions laid down in paragraphs 1 and 2 shall also apply to the following international treaties (Concordats) with the Holy See:
(a) 'Concordato lateranense' of 11 February 1929 between Italy and the Holy See, modified by the agreement, with additional Protocol signed in Rome on 18 February 1984;
(b) Agreement between the Holy See and Spain on legal affairs of 3 January 1979.

21 See Regulation 2116/2004 of 2 December 2004 (*OJEU* L 367, 14 December 2004).

decisions of ecclesiastical authorities.[22] The legislation thus establishes different legal provisions in different countries for a matter that has implications in the area of religious diversity.

(7) Council Directive 2006/112/EC of November 2006 on the common system of value added tax (VAT)[23]

In all the legislative measures analysed thus far, the EU seems to favour respecting the autonomy of Member States in matters of religion, permitting them to establish exceptions to Community legislation. In contrast, the intervention of the European Union is direct in the regulation of the value added tax (VAT). This is hardly surprising given the fact that nearly half of the EU's own resources come from levying a standard percentage on Member States' VAT bases and that a harmonised tax system is an essential component of a single market. This reinforces the hypothesis that the EU's legislative intervention in rights protection is weak compared to its intervention in issues related to the common European market which, in contrast, is quite decisive.

Furthermore, the EU insists on the need to levy uniform tax rates in all Member States, even in charitable organisations. In the case of Spain, the Agreement between the Spanish State and the Holy See on Economic Affairs of 3 January 1979 has proved to be an obstacle to the harmonisation of legislation, as it holds that the purchase of objects intended for worship is not subject to income tax or VAT. This provision, apart from violating the principles of equality and State neutrality, has been the subject of a number of complaints by European institutions, which formally asked Spain to amend its legislation in 2005 under the threat of referral to the Court of Justice.[24]

(8) Council Regulation (EC) No 1099/2009 of 24 September 2009 on the protection of animals at the time of killing[25]

This Regulation, in effect since 1 January 2013, replaces Council Directive 93/119/EC of 22 December 1993. Although the latter provided considerably more protection for animals at the time of killing, it had been applied in vastly different ways by different Member States, which led to serious concerns regarding the well-being of animals that threatened to have an impact on the conditions of competition among business owners.

This new Regulation maintains the exception established by Council Directive 93/119/EC regarding required stunning in the case of religious slaughter; however, it grants a certain amount of leeway to each Member State. Recital 18 states that

> Since Community provisions applicable to religious slaughter have been transposed differently depending on national contexts and considering that national rules take into account dimensions that go beyond the purpose of this Regulation, it is important that derogation from stunning animals prior to slaughter should be maintained, leaving, however, a certain level of subsidiarity to each Member State.

(9) Proposal for a Council Directive on implementing equal treatment between persons irrespective of religion or belief, disability, age or sexual orientation (COM(2008) 426 final, Brussels, 2 July 2008)

On 2 July 2008 the Commission accepted a proposal for a Council Directive on increasing protection from discrimination on the basis of religion or belief, disability, age or sexual orientation outside the professional

---

22 For a detailed analysis, see A Castro Jover, 'La tutela de la libertad religiosa en la Unión Europea y su incidencia en el ordenamiento interno español' in MC Barranco Aviles, O Celador Angon and F Vacas Fernández (eds), *Perspectivas actuales de las fuentes del derecho* (Dykinson 2011) 111–13; J Ferrer Ortiz, 'La eficacia civil del matrimonio canónico y de las decisiones eclesiásticas en el derecho español' (2008) 14 (2) *Revista ius eta praxis* 404–06.

23 *OJEU* L 347, 11 December 2006.

24 The Spanish government renegotiated its agreement with the Holy See: the Catholic Church waived this fiscal advantage, and in exchange, the percentage of the personal income tax of taxpaying physical persons due each year to which it was entitled increased from 0.5 per cent to 0.7 per cent, effective as of 1 January 2007. Protocol 2 of the Agreement stated: 'If Spain's legal and tax system undergoes any substantial modification, both parties will come to an agreement regarding any applicable fiscal advantages and conditions for tax exemption according to the principles of this Agreement.' When Spain joined the European Union, it underwent such a modification, which would have justified a renegotiation of its agreement with the Holy See, but the reform was brought about by pressure from European institutions.

25 *OJEU* L 343, 18 November 2009.

sphere (the Horizontal Directive discussed in § 1.2 of the *Report*). This proposal, which supplements Community legislation in this area,[26] will prohibit discrimination on the grounds mentioned above in the following areas: social protection (including social security and health care), social benefits, education, and access to goods and services, including housing.

The proposal specifies the competences of the Community: it respects the principles of subsidiarity and proportionality, allowing issues such as the organisation of the school system, the content of education courses, the recognition of marital and family status, adoption, reproductive rights, the activities of religious organisations, the presence of religious symbols in schools and the recognition of same-sex marriage to be decided at the national level. The tone of the proposal and the negotiations carried out to date indicate that subsidiarity will occupy a significant position in future legislation in this area.

Conclusion

European Union institutions should play a more proactive role in the promotion and protection of religious diversity and religious freedoms. Thus far, EU intervention has been severely limited by the principle of subsidiarity, among other factors. What's more, it can be said that there is, more than a legal principle, a prevailing idea of subsidiarity in the activities of EU institutions in the field of fundamental rights. This is only decisively overcome when economic aspects or elements of the common market are at stake. Furthermore, and particularly as regards legislative action at the EU level, the domestic margin of appreciation tends to be considerable when determining the scope of freedom of religion, the relationship between States and religious organisations, the protection of religious minorities and the fight against discrimination on religious grounds. An analysis of the European legislative framework related to religious elements provides evidence in this regard.

In this respect, we must encourage what the RELIGARE report calls EU action in its three domains, particularly in adopting more binding legislative instruments. The main difficulty in this field consists of counterbalancing the traditional weight of the principle of subsidiarity. As RELIGARE's final report points out, the European Union's non-interventionist position does not bring us any closer to implementing a minimum standard of protection of the rights of religious minorities throughout the EU. We must continue to work towards establishing the minimum standards of protection that Europe's religious pluralism demands and ensure that there is a minimum degree of protection of freedom of religion that does not depend on the majority legal or cultural traditions of the different Member States.

26 This proposal supplements the existing legislation on non-discrimination within the legal framework of Article 19 of the TFEU. The proposal builds on the Directives currently in force which relate to: establishing a general framework for equal treatment between persons irrespective of religion or belief, disability, age or sexual orientation in employment and occupation (Directive 2000/78/EC of 27 November 2000); implementing the principle of equal treatment between persons irrespective of racial or ethnic origin (Council Directive 2000/43/EC of 29 June 2000); and implementing the principle of equal treatment between men and women in the access to and supply of goods and services (Council Directive 2004/113/EC of 13 December 2004).

Chapter 10
The What, the Why and the How

Russell Sandberg

The RELIGARE project is symptomatic of a wider trend whereby significant attention has been paid recently to the place of religion in the public sphere. At the dawn of the twenty-first century, politicians, judges and decision makers have all focused on questions concerning the extent to which individual and collective religious beliefs ought to be recognised and protected. There have been a number of moral panics concerning religious dress and symbols, the operation of religious courts and tribunals, and clashes between religious freedom and other legal rights such as freedom of expression and the need not to discriminate on grounds of sex and sexual orientation. These moral panics have resulted in public debates and increased academic attention, of which the RELIGARE research forms part. In many respects, this new interest in religious matters was unexpected. It was generally assumed that the social and political influence of religion was declining in modern Westernised societies. And this assumption had been particularly strong in academia. However, the assumptions of old have not been completely discredited. There is still ample evidence of the social decline of religion as shown not only by the decline in attendance experienced by the historical Christian churches, but also by the way in which religiously derived moral teachings are now no longer seen as the norm. The new focus on religion that has occurred in the shadows of the events of 11 September 2001 raises a number of questions. In this chapter, I draw upon my own research on the religion–law–society nexus in England and Wales[1] to suggest some tentative answers to three broad questions: What has occurred? Why has it occurred? and How can we respond both politically and academically? In short, the purpose of this chapter is to take a step back and reflect upon the what, the why and the how of the changing relationship between law, religion and society.

The What

On the face of it, the answer to the first question appears to be straightforward. The answer to what has happened is the 'return of religion'. As Linda Woodhead et al. have noted, 'religion is back on the agenda'.[2] This means that 'religion is no longer dismissed as a private pastime, but is taken more seriously as a public and political force'. I have described this shift as resulting from the politicalisation and problematisation of religion.[3] The term 'politicalisation of religion' refers to the way in which some religious groups have increased the volume of their voices in the public sphere. This trend has been described by the historian Callum Brown, who has observed that in the last decade of the twentieth century, 'in the midst of overall decline in popular religiosity, British religion showed signs of increasing seriousness and militancy'.[4] He wrote that this was 'an uneven and in some ways imperceptible process and one that only became really noticeable in the early twenty-first century'. Brown gave the example of British Catholicism, observing that the Catholic Church 'showed a radically different approach to its position in British life' after the visit of Pope John Paul II to the UK in 1982: it stopped 'keeping its head down' and 'established a new spirit of political and ecumenical engagement … in Britain', which was 'nurtured through media contact'.[5] Indeed, as Brown noted,

---

1 See especially R Sandberg, *Law and Religion* (CUP 2011); R Sandberg, *Religion, Law and Society* (CUP 2014).

2 L Woodhead et al, 'Preface' in L Woodhead, H Kawanami and C Partridge (eds), *Religion in the Modern World* (2nd edn, Routledge 2009) 1.

3 Sandberg (n 1, 2014) ch 5.

4 CG Brown, *Religion and Society in Twentieth-Century Britain* (Pearson 2006) 297.

5 ibid 309.

the growth of technology has been a major factor in enabling religious groups to have their voices heard. The growth of the Internet helped to foster the 'growing opportunities for vigorous minorities', both liberal and conservative, to 'argue their cases, achieve success and push forward agendas'.

This increasing 'politicalisation of religion' occurred against a backdrop of increasing religious pluralism. As Grace Davie has noted, the increase in religious pluralism which came as a result of the wave of immigration in the 1990s challenged 'widely held assumptions about the place of religion in European societies'.[6] She commented that, while the notion that faith is a private matter and should be proscribed from public life was widespread in Europe, 'many of those who are currently arriving in this part of the world have markedly different convictions, and offer – simply by their presence – a challenge to the European way of doing things'. This has meant that 'European societies have been obliged to re-open debates about the place of religion in public as well as private life'.[7] These population changes, this increase in religious pluralism, changed the context within which religion was discussed. These changes furthered the 'politicalisation of religion' and a further development which I have referred to as 'the problematisation of religion'.

The term 'the problematisation of religion' refers to the way in which religion came to be seen as a social problem. It denotes a shift whereby the notion that religions were an invariably benign force for good became questioned and the fact that religious believers were loyal to forms of authority other than the State came to be seen as a problem. The Al-Qaeda terrorist attacks in New York on 11 September 2001 and in London on 7 July 2007 provided an important trigger. Although seeing such atrocities as the turning point whereby religion was placed back on the agenda is too simple an answer, such events clearly had a major impact.[8] The fear of religiously inflicted terrorism was not new. As Woodhead observed, 'religiously inflicted terrorism by the IRA had … been a much more serious threat in Britain for much longer than anything done in the name of Islam – yet this did not shake secular certainties'.[9] The Al-Qaeda terrorist attacks marked a turning point because now fears of religious terrorism and extremism occurred against a backdrop of wider uncertainty: the motivations behind the terror were largely unknown and the fear of terrorism became indistinguishable from wider notions distrusting 'otherness'. The events of September 2001 changed the way in which the West thought and spoke about not only Islam but religion *per se*. This new context shaped the way in which religions operated in public life. Religion was seen as a social problem and attention was afforded to it.

These social changes, summarised as the politicalisation and problematisation of religion, have had an important legal dimension. The identification of religion as a problem has led to the enactment of new laws at both domestic and international levels. This is shown by the increase in attention to religious matters by European Union institutions as documented by the RELIGARE project.[10] In England and Wales, the legal framework concerning religion has been transformed by a wave of legislation and a tide of litigation. I have referred to these legal changes as representing the 'juridification of religion'.[11] Three dimensions of juridification may be identified. The first dimension is 'legal explosion',[12] a process 'through which law comes to regulate an increasing number of different activities'.[13] This includes what Habermas[14] referred to as the 'expansion of law, that is, the legal regulation of new, hitherto informally regulated social matters'. This has clearly occurred in relation to religion. English law now explicitly recognises a right to religious freedom and expressly forbids discrimination on grounds of religion or belief. The last decade has seen a great deal of legislation concerning religion and a great deal of litigation. This has meant that it is now possible in England and Wales to talk of a category of law called 'religion law' in the same way that it is possible to talk

6 G Davie, 'Is Europe an Exceptional Case?' (2006) 23 *The Hedgehog Review* 33.

7 ibid 32.

8 L Woodhead, 'Introduction' in L Woodhead and R Catto (eds), *Religion and Change in Modern Britain* (Routledge 2012) 8.

9 ibid 9.

10 See R McCrea, *Religion and the Public Order of the European Union* (OUP 2010); N Doe, *Law and Religion in Europe* (OUP 2011) ch 10.

11 Sandberg (n 1, 2011) ch 10.

12 G Teubner, 'Juridification: Concepts, Aspects, Limits, Solutions' in G Teubner (ed), *Juridification of Social Spheres* (Walter de Gruyter 1987) 3.

13 LC Blichner and A Molander, 'Mapping Juridification' (2008) 14 (1) *European Law Journal* 36.

14 J Habermas, *The Theory of Communicative Action* (vol 2, Beacon Press 1987) 359.

of 'family law' or 'sports law'.[15] A second and related dimension of juridification is the 'process whereby conflicts increasingly are being solved by or with reference to law'.[16] The increase in the amount of litigation concerning religion is shown clearly by the Case Database maintained by the Law and Religion Scholars Network (LARSN).[17] There has been a dramatic increase in the number of cases concerning religion both in domestic courts and in the European Court of Human Rights. And, although a number of these cases have concerned the interpretation of the new laws concerning religion, a number have questioned the interpretation of older laws in the new post-11 September context.[18] This aspect of the juridification of religion is shown further in the way in which bodies that regulate religion are increasingly adopting a juridical approach.[19] The third dimension of juridification refers to 'legal framing', that is the process 'by which people increasingly tend to think of themselves and others as legal subjects'.[20] 'Legal framing' denotes the way in which reference to law is used outside the courtroom both as a way of solving conflict and also to shape policy.[21] This is clear from the way in which the language of religious rights has begun to enter into the public discourse as a result of the new legal obligations (as evidenced by the number of courses, guidelines and policies which employers and public authorities now have concerning religion) and the media reporting of litigation.

It is ironic that, although the juridification of religion has increased the amount and reach of law concerning religion, there is a feeling among many religious believers that legal protection has decreased rather than increased.[22] This feeling has been perpetuated by a number of 'pressure points' that have arisen in the interpretation of the new body of religion law by the judiciary. The conservative approach taken in many judicial judgments and the simplified reporting of these judgments in the media have stoked fears that English law now disadvantages religious groups. Three particular 'pressure points' may be identified.[23] The first is the way in which the judiciary seem reluctant to recognise that religious rights have been interfered with. Domestic religious freedom claims under Article 9 of the European Convention on Human Rights tend to be dismissed on the grounds that there is no interference with the right rather than because the interference was justified,[24] and indirect discrimination claims concerning religion tend to be dismissed on the grounds that there was no disadvantage rather than by examining whether the disadvantage was justified.[25] This is unfortunate because the question of justification allows consideration of the full merits of the claim within its social context.[26] This is not to say that the 'religion or belief' argument always needs to be successful. However, the 'religion or belief' argument needs to be considered seriously and treated as being as important as other rights. This would occur if the focus in such disputes was the question of justification of interference rather than a simple question of the presence or absence of interference. Telling claimants that there has not been any interference with their religious rights because they could have resigned from their jobs or because that practice does not appear to be obliged by the religion in question has furthered fears that the law is unreceptive to religion. English law has adopted an approach to religious freedom which the RELIGARE report terms 'questionable', an approach which functions to 'relegate religion to the private domain or hold that an employee can always

---

15 Sandberg (n 1, 2011).

16 Blichner and Molander (n 13) 39.

17 See <www.law.cf.ac.uk/clr/networks/lrsn> accessed 27 June 2014.

18 J Rivers, 'The Secularisation of the British Constitution' (2012) 14 *Ecclesiastical Law Journal* 371.

19 This is particularly true of the Charity Commission, on which see PW Edge and JM Loughrey, 'Religious Charities and the Juridification of the Charity Commission' (2001) 21 *Legal Studies* 36.

20 Blichner and Molander (n 13) 39.

21 ibid 44.

22 A national opinion poll carried out by the *Sunday Telegraph* in May 2009 found that three quarters of Christians polled felt there was less religious freedom than 20 years ago <www.telegraph.co.uk/news/religion/5413311/Christians-risk-rejection-and-discrimination-for-their-faith-a-study-claims.html> accessed 27 June 2014. See also the 'Clearing the Ground Inquiry' published by Christians in Parliament <www.eauk.org/clearingtheground/> accessed 27 June 2014; G Carey and A Carey, *We Don't Do God: The Marginalization of Public Faith* (Monarch Books 2012).

23 Sandberg (n 1, 2011) ch 10.

24 ibid ch 5. The turning point in this regard was the decision of the House of Lords in *R (on the Application of Begum) v Headteacher and Governors of Denbigh High School* [2006] UKHL 15.

25 Sandberg (n 1, 2011) ch 6 and in particular the judgment in *Eweida v British Airways* [2010] EWCA Civ 80.

26 See further M Pearson, 'Proportionality: A Way Forward for Resolving Religious Claims' in N Spencer (ed), *Religion and Law* (Theos 2012) 35.

resign from a "voluntary position" in the event of a conflict between professional and religious commitments' (*Report*, 20). Although the European Court of Human Rights has recently clarified the approach which ought to be taken to Article 9,[27] focusing on the Article 9 (2) question of justification as the battleground, it remains to be seen whether domestic courts will correct their conservative and narrow approach.

The second, and related, pressure point has been the increasing tendency of the courts to examine questions of religious doctrine. In some judgments, courts have applied objective criteria to hold that the claimants were under no obligation by reason of their faith's doctrine to manifest their religion in the way they claimed.[28] This contravenes the general principle of English law 'that it is not the business of the courts to intervene in matters of religion'[29] and that 'it is not for the court to embark on an inquiry into the asserted belief' because 'freedom of religion protects the subjective belief of an individual'.[30] Although the European Court of Human Rights has recently reaffirmed that religious freedom protections are not limited only to manifestations of religious belief which are found to be 'central' or 'obligatory' according to doctrinal texts,[31] it remains to be seen what effect this will have upon the domestic jurisprudence.[32] At present, the conservative approach taken by the judiciary has assumed that all adherents to a certain faith share the same beliefs and has excluded religious adherents who have formed beliefs that are not shared by co-religionists or who do not belong to a religious group which has clear religious doctrines. It is not surprising that this unprincipled approach has caused alarm.

The third pressure point is the implicit tension which has developed between the new religion law and older laws protecting religion. The new laws protecting religion now exist alongside much older pieces of legislation, and the assumptions and principles underlying both sets of laws do not easily sit with one another. The old laws were based upon a different premise. They often sought to protect Christianity in general (or the Church of England in particular) as the norm, while providing some degree of toleration for other faiths. Moreover, the legal regulation of religion was characterised by a lightness of touch. The new religion law is different. It is facilitative, seeking to protect religious freedom mainly as an individual right which needs to be balanced against other rights. No special protection is afforded to any one religion, and protection is often afforded to non-religious beliefs. The new legal framework accords utmost importance to the concept of religious equality as the State takes on the role of facilitating the religious marketplace. The RELIGARE report points out that this clash between older and newer legislation concerning religion is common throughout Europe. It is noted that 'a number of paradigms inherited from the past and implicitly reflecting majority religions remain unquestioned in the case law' (*Report*, 12). This is particularly true in England and Wales, where a number of areas of law were historically shaped by Christianity and where the Church of England continues to enjoy a special legal position which has tangible benefits and burdens both at a constitutional and a local level.[33]

Identification of these trends and pressure points provides the answer to the question of 'what has occurred'. The renewed interest in religion – the talk of the 'return of religion' – has arisen as a result of a number of social and legal changes. For convenience these changes may be summarised as being the politicalisation, problematisation and juridification of religion. The interplay of these changes, in a context of increased religious pluralism and moral uncertainties, has meant that, although the amount of law protecting religion has increased, the perception has been that the level of protection has actually decreased. Moreover,

27 See *Eweida and Others v United Kingdom* (2013) 57 EHRR 8, as discussed by Sandberg (n 1, 2014) ch 5; M Hill, 'Religious Symbolism and Conscientious Objection in the Workplace' (2013) 15 *Ecclesiastical Law Journal* 191.

28 See, especially, *R (on the Application of Playfoot (a Child) v Millais School Governing Body* [2007] EWHC Admin 1698 and *Eweida v British Airways* [2010] EWCA Civ 80.

29 Unless 'the parties to the dispute have deliberately left the sphere of matters spiritual over which the religious body has exclusive jurisdiction and engaged in matters that are regulated by the civil courts'; *R (on the Application of E) (Respondent) v Governing Body of JFS* [2009] UKSC 15, paras 157–58.

30 *R v Secretary of State for Education and Employment and Others ex parte Williamson* [2005] UKHL 15, para 22.

31 See *Eweida and Others v United Kingdom* (2013) 57 EHRR 8, as discussed by Sandberg (n 1, 2014) ch 5; Hill (n 27).

32 The judgment in *MBA v Mayor and Burgresses of the London Borough of Merton* [2013] EWCA Civ 1562 suggests that it will have a significant impact in terms of reasoning.

33 See further Sandberg (n 1, 2011) chs 2 and 4.

the interaction between law and religion has become increasingly controversial. The notion that religion is a good thing has become challenged. And the holding of religious beliefs is now seen as being exceptional. This raises our next question: Why have these changes occurred?

The Why

There are a number of reasons why the changes described as the politicalisation, problematisation and juridification of religion have occurred. A social and legal historical analysis is required in order to pinpoint and evaluate a variety of possible causes. However, for current purposes, I want to focus on the extent to which theories of secularisation can provide part of the explanation.[34] Both the legal and sociological approaches to religion have been shaped by the secularisation thesis: the argument that religion, 'seen as a way of thinking, as the performance of particular practices, and as the institutionalisation and organisation of these patterns of thought and action', has lost its *social* influence in Western societies.[35] Law and religion studies have largely paid attention to the way in which the Christian[36] influence upon law has broadly declined, while the sociology of religion has largely been concerned with the social decline of religion. The question that preoccupied the founding fathers of sociology – Karl Marx, Emile Durkheim and Max Weber – was 'how society would manage without religion'.[37] The events of recent years have challenged this central assumption. And this has often caused sociologists of religion to discard talk of the secularisation thesis, often in haste.

However, the 'return' of religion does not debunk the secularisation thesis or, at least, it does not refute sophisticated versions of the thesis which do not argue starkly that God is dead in modern society. As Karel Dobbelaere's work shows, the secularisation thesis refers to a multi-dimensional group of changes that affect social institutions, religious institutions and individuals.[38] The thesis is also historically and geographically specific. As Charles Taylor has put it, the secularisation thesis is a 'subtraction story' in that it only explains the fortunes of those forms of religiosity which were previously dominant.[39] It refers only to what has happened to institutional forms of Christianity. This means that the secularisation thesis cannot provide the entire explanation for how religion, law and society interact today. However, it can still provide part of the explanation.

As I have suggested elsewhere,[40] sociological differences of opinion about the secularisation thesis are often overplayed. Accounts of secularisation in England and Wales largely agree over the basic evidence and largely disagree only in terms of predictions about the future. Reference to legal change provides support for a number of processes of secularisation which began at the time of the Enlightenment and which continue to this day.[41] The impact of these processes is that England and Wales has become a secularised country but not a secular one. This is not only because the processes of secularisation are incomplete, but also because there are a number of exceptions, counter-trends and nuances. For example, reference to law shows that the establishment of the Church of England continues to have an important role at both a constitutional and a local level. It is incontestable, however, that social and legal changes have taken place which have reduced the social role formerly played by the Christian churches.

The RELIGARE findings suggest that 'the majority of national legislatures have made the historic decision to secularise State law' by 'detaching the State and its institutions from religion' (*Report*, 13).

---

34 See further Sandberg (n 1, 2014).

35 B Wilson, *Religion in Secular Society* (Penguin 1966) 14; B Wilson, *Religion in Sociological Perspective* (OUP 1982) 149.

36 Although law and religion scholars have, of course, been interested in how the law affects other religious groups, the focus has nevertheless been on Christianity, reflecting 'Christianity's enduring force' in the legal discourse; D Herman, *An Unfortunate Coincidence: Jews, Jewishness & English Law* (OUP 2011) 175.

37 R Robertson, 'Introduction' in R Robertson (ed), *Sociology of Religion* (Penguin 1969) 12.

38 K Dobbelaere, *Secularization: An Analysis at Three Levels* (Peter Lang 2002).

39 C Taylor *A Secular Age* (Harvard University Press 2007) 22.

40 Sandberg (n 1, 2014).

41 These processes include differentiation, societalisation, rationalisation, individualisation and compartmentalisation. See further Sandberg (n 1, 2014).

Though I would question whether an actual decision was ever made to this effect by English legislators, I agree that this process has taken place. Sociologists of religion have referred to this process as 'social differentiation'.[42] This can be defined as the process whereby specialist institutions develop which take on functions that were previously carried out by one institution. Rather than one specific institution discharging a plethora of functions, a plethora of institutions now discharges specific functions. In relation to religion, social differentiation can therefore be understood as 'the process by which religion and religious institutions become differentiated from other spheres'.[43] It refers to the way in which the church went from being at the centre of social life to becoming just one social institution among others.[44] However, although social differentiation is an important process of secularisation, it is just one of several processes. And even this process is not complete.

Social differentiation can be seen as an important process of what I have referred to as the first wave of secularisation.[45] This refers to the (ongoing) battles of modernity which began with the Enlightenment and which affected mainly the societal level, moving the church away from the centre of social life. However, reference to these developments does not provide the full story of secularisation. Callum Brown has argued that secularisation only really occurred in Britain in the 1960s, when the changing role of women meant that the 'the cycle of inter-generational renewal of Christian affiliation ... was permanently disrupted'.[46] For Brown it was the 1960s that saw the drop in church attendance and membership and in rites of passage such as marriage and funeral rites. And, crucially, it was during this decade that the passing down of Christianity to the young through Sunday schools and the like declined. Brown's work questioned not the extent but the timing of secularisation.[47] However, Brown's thesis does not have to be read in a way which is incompatible with sociological theorists who date secularisation back to the Enlightenment. Rather, Brown's argument can be seen as describing a second wave of secularisation. Secularisation can be seen as a long-term process which includes both the trends that began in the aftermath of the Enlightenment and those of more recent origin which can be traced to the 1960s. The first wave of secularisation can be seen as primarily affecting religious institutions (secularisation at the societal level, to use Dobbelaere's distinction[48]). By contrast, the second wave can be seen as primarily affecting individuals (secularisation at the individual level in Dobbelaere's terms).

This analysis suggests that the social changes which began in the 1960s are an important factor in understanding why the relationship between religion, law and society has developed in the way that it has. As Charles Taylor has pointed out, the 1960s provided 'the hinge moment, at least symbolically', ushering in 'an individuating revolution'.[49] In England and Wales, the Labour Party's victory in the 1945 general election had reflected a common desire that things would be different after the war, and this questioning of the *status quo* escalated following the Suez crisis of 1956. This period witnessed the decline of certainty regarding gender roles, class distinctions and Britain's place in the world; it saw the opening up of the world via the rise of television, the satire boom and the questioning of authority. In short, the 'swinging sixties' experienced the death of deference.[50] And these shifts have escalated in recent decades. Following the end of the Cold War and the collapse of Communism, old certainties continued to collapse. The closing years of the twentieth century and the start of the twenty-first century has been the era of globalisation, the fragmentation of politics, the rise of the Internet and a number of scandals concerning the financial industries, the political classes, the media

42 See, for example, O Tschannen, 'The Secularization Paradigm: A Systemization' (1991) 30 (4) *Journal for the Scientific Study of Religion* 395; R Wallis and S Bruce, 'Secularization: The Orthodox Model' in S Bruce (ed), *Religion and Modernization: Sociologists and Historians Debate the Secularization Thesis* (Clarendon Press 1992) 8.

43 M Hamilton, *The Sociology of Religion* (2nd edn, Routledge 2001) 188.

44 Dobbelaere (n 38) 33.

45 Sandberg (n 1, 2014).

46 CG Brown, *The Death of Christian Britain* (2nd edn, Routledge 2009).

47 S Bruce, 'Secularisation in the UK and the USA' in CG Brown and M Snape (eds), *Secularisation in the Christian World* (Ashgate 2010) 209.

48 Dobbelaere (n 38).

49 C Taylor, *Varieties of Religion Today* (Harvard University Press 2002) 80.

50 H Carpenter, *A Great, Silly Grin: The British Satire Boom of the 1960s* (Perseus Books 2000) 238.

and the historical churches. These changes have resulted in what Charles Taylor[51] and others have referred to as the 'subjective turn'. This refers to the way in which the 'subjectivities of each individual became a, if not the, unique source of significance, meaning and authority'.[52] It describes the increased focus people placed upon the construction and re-construction of personal identities.

Reference to the 'subjective turn' provides both a diagnosis and a cure for the current tensions concerning religion, law and society. It explains that the forms of religiosity which are prospering are those which have accepted the effects of societal secularisation and the importance of the 'subjective turn'.[53] It also provides an explanation for the 'pressure points' that have emerged surrounding the accommodation of religious difference by State actors. These tensions have been perpetuated by a slowness on the part of State actors to recognise the importance of the 'subjective turn'. The new legal framework concerning religion is a product of the 'subjective turn' in that it protects religious freedom as an individual subjective right. The objective binary approaches adopted by judges in the majority of the domestic cases have failed to appreciate this. Judges have required claimants to choose between their religion and their citizenship rights by holding that there was no interference with their religious rights where the claimant could have resigned from his or her job. Judges have assumed a direct, causal link between creedal assent and behaviour by dismissing religious rights claims on the basis that the practice claimed does not appear to be obliged by the religion in question. The 'subjective turn' therefore provides not only the diagnosis but also the cure: the need to recognise religious freedom as a subjective right. This brings us to our third question.

The How

The RELIGARE project proposes two yardsticks against which the way in which countries accommodate religion or belief ought to be measured: 'inclusive State neutrality' and 'justice as even-handedness' (*Report*, 16). Although I agree with this, I think there is an important precursor to these two standards. There is a need for all parties concerned (the State, religious groups, those who are religious and those who are not) to appreciate the effects of the 'subjective turn', to appreciate that people are constantly constructing and re-constructing their identities and performing those identities in different ways according to differing stimuli and in different social situations. This includes people's religious identities. People will draw upon aspects of their religious identities, constantly re-constructing them, in various aspects of social life. This means that their 'religion' is not something that can be consigned to the private sphere; rather it is something which can and will be drawn upon in different contexts in different ways that differ from person to person. Even where people identify themselves with a particular religious tradition, the way in which they draw upon their religious identity is likely to differ from co-religionists. They are likely to make (and re-make) their own interpretations, shaped by their own experiences.

These ideas are not new. They are well expressed in one of the leading (but now often forgotten) British judgments on religious rights, Lord Nicholl's speech in *Williamson*,[54] in which his Lordship stated that 'freedom of religion protects the subjective belief of an individual' since 'religious belief is intensely personal and can easily vary from one individual to another'.[55] This insight has also been reached in the growing literature on legal pluralism. Most notably, Martha-Marie Kleinhans and Roderick A. Macdonald have argued that any traditional accounts of legal pluralism tend to 'view the legal subject only as an abstract "individual"', failing 'to discuss fundamental questions about how legal subjects understand themselves and the law'.[56] They therefore advocate the adoption of 'a critical legal pluralism' where the emphasis 'is on the constructive capacity of the constructed self'.[57] Adopting their work, Codling has gone further to suggest the

51 C Taylor, *The Ethics of Authenticity* (Harvard University Press 1991) 26.

52 P Heelas and L Woodhead, *The Spiritual Revolution* (Blackwell 2005) 3–4.

53 See Sandberg (n 1, 2014) ch 5.

54 *Williamson* (n 30).

55 ibid para 22.

56 MM Kleinhans and RA Macdonald, 'What is a *Critical* Legal Pluralism? (1997) 12 (2) *Canadian Journal of International Law and Society* 36.

57 ibid 39.

need for a 'subjective legal pluralism' which would focus upon 'privileging the narrative account of legal subjects'.[58] These approaches have much in common with the work of Charles Taylor, particularly his work relating to 'identity politics'[59] and his understanding of the 'age of authenticity', in which people constantly negotiate and re-negotiate their identities and what it means to be human through both internal and external dialogue.[60] Indeed, Pascale Fournier's work has made this link explicit, referring to 'liberal-legal pluralism'.[61]

However, as I have argued elsewhere,[62] this argument is most clearly articulated in the work of Ayelet Shachar, particularly her book *Multicultural Jurisdictions*.[63] Shachar's notion of 'joint governance' recognises how people 'jointly belong to more than one community, and will accordingly bear rights and obligations that derive from more than one source of legal authority'.[64] Her work recognises how people of faith are both 'culture-bearers *and* rights-bearers'.[65] Although this notion of 'joint governance' is supported by recent empirical research,[66] it goes against the grain since, as Anne Phillips has pointed out, reference to minority cultures is now 'widely employed in a discourse that denies human agency'.[67] Shachar's approach is innovative in that it recognises that people are 'cultural beings' rather than being 'of a culture'.[68] Her notion of 'joint governance' rests upon the acceptance of 'the complex and multi-layered nature of multicultural identity'.[69] She asserts that we cannot 'remain blind to the web of complex and overlapping affiliations which exist between these competing entities'.[70] Shachar makes a convincing case that this requires activity on the part of the State. She contends that a stance of 'non-intervention' at times 'effectively translates into immunizing wrongful behavior by more powerful parties' and that turning a 'blind eye' to what occurs within religious groups relegates 'these religious traditions to the margins, labelled as unofficial, exotic, or even dangerous (unrecognized) law'.[71] The concept of 'joint governance' requires an 'ongoing interaction between different sources of authority, as a means of improving the situation of traditionally vulnerable insiders without forcing them to adhere to an either/or choice between their culture and their rights'.[72] This argument ties in very neatly with the yardstick of 'justice as even-handedness' proposed by the RELIGARE project, which states that 'what guarantees appropriate protection is not so much justice in the sense of a "hands-off" stance, but rather "even-handedness" between competing interpretations' (*Report*, 12).

Regardless of the terminology involved, it is possible to identify particular practical effects which would result from taking an approach based on 'joint governance' (or recognising 'religious freedom as a subjective right', adopting a 'subjective legal pluralist' perspective or recognising the nature of 'multicultural identities'). In terms of the three 'pressure points' referred to earlier, this approach would encourage courts and tribunals to decide cases according to the question of justification as opposed to the question of interference. It would be accepted that people can hold beliefs and place emphasis upon practices which are not shared by co-religionists. And it would be understood that the fact that a believer can resign from his or her job should

58 AR Codling, 'A Critical Pluralist Analysis of *R (on the Application of Begum) v Headteacher and Governors of Denbigh High School*' (2012) 169 *Law & Justice* 244.

59 C Taylor, 'The Politics of Recognition' in A Guttmann (ed), *Multiculturalism: Examining the Politics of Recognition* (Princeton University Press 1994) 25.

60 Taylor (n 51).

61 P Fournier, *Muslim Marriage in Western Courts: Lost in Transplantation* (Ashgate 2011) 65.

62 R Sandberg et al, 'Britain's Religious Tribunals: "Joint Governance" in Practice' (2013) 33 (2) *Oxford Journal of Legal Studies* 263.

63 A Shachar, *Multicultural Jurisdictions: Cultural Differences and Women's Rights* (CUP 2001).

64 ibid 13.

65 A Shachar, 'Privatizing Diversity: A Cautionary Tale from Religious Arbitration in Family Law' (2008) 9 (2) *Theoretical Inquiries in Law* 593.

66 See Sandberg et al (n 62). This draws upon the findings of Cardiff University's Social Cohesion and Civil Law: Marriage, Divorce and Religious Courts research project. See the project report (G Douglas et al, *Social Cohesion and Civil Law: Marriage, Divorce and Religious Courts* (2011)) and subsequent publications listed at <www.law.cf.ac.uk/clr/research/cohesion.html> accessed 27 June 2014.

67 A Phillips, *Multiculturalism without Culture* (Princeton University Press 2007) 9.

68 ibid 52.

69 Shachar (n 63) 15.

70 ibid 5.

71 Shachar (n 65) 593.

72 Shachar (n 63) 88.

not be sufficient to defeat any religious freedom claim. The role of the State in the twenty-first century is to facilitate religious freedom without favouring any particular form of religion. The detailed proposals in the RELIGARE report provide examples of how this can be achieved (*Report*, 12). The details and implications of the proposals clearly merit careful consideration by policymakers and others who seek practical ways forward.

Moreover, the methodology underlying the RELIGARE report prompts one final reflection. The fusion of legal and sociological methods and approaches by the RELIGARE team underlines the need for interdisciplinary approaches. As I have argued elsewhere,[73] legal or sociological approaches alone cannot adequately grasp the relationship between religion, law and society. An interdisciplinary approach is required, fusing insights from both legal and sociological perspectives. Such an approach is, however, risky. There is a fear that the fusion of different disciplinary approaches will lead to one becoming the master of the other. And the risks of interdisciplinary work increase depending upon how advanced the interdisciplinary process is. Yet, these risks do not mean that interdisciplinary work should not be undertaken. Rather than being fatal to the enterprise, the identification of these risks should inform it. The concerns about interdisciplinary work need to be taken into account in order to improve the enquiry. This will mean that it is vital that the interdisciplinary endeavour builds upon rather than replaces the distinct methodological contributions made by each discipline.[74] The RELIGARE research should therefore provide important inspiration, not only to those grappling with the practical questions concerning the what, the why and the how, but also for the academic study of religion, law and society.

73 Sandberg (n 1, 2014).

74 This requires an instrumental and critical approach to interdisciplinarity whereby the quality of interdisciplinary work is to be determined by the standards usually expected by the disciplines; cf K Huutoniemi, 'Evaluating Interdisciplinary Research' in R Frodeman (ed), *The Oxford Handbook of Interdisciplinarity* (OUP 2010).

Chapter 11

Freedom of Thought, Conscience and Religion: A Policy Priority for the Council of Europe

Stephanos Stavros[1]

The Council of Europe and Religious Diversity

Helping its 47 Member States manage religious diversity is a key activity for the Council of Europe, the Strasbourg-based intergovernmental organisation that defends democracy, human rights and the rule of law across the continent.

Article 9 of its key international treaty, the European Convention on Human Rights (ECHR), guarantees freedom of thought, conscience and religion. The European Court of Human Rights (ECtHR) is often called upon to examine applications by individuals who consider that their rights under this provision have not been respected. Article 9 issues have also been raised with various governments by the Council of Europe's successive Commissioners for Human Rights, as well as in their human rights comments.[2] In its country reports, the European Commission against Racism and Intolerance (ECRI) deals with violence, hate speech, discrimination and prejudice against members of religious groups; it has also issued General Policy Recommendations (GPR) on the problems encountered by two of them.[3] The European Commission for Democracy through Law (the Venice Commission) provides advice to States that are in the process of legislating on Article 9 questions.[4] Religion and belief become topics under the Framework Convention for the Protection of National Minorities when they constitute elements of the protected person's individual identity. The Council of Europe's Committee of Ministers holds an annual exchange on the religious dimension of intercultural dialogue and issued a political declaration on religious freedom on 20 January 2011. Finally, several relevant resolutions and recommendations have been produced by the Parliamentary Assembly[5] and the Congress of Local and Regional Authorities.[6]

The Council of Europe and the Findings of a Project such as RELIGARE

Having attended two RELIGARE events in 2012[7] and having read the summary report carefully, I can confidently say that its findings could be of great relevance for the work of the Council of Europe in the coming years.

1 The views expressed are solely those of the author.

2 See, for example, 'Anti-Muslim Prejudice Hinders Integration' (24 July 2012) <http://humanrightscomment.org/2012/07/24/anti-muslim-prejudice-hinders-integration-5/> accessed 12 June 2014; 'Penalising Women Who Wear the Burqa Does not Liberate Them' (20 July 2011) <http://commissioner.cws.coe.int/tiki-view_blog_post.php?postId=157> accessed 12 June 2014.

3 GPR No. 9, 'The Fight against Antisemitism', see <www.coe.int/t/dghl/monitoring/ecri/activities/GPR/EN/Recommendation_N9/Recommendation_9_en.asp>; and GPR No. 5, 'Combating Intolerance and Discrimination against Muslims', see <www.coe.int/t/dghl/monitoring/ecri/activities/GPR/EN/Recommendation_N5/Recommendation_5_en.asp> both accessed 16 June 2014.

4 On the basis of the 2004 *Guidelines for Legislative Reviews of Laws Affecting Religion or Belief* of the Venice Commission and ODIHR; see <www.venice.coe.int/webforms/documents/default.aspx?pdffile=CDL(2004)061-e> accessed 12 June 2014.

5 On, inter alia, combating religious discrimination; the religious dimension of intercultural dialogue; State, religion, secularity and human rights; freedom of expression and respect for religious beliefs; education and religion; religion, tolerance and democracy; forms of conscientious objection; and Islamophobia and extremism.

6 On, inter alia, inter-faith tensions at the local level and initiatives and responsibilities of local authorities responsible for inter-faith dialogue.

7 The policy dialogue meeting 'Negotiating Religious Pluralism in Europe: Between the European Union and the Council of Europe', organised in Strasbourg on 28 June 2012, and the second part of the conference 'Secularism and Religious Diversity in Europe: Opportunities and Perspectives', held in Brussels on 5 December 2012.

The issues that the project has examined are among the most pressing and topical of our day. So much transpires from the work of one of the Council of Europe's above-mentioned bodies, ECRI, which has been monitoring – for the past five years[8] – Member States' performance in connection with the fight against religious discrimination, antisemitism and intolerance.[9] Many of the recommendations ECRI has addressed to European governments during this period concern unequal access to and conditions of employment, the banning of headscarves and full-face veils, the lack of places of worship and cemeteries, claims to subsidies and communities of believers' special demands. In its summary report, RELIGARE makes – in a well-researched, thoughtful and principled manner – a worthy contribution to all these questions: it debunks a number of myths (in connection with State support); clarifies the theoretical framework (in connection with religion in the workplace and dress codes); illustrates the need for accurate data before taking decisions in complex areas (such as town planning); and asks provocative – if not outright painful – questions (in connection with family law). Moreover, it makes its own set of proposals to domestic authorities and the European Union.

If one had to identify the three Article 9 areas that are most likely to attract particular attention in the near future, these would be (1) reasonable accommodation, (2) discrimination outside the field of employment and (3) the impact of EU accession to the European Convention on Human Rights. All three areas are or could evolve into key concerns for the Council of Europe. It will be argued that the RELIGARE project has a contribution to make in each one of them.

Reasonable Accommodation

There are many reasons why reasonable accommodation will probably become the focus of freedom-of-religion claims. First of all, this would be in the theoretical 'nature of things'. A brief look at ECRI's reports shows that the problems believers are faced with belong to three broad categories. At the risk of oversimplification, these appear to be: (1) being punished for holding beliefs; (2) being restricted in expressing them; and (3) being unable to live an ordinary life because of them.

It is clear that Article 9 of the ECHR should cater for the first category. As the Council of Europe experience – including the case law of the ECtHR[10] – shows, our continent has not yet managed to rid itself of what is undoubtedly the worst form of direct religious persecution. However, one would hope that, with the passage of time, the number of complaints concerning such incidents would diminish.

Under the second category of problems, one finds many issues that concern ways of expressing beliefs that are dear to believers: assembling, preaching, forming communities with legal personality and property, and bringing up one's children in accordance with one's beliefs. Most of the complaints concerning restrictions in expressing religious beliefs could be – and often are[11] – examined under Article 9. However, the ECHR contains a number of provisions that, because of their specialist nature, seem to address them better: Articles 6 (fair trial), 10 (freedom of expression) and 11 (freedom of association), and Articles 1 and 2 of Protocol No. 1 (property and education).

The third category of problems, which is admittedly the most delicate, usually arises because of rules that were not adopted with religious considerations in mind and were meant to apply to everyone (for example,

8 During its fourth country monitoring cycle (2008–2012).

9 ECRI's mandate covers racism, racial discrimination, xenophobia, antisemitism and intolerance (see Article 1 of its Statute). According to its GPR No. 7, 'National Legislation to Combat Racism and Racial Discrimination' (<www.coe.int/t/dghl/monitoring/ecri/activities/gpr/en/recommendation_n7/Recommendation_7_en.asp> accessed 12 June 2014), 'racism' shall mean the belief that grounds such as race, colour, language, religion, nationality or national or ethnic origin justifies contempt for a person or a group of persons, or the notion of superiority of a person or a group of persons. 'Racial discrimination' shall mean any differential treatment, based on grounds such as race, colour, language, religion, nationality or national or ethnic origin, that has no objective and reasonable justification.

10 *Ivanova v Bulgaria*, App no 52435/99 (12 April 2007).

11 See the ECtHR's judgments in *Manoussakis v Greece* (26 September 1996); *Kokkinakis v Greece* (25 May 1993); *Canea Catholic Church v Greece* (16 December 1997); *Grzelak v Poland*, App no 7710/02 (15 June 2010).

the obligation to wear a helmet when driving a scooter[12] or to take part in a school parade[13]). Some believers, however, find it difficult to abide by them because they clash with their beliefs. In order to be able to live ordinary lives, they make claims for exemption. Not surprisingly, today's culturally diverse European societies are witnessing an exponential growth of such claims.

Given what has been explained above in respect of the first two categories of problems, if the freedom-of-religion concept were to retain some of its independent meaning,[14] it would have to evolve so as to provide the basis for addressing some of the believers' communities' demands for special treatment. In order to understand how this could happen, one should look at the kind of claims the Council of Europe has so far shown willingness to accommodate.

One demand for exemption has gained clear recognition: alternatives to military service.[15] However, this is not the case with other claims of conscientious objection – for example, to taxation (for defence spending)[16] or schooling (to the extent that it involves sex education).[17] The ECtHR, at a certain moment in its long history of involvement with complaints raising the third category of problems, seemed on the verge of developing a proper framework for dealing with them. This would be based on the right not to be discriminated against,[18] which 'is also violated when states without an objective and reasonable justification fail to treat differently … situations (that) are significantly different'.[19] In more recent cases, however, the Strasbourg Court seems to have changed tack, returning to its past piecemeal approach and promoting a pragmatic policy of measured concessions under Article 9. For the moment, the scope of this policy appears quite restricted; it applies to particular institutional settings, such as prisons, where individuals have limited control over their lives,[20] or in connection with company policies that pursue – rather inconsistently – goals of lesser importance (such as 'corporate branding or image').[21]

One cannot easily take issue with the Strasbourg's Court's reluctance to apply its policy of measured concessions widely, as the difficulties encountered, when adjudicating in this area, are obvious. It is these difficulties that led the Supreme Court of the United States in 1990 to adopt, in *Employment Division v Smith*,[22] a rather radical stance that allows almost no scope for exceptions from 'generally applicable, neutral laws' under the free-exercise-of-religion clause of the First Amendment to the Constitution. The Supreme Court's approach has the advantage of clarity. However, it empties freedom of religion of much of its potential content.

Is there a way in which Europe can respond to the US approach by pursuing a less uncompromising stance on the basis of a proper theory? On the one hand, the ECtHR could be encouraged to elaborate on *Thlimmenos* by using the concept of indirect discrimination. This concept seems to cover cases where an apparently neutral factor disadvantages – in a disproportionate manner – persons belonging to, inter alia, a religious group, without an objective and reasonable justification.[23]

---

12 No. 7992/77, decision of the European Commission of Human Rights (Commission) of 12 July 1978.

13 See the ECtHR judgment in *Valsamis and Efstratiou v Greece* (18 December 1996).

14 Of course, theoretically, nothing prevents a concept from falling into desuetude – especially since human rights are supposed to be interpreted in the light of modern day (see the ECtHR's judgment in *Tyrer v the United Kingdom* (25 April 1978) para 178).

15 *Bayatyan v Armenia* [GC] App no 23459/03 (7 July 2011); *Ercep v Turkey*, App no 43965/04 (22 November 2011).

16 No 7050/75, Commission decision of 12 October 1978.

17 *Dojan and Others v Germany* (Dec.) App nos 319/08, 2455/08, 7908/10, 8152/10, 8155/10 (13 September 2011).

18 In the enjoyment of Article 9 rights.

19 *Thlimmenos v Greece* [GC] App no 34369/97 (6 April 2000) para 44.

20 *Jakobski v Poland*, App no 18429/06 (7 December 2010).

21 *Eweida and Others v the United Kingdom*, App nos 48420/10, 59842/10, 51671/10, 36516/10 (15 January 2013).

22 494 US 872.

23 See ECRI's GPR No. 7, para 1 (c) in combination with the ECtHR's judgment in *D.H. and Others v the Czech Republic* [GC] App no 57325/00 (3 July 2007) para 175. Requiring that the apparently neutral factor should not disadvantage religious minorities *in a disproportionate manner* is different from allowing proportionality to play its usual role in the 'objective and reasonable justification' test that determines whether any distinction amounts to discrimination (see *DH and Others v the Czech Republic*, ibid). It adds another dimension, in the sense that a neutral, generally applicable rule that pursues a legitimate interest – and, as a result, has an objective and reasonable justification – may be indirectly discriminatory because it disadvantages a member of a religious minority in a disproportionate manner. This would happen if the sacrifice the believer has to make to comply with the rule outweighed the 'harm' that would be caused to the general interest by allowing an exception.

On the other hand, Europe could also look for non-judicial responses to claims for exemption.[24] One or the other Council of Europe body – based on the expertise that the Council has developed in the field of human rights, tolerance and intercultural exchanges – could encourage dialogue between the authorities and believers' communities on these issues. The aim of such dialogue would be to sort out claims that may be accommodated from those that may not. A number of factors could be taken into consideration, including:

- the centrality of the belief put forward to underpin the claim to exemption (in the realm of human rights, the starting point for assessing this would be each person's views; in a process, however, that would not involve the adjudication of individual complaints, it would be easier to juxtapose the person's views with those of the relevant community of believers, in order to test, inter alia, the historical strength of the claim);[25]
- the importance of the general interest pursued by the rule from which an exemption is claimed;
- whether other human rights are at stake (the right to respect for private life would, for example, enter into play when doctors claim the right to refuse to perform lawful abortions, and the right to be free from discrimination would do so when it is sought to refer family-law disputes to arbitration organised by believers' communities);[26]
- whether other claims have been allowed on non-religious grounds;[27]
- whether other religious beliefs have already been accommodated in a similar context (in the course of a non-judicial approach, one would be freer than in adjudication to revisit old debates about the religious origins of some of our generally applicable laws on, for example, the day of rest and holidays).

Arguably, a non-judicial process would be more structured than adjudication. Much of the uncertainty generated by the subjective interpretation of religious beliefs – inherent in individual claims – would be removed. This would serve to contain the process within reasonable limits. Moreover, as shown above, many more relevant elements would be taken in consideration than in the judicial approach. Finally, it would be possible to support the process with serious legal, sociological and religious-studies research. It is obvious that the RELIGARE project has already taken many significant steps in this direction.

The second reason why reasonable accommodation will probably become the focus of freedom-of-religion claims is that it is likely to provide appropriate answers to some of the current 'values' debates on, for example, circumcision and ritual slaughter.

Each of these debates is supposed to involve a balancing of interests between the need to uphold religious beliefs and the need to protect another interest, such as a child's physical integrity or the prevention of animal suffering.[28] However, in today's societies ideas about 'modernity' seem invariably to trump religion. This is amply demonstrated by the fact that, quite often, the debate revolves exclusively around the question of whether animals suffer or not and the degree to which circumcision is beneficial – the end result being that religion is more or less excluded from the equation.

The reasonable accommodation approach could restore some of the weight to religion. For example, even if one were to establish that ritual slaughter results in animal suffering, this would still have to be balanced[29]

---

24 'Freedom of Religion: Lessons from across the Pond?' (1997) 6 *European Human Rights Law Journal* 607–27, contains a call for such a non-judicial response. The present chapter takes on board a number of important developments in the case law of the ECtHR.

25 With the same objective in mind, a distinction would have to be made between systems of belief that resemble what has been traditionally understood as religion and other strongly held views. This happens even in the context of judicial processes (see the ECtHR's judgment in *Eweida and Others v the United Kingdom* (n 21) para 81).

26 All three factors are part of the indirect discrimination equation; however, the balancing exercise would happen on a more general level.

27 This is the only case in which the Supreme Court has indicated that it could reconsider the absolute stance it adopted in *Employment Division v Smith*.

28 Although they could involve claims to exemption from general rules, they are not always framed in such terms. What appears to be sought is the banning of some practices.

29 The ECtHR's judgment in *Cha'are Shalom Ve Tsedek v France* [GC] App no 27417/95 (27 June 2000) accepts this in an unequivocal manner.

against the need to uphold some communities' traditions.[30] Today it might be difficult always to predict the outcome of this balancing exercise. However, whatever happens to each individual claim, it is important to make sure that the global response leaves some place for religion in society. This would be essential to ensure a minimum of social peace. Moreover, it would not necessarily compromise secularism. As Council of Europe organs have made amply clear, separation between 'church' and State and respect for freedom of religion are two distinct notions.[31]

The models put forward by the RELIGARE project – inclusive State neutrality and justice as even-handedness – could provide a way out of the dilemmas often associated with the above 'values' debates. The Council of Europe seeks similar outcomes, albeit more modestly, either through its monitoring processes[32] or through the development of soft law.[33] It goes without saying that academia and policy could – and should – inspire each other.

Discrimination outside the Field of Employment

RELIGARE's summary report refers extensively to the difficulties encountered in having the EU Horizontal Directive adopted. The instrument in question seeks to ban discrimination on grounds of, inter alia, religion or belief in areas that are not covered by Directive 2000/78/EC:[34] social protection, social advantages, education and access to goods and services. There appear to quite a number of sticking points, and the negotiations in Brussels are likely to last for a long time.

However, the countries that sit around the negotiating table in Brussels are already among the addressees of the recommendations made by the Council of Europe in this connection. ECRI's GPR No. 7, for instance, calls upon States to adopt comprehensive civil and administrative legislation that would outlaw unjustified distinctions on the basis of religion 'in all areas'.[35] ECRI's approach is based on the premise that religion, as a ground for hatred and discrimination, should not be treated differently from colour, ethnic origin and race.[36]

It is clear that the Council of Europe's approach is not free of risk.[37] However, the important monitoring work already accomplished in Strasbourg helps contain it. ECRI's country monitoring reports show, for example, that in the field of religious discrimination the focus of the theoretical debate should not only be on religious institutions, which claim autonomy,[38] and faith-based organisations, but also on certain profit-making outfits that allege that neutrality is an essential characteristic of their business ethos.[39] It is encouraging that RELIGARE reaches a similar finding, creating possibilities for additional research, potentially of great relevance.

EU Accession to the European Convention on Human Rights

The prospects of EU accession to the ECHR look today better than ever before. This major development in the European constitutional order will, in all likelihood, have significant impact on many areas of human rights law. The Council of Europe's and the EU's understanding of freedom of thought, conscience and religion will not be left unaffected.

30 Which may be dictated by religious law.

31 *Darby v Sweden*, Commission's opinion (9 May 1989) para 45; *Alujer Fernadnez and Caballero Garcia v Spain* (Dec.) App no 53072/99 (14 June 2001).

32 ECRI has issued recommendations concerning ritual slaughter.

33 See the controversial Parliamentary Assembly Resolution 1952 (2013) on children's right to physical integrity.

34 Of 27 November 2000, establishing a general framework for equal treatment in employment and occupation.

35 para 7.

36 As well as citizenship and language.

37 This is not the place to discuss certain theoretical questions concerning the parallel drawn between religion and race, colour and ethnic origin in the definition of racism in GPR No. 7.

38 See also the ECtHR's judgment in *Sindicatul 'Pastorul cel Bun' v Romania* [GC] App no 2330/09 (9 July 2013).

39 See ECRI's report of 4 December 2013 on Belgium, para 12.

Those following the case law closely know that there are some Article 9 areas in which Strasbourg has adopted a more nuanced, reflective approach than Brussels. Dismissal from faith-based organisations for views or behaviour incompatible with their mandate is one of them.[40]

As already indicated, RELIGARE has called for additional research in this connection. This will certainly facilitate the process of convergence of the two organisations' understanding of this and other freedom of thought, conscience and religion issues, by contributing to the consolidation of the underlying empirical basis and the clarification of the theoretical foundation. Few will doubt that this will be a major gain for both Strasbourg and Brussels.

Other Article 9 Areas Calling for Attention

As shown in the three sections above, projects like RELIGARE can feed in a significant manner into major European policy processes concerning Article 9 issues. Of course, reasonable accommodation, discrimination outside employment and the impact of EU accession are not the only freedom-of-religion questions that are likely to move up on the Council of Europe's agenda in the near future. There are many more, including incitement to religious hatred, reconciling the right not to disclose beliefs with the presence of religion in the public sphere,[41] multiple discrimination, and a host of questions related to religious communities' legal personality and property. The list does not purport to be exhaustive. If anything, its length shows the need for continued dialogue between civil society (including faith-based organisations), national and European policymakers and, of course, academic institutions.

Conclusion

Having concluded on the need for continued dialogue, the only additional comment that ought to be made concerns RELIGARE itself. Without exaggeration, it was a pleasure to be able to participate in such an innovative and well-organised project, which succeeded in pulling together so much experience and good will from so many and diverse sources. The knowledge generated, the tools created and the prospects opened will influence the debate around many important issues in different fora. The Council of Europe, because of the leading role it has traditionally played in the field of freedom of thought, conscience and religion, could very well be one of them.

---

40 ECtHR's judgments in *Schüth v Germany*, App no 1620/03 (23 September 2010); *Obst v Germany*, App no 425/03 (23 September 2010); *Siebenhaar v Germany*, App no 18136/02 (3 February 2011).

41 The sensitive question of equality-data collection inevitably arises in this connection.

Chapter 12
The Relationship between Religious Diversity and Secular Models: An Equality-Based Perspective

Lucy Vickers

In its final report, the RELIGARE project proposes a response to the interplay between religious diversity and secular models, based on 'inclusive State neutrality' and 'justice as even-handedness' (*Report*, 16). The report argues that the notion of the secular public sphere has developed across Europe not so much as a response to the increase in religious diversity, but more as a response to the growth in numbers of those who would identify as 'non-religious'. As the report puts it, 'The hypothesis was that detaching the State and its institutions from religion would ultimately make society in democratic States more inclusive, providing a unitary legal and political framework within which religious and non-religious people can live together' (*Report*, 13). However, as the report goes on to demonstrate, the idea of a secular or neutral public sphere is not always experienced as such by those who identify as religious. In this short piece, I seek to use arguments from an equality perspective to add further weight to this conclusion. In particular, I look at the ways in which so-called neutrality can lead to unequal treatment for members of minority faith groups. I then consider the proposed development of a right to request a reasonable accommodation of religion or belief at work.

As the RELIGARE report notes, strict neutrality has often led in practice to somewhat unequal treatment between different religious groups, because our social organisation can never be truly 'neutral'. There are a number of reasons for this. Most obviously, the dominance of Christianity in European history means that the public sphere is far from neutral, as is well documented in the report: employment law, family law, charity and tax law are all infused with conscious or unconscious preferences towards Christianity.

Yet the ways in which neutrality may fail to be even-handed in its outcomes go beyond this basic inequality; the problem has a number of additional facets. First, a position of State neutrality tends to assume that we can make a clear separation between the public sphere, which remains 'neutral', and the private sphere, where religion is acceptable. However, if we look to the basic tenets of equality jurisprudence, we know that what may look 'neutral' can in practice favour the dominant group: this is the basis for the notion of indirect discrimination on the grounds of sex found in EU law.[1] In the context of gender discrimination it is well established that the 'neutral' norm tends in practice to be a 'male norm', so that neutral rules requiring, for example, that workers must be available to work full time can be indirectly discriminatory on grounds of gender because fewer women than men can comply with them. This can be seen very clearly in the context of religion and belief, where, as noted above, the social organisation is largely 'Christian' rather than neutral. This means that religiously observant Christians will rarely come across work rules and dress codes with which they cannot comply, as Christmas, Easter and Sundays are non-workdays for most. In effect, then, and using the language of gender equality, most workplaces operate according to a set of expectations and in a context which could be termed 'the Christian norm' even though they are not religious in their ethos or organisation.

In addition to the fact that the dominant social organisation accommodates mainstream Christian practice, it can also be argued that Christianity itself has adapted so that it can fit into the 'secular norm' of the 'neutral' social model adopted in much of the EU. This adaptability works at two levels. The first can be illustrated by the example of the adoption by early Christians of pagan winter festivals to celebrate the Christian festival of Christmas. This illustrates the adaptive process through which Christianity has passed; it is not only society which has adapted to Christianity; Christianity, too, has adapted.

1 Equal Treatment Directive 76/207: 'The principle of equal treatment shall mean that there shall be no discrimination whatsoever on grounds of sex either directly or indirectly.'

Moreover, Christianity appears to have developed a theology which allows for greater adaptation to the neutral State. One example of this can be seen in the biblical command to 'give to God what is God's and to Caesar what is Caesar's',[2] a command which allows many Christians relatively easily to reconcile civic duty with religious duty. A second example is the way in which Protestant Christianity in particular has a focus on the mind and its state of 'righteousness' rather than on the body, as expressed in religious practice: orthodoxy rather than orthopraxy. A full theological discussion of these ideas is beyond the scope of this chapter, but put simply, Christianity is based less on religious practice and more on what the individual believes. With a focus on belief, dress codes and dietary rules or prayer rituals tend to be less central as signifiers of religious observance. In contrast, religions such as Judaism and Islam have a greater focus on orthopraxy: a concern for correct religious practice as signifiers of religious adherence. In religious traditions with a focus on orthopraxy, codes of conduct related to attire, diet and prayer are more common and have much greater significance as ways to practise and observe the religion. In many cases it is these practices which then lead to conflict with the secular world. Moreover, many of the practices are based on the idea of setting the religious observer apart from the rest of the world. Dietary laws, for example, sometimes include the prevention of social mixing. It can therefore be very difficult to accommodate such practices within the mainstream, or within the 'secular norm'.

It is arguable, then, that the processes of adaptation between the secularism of the State and Christianity have gone in both directions. In part, the 'world' has adapted to accommodate the dominant religion, but the religion itself has also adapted so that conflicts are reduced: there are few external requirements, such as head covering, for observant Christians to comply with, requirements which might otherwise cause conflict within a secular public sphere. As a result, it can be seen that so-called 'neutral' rules which limit religious manifestation in the public sphere are doubly non-neutral: the rules of minority faiths are less likely to be compatible with mainstream social norms, and minority faiths are also more likely to have visible practices of religious observance, and thus have greater potential to clash with the neutrality of the public sphere in the first place.

Moreover, drawing on the context of gender equality, additional observations can be made about the practical effect of restrictions imposed in the public sphere. For example, it is well recognised that if women's participation at work is to be increased, then some accommodation of the family is needed, whether by way of maternity leave, workplace nursery provision, or other support for working mothers. It could be argued that women's family responsibilities are private matters, best left in the private sphere. If such an argument were accepted, then there would be no need for legally mandated workplace provisions to help meet the needs of working parents. Fortunately, it has been recognised that such an approach does not lead to equal employment terms for women and men. If no accommodation of family life is offered, then many women will not leave their 'personal matters' at home and head out to work: they will stay at home. Many of the hard-won workplace rights such as maternity leave are predicated on the idea that such practical support is necessary if women are to be able to participate in the workplace.

Applied to the grounds of religion and belief, this reasoning suggests that restrictions on religious freedom in the public sphere will do more than have a disproportionate impact on minority religious groups; it will lead to the removal of individuals holding these beliefs from the public sphere, or at least severely hamper attempts to include such individuals in mainstream society. Thus, it is clear that if inclusion of religious minorities is the aim, then some accommodation of religious practice is essential.

These arguments demonstrate that what can look like simple 'State neutrality' may not be experienced as neutral in practice. First, the public sphere is not as neutral as might at first be supposed. Second, the religions themselves are not equally placed in relation to the 'neutral' public space, and so formally equal treatment of religious individuals will not result in the same experience. Third, experience from those working on other grounds of equality demonstrates that a lack of accommodation of difference does not lead to equal participation in public life: it leads to exclusion. Thus, if we exclude the personal from the public sphere, we will end up excluding the person as well.

These considerations based on equality confirm the conclusions of the RELIGARE project that a legal response is needed to ensure that those from minority faiths do not suffer inequalities in their employment

2 Gospel of St Matthew, ch 22 verse 21.

opportunities as a result of a failure by organisations to make any concessions to their religious needs. Of course, any legal response needs to have space for nuanced consideration of some of the complexity involved in regulating religious practice. The response proposed in the report, in the context of the workplace, is the introduction of clearer rights for employees based on a right to request a reasonable accommodation of religion at work. The suggestion is that such a right would bring clarity to the scope of protection for religion, as well as create greater protection, with the onus on employers to justify any refusal to make adjustments to workplace practices in order to accommodate religious practice at work.[3] Such an approach certainly has support, and is adopted in a number of other States, such as the United States and Canada.[4] Its benefits include the fact that it can allow for individualised protection that can reflect the needs of the religious adherents and the context of the particular employer.

However, despite supporting these aims, it is submitted here that such an approach is unnecessary. This is because the outcome of any amendment to the Equality Directive along these lines may be a legal provision that does not, in practice, offer anything beyond that which is available under the current law. The reason for this conclusion is that any right to reasonable accommodation can quite easily be cast as a right not to be indirectly discriminated against. For example, the refusal to accommodate a religious dress code can be cast as a requirement to conform to a secular dress code, which puts the religious adherent at a particular disadvantage. A refusal to accommodate a request for time off work on a Saturday can be cast as a requirement to work on Saturdays, which puts the religious adherent at a particular disadvantage, and so on. In each case, the onus is put on the employer to justify this refusal of religious attire or time off: the right to accommodation is only a right to 'reasonable' accommodation, and so if the employer has a good reason to refuse, the right will not be enforced. Similarly, the requirement regarding working hours or attire may be justified as a proportionate means of achieving a legitimate aim.

To an extent then, a right to request an accommodation of religion at work would not substantially improve the legal protection offered to religious interests in the work context: both legal frameworks offer *prima facie* protection, to the extent that any limitation on religion must be subject to a test of reasonableness or proportionality. The scope of the protection would then turn not on its legal format, but on the standard of review to which any potential justifications are subjected.

Moreover, the two legal frameworks can merge in some respects. This is because it is arguable that a failure to accommodate religion at work can be taken into consideration by the court in assessing whether the employer's requirement constitutes a proportionate means to achieve a legitimate aim. For example, the requirement that staff work on Saturday may be legitimate if it is to ensure adequate staffing at the weekend. But it may not be proportionate to impose this requirement if an easy accommodation can be found, such as an agreement to work on Sunday instead. In effect, then, 'the scope for reasonable accommodation is part of the proportionality assessment'.[5] This is reinforced by the decision in *Eweida v United Kingdom*,[6] where the Strasbourg court suggested that the possibility of changing jobs was to be taken into account in the overall proportionality assessment. It is suggested, then, that in assessing the proportionality of any restriction on religious freedom a court may consider the extent to which it is reasonable to expect the employer to accommodate the employee's right.

These cases suggest that there is no need to create a new right to request a reasonable accommodation to protect religion at work, as suggested by the report. Instead, the language of reasonable accommodation can be incorporated into the interpretation and application of the current indirect discrimination framework.

However, there may be alternative reasons for supporting a move to special provisions governing religious discrimination, based on reasonable accommodation. For example, such provisions would avoid the problem of the 'dilution' of rights. The idea is that the introduction of new and competing grounds of equality can lead to a 'levelling down' or degrading of existing protections, or the introduction of hierarchies among

3 See further K Alidadi, 'Reasonable Accommodations for Religion and Belief: Adding Value to Art. 9 ECHR and the European Union's Anti-Discrimination Approach to Employment?' (2012) 37 (6) *European Law Review* 693–715.

4 ibid; and see M Gibson, 'The God "Dilution"? Religion, Discrimination and the Case for Reasonable Accommodation' (2013) 72 (3) *Cambridge Law Journal* 578–616.

5 *Bull and Another v Hall and Another* [2013] UKSC 73 para 47.

6 (2013) 57 EHRR 213.

protected characteristics. The claims can cut two ways: first, it has been suggested that the right to religious equality is 'diluted' in comparison with, for example, sexual orientation equality.[7] Second, and at the same time, it is argued that the right to religious equality may lead to a reduction or levelling down of protection on grounds such as gender or race.[8] The argument here is based on the fact that standards of scrutiny based on gender and race are particularly high, and there may not be a consensus that such standards should apply to religion and belief equality. For example, a court could decide that matters such as economic cost could justify religious discrimination, but it would be unfortunate if this were to result in a finding that the same were true of sex or race discrimination. The fact that cost can also justify disability discrimination does not run the same risk because the framework of the protection is different: reasonable accommodation rather than indirect discrimination. Hence, the argument for the creation of a special framework to protect the religious interests of employees can be justified in the interests of upholding strict scrutiny standards for gender and race equality.

In either case, the creation of a separate legal framework for religious equality at work, based on a right to request a reasonable accommodation, may serve the useful purpose of avoiding any 'cross-fertilisation' between the protection of religion at work and the protection of other protected characteristics. To the extent that religion is different from other grounds of equality,[9] the creation of a separate legal framework might allow different approaches to develop without the danger of degrading the protection of other groups.

Another benefit of an approach based on accommodation is that, as with the duty to make adjustments which exists as part of European disability discrimination law, a duty to accommodate recognises the fact that changes in the workplace will be very individualised. As with the individualised needs of disabled people, there is a wide variety of religious practices, and so a personalised duty of reasonable accommodation for religious needs may be particularly apt in this context.

Nonetheless, despite these arguments, it is suggested here that the disadvantages of a right to reasonable accommodation outweigh the advantages. One disadvantage is the threat that a separate right to accommodation, introduced in order to avoid any 'levelling down' of gender or race equality protection, serves only to push that threat on to disabled people instead: standards which may develop regarding when an adjustment or accommodation is reasonable may be read across from religion to disability, with the risk that the standard required for disability is diluted.

A second objection is based on the concern that the introduction of a special employment right to protect religion and belief may upset the balance between the secular and the religious in the public sphere.[10] Accommodating religious staff may involve a level of privileging or positive action in favour of religious individuals, and this could amount to a detriment to others, especially if other staff are required to make changes to their working practices. This may cause particularly complex problems given that those who lack a particular belief are protected equally with those who hold the belief. In effect, any accommodation of one religious viewpoint has the potential to be interpreted as discrimination against those of another.[11] Imposing a duty to accommodate religious interests may involve the immediate creation of a corresponding disadvantage for others. Thus, for example, accommodating one person's need to have leave on a Sunday imposes on others the disadvantage of restricted availability of leave.

Thus the introduction of a special legal framework to protect religion at work may end up creating a particular 'advantage' to religion, and may be seen as upsetting the formal balance between religious interests

7 See J Rivers, 'The Secularisation of the British Constitution' (2012) 14 *Ecc LJ* 371, 390.

8 T Loenen, 'Accommodation of Religion and Sex Equality in the Workplace' in K Alidadi, M-C Foblets and J Vrielink (eds), *A Test of Faith? Religious Diversity and Accommodation in the European Workplace* (Ashgate 2012) 119.

9 A full discussion of this contentious point is beyond the scope of this chapter. For some discussion, see M Bell and L Waddingon, 'Reflecting on Inequalities in European Equality Law' (2003) 28 *EL Rev* 349; D Schiek, 'European Union: A New Framework on Equal Treatment of Persons in EC Law?' (2002) 8 *European LJ* 290.

10 R Allen and G Moon, 'Substantive Rights and Equal Treatment in Respect of Religion and Belief: Towards a Better Understanding of the Rights, and their Implications' (2000) *EHRLR* 580, 601.

11 This argument arose in Ireland in case law on the constitutional protection of religion. In *Quinn's Supermarket v Attorney General* [1972] IR 1, it was argued that special exemption for Jewish kosher butchers from the Sunday trading laws was discriminatory against non-Jewish shopkeepers. The argument was not accepted, and the exception was upheld on the basis that it was necessary adequately to protect the freedom of religion of the Jewish community.

and the neutral State. But it is precisely this balance that is necessary for the achievement of both inclusive neutrality and even-handedness as recommended in the RELIGARE report.

In conclusion, the report makes a strong case for improved protection for religious interests in a secular Europe. This case is strengthened by the recognition that detaching the State and its institutions from religion will not of itself lead to a more inclusive society in which religious and non-religious people can live together. Instead, a more flexible approach is needed, with space for religious observance within the public sphere, so that State neutrality can be more inclusive. Comparisons with approaches to gender equality can demonstrate this very clearly. The creation of arrangements at work to enable women to balance private sphere concerns with their work roles has led to greater inclusion of women at work; similarly, encouraging workplaces to adapt to the needs of religious minorities should lead to their greater inclusion in the public space of work. Encouraging some adaptation of workplace rules should not be seen, therefore, as an end to State neutrality, but instead as the development of a more inclusive and even-handed neutrality.

Nonetheless, the mechanism by which a more even-handed approach can be achieved remains contested. It is suggested here that, rather than creating a new right to request a reasonable accommodation, a better approach would be to focus on protecting religion and belief at work through indirect discrimination laws. This approach is particularly beneficial because it contains within it the potential to take into account whether a reasonable accommodation could have been found. Thus a legal framework based on that which is already in existence, with the added ingredient of the concept of reasonable accommodation incorporated within it, is, it is submitted, the best way to achieve the overall objectives of inclusiveness and even-handedness in the context of religious equality at work.

Section 2
On the Reasonable Accommodation Debate

Chapter 13
Reflections on the Recognition of a Right to Reasonable Accommodation in EU Law

Frédérique Ast[1]

Despite their secular character, many aspects of the organisation of our modern European societies derive from Judeo-Christian tradition. This may adversely affect minority religious groups and cause potential tensions particularly within the employment sector.

After three years of remarkable and intense work, the RELIGARE research team thus proposed to amend the Employment Equality Directive (2000/78 Directive)[2] to grant a right to reasonable accommodation to workers on the basis of their religion and belief. This in turn means that an employer, whether public or private, would be required to make reasonable adjustments to the work environment. This duty is 'plainly intended to relieve individuals of the burden of choosing between their jobs and their religious convictions, where such relief will not unduly burden others'.[3] Within the employment sector, the need for religious accommodation most frequently arises where an individual's religious beliefs, observances or practices conflict with a specific task or requirement of the job or the application process. The employer's duty to accommodate will usually entail making a special exception from, or adjustment to, the particular requirement so that the employee or applicant will be able to practise his or her religion. Accommodation requests often relate to work schedules, dress and grooming, or religious expression or practice while at work.

'Engaging with context, and accommodating what otherwise would appear to be irreconcilable world views, will not necessarily satisfy anyone, and it may appear to be the triumph of pragmatism over principle. … But it seems well suited to the social reality of pluralism around religion … today.'[4] One might wonder who could then reasonably oppose this simple and fair principle in a democratic society 'in which diversity [should] not be perceived as a threat but as a source of enrichment'.[5]

First, in fact, such a principle may be hard to square with the constitutional traditions of specific European countries. Secularism and neutrality can place important restrictions on the expression of religion within the scope of public employment. For example, in France, since civil servants represent the State, their conduct must not suggest that the State identifies itself with a particular religion. Therefore, according to a settled administrative case law, public employees are not allowed to display their religious beliefs on the job.[6]

Second, modern and deconfessionalised European countries, based on 'secular' values of equality and human rights, tend to drive faith out of public life. Moreover, many official observers, including the Human Rights Committee, the European Commission against Racism and Intolerance (ECRI) and the Fundamental Rights Agency of the EU, have sounded the alarm about the rise in religious intolerance in Western countries. Even if not alone, Muslims often bear the brunt of a certain public wariness in the

---

1 This article reflects only the opinion of its author, not those of the institution for which she works.

2 Council Directive 2000/78/EC of 27 November 2000 establishing a general framework for equal treatment in employment and occupation, *Official Journal*, L 303, 2/12/2000, 16–22.

3 *Protos v Volkswagen of Am., Inc.*, 797 F.2d 129, 136 (3d Cir. 1986).

4 CF Stychin, 'Faith in the Future: Sexuality, Religion and the Public Sphere' (2009) 29 (4) *OJLS* 729.

5 ECtHR, *Nachova and Others v Bulgaria*, 6 July 2005, nos 43577/98 and 43579/98, para 145.

6 Council of State 3 May 2000, *Marteaux*, no 217017. The French Council of State has also held that a civil servant violated this duty of neutrality when his professional e-mail address appeared on the website of an association related to the Unification Church (founded by the Korean Sun Myung Moon), even in the absence of proselytising behaviour (Council of State 15 October 2003 *Jean-Philippe M.*, no 246215). It also upheld the decision to suspend a postal worker for six months because he had given out religious leaflets to the public at the counter (Council of State 19 February 2009 *Christophe A.*, no 311633).

aftermath of 11 September, which constitutes a new form of 'McCarthyism' or 'cultural racism'.[7] Besides, some European countries do deal with radical movements and sectarian abuse. Such a context creates and perpetuates prejudicial stereotypes of religion, such as that it promotes gender inequality, backwardness, oppression, fundamentalism or extremism. It seems that we are losing, in the twenty-first century, what was previously taken for granted and yet is one of the fundamental values of our modern societies, that is the freedom of religion.

In this context, some employers may therefore be wary of religion coming to the fore. Some may wish to confine religious practice entirely to the private sphere. They may consider that it is not their responsibility to adjust to the religious needs of their employees in their businesses, or they may refuse the display of religious symbols such as the headscarf to protect a certain corporate image.

This chapter aims to discuss whether the RELIGARE proposal is necessary, appropriate and feasible. This implies, on the one hand, reviewing existing protections and examining their potential pitfalls and, on the other hand, anticipating the effect that the recognition of a right to reasonable accommodation would have on the EU system.

Existing Legal Protections Enabling Reasonable Accommodation of Religious Needs in Europe

At present, the right to reasonable accommodation within the scope of employment is provided only to disabled workers under EU law.[8] Moreover, even if some national measures allow for religious accommodation in specific cases, such as the accommodation of days off in the public sector in France, very few explicit general reasonable accommodation duties extending beyond disability have been adopted around Europe.[9] Despite the fact that EU law does not provide for a similar provision regarding religion, indirect discrimination is used as a legal tool to combat the exclusion created by dominant practices.[10] Human rights law and, in particular, the right to freely exercise one's freedom of religion may also require adjusting a general rule to specific needs.

We might begin by briefly reminding the reader about the set of rules relating to workers' freedom of religion and the protection of religious rights in Europe. Even if this chapter does not aim at being exhaustive, there is, on the one hand, the binding Charter of Fundamental Rights of the European Union[11] enshrining the freedom of religion and the right not to be discriminated against and, on the other hand, the 2000/78 Employment Equality Directive, aimed at combating both direct religious discrimination and indirect religious discrimination. The European Convention on Human Rights (ECHR), ratified by all EU Member States, also prohibits religious discrimination in relation to the rights and freedoms safeguarded by the other substantive provisions of the Convention and its Protocols (Article 14 combined with Article 9 ECHR). Its Article 9 also enshrines freedom of religion as

7 Y Shooman and R Spielhaus, 'The Concept of the Muslim Enemy in the Public Discourse' in J Cesar (ed), *Muslims in the West after 9/11: Religion, Politics, and Law* (Routledge 2010) 198–228.

8 Article 5 of 2000/78 Directive states: 'In order to guarantee compliance with the principle of equal treatment in relation to persons with disabilities, reasonable accommodation shall be provided. This means that employers shall take appropriate measures, where needed in a particular case, to enable a person with a disability to have access to, participate in, or advance in employment, or to undergo training, unless such measures would impose a disproportionate burden on the employer. This burden shall not be disproportionate when it is sufficiently remedied by measures existing within the framework of the disability policy of the Member State concerned.'

9 See also Art. 5.4 of the Flemish Decree on Proportionate Participation on the Labour Market of 8 May 2002 relating to a general duty of reasonable accommodations for various 'risk groups' (*kansengroepen*), as mentioned in K Alidadi, 'Reasonable Accommodations for Religion and Belief: Adding Value to Article 9 ECHR and the European Union's Anti-Discrimination Approach to Employment?' (2012) 37 *European Law Review* 693–715 <www.rechten.unimaas.nl/iuscommune/prize/pdf/2013_Alidadi_2013.pdf> accessed June 2014.

10 On this issue, see F Ast, 'Indirect Discrimination as a Means of Protecting Pluralism: Challenges and Limits' in Council of Europe (ed), *Institutional Accommodation and the Citizen: Legal and Political Interaction in a Pluralist Society, Trends in Social Cohesion* no. 21 (Council of Europe Publishing 2009) 85–109.

11 For the full text, refer to <http://eur-lex.europa.eu/LexUriServ/LexUriServ.do?uri=OJ:C:2010:083:0389:0403:en:PDF> accessed June 2014.

> one of the foundations of a 'democratic society' within the meaning of the Convention. ... It is one of the most vital elements that go to make up the identity of believers and their conception of life, but it is also a precious asset for atheists, agnostics, sceptics and the unconcerned. The pluralism indissociable from a democratic society, which has been dearly won over the centuries, depends on it.[12]

Reasonable Accommodation Adjudicated on the Basis of Human Rights Law around Europe: The Eweida Case

In the eagerly awaited *Eweida* case,[13] the European Court concluded that the United Kingdom had failed to comply with the positive obligation, implied in Article 14 of the ECHR, 'to treat differently persons whose situations are significantly different'.[14] It implicitly found that the restriction implemented by British Airways on the wearing of jewellery by its employees should have been adjusted to accommodate Christian employees wanting to visibly wear a Christian cross.

In this case, a member of the check-in staff and practising Coptic Christian complained about restrictions placed by her employer, British Airways, on her wearing of a cross visibly around her neck. British Airways required all their staff in contact with the public to wear a uniform. According to the uniform guidelines that were in place at the time,

> any accessory or clothing item that the employee is required to have for mandatory religious reasons should at all times be covered up by the uniform. If however this is impossible to do given the nature of the item and the way it is to be worn, then approval [is] required through local management as to the suitability of the design to ensure compliance with the uniform standards, unless such approval is already contained in the uniform guidelines. ... No other items are acceptable to be worn with the uniform. [Employees] will be required to remove any item of jewellery that does not conform to the above regulations.[15]

British Airways recognised certain items of unconcealable clothing as mandatory in certain religions, and therefore authorised, for example, male Sikh employees to wear a dark blue or white turban and to display the Sikh bracelet in summer if they obtained authorisation to wear a short-sleeved shirt. Female Muslim ground staff members were also authorised to wear headscarves in British Airways approved colours.

The applicant was offered a non-customer-facing role in which she could have worn the cross, but she declined and remained at home without pay. Ms Eweida was eventually reinstated in her job after the review of her employer's uniform policy.

When assessing the fair balance struck between the competing interests of the individual and of the community as a whole, the Court concluded that there was no evidence of any real encroachment on the interests of others, such as the employer's wish to project a certain corporate image. Ms Eweida's cross was discreet and there was no evidence that it would have detracted from professional appearance or harmed the brand. In light of this conclusion, it was not considered necessary to separately examine the applicant's complaint under Article 14 (right to non-discrimination) taken in conjunction with Article 9 (freedom of religion).

Reasonable Accommodation Adjudicated on the Basis of Discrimination Law around Europe

Direct religious discrimination refers to differential treatment based on religion or belief. The primary reason for prohibiting direct discrimination is to correct individual deviant behaviour and punish the perpetrators. Indirect discrimination cases involve no-fault objective liability. There is indirect discrimination when any provision, criterion or practice which is neutral on its face is liable to adversely affect workers on the grounds of their religion. Indirect discrimination arises solely from a concern to comply with structural requirements.

12 ECtHR, *Kokkinakis v Greece*, 25 May 1993, para 31, Series A no 260A.
13 ECtHR, *Eweida v United Kingdom*, 15 January 2013, App no 48420/10.
14 ibid para 87.
15 ibid para 10.

The prohibition against indirect discrimination is intended to home in on standards and practices that are so deeply rooted in our social structures that the economic and social partners no longer even have to consciously choose to act in a discriminatory manner. It is enough for them to comply with their organisations' operational standards, which discriminate for them. The indirect discrimination mechanism, precisely, prevents individuals from taking advantage of the existence of discriminatory structures created by others. The purpose of prohibiting indirect discrimination fits in with a 'redistributive justice' rationale, endeavouring to compensate victims of a social structure. Indirect discrimination identifies the existence of differences in the situations facing specific individuals or groups of individuals and takes their specific needs into account. This differentiation overturns the formally egalitarian social constructs in order to achieve genuine equality of treatment by adjusting the rules.

There are many cases around Europe where national equality bodies and courts have already granted an implicit right to reasonable accommodation for religious practices or beliefs within the scope of employment and beyond.

In France

In its Decision no. 2007–301 of 13 November 2007, the French equality body, the HALDE (now replaced by the Defender of Rights), dealt with the refusal of an employer to authorise the absence of his employees for the Eid al-Adha, a one-day Muslim holiday, despite the fact that he authorised the absence of his Jewish employees on Yom Kippur. The HALDE held that the Labour Code provides for a subtle balance between the freedom of religion and the interests of the company. If discrimination based on religious grounds is prohibited during the employment contract, restrictions can be authorised only if they are justified and proportionate in regard to the organisation of work within the company. Therefore, the employer must justify, by reference to factors unrelated to any discrimination, the refusal to authorise the absence of an employee on a holy day. The HALDE thus implicitly acknowledged that any worker should normally benefit from days off in order to fulfil religious requirements, the only limit being the proper organisation of the service in which he or she works.

As for the practice of Ramadan, in 2010 a municipality requested the HALDE's opinion about the legal framework applicable to Muslim children. It should be recalled that Ramadan fell during the summer 2010. The issue was therefore raised of the compatibility of fasting with the normal activities and proper functioning of public leisure centres (a public service providing activities to children during the summertime, during other school holidays and after school). In its Decision no. 2011–69 of 21 March 2011, the HALDE concluded that fasting for Ramadan was not necessarily or inherently risky. It affirmed that the systematic exclusion of fasting children from activities provided by public leisure centres seemed disproportionate to the legitimate aim of security. A concrete analysis of the real risks for the children's safety was necessary, taking into account the specific context, and particularly the sport or recreational activities in question. The HALDE recommended further that, if it were determined that fasting represented a genuine safety risk, alternative activities compatible with respect for the obligation to fast should be proposed to the children. Moreover, when the children are present at a public leisure centre for several days, meals should be provided to the children outside of fasting periods unless exceptional circumstances render doing so impossible.

In the Netherlands

The Dutch Equality Commission has held that a restaurant dress code prohibiting any kind of headgear is discriminatory against Muslim women. It considered that the restaurant owner in question could have attracted a high-quality clientele with less coercive measures, such as requiring 'appropriate clothing' or prohibiting caps or sports clothing.[16] Setting out these alternatives therefore provides the restaurant owner with useful information on how to put an end to a discriminatory practice.

---

16 Opinion 2004–112 of the Commissie Gelijke Behandling of 4 September 2004, quoted in C Tobler, 'Limits and Potential of the Concept of Indirect Discrimination' (Office for Official Publications of the European Communities, September 2008) esp. 58; see also D Schiek, 'Indirect Discrimination' in D Schiek, L Waddington and M Bell (eds), *Non Discrimination Law* (Art Publishing 2007) 323–475, esp. 429–30.

In the United Kingdom

In the *Kumari Singh* case,[17] the British High Court granted a Sikh girl the right to wear a *kara* (a 5 mm-wide steel bracelet, one of the symbols of the Sikh religion) even though her school's rules prohibited the wearing of jewellery for safety reasons. The British Court ruled that exempting this pupil from the school rules was an appropriate measure. The High Court thus implicitly condemned the school's makeshift solution of authorising the pupil to wear the *kara* provided that she remained isolated from the other pupils while on the school premises.[18] The Court concluded that the school's actions constituted indirect discrimination on the basis of religion and race.

In the ECtHR law: the Thlimmenos case law

The European Court of Human Rights (ECtHR) has also had the opportunity to grant reasonable accommodation within the employment sector, even if it does not define it as such. For example, in its *Thlimmenos v Greece* judgment,[19] the ECtHR addressed a case in which a Jehovah's Witness complained of being excluded from the profession of chartered accountant because of a criminal conviction. The applicant had been sentenced for refusing to carry out his mandatory military service on the grounds of his religious convictions. The Strasbourg Court, sitting in Grand Chamber, ruled that the applicant was in a clearly different situation from other individuals found guilty of serious crimes because 'a conviction for refusing on religious or philosophical grounds to wear the military uniform cannot imply any dishonesty or moral turpitude likely to undermine the offender's ability to exercise this profession'. The Court came to the verdict of religious discrimination because the legislation had failed to introduce 'appropriate exceptions to the rule barring persons convicted of a serious crime from the profession of chartered accountants'. This case law therefore requires the State to define the types of criminal convictions that do not prevent those concerned from exercising the profession of chartered accountant.

The aforementioned examples show that in Europe there are alternative ways to address the issue of reasonable accommodation: on the basis of indirect discrimination or on human rights law. The obligation of differential treatment deriving from the prohibition of any kind of indirect discrimination more or less corresponds to the Canadian legal obligation of reasonable accommodation. Indeed, the Canadian Supreme Court conceives the right to reasonable accommodation as a corollary to the right to equality. Since its *O'Malley v Simpsons-Sears* judgment,[20] the Canadian Supreme Court has enshrined 'a legal obligation applicable in a situation of discrimination, consisting in adapting a standard or practice of universal scope within reasonable limits by granting differential treatment to an individual who would otherwise be penalised by such standard or practice'.[21] The limit of this obligation is 'undue hardship'. The lack of recognition by EU legislation of any right to reasonable accommodation for cultural and religious groups does not alter this fact. Nevertheless, this piece of protection may not appear as sufficient as need be.

The Shortcomings of the Existing Legal Framework in Europe

Alidadi has pointed out that granting accommodation as a consequence of indirect discrimination may entail serious pitfalls.[22] She argues that indirect discrimination law requires all persons claiming the right to a differential treatment to prove that they suffer from a group disadvantage. Moreover, such discrepancy is only

17 High Court of Justice, Administrative Court, 29 July 2008, *The Queen on the Application of Sarika Watkins-Singh (a Child Acting by Sanita Kumari Singh, her Mother and Litigation Friend) v the Governing Body of Aberdare Girls High School and Rhondda Cynon Taf Unitary Authority* (2008) EWHC 1865 (Admin).

18 This solution is very similar to that adopted by the South African Constitutional Court, which condemned a refusal to grant a school dress code exemption to a Tamil girl who wished to wear a ring in her nose as a symbol of her cultural and religious identity; *MEC for Kwazulu-Natal, School Liaison Officer and Others v Pillay*, CCT 51/06 (2007) ZACC 21.

19 ECtHR, *Thlimmenos v Greece*, 6 April 2000, App no 34369/97.

20 Supreme Court, *Ontario Commission of Human Rights and Theresa O'Malley (Vincent) v Simpsons-Sears Ltd* (1985) 2 SCR 536, 17 December 1985.

21 This right can now also be invoked on the basis of a finding of direct discrimination; Supreme Court, *British Columbia (Public Service Employee Religions Commission) v BCGSEU* (1999) 3 SCR 3, 22 February 1999.

22 Alidadi (n 9).

accepted if it is objectively justified as being necessary and proportionate for a legitimate aim. The judicial assessment relating to the justification of indirect discrimination leads to a wide variety of solutions, which may sometimes appear inconsistent.

The Prima Facie Evidence of a Group Disadvantage

The issue of evidence of indirect discrimination was at stake in the aforementioned *Eweida* case. The English tribunals and courts held that Ms Eweida, who wanted to wear a visible Christian cross in breach of the uniform guidelines, had failed to produce evidence of a group disadvantage on the part of Christians. She had only demonstrated a disadvantage to herself arising out of her desire to manifest her Christian religion in a certain way. The Court of Appeal endorsed the approach of the Employment Appeal Tribunal by asserting that 'in order for indirect discrimination to be established, it must be possible to make some general statements which would be true about a religious group such that an employer ought to reasonably be able to appreciate that any particular provision may have a disparate adverse impact on the group'. It noted that, of the uniformed work force of 30,000, none had ever requested permission to display a cross necklace except for Ms Eweida.[23] For some seven years no one, not even Ms Eweida, had ever complained about the prohibition against jewellery.[24]

First, this tempting reasoning should be critically re-examined in light of EU law. In fact, gross statistical disparities can constitute *prima facie* proof of a practice of discrimination, but according to EU law, this is only a means to provide evidence of discrimination. It is not necessary to demonstrate disparate impact through statistical data because disparate treatment may be sufficient in many cases. The European Court of Justice thus stated, in a case of indirect discrimination based on nationality, that

> unless objectively justified and proportionate to its aim, a provision of national law must be regarded as indirectly discriminatory if it is *intrinsically liable* to affect migrant workers more than national workers and if there is a consequent risk that it will place the former at a particular disadvantage. It is not necessary in this respect to find that the provision in question does in practice affect a substantially higher proportion of migrant workers. It is sufficient that it is liable to have such an effect.[25]

According to this comparative test, it seems rather logical that the prohibition against wearing jewellery would necessarily put at a disadvantage those who believe that they must wear a visible cross to be in accordance with their genuine faith. To what extent this belief is shared within the Christian community is not an issue the courts would be competent to address.

Second, the reasoning of the British courts was overturned by the European Court majority. It did not consider this case to be a matter of discrimination, but a mere issue of human rights law and its impact on the respect of freedom of religion.

> The ECtHR's decision now calls into question the whole concept of group disadvantage as a gateway to the law's protection. Now, arguably any interference with the way you manifest your own personal beliefs, regardless of whether anyone else feels the same way, triggers article 9 and the employer should be required to show justification.[26]

In my opinion, the main pitfall of indirect discrimination described by Alidadi may not be as critical as it seems. EU law may consider it sufficient, as *prima facie* evidence of indirect discrimination, to show that a

---

23 *Eweida v British Airways Plc* [2010] EWCA Civ 80 (12 February 2010) <www.bailii.org/ew/cases/EWCA/Civ/2010/80.html> accessed June 2014.

24 After hearing a Christian theologian assert that the Christian Church did not require believers to wear a cross, the Court held that it was then a personal decision by Ms Eweida, and there was no evidence of other Christians at British Airways being disadvantaged. Such an analysis is not in compliance with the subjective definition of religion usually referred to in Europe, the United States and Canada.

25 ECJ, *John O'Flynn v Adjudication Officer*, 23 May 1996, Case C-237/94, paras 20 and 21.

26 Markleham, 'Eweida: What it All Means', posted on Markleham's blog on 16 January 2013 <http://mrsmarkleham.wordpress.com/2013/01/16/eweida-what-it-all-means/> accessed June 2014.

practice prohibiting any specific expression of religion is intrinsically liable to put a group of workers who are fervent and sincere believers at a disadvantage compared to other workers. In any event, case law shows that there are ways to overcome the evidence hurdle. The holder of a right to reasonable accommodation, however, is not required to demonstrate that he or she has been discriminated against in order to obtain accommodating exceptions from his or her employer. This constitutes an important advantage.

Besides, there is another issue arising from the use of indirect discrimination or human rights law to provide reasonable accommodation on the grounds of religion. It is the existence of random case law around Europe. The use of indirect discrimination is subject to appraisals, which can vary, or indeed diverge. Depending on the legal, social and societal cultures, an identical situation may be reassessed to give rise to reasonable accommodation or, on the contrary, be preserved as its stands despite its exclusive effects.

Heterogeneous Protection of Religious Needs

To date, the Court of Justice of the European Union has had no opportunity to express its views in any preliminary ruling concerning the interpretation of 2000/78 Directive on religious discrimination. Nevertheless, we would like to recall the old *Vivien Prais* judgement,[27] where the European Court of Justice ruled, on the basis of the equal treatment principle, that the EC administration was required to hold competitive examinations on dates not coinciding with religious festivals, where possible. This is a tentative case law, although isolated, to accommodate religious needs at the EU level.

The indirect discrimination test assesses whether the neutral measure, practice or provision is justified and whether it is appropriate and proportionate. The proportionality notion having been weighed differently in each case, we sometimes end up with judicial decisions that can appear quite inconsistent. Employers may therefore feel at a loss to determine whether or not they should grant reasonable accommodation in their situation. For example, in the United Kingdom, an employment tribunal ruled that a Muslim security guard did not suffer indirect discrimination when his employer refused him permission to leave work early on a Friday.[28] On the contrary, another tribunal decided that a Christian care worker did suffer indirect discrimination when her employer required her to work a Sunday shift.[29]

Another striking example is the lack of uniformity relating to the legal protection of Muslim women in Europe.[30] This concerns not only the public employment field, where the neutrality of the State may limit the wearing of religious symbols in some countries, but also affects Muslim women within the private sector. For example, the Danish Supreme Court (Højesteret) held that clothing guidelines of a department store (the well-known Føtex chain) that aimed at creating a religious-neutral workplace were not discriminatory on the basis of religion. Although it admitted that such a dress code mainly affected Muslim women, the differential treatment was found objectively justified and proportionate.[31] A Belgian Labour Court (Cour du Travail) came to the same conclusion about the dismissal of a female employee working in a bookshop for non-compliance with clear dress guidelines. It explained that any freedom may be limited where religious practices are 'likely to lead to chaos'. The dismissal was found justified because the dress code was applicable to every worker and supported a neutral image of the company.[32]

27 ECJ, *Vivien Prais*, Case C-130/75.

28 *Cherfi v G4S Security Services Limited*, EAT Case no 0379/10/DM, 24 May 2011.

29 *Williams-Drabble v Pathway Care Solutions* [2004] ET Case no 2601718/2004, 2 December 2004, mentioned by A Donald, 'Advancing Debate about Religion or Belief, Equality and Human Rights: Grounds for Optimism?' (2013) 2 (1) *Oxford Journal of Law and Religion* 50–71.

30 For illustrations of this variety, see N Doe, *Law and Religion in Europe: A Comparative Introduction* (OUP 2011); I Rorive, 'Religious Symbols in the Public Space: In Search of a European Answer' (2009) 30 *Cardozo Law Review* 2669–97.

31 Danish Supreme Court, 21 July 2005 (Case 22/2004), U.2005.1265H; compare with the 2000 judgment concluding to indirect discrimination on the basis of religion. This case was about a veiled girl who was denied traineeship in a department store for non-observance of the dress code. The guidelines did not, however, specify that the employees should be dressed uniformly, but that the employees should be dressed in a 'business-like' and 'nice' way. The plaintiff was awarded 10,000 DKR in compensation (Eastern High Court, 10 August 2000, U.2000.2350Ø).

32 Brussels Labour Court of Appeal, 15 January 2008, *E.F. v SA Club*, RG no 48695.

By contrast, a German Labour Court ruled as discriminatory on the basis of religion the dismissal of a Muslim nurse wearing the headscarf in a Catholic hospital because she was capable of fulfilling her tasks regardless of her headgear.[33] Adopting the observations of the HALDE, the Paris Criminal Court of Appeal (Cour d'appel, chambre correctionnelle) convicted a private training centre of discrimination because it excluded Muslim women wearing the headscarf.[34]

More surprisingly, the same situation may lead to diametrically opposed solutions. For example, the dismissal of a receptionist working in a private company because she was wearing a headscarf was considered justified by Belgian courts but discriminatory in France.[35] It sometimes happens in one and the same case. We think, for example, of the so-called *Baby-Loup* 'saga',[36] concerning the dismissal for serious misconduct of a veiled woman working as a deputy director in a private day-nursery (called Baby-Loup). The decisions of the lower courts (the Mantes-la-Jolie Labour Tribunal and the Court of Appeal of Versailles) upholding this dismissal were eventually overturned by the Court of Cassation. This decision was, however, recently quashed by the Court of Appeal of Paris despite the legal principle under French law that lower courts to which a case is referred back after an appeal in cassation must abide by the settled point of law. Another appeal is likely in this case, which has gripped France for five years. The French Defender of Rights has asked the government for a clarification of the legal framework.

Moreover, the ECtHR case law not only appears fragmented, but also restrictive. The Strasbourg Court has consistently held that the legitimate exercise and enjoyment of the right to freedom of religion is not absolute. It shall not authorise any individual to be exempted from the application of general law. First, the Court gives a wide margin of appreciation to States Parties. Second, it has, on many occasions, ruled that the 'pressing social needs' provided for in Article 9 paragraph 2 of the ECHR may justify maintaining the common rule despite its exclusive effects on specific groups of persons. These may refer to respect of the secularism principle, protection of the rights and freedoms of others, gender equality, public order, health and safety, and so on. Until now, with a few exceptions, most applicants challenging the prohibition on religious signs before the Strasbourg Court have been unsuccessful. The Court has considered it justified to apply the headscarf ban to a teacher[37] and to prohibit a nurse within the public sector from displaying a visible cross.[38] Thus far, the same applies to workers who seek to accommodate their working time or the main functions of their employment contracts to their religious requirements.[39]

Moreover, in its *Dahlab* judgment,[40] the ECtHR held that the headscarf is a 'powerful external symbol' and that

> it might have some kind of proselytising effect, seeing that it appears to be imposed on women by a precept which is laid down in the Koran and which … is hard to square with the principle of gender equality. It

---

33 Cologne Labour Court, 6 March 2008, 19 Ca 7222/07 and Cologne Land Labour Court, 3 December 2008, 3 Ca 785/08, quoted by Doe (n 30).

34 HALDE, Decision no 2009–339 of 28 September 2009 and Paris Court of Appeal, 8 June 2010, *Benkirane*, n 08/08286; for a comment, see S Pradelle, 'L'interdiction du port du voile dans l'enseignement supérieur peut être le signe d'une discrimination' (2011) 2 *AJ P* 79 and seq.

35 Antwerp Labour Court of Appeal, 14 January 2008, *Centre for Equal Opportunities and Opposition to Racism v NV G4S Security Services and Samira Achbita*, no 53282 Comp. Paris Court of Appeal, 19 June 2003, *Teleperformance v Tahri* (Ms Tahri had, however, always worn the veil, even during the recruitment interview and during the 18 months she worked with the company, whereas Ms Achbita declared to her supervisor that she intended to wear a headscarf after she had already worked in the company for years).

36 B Bossu, 'Affaire Baby-Loup: le retour à la case départ' (19 December 2013) 51 *La Semaine Juridique Entreprise et Affaires* 1710.

37 ECtHR, *Dahlab v Switzerland*, 15 February 2001, App no 42393/98.

38 ECtHR, *Chaplin v United Kingdom*, 15 January 2013, App no 59842/10.

39 ECtHR, *Konttinen v Finland*, 3 December 1996, App no 24949/94; ECtHR, *Sessa v Italy*, 3 April 2012, App no 28790/08 concerning the refusal to adjourn a hearing listed on the date of Yom Kippur and subsequent inability of a Jewish lawyer to attend the hearing four months later. ECtHR, *McFarlane and Ladele v United Kingdom*, 15 January, App nos 51671/10 and 36516/10.

40 ECtHR, *Dahlab v Switzerland*, App no 42393/98; see also ECtHR (GC), *Şahin v Turkey*, 10 November 2005, App no 44774/98.

> therefore appears difficult to reconcile the wearing of an Islamic headscarf with the message of tolerance, respect for others, and above all, equality and non-discrimination.

On the contrary, the Grand Chamber in *Lautsi* decided that even if the crucifix should be construed as a 'Christian sign conferring on the country's majority religion preponderant visibility', its display in the State-school classrooms in Italy was in itself 'insufficient to denote a process of indoctrination' on the respondent State's part.[41] Many authors have criticised the paternalistic approach of the Court to Muslim women and its tendency to overvalue the majority culture. Dissenting judges also denounced 'this little understanding of religious minorities' concerns'[42] by accepting the *de facto* situation where an applicant has to choose between his religious duties and his professional duties.

Would extending the current protection granted to disabled persons in EU law to religious minorities end these very divergent solutions to managing diversity around Europe?

The Potential Input of New EU Legislation Providing for a Right to Reasonable Accommodation

All the aforementioned judicial examples show that Europe is not completely out of step with, for example, Canadian law when reasonable accommodation of religious requirements is at stake. To what extent would the introduction of a right to reasonable accommodation improve EU protection of religious minorities? It can be argued that it would bypass the hurdle faced by victims of bringing *prima facie* evidence of indirect discrimination. It would help courts and tribunals converge on a clear goal and restrict the considerable diversity of judicial solutions that exists throughout Europe.

The Advantage of 'Short-Circuiting' Discrimination Law

By guaranteeing a right to reasonable accommodation, the legislature intends to raise protection against specified forms of discrimination to the rank of substantive protection. This formulation of protection no longer comes under the category of the right to non-discrimination, but is governed by a different set of legal rules. The rights-holders no longer have to prove that they have been discriminated against in order to secure special treatment. They enjoy an individual right provided for by law, whose application they can simply demand, leaving it to the party challenged (for example, the employer) to demonstrate, if it can, that it cannot legitimately accede to the demand.

So far, some groups that are traditionally considered vulnerable have been granted this kind of protection. This applies, for instance, to people with disabilities, for whom employers must provide reasonable accommodation by taking appropriate measures, where needed in a particular case, unless such measures would impose a disproportionate burden on the employers.[43] It can also apply to pregnant women, whose employers must take the necessary measures to ensure that, by temporarily adjusting the working conditions and/or the working hours, the workers in question are not exposed to certain risks during their pregnancy.[44]

These cases concern a positive obligation established by legislation. In some cases such 'short-circuiting' of the right to non-discrimination can even necessitate an accommodation that is no longer merely reasonable. This applies to the fundamental right of an accused person who does not understand or speak the language used by the court, set out in Article 6(3)(e) of the ECHR, to the free assistance of an interpreter.[45]

---

41 ECtHR (GC), *Lautsi v Italy*, 18 March 2011, App no 30814/06.

42 Report to the dissenting opinion of Judges Tulkens, Popovic and Keller in the aforementioned case *Sessa v Italy*.

43 Article 5 of 2000/78 Directive.

44 Article 5 of Council Directive 92/85/EEC of 19 October 1992 on the introduction of measures to encourage improvements in the safety and health at work of pregnant workers and workers who have recently given birth or are breastfeeding, *Official Journal*, L 348, 28/11/1992, 1.

45 However, this provision 'does not go so far as to require a written translation of all items of written evidence or official documents in the procedure. The interpretation assistance provided should be such as to enable the defendant to have knowledge of the case against him and to defend himself, notably by being able to put before the court his version of

In US federal law, an employer is already required to reasonably accommodate an employee's religious beliefs or practices, unless doing so would cause more than a minimal burden on the operations of the employer's business. Reasonable accommodation without undue hardship is expressly provided for in section 701(j) of Title VII of the Civil Rights Act of 1964 as amended in 1972.

This provision makes it unlawful for an employer to fail to reasonably accommodate the religious practices of an employee or prospective employee, unless the employer demonstrates that accommodation would result in undue hardship in the running of the business. The term 'religion' includes all aspects of religious observance and practice, as well as belief. A similar provision was then added to the 1990 Americans with Disabilities Act.[46] This provides a common approach for employers to reconcile contradictory employment tasks with workers' religious needs. This is not the case in EU law yet.

A Common Approach to Religious Groups' Concerns?

As mentioned earlier, the Court of Justice of the European Union unfortunately had no opportunity to rule on cases of religious discrimination over the last decade. Had it done so, it would have given a uniform interpretation of EU law in this respect, that is, all the Member States would have had to comply with it. As it stands, we have no real clue whether the Court of Justice of the European Union would actually interpret the indirect discrimination concept in a proactive way regarding religion. Depending on the cases submitted, it could give binding guidelines on the wearing of religious symbols at work or on the conciliation between religious needs and the requirements of the employment contract.

In my opinion, it is the harnessing of the indirect discrimination concept rather than the concept itself that can help pinpoint different shades of responses to the question of respect for diversity. The public outcry inspired by any decision that can be interpreted as affording unjustifiable preferential treatment seems to restrain judicial initiative in this field.

In fact, it happens that some courts do self-censor the real motives underlying their decisions to accommodate the cultural and social reality of religious requirements. They simply leave it unsaid. As an example, the Paris Court of Appeal did not draw any legal conclusions from certified reports demonstrating that a restaurant managed by a Muslim was closed during Ramadan.[47] Another example of this kind of 'taboo' can be found in the interim order of the presiding judge of a Court of Assizes, postponing a trial until after Ramadan.[48] In doing so, he granted a request of the defendant, a Muslim who was fasting and who argued that he would not, as a consequence, be 'fully able to defend himself'. The judge explained his decision merely as a way to 'meet the needs of a sound administration of justice'. Furthermore, French courts permit ritual practices like circumcision, practised by Jews and Muslims, to be carried out in public hospitals.[49] Hence, no doctor or accredited *mohel* has ever been convicted on the basis of Article 222–1 of the Penal Code, which prohibits inflicting physical harm on individuals, for performing ritual circumcision, contrary to cases of excision.[50]

---

the events.' (ECtHR, *Kamasinski v Austria*, 19 December 1989, App no 9783/82; see also ECtHR, *Lagerblom v Sweden*, 14 January 2003, App no 26891/95).

46 Concerning this right within the employment sector, see Section 12111 ('Definitions') para 9: 'The term "reasonable accommodation" may include (A) making existing facilities used by employees readily accessible to and usable by individuals with disabilities; and (B) job restructuring, part-time or modified work schedules, reassignment to a vacant position, acquisition or modification of equipment or devices, appropriate adjustment or modifications of examinations, training materials or policies, the provision of qualified readers or interpreters, and other similar accommodations for individuals with disabilities.'

47 Paris Court of Appeal, 20 December 2007, *Ghoufali c/ SCI Immobess*, no 07/00211.

48 'Un procès renvoyé pour cause de ramadan' *Le Figaro* (4 September 2008); *Le Monde* (5 September 2008).

49 Council of State, 3 November 1997, *Hopital Joseph-Imbert d'Arles*, *Revue Française de Droit Administratif*, Jan–Feb. 1998, 90.

50 In a case related to an ill-fated circumcision performed on a baby by a person without French medical qualifications, the prosecutor of Lille noted that such a customary practice could not be assimilated to a surgical act and that he could not prosecute the person who had performed the circumcision for negligence, since the law does not require the hospitalisation of children for circumcision, and the United Nations does not consider circumcision to be genital mutilation. The Court of Appeal of Douai upheld the decision to acquit the accused on 15 June 2010 (Mazen M. Case). Compare with

In this context, an explicit right to reasonable accommodation may in some ways help remove inconsistencies. Nevertheless, it would not bring any uniformity at the EU level because the reasonable accommodation test implies, by nature, a concrete case-by-case analysis of undue hardship. Therefore, depending on the circumstances and the context, tribunals and courts may rule on cases in different ways. Moreover, the mere notion of undue hardship can be interpreted in different ways. For example, the United States Supreme Court stated that a *de minimis* cost could be deemed excessive,[51] whereas the Canadian Supreme Court opted for a more demanding test: 'more than mere negligible effort is required to satisfy the duty to accommodate. The use of the term "undue" infers that some hardship is acceptable; it is only "undue" hardship that satisfies this test.'[52]

Even if the recognition of a right to reasonable accommodation would not resolve everything, it would indeed demonstrate clear and strong political will towards the protection of minority religious groups. It would legitimise courts' decisions to provide stimuli to this end, calling for the requisite reforms or even revolutions.

A parallel can be made with the legal protection of homosexuals under EU law. In 1998, the European Court appeared reluctant to grant specific protection of homosexuals' rights and called for the intervention of the legislature to adopt, if appropriate, measures to that effect.[53] This was done two years later within the provisions of the 2000/78 Directive, which expressly prohibits discrimination on the grounds of sexual orientation within the employment sector. This piece of legislation was indeed a new step towards the recognition of subjective rights for same-sex couples under EU law and is fully implemented by the Court.[54]

In a system of law which is not a pure common law system (as the EU is not), it is not usual to give the courts full responsibility for deciding whether the collective rule should be imposed on all or whether some individuals or groups should enjoy special regulations. The judges may need some support from the legislature to move forward, especially on sensitive issues like religion. A full-scale democratic debate leading to some sort of consensus would indeed be very welcome. The question is whether it is possible to build a consensus among 28 States on religion and how to accommodate religious needs within not only the private but also the public employment sector.

The Feasibility of the RELIGARE Recommendation

The current 2000/78 Directive is based on ex Article 13 of the Treaty Establishing the European Community. Since the Lisbon Treaty entered into force, any reform of this legislative text should now be based on Article 19 of the Treaty on the Functioning of the European Union (TFEU). This provision requires not only the consent of the European Parliament, but also the unanimity of the Council. Twenty-eight countries would therefore need to agree on such a proposal, which may be difficult, if not impossible in the current context. According to the settled ECtHR case law, there is little or no consensus within Europe on how to treat religious symbols and requirements, whether in the private or the public sphere. It may therefore be difficult to reach unanimity on a right to reasonable accommodation in the religious sphere.

It is true that the EU anti-discrimination legislation, namely the Race Directive[55] and the Equal Employment Directive, was adopted unanimously in the early 2000s and that all the existing Member States decided to prohibit direct and indirect religious discrimination in the field of employment at that time. But that was before the addition of the 10 Central and Eastern European countries. Moreover, the sudden surge in

---

the German situation: 'Cutting Controversy: German Court Sets New Circumcision Rules' (*Spiegel*, 27 September 2013) <www.spiegel.de/international/germany/new-circumcision-ruling-requires-doctors-to-discuss-procedure-a-924984.html> accessed June 2014.

51 *Trans World Airlines v Hardison*, 432 US 63 (1977).

52 *Central Okanagan School District No. 23 v Renaud* [1992] 2 SCR 970, 984.

53 ECJ, *Lisa Jacqueline Grant v South-West Trains Ltd*, 17 February 1998, Case C-249/96.

54 ECJ, *Maruko*, 1 April 2008, Case C-267/06; ECJ, *Römer*, 10 May 2011, Case C147/08; CJEU, *Hay v Crédit Agricole*, 12 December 2013, Case C-267/12.

55 Council Directive 2000/43/EC of 29 June 2000 implementing the principle of equal treatment between persons irrespective of racial or ethnic origin, *Official Journal*, L 180, 19/07/2000, 22–26.

combating discrimination seems now to be running out of steam. The financial, economic and political crisis Europe is now facing definitely has a negative impact on the EU agenda when it comes to discrimination.

An illustration of this situation is the bleak future faced by the so-called Horizontal Directive proposal concerning discrimination beyond employment.[56] No consensus seems to be in sight after five years of discussions. While most Member States agreed that work should continue in the interest of strengthening anti-discrimination legislation, some of them have maintained reservations regarding the proposal.[57] There are a variety of reasons for these blocks. Some delegations question the need for such an initiative, which they consider an infringement on national competence and in conflict with the principles of subsidiarity and proportionality. But this opposition to the new Directive is more than purely technical. It is highly political.

Pleading for substantive equality may have significant ideological implications. As Bosset explains,[58] discrimination has deep and ancient roots; it has progressively helped design the social fabric of our society. It has determined the way we conceive and allocate the 'normal' and 'fair' place of individuals in society. Fighting discrimination may overturn our social equilibriums and overhaul our conceptions of social cohesion. It is thus not surprising that a complete implementation of discrimination law is likely to encounter resistance.

Nevertheless, the current 2000/78 Directive expressly limits the right to reasonable accommodation to disabled workers. In its explanatory memorandum, the Commission stated 'the principle of equal treatment as applied in the context of disability entails an identification and removal of barriers in the way of persons with disabilities who, with reasonable accommodation, are able to perform the essential functions of a job'. The Commission thus stressed that 'the concept has become central to the construction of modern legislation combating disability-based discrimination and is also expressly recognised at an international level'. It referred to existing national laws in the UK, Sweden and Ireland,[59] as well as to the UN Standard Rules.[60] The EU law is in this respect the reflection of a general consensus that is now enshrined within the UN Convention on the Rights of Persons with Disabilities.

The fact that the right to reasonable accommodation as provided by EU legislation for the disabled has not been extended to include religion cannot be seen as simple negligence, given that such a right was first introduced in the United States and Canada in the context of religious discrimination before being extended to other categories of persons.[61] By restricting this right to disabled workers, I suggest that the EU legislature implicitly finds it neither appropriate nor necessary to extend this right to workers belonging to religious minorities. The twin fears of encouraging communitarianism and of challenges to the law as a general standard are likely to curb the process of adopting and implementing reasonable accommodation rights in Europe.

At this stage, I am therefore quite sceptical about the feasibility of legislative reform of the Equality Employment Directive aimed at introducing a right to reasonable accommodation on the grounds of religion in EU law, as the RELIGARE team have recommended. I have, however, shown in this chapter that the existing legal framework is not completely blank, and that there are alternative legal tools to draw upon for pragmatic solutions in Europe. Moreover, accommodating religious needs can be accomplished in the meantime through a bottom-up process. 'Pragmatic solutions will be preferred to ideological stalemates. This

56 'Proposal for a Council Directive on Implementing the Principle of Equal Treatment between Persons Irrespective of Religion or Belief, Disability, Age or Sexual Orientation', COM(2008) 426 final, 2 July 2008.

57 Concerning the evolution of the procedure, see <www.europarl.europa.eu/oeil/popups/ficheprocedure.do?reference=2008/0140(APP)&l=EN> accessed June 2014.

58 P Bosset, 'Les mesures législatives de lutte contre la discrimination raciale au Québec. Un bilan institutionnel' (2005) 17 (2) *Nouvelles Pratiques Sociales* 15–30 <www.erudit.org/revue/nps/2005/v17/n2/011224ar.html> accessed June 2014.

59 The UK Disability Discrimination Act 1995; the Swedish Act on Discrimination of People with Disabilities 1999; Ireland's Employment Equality Bill 1997.

60 At that time, the Commission referred to the UN Standard Rules on the Equalisation of Opportunities for Persons with Disabilities ('the Standard Rules') and the UN Committee on Economic, Cultural and Social Rights' understanding of the notion of discrimination contained within the International Covenant on Economic, Social and Cultural Rights (General Comment, 1994).

61 E Bribosia, J Ringelheim and I Rorive, 'Aménager la diversité: Le droit à l'égalité face à la pluralité religieuse' (2009) 78 *Revue Trimestrielle des Droits de l'Homme* 319–73.

is pluralism at the coalface, in which purity is foregone, solutions may not be pleasing to participants, and agreements are contingent and partial.'[62]

As the RELIGARE recommendation may go unheeded, I would thus recommend that EU institutions launch and subsidise a large-scale study of the existing good practices around Europe in order to get a better idea of how employers manage religious diversity in the workplace. This would subsequently help the European Commission, the European Parliament and even the EU Fundamental Rights Agency draw EU guidelines based at least on the lowest and most uncontroversial common denominator, if one exists. In this respect, the EU should take inspiration from the American Equal Employment Opportunity Commission's practice. The EEOC has given examples of some common religious accommodations that include flexible scheduling, voluntary shift substitutions or swaps, job reassignments and modifications to workplace policies or practices.[63]

Moreover, the EU could also take a more holistic approach to religious discrimination in Europe, which is still disconnected from other forms of inequalities. Most of the time, it does not fully include the gender perspective or the origin background of the victims.[64] The current approach requiring 'the persons to slot themselves into rigid compartments or categories'[65] does not fully correspond to reality and is often inappropriate, misleading and even counterproductive in the fight against discrimination. EU non-discrimination law may thus fail to address the real question, which has less to do with any characteristic inherent in individuals than with the disadvantages and stigmatisation suffered by particular individuals in society.

62 Donald (n 29) <http://ojlr.oxfordjournals.org/content/2/1/50.full.pdf+html> accessed June 2014.

63 EEOC, *Guidelines on Discrimination Because of Religion*, 29 CFR Part 1605, 31 October 1980, as amended at 74 FR 3430, 21 January 2009 <www.gpo.gov/fdsys/pkg/CFR-2011-title29-vol4/xml/CFR-2011-title29-vol4-part1605.xml> accessed June 2014. See also the *Compliance Manual, Section 12: Religious Discrimination (2008)* <www.eeoc.gov/policy/docs/religion.pdf> accessed June 2014.

64 See F Ast and R Spielhaus, 'Tackling Double Victimization of Muslim Women in Europe: The Intersectional Response' (2012) 16 *Mediterranean Journal of Human Rights* 357–82.

65 Ontario Human Rights Commission, 'An Intersectional Approach to Discrimination: Addressing Multiple Grounds in Human Rights Claims', Discussion Paper, 5, October 2001 <http://www.ohrc.on.ca/sites/default/files/attachments/An_intersectional_approach_to_discrimination%3A_Addressing_multiple_grounds_in_human_rights_claims.pdf> accessed 22 August 2014.

Chapter 14
The Reasonable Accommodation of Conservative Religious Beliefs and the Protection of LGBT Rights at the Workplace

Peter Cumper

Introduction

When is it reasonable for a person's religion or beliefs to be accommodated at the workplace? This is a question that has recently generated much discussion and, with the publication of the RELIGARE report, the debate on reasonable accommodation seems set to continue.

An obvious issue of contention in this regard concerns the determination of what is meant by *reasonable* accommodation. The parameters of the debate have long tended to focus on the cost and administrative implications of reasonable accommodation for employers and employees (respectively). However, in recent years, an equally significant issue has emerged – the emotive relationship between religious freedom and the principle of equality. This has led to questions such as whether a liberal State should ever facilitate the reasonable accommodation of a person's religion or beliefs at the workplace if, in so doing, it might lead to the erosion of the dignity of another worker (or group of workers). Indeed, more specifically, attention has recently been focused on whether the accommodation of an employee's religiously conservative beliefs can ever be justified if such a policy were potentially to risk undermining respect for lesbian/gay/bisexual/transgender (LGBT) rights.

In seeking to examine such contentious and topical issues, this chapter aims to explore the boundaries of the proposal advanced by RELIGARE for the recognition of the principle 'of *legally enshrined* reasonable accommodation on the basis of religion and belief in the workplace' (*Report*, 19). In particular, given that the RELIGARE project was underpinned by 'the search for a balance between the protection of the freedom of religion and belief, on the one hand, and the principle of equal treatment and non-discrimination on the other' (*Report*, 17), this chapter will focus on the often controversial relationship between religious and LGBT rights at the workplace.

The chapter starts with a brief examination of *Eweida and Others v the United Kingdom*[1] – a case recently decided by the European Court of Human Rights in which two (of the four) Christian applicants (Ladele and McFarlane) sought accommodation at the workplace of their religiously motivated reservations about homosexuality. This case will be used to highlight an issue of increasing contemporary relevance in European public life[2] – the challenge facing law- and policymakers of having to strike an appropriate balance between protecting the rights of conservative religious employees and those of LGBT workers. In examining this issue the chapter's focus is confined mainly to the submission of two propositions.

First, I challenge the contention of those who object to *any* workplace accommodation of conservative religious attitudes to homosexuality on the basis that such 'religious' beliefs are akin to socially objectionable 'racist' ones. While acknowledging that many religious traditions have had[3] – or continue to have[4] – a shocking

1 *Eweida and Others v the United Kingdom*, App nos 48420/10, 36516/10, 51671/10, 59842/10. HUDOC (2013).

2 On this generally see, for example, J Habermas and J Ratzinger, *The Dialectics of Secularization: On Reason and Religion* (Ignatius Press 2007).

3 See, for example, L Crompton, *Homosexuality and Civilization* (Harvard 2006); J Mark, *The Invention of Sodomy in Christian Theology* (University of Chicago Press 1997).

4 Homosexuality remains a criminal offence in more than 70 countries, mainly in Africa, Asia and the Middle East. See <www.government.nl/issues/gay-rights/lgbt-rights-worldwide> accessed 27 June 2014. See also M Badgett and J Frank (eds), *Sexual Orientation Discrimination: An International Perspective* (Routledge 2007).

history of having failed to respect LGBT rights, I argue that there are nonetheless significant distinctions to be drawn between racist beliefs and conservative religious beliefs in this regard.

Second, with a significant number of high-profile court cases having recently involved acrimonious disputes between members of religious and LGBT groups, I suggest that more attention needs to be focused on the development of informal dispute resolution strategies that could assist in supplementing existing legal remedies. Such strategies might conceivably reduce some of the tensions that are commonly associated with litigation by helping to foster dialogue, and potentially assist in the discovery of shared values between conservative faith and LGBT organisations.

The Workplace – a Battleground for Religion and Belief

There has, in recent years, been a dramatic increase in the number of employment disputes with what might be termed a 'religious dimension'. In some such cases, litigants have wished to be protected *from* the influence of religion[5] – such as, for example, in a recent British case where an employer's imposition of restrictions on a Christian doctor, banning him from making reference to his beliefs in professional communications, was held to be lawful.[6] However, by the same token, a significant number of employment disputes have also tended to involve applications from those who wish to invoke the principle of freedom *of* religion at the workplace.[7] The occasions where employees have sought *positive* accommodation of their religious beliefs at the workplace have certainly, in the last couple of decades, been frequent and contentious.[8] They have ranged from controversies surrounding the non-recognition by employers of prayer times,[9] holy days,[10] religious dress[11] and displays of religious symbols,[12] to less 'predictable' areas of conflict, such as retail staff being unwilling to sell pork or alcohol,[13] and even a professional footballer refusing, for a time, to wear the logo of

5 Article 9 of the ECHR (n 9, below) has been interpreted as guaranteeing the 'freedom to hold or not to hold religious beliefs and to practise or not to practise a religion': *Grzelak v Poland* HUDOC (2010) para 85.

6 See *Drew v Walsall Healthcare NHS Trust* [2013] UKEAT 0378_12_2009 (20 September 2013).

7 See Article 9 of the ECHR, which provides that:

> (1) Everyone has the right to freedom of thought, conscience and religion; this right includes freedom to change his religion or belief and freedom, either alone or in community with others and in public or private, to manifest his religion or belief, in worship, teaching, practice and observance.
>
> (2) Freedom to manifest one's religion or beliefs shall be subject only to such limitations as are prescribed by law, and are necessary in a democratic society in the interests of public safety, for the protection of public order, health or morals, or for the protection of the rights and freedoms of others.

8 On the issue of the working week being still largely based on the Christian calendar see, for example, G Alexis, 'Not Christian, but Nonetheless Qualified: The Secular Workplace – Whose Hardship?' (2011) 3 (1) *Journal of Religion and Business Ethics* 1, who argues (albeit in the context of the US) that employees who are immigrants from non-Christian, non-Western cultures 'are at a disadvantage in the so-called secular U.S. workplace because it in truth represents a bastion of secularized Christianity'.

9 See, for example, *Ahmad v UK*, no 8160/78, 22 DR 27 (1981); 4 EHRR 126 at 135, where the European Commission rejected a Muslim teacher's request for an extended Friday lunch-break so that he could attend a mosque for prayers, on the basis that the applicant 'remained free to resign if and when he found that his teaching obligations conflicted with his religious duties'.

10 See, for example, Stedman v UK, no 29107/95, 23 EHRR CD 168 (1997), where the complaint of a Christian employee who refused to work on Sundays was rejected on the basis of the 'free to resign' test, applied in *Ahmad* (n 9). This test has been subsequently repudiated by the European Court in *Eweida* (n 1).

11 See, for example, *Dahlab v Switzerland*, no 42393/98, ECHR 2001-V, 15 February 2001, where the European Court held that the State's actions in banning a female teacher from wearing the Islamic veil in a primary school had been justified (under Article 9(2) of the ECHR), on account of the need to guarantee religious neutrality in the classroom of a multi-faith society. See also *Leyla Şahin v Turkey*, 2005-XI, 44 EHRR 99, para 115, GC.

12 See, for example, *Eweida and Others v UK* (2013) (n 1) para 94, where the European Court held that there had been a violation of Article 9 of the ECHR in relation to Eweida (a British Airways employee), on account of the State's failure to protect, sufficiently, her right to manifest her religion by wearing a Christian cross around her neck at work.

13 See, for example, 'M&S Apologises after Muslim Assistant Refused to Sell Customer Alcohol' (*The Guardian*, 23 December 2013) <www.theguardian.com/business/2013/dec/23/marks-and-spencer-muslim-alcohol> accessed 27 June 2014.

his club's sponsor (a money lending company) on the team's shirt.[14] While these scenarios raise a plethora of issues in relation to the accommodation of religious belief at the workplace,[15] few of them are as controversial as the one that is the primary focus of this chapter: the task facing law- and policymakers of having to consider requests for the accommodation of conservative religious beliefs that elevate heterosexual relationships above LGBT ones.

Religious Perspectives and LGBT Rights in Context

It is important from the very onset to observe that attitudes to LGBT practices vary tremendously among people of faith. Accordingly, it is wrong to regard cases such as *Eweida and Others v UK* as being merely conflicts between LGBT rights and freedom of religion *per se*. Such characterisations are fallacious, as seen from the fact that there are at least three different responses from people of faith to matters pertaining to sexual orientation.

First, there are the positive faith advocates of LGBT relationships – usually from liberal Christian and Jewish traditions in the United States and Western Europe – who embrace and celebrate sexual diversity and as a gift from God.[16] Those who come within this category are typically very supportive of human rights and equality laws, so are not the primary focus of this chapter.

Second, in total contrast, there are faith groups who unambiguously regard homosexuality as being anathema to their religious beliefs, and whose intolerance of it means that they are willing to condone discrimination, and even violence, against homosexuals.[17] Few would object to the fact that manifestations of such hateful beliefs are expressly prohibited under European and international human rights law.[18] But if such groups were ever to seek accommodation of their homophobic convictions at the workplace – by, for example, claiming that they had a right to target LGBT colleagues specifically for proselytism – it is inconceivable that their beliefs would be accommodated, not least because gay rights have been recognised by the European Courts of Human Rights[19] and Justice,[20] while employees are protected from discrimination and harassment under EU law.[21]

A third group – and the one that is the primary focus of this chapter – includes those who maintain that, as a result of their conservative religious beliefs, they are opposed to 'homosexuality' as a practice, but not to 'homosexuals'.[22] For many LGBT groups any such distinction is spurious, although it has been

14 See 'Papiss Cissé Refuses to Wear Newcastle's Wonga-Branded Shirt' (*The Guardian*, 17 July 2013) <www.theguardian.com/football/2013/jul/17/papiss-cisse-newcastle-wonga-shirt> accessed 27 June 2014.

15 On such issues generally see, for example, K Alidadi, M-C Foblets and J Vrielink (eds), *A Test of Faith? Religious Diversity and Accommodation in the European Workplace* (Ashgate 2012).

16 See, for example, J Creech, *Adam's Gift: A Memoir of a Pastor's Calling to Defy the Church's Persecution of Lesbians and Gays* (Duke University Press 2011); D Shneer and C Aviv (eds), *Queer Jews* (Routledge 2002).

17 On holy texts within the Judaeo-Christian tradition that condemn homosexuality and even sanction the murder of homosexuals, see, for example, Leviticus 18:22 and 20:13. While most Biblical scholars currently maintain that such verses must be interpreted within their proper historical context (see, for example, R Scroggs, *Homosexuality and the New Testament* (Fortress 1983)), Christian theology nonetheless continues to be used to justify anti-gay laws in some parts of the world (for example, Uganda, Nigeria, Malawi and Zambia). More generally, on the relationship between Islam and homosexuality see, for example, K Duran, 'Homosexuality and Islam' in Arlene Swidler (ed), *Homosexuality and World Religion* (Trinity Press 1993) 181–98.

18 See, for example, Art 9(2) of the ECHR 1950 and Article 18(3) of the International Covenant on Civil and Political Rights (1966).

19 See, for example, *Vallianatos & Ors v Greece* [2013] ECHR (GC) 1110, on the prohibition of discrimination between different-sex and same-sex couples; *Dudgeon v United Kingdom* (1981) 4 EHRR 149, on a successful challenge to a ban on consensual sex between adult men; and *Sutherland v UK* (1996), App no 25186/94, which established the need to equalise the age of consent for gay and heterosexual men.

20 See, for example, *Frédéric Hay v Crédit Agricole Mutuel de Charente-Maritime et des Deux-Sèvres* [2013] EUECJ C-267/12, where the European Court of Justice held that same-sex couples who enter into registered partnerships are entitled to the same workplace benefits as married employees.

21 See, for example, Council Directive 2000/78/EC, which prohibits various forms of discrimination on the grounds of one's religion or belief.

22 See, for example, S Grenz, *Welcoming but Not Affirming: An Evangelical Response to Homosexuality* (John Knox Press 1998).

claimed 'that some intrinsic religious individuals apparently are able to make the distinction between "sin and sinner"'.[23] This 'love the sinner, hate the sin' distinction is controversial, not least because it potentially offers a cloak under which homophobia can hide – yet it is noticeable that a variant of this view has recently been evident in the response of some mainstream Christian groups to the same-sex marriage debate, with opprobrium reserved for gay marriage rather than gay people.[24] While clearly deficient in many respects, this approach is nonetheless one way of possibly differentiating between the hateful homophobe, whose convictions should never be accommodated, and the conservative faith applicant, whose beliefs are worthy of serious consideration in a liberal democracy that is willing to accept diversity in its many different forms.

The boundaries of the three classifications above are inevitably fluid and open to challenge. Yet notwithstanding such considerations, one thing seems clear – there is a correlation between negative attitudes towards LGBT people and conservative forms of religiosity.[25] This association makes the task of balancing certain faith and LGBT interests a particularly difficult one, and it lay at the very heart of the challenge recently faced by the European Court of Human Rights (ECtHR) in *Eweida and Others v UK*.[26]

Managing Conservative Faith and LGBT Interests at the Workplace

In *Eweida and Others v UK*, the ECtHR considered, inter alia, the applications of two religiously conservative Christians – Lillian Ladele and Gary McFarlane. They sought to challenge the failure of their respective employers to accommodate their beliefs at the workplace, and argued that, as a result of this non-accommodation, they had each been victims of religious discrimination. Ladele, a registrar of births, deaths and marriages for the London Borough of Islington, had refused to officiate at civil partnership ceremonies on grounds of religious conscience[27] – and McFarlane, a relationship counsellor for the charity Relate, had objected (again on the grounds of religious belief) to offering psycho-sexual counselling to same-sex couples.

The ECtHR, in rejecting each of their applications, held that the State had a wide margin of appreciation in seeking to take account of the applicants' right to manifest their beliefs at work, particularly given the duty of employers to protect the rights of others.[28] It was held by the Court that, on the facts of *Ladele* and *McFarlane*, the right balance had been struck on account of the employers' clear policies to promote equal opportunities, and the related ban on employees from acting in a way that might discriminate against others (for example, their LGBT co-workers).[29]

A salient characteristic of the ECtHR's rejection of these two applications was its heavy reliance on the principle of the margin of appreciation. By adjudicating in a way that narrowly limited its analysis to the facts of the case, the Court refrained from offering any general guidance as to the possible limits of accommodating conservative religious beliefs at the European workplace. On one level the ECtHR's approach is perfectly

23 See S Veenvliet, 'Intrinsic Religious Orientation and Religious Teaching: Differential Judgments toward Same-Gender Sexual Behavior and Gay Men and Lesbians' (2008) 18 (1) *International Journal for the Psychology of Religion* 53.

24 A case in point is the speech of the Archbishop of Canterbury (Justin Welby) made during the passage of recently enacted legislation on same-sex marriage in England and Wales, where he restated his opposition to same-sex marriage, but acknowledged that 'the church has often not served the LGBT communities in the way it should': HL Hansard, 3 June 2013, col. 953. See also the Church of England's pastoral letter of care and support for people, regardless of their sexual orientation <www.anglicannetwork.ca/pdf/dromantine_communique_02_2005_aec.pdf> accessed 27 June 2014.

25 For example, on claims that religiously conservative Protestants are the most negative in their attitudes towards lesbians and gay men, in contrast to the more positive perspectives of those from atheist, agnostic and Jewish traditions, see B Newman, 'Lesbians, Gays and Religion: Strategies for Challenging Belief Systems' (2002) 6 (3–4) *Journal of Lesbian Studies* 87–98. See also A Fulton, R Gorsuch and E Maynard, 'Religious Orientation, Antihomosexual Sentiment, and Fundamentalism among Christians' (1999) 38 (1) *Journal for the Scientific Study of Religion* 14–22.

26 *Eweida v UK* (n 1).

27 Introduced by the Civil Partnership Act 2004, civil partnerships afforded same-sex couples in the UK a legal status similar to that traditionally vested on married couples, as well as many of the same rights and responsibilities.

28 *Eweida* (n 1) para 105.

29 ibid paras 106, 109.

understandable, because given the highly emotive nature of the subject matter, the Court was almost certainly reluctant to find itself drawn into such a politically controversial area. Yet, on another level, the Court's approach is regrettable because it meant that an opportunity was probably missed for offering guidance to (other) law- and policymakers charged with having to balance conservative religious beliefs and LGBT rights in contemporary Europe.

In spite of the fact that the ECtHR dismissed the applications of Ladele and McFarlane, it is apposite to bear in mind that, in factual terms, their applications were quite different in two respects. For a start, while McFarlane was fully aware of the fact that he was under a positive duty to promote equality at the beginning of his time of employment with Relate (that is, by providing sex therapy both to opposite *and* to same-sex couples), there was no way that Ladele could have known, when accepting a job as a registrar with Islington Council, that one day legislation permitting civil partnerships would be passed and that, as a consequence, she would be then required to officiate at such ceremonies. Furthermore, a second factual difference between Ladele and McFarlane relates to the ease by which their respective employers could have accommodated their religious beliefs. Whereas McFarlane's request not to offer psycho-sexual counselling to same-sex couples was precluded by Relate's commitment to providing a service without discrimination (that is, it would not have been possible to filter clients on the basis of their sexual orientation), Islington Council could have chosen, had it so wished, to excuse Ladele from officiating at civil-partnership ceremonies by letting her undertake alternative duties – an option that some other councils had provided for their registrars who shared Ladele's concerns. As a consequence it has been suggested that Ladele was the 'real loser' in the case,[30] sentiments doubtlessly echoed by the Christian Institute, one of Ladele's key backers, which has described the European Court's ruling (and its subsequent refusal to refer the case to the Grand Chamber) as confirming their 'fears that people with Christian beliefs about marriage will be penalised in the workplace'.[31] Moreover, with claims that Ladele's application was rejected because she found herself on 'the wrong side of the line' of a 'state-sponsored sexual orthodoxy',[32] her case highlights the challenge of determining the extent to which conservative religious beliefs should be accommodated at the workplace in an increasingly secular age.

The Limits of Reasonable Accommodation: Conservative Religious Beliefs and LGBT Rights

From academics[33] and pressure groups[34] to politicians[35] and State-funded public bodies,[36] the question of whether the State should make provision for the reasonable accommodation of a person's religious beliefs at the workplace has garnered contributions from a range of different sources. Applicants such as Ladele would wish to answer such a question in the affirmative, whereas a commonly made argument against

30 M Hill, 'Lillian Ladele is the Real Loser in Christian Discrimination Rulings' (*The Guardian*, 17 January 2013) <www.theguardian.com/commentisfree/belief/2013/jan/17/lillian-ladele-loser-christian-discrimination-rulings> accessed 27 June 2014. See also M Hill, 'Religious Symbolism and Conscientious Objection in the Workplace: An Evaluation of Strasbourg's Judgment in *Eweida and Others v United Kingdom*' (2013) 15 (2) *Ecclesiastical Law Journal* 191–203.

31 <www.christian.org.uk/news/christian-registrar-denied-european-court-appeal/> accessed 27 June 2014.

32 Julian Rivers, as cited by A Donald et al, *Religion or Belief, Equality and Human Rights in England and Wales*, Equality and Human Rights Commission, Research report 84 (2012) 87 <www.equalityhumanrights.com/uploaded_files/research/rr84_final_opt.pdf> accessed 27 June 2014.

33 See, for example, K Alidadi, 'Reasonable Accommodations for Religion and Belief: Adding Value to Art.9 ECHR and the European Union's Anti-Discrimination Approach to Employment?' (2012) 37 (6) *European Law Review*, 693–715; E Bribosia, J Ringelheim and I Rorive, 'Reasonable Accommodation for Religious Minorities: A Promising Concept for European Antidiscrimination Law' (2010) 17 *Maastricht J Eur & Comp L* 137; A Somek, *Engineering Equality* (OUP 2011) 183–84.

34 See, for example, <www.secularism.org.uk/uploads/nss-response-to-ehrc-consultation-on-intervention-in-religious-discrimination-cases-at-ecthr.pdf> accessed 27 June 2014.

35 See, for example, Christians in Parliament, *Clearing the Ground* (2012) <www.eauk.org/current-affairs/publications/clearing-the-ground.cfm> accessed 27 June 2014.

36 See, for example, Equality and Human Rights Commission <www.equalityhumanrights.com/news/2011/july/commission-proposes-reasonable-accommodation-for-religion-or-belief-is-needed/>.

such accommodation is that claims of religious conscience should not be afforded any special right of exemption (or accommodation) from generally applicable legal obligations,[37] and that there is nothing quintessentially special about religious belief in terms of its accommodation in public life.[38] By advocating the recognition 'of *legally enshrined* reasonable accommodation on the basis of religion *and* belief in the workplace' (second emphasis added) (*Report*, 19), the RELIGARE report accepts that certain religious or equivalent secular beliefs should, in principle, be so accommodated. But what are the permissible limits of such accommodation? In seeking to examine this question, it is perhaps useful to return, briefly, to the facts of *Ladele*. For example, what if Islington Council had accommodated Ladele's *religiously* motivated claim? Had this been the case, would it have also then been required to accommodate a range of other seemingly comparable requests – such as that of a registrar who was unwilling, say, to marry inter-racial couples on *racist* grounds? In other words, was there a risk that any such accommodation of religious belief would have opened the floodgates for the accommodation of other (less palatable) forms of belief, such as white supremacist or racist world views?

At first glance there might seem to be a compelling case for treating an avowedly religious registrar no differently from a *racist* one.[39] However, on closer inspection, these apparently similar scenarios can perhaps be distinguished on four grounds.

A first distinction between race and religion in this regard relates to the nature of the motivation of the relevant actor. Thus, for example, the avowedly racist registrar who refuses to marry inter-racial couples is likely to be doing so on the basis of a secular political philosophy that has little connection with the metaphysics of an ultimate reality,[40] or what John Hick calls 'a human response to the transcendent'.[41] In contrast, however, the motivation of *religious* registrars like Ladele will typically be much more complicated and multi-faceted.[42] For example, they may not just genuinely believe that it is 'spiritually' wrong for them to conduct such same-sex unions, but that, if they were to do so, there is a risk of them being subject to the divine wrath of an omnipotent deity in an afterlife.[43] In our largely secular age it is of course tempting to sneer at such bizarre and irrational considerations, yet in recent years there have been occasions where litigants have made the case for the accommodation of their religious belief on the basis of such fears.[44] Accordingly, the *consequences* of undertaking work-related duties that rest uneasily with one's conscience are potentially much

---

37 A powerful case is made against religious exemptions by Brian Leiter in *Why Tolerate Religion?* (Princeton University Press 2013).

38 On this debate generally see, for example, G Cornelissen, 'Belief-Based Exemptions: Are Religious Beliefs Special?' (2012) 25 (1) *Ratio Juris* 85–109; M McGann, 'Equal Treatment and Exceptions' (2012) 38 (1) *Social Theory and Practice* 1–32; Y Nehushtan, 'Religious Conscientious Exceptions' (2011) 30 (2) *Law and Philosophy* 143–66; MP Ferretti, 'Exemptions for Whom? On the Relevant Focus of Egalitarian Concern' (2009) 15 (3) *Res Publica* 269–87; S Bedi, 'Debate: What is so Special about Religion? The Dilemma of the Religious Exemption' (2007) 15 (2) *Journal of Political Philosophy* 235–49.

39 On claims of parallels between Rosa Parks, racial discrimination and the actions of Ladele, see R McCrea, 'Strasbourg Judgment in *Eweida and Others v the United Kingdom*' <http://ukconstitutionallaw.org/2013/01/16/ronan-mccrea-strasbourg-judgement-in-eweida-and-others-v-united-kingdom/> accessed 27 June 2014.

40 On racist motives generally see, for example, G Schutte, *What Racists Believe: Race Relations in South Africa and the United States* (Sage 1995); R McVeigh, 'Structured Ignorance and Organized Racism in the United States' (2004) 82 (3) *Social Forces* 895–936.

41 J Hick, *An Interpretation of Religion: Human Responses to the Transcendent* (Palgrave Macmillan 2004).

42 The possibility of religiously inspired forms of racism is acknowledged – such as by virtue of the membership, say, of a white supremacist church – but such organisations, which are largely confined to the US, are numerically very small, and their teachings are condemned by all mainstream Christian denominations.

43 For example, there is evidence to suggest that, among Christian denominations, 'fundamentalist Protestants' have the strongest belief in notions of heaven and hell; J Exline, 'Belief in Heaven and Hell among Christians in the United States: Denominational Differences and Clinical Implications' (2003) 47 (2) *OMEGA – Journal of Death and Dying* 155–68. Moreover, the fear of possible punishment in an afterlife is not unique to Christianity. See, for example, N Ghorbani, P Watson and K Shahmohamadi, 'Afterlife Motivation Scale: Correlations with Maladjustment and Incremental Validity in Iranian Muslims' (2008) 18 (1) *The International Journal for the Psychology of Religion* 22–35.

44 See, for example, *R (on the application of Ghai) v Newcastle City Council (Ramgharia Gurdwara, Hitchin and Another Intervening)* [2010] EWCA Civ 59, where fears of punishment in an afterlife underpinned the applicant's request (subsequently accepted by the UK's Court of Appeal) to be cremated on a Hindu funeral pyre.

greater for the religiously conservative registrar than for the racist registrar whose motivation is typically based on a secular racist world view.[45]

Secondly, a key difference between religion and race for the purposes of this discussion is demonstrated by the fact that reasonable accommodation has long been associated with the manifestation of religious beliefs – but not racist ones – at the workplace. A case in point relates to employees' rights in the field of medical law. After all, legally enshrined conscience clauses have often afforded respect to the religious convictions of health-care professionals,[46] most notably in relation to abortion.[47] For example, a Scottish Court recently found for two midwives who objected, on the basis of their Catholic faith, to participating in the termination of pregnancies,[48] whereas no such accommodation would have been made for the beliefs of, say, midwives wishing to so act on racial grounds. By the same token, additional parallels can be drawn with the area of conscientious objection to military service. For example, while the ECtHR would almost certainly reject any request to accommodate the beliefs of, say, a racist soldier who objected to undertaking military service on account of his/her refusal to kill people of the same skin colour, the Court has, in recent years, shown itself to be increasingly willing to attach considerable weight to the wishes of those who object to military service on the grounds of a religious or philosophical belief.[49]

A third difference between race and religion in this context relates to an employee's sense of identity. While racists may identify with other racists by virtue of the same skin colour[50] or even a shared pastime,[51] the extent to which their intolerance of other races may directly provide them with a deep-rooted sense of personal identity is questionable,[52] in contrast, say, to zealous religious devotees, whose sense of self is often powerfully shaped by their faith.[53] Scholars have long commented on the correlation between a person's religious beliefs and his or her sense of identity,[54] with even the European Court of Human Rights having acknowledged that, for a significant number of people, religion remains 'one of the most vital elements that go to make up [their] identity'.[55] Therefore, the legal obligation on, say, registrars from a conservative religious tradition to undertake a task which, for them, raises fundamental issues of conscience, potentially strikes at the heart of their very identity in a way that is unlikely to so affect a comparable racist employee.

And finally, there is an obvious difference in societal attitudes to forms of intolerance based on race and those based on religion. For example, were a council registrar to refuse to marry a couple on racial grounds, she/he would almost inevitably face widespread public scorn, but this appears not to have been the case

45 Admittedly, while some racist political philosophies, such as fascism (*X v Italy No 6741/74*, 5 DR 83 (1976)) and neo-Nazi principles *(X v Austria No 1747/62*, 13 CD 42 (1963)), have on occasion been held to constitute 'beliefs' for the purposes of Article 9 of the ECHR, they can nonetheless be distinguished – at least on one level – from 'religions' on the basis of their lack of relevance to matters generally pertaining to spirituality or metaphysics.

46 See, for example, D Weinstock, 'Conscientious Refusal and Health Professionals: Does Religion Make a Difference?' (2014) 28 (1) *Bioethics* 8–15; and L Ross and T Aspinwall, 'Religious Exemptions to the Immunization Statutes: Balancing Public Health and Religious Freedom' (1997) 25 (2–3) *Journal of Law, Medicine and Ethics* 202–09.

47 See, for example, in the context of the UK, The Abortion Act 1967, s 4(1); *Janaway v Salford Health Authority* [1989] AC 537, HL.

48 See *Doogan & Anor v NHS Greater Glasgow & Clyde Health Board* [2013] Scot CS CSIH 36.

49 See, for example, *Bayatyan v Armenia*, no 23459/03 [2011] ECtHR (GC) 1095 (7 July 2011); *Ercep v Turkey* (no 43965/04) 22 November 2011 (HUDOC).

50 See generally B Fields, 'Whiteness, Racism and Identity' (2001) 60 *International Labor and Working-Class History* 48–56.

51 See, for example, P Dimeo and G Finn, 'Racism, National Identity and Scottish Football' [2001] *Race, Sport and British Society* 29–48.

52 See, for example, B Dobratz, 'The Role of Religion in the Collective Identity of the White Racialist Movement' (2001) 40 (2) *Journal for the Scientific Study of Religion* 287–302, who found that differences of religion between white racialist groups were likely to make such groups potentially antagonistic to each other.

53 See, for example, B Parekh, 'Religion and Public Life' in T Modood (ed), *Church, State and Religious Minorities* (PSI 1997) 21.

54 See, for example, V Kahani-Hopkins and N Hopkins, '"Representing" British Muslims: The Strategic Dimension to Identity Construction' (2002) 25 (2) *Ethnic and Racial Studies* 288–309; A Saeed, N Blain and D Forbes, 'New Ethnic and National Questions in Scotland: Post-British Identities among Glasgow Pakistani Teenagers' (1999) 22 (5) *Ethnic and Racial Studies* 821–44.

55 *Kokkinakis v Greece* (1994) 17 EHRR 397, para 31.

with Lillian Ladele who – at least in some quarters of the press – has been portrayed in sympathetic terms.[56] Furthermore, the suggestion that her religiously inspired actions are akin to those of a racist registrar is particularly ironic, not least because Lillian Ladele is a black British woman from a Nigerian background. Indeed, in this respect, it is striking that a significant number of the religiously motivated applicants in these 'faith/LGBT' cases are themselves of ethnic minority origin. After all, of Ladele's co-applicants in *Eweida*, Gary McFarlane is also black, while Nadia Eweida, who grew up in Egypt, is a Coptic Christian. With some of the fastest growing religious groups in Europe being black evangelical churches that eschew a liberal approach to LGBT issues,[57] any suggestion that conservative religious attitudes to LGBT rights are akin to racist beliefs is unlikely to be well received in many of the very communities that have experienced the evils of racism.

Reasonable Accommodation, Faith, LGBT Rights – Where Do We Go from Here?

The publication of the RELIGARE report provides an ideal opportunity for generating wider debate, not merely on the specific issue of whether there are differences between race and religion in the context of a State official who objects to providing services to a specific section of the public, but also on the more general relationship between manifestations of faith and LGBT rights at the workplace. In addition, the report provides a fresh opportunity to consider how a Europe that is increasingly accepting of same-sex relationships should respond to those who, on religious grounds, wish to elevate heterosexual relationships above homosexual ones.

One commonly expressed view is that litigants such as Ladele are little more than 'awkward customers',[58] who should either confine their beliefs to the private sphere, or swiftly accept the moral authority of judges' rulings on LGBT rights. Yet neither scenario is foreseeable. In relation to the former it is hard to imagine that large numbers of morally conservative believers will suddenly retreat from public life or refrain from seeking employment in certain contentious areas, not least because their sacred texts often exhort them to express their beliefs in the public domain.[59] And with regard to the latter, there is no evidence to suggest that the members of such religious groups are – even in the wake of frequent defeats under Article 9 of the ECHR – any more likely to adopt a liberal stance to LGBT rights. On the contrary, if anything, it seems that cases such as *Ladele* and *McFarlane* have convinced many religious conservatives of the legitimacy of their cause.[60]

Recent judicial interpretation of human rights and equality legislation appears to have created the impression, in some communities, that secular judges are using human rights law to trample religious freedoms.[61] For example, in cases involving conservative Christians – ranging from bed-and-breakfast owners refusing to provide a double room to two gay men in a civil partnership[62] to a married couple being rejected as prospective foster carers because of their views about homosexuality[63] – there has generally been one

56 See, for example, M Judge, 'The Forgotten Bullying of the Registrar Who Dared to Believe in Marriage' (*The Huffington Post*, 1 June 2013) <www.huffingtonpost.co.uk/mike-judge/the-forgotten-bullying-of-registrar-who-dared-believe-in-marriage_b_3364349.html> accessed 27 June 2014.

57 See, for example, Brierley Consultancy, 'London's Churches are Growing' (2013) <www.brierleyconsultancy.com/images/londonchurches.pdf> accessed 27 June 2014.

58 See, for example, *The Guardian*, Editorial (15 January 2013): 'The quartet of devout appellants considered by Strasbourg … might, putting it politely, be described as awkward customers' <www.theguardian.com/commentisfree/2013/jan/15/religious-freedom-strasbourg> accessed 27 June 2014.

59 See, for example, Matthew 5:13–16, which enjoins believers to be like 'salt and light' for the world.

60 For example, see the criticisms of the former Archbishop of Canterbury, Lord Carey, in *McFarlane v Relate Avon Ltd* [2010] EWCA Civ B1, at para 17. See also 'Pope Condemns Gay Equality Laws ahead of First UK Visit' (*The Guardian*, 1 February 2010) <www.theguardian.com/world/2010/feb/01/pope-condemns-british-equality-bill> accessed 27 June 2014.

61 See, for example, R Trigg, *Equality, Freedom and Religion* (OUP 2012) 121.

62 See, for example, *Bull and Another v Hall and Another* [2013] UKSC 73.

63 See *Johns v Derby City Council and Equality and Human Rights Commission* (intervening) [2011] EWHC 375 (Admin).

outcome: the conservative faith litigants have lost. Accordingly, there appears to be a strong belief in some Christian circles that human rights norms are akin to a 'Trojan horse', being more likely to undermine, rather than protect, religious freedom.[64]

While it could be argued that the apparent alienation of some obdurate religious believers is of little (if any) public consequence, it is suggested that there are, nonetheless, three reasons why it may be prudent not to ignore this state of affairs. To begin with, it is surely a matter of concern if a potentially significant section of society – be it religious or secular – appears to lack confidence in the nation's human rights laws. Furthermore, the risk cannot be discounted that, at some point in the future, members of other faiths will bring cases of the kind that have been recently brought by conservative Christians – a salutary consideration being that Muslim leaders recently joined forces with some Christian churches to oppose the enactment of same-sex marriage legislation in the UK.[65] And finally, it is significant that – in relation to LGBT rights – not merely have some faith groups evidently been impervious to the influence of equality laws, enacted with the aim of eliminating intolerance,[66] but that, from the perspective of certain faith communities themselves, such laws have exacerbated intercommunal tensions.

In acknowledging the limitations of equality and human rights laws when it comes to changing the attitudes of obdurate believers,[67] there is a strong case for focusing attention on the potential contribution of 'non-legal' strategies as a way of resolving disputes or helping to defuse tensions between some faith and LGBT groups at the workplace. At first glance it might appear that any rapprochement in this regard between the very people who have often been 'the catalysts behind anti-gay-rights initiatives'[68] and LGBT communities would be impossible. However, on closer analysis, it is axiomatic that a number of basic values are shared by conservative faith and LGBT groups. These include 'dignity',[69] 'compassion'[70] and 'empathy'[71] – all being values that, individually and collectively, can help to provide a useful foundation for the resolution of disputes in the field of human rights.[72]

In a previous generation Mahatma Gandhi is believed to have said to a Christian missionary, 'I would suggest that you study non-Christian religions and culture more sympathetically in order to find the good that is in them, so you might have a more sympathetic approach to the people'.[73] Perhaps similar sentiments could apply to contemporary faith–LGBT dialogue. An ability to stand in the shoes of 'the other' is certainly a crucial prerequisite for effective dialogue.[74] Thus, were it possible for conservative religious believers to make a leap of 'imaginative identification',[75] enabling them to view the universe from an LGBT perspective – and vice versa – the number of disputes requiring adjudication in the court-room might be reduced, and some of the 'fear' that often underlies such disputes could be diminished.[76]

---

64 See 'Human Rights Act Undermines Christian Values Warns Bishop', *The Sunday Telegraph* (1 October 2000) 1.

65 See 'British Imams and Muslim Leaders Speak out against the Marriage (Same Sex Couples) Bill' (*The Daily Telegraph*, 18 May 2013) <www.telegraph.co.uk/comment/letters/10065280/Muslim-leaders-stand-against-gay-marriage.html> accessed 27 June 2014.

66 On what has been (sardonically) referred to as creating a world 'inhabited by better people', see, for example, Somek (n 33) 15.

67 On the impact of the legal as a vehicle for changing social attitudes generally, see, for example, T Tyler, *Why People Obey the Law* (Princeton University Press 1990); H Tang et al, 'Changes of Attitudes and Patronage Behaviors in Response to a Smoke-Free Bar Law' (2003) 93 (4) *American Journal of Public Health* 611–17.

68 ML Rubinstein, 'Gay Rights and Religion: A Doctrinal Approach to the Argument that Anti-Gay-Rights Initiatives Violate the Establishment Clause' (1995) 46 *Hastings Law Journal* 1585.

69 C McRudden, 'Religion, Human Rights, Equality and the Public Sphere' (2011) 13 (1) *Ecclesiastical Law Journal* 26–38.

70 M Nussbaum, 'Compassion: The Basic Social Emotion' (1996) 13 (1) *Social Philosophy & Policy* 27–58.

71 L Hunt, *Inventing Human Rights: A History* (Norton 2007).

72 See, for example, C Gearty, *Can Human Rights Survive (The Hamlyn Lectures)* (CUP 2006) 43.

73 B McLaren, *Why Did Jesus, Moses, the Buddha and Mohammed Cross the Road?* (Hodder and Stoughton 2012) 253.

74 On this generally see R Rorty, 'Human Rights, Rationality, and Sentimentality' <www.nyu.edu/classes/gmoran/3RORTY.pdf> accessed 27 June 2014.

75 R Rorty, *Contingency Irony and Solidarity* (CUP 1989) 93.

76 On this generally see, for example, M Nussbaum, *The New Religious Intolerance: Overcoming the Politics of Fear in an Anxious Age* (Harvard University Press 2012) 3, who suggests that, in overcoming the phenomenon of fear there

In seeking to facilitate this noble aim, it is perhaps worth considering hitherto unconsidered alternatives by thinking 'outside the box'. This could include looking further afield to see whether there are, for example, any lessons to be learnt from what has been termed the 'applied legal storytelling' model in the United States.[77] This model has seen legal scholars using narratives to build on such commonly held values as empathy in order to better connect parties in a range of areas as diverse as criminal justice,[78] corporate responsibility,[79] terrorism[80] and the rights of the child.[81] Thus, by seeking to promote intergroup dialogue through the construction of personal narratives, scholars in this field have recognised that the law is not the only mechanism for the successful resolution of disputes or shaping of positive social attitudes.[82] Accordingly, with suggestions that the construction of narratives has been an important tool in highlighting racial intolerance and discrimination,[83] it is possible that such a 'storytelling' strategy could generate interest in the challenge of fostering (largely unheard of) faith/LGBT engagement in parts of contemporary Europe.

It is, of course, axiomatic that tensions between conservative faith and LGBT communities are deep seated, so it would be naive to expect any seismic attitudinal changes in the foreseeable future. Yet, by the same token, the chances of dialogue between some religious groups and LGBT communities have increased in recent years on account of a fresh willingness by people of faith, in at least some parts of the world, to take account of LGBT rights.[84] For example, various factors appear to suggest that reform is taking place, particularly within the Christian tradition. These factors include: the emergence of Christian groups that see LGBT rights as being fully compatible with their faith;[85] the increasing willingness of some Christian leaders to 'defy' conservative church teaching on LGBT matters;[86] a new desire on the part of some senior Christian leaders (for example, Pope Francis[87] and the Archbishop of Canterbury[88]) to reach out to homosexuals; and even reports that certain denominations which have, to date, officially resisted recognition of same-sex marriage are now considering offering '"weddings in all but name" for same sex-couples'.[89] Admittedly, these

---

needs to be 'a systematic cultivation of … the imaginative capacity … to see how the world looks from the point of view of a person different in religion or ethnicity'.

77 A Robbins, 'An Introduction to Applied Legal Storytelling' (2008) 14 *Legal Writing* 17.

78 See, for example, L Olsen-Fulero and SM Fulero, 'An Empathy-Complexity Theory of Rape Juror Story Making' (1997) 3 *Psychol Pub Policy and Law* 402; SE Sundby, 'The Capital Jury and Empathy: The Problem of Worthy and Unworthy Victims' (2002–2003) 88 *Cornell Law Review* 343.

79 See, for example, JL Schroeder, 'Economic Rationality, Empathy, and Corporate Responsibility' (2002) 70 *Geo Wash L Rev* 875.

80 See, for example, WD Casebeer, 'Identity, Culture and Stories: Empathy and the War on Terrorism' (2008) 9 *Minn L L Sci & Tech* 653; MD Falkoff, 'Conspiracy to Commit Poetry: Empathetic Lawyering at Guantanamo Bay' (2007) 6 *Seattle Journal for Social Justice* 3.

81 See, for example, S Nauss Exon, 'The Best Interest of the Child: Going beyond Legalize to Empathize with a Client's Leap of Faith' (2003–2004) 24 *UC Davis Journal of Juvenile Law and Policy* 1.

82 See, for example, R Delgado, 'Storytelling for Oppositionists and Others: A Plea for Narrative' (1989) 87 *Michigan Law Review* 2411; K Abrams, 'Hearing the Call of Stories' (1991) 79 *Cal L Rev* 971.

83 See, for example, M Matsuda, 'Public Response to Racist Speech: Considering the Victim's Story' (1989) 87 *Mich L Rev* 2320; J Suggs, *Whispered Consolations: Law and Narrative in African American Life* (University of Michigan Press 2000); C Haney, 'Condemning the Other in Death Penalty Trials: Biographical Racism, Structural Mitigation, and the Empathic Divide' (2004) 53 *DePaul L Rev* 1557.

84 See, for example, <http://publicreligion.org/research/2011/03/for-catholics-open-attitudes-on-gay-issues/> accessed 27 June 2014.

85 See, for example, LW Countryman and M Ritley, *Gifted by Otherness: Gay and Lesbian Christians in the Church* (Morehouse Publishing 2001).

86 J Creech, *Adam's Gift: A Memoir of a Pastor's Calling to Defy the Church's Persecution of Lesbians and Gays* (Duke University Press 2011).

87 See, for example, 'Pope Francis Calls for Catholic Church Re-Think on Gay Parents' (*The Huffington Post*, 1 May 2014) <www.huffingtonpost.com/2014/01/05/pope-francis-gay-parents-_n_4542026.html> accessed 27 June 2014.

88 See, for example, 'Archbishop Urges Christians to "Repent" over "Wicked" Attitude to Homosexuality' (*The Daily Telegraph*, 28 August 2013) <www.telegraph.co.uk/news/religion/10271438/Archbishop-urges-Christians-to-repent-over-wicked-attitude-to-homosexuality.html> accessed 27 June 2014.

89 See 'Church of England Considers "Weddings in all but Name" for Same Sex Couples' (*The Daily Telegraph*, 28 November 2013) <www.telegraph.co.uk/news/religion/10481921/Church-of-England-considers-weddings-in-all-but-name-for-same-sex-couples.html> accessed 27 June 2014.

factors are counterbalanced by the fact that faith groups in Eastern Europe tend to be much less receptive to any recognition of LGBT rights than their Western European counterparts,[90] and that this greater acceptance of homosexuality by some (Western) Christian traditions has not been matched by any significant 'internal' transformation in faiths such as Islam.[91] Nonetheless, with evidence suggesting that attitudes to LGBT issues are softening among many evangelical Christians[92] and that young people are more accepting of gay rights than their elders,[93] it is possible that, in the future, hostility to LGBT rights will, like racism is today, be officially condemned by many mainstream denominations, thereby potentially obviating the courts of the need to adjudicate (at least so often) in this most emotive of areas.

Conclusion

Human rights and equalities laws in Europe have played, and continue to play, a crucial role in eliminating intolerance and discrimination. Yet, as has been argued above, they have certain limitations, especially when it comes to the highly emotive relationship between conservative tenets of faith and human sexuality. In this regard, many of the RELIGARE proposals, such as those that 'encourage platforms for exchange of "good business" practices in respect of granting requests for religious accommodation ... across EU Member States' are potentially extremely valuable (*Report*, 22). After all, there is evidently a need for innovative strategies that may assist in facilitating better relations between all relevant parties – and might also help, for example, to assuage the fears of those who are concerned about their religious freedom being threatened by the State affording equal rights to LGBT communities, without undermining or jeopardising hard-won LGBT rights.

With a significant increase in the number of national legislatures and courts in Europe that have afforded recognition to same-sex marriage in recent years,[94] the likelihood that other State officials, on the grounds of faith, will refuse to officiate at such marriage ceremonies increases. Whereas in *Ladele* it was a conservative Christian who (unsuccessfully) sought reasonable accommodation of her religious beliefs, on another occasion it could be a Muslim or an orthodox Jewish public servant who refuses to undertake certain work-related duties. In situations of this kind the risk of social disharmony might possibly be mitigated if there were appropriate fora to assist in the 'informal' resolution of resultant conflicts, thereby obviating the need for litigation. But in the apparent absence of any such scenario, the risk remains of Europe's judges finding themselves increasingly mired in acrimonious disputes between conservative religious and LGBT groups, with tensions further heightened by well-reported (and generally unfounded) claims of religious persecution. In these circumstances the 'winners' will be determined by the courts – but the real 'loser' could be the advancement of a fair and effective European equalities agenda.

90 See, for example, 'Eastern and Western Europe Divided over Gay Marriage, Homosexuality' <www.pewresearch.org/fact-tank/2013/12/12/eastern-and-western-europe-divided-over-gay-marriage-homosexuality/> accessed 27 June 2014.

91 While some have questioned the traditional interpretation of the Quran that forbids homosexual activity (see, for example, S Kugle, *Homosexuality in Islam: Critical Reflection on Gay, Lesbian, and Transgender Muslims* (Oneworld 2010)), the dominant view among Muslims is that same-sex relationships are incompatible with Islam.

92 See, for example, Baylor University, 'The "Messy Middle": Many Evangelicals are Ambivalent about Homosexuality and Civil Unions for Gays, Baylor Study Shows' (2013) <www.baylor.edu/mediacommunications/news.php?action=story&story=131931>.

93 See, for example, Lancaster University, 'Over 60s and under 50s Sharply Divided on B&B Gay Discrimination, New Survey Shows' (2013) <www.religionandsociety.org.uk/uploads/docs/2013_10/1381315862_Christian_B&B_poll_Press_Release.pdf> accessed 27 June 2014.

94 See generally K Boele-Woelki and A Fuchs (eds), *Legal Recognition of Same-Sex Relationships in Europe* (Intersentia 2012).

Chapter 15

The Effective Protection of the Freedom of Religion: The ECtHR's Variable Margin of Appreciation Regarding Religion–State Relations and the Rule of Law

Kristin Henrard

Introduction

Globalisation and related migration streams in combination with diversification of particular religious movements and the emergence of entirely new religious movements lead to ever increasing levels of religious diversity. Not surprisingly, and as confirmed by the RELIGARE project report, States are increasingly confronted with difficult, often controversial questions pertaining to their relationship to religion, particularly religious movements, their institutions and the manifestation of religion in the public sphere.[1]

The RELIGARE report highlights in this respect controversies about State support and State discrimination against new confessional groups and churches and the contours of the individual and collective right to freedom of religion. The recommendations call for the development of a coherent policy framework by EU institutions that would guide the Member States. In this respect it is good to recall that the European Convention on Human Rights (ECHR) and the multiple obligations it enshrines are not only binding on all EU Member States, but that the EU itself also recognises that fundamental rights as guaranteed by the ECHR constitute general principles of EU law by which it is bound.[2] Hence, the ECHR, as interpreted by the European Court of Human Rights (ECtHR), determines the outer framework for policy decisions of the EU institutions and the Member States. In relation to religion, it is thus relevant to the ECtHR's jurisprudence on the freedom of religion as enshrined in Article 9 of the ECHR (and its educational dimension – framed as the rights of the parents – in Article 2 of the first additional protocol) and the prohibition against discrimination on grounds of religion as laid out in Article 14, adding an important non-discrimination gloss.[3]

One of the central lines of jurisprudence of the Court concerns the need for the Convention to be interpreted in a manner which renders its rights 'practical and effective, not theoretical and illusory'.[4] Effective protection of fundamental rights can also be related to important interpretative principles, most notably the injunction that the scope of application of fundamental rights should be interpreted generously, while the scope of legitimate limitations should be interpreted narrowly.[5] A system with the protection of fundamental rights as its foundational rationale obviously considers protection of human rights as the baseline, while limitations on human rights are the exception. This also implies that once something falls within the scope of application of a fundamental right, it needs to be protected. Only when public authorities have good and specific reasons to limit the enjoyment of these rights are they allowed to do so. Arguably this points to a rather high level

1 See also K Henrard, *The Ambiguous Relationship between Religious Minorities and Fundamental (Minority) Rights* (Boom Eleven International 2011) 7.

2 See Article 6(3) TFEU and Article 52(3) EU Charter of Fundamental Rights.

3 See also F Tulkens, 'The European Convention on Human Rights and Church–State Relations: Pluralism vs. Pluralism' (2009) 30 *Cardozo Law Review* 2575.

4 Two examples of prominent Grand Chamber judgments are *Bayatyan v Armenia*, 7 July 2011, para 98, and *Chassagnou and Others v France*, 24 April 1999, para 100. See also A Mowbray, 'The Creativity of the European Court of Human Rights' (2005) 5 *Human Rights Law Review* 57–79, 78; O Spiermann, 'Twentieth Century Internationalism in Law' (2008) 18 *EJIL* 785–814, 802.

5 N Jayawickrama, *The Judicial Application of Human Rights Law: National, Regional and International Jurisprudence* (CUP 2002) 184.

of scrutiny as a baseline.[6] Put differently, the ECtHR should make sure that States respect the conditions for legitimate limitations so that these limitations do not amount to violations of the rights concerned. Of central importance is that a limitation be proportionate to the legitimate aim it is supposed to realise.[7] The effective protection of the freedom crucially depends, then, on the level of scrutiny adopted by the supervisor in relation to the proportionality test. When the level of scrutiny is high, the level of protection of the right concerned is high, and the discretion left to States (by the supervisor) is narrow.

Nevertheless, early on the ECtHR has devised the margin of appreciation doctrine, following which States are granted a certain amount of discretion in assessing (and deciding) whether restrictions and limitations are indeed proportionate, and more generally in the way in which they fulfil their obligations under the Convention.[8] This discretion would be justified because of the subsidiary nature of the supervision exercised by the Court, as the contracting parties carry the primary responsibility. Furthermore, the national authorities would be better placed to assess what limitations or restrictions would be reasonable and appropriate given the specific local particularities.[9] The RELIGARE project report does acknowledge that the margin of appreciation is not unlimited, but it nevertheless appears to limit the Court's scrutiny of the national decision-making processes in terms of 'due process' (*Report*, 50). However, the argumentation here proceeds on a richer baseline scrutiny that attaches more weight to the substance of the balancing.[10] Following this view, the determination of the level of scrutiny and its corollary, the width of the margin of appreciation, deserves more attention than the RELIGARE report acknowledges.

Several steady lines of jurisprudence arguably point to the appropriateness of a vigorous protection of the freedom of religion for the diversity of religious groups present in a particular State, which would imply a narrow margin of appreciation for States. Not only is the freedom of religion qualified as one of the cornerstones of a democratic society, and religious pluralism is recognised by the Court as one of the central principles of the freedom of religion,[11] religion is also considered to be one of the most vital components of the identity of believers.[12] In relation to religious pluralism, the Court furthermore emphasises that States are supposed to be neutral and impartial organisers of the means necessary for the exercise of various religions, faiths and beliefs, while their overall role is meant to be conducive to religious harmony and tolerance.[13]

The Court has, however, chosen to focus on the alleged lack of a common European standard regarding religion–State relations to grant States a wide margin of appreciation in these matters.[14] This wide margin of appreciation for States goes hand in hand with lenient scrutiny, not only regarding the assessment of alleged interferences with the freedom of religion, but also concerning the alleged lack of fulfilment of positive obligations aimed at the effective protection and accommodation of freedom of religion.[15] Consequently, the freedom to manifest one's religion is in several respects not protected effectively enough.[16]

---

6 G Itzcovich, 'One, None and One Hundred Thousand Margins of Appreciations: The Lautsi Case' (2013) *Human Rights Law Review* 7–17, 10.

7 M Kumm, 'Democracy is not Enough: Rights, Proportionality and the Point of Judicial Review' in M Klatt (ed), *The Legal Philosophy of Robert Alexy* (OUP 2009) 1.

8 JA Brauch, 'The Margin of Appreciation and the Jurisprudence of the European Court of Human Rights: Threat to the Rule of Law' (2005) 11 *Columbia Journal of European Law* 115.

9 Y Arai-Takahashi, 'The Margin of Appreciation Doctrine: A Theoretical Analysis of Strasbourg's Variable Geometry' in A Follesdal, B Peters and G Ulfstein (eds), *Constituting Europe: The ECtHR in a National, European and Global Context* (CUP 2013) 62–105, 62–63; D Spielmann, 'Allowing the Right Margin: The European Court of Human Rights and the National Margin of Appreciation Doctrine: Waiver or Subsidiarity of European Review?' (2012) CELS Working Paper Series 4–5.

10 For a more elaborate discussion, see K Henrard, 'A Critical Appraisal of the Margin of Appreciation Left to States Pertaining to "Church–State Relations" under the Jurisprudence of the ECtHR' in K Alidadi, M-C Foblets and J Vrielink (eds), *A Test of Faith? Religious Diversity and Accommodation in the European Workplace* (Ashgate 2012) 59–86.

11 *Nolan and K. v Russia*, 12 February 2009, para 73.

12 *Kokkinakis v Greece*, 25 May 1993, para 31.

13 Tulkens (n 3).

14 ibid 2557–78.

15 A Hambler, 'A Private Matter? Evolving Approaches to the Freedom to Manifest Religious Convictions in the Workplace' (2008) 3 *Religion and Human Rights* 111–33, 121–24.

16 Tulkens (n 3) 2577–78; S Rorive, 'Religious Symbols in the Public Space: In Search of a European Answer' (2008–2009) 30 *Cardozo Law Review* 2669–98, 2682.

Strikingly, the Court has never even hinted at an attempt to identify the contours of the concept 'religion–State relations'. When one considers the different strands of jurisprudence that are put in this frame of analysis, though, it seems almost like a term that encompasses all cases pertaining to the freedom to manifest one's religion (including in the educational sphere). Although there has been no official revocation or reversal of this line of jurisprudence, the Court's reasoning in several cases over the past few years has led to cautious suggestions of a shift in the jurisprudence away from a broad margin of appreciation regarding 'religion–State relations'. It has even been intimated that the Court appears to be elaborating a coherent (overarching) theory regarding rights, religion and the public sphere.[17] However, on closer scrutiny it is simply not possible to make such a general statement. This is also related to the sheer breadth of issues that the Court's jurisprudence marks as concerning 'religion–State relations'.

This chapter aims to demonstrate that in fact the Court adopts different levels of scrutiny for distinctive sub-themes of 'religion–State relations' (several of which concern the controversies enumerated above), without, however, making this differentiation explicit, let alone identifying the relevant variables in this respect. As space constraints do not allow me to cover this topic comprehensively, in the following analysis I will limit myself to identifying various themes for which the Court has already reduced States' margin of appreciation in religious matters, more particularly concerning the registration of religions/churches, respect for church autonomy, and respect for conscientious objectors. At the same time the analysis shows that, in regard to several other religious matters, attempts to reduce States' margin of appreciation have not been successful, including in the protection of the fundamental rights of members of churches and duties of reasonable accommodation in the employment sphere. Because these differential margins of appreciation are not acknowledged, let alone argued and justified, they go hand in hand with an extensive degree of unpredictability. This unpredictability threatens not only the rule of law, the hallmark of the ECtHR system, but also the emergence of a coherent policy framework as envisaged by the RELIGARE report. Consequently, a fuller, more transparent and consistent argumentation of the Court's determination of the width of the margin of appreciation concerning 'religion–State relations' is advocated here.

The Rule of Law and Legal Certainty versus Unpredictable Margins of Appreciation

In addition to the fundamental concerns about the margin of appreciation hinted at above,[18] the Court is regularly criticised for the way in which it uses the margin of appreciation doctrine. A sustained criticism has been voiced regarding the inconsistent way in which the Court uses this doctrine, and also the various factors that it has identified as influencing the width of the margin in concrete instances. The Court has indeed identified several factors that determine the width of the margin of appreciation, which in theory could bring more precision to its application.[19] However, overall the Court's reasoning on the width of the margin of appreciation is rather shallow. The Court does not use these factors in any systematic way, and often does not really argue why it focuses on only one factor while others are in play, or why it attaches preponderant weight to one over the other factors.[20]

Unsurprisingly, a recurring criticism concerns the inconsistencies in the application of the doctrine on the margin of appreciation.[21] Arai-Takahashi notes in this respect that 'inconsistent and opaque modality of operation ... might stultify rationality expectations'.[22] Indeed, a lot of uncertainty remains about the width of the margin of appreciation, thus making accurate predictions in this respect extremely difficult if not

17 J Ringelheim, 'Rights, Religion and the Public Sphere: The European Court of Human Rights in Search of a Theory?' in C Ungureanu and L Zucca (eds), *A European Dilemma: Religion and the Public Sphere* (CUP 2012) 283–304, 303–04.

18 See also Henrard (n 10).

19 Brauch (n 8) 127.

20 P Mahoney, 'Marvellous Richness of Diversity or Invidious Cultural Relativism?' (1998) 19 *Human Rights Law Journal* 4; J Kratochvil, 'The Inflation of the Margin of Appreciation by the European Court of Human Rights' (2011) 29 *Netherlands Quarterly of Human Rights* 324–57, 357.

21 Kratochvil (n 20) 336–43; P Gallagher, 'The European Convention on Human Rights and the Margin of Appreciation' (2012) UCD Working Papers in Law, Criminology & Socio-Legal Studies Research Paper No. 52/2011, 11–21.

22 Arai-Takahashi (n 9) 79–80.

impossible (including when various relevant factors are in play but they pull in opposite directions).[23] The resulting lack of legal certainty is said to have a corrosive effect on the rule of law,[24] and the margin of appreciation doctrine of the Court has even been called a threat to the rule of law.[25]

This tension between one of the most prominent and central lines of jurisprudence of the Court[26] and the rule of law is particularly problematic since the rule of law is considered to be one of the core values of the Council of Europe.[27] The Committee of Ministers of the Council of Europe has underscored that the rule of law implies that the highest courts in particular need to ensure the coherence of their case law.[28] Furthermore, the Court itself claims the rule of law to be inherent in all articles of the Convention and furthermore uses the rule of law as a fundamental guiding principle to the application and interpretation of the Convention.[29]

Analysis of a Range of Cases on the Freedom of Religion: *De facto* Differential Margins of Appreciation for Distinctive Themes of 'Religion–State Relations'

The following analysis of case law does not purport to cover all distinctive lines of jurisprudence (one way or the other) concerning 'religion–State relations'. The aim is rather to expose the different degrees to which the Court is (*de facto*) ready to narrow the margin of appreciation of States in cases on particular sub-themes of 'religion–State relations'. To this effect the case law regarding registration, recognition and cooperation schemes, church autonomy and conscientious objectors, on the one hand, is juxtaposed with the case law on reasonable accommodation and fundamental rights of church personnel on the other.

Registration, Recognition and Cooperation Schemes

It is quite striking that the strongest example of a line of jurisprudence which restricts the margin of appreciation of States actually concerns systems pertaining to registration and especially cooperation schemes with recognised religions having a special status and rights,[30] an area which clearly and directly concerns 'religion–State relations'. Indeed, while public authorities may not be under an obligation to provide an identical legal status to all religions and religious communities in their territory,[31] the Court is increasingly demanding about the non-discriminatory content of the conditions and criteria for such registration and cooperation, as well as about the transparency of the process.[32]

It is furthermore striking that exactly in a case on this specific theme, where the Court does not grant States a wide margin of appreciation, the Court is ready to acknowledge (again) that religion is a suspect ground of differentiation. In its *Savez crkava* judgment the Court held indeed that the criteria for religious groups to obtain a special status, entitling them to various rights and privileges, call for particular scrutiny.[33] This seems

23 MR Hutchinson, 'The Margin of Appreciation Doctrine in the European Court of Human Rights' (1999) 48 *International and Comparative Law Quarterly* 638–50, 641.

24 Arai-Takahashi (n 9) 80.

25 Brauch (n 8) 124; J Christoffersen, *Fair Balance: Proportionality, Subsidiarity and Primarity in the ECHR* (Martinus Nijhoff 2009) 265 ff.

26 Brauch (n 8) 119.

27 Committee of Ministers (CM), *The Council of Europe and the Rule of Law: An Overview* (CM 2008) 170, para 23; Brauch (n 8) 122.

28 European Commission for Democracy through Law, *Report on the Rule of Law*, CDL-AD(2011)003 Rev, paras 44, 50; see also Brauch (n 8) 125.

29 See *Golder v The United Kingdom*, 21 February 1975, para 34; CM (n 27) 170, para 34; S Greer, 'The Legal and Constitutional Impact of the European Convention on Human Rights in the UK' in R Arnold (ed), *The Universalism of Human Rights* (Ius Gentium: Comparative Perspectives on Law and Justice 2013) 189–207, 195.

30 S Langlaude, 'Indoctrination, Secularism, Religious Liberty and the ECHR' (2006) 55 *International and Comparative Law Quarterly* 929–44, 939.

31 Tulkens (n 3) 2585–86.

32 See, inter alia, *Jehovas Zeugen in Österreich v Austria*, 25 September 2012, para 92; *Koppi v Austria*, 10 December 2009, para 33; *Lang v Austria*, 19 March 2009, paras 30–31.

33 *Savez crkava 'Riječ života' and Others v Croatia*, 9 December 2010, para 88.

to confirm the link that was intimated between, on the one hand, the width of the margin of appreciation for religion–State relations and, on the other hand, the recognition of the suspect nature of religion as a ground of differentiation.[34] Indeed, as long as the Court chooses to hold on to the broad margin for religion–State relations, it cannot explicitly acknowledge religion as a suspect class. Conversely, to the extent that the Court acknowledges religion as a suspect class, it arguably signals that it is ready to relinquish its long-standing line of jurisprudence on a broad margin for States concerning religion–State relations. However, as is further explained below, in the seminal *Eweida* judgement,[35] the Court arguably signals that it is not ready yet to develop a clear line of jurisprudence on the suspect nature of religion as a ground of differentiation.

Church Autonomy

A strong line of jurisprudence also exists regarding State duties to respect church autonomy, thus constraining possible State interference in terms of the internal organisation, tensions and possible schisms within religions or religious structures and related leadership struggles.[36] The way State authorities relate to religious institutions and structures clearly concerns religion–State relations. Nevertheless, in this line of case law, the Court either does not talk about the margin of appreciation at all,[37] or merely identifies a 'certain margin of appreciation' for States.[38] Strikingly, insofar as the Court argues the margin of appreciation, it determines the scope not in light of the limited European consensus regarding religion–State relations, but instead by 'what is at stake, namely the need to maintain true religious pluralism, which is inherent in the concept of a democratic society'.[39] The Court furthermore focuses in this respect on State duties of neutrality and impartiality that need to be respected.[40] In other words, in matters pertaining to internal structures, possible schisms and leadership battles, the Court does not grant States a wide margin of appreciation, but *de facto* proceeds to apply strict scrutiny.

Limits to church autonomy: the effective protection of fundamental rights of members and personnel?

Respecting the autonomy of churches and religions is indeed important to effectuate the collective aspect of the freedom to manifest one's religion and thus contributes in this respect to the effective protection of the freedom of religion. However, there is arguably a limit to the extent to which the protection of church autonomy can be allowed to reduce the effective protection of the fundamental rights of their members and/or their personnel, particularly the right to respect for private and family life. The Court is increasingly confronted with cases revolving around the conflict between the collective dimension of the freedom of religion on the one hand, and fundamental rights to respect for private and family life and also the right to establish and take part in trade unions, on the other. The critical question to be addressed in these cases is whether, in light of the State duty to respect church autonomy, it would be legitimate for States to interfere (through their national courts) in decisions by the church hierarchy that constitute disproportionate interference with the fundamental rights of (some of) its members. Would States' positive obligations to ensure the enjoyment of fundamental rights between private parties not come into play?[41] Or does the Court's position in this regard reflect again the extraordinary position of religion and churches in Europe's conceptualisation of society?[42]

34 Henrard (n 1).

35 *Eweida and Others v the United Kingdom*, 15 January 2013.

36 See J Martinez-Torron, 'Freedom of Religion in the European Convention on Human Rights under the Influence of Different European Traditions' in MA Glendon and H Zacher (eds), *Universal Rights in a World of Diversity: The Case of Religious Freedom* (Pontifical Academy of Social Sciences 2012) 329–55, 334–35, <www.pass.va/content/dam/scienzesociali/pdf/acta17/acta17-martineztorron.pdf> accessed 26 June 2014; Langlaude (n 30) 938; Tulkens (n 3) 2580–82.

37 See, for example, *Hasan and Chaush v Bulgaria*, 26 October 2000, paras 75–89; *Agga v Greece*, 25 January 2000, paras 56–61.

38 *Metropolitan Church of Bessarabia and Others v Moldova*, 13 December 2001, para 119.

39 ibid.

40 ibid paras 116 and 123.

41 See JD Van den Vyver, 'State Interference in the Internal Affairs of Religious Institutions' (2012) 26 *Emory International Law Review* 1–6, 6.

42 See J Temperman, 'Are State Churches Contrary to International Law?' (2013) 2 *Oxford Journal of Law and Religion* 119–49, 122 and 148–49.

While the Court tends to grant States a wide margin of appreciation when deciding how to deal with conflicting rights, this was not the line adopted in the first cases regarding decisions by religious authorities (church hierarchy) to dismiss (or, in some cases, not to extend the contracts of) persons employed as clergy or in a position which is inherently tied up with a particular religion or church. In the first cases of this kind,[43] the national (German) labour courts all decided to confirm the decision of the church hierarchy. The dismissals (in these cases, non-renewals) were all related to an act, behaviour or expression that was not in line with the religious dogma and related obligations of loyalty concerned, but did engage the person's concerned right to private and family life.[44] The Court adopted in all these cases a similar approach of 'ad hoc balancing', emphasising the need for national courts to explicitly and thoroughly balance the different interests at stake. The ECtHR concluded only in *Schüth* that the church's actions amounted to a violation because in that case the national Court had not sufficiently considered the interests of the individual member.[45]

However, in a similar 2012 case against Spain, the ECtHR adopted a radically different approach by accepting the categorical balancing by the Spanish courts in favour of church autonomy.[46] The Constitutional Court held that it was not competent to judge the reasons for the dismissal as these were 'exclusively religious', and the State was bound by its duty of religious neutrality (para 81). According to Spanish law the church authorities still had to respect fundamental rights (para 81), but this seems to be 'assumed' when a decision is based on exclusively religious reasons (para 84). The ECtHR accepts this reasoning of the national courts as sufficiently weighing the diverging interests (of individual members of a church and the church: para 82), while underscoring that the autonomous existence of religious communities is an issue at the very heart of the protection that Article 9 affords (para 80). In other words, in this judgment the Court does revert to the broad margin of appreciation of States when weighing up conflicting rights (para 78). It actually accepts that heightened duties of loyalty can legitimately be imposed on clergy, given the special bond of trust between a church and its religious personnel (paras 84–87). The reasoning by the Court appears to indicate that church authorities have reduced obligations to respect the fundamental rights of their personnel. Not surprisingly, this judgment has been criticised for giving disproportionate weight to the autonomous existence of religious communities, possibly excluding particular employees from protection against discrimination under employment law.[47]

Similarly, the Grand Chamber judgment in *Sindicatul 'Păstorul cel Bun' v Romania* seems to allow States to put the collective dimension of the freedom of religion and the autonomy of religious community hierarchically above the fundamental rights of members of that community.[48] While the Court in the latter case does not approve of categorical balancing by national courts, it does allow States to attach a lot of weight to the principle of church autonomy and the duty of State neutrality. The Court even accepts the national choice to allow churches to decide whether or not to allow trade union rights for their personnel (paras 163 and 164–68). Throughout the Court's reasoning it is obvious that it is intent on granting the State a broad margin of appreciation in the matter. Indeed, the Court identifies no less than four reasons why this should be so in regard to trade union rights of particular clergy members of a religious movement: because there is no consensus on trade union rights for clergy (para 61); because a State can choose how to protect trade union rights of employees (para 133); because it concerns two conflicting convention rights (para 160); and because it concerns church–State relations, about which there is no European consensus (para 171).

Arguably these cases all concern the sensitive question of the protection of dissenters within a particular religious group or structure who do not want to leave the religious group but rather want better protection of their fundamental rights. Such 'constructive' minorities are undoubtedly a vulnerable group, the protection of whose rights requires special regard. Religious autonomy should arguably not be glorified to such an extent

43 *Obst v Germany*, 23 September 2010; *Schüth v Germany*, 23 September 2010; *Siebenhaar v Germany*, 3 February 2011.

44 Martinez-Torron (n 36) 337.

45 See Van den Vyver (n 41) 4–8; but see also Martinez-Torron (n 36) 338–41.

46 *Fernández Martínez v Spain*, 15 May 2012. See S Smet, *Fernández Martínez v Spain: Towards a Ministerial Exception for Europe?* (2012) 4–5 <http://strasbourgobservers.com/2012/05/24/fernandez-martinez-v-spain-towards-a-ministerial-exception-in-europe/> accessed 26 June 2014.

47 Smet (n 46) 5.

48 *Sindicatul 'Păstorul cel Bun' v Romania*, 9 July 2013.

that religious organisations would be absolved from respecting the fundamental rights of their members. One can hope the Grand Chamber judgment in *Fernández Martínez* will develop into a more explicit and elaborate reasoning about the width of the margin of appreciation, thereby providing some guidance to the States Parties in this sensitive matter (ultimately contributing to legal certainty and thus the rule of law – see also below).

Conscientious Objection to Military Service

A third line of jurisprudence which is arguably rather consistent concerns the protection of conscientious objectors (to military service) and is set in place by the judgment of the Grand Chamber in the *Bayatyan* case.[49] The way in which a State deals with persons who object to military service on the grounds of their religious or philosophical convictions can indeed be considered an issue of the relationship between State and (the manifestation of) religion.

Bayatyan is a good example of a reversal of jurisprudence that is extensively and explicitly argued by the Court. In the past, the former European Commission on Human Rights chose an easy way out of controversies pertaining to conscientious objection and State obligations in this respect under the ECHR. It tackled the tricky question by establishing an awkward link between Article 9 and Article 4 on the prohibition against forced or compulsory labour. Because neither military service nor alternative civilian service could be considered forced or compulsory labour in the sense of Article 4 of the ECHR, and because Article 4, para 3(b) reads 'any service of a military character or, in cases of conscientious objectors, in countries where they are recognized', conscientious objection to those services did not according to the Commission fall within the scope of application of or protection by Article 9 of the ECHR. In other words, the ECHR would leave the choice of recognising conscientious objectors to each contracting party.[50]

In 2011 the Grand Chamber in *Bayatyan* finally acknowledged the flaws in the above reasoning and reversed that line of jurisprudence[51] by highlighting that it was not the purpose of Article 4 of the ECHR to limit the protective scope of Article 9 (paras 100–101). The Court also drew on the living instrument doctrine in this respect, highlighting that there have been 'important developments both in the domestic legal systems of Council of Europe Member States and internationally', arguably establishing a clear trend and virtually general consensus to recognise the right to conscientious objection (paras 101–109).

When assessing whether the interference with the freedom to manifest one's religion was legitimate or amounted to a violation, the Court did not resort to the broad margin of appreciation concerning religion–State relations. It started by saying that States have a certain margin of appreciation in deciding whether and to what extent an interference is necessary (para 121). The Court went on to establish the scope of the margin in relation to two factors: (1) what is at stake, namely the need to maintain true religious pluralism, and (2) a nearly general consensus to accommodate conscientious objectors (paras 122–23). Consequently, when a State is not in line with this consensus, it has 'only a limited margin of appreciation and must advance convincing and compelling reasons' (para 123). Ultimately, the Court in Grand Chamber formation concluded that the Armenian State had violated Article 9 (para 128).

While the Court did not explicitly denounce the broad margin of appreciation doctrine for religion–State relations because there would be no European consensus on the matter, it clearly chose to focus on a matter about which there *is* European consensus, namely the need to accommodate conscientious objectors. The Court furthermore attached weight to a different factor, namely 'what is at stake', and chose to identify 'the need to maintain true religious pluralism' as a stake which (similarly) merits only a narrow margin of appreciation. In other words, the Court did not address the question of the width of the margin of appreciation for religion–State relations, but *de facto* evaluated a matter concerning 'religion–State relations' in a rather strict way. This case clearly demonstrates how it is always a choice by the Court to focus on one or another factor to determine the width of the margin of appreciation. The Court's smart use of 'accepted' and non-controversial factors for this determination arguably facilitates the acceptance of the

49 *Bayatyan v Armenia*, 7 July 2011.

50 P Muzny, 'Bayatyan v Armenia: The Grand Chamber Renders a Grand Judgment' (2012) 12 *Human Rights Law Review* 135–47, 140.

51 ibid 140.

outcome by the Member States, even when their *de facto* margin of appreciation concerning religion–State relations is reduced.

Reasonable Accommodation Regarding Religion (in the Workplace): Holidays, Symbols and so on

Whether – and to what extent – religious diversity should be accommodated has been discussed in several respects, including religious holy days and weekly days of rest (and related church attendance), dietary restrictions, religious symbols individuals might want to wear and other religiously inspired acts that individuals might want to perform. Duties of reasonable accommodation on grounds of religion are in two respects important for the effective protection of fundamental rights: first, for an effective enjoyment of the freedom to manifest one's religion, and second, in order to obtain equal opportunities regarding effective access to employment, education and other (public) services.[52] The latter concerns an interpretation of the prohibition against discrimination which embraces substantive or real equality (often in combination with socio-economic rights), and has been extensively discussed elsewhere.[53] The focus here will be on duties to accommodate religious diversity in terms of the freedom of religion, and actually concerns the doctrine of positive obligations and its ultimate aim of effective protection of fundamental rights.[54] For example, regarding the wearing of a headscarf in State schools, duties (positive obligations) of reasonable accommodation would arise to ensure the full enjoyment of the freedom to manifest one's religion and also one's effective access to education. When the school is a private school, there is still the question of positive State obligations, but this time aimed at the regulation of private action: should States (through legislation and/or case law) impose duties of reasonable accommodation on employers, service providers and the like to ensure that the convention rights are reasonably safeguarded in relations between private parties?

Traditionally the supervisory bodies of the ECtHR have not been eager to develop duties to accommodate religious diversity.[55] This was most clearly visible in relation to cases pertaining to the work environment,[56] where most cases implying claims for such accommodation originated. In the meantime, an ever-growing string of themes and claims can be recognised in accommodation language and can be considered claims for reasonable accommodation, both in and outside the work environment. The following paragraphs set out to capture the jurisprudence of the Court in relation to claims to (reasonable) accommodation, while identifying relevant distinctions as to themes and contexts in which these demands are made: absences from work for or scheduling of particular activities in order to respect religious observances and holidays, wearing religious symbols at work, refusal to provide services for religious reasons and so forth.

Regarding the work environment there is indeed a steady line of jurisprudence of the former European Commission on Human Rights suggesting that unauthorised absences from work for religious reasons are not protected under freedom of religion.[57] Several strands of reasoning were adopted to argue that sanctions for these unauthorised absences did not amount to violations of the freedom to manifest one's religion: (1) the unauthorised absence from work might have been motivated or inspired by religion but would not amount to a manifestation of religion; (2) there would not be an interference with the freedom to manifest one's religion because either the sanctions were not causally related to the manifestation of a religion and were merely

52 P Bosset and M-C Foblets, 'Accommodating Diversity in Québec and Europe: Different Concepts, Similar Results?' in *Institutional Accommodation and the Citizen: Legal and Political Interaction in a Pluralist Society* (Council of Europe 2010) 37–66, 37.

53 See also K Henrard, 'Duties of Reasonable Accommodation in Relation to Religion and the European Court of Human Rights: A Closer Look at the Prohibition of Discrimination, the Freedom of Religion and Related Duties of State Neutrality' (2012) 5 *ELR* 5–25; K Alidadi, 'Reasonable Accommodations for Religion and Belief: Adding Value to Article 9 ECHR and the European Union's Anti-Discrimination Approach to Employment?' (2012) 6 *European Law Review* 693–715.

54 K Boyle, 'Freedom of Religion in International Law' in J Rehman and SC Breau (eds), *Religion, Human Rights and International Law: A Critical Examination of Islamic State Practice* (Martinus Nijhoff 2007) 23–51, 29; Henrard (n 1) 55–56.

55 See, inter alia, Alidadi (n 53) 703; Henrard (n 53).

56 Alidadi (n 53) 704–06.

57 Prominent cases include *Konttinen v Finland*, 3 December 1996 and *Stedman v the United Kingdom*, 9 April 1997.

imposed because an employee had not fulfilled his or her contractual obligations, or these sanctions did not make it impossible to manifest one's religion because the employee could avoid these hurdles by resigning and seeking employment elsewhere (the so-called specific situation rule or the freedom to resign).[58] In 2006 the Court *de facto* confirmed this reasoning when it similarly denied that unauthorised absence from work for religious reasons would amount to a manifestation of one's religion, and even if it would qualify as a manifestation, there would not be an interference with the freedom to manifest one's religion.[59] The Court explicitly pointed out that 'there is no right as such under Article 9 to have leave from work for particular religious holidays'.[60]

The decision in *Francesco Sessa v Italy* (3 April 2012) might not be directly related to sanctions for not respecting working hours, but it does pertain to the timing of work, more particularly the scheduling of hearing days for a lawyer's case. The Court ruled that a complaint about a refusal to adjourn a case because the hearing date would otherwise collide with a most important Jewish holiday was manifestly ill-founded and thus inadmissible. According to the Court, there would not be an interference with the freedom to manifest one's religion, because the lawyer was not pressured into not observing the holiday concerned.

Interestingly, the preceding lines of argumentation of the Commission and the Court did not mention the margin of appreciation and were actually focused on the earlier stages of analysis regarding the existence of a manifestation of a religion and/or an interference with this manifestation. Nevertheless, this reasoning can also ultimately be argued to reveal an apparent reluctance of the supervisory bodies to impose far-reaching positive obligations on States in relation to the freedom of religion,[61] leaving the choice of how to deal with these requests more or less to the discretion or appreciation of the States themselves.[62]

The more recent case of *Eweida* does not send an explicit and clear signal in terms of the margin of appreciation the Court is leaving States regarding 'religion–State relations'. The judgment implies important shifts in the jurisprudence, which arguably heighten the protection of the freedom of religion and religious diversity, but at the same time leaves States extensive discretion in matters relating to the place of religion in the work environment. This case is actually a compilation of four cases, all of which concern State duties in relation to the accommodation of religion and religious diversity in the work environment, without touching on unauthorised absences from work in order to respect religious holy days or days of rest. Two concern the wearing of the cross during work time, and two the refusal to provide services to same-sex couples.

Eweida is extremely important in that it reverses the traditional jurisprudence exhibiting a narrow understanding of what amounts to a manifestation of religion, or an interference with such a manifestation, squarely leaving the important decisions to be made in terms of the doctrine of legitimate limitations, and especially the proportionality principle.[63] At first sight this carries the promise that the Court is willing to adopt a more demanding level of scrutiny. However, on closer inspection the Court's (superficial) proportionality reasoning actually points to the opposite. The prohibition against the nurse's wearing a cross at work was all too easily accepted once the government invoked the protection of health and safety of the patients, as if there were no subsidiarity considerations and as if this limitation analysis does not depend on all relevant circumstances. In the two cases concerning the refusal to provide services to same-sex couples, the Court similarly ducks any explicit reasoning and hides behind the broad margin of appreciation of States regarding conflicting rights. In other words, the Court is not repeating the mantra of the broad margin of appreciation regarding 'religion–State relations', but it *de facto* still leaves States wide-ranging discretion in these matters. Not surprisingly, this resulted in a finding of non-violation in three of the four cases, while the one case where the Court did conclude that a violation had occurred (wearing of the cross by a desk officer of British Airways), the employer concerned had already admitted its fault and changed policy.

---

58 SO Chaib, 'Religious Accommodation in the Workplace: Improving the Legal Reasoning of the European Court of Human Rights' in K Alidadi et al (n 10) 33–58, 38–41.

59 *Kosteski v the Former Yugoslav Republic of Macedonia*, 13 April 2006, paras 37–38.

60 ibid para 45.

61 Henrard (n 1) 55–56.

62 J Ringelheim, *Diversité culturelle et droits de l'homme: l'émergence de la problématique des minorités dans le droit de la convention européenne des droits de l'homme* (Bruylant 2006) 169.

63 M Pearson, 'Article 9 at a Crossroads: Interference before and after Eweida' (2013) 13 *Human Rights Law Review* 580–602, 589, 595–96.

This reading of *Eweida* could also explain why the Court chose to ignore in this case the explicit argument of one of the claimants that religion would be a suspect ground of differentiation. Since a broad margin of appreciation for religion–State relations cannot be reconciled with a narrow margin of appreciation for differentiations on grounds of religion (religion being suspect), the former can only be maintained when one denies (or ignores) the latter. Put differently, the reasoning in *Eweida* arguably indicates that the Court is not yet willing and ready to adopt strict scrutiny towards States' decisions that concern, to use a phrase frequently employed by the Court, the 'delicate relations between the churches/religions and the State', especially regarding the work environment.

Concluding Recommendations: A Call for a More Transparent Operationalisation of the Margin of Appreciation Regarding 'Religion–State Relations'

The case law analysis has revealed seemingly different baselines for distinctive aspects of the umbrella term 'religion–State relations' that are neither addressed nor explained by the ECtHR. In order not to frustrate typical rule of law demands about predictability and legal certainty, the differentiation in the breadth of the margin of appreciation needs to be argued explicitly. Indeed, it is always a question of choice whether one focuses on the factor(s) that point towards a broad margin or to those that point to a narrow margin of appreciation. Considering the lack of explicit reasoning and the resulting tension with legal certainty and the rule of law, the Court is urged to be more transparent in how it operationalises the margin of appreciation regarding 'religion–State relations', acknowledging the different lines encompassed by this term, and within each line identifying the relevant factors and the way these relate to one another.[64]

In addition to problems in terms of predictability and legal certainty, the Court has been criticised for using the (broad) margin of appreciation to avoid having to take an explicit stance in controversial matters,[65] thus using the margin of appreciation as a substitute for coherent legal analysis of the issues at stake.[66] This 'practice' carries the danger of making decisions that are inadequately backed up by explicit, clear analysis and application of the Convention,[67] and ultimately threatens the very legitimacy that the Court is trying to secure through the use of the margin of appreciation doctrine.[68]

If the Court were to follow the recommendation to argue its determination of the scope of the margin of appreciation fully, consistently and explicitly, it would not only be in line with the rule of law, but it would also strengthen its legitimacy by showing that it 'justif[ies] its decisions according to a scheme of principles that represents an intelligible and coherent vision of justice'.[69] This type of reasoning would furthermore contribute to the emergence of a coherent policy framework in relation to religious diversity because it would enable the Court to provide more guidance to States (and the EU institutions) on how to realise their overarching obligations of (religious) neutrality and impartiality in ways that would further the effective protection of the freedom of religion[70] and would strengthen the effective protection against discrimination on grounds of religion.

64 See also G Letsas, 'Strasbourg's Interpretive Ethic: Lessons for the International Lawyer' (2010) 21 *EJIL* 509–41, 540–41; Kratochvil (n 20) 244.

65 Brauch (n 8) 138 (and 149).

66 See also Hutchinson (n 23) 641.

67 ibid.

68 Arai-Takahashi (n 9) 80; see also K Dzehtsiarou, 'European Consensus and the Evolutive Interpretation of the European Convention on Human Rights' (2011) 12 *German Law Journal* 1730–45, 1734–35.

69 Letsas (n 64) 540–41.

70 C Evans, *Freedom of Religion under the ECHR* (OUP 2001).

Chapter 16
Religious Accommodation and Inclusive Even-Handedness

Cécile Laborde

The RELIGARE report makes a convincing, well-supported case for the accommodation of a number of religiously motivated demands in the public spheres of European countries. The following comments are directed at the theoretical framework underpinning these recommendations. I aim to assess the theory of 'inclusive even-handedness' (hereafter IEH) from the point of view of the political philosophy of justice in diverse societies.

While I agree with the practical recommendations of the report, I raise some questions about the normative framework that justifies them. In brief, my argument will be that while IEH is essential for rectifying some inequalities between members of majority and minority religions, it cannot serve as an overarching framework for an egalitarian theory of religious and philosophical diversity.

Inclusive Even-Handedness Defined

We can distinguish two distinct senses of IEH: procedural and substantive.

Procedurally, IEH points towards a deliberative, dialogical approach to the management of diversity rather than a top-down, one-sided approach. Clearly, this is an attractive and cogent way of thinking about lawmaking and conflict management in diverse societies. It neatly tallies with a contextualist requirement that all facts relevant to a case be taken into account. It also warns against the risks of premature legislation or judicialisation of conflicts. So, for example, it should not have been necessary to involve a judge to reach the agreement that a woman wearing *hijab* can wear headphones under her *hijab*. Such pragmatic, commonsensical solutions can be found through minimal dialogue.

Substantively, IEH points to real, as opposed to formal, equality of treatment. This too is an important idea: evidently, treating people as equals does not always require that they be treated identically. As Aristotle said long ago, we should treat similar cases the same, and different cases differently. Now the question arises: How do we know what is relevantly different? The RELIGARE report suggests where to look for an answer to this question. Majorities and minorities fare differently under current European law and practice. In particular, members of religious minorities face disproportionate burdens in the exercise of their religious rights. Because European public spheres are culturally Christian, the structure of the week, dress codes, rituals of marriage and family law, and systems of recognised religions remain profoundly marked by that heritage. IEH therefore demands that, when possible, we compensate for this disadvantage and rectify this indirect discrimination.

For example, in European public spheres today, it is difficult for a Muslim to go to prayers at the mosque on Fridays if he or she is tied to a normal work week. For a Christian wishing to go to church on Sunday, no such difficulty arises. This is the incontrovertible sense in which European public spheres are not religiously neutral. A secular law or norm can be neutral on its face, yet indirectly discriminatory.[1]

IEH is well equipped to address such inequalities of treatment between majority and minority religions. It compensates for the costs which arise, not from the practice of religion itself (so the costs of a pilgrimage, for example, should be supported by the pilgrim and not by the community at large), but rather out of the interaction between the cultural norms of a given society and the exercise of basic religious rights by minorities. IEH, then, demands that we distinguish clearly between the 'internal' costs of religious practice

1 C Laborde, *Critical Republicanism: The Hijab Controversy and Political Philosophy* (OUP 2008) ch 4.

(for example pilgrimage) and the 'external' costs which result from the conflict between the religious practice and the structure of the environment.[2]

Substantive Equality?

Let us look in more detail at the kind of equality this is. The report introduces 'substantive equality' as the aim of IEH (*Report*, 19). Yet this is a problematic idea. Substantive equality refers to the idea that what should be equalised is the success of different groups in pursuing the aims they happen to have in, say, living their religious lives. This can also be called equality of outcome. Yet, when we rectify inequalities of treatment between members of majority and minority religion, what we should equalise is not the actual success at realising particular goals, but the basic opportunities of all to participate in the workplace, have access to education, move around freely and so on, without having to bear disproportionate burdens in the exercise of their freedom of religion rights.

It is important to grasp the difference between the two notions. First, what should be equalised in a liberal society is not 'success in living one's religious life', but the basic socio-economic, educational and political opportunities that are due to all as citizens. Second, it is not the relative status of religious groups as *groups* that should be equalised, but the basic opportunities of *individuals*. From this point of view, a ban on religious dress in the workplace does not infringe on substantive religious equality – a problematic notion in any case – but rather on basic individual rights to, for example, work and education.

Liberal States should aim not to equalise the status of religious groups; rather, the focus should be on the status of individuals within the groups, making sure that members of every minority have a roughly equal set of basic opportunities. But we need to adopt a culturally sensitive definition of what it means to have an 'opportunity' to work.[3] In particular, what we should seek is the equal right of all to take up basic opportunities of social participation without having to suffer unreasonable burdens on the exercise of their religion. So if I wear a *hijab* and am therefore prevented from working in a supermarket because of the prejudices and intransigence of my employer, I could be said not to enjoy a *real opportunity* to work.

Under IEH properly conceived, then, religious demands can be accommodated when the costs of accommodation are low or fairly distributed, when they do not challenge the point of the law or regulation, and when the point is to equalise opportunity sets for individuals so they can combine the exercise of basic religious rights and the pursuit of work, educational, socio-economic and political opportunities in their societies.

Note that there is another argument, unrelated to issues of recognition and equality, that militates against (even-handed) public support of religion as such. It is the fear, articulated by early modern critics of State-supported religion, that State support of religion will not foster religious vitality, but rather suppress it. The current enthusiasm for State support of religion in Europe has lost sight of this basic liberal insight – that supported, funded and established religion loses its independence, vitality and critical spirit.

Three Internal Limits

Does IEH, however, always demand the accommodation of religious demands? It does not. We can distinguish three cases.

First, in many cases, what equality demands is not accommodation or exemption, but simply modification or annulment of the law or regulation. For example, schools or companies can change their uniform policy (for example, by not requiring that employees be bare-headed) instead of accommodating religious demands on a case-by-case basis. So instead of accommodation, we can often seek a more equal formal law applying to all.

2 P Jones, 'Bearing the Consequences of Belief' (1994) (2) 1 *Journal of Political Philosophy* 24–43.

3 D Miller, 'Liberalism, Equal Opportunities and Cultural Commitments' in P Kelly (ed), *Multiculturalism Reconsidered: Culture and Equality and Its Critics* (Polity Press 2002).

Second, at times equalising will involve equalising 'downwards' rather than 'upwards'. So instead of extending some privileges of recognition to minority groups, equality might require that existing privileges be removed. One topical example is the current debate about the presence of bishops in the UK House of Lords. One influential argument here is that the interests of democratic representation may best be served by not entrenching religious representation within democratic assemblies.

Third, and as is made clear in the RELIGARE report, the advantages of accommodation need to be weighed – through careful balancing or proportionality analyses – against the costs of accommodation on the one hand, and, on the other hand, the compelling interest States might have for enforcing the same rule for all. For example, as is argued in the report, there is probably no compelling State interest in forcing people to show their faces in the public space *lato sensu*. However, there might be such an interest in banning face veils in key parts of the public sphere – when people act as civil servants, or appear before a judge. More attention needs to be given to conflicting demands in different spaces and to the different functions and roles people may occupy.

Having defined the scope and limits of IEH, I now turn to a more fundamental examination of the exact place of IEH in a conception of justice suitable for pluralist societies.

Three External Limits

IEH cannot be an overarching normative framework for three reasons. First, it would be implausible to say that just law is always even-handed law. Imagine an employer who openly discriminates against Muslims or homosexuals. We do not want the law – or the judge – to be even-handed in dealing with the employer and the discriminated party. It is not clear, in such cases, what work IEH does. As the report points out, human rights, gender or sexuality equality norms often rightly trump even-handedness, including in tricky cases of private international law (for example, family law).

Second, IEH exponents sometimes assume (or write as if they assume) that secular law is nothing but established Christian law. On that view, equality would demand the 'dis-establishment' of secular–Christian law and equal distribution of privileges and advantages among Christians, Jews, Muslims and so forth. But – as the report's recommendations about human rights and gender equality reveal – many secular norms are not (just) Christian and ethnocentric. And, in fact, secular law and norms are challenged by some Christian groups, who object to the pervasive impact of secular norms of equality and non-discrimination on their internal organisation. Here the notion of IEH does not give sufficient guidelines for thinking about the relationship between civil law and religious rules.

Third, and closely connected, IEH does not tell us how to balance the collective rights of religious associations and the rights of individual members or of the recipients of the services they provide. How far should religious associations be allowed to discriminate against non-religionists, women or homosexuals? This is already a huge issue in the United States, where faith-based associations provide a wide range of public services, from advice to pregnant women to sport facilities, education and commercial activities. The recent Supreme Court decision *Hosanna-Tabor*, for example, extended the ministerial exemption (the right to be exempted from discrimination legislation in the appointment of clergy) to all employees of religious associations.

In sum, IEH is very useful to help us think about equality between members of different religious groups when such equality is compromised by the cultural and religious bias of existing institutions. It draws our attention to the invisible, insidious processes of discrimination, domination and racialisation of religious minorities. But we should resist the tendency to assume that the notion will, in and of itself, also help in addressing trickier cases of reconciliation or balance between conflicting rights – non-discrimination, gender equality, associational rights and so forth. I am sceptical of IEH's capacity to do this. We need a more complex theory of what justice for members of religious minorities, and other members of society, requires.

Chapter 17
Reasonable Accommodation for Religion and Belief: Can it Be Accommodated in EU Law without an Express Duty?

Andreas Stein[1]

Introduction

One of the key findings of the RELIGARE project is that an analysis of the existing legal framework at the European level – both in terms of the European Convention on Human Rights (ECHR) and of EU anti-discrimination legislation – reveals gaps which make it difficult to ensure reasonable accommodation on the basis of religion and belief in the workplace (*Report*, 19). Accordingly, it is recommended to EU policymakers to amend Directive 2000/78/EC (the Employment Equality Directive)[2] to add an explicit right for employees 'to request reasonable accommodation on the basis of religious beliefs, practices and observances unless such accommodation would result in a demonstrated disproportionate distribution of burden or cost' (*Report*, 22).

It is the purpose of this chapter to critically review the suggested benefits of such an express duty of reasonable accommodation in addition to the protection provided by the Employment Equality Directive. This assessment will be carried out against the backdrop of the political and legal environment for the adoption of new EU anti-discrimination legislation, which has been immensely difficult in the recent past and is unlikely to fundamentally change in the near future. Measures to combat discrimination on grounds of religion and belief based on Article 19 of the Treaty on the Functioning of the European Union (TFEU) require unanimity in the Council and can thus be effectively vetoed by any single Member State. The European Commission's proposal for a Horizontal Directive that would prohibit discrimination on, inter alia, grounds of religion and belief outside employment was made in 2008 and has now been stalled in negotiations for more than five years.[3] Given the generally sensitive nature of matters of religion and belief and the drastically different traditions and approaches to dealing with such matters across Member States, it is not difficult to predict that gaining unanimous approval of the insertion of a duty of reasonable accommodation in the Employment Equality Directive or in the proposed directive applying outside the area of employment[4] would represent a challenging endeavour.

In these circumstances, I would submit as a starting point that a proposal for an amendment to the existing legal framework should only be considered where it holds the potential for a clear improvement over the present situation or, in other words, where the objective of a duty of reasonable accommodation cannot be achieved with the tools already available under the Employment Equality Directive. In that context, a particular focus will be placed on the question whether and to what extent the prohibition against indirect discrimination constitutes a functional equivalent to an obligation of reasonable accommodation. I will further briefly try to shed some light on the link between fundamental rights law and reasonable accommodation and

1 The author is an official of the European Commission. This article exclusively reflects his personal views.

2 Council Directive 2000/78/EC of 27 November 2000 establishing a general framework for equal treatment in employment and occupation; OJ L 303 of 2 December 2000, 16.

3 'Proposal for a Council Directive on Implementing the Principle of Equal Treatment between Persons Irrespective of Religion or Belief, Disability, Age or Sexual Orientation', COM(2008) 426 final of 2 July 2008.

4 The RELIGARE findings are limited to the realm of employment, but it has to be assumed that this is explained by the current limited scope of EU legislation and that the same recommendations would also apply in the areas of education (where problems very similar to those encountered in employment often arise, for example relating to religious dress or time off for religious holidays) or in access to goods and services.

to analyse the impact of the introduction of an explicit duty of reasonable accommodation in the US and in Canada, before drawing some tentative conclusions.

Reasonable Accommodation and Indirect Discrimination: Two Sides of the Same Coin?

It is generally acknowledged[5] that from a conceptual point of view a duty of reasonable accommodation is closely related to the notion of indirect discrimination as laid down in the Employment Equality Directive.[6] While the same directive establishes in its Article 5 a duty of reasonable accommodation (only) on the grounds of disability without formally requiring demonstration of discrimination in the absence of measures to accommodate, the introduction to that provision makes it explicit that this duty is introduced in order to guarantee compliance with the principle of equal treatment (and the prohibition of discrimination). And although it is true that reasonable accommodation is not an equivalent to indirect discrimination in the narrower sense of the term, but rather a means to either prevent or rectify indirect discrimination, this change in perspective should not be translated into a substantive conceptual difference. Where apparently neutral rules, for example regarding working hours or work uniforms, have a detrimental effect on those whose religion or belief implies particular requirements, the failure to accommodate a request for different treatment may amount to indirect discrimination unless the refusal to accommodate can be reasonably justified.[7] This would not necessarily appear to require a particularly dynamic or extensive interpretation of the concept of indirect discrimination, but can be concluded on the basis of existing EU legislation and case law. Where a seemingly neutral practice prohibiting any head covering places employees of a certain belief at a disadvantage, it qualifies as indirect discrimination and is therefore prohibited unless it can be demonstrated that this practice is justified by a legitimate aim and that the means to achieve that aim are appropriate and necessary.

It is very difficult to spot any considerable difference of substance to the logic of reasonable accommodation in terms of both the standards to be applied and the procedural requirements, particularly in relation to the burden of proof. In both cases the onus is first on the person claiming reasonable accommodation to show a conflict between work requirements and religious commitments which would require a derogation from work requirements in order to be able to honour religious commitments.[8] This onus can be discharged (with an express duty of reasonable accommodation) by showing that the derogation is needed[9] to follow the religious rules and practices in question or (without such express duty) by showing that the work requirement is incompatible with such rules or practices and therefore places persons wishing to follow them at a particular disadvantage. No considerable difference is detectable in the nature of the information that needs to be provided.

Once that is done the onus shifts to the employer. Where an explicit duty of reasonable accommodation exists, the employer needs to show (and prove) that the requested accommodation would impose a disproportionate burden in order to prevail. Without such express obligation the employer would have to prove that, in spite of the adverse effect on followers of a particular belief, there is no prohibited discrimination.

5 See, for example, E Bribosia and I Rorive, 'Reasonable Accommodation beyond Disability in Europe? European Network of Legal Experts in the Non-Discrimination Field' (2013) 9, <http://ec.europa.eu/justice/discrimination/files/reasonable_accommodation_beyond_disability_in_europe_en.pdf#h2–7> accessed 27 June 2014; K Alidadi, 'Reasonable Accommodation for Religion and Belief: Adding Value to Article 9 ECHR and the European Union's Anti-Discrimination Approach to Employment?' (2012) 37 (6) *European Law Review* 693–715, 707, both of which describe them as functional equivalents in spite of some differences.

6 Defined in the Employment Equality Directive for, inter alia, religion and belief as occurring where an apparently neutral provision, criterion or practice would put persons having a particular religion or belief at a particular disadvantage compared with other persons unless that provision, criterion or practice is objectively justified by a legitimate aim and the means of achieving that aim are appropriate and necessary.

7 L Vickers, 'Religion and Belief Discrimination in Employment – the EU Law' (European Commission, Directorate-General for Employment, Social Affairs and Equal Opportunities Unit G.2 2006) 21, <http://bookshop.europa.eu/en/religion-and-belief-discrimination-in-employment-pbKE7606351/> accessed 27 June 2014.

8 E Bribosia, J Ringelheim and I Rorive describe the requirements under Canadian law; see 'Reasonable Accommodation for Religious Minorities: A Promising Concept for European Antidiscrimination Law?' (2010) 17 (2) *Maastricht Journal of European and Comparative Law* 137–61, 149.

9 This is the terminology used in Article 5 of the Employment Equality Directive for disability.

The employer can do this by showing that the challenged practice is justified by a legitimate aim and that the means to achieve that aim are appropriate and necessary. It is quite self-explanatory that the key element in both tests is a proportionality assessment, and the material difference between both tests appears to be marginal at best. Where an employer has to show the appropriateness and necessity of the work requirement, the proportionality assessment includes the question of whether another more flexible measure allowing employees to observe religious commitments (such as a limited derogation from general dress rules) is sufficient in order to achieve the legitimate objective. Where that is the case the practice in question cannot be justified, amounts to prohibited indirect discrimination, and needs to be ended or modified. In the same circumstances it would appear impossible for the employer to show that a reasonable accommodation would result in a disproportionate burden simply because the same objective can be reached without strictly imposing the rule in question without exception.

This striking parallelism between the mere application of the concept of indirect discrimination as already firmly established in EU law and the introduction of a new explicit rule on reasonable accommodation cannot come as a surprise if one considers the history of the principle of reasonable accommodation. Canada, the country in which this concept has been developed and applied most broadly, not only in the areas of disability (as in the EU) or disability and religion (as in the US), but for all grounds of discrimination, is a case in point here.

The landmark 1985 judgment by the Canadian Supreme Court on the duty of reasonable accommodation[10] is not a decision interpreting a statutory obligation to that effect, but first and foremost a ruling recognising the prohibition against indirect discrimination in cases where a rule does not directly and intentionally discriminate on grounds of religion but, despite being neutral on its face, has 'adverse effects' for those of a certain creed. The major part of the reasoning is dedicated to the recognition of such 'adverse effect discrimination' as discrimination prohibited by Canadian legislation without a requirement of discriminatory intent (the ruling itself did not specifically refer to indirect discrimination at the time).[11] Reasonable accommodation comes into play not as an independent concept in its own right, but only where the Supreme Court considers the consequences of the finding of indirect discrimination. It is here that the Court establishes a difference between direct discrimination, where the discriminatory rule is simply struck down, and adverse effect discrimination, where the solution is not as simple given the fact that the working rule in question (in that case a requirement to work in a department store on Saturdays, which collided with the Sabbath requirements of an employee who was a Seventh-Day Adventist) was neutral and free from discriminatory intent. It was in this specific context that the Supreme Court concluded that anti-discrimination legislation had to be construed and flexibly applied to protect the right of the employee who is subject to discrimination and also to protect the right of the employer to proceed with the lawful conduct of his business. It then drew inspiration from the US statutes and case law to introduce a duty of reasonable accommodation without any statutory obligation in the Canadian legislation.

The inextricable link between the concept of indirect discrimination and the logic of reasonable accommodation, and the fact that reasonable accommodation is an emanation of indirect discrimination, is very well summarised where the Canadian Supreme Court presents the question which it later answers in the affirmative:

> [T]he duty to accommodate, referred to in the American cases, provide[s] that where it is shown that a working rule has caused discrimination it is incumbent upon the employer to make a reasonable effort to accommodate the religious needs of the employee, short of undue hardship to the employer in the conduct of his business. There is no express statutory base for such a proposition in the Code. Hence, the vacuum in the Code and the question: Should such a doctrine be imported to fill it?[12]

The logic of reasonable accommodation is thus not only nothing distinct from the concept of indirect discrimination. In the reasoning of the Canadian Supreme Court, it presupposes the existence of indirect

10 *Ontario Human Rights Commission and O'Malley v Simpsons-Sears* [1985] 2 SCR 536.

11 Paras 12–18 of the judgment.

12 Para 20 of the judgment.

discrimination and is a principle guiding the amendments that have to be made to a rule to remedy (or prevent) such discrimination.

It is also noteworthy that the Canadian Supreme Court established this principle without an express reference in legislation. Even in the wake of this ruling no express duty of reasonable accommodation along the lines of Article 5 of the Employment Equality Directive has been comprehensively incorporated into the relevant Canadian legislation. After its establishment in case law it was explicitly referred to in some but not all the relevant human rights statutes.[13] It is further noteworthy how the duty is concretely framed where it is stipulated. In particular, in the Canadian Human Rights Act, reasonable accommodation is enshrined as a general principle in the provision setting out the purpose of the Act,[14] and is further mentioned only in the context of the need to demonstrate a *bona fide* occupational requirement and the undue hardship that would result from an accommodation or, on the other hand, to provide justification for differential treatment.[15] It is clear from both references that the idea of reasonable accommodation has not been devised as a separate enforceable obligation, but remains firmly rooted in the concept of indirect discrimination from which it was derived in the case law.[16]

Somewhat similarly, Title VII of the US Civil Rights Act establishes the employers' obligation to make reasonable accommodation for the religious observances of their employees not through an express duty to that effect, but through a definition of the term 'religion', which includes the notion of accommodation[17] and thus makes it clear in the context of the legal construction of the Act that the refusal of reasonable accommodation short of incurring undue hardship constitutes prohibited (indirect) discrimination.[18]

Given that a closer look at the history and construction of reasonable accommodation in the US and in Canada tends to confirm that this notion is an emanation of the concept of indirect discrimination, it appears to be more than just arguable[19] that a duty of reasonable accommodation on the basis of the prohibition of indirect discrimination can be construed under the existing Employment Equality Directive. The Court of Justice of the European Union has never rejected such an interpretation; it has simply not had an opportunity yet to pronounce on this dimension of the prohibition of indirect discrimination on grounds of religion and belief. Against that background it is reasonable to enquire about the legal reasoning underpinning the suggestion that an express duty under EU law and thus an amendment of the Directive is necessary.

The main argument advanced in that context appears to be the fact that a finding of indirect discrimination as defined under EU law requires a *group* disadvantage as established by a comparison exercise, in contrast to the duty of reasonable accommodation as framed in Article 5 of the Employment Equality Directive, which focuses more specifically on the particularities of an individual in a given situation.[20] This consideration does not seem to carry too much weight since the religious commitments at issue in reasonable accommodation

13 See Bribosia, Ringelheim and Rorive (n 8) 145.

14 Section 2 reads: 'The purpose of this Act is to extend the laws in Canada to give effect, within the purview of matters coming within the legislative authority of Parliament, to the principle that all individuals should have an opportunity equal with other individuals to make for themselves the lives that they are able and wish to have and *to have their needs accommodated*, consistent with their duties and obligations as members of society, without being hindered in or prevented from doing so by discriminatory practices based on race, national or ethnic origin, colour, religion, age, sex, sexual orientation, marital status, family status, disability or conviction for an offence for which a pardon has been granted or in respect of which a record suspension has been ordered' (emphasis added).

15 According to Section 15(2), for any practice to be recognised as based on a *bona fide* occupational requirement or having a *bona fide* justification, 'it must be established that accommodation of the needs of an individual or a class of individuals affected would impose undue hardship on the person who would have to accommodate those needs, considering health, safety and cost'.

16 Bribosia and Rorive (n 5) 14 and 17; they also confirm that for the legal duty of accommodation to arise, discrimination based on grounds prohibited by the Canadian Human Rights Act must first be established.

17 Para 701(j) reads: 'The term "religion" includes all aspects of religious observance and practice, as well as belief, *unless an employer demonstrates that he is unable to reasonably accommodate to an employee's or prospective employee's religious observance or practice without undue hardship on the conduct of the employer's business*' (emphasis added).

18 This approach is even clearer in the 1990 Americans with Disabilities Act, which stipulates in its Section 12112(b)(5)(A) that discrimination on the basis of disability includes not making reasonable accommodations to the known limitations of an otherwise qualified individual with a disability who is an applicant or employee, unless it can be demonstrated that the accommodation would impose an undue hardship on the operation of the business.

19 See Vickers (n 7) 22.

20 Alidadi (n 5) 707; Bribosia and Rorive (n 5) 40.

cases and relating to religious dress, religious holidays and festivities and certain forms of (required or prohibited) conduct are typically the commitments of at least a certain (often orthodox) group of followers of a faith. It seems difficult if not impossible to dismiss any of the cases that have been researched in the context of the RELIGARE project[21] because of the lack of a group dimension. In fact, it is the rather individual nature of limitations and impairments caused by the specific condition of an individual's disability in the face of an infinite number of specific occupational requirements which militates in favour of an individual approach to reasonable accommodation in that area,[22] in contrast to religious commitments, which appear to be more group-based by definition.[23]

It is true that in the *Eweida* case recently decided by the ECtHR concerning an employee who wanted to visibly wear a cross as a sign of her commitment to her faith contrary to her employer's work uniform code,[24] the UK courts concluded that the concept of indirect discrimination implies discrimination against a defined group and that the applicant had not established evidence of a group disadvantage.[25] However, it would not appear to be an insurmountable obstacle to show that the wearing of a cross is a widely practised manifestation of belief.[26] Rather, there may be reason to believe that the UK courts took an overly restrictive view of the requirements for the establishment of a *prima facie* case of indirect discrimination in this case.[27]

This takes us to the second argument repeatedly offered to argue that an implicit duty of reasonable accommodation arising from the prohibition of indirect discrimination is insufficient and an express provision to that effect is necessary. That argument is the complexity of the concept of indirect discrimination. It is contended that this concept is still not correctly understood and applied by courts in many Member States and is therefore still surrounded by considerable legal uncertainty, which hampers the effectiveness of its application in daily life and makes it a second-best solution when compared to a straightforward explicit duty of reasonable accommodation.[28] Without trying to belittle the intricacy of the concept of indirect discrimination, it appears to be somewhat doubtful that the concept of reasonable accommodation is really superior in terms of the simplicity of its day-to-day application, especially in the light of the close correlation between the two concepts and the pivotal role of a proportionality assessment that essentially stays the same whether it is carried out under the heading of 'appropriate and necessary means to achieve a legitimate objective' or under the heading of 'disproportionate burden'.[29] These considerations aside, any finding of shortcomings in the accurate implementation of the prohibition of indirect discrimination would provide a strong incentive

---

21 An illustrative list of examples is also provided by Alidadi (n 5) 697.

22 L Waddington, 'Reasonable Accommodation: Time to Extend the Duty to Accommodate Beyond Disability?' (2011) 38 *NJCM Bulletin: Nederlands Tijdschrift voor de Mensenrechten* 186–98. Waddington highlights on p. 188 the need for an individualised analysis both in terms of the abilities of the recipient of the accommodation and the work-related skills and activities that are required.

23 ibid 194. This difference cannot be convincingly challenged by the statement of Alidadi (n 5) 709, that there are many examples of disability accommodation that would benefit a group of people and that in religious matters the trend towards individualisation calls for increasingly individualised solutions. The fact remains that the very notion of religion typically has a defining community/group dimension that would make it appear a rather exceptional situation for a certain practice by an employer to potentially affect only one individual person and not a certain (albeit perhaps small) group.

24 ECtHR (Fourth Section), *Eweida and Others v The United Kingdom*, judgment of 15 January 2013 (App nos 48420/10, 59842/10, 51671/10 and 36516/10). See the section 'The Impact of Fundamental Rights Law', below, for further consideration of that decision.

25 See paras 14–16 of the judgment. However, the UK Court of Appeal also argued in the alternative that a neutral rule putting a group of Christians at a disadvantage would be justified and therefore not amount to prohibited indirect discrimination.

26 All the more so as a practically identical case of another employee, Ms Chaplin, was pending in the UK at the same time and was eventually decided by the ECtHR in the same judgment, albeit with a different outcome.

27 The Employment Appeal Tribunal's reference to the need for a 'defined' group may point in the direction of the necessity of a commandment of a particular confession or a scriptural requirement. On the impact of the *Eweida* ruling on the interpretation of the Employment Equality Directive and national anti-discrimination law, see the section 'The Impact of Fundamental Rights Law', below.

28 Alidadi (n 5) 708; Bribosia and Rorive (n 5) 40.

29 The information provided under the section 'An Express Duty of Reasonable Accommodation: A Guarantee of Progress?', below, on the US and Canadian case law should testify to comparable levels of complexity. Waddington (n 22) 188, also points out the complexity of a duty of reasonable accommodation.

to insist on its proper use and interpretation and provide further clarifications, including through referrals for preliminary rulings. This avenue of further refining a concept that has been present in EU law for decades and has given rise to a substantial amount of case law does not appear to hold lesser prospects even from a purely legal perspective than the introduction of a new notion with its own (and new) intricacies.

The Impact of Fundamental Rights Law

It would go beyond the scope of this chapter to even attempt to take a thorough look at the extent to which the logic, if not the language, of reasonable accommodation has been recognised in the case law on the interpretation of the ECHR. But even a rather superficial analysis indicates that the 2013 judgment in the *Eweida* case marks a turning point.

In the landmark decision *Thlimmenos v Greece*,[30] a case concerning Greek legislation that barred a Jehovah's Witness from appointment to a post of chartered accountant because of a criminal conviction for his religiously motivated conscientious objection to military service, the ECtHR recognised for the first time that the principle of non-discrimination laid down in Article 14 ECHR not only prohibits the State from treating people who are in analogous situations differently, but also proscribes the *failure*, without an objective and reasonable justification, to treat differently persons whose situations are significantly different. On that basis it concluded that the Greek State had violated the applicant's right not to be discriminated against by its failure to introduce appropriate exceptions for offences committed exclusively because of religious beliefs to the rule barring persons convicted of a serious crime from access to the profession of chartered accountant.[31] It is generally acknowledged that this decision is based on the logic of reasonable accommodation, although this term is not used.[32]

The reason for discontent among the proponents of reasonable accommodation was less of a terminological nature and more rooted in the ECtHR case law on Article 9 ECHR protecting the freedom of thought, conscience and religion, which did not embrace that same logic. In fact, in cases concerning employment relationships the ECtHR generally did not even reach the stage of assessing the justification of an interference with the freedom to manifest a belief (which is governed by Article 9(2) ECHR), but denied any interference with that freedom. In a number of cases that did in fact concern requests for reasonable accommodation (such as requests concerning time off for prayers or the rescheduling of court hearings that fell on religious holidays), the ECtHR routinely applied the doctrine that, where a person is able to take steps to circumvent a limitation placed on the freedom to manifest religion or belief, there is no interference with the right under Article 9 ECHR and thus no requirement for a justification. In cases involving restrictions placed by employers on an employee's ability to observe religious practice, the possibility of resigning from the job and changing employment was interpreted as such a circumvention which excluded interference with Article 9 ECHR.[33]

While the *Thlimmenos* judgment did not have an immediate impact on this line taken by the ECtHR, the Court has now clearly departed from its earlier case law and embarked on a new path in *Eweida*. In that decision the Court noted that it had not adopted a similarly restrictive approach to the finding of interference in respect of employment sanctions imposed on individuals because they exercised other rights protected by the ECHR, such as the right to freedom of expression or the right to respect for private life. It concluded with the statement of principle that

> given the importance in a democratic society of freedom of religion, the Court considers that, where an individual complains of a restriction on freedom of religion in the workplace, rather than holding that the possibility of changing job would negate all interference with the right, the better approach would be to weigh that possibility in the overall balance when considering whether or not the restriction was proportionate.[34]

30 ECtHR (Grand Chamber) *Thlimmenos v Greece*, 6 April 2000, 31 EHRR 15.

31 Paras 44 and 48 of the judgment.

32 Bribosia and Rorive (n 5) 24.

33 See the description by the ECtHR in *Eweida*, para 83; Alidadi (n 5) 703–04; Bribosia and Rorive (n 5), 21–26, all with numerous case references.

34 Para 83 of the judgment.

On the basis of this new approach the ECtHR scrutinised whether or not the UK, which was obviously not directly responsible for any limitations imposed by a private employer, had complied with the positive obligation on State authorities under the Convention to secure the rights under Article 9 to those within their jurisdiction.[35] And after carrying out a proportionality test the Court held that, even taking into account the margin of appreciation enjoyed by the Contracting States, the UK courts had accorded too much weight to the employer's legitimate aim of projecting a certain corporate image through its uniform policy in the exercise of balancing it with the applicant's desire to manifest her belief by wearing a discreet cross that was visible but could not have detracted from her professional appearance. Consequently, it was concluded that the domestic authorities had failed to sufficiently protect the applicant's right to manifest her religion.[36]

Although that case was decided on the basis of Article 9 ECHR only, the Court itself clarified, in relation to another applicant in the same decision, that the proportionality assessment would be similar when analysing the same circumstances in the context of the non-discrimination provision of Article 14 ECHR.[37] The ECtHR seems to have come to an interpretation of both provisions that, without specifically referring to either reasonable accommodation or even the concept of indirect discrimination, amounts to a proportionality test incorporating the logic of reasonable accommodation.[38]

While that is of substantial significance in and of itself, the interesting question from an EU law perspective is whether and how these developments may affect the interpretation of Member State obligations under the Employment Equality Directive.[39] In that context the positive obligation of all EU Member States as Contracting States of the ECHR – and of the EU itself as soon as it has become a Contracting Party – to secure the rights of individuals under Article 9 may assume particular importance. The right to manifest one's belief as protected by Article 9 ECHR is an individual fundamental right free of any collective or group connotation. If Member States and the EU are required to protect that freedom by safeguarding proportionality in any interference with it by employers, they will have to do so by applying the relevant domestic or EU law construed in compliance with this obligation under the ECHR. Even if one were to consider that the necessity of a group disadvantage for the finding of indirect discrimination under the Directive implied shortcomings concerning the functional equivalence of that concept to an express duty of reasonable accommodation,[40] it would appear reasonable that the Convention imposes an interpretation of the Directive that ensures compliance with this obligation by relaxing requirements concerning the group dimension of the disadvantage.[41] If necessary the obligations under the ECHR as now construed by the ECtHR could therefore provide further assistance in supporting or requiring an interpretation of the concept of indirect discrimination under the Directive which guarantees the right to reasonable accommodation without an explicit obligation to that effect.

---

35 See para 84 of the judgment on the nature of this positive obligation.

36 Paras 89–95 of the judgment; the outcome was different for the second applicant, Ms Chaplin, a nurse who made a similar request to visibly wear a cross (paras 96–101). In the same judgment the ECtHR failed to detect disproportionality on health and safety grounds in the operation of a hospital.

37 Para 101, where the ECtHR held that the test is in fact so similar that after rejecting a breach of Article 9 ECHR, a fully fledged assessment of Article 14 ECHR was no longer necessary ('it considers that the factors to be weighed in the balance when assessing the proportionality of the measure under Article 14 taken in conjunction with Article 9 would be similar and that there is no basis on which it can find a violation of Article 14 either in this case').

38 The same phenomenon can be observed at the national level. The recent decision by the German Federal Administrative Court of 11 September 2013 (BVerwG 6 C 25.12) can serve as an illustration. In this case the possibility of wearing a bathing suit fully covering the whole body was considered a sufficient reasonable accommodation (without using this terminology) for a female Muslim student to participate in coeducational swimming lessons at school, thus rejecting a full dispensation from such lessons.

39 Or possibly under the Charter of Fundamental Rights of the European Union.

40 See the section 'Reasonable Accommodation and Indirect Discrimination: Two Sides of the Same Coin?', above.

41 After all, the wording of Article 2(2)(b) of the Directive, which defines indirect discrimination as practices which would put persons having a particular religion or belief at a particular disadvantage compared with other persons, appears to contain some openness as to the precise meaning of the use of the plural ('persons') in terms of a group disadvantage. It may well be of relevance in this context that religion and belief are the only prohibited grounds of discrimination that directly correspond to the exercise of a specific individual fundamental right.

An Express Duty of Reasonable Accommodation: A Guarantee of Progress?

Finally, I would like to briefly examine the justification of the expectation or hope that an amendment of EU law to stipulate an express duty of reasonable accommodation for religion or belief would necessarily lead to better outcomes than an approach based on the prohibition of indirect discrimination in terms of an appropriate weight accorded to the recognition of religious observance. The best way to do that would appear to be a look at the experience in the countries that have stipulated such a duty in their legislation, that is, the US and Canada.

The leading decision of the US Supreme Court concerning the interpretation of the duty of reasonable accommodation, and in particular the concept of undue hardship limiting this duty, is *TWA v Hardison*,[42] concerning a shift worker in a department operating around the clock who wanted to refrain from working on Saturdays in order to observe the Sabbath and was eventually dismissed after refusing to work during a designated shift. In its ruling the Supreme Court opted for a very extensive interpretation of what constitutes an undue hardship, and held that any requirement for the employer to bear more than a *de minimis* cost in order to give the claimant Saturdays off would represent such an undue hardship.[43] This is in contrast with the definition provided for the same concept in the context of disability defined in the Americans with Disabilities Act as an 'action requiring significant difficulty or expense',[44] and it also appears to go significantly beyond both the notion of 'disproportionate burden' in the Employment Equality Directive and the standards usually applied in the proportionality assessment for the justification of indirect discrimination under EU law. What is more, the US Supreme Court, irrespective of the cost dimension, made a statement of principle that the duty of reasonable accommodation cannot be interpreted as implying a justification for unequal treatment of workers, granting a privilege to those who want Saturdays off for religious reasons over those who have other strong but perhaps non-religious reasons for not wanting to work on weekends which would 'require an employer to discriminate against some employees in order to enable others to observe their Sabbath'.[45]

This restrictive view of the duty of reasonable accommodation was harshly criticised by Justice Marshall in his dissenting opinion as dealing a fatal blow to the accommodation of work requirements to religious practices and effectively nullifying the statutory obligation. Marshall not only called into question the construction of undue hardship, but also pointed out that the accommodation issue by definition only arises when a neutral rule of general applicability conflicts with the religious practices of a particular employee, and that therefore any exemption will always result in a privilege allocated according to religious beliefs.[46]

Without exaggerating the comparability of the legal situations in the US and the EU, the US example does, in my view, demonstrate that the mere existence of a duty of reasonable accommodation does not *per se* imply a higher level of protection. The statutory obligation as construed by the US Supreme Court, which excludes the right to accommodation wherever any competing rights and interests of other employees are at play and whenever it would have more than a *de minimis* cost, would appear to at least possibly lag behind the current level of protection under EU law without such an express duty. The US case law also illustrates the considerable complexity of the concept of reasonable accommodation and undue hardship or disproportionate burden, and the very real possibility of its different interpretation for different grounds of discrimination.[47] Against that background it is not easy to see why the danger of incorrect and inconsistent interpretation of the concept of indirect discrimination, one of the arguments used to advocate a duty of reasonable accommodation, would be significantly reduced in the event of the introduction of such a duty.

---

42 432 US 63 (1977).

43 Both of the options considered reasonable by the Court of Appeals – having a supervisor or another worker on duty elsewhere fill in for the claimant and replacing the claimant with another worker requiring overtime pay – were dismissed as undue hardship, the former on the basis of loss of efficiency, the latter for the additional expense it would cause.

44 Americans with Disabilities Act (1990), 42 USC, para 12111(10).

45 *TWA v Hardison* (n 42) at 84–85 but also at 81. A collective agreement regulating the allocation of shifts, from which a derogation would have been necessary, was of relevance in this case, but the principles established by the Supreme Court are not limited to this particular setting.

46 *TWA v Hardison* (n 42) 86ff.

47 Waddington (n 22) 191, points to the risk of confusion and legal uncertainty resulting from the application of different standards in different areas.

The evolution of the duty of reasonable accommodation under Canadian law shows the whole breadth of the spectrum of the possible interpretation of this type of obligation. The Canadian Supreme Court has unequivocally rejected the *de minimis* standard as applied in the US[48] and has generally held that in order to invoke undue hardship, including in relation to (potential) clashing rights of other employees, the mere hypothesis of a certain cost or of a disruption of a company's organisation is not sufficient; concrete evidence needs to be presented.[49] More recently, the Canadian Supreme Court has limited the scope of the duty of reasonable accommodation to some extent by deciding that it does not apply where a legislative measure of general application is involved.[50] While the Canadian example demonstrates a considerably farther-reaching and more extensive interpretation of the concept of reasonable accommodation, the comparison of the situations in Canada and the US also showcases that it is less the existence of an express obligation than the spirit in which it is applied that is decisive for its real effects and for its value added. The same could be said about the concept of indirect discrimination, which possesses the potential to incorporate the logic of reasonable accommodation.

Conclusions

It has not been the purpose of this chapter to categorically deny any value added of an express duty of reasonable accommodation for religion and belief under EU anti-discrimination law. In particular, considerations outside the strictly legal purview, such as the political message of an explicit provision[51] and the practical effect of framing such a duty without necessarily having to raise the issue whether an employer is indirectly discriminating against some employees, would have to be taken into account in weighing the existence of such a value added.

Rather, the intention was to examine whether the recommendation in the RELIGARE final report to introduce such a duty in the Employment Equality Directive is the indispensable and only means to achieve the objective of a fair balancing of religious commitments of employees with both the business needs of the employer and the clashing rights or needs of other employees.

Against the backdrop of limited prospects for amendments to the Employment Equality Directive in the near future, the analysis of the notion of reasonable accommodation, in particular its conceptual history and development as a corollary of indirect discrimination, suggests that the objectives of a duty of reasonable accommodation could be achieved by the application of the existing rules on indirect discrimination to a very large or even to the same extent.

At the same time, the US example shows that an express duty of reasonable accommodation is not *per se* a panacea that can bring about an adequate recognition of faith-based practices in the workplace. Hard cases will always remain hard, and the final outcome will always depend on the proportionality analysis that is the key feature in the assessment of both indirect discrimination and a disproportionate burden.

In the light of these circumstances, advocacy should not focus entirely on new legislation and neglect the considerable potential of the legislation already in place. A key problem appears to reside not so much in the inadequacy of the concept of indirect discrimination to address issues of reasonable accommodation,

48 In *Central Okanagan School District No. 23 v Renaud* [1992] 2 SCR 970, 984.

49 See Bribosia, Ringelheim and Rorive (n 8) 146–50 for a detailed description of the Canadian case law.

50 In *Alberta v Hutterian Brethren of Wilson Colony* [2009] 2 SCR 567, the members of a religious community challenged a regulation obliging them to display a photo on the driver's license on the basis of their belief that the Second Commandment prohibited them from having their photograph willingly taken. The Supreme Court held in paras 67–71 that the concept of reasonable accommodation, which envisions a dynamic process of adjustment of the relationship between two parties – most commonly an employer and employee – is not suitable for the very different relationship that pertains between a legislature and the people subject to its laws. However, it carried out a proportionality assessment taking into account the legitimate objective of the legislation and its impact on the religious freedom of the claimants, and it is not clear whether the outcome of that process would have been any different from applying the concept of reasonable accommodation.

51 If one extended the duty of reasonable accommodation beyond its current scope of disability, where some specific considerations appear to be relevant, one would have to answer the question why such a duty should exist only for religion and belief, and not also for the other grounds of discrimination, in particular age.

but in the fact that this has not been sufficiently tested yet. Given the number of cases examined in the context of the RELIGARE project and the obvious link of the accommodation requested to matters of indirect discrimination as covered by the Employment Equality Directive and its transposition in Member States, it is rather surprising that this dimension is rarely invoked, that no preliminary questions have yet been referred to the CJEU, and that cases are argued rather in terms of fundamental rights and eventually taken to the ECtHR.[52]

The CJEU has only once had the opportunity to pronounce on a matter of reasonable accommodation, and that was in 1976, long before the adoption of any EU legislation protecting against discrimination on grounds of religion and belief. In *Prais*,[53] the plaintiff had complained about scheduling a written test in a competition for recruitment on a Jewish holiday during which she was not permitted to travel or write and could thus not participate. On the basis of general considerations in the absence of specific legislation, the Court carried out a balancing exercise weighing the interest of candidates of a certain creed for whom a certain date would be unsuitable against the principle of equality requiring that written tests shall be administered under the same conditions and on the same date for all candidates. It came to the conclusion that where a candidate informs the competent authority that certain dates are impossible for religious reasons, this should be taken into account and an attempt should be made to avoid those dates. Where the authority has not been (made) aware in good time of such difficulties, the Court held that it is justified to refuse offering an alternative date, particularly if other candidates have already been convoked for the test.

Admittedly this is an application of the logic of reasonable accommodation in a somewhat embryonic form, but it is a starting point. Further trying to build on this first precedent, on a solid basis of existing anti-discrimination legislation and settled case law on indirect discrimination in general, should not be neglected or dismissed in order to place one's hope in an amendment to the Employment Equality Directive, which is not very likely to materialise any time soon.

52 It is rather striking, for example, that this also happened even in the recent *Eweida* case, which was argued before UK courts within the framework of anti-discrimination legislation.

53 *Vivien Prais v Council of the European Communities*, 27 October 1976, Case C-130/75, ECR [1976] 1589.

Section 3
Seeing Religious Diversity in Context

Chapter 18
Seeking Soft Measures: Complementing Law and Policy as a Strategy for Responding to Diversity

Lori G. Beaman[1]

The management of religious diversity has become a central preoccupation in a number of liberal democracies. The seriousness with which this broad topic is being treated is evidenced in part by the commitment of large amounts of research funding to projects that study religious diversity, including those that identify problems, explore solutions and make recommendations. Examples of such projects include, of course, RELIGARE, but also the Religion and Society Research Programme in the United Kingdom, IMPACT in Sweden, NOREL in Norway and NRP 58 in Switzerland. Sometimes the recommendations made by such projects take the form of legislative or policy directives or suggestions. The focus of this volume is the document prepared by the members of the RELIGARE project as a result of their intensive examination of religious diversity and its management in 10 countries. Part of their mandate was to prepare a series of recommendations that could inform European policy and law on the management of diversity.

In addition to these law- and policy-focused recommendations, the final RELIGARE report includes mention of something that might go largely unnoticed, given the rather strong focus on law in the programme of research that has been carried out. Rather than focusing on law and policy, the discussion in this chapter proposes an alternative or complementary tack. The RELIGARE report supports a normative stance that emphasises developing 'a concept of *equality* which requires (mutual) adaptation and change' as opposed to 'requiring people to conform to existing norms',[2] and follows up by stating:

> In light of these normative choices, the mode of handling issues or conflicts (through judicial, legislative or regulatory means, or simply through the use of certain voluntary (good) practices) is not irrelevant. *Soft measures* should be complementary to more ambitious proposals for legislative change in a volatile environment. (*Report*, 19, emphasis added)

In this chapter I argue that in fact these 'soft measures' should lead the conversation about the management of diversity; that they are tied up with the vision of equality mentioned in the same quotation; and that, indeed, the very notion of diversity as something to be managed needs to be re-thought, particularly in relation to the oscillations people experience in relation to their religious lives and the identity rigidity that characterises intellectual imaginings of religion.[3]

Soft Measures

What exactly is meant by 'soft measures'? Although the report does not elaborate on this, I argue that soft measures noted by RELIGARE are to be found at the level of everyday interaction between people as they go

1 I would like to acknowledge the support of the Religion and Diversity Project in the preparation of this chapter as well as the ongoing financial support of my research through my Canada Research Chair in the Contextualization of Religion in a Diverse Canada. I am also grateful to Marianne Abou-Hamad for her editorial assistance.

2 The authors of the RELIGARE report have borrowed the preceding quotes from S Fredman, 'Disability Equality: A Challenge to the Existing Anti-Discrimination Paradigm?' in A Lawson and C Gooding (eds), *Disability Rights in Europe: From Theory to Practice* (Hart Publishing 2005) 203.

3 A-S Lamine, 'Singular Pluralities: A Critical Review of Religious Pluralism' (2013) 4 (1) *Religion and Society: Advances in Research* 150–66.

about their day-to-day lives. As a site for research these everyday interactions, or 'non-events', remain largely unexplored in projects on the management of religious diversity. In short, despite the incidents of disagreement, conflict and prejudice that seem to provide the foundational place from which many of us are considering religious diversity, there is a parallel world of the everyday in which people work out religious difference, often as one of many pieces of their identity 'package'. The incidents of people working out religious difference often occur in such mundane circumstances that they are frequently overlooked by those of us seeking to puzzle through the 'new diversity'. Yet, it is these strategies of negotiation and navigation employed by so-called ordinary people that offer a potential map and alternative narrative to the current one of religious diversity as a problem to be managed. To put this in public policy terms, the ways that religious diversity is worked through can assist in the formulation of best practices, which may be translated into more formal legal or policy measures, but may simply remain at the local level as a strategy for enacting this mutual version of equality.

In many instances, such strategies are so local and so context specific that translating them into a broader formulation of 'best practices' may be extremely challenging, if not impossible. This is not, however, a good justification for dismissing them or ignoring them. Varied strategies of navigating religious difference can, at the very least, offer master narratives of positive encounters of those who are religiously different. There is an abundance of negative narratives, while stories of positive interaction are rarely researched, reported on in the media or drawn from by policy- and lawmakers in their formulations of responses to the 'problem' of diversity.

Diversity and the idea of religious difference also include those who describe themselves as 'nones'. It is between nones and the religious where there is often an under-recognised potential for tension, disrespect, conflict and even hatred. Given the increasing number of religious nones, the potential for conflict between the 'religious' and the 'non-religious' should not be underestimated. Certainly, cases like *Lautsi*[4] in Italy, which eventually went before the Grand Chamber, and *Saguenay*[5] in Canada, which is on its way to the Supreme Court of Canada, are illustrations of this contest between a religious majority (in both cases presenting itself as 'culture and heritage' and 'universal values') and religious nones, in these cases specifically atheists. Both of these cases involve contests over the display of religious symbols in State-controlled spaces (a school and a municipal council chamber).

As previously mentioned, it is soft measures (not law, legislation and policy) that should lead in the discussion of religious diversity. Thus, we may want to challenge the very term 'soft measures'. Those who live with diversity, while often doing so with no fuss or thought that what they are doing can even be called negotiation or navigation, are doing the hard work of creating and maintaining an inclusive society. By calling these soft measures (presumably part of a soft/hard binary), we risk creating a hierarchy that minimises the creativity, generosity and flexibility of people as they innovatively respond to those who may not share their beliefs and practices, whether religious or non-religious. The grounded wisdom of everyday strategies of diversity navigation is as important as the grand pronouncements of law and policy.

There are two key features of the sorts of interactions included in the everyday navigation of religious difference that are foundational to soft measures: first, religious identity is only one part of such interactions, and, in fact, sometimes only a very minor part. Second, in the process of interacting, people are often focused on similarities which arise from shared experiences or identity points other than religion, or a combination of both. Similarity exists on a continuum between sameness and difference; both identities and points of similarity are extremely fluid, which allows for the sort of navigation that comprises soft measures. So, for example, a shared experience as neighbours, parents or women may characterise an interaction and serve to bypass religious difference. Highlighting religious identity may foreclose the possibility of other identity markers acting to bridge difference.

Soft Measures, Law and Equality

The RELIGARE report's mention of equality notes that it requires mutual adaptation and change. The reconstitution of equality as a conceptual tool is, as the report notes, an important task. But is this version

4 See *Lautsi v Italy*, ECHR 2009, no 30814/06; *Lautsi and Others v Italy*, ECHR 2011, no 30814/06.

5 *Saguenay (Ville de) v Mouvement Laïque Québécois*, 2013 QCCA 936.

of equality to be found in law? The legal notion of equality varies depending on the social context in which it is situated. In the European context, equality is, for the most part, imagined as being 'sameness' and thus relies on a very formal notion of equality. The French notion of *laïcité* is premised on such a formal idea of equality, as is in fact the republican notion of citizenship. Such formal notions stand in contrast to substantive understandings of equality, which recognise that it may be achieved through differential treatment. Sometimes, for example, historical wrongs must be addressed or structural impediments to equality must be balanced. This more responsive approach to inequality is frequently characterised by majorities as being unfair to them, as exceptions, as accommodations or as special treatment.

It is not, however, these legal understandings of equality that are of most interest in relation to the 'soft measures' advocated by the RELIGARE report. More important is the idea of an equality that requires mutual adaptation and change and is located in the space of everyday interactions in which people perceive each other as equals, enacting an ethic of respect, caring, consideration, neighbourliness, flexibility and a recognition of similarity rather than an emphasis on either sameness or difference. This equality, intimately tied up with the notion of 'soft measures', is something I have called 'deep equality' in other contexts.[6] It is relational, enacted in day-to-day relations between people as they encounter each other in the course of ordinary life.

What is the relationship between the notion of soft measures, equality and law? The RELIGARE proposal is clear that soft measures are to be complementary to legal and policy attempts to regulate religious diversity. This relationship between the role of law in the regulation of religious diversity and the possibility of citizen action is an ongoing element of public discussions. For example, when the government of the Canadian province of Québec established a commission to examine increased diversity in the province and a perceived problem of 'too much accommodation' (known as the Bouchard–Taylor Commission), some of the groups and individuals who made public submissions to the commission (there were 900 such submissions) suggested that law was being overused in the resolution of disputes about 'reasonable accommodation'. In their report the commissioners, Gérard Bouchard and Charles Taylor, responded to this theme by suggesting that citizens should, instead of turning to the law, engage in a strategy of 'concerted adjustment' to resolve disputes.[7] There was no evidence of an actual abuse or overuse of the law and the human rights protections offered in relation to freedom of religion, so such a suggestion seems to have been made to create a sense of action around a problem that was not, in fact, a problem.

Encouraging an attitude that sees law as somehow intrusive or inappropriate in cases of human rights abuses is not a particularly desirable direction. It can have the effect of leaving vulnerable people and groups feeling isolated and without any recourse for unjust treatment. But the sentiment behind the idea that people should work among themselves to resolve disputes about religious difference is one that, if taken in a slightly different direction, could be helpful. In recognising that power relations are often unequal between employers and employees, and between some immigrants and those who perceive themselves to be 'original' members of some societies, it is important to ensure that law can afford protections for unjust treatment of vulnerable people, who are often minority members of society. However, it is also important to recognise that religious difference and needs are often simply negotiated or navigated in the course of day-to-day life. Religious difference or needs frequently do not reach a dispute stage, but are simply part of the multiple negotiations that happen between people as they encounter each other. It is this working out, and a close examination of how those agreements, which are often tacit or *de facto*, are embedded in day-to-day practices, that can constitute what the RELIGARE report has termed 'soft measures'. It is these measures that cultivate a sense of belonging and inclusiveness, no matter what the 'status' of the parties involved.

6 See LG Beaman, '"It Was All Slightly Unreal": What's Wrong with Tolerance and Accommodation in the Adjudication of Religious Freedom?' (2011) 23 (2) *Canadian Journal of Women and Law* 442–63; LG Beaman, 'Alternatives to Reasonable Accommodation' in LG Beaman (ed), *Reasonable Accommodation: Managing Religious Diversity* (UBC Press 2012) 208–23; LG Beaman, 'Deep Equality: Moving beyond Tolerance and Accommodation' and 'Response' (winter 2012) *Impetus* <www.luthercollege.edu/impetus> accessed 27 June 2014; LG Beaman, 'Tolerance and Accommodation as Vestiges of Empire' in B Berman, R Bhargava and A Laliberté (eds), *Secular States and Religious Diversity* (UBC Press 2013) 120–35; LG Beaman, 'Woven Together: Advocacy and Research as Complementary' (2014) 44 (2) *Religion* 276–88.

7 G Bouchard and C Taylor, *Building the Future: A Time for Reconciliation* (Government of Québec 2008) 19.

Deflecting Diversity

The assumptions underlying the focus on religious diversity in public policy and research include the notion that diversity is a problem to be solved; that it inevitably presents conflict or tension; that religious diversity is constituted by different religious groups and individuals with discrete and separate identities; and that the site of research is the problem or what is not working rather than what might be working. These assumptions raise an important question: to what extent is public policy and even law being formulated on the basis of the most difficult and least common experiences and incidents? This in turn raises another issue: should best practices, which are essentially what policy and law should reflect, be based on the everyday negotiation of religious difference rather than on that minority of cases that are problematic?

At the conclusion of their Danish Pluralism Project, which began in 2002, Ahlin et al. reflected on the work that the concept of diversity was doing in their examination of religion in Denmark.[8] They noted in particular that the concepts of religious pluralism and religious diversity may be based on unsustainable assumptions about the stability of the relationship between 'religion and religious adherents and clear-cut boundaries between religious groups'.[9] Certainly religion as it is often used by social scientists, humanities scholars, policymakers and those who work in law, has taken on this air, floating disconnectedly from the practices of day-to-day life that are so difficult to describe given our current conceptual repertoire. Given the fluidity with which religious identities manifest in social life, as well as the growing number of people who describe themselves as religious nones, the observations of Ahlin et al. must be taken as a serious call to reconfigure the ways that religion is studied.[10]

A recent survey commissioned by the Religion and Society Programme based in the United Kingdom and conducted by YouGov offers insights relevant to the emphasis on difference embedded in diversity 'management'.[11] The survey explored attitudes among religious groups towards three contentious issues: abortion, euthanasia and same-sex marriage. Rather than finding significant disparities between religious groups, the study found that the vast majority of people, whether religious or not, held similar beliefs about all of these issues. There was, the survey found, a relatively small group (about 9 per cent of the population), spread across religious traditions but with a greater concentration of Baptists and Muslims, who shared a position in opposition to the vast majority of the population. Linda Woodhead, the director of the Religion and Society Programme, calls this the 'moral minority'.[12] However, being male and voting Conservative turned out to be better predictors of a narrow view of these family-related issues than belonging to that moral minority.[13] The point is, most people are similar in their values and thus an emphasis on difference, whether because of religion or other factors, plays to a conceptualisation of diversity and its potential challenges that may be misguided at best. Further, such an overemphasis can reinforce negative narratives that create a sense of a problem in need of a solution. In fact, most people simply get along most of the time.

To put it in Foucauldian terms, the demarcation of the problem of diversity has in part created the problem of diversity. In our haste to solve the problems of diversity and to formulate legal solutions, we have forgotten to examine the many ways in which people work together to resolve any difference. And sometimes they do not even 'work' at it – it simply happens. These non-events are the most difficult to track because they are based in an ease of relations that obscures the identification of the interaction with the notion of a problem.

8 L Ahlin, J Borup, M Qvortrup Fibiger, L Kühle, V Mortensen and R Dybdal Pedersen, 'Religious Diversity and Pluralism: Empirical Data and Theoretical Reflections from the Danish Pluralism Project' (2012) 27 (3) *Journal of Contemporary Religion* 403–18.

9 ibid 403.

10 L Woodhead, 'Five Concepts of Religion' (2011) 21 (1) *International Review of Sociology* 121–43.

11 L Woodhead, 'Westminster Faith Debates: Research' (*Faithdebates.org*, 2013) <http://faithdebates.org.uk/research/> accessed 27 June 2014.

12 L Woodhead, 'Note from across the Pond: Church–State Separation isn't for Everyone' (*Religion Dispatches*, 12 August 2013) <http://religiondispatches.org/note-from-across-the-pond-church-state-separation-isnt-for-everyone/> accessed 27 June 2014.

13 L Woodhead, 'Press Release Westminster Faith Debate 4: Old Tory Men Have the Narrowest View of Family' (*Religion and Society*, 27 March 2013) <www.religionandsociety.org.uk/events/programme_events/show/press_release_westminster_faith_debate_4_old_tory_men_have_the_narrowest_view_of_family> accessed 27 June 2014.

Conclusions

If 'hard measures' are the response to diversity found in law and policy, then we may want to rethink the role they are playing in discussions about difference and religion. To be sure, difference between people and groups exists and can and does cause tension, conflict and violence. But to base a general approach to religious diversity on examples of 'what went wrong' rather than on those strategies and interactions that model 'what went right' risks exacerbating difference, overemphasising religious identity and creating problems rather than solving them. In their report the RELIGARE team notes, 'The sociological interviews, for their part, show where there is need for clearer and more explicit justification on the part of legislatures and why, in recent years, some actions in particular have given rise to critical comments' (*Report*, 12). Although we must read between the lines to discern the critical comments that emerged from the sociological data, we might guess that poorly explained and justified laws attract the attention (and critical commentary) of religious minorities, majorities and the non-religious. In part this is because actions that are based in conflict experience do not speak to the experience of many people, no matter how they are socially situated. Moreover, developing social policy and law that reflect positive social practices, and being clear about their basis, may offer the key to deflecting the critical comments mentioned in the report. In other words, mapping positive interactions and creating a narrative that is an alternative to the problem-based one upon which much diversity research relies can shift the focus to the soft measures and away from the hard alternatives like law. Although the State has a role to play in navigating difference, law's heavy-handed approach can exacerbate rather than help in the management of diversity.

Chapter 19
Traditional African Religions: Culture or Religion?

Tom Bennett

Introduction

This chapter concerns traditional African religions (TARs), with specific reference to their fate under South Africa's new democratic constitution.[1] The country is now firmly committed to a path of both religious and cultural diversity,[2] and non-discrimination on the basis of, inter alia, race, religion or culture.[3] The policy on diversity was set in place by the Interim Constitution (1993),[4] and affirmed in several subsequent court decisions.[5]

The duty to respect cultural and religious pluralism has been interpreted to mean more than mere tolerance: the State and other concerned bodies are obliged to engage actively in maintaining and promoting diversity.[6] In this regard, South African courts would echo sentiments in Europe: that protecting the security, lifestyles and identities of minority groups serves ultimately not only the interests of the minorities themselves but also the wider society.[7]

Those adhering to a TAR in South Africa probably constitute only 0.3 per cent of the population. By far the majority (approximately 86 per cent) claim membership in a Christian denomination, in particular membership in one of the independent African churches.[8] In light of the minority status of TARs, the constitutional principles of non-discrimination and freedom of religion might have been expected to have a significant bearing on TARs, but this has not necessarily been the case.

In South Africa – and elsewhere in Africa – talk of religion normally implies one of the main monotheisms: Judaism, Islam or Christianity. TARs are generally overlooked because courts, lawyers and even the people themselves are inured to thinking of TARs as matters of culture.[9] This tendency is due in large part to a persistent prejudice resulting from many years of missionary and colonial activity.[10] As a result, TARs are taken less seriously than other religions.

The primacy of religion in European thought, and indeed the distinction between religion and culture, is evident in the history of the human rights movement.[11] Freedom to live and worship according to the dictates of one's faith was one of the earliest rights to be given legal force in Europe. A right to culture appeared only much later, during the late eighteenth and early nineteenth centuries, when it was taken to mean a freedom to pursue an intellectual or artistic endeavour, akin to a freedom of expression.[12] A later meaning, which is the

1 With its remarkably progressive Bill of Rights (Chapter 2 of the 1996 Constitution).

2 See *Christian Education, South Africa v Minister of Education*, 2000 (4) SA 757 (CC) para 24, for example.

3 Section 9 of the Constitution.

4 Constitutional Principle XI, as read with section 71(1)(a) of Act 200 of 1993, Schedule 4.

5 Beginning with *Ryland v Edros*, 1997 (2) SA 690 (C) 17–18.

6 *MEC for Education, KwaZulu-Natal, and Others v Pillay*, 2008 (1) SA 474 (CC) para 65.

7 *Chapman v UK* [GC] no 27238/95 §93 ECHR 2001-I. See also *Muñoz Díaz v Spain*, no 49151/07 para 59 2009 ECHR.

8 See *Statistics South Africa Primary Tables of South Africa Census '96 and 2001 Compared* (2001) <www.statssa.gov.za/census01/html/RSAPrimary.pdf> accessed 11 November 2013.

9 As, for example, in the recent dispute about the burial place for the Mandela ancestors; B Horner, 'Row over Mandela's Last Resting Place', *Sunday Times* (Johannesburg, 29 May 2011) 1. See *Mandela and Others v Dalibhunga (Mandela) and Others* (1552/13) [2013] ZAECMHC 7 (3 July 2013).

10 In this regard, even the definition of African religions has been largely determined by colonial discourse; HP Müller, 'The Invention of Religion: Aspects of the South African Case' (2000) 26 *Social Dynamics* 56, 64.

11 See T Banchoff and R Wuthnow, 'Introduction' in T Banchoff and R Wuthnow (eds), *Religion and the Global Politics of Human Rights* (OUP 2011) 6.

12 See Article 15(1)(a) and (c) of the International Covenant on Civil and Political Rights (1966).

concern of much of today's litigation, denoted a people's store of knowledge, beliefs, arts, morals, laws and customs.[13] In this sense, culture functions to distinguish one group from another.[14]

This chapter explores both the reasons for classifying TARs as culture and the consequences of doing so. The fate of TARs in South Africa may therefore be instructive for law- and policymakers in Europe, both with regard to Africans who happen to be present in Europe and profess a TAR, and with regard to other belief systems – such as Buddhism – which do not conform to Eurocentric conceptions of religion.

An Example of a Traditional African Religion

In order to understand the European reaction to TARs, a brief description will be given of the main features of the religion of the amaPondo,[15] a group of isiXhosa speakers from the Eastern Cape Province of South Africa.[16] These people, in common with nearly all those of southern Africa, used to (and still do) believe in the existence of a single, supreme being: uThixo. In writings about isiXhosa religious beliefs, however, the supreme being usually goes unnoticed, because it is a *deus otiosus*, and is therefore too remote from everyday life to be concerned with the doings of individuals.[17] In consequence, the living do not call upon uThixo to intervene in their lives, nor do they have special rituals dedicated to its worship.[18] These are features that inevitably result in an unfavourable comparison with the God of the Abrahamic faiths.

Instead, the spirits of deceased clan members exert the most immediate influence in daily life. These beings are sources of wisdom, authority and security. Their presence is most strongly felt when they visit retribution on people who infringe the accepted standards of good conduct (the moral code of *ubuntu*).[19] While the ancestors may be those of the recently or long departed, not all those who die are destined to be taken into the spirit realm. People who lived a life of *ubuntu* are preferred,[20] while the fate of children who were too young to become properly socialised is left vague.[21]

Veneration of the ancestors involves recognition of a form of life after death, together with the notion of a spirit or 'soul' (*ithongo*).[22] Some months after a person has died, the family calls his or her *ithongo* back to the homestead, when the deceased's estate can then be distributed and the spirit laid to rest. From then on, the spirit is free to join all the other departed who constitute the patrilineal clan. Communication with the spirit world is maintained by the performance of certain rituals, one of which requires the slaughter of animals.[23]

---

13 In other words, everything that humans acquire by virtue of being members of society. This definition is taken from the founder of cultural anthropology, EB Tylor, *Primitive Culture: Researches into the Development of Mythology, Philosophy, Religion, Language, Art and Custom* (1st vol, 4th edn, John Murray 1920) 1. See H Strydom, 'The International and Public Law Debate on Cultural Relativism and Cultural Identity: Origin and Implication' (1996) 21 *SA Yearbook of Int L* 1, 4ff.

14 Hence, culture is inherently oppositional, and consciousness of culture arises only through close interaction between two or more social groups; EE Roosens, *Creating Ethnicity: The Process of Ethnogenesis* (Sage 1989) 12.

15 This system obviously cannot stand for the rest of Africa, but it does contain certain features that are evident in many other TARs.

16 This account is taken from M Hunter, *Reaction to Conquest: Effects of Contact with Europeans on the Pondo of South Africa* (OUP 1936) and FH Kuckertz, *Creating Order: The Image of the Homestead in Mpondo Social Life* (Wits University Press 1990). Both works are dated, but are useful in that they took careful note of the effects of colonisation and labour migration on Pondo culture.

17 Although some peoples in South Africa accord the supreme being power to determine the workings of nature. See WD Hammond-Tooke, 'World View I: A System of Beliefs' in WD Hammond-Tooke (ed), *The Bantu-Speaking Peoples of Southern Africa* (2nd edn, Routledge & Kegan Paul 1974) 320–21.

18 ibid 319.

19 ibid ch 10.

20 *uBuntu* is the foundational concept of the indigenous systems of ethics in South Africa; TW Bennett and J Patrick, 'Ubuntu, the Ethics of Traditional Religions' in TW Bennett (ed), *Traditional African Religions in South African Law* (UCT Press 2011) 223ff.

21 Hunter (n16) 231.

22 ibid 232.

23 See VW Turner, *The Ritual Process* (University of Chicago Press 1969) ch 1 on the Ndembu of Zambia.

Apart from the ancestors, the traditional African pantheon had room for other lesser spirit beings, both benign and malign. Their powers were generally tied to special places and objects.[24] More important, however, was (and still is) a pervasive belief in witchcraft. Practitioners of the dark arts can be detected through physical stigmata, aberrant social behaviour and association with animal familiars. In some systems, individuals are thought to have the power to attract and exploit spiritual forces actively; in others, they are thought to be born with it. In either event, witches are seen as a prime source of evil, whether in the social or the natural world.[25]

Belief in the power of ancestors, spirits and witches places TARs at the lower end of an evolutionary scale of religions that was widely used in European writings about exotic belief systems.[26] According to this idea, 'religion' was thought to have progressed from animism to ancestor worship to polytheism and, from there, to the pinnacle of development: monotheism. In terms of such thinking, the central elements of African belief were put down to simple animism or outright superstition.[27]

As it happens, TARs such as the one described above are disappearing. Because the integrity of a TAR depends on orthopraxis rather than orthodoxy,[28] ritual veneration of the ancestors is a critically important issue. It is difficult to sustain, however, in the overcrowded cities that are now home to over half of the South African population.[29] On the one hand, the keeping and slaughter of the livestock needed to perform veneration rituals are prohibited in urban areas,[30] and, on the other, the anonymity and transience of modern city life cuts people off from the rural surroundings that were home to their ancestors.[31]

Perhaps the most important reason for the decline of TARs, however, is their syncretistic outlook, which makes them susceptible to assimilation by proselytising monotheisms.[32] In this regard, it is difficult to determine whether particular belief systems are now TARs or Christian, since most of those professing Christianity belong to one of the African independent churches.[33] These groups, which feature faith healing, revelation through dreams and baptism in rivers, have synthesised elements of both Christianity and the TARs. So it has come about that Africa's indigenous religions seldom exist in a pure form.[34]

The Fate of Traditional African Religions under Colonialism

With colonial penetration of Africa began a tendency to classify TARs as matters of culture. A typical colonial propensity, and one that is probably inescapable when people attempt to come to terms with alien data, was to overgeneralise.[35] In the process, the data were then reduced to whatever categories were available in the

24 See further JS Mbiti, *Concepts of God in Africa* (SPCK 1970) 3–16, 114–27 and 220–33.

25 Hunter (n 16) 275ff.

26 This scale of development derives from Tylor (n 13) 1.

27 This term is generally used to denigrate a supposedly deficient belief of others. See footnote 60 below.

28 W Menski, *Comparative Law in a Global Context: The Legal Systems of Asia and Africa* (2nd edn, CUP 2006) 414–15.

29 See, for instance, Hunter (n 16) 455–58, 487 and 488–96. cf BA Pauw, 'Ancestor Beliefs and Rituals among Urban Africans' (1974) 33 *African Studies* 99, 99ff.

30 Hunter (n 16) 537, 547–48.

31 I Hofmeyr, *'We Spend Our Years as a Tale that is Told': Oral Historical Narrative in a South African Chiefdom* (Wits University Press 1993) 159–60.

32 See, for example, BA Pauw, 'The Influence of Christianity' in WD Hammond-Tooke (ed), *The Bantu-Speaking Peoples of Southern Africa* (2nd edn, Routledge & Kegan Paul 1974) 415ff.

33 The Zionist Christian Church, for instance, is the largest denomination in South Africa, accounting for 11.1 per cent of the country's population in 2001; *Statistics South Africa* (n 8) 28. See JP Kiernan, 'African Traditional Religions in South Africa' in M Prozesky and J de Gruchy (eds), *Living Faiths in South Africa* (David Philip 1995) 15ff; D Chidester, *Religions of South Africa* (Routledge 1992) 112–47.

34 See figures given by the Pew Forum working on estimates from the World Religion Database; Pew Research Religion and Public Life Forum, 'Islam and Christianity in Sub-Saharan Africa' (pewforum.org, 15 April 2010), <http://features.pewforum.org/africa/> accessed 4 November 2013.

35 J Amoah and TW Bennett, 'The Freedoms of Religion and Culture under the South African Constitution: Do Traditional African Religions Enjoy Equal Treatment?' (2008) 8 *Afr Hum Rts LJ* 357, 360.

observers' own conceptual repertoire. In the case of TARs, the two most obvious categories were animism and ancestor 'worship'.[36]

Certain Christian missionaries in southern Africa went even further to say that Africans had no religion at all.[37] Admittedly, the vernacular languages had no specific word that could be translated as 'religion', but the missionaries' evangelical background led them to believe that a true religion required the worship of a god (or gods) or, at the very least, an explanation for the existence and meaning of humanity.[38] These were not qualities that they could see in the TARs.

Unfortunately, the very nature of Africa's indigenous religions made them vulnerable to this type of assessment. Their observance was not prescribed by set canons of belief; they were not administered by professional clerical institutions; they made no claim to a universal validity, nor did they pose an apocalyptic contest between sin and virtue, justification in a final judgment or an eternal salvation. Instead, they appeared to outsiders as collections of esoteric rituals, with little coherence or system, and thus inferior to the familiar monotheisms.[39]

The fact that African religions functioned in terms of an oral tradition interposed another negative influence on European perceptions.[40] Indeed, it is obvious that an oral culture will frame knowledge and experience in ways quite different to a literate tradition. Without writing, it is more difficult to differentiate particular systems of knowledge. In the case of TARs, for instance, one of the consequences was an absence of canonical texts and a codified system of morality.[41] This, in part, accounted for the absence of ideas of an orthodoxy (and the corresponding heterodoxy). Even worse, from a Western perspective, the illiterate bore an indelible mark of the primitive.

Linked to the above, and perhaps the most serious shortcoming in TARs, was their failure to draw a clear distinction between the sacred and the profane.[42] If a society does not differentiate (sacred) belief from (profane) knowledge, it has no need for a professional class to analyse and interpret a specialist subject. Admittedly, the conduct of rituals might require particular skills, and might also entail privileged access to supernatural powers. In fact, the practice of most TARs requires diviners, spirit mediums and 'witch doctors' (who specialise in the detection of malevolent forces). But, notwithstanding these expert groups, there was no authoritative body specifically qualified to pronounce on matters of faith and orthodoxy.[43]

Syncretism was a final, complicating factor concerning the colonial – and even current – perceptions of TARs. These religions are not driven by a need to proselytise to the non-believers. To the contrary, they are open to proselytising influences, leaving their adherents susceptible to absorption into Islam or Christianity. These, the two major missionary faiths in Africa, were driven to preach a 'true' belief on the understanding that potential converts were either damned or lacking a proper faith.[44]

In the case of Christianity, the evangelical churches were supported by the policy of the colonial States,[45] because the only plausible justification for conquering Africa was a need to persuade the 'natives' to accept the

36 A better term is 'veneration'. When described as 'worship', the practice is subtly denigrated since, in terms of monotheistic belief, ancestors are clearly misplaced as subjects of prayer and reverence.

37 L Alberti, *Ludwig Alberti's Account of the Tribal Life and Customs of the Xhosa in 1807* (William Fehr tr, AA Balkema 1968) 47; E Casalis, *The Basutos, or Twenty-Three Years in South Africa* (James Nisbet 1861) 238.

38 *Christian Education South Africa v Minister of Justice*, 1999 (4) SA 1092 (SE) 1100.

39 These generalisations refer to the religions of southern Africa. The TARs of West Africa would provide many exceptions, and, of course, the Orthodox Church in Ethiopia and the Coptic Church in Egypt would confound most of what is said in the text.

40 The matters enumerated here are derived from F von Benda-Beckmann, 'Who's Afraid of Legal Pluralism' (2002) 47 *J Legal Pluralism & Unofficial L* 37, 49–50, with reference to systems of customary law.

41 See, in this regard, G Obeyesekere, *Medusa's Hair: An Essay on Personal Symbols and Religious Experience* (University of Chicago Press 1981) 82–83.

42 This absence in itself meant that believers could have no notion of a theological doctrine; Hammond-Tooke (n 17) 319.

43 D Chidester, C Kwenda and R Petty, *African Traditional Religion in South Africa: An Annotated Bibliography* (ABC-CLIO 1997) 7.

44 B Tlhagale, 'Inculturation: Bringing the African Culture into the Church' (2000) 14 *Emory Int L Rev* 1249.

45 C Villa-Vicencio and P Grassow, *Christianity and the Colonisation of South Africa, 1487–1883* (vol 1, Unisa Press 2009) xi, and its companion, JW de Gruchy, *Christianity and the Modernisation of South Africa, 1867–1936* (Unisa Press 2009) provide commentary and documents on the spread of Christianity in South Africa.

enlightening influences of Christian belief.[46] This policy was complemented by evolutionist thinking which claimed that, when suitably educated, Africans would abandon their former ways in favour of a superior European model.[47]

Religion under the South African Constitution

South Africa's 1996 Constitution maintains a separation of church and State, together with a conditional pluralism mediated by the State.[48] On this basis, the courts have built a positive 'jurisprudence of accommodation' which 'celebrates "otherness" beyond the confines of mere tolerance or even magnanimous recognition and acceptance'.[49]

Freedom of religion and culture is guaranteed in the Bill of Rights, both separately and in conjunction with one another. Separate protection is given in sections 15(1) and 30. The former deals only with religion: '[e]veryone has the right to freedom of conscience, religion, thought, belief and opinion'. The latter deals with culture (and language): everyone has 'the right to … participate in the cultural life of their choice'. Section 31(1) deals with the two together: 'Persons belonging to a cultural, religious or linguistic community may not be denied the right, with other members of that community … to enjoy their culture [and] practise their religion.'

Although the freedoms guaranteed in these sections may be similar, the three provisions have significant differences. Section 15 protects an individual's subjective right to hold whatever faith or belief he or she has chosen, whereas section 31(1) gives individuals an objective right to participate in a religion or culture of choice. Section 30, which pertains to culture (and language), also guarantees the objective right to participate in a culture (or language) of choice. Both sections 30 and 31(1) are associative rights, since exercise of a culture (like a language, but unlike a belief or religion) presupposes the existence of a community of individuals sharing the same practices.[50]

In the case of freedom of religion, the courts have distinguished the following three rights: '(a) to have a belief, (b) to express that belief publicly and (c) to manifest that belief by worship and practice, teaching and dissemination.'[51] For obvious reasons, the first component is not readily amenable to legal regulation, whereas the second and third, which are protected in conjunction with culture, are easier to assess and control. What is more, sections 30 and 31(2) provide explicitly that the rights they specify 'may not be exercised in a manner inconsistent with any provision of the Bill of Rights'.[52]

Sections 15, 30 and 31 must be read in conjunction with section 9, an all-important provision on the right to equal treatment.[53] This provides the main legal basis for maintaining religious pluralism. Although section 9 ostensibly seeks to protect individuals, groups also benefit, and so, too, do the religions and cultures

---

46 Lord Hailey *An African Survey: A Study of Problems Arising in Africa South of the Sahara* (OUP 1938) 68–102.

47 See Makua wa Mutua, 'Limitations on Religious Rights: Problematizing Religious Freedom in the African Context' (1999) 5 *Buff Hum Rts L Rev* 75, 96–97.

48 *Ryland v Edros*, 1997 (2) SA 690 (C) 703; *Prince v President, Cape Law Society, and Others*, 2002 (2) SA 794 (CC) para 42; *Taylor v Kurtstag NO and Others*, 2005 (1) SA 362 (W) para 39; *Singh v Ramparsad*, 2007 (3) SA 445 (D) para 50. cf the fourth RELIGARE model of non-establishment and conditional pluralism (*Report*, 13–14).

49 LM du Plessis, 'The Constitutional Framework for the Protection of Religious and Related Rights in South Africa' in Bennett (n 20) 90, 99 with reference to *MEC for Education: KwaZulu Natal and Others v Pillay and Others*, 2008 (1) SA 474 (CC).

50 *Pillay* (n 6) paras 145–46 per J O'Regan.

51 I Currie and J De Waal, *Bill of Rights Handbook* (5th edn, Juta 2005) 339.

52 This 'internal limitation clause' is reinforced by section 36(1), the general limitation clause, which provides that all the rights in the Constitution 'may be limited only in terms of law of general application to the extent that the limitation is reasonable and justifiable in an open and democratic society based on human dignity, equality and freedom, taking into account all relevant factors'.

53 Section 9(1) provides that: 'Everyone is equal before the law and has the right to equal protection and benefit of the law.' Subsection (3) continues: 'The state may not unfairly discriminate directly or indirectly against anyone on one or more grounds, including race, gender, sex, pregnancy, marital status, ethnic or social origin, colour, sexual orientation, age, disability, religion, conscience, belief, culture, language and birth.'

associated with those groups. On this understanding, the court in *Ryland v Edros*[54] held that Islamic marriages were entitled to recognition on the ground that the State was obliged to promote diversity, and thereby accord equal treatment to all the country's cultures and faiths.[55]

Another all-important provision gives the Bill of Rights horizontal application. Section 8(2) provides that: 'A provision of the Bill of Rights binds a natural or a juristic person if, and to the extent that, it is applicable, taking into account the nature of the right and the nature of any duty imposed by the right.' As a result, individuals have been able to assert their freedom of religion or culture against other individuals or religious bodies.[56]

As it happens, TARs, *as religions*, have attracted very little attention in the law. Not only have they been subsumed under the rites of the independent African churches, but they have also been treated as aspects of culture. For instance, in most legal systems, rites of circumcision, marriage or death occasion questions of religious freedom and equal treatment, but in South Africa these events are regarded as matters of culture, not religion.

Circumcision is a notable case in point. Although considered a religious rite in Islam and Judaism, circumcision in accordance with a traditional belief system is discussed in terms of health and culture.[57] The same is true of marriage. Again, although seen by the monotheisms as a sacrament, marriage is considered a cultural matter when celebrated by traditional African rites. Accordingly, in a project undertaken by the South African Law Reform Commission to reform the indigenous law of marriage, lawmakers paid scant attention to traditional beliefs.[58]

When TARs did feature in the law, which was generally in criminal cases, they appeared in terms of 'superstitious beliefs'. For instance, when accused persons claimed to have acted under the power of spirits or witches,[59] the courts responded by calling their beliefs mere superstition[60] or some other form of aberration. The beliefs were not treated as part of an acceptable religious system. Cases involving ritual slaughter – a recent *cause célèbre* being the slaughter of a bull to celebrate the Zulu first fruits ceremony[61] – were poised awkwardly on the cusp of religion and culture.

Conclusion: The Consequences

The tendency to talk of traditional African belief systems as culture is perhaps instructive for the RELIGARE project in two respects. First, it demonstrates the no doubt obvious point that majority religions are better understood and therefore better protected than others. In Europe, the dominance of Christianity, the religion of

54 1997 (2) SA 690 (C).

55 cf *S v Lawrence*, 1997 (4) SA 1176 (CC) para 122. It is somewhat surprising, however, to discover that the right to equal treatment has received negligible mention in relation to religion: LM du Plessis, 'Freedom *of* Religion or Freedom *from* Religion? An Overview of Issues Pertinent to the Constitutional Protection of Religious Rights and Freedom in "the New South Africa"' (2001) *BYU L Rev* 439, 450–51. An exception was the decision in *MEC for Education: KwaZulu Natal and Others v Pillay and Others*, 2008 (1) SA 474 (CC).

56 As in *Nkosi v Bührmann*, 2002 (1) SA 372 (SCA), which concerned the right to bury family members on another person's property.

57 Section 12 of the Children's Act 38 of 2005 and Circumcision Schools Act 6 of 1996. See DJ Ncayiyana, 'Astonishing Indifference to Deaths Due to Botched Ritual Circumcision' (2003) 98 *SAMJ* 545; J Sloth-Nielsen, 'A Foreskin too Far? Religious, Medical or Customary Circumcision and the Children's Act 38 of 2005 in the Context of HIV/AIDS' (2012) 16 *Law, Democracy & Development* 69ff.

58 In the Commission's preparatory works, religion was hardly mentioned; Law Reform Commission, *Report on Customary Marriages* (Project 90, Government Printer 1998) para 4.4.5ff. In this respect, the Commission was following a pattern of thinking already well-established in the courts: the 'religious element' of marriage was mere custom, of no greater consequence than 'music, singing or a wedding reception'. See, for example, *Sila and Another v Masuku*, 1937 Native Appeal Court (N&T) 121, 123.

59 See J Burchell, *Principles of Criminal Law* (3rd edn, Juta & Co 2005) 535 and 536.

60 See, for example, the famous case of *R v Mbombela*, 1933 AD 269.

61 *Smith NO and Others v His Majesty King Goodwill Zwelithini and Others*, Case (10237/2009) [2009] ZAKZPHC 75 (4 December 2009). See also the case of Tony Yengeni, former Chief Whip of South Africa's governing party, the ANC, which attracted much media attention; L Feni, 'Wave of Support for Yengeni's Bull Ritual', *Daily Dispatch* (East London, 25 January 2007) 3.

the majority, secured it a privileged position. In Africa, however, the religions of the majority were condemned to an inferior status through colonialism and the influence of proselytising monotheisms.

Second, and more importantly, the confounding of religion and culture shows that significant – albeit implicit – consequences may ensue for forensic strategy. South Africa is ostensibly committed to protecting and promoting cultural, linguistic and religious diversity, and, in principle, none of these rights may be considered of greater value than the other. In fact, the courts have declared that the Constitution admits of no hierarchy in the Bill of Rights.[62] Nevertheless, in practice, religion is deemed to be a more important matter.[63]

The RELIGARE project team has made the same observation in its analysis of European case law, and, indeed, the instruments dealing with religion and culture give the former a patently higher degree of protection.[64] In this regard, the right to culture was initially protected only indirectly via provisions guaranteeing the usual civil and political rights.[65] As a self-standing issue, the right emerged only recently,[66] but even then only under the rubric of minority protection.[67]

For reasons of history and demography, culture poses a challenge to national integrity in Europe, which suggests a need for closer control. The Preamble to the European Charter, for instance, provides that an expression of cultural diversity must take place within the framework of national sovereignty.[68] South Africa, on the other hand, has been a unified State for over a century, during which claims to cultural freedom have posed little threat to national identity.

It is, of course, extraordinarily difficult to separate religion and culture, since the two concepts have a close and symbiotic relationship, and they often overlap.[69] Religion may therefore function as a marker of culture, and culture of religion.[70] Nevertheless, differences become apparent in the course of litigation.

For example, a claim to religious freedom will benefit from the doctrine of 'non-entanglement', which obliges the State to adopt a neutral stance.[71] The court must therefore not become involved in a dispute over dogma,[72] and, unless absolutely necessary, may not impose a secular law on a religious community.[73] No such scruples constrain the courts in their dealings with culture.

62 *The Citizen 1978 (Pty) Ltd and Others v McBride*, 2011 (4) SA 191 (CC) para 148; *SA Broadcasting Corp Ltd v National Director of Public Prosecutions and Others*, 2007 (1) SA 523 (CC) paras 55, 91 and 125; *S v Mamabolo (E TV and Others Intervening*, 2001 (3) SA 409 (CC) para 14.

63 An interesting example is supplied by a leading South African case, *Christian Education, South Africa v Minister of Education*, 2000 (4) SA 757 (CC), where the applicants began by arguing that their right to impose corporal punishment in schools was based on both the rights to religion and culture, but ultimately proceeded only on the basis of religion.

64 In South Africa, the Bill of Rights makes express provision for both, while the European instruments give primacy to religion; see Article 9 of the Convention on Human Rights (1950).

65 Such as freedom of association (*Sidiropoulos and Others v Greece*, no 26695/95 ECHR 1998-IV) and non-discrimination (*Cyprus v Turkey* [GC] no 25781/94 paras 241–47 ECHR 2001-IV). It is notable, therefore, that culture is not explicitly protected under Article 14 of the European Convention, but only by implication of the terms 'on any ground such as …'. See, too, Article 1 of Protocol No 12 (which entered into force in 2009).

66 Article 22 of the Charter of Fundamental Rights of the European Union (2000) obliges the Union to 'respect cultural, religious and linguistic diversity'.

67 See the Framework Convention for the Protection of National Minorities (1995). The authors of the South African Bill of Rights deliberately eschewed use of the term 'minority' when referring to cultural rights – the term might prejudice a claimant's right because the African population is, paradoxically, a numerical majority, but a cultural minority. See *Ex Parte Gauteng Provincial Legislature: In re dispute concerning the constitutionality of certain provisions of the Gauteng School Education Bill 1995*, 1996 (3) SA 165 (CC) para 81.

68 See D Kugelmann 'The Protection of Minorities and Indigenous Peoples Respecting Cultural Diversity' (2007) 11 *Max Planck Yearbook of UN Law* 233, 240.

69 See JM Donovan, 'God is as God Does: Law, Anthropology, and the Definition of "Religion"' (1995) 6 *Seton Hall Const LJ* 23, 70ff regarding the legal and anthropological approaches.

70 Müller (n 10) 62–63. This process of blending is familiar to Christian missionaries, since African culture has often been used as a medium for communicating the gospel message; B Tlhagale, 'Inculturation: Bringing the African Culture into the Church' (2000) 14 *Emory Int'l L Rev* 1249.

71 For Europe, see *Lautsi and Others v Italy* (App no 30814/06) para 60.

72 See cases in footnote 48.

73 *Worcester Muslim Jamaa v Nazeem Valley and Others*, 2001 JDR 0733 (C) para 109. For Europe, see *Jehovah's Witnesses of Moscow and Others v Russia*, no 302/02 ECHR 2010; *Pretty v UK*, no 2346/02 para 62ff ECHR 2002 III; *Leyla Şahin v Turkey*, no 44774/98 ECHR 2004.

The advantages to basing a claim on religion rather than culture must be weighed against certain significant disadvantages. If the existence of a religion or the affiliation of an adherent is at stake, the claimant will be put to a more demanding set of proofs. Thus, a party – whether an individual or group – wishing to argue freedom of religion may be called upon to prove the existence of the religion in question, as well as his or her affiliation to it.[74]

This issue entails two inquiries, one objective and the other subjective.[75] The former presupposes that certain universally applicable characteristics exist to denote a *bona fide* 'religion'[76] (the believer, however, is not obliged to prove that the idea in question is true or credible[77]). We are, of course, on dangerous ground when we assume that there are universally valid definitions for such social institutions as religion.[78] The definition inevitably leads to a search for such essential characteristics as belief in a supreme being[79] or a sense of the sacred.[80] All too often, these quests turn out to be misguided, because thinking in essentialist terms introduces the danger of the observer's preconceptions determining the nature of the subject under study.[81]

If the existence of an accepted religion can be established, the claimant must then demonstrate his or her subjective belief in it. Furthermore, in order to fend off an accusation that the claim is false or opportunistic, proof must be adduced that the belief is sincere.[82] This highly subjective requirement is likely, of course, to be difficult to fulfil.

As yet, neither the bias against culture nor the procedural consequences seem to have been remarked on in the courts or deliberately exploited in the tactics of litigation. Nor have we seen any judicial pronouncements on the definition of culture or religion, although it may, formally at least, be necessary for evidentiary purposes.[83] The well-nigh impossible task of definition may be soluble only on a functional basis: culture is broader than religion, for it embraces everything that marks humans as social beings, whereas religion is not a necessary requirement of social life.

In any event, the disparity in the status of the rights to religion and culture may, in time, be corrected. As societies, such as those in Europe, grow more secular in outlook, less importance may be attached to religion, while culture may correspondingly become more important, as minority groups struggle to maintain their identities. A parallel process may also ensue, as became evident in the judgment of the *Lautsi II* case regarding the crucifix:[84] secularism may result in the assimilation of certain rites and symbols to national heritage, thereby depriving them of a sacred or religious meaning.

---

74 G van der Schyff, 'The Legal Definition of Religion and its Application' (2002) 119 *SALJ* 288, 292. See further PG Danchin, 'Islam in the Secular Nomos of the European Court of Human Rights' (2011) 32 *Michigan J Int Law* 663.

75 *Christian Education South Africa v Minister of Justice*, 1999 (4) SA 1092 (SE) 1100. Some cases seem to favour the subjective approach, with the qualification that the belief must be sincere; *MEC for Education, KwaZulu-Natal v Pillay*, 2008 (1) SA 474 (CC) para 52. For Europe, see *Moscow Branch of the Salvation Army v Russia*, no 72881/01 paras 74 and 75 ECHR 2006 XI; *Hasan and Chaush v Bulgaria* [GC] no 30985/96 para 62 ECHR 2000-XI; *Religionsgemeinschaft der Zeugen Jehovas and Others v Austria*, no 40825/98 para 61 ECHR 2008.

76 Van der Schyff (n 74) 290 provides a list of the characteristics of a religion.

77 Although he or she may be required that show that it is *central* to the faith being examined; *Prince v President, Cape Law Society*, 2002 (2) SA 794 (CC) para 42.

78 According to some scholars, the process of definition is a futile exercise because religion cannot be defined. See GC Freeman, 'The Misguided Search for the Constitutional Definition of "Religion"' (1983) 71 *Geo LJ* 1519ff; TJ Gunn, 'The Complexity of Religion and the Definition of "Religion" in International Law' (2003) 16 *Harv Hum Rts J* 189, 191. Donovan (n 69) 28 goes so far as to say that the exercise is unconstitutional.

79 See Freeman (n 78) 1553. Donovan (n 69) 60–61 cites the list of features prepared by the US Internal Revenue Service.

80 A factor which is critical to Durkheim's *The Elementary Forms of the Religious Life* (Carol Cosman tr, first published 1912, OUP 2001). See Donovan (n 69) 73.

81 *MEC for Education: KwaZulu Natal and Others v Pillay and Others*, 2008 (1) SA 474 (CC) para 52 per J O'Regan citing S Benhabib, *The Claims of Culture: Equality and Diversity in the Global Era* (Princeton University Press 2002) 5.

82 M du Plessis, 'Doing Damage to Freedom of Religion' (2000) 11 *Stell L Rev* 297 and Van der Schyff (n 74) 292. cf *Pillay* (n 6) especially para 154. For Canada, see *Multani v Commission Scolaire Marguerite-Bourgeoys* [2006] 1 SCR 256 paras 33ff; for Europe, see *Eweida and Others v UK*, nos 48420/10, 59842/10, 51671/10 and 36516/10 ECHR 2013.

83 cf C Rautenbach, 'Unkhosi Ukweshwama: Revival of a Zulu Festival in Celebration of the Universe's Rites of Passage' in Bennett (n 20) 63, 67–75; *MEC for Education, KwaZulu-Natal, and Others v Pillay*, 2008 (1) SA 474 (CC) paras 150 and 152 per J O'Regan regarding the definition of culture. cf further the difficulties experienced by the court in *Campbell and Cosans v UK*, no 7511/76; 7743/76 §36 ECHR 1982.

84 *Lautsi and Others v Italy* [GC] no 30814/06 paras 15–16 ECHR 2011.

Chapter 20
Notes towards Connecting the Disconnect: The Role of the Religion–National Identity Link

Effie Fokas

This chapter engages with insights arising from the RELIGARE project regarding the topic of State neutrality. The project usefully frames the topic within the various historical contexts in which religion–State regimes were formed, on the one hand, and the disconnect between these historical contexts and the present situations across Europe, on the other.

This disconnect is expressed in the project's final report as follows:

> in a rapidly globalising world, one can observe in Europe both a de-traditionalisation, in the form of the rise of the 'unchurched', and an emergence of new religious movements and alternative, non-institutionalised spiritualities. … Is the gap between an increasingly unchurched majority sentiment and the legal regulation of religion still in force evidence of hypocrisy, ethnocentrism, or perhaps just *bona fide* neglect of a developing trend? And what legitimate policy aims in this changing societal context still remain? (*Report*, 13)

The project's final report suggests an emphasis on the latter question rather than the former, and thus engages mostly with policy responses rather than with the 'why' questions behind this disconnect.

In a nutshell, a main proposed policy response centres around implementation of 'inclusive State neutrality' and 'justice as even-handedness'. Summarising the main argument regarding religion–State relations in their final report, the RELIGARE team explain that 'inclusive State neutrality' and 'justice as even-handedness', when taken together, mean that the State's policy in granting recognition to religions, beliefs and practices should be fair to all. The underlying principle of this approach is *respect* (*Report*, 16).

Though this concept is certainly healthy and desirable, the RELIGARE report falls short of examining the factors and mechanisms which challenge this neat combination of inclusive State neutrality and even-handedness in practice, particularly at the local and national levels. For the purposes of achieving *substantive change* at the local and national levels, these proposals seem rather vague and somewhat distanced from the practical barriers to their implementation, such as intense lobbying of the State by majority religious groups, where applicable and effective, and the political costs feared by politicians.

Addressing such problems requires attention to 'why' questions such as those set out by the RELIGARE team, including the question quoted above about the reasons behind 'the gap between an increasingly unchurched majority sentiment and the legal regulation of religion'. The answers to this question, for different national- and local-level contexts, are in and of themselves interesting for scholars. But for effective policymaking purposes, they are *essential*, especially at those national and local levels. Without such insights into the problems at hand, and the factors and mechanisms keeping these problems in place on the ground, concepts such as 'inclusive State neutrality' and 'even-handedness' may be too far removed from the realities on the ground to be effective.

One important place to look for explanations of the disconnect between historically embedded religion–State regimes and the present situation of religious diversity and patterns of secularity across Europe is the relationship between religion and national identity – a connection often overlooked and certainly underplayed in much discussion of Western European contexts. The connection between religion and national identity is assumed in many Eastern European countries (for example, Poland), and is particularly conspicuous in contexts where the majority of the population is Orthodox.[1] But the religion–national identity

1 This was the topic of a European Commission-funded study conducted by the author between 2010 and 2013, entitled Pluralism and Religious Freedom in Majority Orthodox Contexts (PLUREL). A monograph with the project results is currently in preparation.

link in most of Western Europe is often conceived of as 'merely' manifested in all kinds of symbols around us, including flags, anthems, depictions on currency, and so on, much like Michael Billig's description of 'banal nationalism'.[2] Nationalism, when seen from a 'Western European perspective', is something to be found at the periphery among separatists, extremists, guerrilla figures and so on, but not among 'us'. So too, vestiges of a strong relationship between religion and national identity (whether positive, as in the Norwegian case, or negative, as in the French case) are likewise often overlooked or downplayed, though this relationship still permeates so much, in both Eastern and Western European contexts, in terms of religion–State relations and State policies towards religion(s) (majority and non, atheistic and so on).

A religion–national identity link underlies a number of 'invisible national norms' at play which sometimes lead to tensions between majority and minority communities[3] – for example, the Swedish case of the taken-for-grantedness of using church buildings for public school functions and ceremonies. The question is where do these banal manifestations of a majority religion (or majority *non*-religion, as the case may be) stop being banal and actually impinge upon the religious freedom of religious minorities or non-religious groups? As Billig notes, banal does not imply benign.[4] A lot more than we realise, I think, falls within a grey area between the benign and the pernicious. Normative statements about that grey area are unlikely to be helpful; instead, I suggest a deeper awareness of its existence and of its repercussions, potential and real.

This attention to religion and national identity follows the reasoning prevalent in David Martin's work since his 1978 *A General Theory of Secularisation*.[5] It is also heavily influenced by my experience of the Greek situation, a context in which there are in fact formal links between church and State, but predominant conceptions of Greek national identity as intrinsically linked to the Orthodox faith are far more formative of responses to religious minorities. Such conceptions are significantly deeper and, I submit, more consequential (in a negative sense, for religious minorities) than the formal links between church and State. The relationship between religion and national identity in the Greek case has been painstakingly and calculatingly maintained through 'the production and reproduction of collective memory managed and maintained by clergy, theologians and academics, propagated through official speeches, commemorative acts and other media and then duplicated through the school curriculum and holidays'.[6] The religion–national identity link is also maintained through politicians' yielding to church pressure, particularly around election time. And the religion–national identity link is, arguably, the main and most steadfast buttress of the strong ties between church and State in Greece.[7]

In the Greek case, the relationship between religion and national identity is the main reason why, as a representative of the Greek ombudsman put it, 'Kokkinakis is in the drawer'.[8] His reference is to the 1993 European Court of Human Rights case of a Greek Jehovah's Witness, Minos Kokkinakis, against the Greek State, after he was imprisoned for proselytism. The ombudsman's representative delivered this statement as a positive matter: police no longer send Jehovah's Witnesses to jail in Greece, he said, because they have the Kokkinakis case in their desk drawer, in order to justify to complainants why the Jehovah's Witness in question could not be sent to jail, and of course to remind themselves of the same thing. But from a different perspective, namely, that of religious minorities, the *drawer* is not a particularly prominent or effective

2 M Billig, *Banal Nationalism* (Sage 1995).

3 P Pettersson and N Edgardh, 'Welfare and Values in Europe: Transitions Related to Religion, Minorities and Gender (WaVE). Gävle (Sweden) Case Study Report' (2008), available at <http://uu.diva-portal.org/smash/record.jsf?searchId=1&pid=diva2:303178> accessed 21 June 2014.

4 Billig (n 2) 6. Here the parallels with Billig's arguments end, as Billig's focus is on the ideological means by which nation-States are reproduced.

5 D Martin, *A General Theory of Secularization* (Harper & Row 1978).

6 V Roudometof, 'The Evolution of Greek Orthodoxy in the Context of World Historical Globalization' in V Roudometof and V Makrides (eds), *Orthodox Christianity in 21st Century Greece: The Role of Religion in Politics, Ethnicity and Culture* (Ashgate 2010) 29.

7 E Fokas, 'Greek Orthodoxy and European Identity' in A Mitsos and E Mossialos (eds), *Contemporary Greece and Europe* (Ashgate 2000) 275–302; E Fokas, 'Greece: Religion, Nation and European Identity' in H Gulalp (ed), *Citizenship and Ethnic Conflict: Challenging the Nation-State* (Routledge 2006) 39–60.

8 Personal interview, 14 January 2013.

place for Kokkinakis to be: it should be on the *books*, in the legislation.[9] Instead, the 1938 law forbidding proselytism, which dates back to a period of Greek dictatorship, is still formally in effect. And this because politicians dare not face the wrath of church leaders (who have a proven ability to mobilise masses on the basis of the religion–national identity link) by proposing a change to the proselytism law.

A focus on the relationship between religion and national identity need not entail a strict path-dependency approach. Although historical factors influencing the relationship between religion and national identity are critical in each national case, certainly there is room for change and, in fact, radical change, in terms of the repercussions of that link for those not belonging to the majority religion. And this is where a significant challenge lies – designing policy responses tailored with that religion–national identity link in mind, delivered in a way somehow conducive to circumventing potential negative reactions based on claimed threats to national identity.

Reactions to Islam constitute one sure-fire place to look in Western Europe for the policy impact of religion–national identity links.[10] At the present juncture in nations across Western Europe, we see instances of crises in national identity transmuting into crises to do with the Muslim presence and vice versa – crises having to do with the Muslim presence transmute into national identity crises.

The 'myth' of a threat to national identity represented by the religious 'other' (Greece), or by the religious in general (France), or by the secular (in the UK, for example, in certain reactions to a robust humanist lobby) is politically expedient for those who propagate such myths; they are very powerful mobilising factors.[11] A case in point is former French president Nicolas Sarkozy's launching of a national debate on French national identity at the end of 2009.[12] 'It's a familiar story', writes one French commentator. 'Every time France is in trouble, and when its politicians are in need of public support, they reach for a supposedly unfailing remedy: the nation.'[13] In an environment of high unemployment and popular dissatisfaction with the political status quo and, critically, ahead of regional elections, 'politicians find it easier to instil fear of a *burqa* than search for more than band-aid solutions to economic and social problems'.[14] In the speech launching the debate on national identity, Sarkozy declared that 'France is diverse and always has been … but there is no place in France for the *burqa* or for the enslavement of women. … To become French means to adhere to a form of civilisation, to values and customs.'[15]

It is also important to understand how links between religion and national identity can bridge national and European policy areas. For example, it was in early November 2009 that the Italian State argued, unsuccessfully, in the European Court of Human Rights (ECtHR) *Lautsi v Italy* case, that the crucifix is a symbol of Italian national identity and, as such, should be allowed in public schools. And later that same month, also with reference to national identity, the Swiss passed a law banning the building of minarets. In March of 2011, the Grand Chamber of the ECtHR reversed the earlier *Lautsi* decision, and in July of 2011, the ECtHR refrained from addressing the Swiss minaret ban case by declaring it inadmissible to the Court. All of the above of course is intimately connected to the 'margin of appreciation' afforded by the Court to the defendant States in determining whether a particular restriction of a right is required ('necessary in a democratic society') in the given circumstance,[16] and the subsidiary role of the Court (now buttressed by the inclusion of Protocol 15 in the European Convention on Human Rights in 2013). Both of these concepts and the politicisation around them are closely linked to national identity concerns.

---

9 Of course, in theory *Kokkinakis* could be on the books but not in the drawer, and with more adverse effects for religious minority groups.

10 Here I build on ideas developed in E Fokas, 'Islam in Europe: The Unexceptional Case' 2011 (24) 1 *Nordic Journal of Religion and Society* 1–17.

11 This point is borrowed from Fred Halliday's writings about the myth of the Islamic threat; see F Halliday, *Islam and the Myth of Confrontation* (I.B. Tauris 1996).

12 See 'Débat sur l'Identité Nationale' (2010), available at <http://www.liberation.fr/politiques/2009/11/12/sarkozy-le-debat-sur-l-identite-nationale-est-un-debat-noble_593263> accessed 30 June 2014.

13 P de Beer, 'France: Identity in Question' (*Open Democracy*, 12 December 2009) <www.opendemocracy.net/patrice-de-beer/france-identity-in-question> accessed 21 June 2014.

14 P de Beer, 'France's Other Worlds: Burqa and Abyss' (*Open Democracy*, 3 March 2010) <www.opendemocracy.net/patrice-de-beer/frances-other-worlds-burqa-and-abyss> accessed 21 June 2014.

15 de Beer (n 13).

16 C Evans, *Freedom of Religion under the European Convention on Human Rights* (OUP 2001) 142.

As Mancini notes,[17] 'the collective reputation of a court depends, to a large extent, on the audience at which its opinions are aimed. ... If a court's interpretations deeply differ from the convictions of the people, the people will start resisting judicial decisions.' States' handling of religious matters (often) reflects grassroots-level demands, expectations and mobilisations which, in turn, are (often) embedded in predominant conceptions of religion in relation to national identity[18] and (sometimes) in nationalism infused with religion or with a religious agenda.[19] Meanwhile, these European publics tend to anticipate subsidiarity in matters of national identity and religion.

In the RELIGARE final report, the authors note that a number of paradigms inherited from the past regarding (majority) religion remain unquestioned in the case law (*Report*, 12), and they introduce recommendations which call for a more direct and active role for EU institutions in developing 'a coherent policy framework that would strengthen the combat in Europe against discrimination on the basis of religion or belief in a way that is compatible with a democratic understanding of the functioning of pluralist democracies' (*Report*, 12). The modest aim of the present contribution is to focus our attention on how national identity concerns, in their relation (positive or negative) to religion, intertwined with inherent tensions between democracy, pluralism and subsidiarity, can serve as formidable factors in both national- and European-level efforts to secure and promote religious freedoms in case law and beyond.

17 S Mancini, 'The Crucifix Rage: Supranational Constitutionalism Bumps against the Counter-Majoritarian Difficulty' (2010) 6 (1) *European Constitutional Law Review* 26.

18 This is the subject of an ERC-funded project currently underway (2014–2019), Directions in Religious Pluralism in Europe: Grassroots Mobilisations in the Shadow of European Court of Human Rights Religious Freedom Jurisprudence (GRASSROOTSMOBILISE).

19 When we speak of 'religious nationalism', care must be taken to distinguish, on a case by case basis, between nationalism reflecting religious agendas and nationalism infused with religious language but devoid of religious substance. Rogers Brubaker makes this point eloquently; R Brubaker, 'Religion and Nationalism: Four Approaches' (2012) 18 (1) *Nations and Nationalism* 2–20.

Chapter 21
The 'Inclusive State Neutrality' Normative Paradigm

Eugenia Relaño Pastor

> Freedom sees in religion the companion of its struggles and its triumphs, the cradle of its infancy, and the divine source of its rights. It considers religion as the safeguard of mores, and mores as the guarantee of laws and the pledge of its duration.
>
> – Alexis de Tocqueville, *Democracy in America* (1835)

The Religare project has identified as the main conundrum of religious pluralism in the European Union how to strike a balance between the application of non-discrimination norms and the protection of the right to freedom of religion and belief, taking into account the need to both promote diversity and respect the national context of the Member States.

This pressing question arises in many areas of public life in which the non-discrimination principle and freedom of religion converge: the workplace, family law, access to and use of public spaces and State support of religious communities. The questions related to each area are followed by particular RELIGARE recommendations addressed both to domestic authorities and to the EU institutions. The RELIGARE project's overall goal was to develop a coherent policy framework to combat discrimination on the basis of religion or belief in Europe. In order to achieve this goal, the specific and precise recommendations rely on some hypotheses that require forward thinking.

Section 1.1 of the RELIGARE report notes that the historic decision in most European countries to secularise State law was based on the hypothesis 'that detaching the State and its institutions from religion would ultimately make society in democratic States more inclusive, providing a unitary legal and political framework within which religious and non-religious people can live together'. The report further states that 'one can observe in Europe both a de-traditionalisation in the form of the rise of the "unchurched" and an emergence of new religious movements and alternative, non-institutionalised spiritualities' (*Report*, 13). I would like to make some comments on these two statements.

Detaching the State from Religion: Rethinking the 'Overarching Principle' for Managing Religious Diversity

> The starting points of liberal theorizing are never neutral between conceptions of the human good; they are always liberal starting points. And the inclusiveness of the debates within liberalism as to the fundamental principles of liberal justice reinforces the view that liberal theory is best understood, not at all as an attempt to find a rationality independent of tradition, but as itself the articulation of an historically developed and developing set of social institutions and forms of activity, that is, as the voice of a tradition. Like other traditions, liberalism has internal to it its own standards of rational justification. Like other traditions, liberalism has its set of authoritative texts and its disputes over their interpretation. Like other traditions, liberalism expresses itself socially through a particular kind of hierarchy.
>
> – Alasdair MacIntyre, *Whose Justice? Which Rationality?* (1988)

The hypothesis mentioned above addresses the interaction between the State and religions. The RELIGARE project proposes two yardsticks to manage conflicts between the State and religions: 'inclusive State neutrality' and 'justice as even-handedness'. The combination of the two will develop a substantive understanding of equality, one which improves inclusivity in practice. And, in order to achieve both real equality and inclusivity, the project avoids 'strict neutrality' and suggests a concept of 'inclusive State neutrality', which 'offers an overarching framework for "managing" competing claims on the public space, including those of religions and beliefs, in a way that recognises their roles and their right to make claims' (*Report*, 16). My concern is how and on what to base the 'neutral' overarching framework. Should the overarching framework be grounded on 'common societal norms' or 'common values' or on 'a comprehensive liberal secularism' or on 'European citizenship'? The foundation and legitimacy given to the so-called 'overarching framework' will probably have an effect on the extent to which it will result in a more equal society (which would realise the non-discrimination principle) and a more inclusive one (which would guarantee an effective religious freedom).

In many European countries the principle of neutrality is based on an ideological and cultural understanding of secularisation. The idea that religion cannot play a role in the general well-being of societies is common throughout Europe. In France and in Switzerland there are clear signs of increasingly restrictive approaches to religious freedom, in the form of restrictions on religious symbols in schools. The ongoing controversy related to the wearing of the *hijab*, frequent outcries over cartoons in magazines and newspapers, radical preaching in mosques, the demand for separate Muslim religious education, the use and growth of shariah courts, and the Swiss prohibition on the construction of minarets: all these issues are manifestations of the tension between minority claims and European conceptions of secularism.[1] Liberalism itself becomes an identity for modern secular people, with the liberal and civic integration presented in terms of inflexible cultural–national frames reproducing hierarchies of good culture versus bad culture, good religion versus bad religion. European societies like to present themselves as communities based on good citizenship, as opposed to other religiously based societies.

From that perspective, the secularisation of the principle of neutrality means to understand cultural diversity as something that occurs in private space (as separate from public space). The majority rules have responded to the idea of cultural diversity from the position that the State is culturally neutral and people are free to act as they like so long as it is done within the private sphere.[2] Cultural diversity then becomes an extension of the principles of secularism, yet secularism as such has been highly contested by minority communities living in liberal democracies. Hence, the secularism of liberal democratic States can no longer simply be taken for granted.[3]

However, to build up an 'inclusive State neutrality' as a yardstick or as a normative paradigm, the recognition of diversity must be understood as the key to dealing with multiple collective identities.[4] Furthermore, since the law, as a cultural phenomenon, tends to reflect the cultural attitude of the majority, the management of diversity today requires that certain concepts be reviewed, among them the concept of citizenship, as well as a redefinition of the means by which laws are produced.

French Republican Secularism and the Liberal Secularism of Rawls and Habermas

Take, for example, the French ban on religious symbols in public schools. Social anthropologist John Bowen indicates that the public debate made it clear that the ban on wearing religious symbols in public schools was 'aimed at keeping Muslim girls from wearing headscarves in public schools'.[5] Bowen engages in an 'anthropology of public reasoning' to discern the significance of the debate about headscarves in France. He approaches this issue by asking 'how French public figures understand the proper relationships among

1 HA Hellyer, *Muslims of Europe: The 'Other' Europeans* (Edinburgh University Press 2009).

2 R Zapata-Barrero, *Citizenship Policies in the Age of Diversity: Europe at the Crossroads* (Fundación CIDOB 2009) 8.

3 V Bader, *Secularism or Democracy? Associational Governance of Religious Diversity* (Amsterdam University Press 2008).

4 F Palermo, 'Soluciones jurídicas a sociedades complejas. El Derecho de la diversidad' in E Ruíz Vieytez (ed), *Derechos humanos y diversidad. Nuevos desafíos para las sociedades plurales* (Diputación Foral de Gipuzkoa 2008) 75–97, 81. As Kymlicka points out, 'Public values and constitutional norms of tolerance and equality, and individual freedom, underpinned by the human rights revolution, all push in the direction of multiculturalism. … That minority rights, liberal democracy and human rights can coexist is now a fixed point in both domestic constitutions and international law. There is no credible alternative to multiculturalism in these contexts'; W Kymlicka, 'The Rise and Fall of Multiculturalism? New Debates on Inclusion and Accommodation in Diverse Societies' in S Vertovec and S Wesendorf (eds), *The Multiculturalism Backlash: European Discourses, Policies and Practices* (Routledge 2009) 46.

5 JR Bowen, *Why the French Don't Like Headscarves: Islam, the State and Public Space* (Princeton University Press 2007) 1.

religion, the state, and the individual, and how they justify their arguments and policies in terms of concepts such as *laïcité*, Republicanism, and equality'.[6] From his analysis, he discovers that the headscarf issue is consistently linked to 'three other social problems identified by public officials, journalists, and intellectuals: communalism, Islamism, and sexism'.[7] All three of these issues relate to the failure of Muslim immigrants to fulfil the French republican expectations of integrating into French culture and adopting 'French' republican values.

For instance, Bowen defines 'communalism (*communautarisme*)' as 'the closing of ethnically defined communities on themselves … and the refusal of integration'.[8] He notes a parallel between the 'Jacobin' impulse after the 1789 Revolution to attack guilds and religious orders as impeding common values and the contemporary criticism of Muslim groups.[9] Muslim groups are likewise criticised for constraining Muslims 'both by requiring them to follow certain rules (requiring girls to wear scarves) and by keeping them from participating in emancipation through immersion in state institutions', and for following 'a different authority than that of the French state'.[10] Bowen finds another revealing pattern in French explanations of *laïcité*. His interviews and conversations reveal that the French held a collective narrative of French citizenship. This narrative helps explain the republican character of French secularism.[11] The French narrative emphasises a 'republican polis' going back to the Greeks which holds that the key function of the State is to facilitate virtue and the good life.[12] French secularism further underlines the republican 'idea that one finds both liberty and order only through the intervention of the state'.[13]

The French notions of *laïcité*, republicanism and equality could be interpreted as mere political aspirations that the French value more than religious liberty. They go to the heart of French and European identity. The French narrative only includes those who are, for the most part, ethnically French and Christian or 'post-Christian'.[14]

The anthropologist Talal Asad emphasises that 'to the extent that "France" embodies the Jacobin narrative, it essentially represents the Christian and post-Christian citizens who are constituted by it'.[15] He further claims that 'the problem of understanding Islam in Europe is primarily … a matter of understanding how "Europe" is conceptualized by Europeans. Europe (and the nation-states of which it is constituted) is ideologically constructed in such a way that Muslim immigrants cannot be satisfactorily represented in it.'[16] Asad highlights that Europeans believe that 'real Europeans acquire their individual identities from the character of their civilization', so that inhabitants 'without that civilizational essence' are not '"really" or "fully" European'.[17] Although not specifically identifying French secularism as a religion, Asad's comments suggest that French secularism is the 'religion of the rule' that the French government imposes on its citizens to promote social stability. He stresses that the Muslim headscarf symbolises the perceived Islamic threat to 'the secular character of the French Republic'.[18] As Modak-Truran points out,

> the French government seems to have missed the chief lessons learned from the wars of religion. Coercing uniformity of belief and practice under the pre-modern paradigm arguably triggered and certainly fueled the wars of religion. … French secularism constitutes a comprehensive or religious conviction about authentic human existence because it defines how citizens ought to live and dress in the public realm and specifies

6 ibid 3.

7 ibid 155.

8 ibid 156.

9 ibid 160.

10 ibid.

11 ibid 19.

12 ibid 15–16.

13 ibid 15. See JR Bowen, *Can Islam be French? Pluralism and Pragmatism in a Secularist State* (Princeton University Press 2010) 196–97.

14 MC Modak-Truran, 'Beyond Theocracy and Secularism (Part I): Toward a New Paradigm for Law and Religion' (2007–2008) 27 *Mississippi College Law Review* 159–233, 218.

15 T Asad, *Formations of the Secular: Christianity, Islam, Modernity* (Stanford University Press 2003) 175.

16 ibid 159.

17 ibid 168.

18 ibid 94.

> common values and interests for French citizens. ... All French citizens must embrace the genealogy of French secularism and recognize its comprehensive priority over private or personal genealogies including religious ones.[19]

The French republican secularism is similar to the liberal secularism of Rawls and Habermas. Both philosophers make similar comprehensive demands. Rawls requires sacrificing religious justifications in order to allow 'political' values to be the sole justification of the law. He remarks that contemporary liberals appeal to the idea of neutrality to suggest how we might deal with conflicts arising from citizens' diverse views of the good. The main idea is that political principles, procedures and State institutions should not favour any particular comprehensive conception of the good.[20] Liberal legitimacy depends on securing the reciprocal agreement of citizens who may have diverse and even incommensurable moral and social beliefs and values. In *Political Liberalism*, Rawls defends neutrality on the grounds both that it is the principle that rational agents would ideally choose and that it is a widely held norm in liberal States.[21] Rawlsian neutrality requires that citizens and legislators adhere to the norm of public reason in debating political principles. So the reasons that citizens and legislators supply as justifications for political principles must be widely acceptable and reasonable.[22] Rawls's *ideal of reasonableness* marginalises the perspective of those who view their group identity and their comprehensive views as links to their political convictions. Reasonable citizens will refrain, by definition, from making truth claims about their own private views or beliefs. This notion of reasonableness is based on the assumption that citizens have two views, a comprehensive one and a political one.[23] Against Rawls's position it is possible to imagine reasonable political dialogue in which citizens present their concerns by appealing to their beliefs, for example, Native American claims over land use. In the case of *Lyng*,[24] an association of Native Americans tried to prevent the United States Forest Service from building a road through an area that historically had been intended for their religious activities. The construction of the road meant 'virtually destroying the opportunity for Indians to practice their religion'.[25]

Habermas similarly maintains the independence of law from religion. In hard cases, Habermas requires judges to rely solely on legal paradigms as the basis for their decisions rather than personal moral, political, or religious beliefs. According to Habermas, comprehensive and religious convictions are not rational because they cannot be intersubjectively validated. Both Rawls and Habermas require citizens and public officials to give up their comprehensive convictions as the comprehensive condition of validity and to accept a liberal secularism (a comprehensive denial of comprehensive convictions). Only those already subscribing to liberal secularism like Rawls and Habermas will find this position 'neutral' among religious convictions as required by the secular paradigm. Therefore the secularisation of the principle of neutrality would imply that the State impose a comprehensive liberal secularism on the citizens whether they agree or not.

---

19 Modak-Truran (n 14) 220–21.

20 Rawls articulated how to respond to diversity in a section of *Political Liberalism*. Considering the objection that certain ways of life and conceptions of the good may not flourish, or even survive, in the political order that he defends, Rawls responds by questioning whether public institutions should have as their aim the promotion or maintenance of any particular form of life. Instead, he argues, public institutions should establish 'a just basic structure within which permissible forms of life have a fair opportunity to maintain themselves and to gain adherents over time'. On this view, the key requirement is not to achieve a particular outcome such as convergence or maintenance. Rather, the responsibility of public institutions is to ensure that different ways of life, and conceptions of the good, struggle for survival and success under 'background conditions' that are fair. See J Rawls, *Political Liberalism* (Columbia University Press 1996) 198–99.

21 Many recent liberal theorists have argued that State neutrality is supported by a metaphysical thesis about value, namely pluralism, which asserts that there are some conceptions of the good life which neither form a hierarchy nor represent versions of a single good. It is, however, doubtful whether neutrality is supported by pluralism; indeed, it may in some cases be precluded by it; see G Newly, 'Metaphysics Postponed: Liberalism, Pluralism, and Neutrality' (1997) 45 *Political Studies* 296–311.

22 For a discussion of Rawls's liberal principle and reasonable citizens, see S Cabulea May, 'Religious Democracy and the Liberal Principle of Legitimacy' (2009) 37 (2) *Philosophy and Public Affairs* 136–70.

23 Rawls (n 20) 140.

24 *Lyng v Northwest Indian Cemetery Protective Association* (1988) 485 US 439.

25 J Choper, 'The Rise and Decline of the Constitutional Protection of Religious Liberty' (1991) 70 *Nebraska Law Journal* 660.

All three forms of secularism (Rawls's, Habermas's and French secularism) maintain a unitary legitimation for the law based on a particular understanding of secularism and require the State to enforce compliance with that secularism. The price of secularity for Rawls, Habermas and French secularism includes rejecting religious convictions as not rational so that everyone can accept the same 'rational' foundation for the law. These proposals for a unitary secular foundation of the State attempted to replace traditional religious convictions with secular comprehensive convictions under the illusion of a secularisation of the principle of neutrality.

Liberal Secularism in the United States

The United States Constitution and its parts have been fertile ground for the production of metaphors. Perhaps most well-known, the Free Speech Clause has been the stage for an ongoing debate over the metaphor of the 'marketplace of ideas', and the most important and controversial metaphor for understanding the interaction of church and State has been Thomas Jefferson's description of the Establishment Clause as 'building a wall of separation between Church and State'. Two clauses of the First Amendment (the Establishment Clause and the Free Exercise Clause) offer a legitimate, consistent and doctrinally valuable way of resolving some of the most pressing issues in the law of church and State. An analysis of the Establishment Clause violations in jurisprudence reveals the adoption of both paradigms in the case law: the liberal secularism paradigm, such as French republicanism, and a more 'inclusive State neutrality' paradigm. The latter has been incorporated into the American context as a republican form of secularism.

The Establishment Clause reads, 'Congress shall make no law respecting an establishment of religion'. There is substantial disagreement among the Supreme Court justices about the scope of the Establishment Clause.[26] Scholars have often identified three main positions taken by the justices (strict separation, neutrality and accommodation) in their interpretations of the Establishment Clause. These theoretical positions have influenced the justices' decisions quite substantially.[27]

Despite this disagreement, there has been long-standing agreement among the justices as to the most basic parameters of the Establishment Clause. At least, the Establishment Clause appears to prohibit the State from explicitly embracing a particular religious justification for the law. In the first case applying the Establishment Clause to a State statute (*Everson v Board of Education*), the Court articulated a strict separation position in stating that 'the "establishment of religion" clause of the First Amendment means at least this: Neither a state nor the Federal Government can set up a church. Neither can pass laws which aid one religion, aid all religions, or prefer one religion over another.'[28] The *Everson* majority said that it was not unconstitutional for New Jersey to permit parents of students to be reimbursed for the out-of-pocket cost of school transportation, including reimbursing the parents of students attending religious schools. In *Lee v Weisman*, Justice Kennedy, who advocates substantial accommodation of religion by the State, has declared that 'it is beyond dispute that, at a minimum, the Constitution guarantees that government may not coerce anyone to support or participate in religion or its exercise, or otherwise act in a way which "establishes a [State] religion or religious faith, or tends to do so"'.[29] This minimal understanding of the Establishment Clause would prohibit the State from embracing a form of secularism such as the French, Habermasian and Rawlsian ones. However, the Supreme Court has recognised some exceptions to the prohibition on the State endorsement of specific religious

26 E Relaño Pastor, 'Las desventajas del principio de neutralidad en Estados Unidos: una relectura de la cláusula de no establecimiento' (2003) 3 *Quaderni di Diritto e Politica Ecclesiastica* 844.

27 S Monsma, 'Substantive Neutrality as a Basis for Free Exercise–No Establishment Common Ground' (2000) 42 *Journal of Church and State* 27. For Laycock, 'substantive neutrality' means 'the religion clauses require government to minimize the extent to which it either encourages or discourages religious belief or disbelief, practice or non practice, observance or no observance'; D Laycock, 'Formal, Substantive, and Disaggregated Neutrality towards Religion' (1990) 39 *DePaul Law Review* 1001. McConnell noted as well: 'My position is that government must "single out" religion in both free exercise and establishment contexts, with the goal of approximating a substantive neutrality in a religiously pluralistic culture'; M McConnell, 'Accommodation of Religion: An Update and a Response to the Critics' (1992) 60 *George Washington Law Review* 710.

28 *Everson v Board of Education* (1947) 330 US 1, 15.

29 *Lee v Weisman* (1992) 505 US 577, 587 (quoting *Lynch v Donnelly*, 465 US at 678).

convictions like the national motto 'In God We Trust' because these exceptions deal with historic recognition of religion and do not rely on religion as a justification for government decision making.[30]

The approaches of the Supreme Court to the interpretation of the Establishment Clause provide important clues to elaborate an inclusive State neutrality paradigm in which diversity could be promoted. The Supreme Court has interpreted the Establishment Clause to require that laws have a *secular purpose* and a *primarily secular effect*. Under *Lemon v Kurtzman*,[31] the Supreme Court described three tests (the Lemon test) that all must be met for a statute to pass an Establishment Clause challenge: 'First, the statute must have a secular legislative purpose; second, its principal or primary effect must be one that neither advances nor inhibits religion …; and finally, the statute must not foster "an excessive government entanglement with religion"'.[32] Although the Court has not formally repudiated the Lemon test, a majority of the justices sitting since 1997 have criticised it, and it has not been relied on by a majority to invalidate any practice since early 1985.[33]

In place of the Lemon test, many of the justices have embraced the 'endorsement test', which was originally proposed by Justice O'Connor in her concurring opinion in *Lynch v Donnelly*.[34] The endorsement test has two prongs: (1) the 'purpose prong asks whether government's actual purpose is to endorse or disapprove of religion'; and (2) 'the effect prong asks whether, irrespective of government's actual purpose, the practice under review in fact conveys a message of endorsement or disapproval'.[35] With respect to the *purpose prong*, Justice O'Connor has argued that 'the secular purpose requirement alone may rarely be determinative in striking down a statute', but that 'it reminds government that when it acts it should do so without endorsing a particular religious belief or practice that all citizens do not share'.[36] And, with respect to the *effect prong*, Justice O'Connor emphasised that 'what is crucial is that a government practice not have the effect of communicating a message of government endorsement or disapproval of religion'.[37] Under the endorsement test, adopting a comprehensive secularism as the justification for government activity would constitute a religious purpose and thereby violate the Establishment Clause. The above notwithstanding, requiring that the law have 'secular purpose' does not prohibit the law from implying a plurality of convictions as a foundation for the law.

The effect prong of the 'endorsement test' is very important to reinforce an inclusive State neutrality. If the government sends a message of endorsement of one particular religion or if government action has the negative effect of communicating a message of exclusion of one particular religion, the Establishment Clause could be violated.[38]

Consequently, from the analysis of the French secularist and the US jurisprudence approaches to the neutrality principle, an inclusive State neutrality paradigm should take into account that (1) the legitimation of law depends on the plurality of religious and comprehensive convictions in the culture; (2) the law should always have a secular purpose; and (3) government action should not endorse or disapprove any religion in order to coerce either believers or non-believers by singling them out as outsiders.

Tolerance as a Manifestation of Liberal Secularism

Previously it was noted that the law, as a cultural phenomenon, tends to reflect the cultural attitude of the majority. An analysis of conflicts between religious difference and the constitutional rule of law will reveal that such conflicts (between religious freedom or religious equality and other constitutional rights) are frequently resolved via the idea of tolerance.

---

30 Modak-Truran (n 14) 225.

31 *Lemon v Kurtzman* (1971) 403 US 602.

32 ibid 612–13.

33 The Supreme Court advocated abandoning the Lemon test in *Agostini v Felton* (1997) 571 US.

34 *Lynch v Donnelly* (1984) 465 US 668.

35 ibid 690.

36 *Wallace v Jaffree* (1985) 472 US 38, 108 at 75–76 (J O'Connor, concurring).

37 *Lynch* (n 34) 692 (J O'Connor, concurring).

38 Justices applied the endorsement test in their analysis of whether a creche in the county courthouse and a menorah in front of a city-county building constituted an establishment of religion in *County of Allegheny v ACLU* (1989) 492 US 573, 579 (holding that the creche violated the Establishment Clause but that the menorah did not). The Supreme Court elaboration of the coercion test in *County of Allegheny* was later developed in *Lee v Weisman* (1992) 505 US 577.

A religiously diverse society is one which can accommodate a wide variety of beliefs, diversity of customs and codes of conduct. In US and Canadian case law, as well as in European case law, freedom of religion is an ideal that revolves around the notion of tolerance. Particularly difficult cases should be decided by looking at the limits on freedom of religion and whether such limits may be justified in order to protect broad social interests or the rights of others. We can illustrate this statement with examples from Canadian and European case law.

The case of *Multani* is an interesting example in the Canadian case law of apparent legal tolerance, in part because it also contains a passionate plea by the Court for the importance of religious tolerance in Canadian society and the need to teach this value to Canadian youth.[39] *Multani* involved an Orthodox Sikh boy who felt that his faith required him to wear a *kirpan*, a small ceremonial dagger, at all times.[40] His school issued an absolute prohibition on wearing the *kirpan* at school on the basis of a policy which prohibited students from carrying any 'weapons and dangerous objects'. Given that it was the product of a sincerely held religious belief, the Court had no difficulty finding that the policy offended Multani's right to freedom of religion as guaranteed in Section 2(a) of the Canadian Charter of Rights and Freedoms. The bulk of the analysis turned on Section 1 (limitations to constitutional rights). Although the school board argued that the prohibition was justified as a safety measure and that the presence of the *kirpan* could have an adverse impact on the school environment, the Court concluded that this absolute prohibition was not a proportional limit on Multani's religious right.[41] Dismissing the safety concern as ill-founded, the Court noted that there was no history of *kirpan*-related violence and that Multani had already agreed to wear the *kirpan* under his clothes sewn in a cloth envelope. So this religious practice is entitled to legal tolerance.[42] The Court even emphasised that 'religious tolerance is a very important value of Canadian society'.[43] *Multani* holds that this religious difference will be 'tolerated', but the underlying message is that it will be tolerated because it conforms to the law's understanding of religion, which means it conforms to a particular cultural system.

Similar legal reasoning can be seen in case laws regarding religious symbols in schools. A comparative analysis of the reactions of courts and legislatures confronted with conflicts – such as when the limitation on the right to wear religious symbols in schools is justified in the name of other rights, or the conflict arising when a religious symbol such as the crucifix is used as the 'public language' of identity by public authorities and against minorities' religious feelings – shows a tendency to minimise pluralism.[44] In both types of conflicts of majority versus minority rights over religious symbols, courts and legislatures tend to secularise the meaning of religious symbols, interpreting them according to the prejudices and claims of the majority.

On the one hand, the religious meaning of majority (Christian) symbols is watered down and interpreted in 'cultural' terms, not as a symbol of a given religion. Cases in several countries (including Switzerland, Germany and Italy) on the display of the crucifix show a number of surprising analogies.[45] In these cases the courts made a choice among the various possible meanings of the crucifix and picked the following one: the crucifix may be displayed in State schools because it does not clash with the principle of secularism. Interpreting the crucifix as a cultural symbol has the advantage of the consensus: the number of those who

---

39 WJ Smith, 'Private Beliefs and Public Safety: The Supreme Court Strikes Down a Total Ban on the Kirpan in Schools as Unreasonable' (2006) 16 *Education & Law Journal* 83–112; AN Crawford, 'Learning Lessons from Multani: Considering Canada's Response to Religious Garb Issues in Public Schools' (2007) 36 *Georgia Journal of International and Comparative Law* 159–88.

40 *Multani v Commission Scolaire Marguerite-Bourgeoys* (2006) 1 SCR 256.

41 ibid para 6.

42 Crawford (n 39) 169.

43 'Religious tolerance is a very important value of Canadian society. If some students consider it unfair that Gurbaj Singh may wear his kirpan to school while they are not allowed to have knives in their possession, it is incumbent on the schools to discharge their obligation to instil in their students this value that is … at the very foundation of our democracy'; see *Multani* (n 40) para 76.

44 S Mancini, 'The Power of Symbols as Power: Secularism and Religion as Guarantors of Cultural Convergence' (2009) 30 *Cardozo Law Review* 203.

45 P Veronesi, 'La Corte costituzionale, il Tar e il crocifisso: il seguito dell'ordinanza n. 389/2004'; B Randazzo, 'Laicità "positiva" e crocifisso nelle aule scolastiche: incostituzionalità dell'obbligo di esposizione e incostituzionalità dell'obbligo di rimozione'; S Ceccanti, 'Crocifisso: dopo l'ordinanza 389/2004. I veri problemi nascono ora'; all available at <www.forumcostituzionale.it> accessed 30 June 2014.

supposedly share the same national/cultural identity is much larger than those who actually believe in the tenets of the Catholic religion. The Bavarian judges justified any possible discriminatory effect by balancing the positive freedom of religion of the majority with the negative one of religious minorities. And the Italian judges justified the discriminatory effect by stating that Christianity, unlike other denominations, is naturally inclusive and contains the idea of tolerance and freedom in such a way that Christianity overlaps with democracy, while other religions do not.[46]

On the other hand, minority (and particularly Islamic) symbols are interpreted as expressions of cultural and political values which are at odds with liberal and democratic values. The mechanism is analogous to the one applied by the Italian and Bavarian judges in the crucifix cases but, unlike in the latter, the conclusion in cases involving Islamic symbols is that they cannot be legitimately displayed because they are associated with beliefs and behaviour contradicting the essential values that the State should promote. This is the primary reasoning applied by the European Court in its 'veil jurisprudence'.[47] In deciding such cases, the European Court, while relying on the doctrine of the margin of appreciation, has interpreted the *hijab* as a religious symbol which cannot be reconciled with Western values. In *Şahin*, the Court observed that 'the principle of secularism … is the paramount consideration underlying the ban on the wearing of religious symbols in universities'.[48]

From the cases mentioned, one can conclude that the constitutional rule of law is, in itself, a cultural system. Putting law 'above' culture in this way means that the tools used by the law (tools of 'tolerance' and 'accommodation') are themselves seen as distinct from any particular cultural system, when in fact they are not. When asking if a limit on religious freedom is justified, the question is assessed within the values, assumptions and symbolic commitments of the rule of law itself. Therefore law's conception of religion comes strongly into play.

The limit on tolerance is justified owing to the commitments, values and overarching objectives of the rule of law. If the limit on tolerance is not justified, the reason is the same. Law always vindicates its own cultural understandings. Thus, law's encounter with religion takes an assimilationist mode of cross-cultural encounter. Law tolerates that which is different only so long as it is not so different that it challenges the organising norms, commitments, practices and symbols of the constitutional rule of law.[49]

The Rise of the 'Unchurched' and the Emergence of New Religious Movements

The difficulty of defining 'religion' in any comprehensive way, or with any pretension to universality, is a long-standing one. Indeed, one might say that the entire disciplines of the history and sociology of religion in the modern period, since their emergence in the late eighteenth century, have been built in large part around this difficulty. As has been previously noted, it is impossible to avoid the conclusion that secularism itself is not simply a word that defines a negative condition (the absence of religious belief), but is rather a term that has almost as much ambiguity and difficulty as 'religion'.

The heteronomy of religion has been transformed into the autonomy of individual identity. The postmodern version of religion is focused more on a personal interiority of feelings than on religious behaviour, attitudes or an attachment to a collective religious order. Western case law has abandoned all attempts to determine a concept of religion that would reach beyond the subjective feeling of individuals who invoke the right to religious freedom. In the end, it is no longer possible to arrive at a definition of what a religion is. Consequently, the criteria for the limits to religious freedom cannot be formulated in a specific manner that could be adapted to a collective understanding because it is difficult to evaluate personal religious feelings in a rational way.

46 *Lautsi v Italy*, App no 30814/06 (2011) ECtHR (GC). R Bin, G Brunelli, A Pugiotto and P Veronesi (eds), *La laicità crocifissa? Il nodo costituzionale di simboli religiosi nei luoghi pubblici* (Torino 2004); G Brunelli, 'Simboli collettivi e segni individuali di appartenenza religiosa: le regole della neutralità, Testo provvisorio della relazione al Convegno annuale dell'Associazione italiana dei costituzionalisti su Problemi della laicità agli inizi del secolo XXI' (Napoli 26–27 ottobre 2007); see <www.associazionedeicostituzionalisti.it> accessed 30 June 2014.

47 *Leyla Şahin v Turkey*, judgment of 10 November 2005 and *Dahlab v Switzerland*, judgment of 15 February 2001.

48 *Şahin* (n 47) para 116.

49 B Berger, 'The Cultural Limits of Legal Tolerance' (2008) 21 *Canadian Journal of Law and Jurisprudence* 245–77.

At the same time, religious freedom as a public, mainly collective, institution has been transformed into a fragment of a diffuse 'right to identity' that blurs the line between the public and private domains and demands a 'right of recognition' by public authorities. Members of religious minorities are demanding not only equality and non-discrimination as individuals, but also the legal recognition of their collective identities. Their claims to cultural protection and accommodation are necessarily philosophical, political, moral and (both constitutionally and normatively) legal. There are certain demands for recognition of the existence and validity of systems of rules parallel to that of the State, particularly religious legal systems. This can be illustrated by reference to the controversy surrounding the possible application of religious law by the Ontario courts in family arbitration cases. Recognition of legal systems parallel to those of the State raises much more fundamental questions. This conflict also emerged in the United Kingdom (regarding arbitration tribunals), provoking great alarm because they were called 'shariah courts' even though this was merely an approach to managing private affairs authorised under ordinary law.[50]

The 'conflict of norms' of religious rules and law has been addressed in American jurisprudence and doctrine. In his classic foreword to the 1982 Supreme Court Term,[51] Robert Cover argued that a case such as *Bob Jones University v United States*[52] generates a series of paradoxes and binary oppositions as it seeks to resolve apparently opposing demands for freedom and autonomy: on the one hand, world-creating 'paideic' systems of normative life that are the product of strong 'culture-specific designs of particularistic meaning' and, on the other hand, the preservation of abstract universal norms that are justified by the need to ensure the coexistence of worlds of strong normative meaning. Differences in society arise immediately as challenges are made to the illusion of the identification of order with truth. In order to maintain 'paideic' unity, dissenters advancing 'flowers of normative meaning' are expelled and exiled (or worse), leading to the sectarian separation of communities, now within their own paideic nomoi.[53]

The famous case of the Amish decided by the United States Supreme Court in 1972 might be a good example.[54] Here we are confronted with a religious and cultural community that has existed in the United States for centuries. The preservation of the group within American society is a value that has to be taken seriously: there is even a practice of opening the traditional community for an 'exit' option, the so-called time of *rumspringa*, which means that a young member can decide by himself or herself whether he or she prefers the traditional way of life to postmodern alternatives. This may be an illusionary 'free' decision, but regardless, this is a kind of 'conflict of norms' or a 'collision of rules' that links the traditional community with a secular liberal society. Therefore the concern about the rise of a 'parallel society' in the United States was not seen as a threat to the internal order of the society, as it might have been in Europe.

The Preamble of the Charter of Fundamental Rights of the European Union declares that 'The Union contributes to the preservation and to the development of these common values while respecting the diversity of the cultures and traditions of the peoples of Europe'. Taking this into consideration along with Article 22 of the Charter, entitled Cultural, Religious and Linguistic Diversity, which stresses that 'The Union shall respect cultural, religious and linguistic diversity', the future challenge will be to analyse whether an inclusive State neutrality paradigm includes the recognition of normative parallel religious orders in the European context.

50 In 2004 a report to the Attorney General of Ontario was sympathetic to family arbitration based on the principles of religious law, though subject to various legal safeguards. However, after all the public controversy, the Ontario government finally opted for the opposite approach, and even made the conditions under which family disputes could be submitted for arbitration much stricter (see Family Statute Law Amendment Act, S O 2006, c 1).

51 R Cover, 'The Supreme Court, 1982 Term – Foreword: Nomos and Narrative' in M Minow et al (eds), *Narrative, Violence and the Law: The Essays of Robert Cover* (University of Michigan Press 1993) 95 (originally published in *Harvard Law Review* (1983) 4).

52 *Bob Jones U. v U.S.* (1983) 103 S Ct 2017 (raising the question of whether a religious school discriminating on the basis of race could be denied tax-exempt status by the IRS).

53 Cover (n 51) 109.

54 *Wisconsin v Yoder* (1972) 406 US 205.

Chapter 22
RELIGARE: Reflections on Research and Policy Recommendations

Adam B. Seligman

What I hope we can all learn from the RELIGARE project is a renewed understanding of the primacy of experience and what I would like to call 'embodied knowledge' over abstract and generalised theories and presuppositions. We must – I would suggest – be ever so attentive to context, to particularities and, in fact, to very specific histories and traditions as we carry out our research, and even more so as we endeavour to give concrete policy suggestions – which is a goal I suggest we treat with utmost seriousness. Moreover, this attention to context and language must not be restricted to the subject of our research, but also to the default, taken-for-granted and often unproblematised assumptions of the research itself.

Let me give a brief example and begin with that difficult, yet taken-for-granted reality of the secular or secularism, or for that matter of religion – which purports to be the object of our studies. I would like to argue that both religion and secularism are concepts that developed in a very particular and Christian context and can be used, helpfully, to describe aspects and periods in the coming to be of Christian civilisation. They do not, however, serve us well when we come to discuss, analyse and understand other traditional civilisations or other civilisations within which tradition is changing and being re-negotiated – including such civilisational 'enclaves' (shall we call them) existing within Europe.

What for example is a secular Jew? What of a Jew who observes no commandments, goes to synagogue only on Yom Kippur and does not otherwise maintain any traditional practices? Is he secular, or partially religious or simply confused? How do we characterise China with a population of 1.3 billion? Inglehart has characterised China as the most irreligious country in the world.[1] But if we consider the proliferation of spirit cults and other forms of worship it becomes clear that this is not secularism in any usual sense of the term.[2] What of the case of Islam? What of the individual or community whose observance of traditional commandments is partial, or almost non-existent? What of the Muslim who eats during Ramadan – but only in private, in hiding, away from communal eyes? Is he secular or hypocritical? What of she who does not eat during Ramadan but does drink wine occasionally? What of those communities in Central Asia who celebrate the Eid by drinking vodka? Are these people secularists or sinners or ignorant? Or are they, as are so many, engaged in the never-ending movements, interpretation and transformation of their tradition that is always continually being negotiated and negotiated anew by communities and individuals over the course of time?

I would in fact claim that secularism is a very particular moment in the Christian process of negotiating its own tradition – as was the Protestant Reformation and as is the phenomenon of Christian fundamentalism. All are particular moments in the way the concrete practice of tradition mediates, transforms and negotiates the tradition of practices that define any civilisational endeavour. That a particular moment of this negotiation in Christianity is understood in terms of secularism has much to do with the privileging of belief over practice, of faith over works and of *Innerlichkeit* (inner belief) over external practice that has been part of Christianity from its origins (as evinced in its rejection of Jewish law and its unique allegorical way of reading and interpreting scripture) and which received particular emphasis during the Protestant Reformation of the sixteenth century. Secularism as unbelief is thus the complement of tradition understood primarily in terms of belief rather than practice. The consequent use – I would say, misuse – of this term to characterise other civilisational

---

1 R Inglehart, *Human Values and Beliefs: A Cross-Cultural Sourcebook* (University of Michigan Press 1998) 5–9, 5–175, 5–234.

2 R Weller, 'Worship, Teachings and State Power in China and Taiwan' in W Kirby (ed), *Realms of Freedom in Modern China* (Stanford University Press 2004) 285–314, 285–88.

endeavours – the Jewish, the Islamic, the Hindu, Confucian and so on – is simply the spoils of war as it were: a consequent of the power differentials between the Christian, Jewish, Islamic, Indian and Chinese civilisations. Indeed, as I have already hinted at, I would much prefer to replace the dichotomy of religion/secular with that of tradition of practices/practice of tradition, which is a more structural, less particularistic, historicist and Whiggish way of conceptualising what is usually understood as the dichotomy between religious and secular individuals, cultures and communities.

We must also recall that Europe is the 'secular' exception in a world that is overwhelmingly 'religious'. Or, in the terms I am offering here, European civilisation is the one where traditional practices have been most abandoned and rejected, a fact that can be ascertained by visiting any of the churches of Europe and calculating the average age of those in attendance on any given Sunday. Moreover, this rejection of tradition is intimately tied up with the overwhelming terms of collective identity. In fact, the two phenomena may well be related. The Peace of Westphalia and the concept of *cuius regio, eius religio* ('whose realm, his religion', meaning the religion of the ruler determined the religion of his subjects) may be central here. Europe, which was Christian, became rather a continent of nation-States and in different ways traditional practices were subsumed within new national identities. I note this because it brings us directly to one of what I believe to be the great fallacies of social scientific research on what we call religious phenomena today – and that is the study of religion in terms of identity. This is in fact the primary language that social scientists have to discuss what goes under the rubric of religion. As social scientists are not generally the followers of any sacred tradition, they can but translate the behaviour, attitudes and dispositions that they find into language that they understand, and the result is our rather simplistic understanding of sacred traditions in terms of the eminently modern problem of identity – whether of individuals or collectivities. From identity we can of course develop increasing concerns with authenticity, fundamentalism, collective boundaries, value orientations, preferences and a host of additional conceptual categories which are, at the end of the day, nothing but our own attempt to translate a set of sacred practices into the languages of the secular, social sciences.

There is nothing inherently 'wrong' with this, other than that it does not get anywhere near the phenomena that it presumes to explain. For observant Muslims or Jews or Jains or Sikhs do not, at the end of the day, 'do' identity or 'do' religion when going about their daily rituals. Rather they are following a tradition, a way of being: both *halacha* in Judaism and shariah in Islam mean way or path. Christianity is also referred to that way in the Acts of the Apostles. That today, under the onslaught of modernity and modern conceptualisations, many Jews and Muslims also conceive of themselves as 'doing' identity (not to mention identity politics) is precisely what has given rise to phenomena that we term 'fundamentalist'. But here again, we do not really observe the reality in question – rather, we translate it into categories convenient to our way of thinking. What often goes unremarked is that the roots of this so-called fundamentalism are of the same stuff as the ideology of the social sciences – that is a secular ideology focused on individual and group identity and the realisation or, as with nineteenth-century romantic nationalism, the expressive realisation of both. Hence the suicide bomber who leaves a note that begins not *Bismillah*, that is, 'In the name of Allah', but 'In my name and the name of my family'. This is precisely religion as a modern ideology – sharing the same conceptual framework as our own social scientific inquiry. It does not, however, even begin to encompass the meaning or perhaps meanings held by what we term religion from time out of mind.

What was meant by religion before the contemporary period was not a value, not a preference and definitely not an identity.[3] What is taken for religion by social scientists, but has for billions of people in the world been understood as their own sacred traditions, is in fact a response to the problem of Being. The fact that most social scientists no longer understand this as a problem and a perpetual challenge to the human endeavour leads them to a critical methodological error – they impute their own etic categories to their informants and treat their own categories as emic ones. They construct great edifices of theory, but the explanatory potential of these theoretical edifices is severely compromised. Essentially, social scientists, working with a model of the self as autonomous moral decisor, that is, with a model of the liberal self, cannot really conceive of a social agent as anything but an entity that either has or does not have something – in this case, choices – or as an agent who effects actions – that is, who makes or does things. We have preferences

3 J Mitchell, 'Religion is not a Preference' (2007) 69 (2) *The Journal of Politics* 351–62.

and we make choices based on these preferences. The great debates within the social sciences are of course over the sources of these preferences – whether in some sort of collective conscience, or in a more Humean or perhaps even Hobbesian calculus of individual interests. No one, however, doubts the existence of choice and the autonomy of the agent who chooses.

What I have tried to hint at, no more than hint at, in the above remarks is that this itself is a very particular construction of self, no more or less reasonable than any other – but one that perhaps leaves us in the dark about the motivations, understandings and existence of billions of individuals, today and in the past, who do not understand themselves to be morally autonomous actors, but rather see themselves as acting out heteronomously imposed norms where the only choice is to observe God's commands or not. This is, of course, a good distance from the type of choice that rational actor theories, or even more culturalist readings of the self, understand to be at the core of social action.

Let me give a very simple example of the type of problem that may ensue from this sort of confusion between the language of social science and that of religious individuals. We talk much in Europe and the United States today of 'religious symbols' – the headscarf worn by some women, or the kippah (yarmulke) worn by some Jewish men or the crucifix worn around the neck are referred to as 'religious symbols'. This is fine so long as we recall that they are symbols not for the wearer, but for the observer or the jurist, especially for the secular observer or jurist. For such an observer this headscarf or kippah or cross is a 'sign' or 'symbol' of the wearer's religious commitment: it references a reality beyond the sign and that reality is immanent, has to do with social status, background and all so many other ideas that the observer imputes to the bearer and which may or may not be correct. For the wearer of the headscarf or kippah or cross, however, these are not symbols (or not necessarily symbols, though they may be) – they are rather acts of piety, obligations, rightly or wrongly taken on out of one's understanding of tradition's demands. They are not a 'sign' or 'symbol' of some other reality, but are themselves a religious act, and they do not so much reference another reality as partake in one – and that one is transcendent rather than immanent. Good research, then, would in fact distinguish three different realities: that of the observer, that of the wearer, and the interstitial realm between them, which is often, in fact, a political one. This is what I mean by paying attention to particular contexts and local meanings, as well as which aspects of reality are indeed shared and which are not.

Based on the above examples, I would thus like to suggest that the very use of the concept of secularism in contrast to something which is 'religious' as the meta-frame of our analysis betrays a particular historical, religious and perhaps even ideological heritage that, of necessity, clouds one's glasses and skews one's assumptions when approaching the world of social phenomena. Remember please that the very term religion does not exist in other civilisations; it originated as a concept in Roman law, and carries with it a very particular cultural baggage and no end of ambiguous meaning from the period of late antiquity onward. Lucretius used it differently from Cicero.[4] In the pre-Christian era it was best understood as an adjective rather than as a substantive (if something was *religio* for me, it meant that it was mighty incumbent on me to do it). With the Church fathers – Lactantius and of course, later Augustine – *religio* really becomes the way to posit boundaries and distinguish between the followers of the true religion (Christianity) and of false practices and beliefs. It is, if you will, a full-fledged ideology, *avant la lettre*, and we must be wary of incorporating those ideological assumptions into our own research programmes.

If we wished, we could continue this type of analysis into so many of the other concepts that are central to the RELIGARE project: not only secularism, religion and identity, but also diversity, recognition and autonomy, not to mention our distinction between the public and the private spheres. All of these concepts are tied to particular historical, juridical, linguistic and socio-political developments that makes their use as universal categories of social scientific analysis problematic at best. The ways in which the public and private realms are parsed in different cultures are, for example, vastly divergent, let alone the different valuations given to one or the other as spheres of virtue and the realisation of the good. Yet, it is also the case that careful inquiry into particular traditions will find areas of significant overlap or functional equivalence between different legal traditions. For example, the distinction we make between public and private law can also be found in other traditions, albeit called by different names. So, for example, the distinction in Jewish law between laws of monetary damages and those of religious prohibitions (which include but are not limited to

4 WC Smith, *The Meaning and End of Religion* (Fortress Press 1991) 21–23.

what we would term the obligations of public order) roughly parallels the distinction we make between tort law and what we would call criminal law.[5] Moreover, the millennia-old understanding that local communities may enact a ruling that would override Biblical or Talmudic law in the matter of torts makes a hash of any easy identification of secularisation with autonomy, modernity, civic society and so on. I imagine similar distinctions exist in other traditions as well, though I am not familiar with them. What I am trying to get at, however, is that we must understand law as a language, not just as the expression of political will, and, as a language, it is a mode of communication between individuals, communities and histories, here in Europe and beyond. We must, therefore, not only develop our capacities for translation across these languages, but also a sense of history – of communities, of laws, of communal relations, of different ideas and the importance of tradition to different social actors and communities – and recognise how this affects policy and how policy could be understood, interpreted and, of course, implemented.

Again and again, recognition of local context must act as a corrective to more abstract and generalised systems of meaning and normative assessment, much perhaps in the way that Aristotle referenced a certain builders' rule used on the island of Lesbos that was made of lead and so provided a measure that was itself moulded to its circumstances and context rather than one independent of all context and particularity (he used this, by the way, as an analogy for the workings of equity in law).

Such an approach will focus our work on particularities and hence on what is, in essence, experience. In this it should call to mind the advice of John Dewey, the American pragmatist philosopher, who taught us that experience is the central component in thinking.[6] 'To learn from experience', he tells us, 'is to make a backward and forward connection between what we do to things and what we enjoy and suffer from things in consequence. Under such conditions, doing becomes a trying; an experiment with the world to find out what it is like.' In this process, we cannot separate the intellect from experience. Indeed, the attempt to force such separation leaves us with disembodied, abstract knowledge that all too often emphasises things rather than the relations or connections between them. Such knowledge, however, offers little help in our attempt to connect the multitude of disconnected data that the world presents into a framework of meaning. Meaning rests not on the knowledge of 'things' but on the relations between them, that is, between us. We can assess these relations, as Dewey argued, only through experience, because only through experience do we bring the relevant relations between things into any sensible sort of juxtaposition.

In the construction of a shared social world, which includes those who are different, challenging, unknown and even threatening and which was, I submit, the ultimate aim of the RELIGARE project, we benefit from being open to experience rather than falling back on preconceived ideas and abstract forms of knowledge. We must enter a process that can only be realised through a slow, cumulative and not always conscious process of straddling the boundaries of our existing and developing modes of thought through the challenges of shared action and experience. In so doing, we may come to recognise the only partial, fragile, mutable and heavily freighted nature of the interpretive and notational frames that we bring to our experiences, even as we overcome them in our newly shared human encounters.

In short, if, now that the academic work of the RELIGARE project has been completed, its more long-term promise is to be fulfilled and its explicitly articulated aims of 'encouraging a critical debate between secular assumptions and practical realities' and of 'a new understanding of the paradigm of secularisation in Europe' are to be realised, the recipients of the project's analyses and recommendations must be willing to engage critically with ways of seeing, understanding and living different from their own and, in so doing, subject their own presuppositions to continual critique and self-reflective inquiry.

I would like to conclude with a reminder of some fundamental insights that the social sciences have bequeathed us – to help in our understanding not only of the 'other', but of ourselves as well:

1. Knowledge is collective, not individual. What we know, we know collectively, as part of a group. Our categories, ways of understanding, moral judgments, boundaries of what is permissible and prohibited, basic frames of meanings, fears and desires – all these are, in a strong sense, social. We hold them together with others and not simply as individual beliefs.

5 M Elon, *Jewish Law: History, Sources, Principles* (vol 2, Jewish Publication Society 1994) 1004.
6 J Dewey, *Democracy and Education* (Dover Publications 2004) 134, 137.

2. As knowledge is collective, an important part of what it is we know is bound up with who it is that we trust. In most cases we are called upon to grant moral credit to some source in matters which are, by their nature, almost always morally ambiguous. We may not dispute any particular 'fact' or 'set of facts' (the building of a mosque in lower Manhattan, the knifing of a marcher in a gay pride parade in Jerusalem, the murder of a Jew in Paris, the establishment of hidden cameras in the Muslim neighbourhoods of Birmingham), but the frame of the act, the set of relevant external bits of information and histories needed to explain them will frequently be decided on the basis of our group belonging and the moral credit that we, as members of one or another group, grant to the act of inclusion or exclusion of information as relevant or irrelevant to this particular case.
3. These communities within which moral credit is granted (and thus where the very structuring of our knowledge is developed) tend to be what many call 'communities of belonging'. This is no less true of secular communities or, for that matter, scientific communities which have their own beliefs, codes and myths – not to mention ideologies. By the nature of the case, communities of belonging are not universal, but are bounded (just as families are bounded); they have their own histories and their own trajectories, their own languages and jokes, their own obligations, taken-for-granted worlds, their own flavours and smells – their own understandings of home. They may be more or less open, more or less ascribed, their boundaries may be more or less permeable, but they do have boundaries and always define some 'us' as against some 'other'.
4. These communities are real, live, active entities within which human actors are born, thrive, live, die and make sense (or don't) of their worlds and the worlds of others. We cannot live without these communities and, despite all dangers that arise from them, there is no possibility of human life or achievement outside of them.
5. Consequently, we must recognise that many of our substantive differences are precisely the markers of these different communities of belonging that define who we are and provide the settings in which we live our lives and where we feel most secure.
6. The ultimate aim of RELIGARE's policy recommendations should be understood as an attempt to build trust and hence a common store of knowledge across different communities. It remains to be seen, however, if the frameworks of knowledge provided by a group of scholars, themselves members of different communities of belonging, can aid in the building of trust and the construction of a shared frame of reference that can be drawn upon when events that may divide different communities threaten the ability of our fellow citizens to live their differences together.
7. The extent to which the RELIGARE recommendations facilitate the granting of moral credit to the other, to him or her who is not a member of one's own group, and so share with him or her some common frame of understanding and knowledge despite being members in very different communities, tied to different myths, obliged by different commandments and loyal to different particularities, will be, ultimately, the mark of the project's success or failure.
8. Going beyond the confines of this project, we should all remain mindful of the need of different European communities to share experience and so find the way to build trust even as they remain loyal to their own particular communities of trust, belonging and knowledge. Shared experience and what I would call 'embodied knowledge' can provide the necessary bases for constructing (what are, by definition, new) frames of knowledge across our different communities of belonging.

At the end of the day, the real importance of the RELIGARE project is to help us reformulate our moral universe. If we can meet that challenge, we can also, I believe, wrest our existing prejudices *vis-à-vis* the other from the taken-for-granted worlds of our own communal belonging. In such a manner, both our research and policy recommendations will indeed contribute to greater integration and the ability to truly develop modes of 'living together differently' in a rapidly changing Europe.

Section 4
Religious and Philosophical Diversity and Secularism: Questioning Normativity

Chapter 23
Religion in the European Union: Comments on the RELIGARE Project

Christian Joppke

The RELIGARE project (as summarised in the *Report*) provides an impressive state-of-the-art review of the law and policy on religion in the European Union, along with many useful recommendations for how to improve things, mostly by way of expanding the scope of an existing EU law that touches on religion only indirectly (as being the subject or object of discrimination and as potentially impeding free movement). The usual point of entry to discussions of religion in the EU is to stress the great diversity of approaches that relate religion and State across Europe, from separationist (France) to various forms of establishment (for example England) to public recognition of several religions (for example Germany). This diversity and the controlling power of national law over church and religious affairs is affirmed in Article 17 of the Treaty on the Functioning of the European Union (TFEU), which mandates that the EU 'respect' the national regimes and religious laws in place, and at most allows the EU to maintain a 'dialogue' with religious organisations. This Article 17, however, is to a degree a defensive measure by Europe's churches to immunise themselves against the reach of EU anti-discrimination law, which threatens the organisational autonomy that is often a cloak for internal discrimination against women, members of other religions and non-religious individuals, especially in the critical domain of employment.

The RELIGARE authors define as the key challenge in dealing with religion in the EU to 'strike a balance between the application of non-discrimination norms … and the protection of the right to freedom of religion and belief' (*Report*, 11). This is well framed indeed. The clash between anti-discrimination (or equality) and religious liberty norms is particularly pertinent in the employment domain. While the RELIGARE project pays equal attention to conflict issues across sectors, from employment and family law to access to public spaces and State funding, which appears to me a very plausible way of mapping the field, I found the dilemmas exposed with respect to employment particularly new and noteworthy. This is partially conditioned by new case law in this area, especially the 2013 European Court of Human Rights (ECtHR) decision on *Eweida and Others v the United Kingdom*. Previously it seemed that religious conflicts in the workplace were mostly limited to minority religions (particularly Islam) not attuned to the implicitly Christian structuring of time and space, and it seemed that the trend across Europe was towards inclusive and liberal solutions in the context of increasingly flexible and protective labour laws.[1] The picture given by RELIGARE is less comforting, but interestingly more in the direction of more aggressive religious demands than of rampant religious discrimination. Note that *Eweida and Others* does not deal with the usual suspects – Muslims – but with Christians who find their religious precepts violated or offended at the workplace, from a British Airways employee rather appallingly fired for wearing a large crucifix around her neck (and rightly winning her case in court) to the rather more exotic case of a civil servant refusing to register same-sex marriages out of religiously condoned homophobia (she rightly lost her case). With respect to the latter, you find a completely new turn in which religious liberty rights are no longer working in sync with anti-discrimination rights, so that religious claimants can no longer pick and choose and/or be doubly protected by ECHR human rights and EU anti-discrimination law. Instead, rather worryingly, you now find religious liberty used as license to discriminate, in this case against homosexuals.

Without spelling out the details, the RELIGARE report lists similar employment cases of religionists refusing to handle alcohol or pork, refusing to shake hands with people of the opposite sex, challenging female superiors (*qua* women), or seeking to be excused from parties at work, among other cases (*Report*,

1 See F Dassetto, S Ferrari and B Maréchal, *Islam in the European Union* (European Parliament 2007) 49–51.

18). These are all cases of religion as a threat to the social contract, and – here is my first critique – I would have appreciated a clearer statement of the RELIGARE researchers' position on this. Instead, upon listing these extreme cases of religious licentiousness, one reads that there was an 'overwhelming consensus among respondents (including, notably, secular respondents) ... that in the workplace employers should try to accommodate the religious practices of employees' (*Report*, 18). And instead of explicating soberly what makes these 'hard cases' *hard* (to me they appear not 'hard' at all, but obvious abuses of religious liberty rights), the authors seek refuge in a vaguely defined 'reasonable accommodation' approach. But one does not learn (at least not in this document) whether this is alternative or complementary to human rights or anti-discrimination rights, and what the added value of 'reasonable accommodation' should be. In effect, 'reasonable accommodation' boils down to the admonition that 'Europe should not require an *assimilative approach* to religion in the workplace' (*Report*, 21; emphasis in the original). This is a strange conclusion that misconstrues the real issue at stake: the clash of religious liberty rights with concerns to protect not only third party interests, but also the social contract at large.

I wonder here whether the project authors have the appropriate conceptual framework at hand to handle the problem of conflicting highest-order ('constitutional') principles and interests. Normatively, the lead concepts are 'inclusive State neutrality' and 'justice as even-handedness'. The meaning of 'inclusive State neutrality' is fairly clear: it is a rejection of French-style 'strict separation', which might entail 'hostility' to religion (*Report*, 16). Within the diverse canvas of European religion–State relations, a clear preference is thus expressed for a German-style public recognition regime, though one that does not entail any preference for majority religions (as the German religion–State regime still does, denying the privileged 'corporation under public law' status to organised Islam). The second normative lead concept, 'justice as even-handedness', is much less clear. In particular, its added value to 'inclusive State neutrality' remains opaque – the latter already entails an inclusive and equal approach to religions (in the plural), for which 'justice as even-handedness' would be just another term. I take the thrust of 'justice as even-handedness' to be the favouring of a context-sensitive rather than rigidly principled approach to religious claims and conflicts – though, to repeat, this is nowhere clearly laid out. Whatever the exact meaning of each, both principles combined boil down to the maxim that the 'State's policy should be fair to all in granting recognition to religions, beliefs and practices', and that 'the principle is respect' (*Report*, 9). Tellingly, the only limit to this is said to be 'the fundamental rights of others'. No mention is made of more societal limiting principles such as 'public order, health, or morals', as outlined in the religious liberty clause of the European Convention on Human Rights (Article 9). This omission appears to be deliberate. This is because the RELIGARE authors admit that the two yardsticks of 'inclusive State neutrality' and 'justice as even-handedness' are 'to advance' minority concerns, and to read the 'freedom of religion and belief' as 'primarily … a fundamental right of minorities' (*Report*, 50). It is true that 'public order' and 'morality' are vague and legally questionable terms, the former defensible in our human rights era only in clearly demarcated and limited 'security' terms (that in effect approximate the protection of liberty), and the latter perhaps not defensible at all (even though 'morality' restrictions are having a strangely ambivalent revival in the context of accommodating – or repudiating – some Islamic claims in Western societies[2]). But my point is that a conceptual framework geared to be maximally minority sensitive and protective of religious liberties is rather limited to take in either possible conflicts between minority and majority concerns, or public order and social contract considerations that may sometimes require trumping overzealous religious liberty demands.

Having said this, an alternative to the RELIGARE report's point of entry to the religion–State problematique in Europe – that is, referring to a diversity of national approaches (from French to German and so on), and then normatively siding with one of them (in this case, an idealised German 'inclusive State neutrality' approach) – would be to stress the commonalities of a 'European model' that outweigh national variations (which, of course, continue to exist). Dassetto, Ferrari and Maréchal have taken this line, defining the European model in three points: (1) the protection of religious freedoms; (2) autonomy of religious communities; and (3) cooperation between State and religious communities.[3] Dassetto et al. thus come to the optimistic conclusion that the 'legal systems of the European Union countries have the necessary instruments to deal with … (the)

2 See C Joppke, 'Islam and the Legal Enforcement of Morality', unpublished manuscript (2013).

3 See Dassetto et al (n 1).

problems' raised by the need to integrate minority religions, especially Islam. The fact that, on the basis of (1) and (2), Europe does fairly well in dealing with religion, especially new minority religions imported by immigration, is sometimes lost on American observers[4] no less than on the RELIGARE authors, who paint a rather more sombre picture of 'religious discrimination' as 'still a serious problem' (*Report*, 12). Of course, much of this discrimination is more situated horizontally between civic actors than between State and citizens, so that a good report card on the latter (the focus of Dassetto et al.) need not entail the same for the former. But still, in light of the findings of Dassetto et al., any other than an overall liberal and inclusive picture of the handling of religious (minority) claims in European States would require the burden of proof.

The crux in Europe seems to be not the protection of religious freedom or the autonomy of religious organisations,[5] but the State's 'cooperation' with organised religion. Only this third principle of the 'European model' makes Europe combined different from the United States, where any 'cooperation' between State and religion founders on the constitutional Establishment Clause (perhaps more accurately, the No-Establishment Clause) that classically requires a 'wall of separation' between State and religion (though an increasingly conservative Supreme Court under the sway of the Christian Right has taken large bites out of the 'wall of separation', slowly but steadily moving the American separation regime closer to Europe's cooperation regimes). Whereas in America church and State were separate from the start, in Europe State and church fought for supremacy through the centuries. As a result, and France is only a partial exception to this, privileged 'cooperation' with the State is the price for the churches having lost this fight and conceding the sovereignty of the secular State. As Dassetto et al. judiciously submit, this cooperation is to be 'undiscriminating' but 'not indiscriminate'; it is controlled by 'the values on which the political system and social peace are based: dignity of the human being, democratic citizenship, freedom of conscience, equality, and so on'. In other words, respect for liberal State values is the precondition for organised religion to 'cooperate' with the State.

This, of course, is a controversial position, particularly with respect to sects and new minority religions that clamour for equal treatment by the State. For one, the German Federal Constitutional Court, in its important 2000 decision on Jehovah's Witnesses, has ruled out any values-based selectivity on the part of the German State when granting to religious groups the highly coveted status of 'corporation under public law' (which entails important tax and other privileges to the respective groups). No deeper 'loyalty' to the Constitution could be expected of claimants for public law status, the court argued in this landmark decision; the only thing that could be constitutionally expected is a thin and procedural 'fidelity to the law' (*Rechtstreue*) that amounts to not smashing windows or throwing bombs (that is, not breaking the law). Now, the German State could, in principle, be forced to 'cooperate' with religious groups that repudiate the basic values and principles of the liberal–democratic State, as Jehovah's Witnesses very openly do, and as many Islamic organisations (like the expediently court-going Milli Görüş, spin-off of the mildly Islamist Refah Party in Turkey) are also suspected of doing.[6] One of the most delicate issues in religion–State relations in Germany today (taken here as an exemplar of a European 'cooperation' regime) is whether the increasingly dated 'corporation under public law' privileges to churches and non-Christian religious groups are sustainable, or whether it would be preferable, considering the high degree of secularisation of German society and the existence of a plethora of non-religious civil society organisations categorically denied public law privileges, to fold *all* of them back, French-style, to the same status of 'associations under private law'. This, surely, would be a victory for equality! Unfortunately, the 'inclusive State neutrality' frame of RELIGARE, which entails a preference for religion over non-religion, does not allow even grasping this issue, and the report is consequently mute on it and similar 'cooperation' problems. Instead, there seems to be a well-meant preference for 'cooperation' as such, without any reflection on the terms of this cooperation and the dilemmas possibly generated by it.

Finally, and connected to the last point, what does 'inclusive State neutrality' entail for the tallying of majority and minority religions? 'Inclusiveness', after all, should not be a privilege of the minorities (though this is, of course, the thrust of RELIGARE, as flagged by its lead concept of 'inclusive State neutrality'). The RELIGARE report briefly mentions, but does not at all elaborate on, the enigmatic *Lautsi* decisions of

4 See, for example, M Nussbaum, *The New Religious Intolerance* (Harvard University Press 2012).

5 That is, the first and second principles of the 'European model' as presented in Dassetto et al (n 1).

6 See C Joppke and J Torpey, *Legal Integration of Islam: A Transatlantic Comparison* (Harvard University Press 2013) ch 3.

the European Court of Human Rights, first rejecting the Christian crucifix in Italian public schools for the sake of secularism and State neutrality (in a small chamber decision of 2009), but later reversing course for the sake of Christianity as an 'identity-linked value' of the Italian State, while formally hiding behind the court's trademark 'margin of appreciation' doctrine that leaves prickly cultural and religious issues for the national lawmakers to decide (in the Grand Chamber decision of 2011). *Lautsi II* may have been legally badly argued (I leave that to the lawyers to decide),[7] but it still seems the politically right decision, welcomed by the great majority of Italians and without measurable (non-symbolic) costs for Italy's religious minorities, which seem not to be impaired in their religious liberties in an overall 'pluralist' Italian school environment. Can a European State be partial to the majority religion *qua* religion (as long as no measurable discrimination is thereby created for minority religions), or is a majority preference in need of being reduced to a cultural preference because, after all, the liberal State must be neutral on religion (which is what makes it 'liberal' in the first place)? The annoyingly short and evasive court opinion in *Lautsi II* allows for either interpretation (though I hold the cultural preference interpretation to be more plausible).[8] Judges may be pardoned for ducking grand philosophical questions, especially in the present populist climate that has no patience for 'juristocracy'. But I would have expected from a state-of-the-art review on 'Religion in the European Union', which assembles some of Europe's brightest academics on religion and law issues, more of a sustained reflection on the contents and limitations of the secular and secularism in contemporary Europe.

7 See L Zucca, *A Secular Europe: Law and Religion in the European Constitutional Landscape* (OUP 2012).
8 See C Joppke, 'A Christian Identity for the Liberal State?' (2013) 64 (4) *British Journal of Sociology* 597–616.

Chapter 24
RELIGARE: The Central Conflict

Lorenzo Zucca

The RELIGARE project is one of the largest, most sustained attempts to come to grips with a central dilemma faced by all European States: How can we promote freedom of religion while preventing discrimination between religions and between religious and non-religious people? This question is particularly acute because the secular State is expected to treat everyone (that is, religious and non-religious people) neutrally, that is to say, in a way that does not give preference to an individual or a group on the basis of her beliefs. This dilemma can be presented in a simplified way as a conflict between liberty and equality.[1]

Theories of freedom of religion do not help to solve this conflict at its roots. The main contrast is between liberty-based and equality-based theories of freedom of religion.[2] Liberty-based theories of freedom of religion have an underlying assumption that the State is to be suspected of unduly interfering with consciences.[3] This means that freedom of religion should be conceptualised as freedom of conscience, and as such it has extra protected status. Equality-based theories of freedom of religion argue that the State can provide a scheme of fair liberties to all citizens.[4] Within such a framework, freedom of religion is but another freedom, like free speech or assembly. On this view, freedom of religion does not have extra special protection. Crucially, it also means that freedom of religion can be equated with or reduced to other types of freedom.[5]

Theories of freedom of religion do not deal with this conflict, but aim to define it away. The RELIGARE project rightly insists that more can be done to understand the dilemma and to see it at play in different contexts rather than ride roughshod over it. The project also usefully stresses the importance of evaluating the role of the EU in the context of the exercise of religious freedom. The recent revival of religion in Europe is a transnational issue that cannot be easily solved at the national level. It is crucial that all supranational and international players be involved in understanding and dealing with it.[6]

Where I do part company with the report is at its normative level, more specifically, with the key principles that it singles out: 'inclusive State neutrality' and 'justice as even-handedness'. To briefly state my position, I believe that neutrality is part of the problem, not part of the solution.[7] There is no value-neutral way of choosing between liberty and equality.[8] Rather than proposing a normative solution to the dilemma, I present a genealogical explanation of the roots of the problem. The difference between these two avenues is that the

1 For a critique of neutrality, see L Zucca, *A Secular Europe: Law and Religion in the European Constitutional Landscape* (OUP 2012).

2 For the distinction between liberty-based and equality-based theories of freedom of religion, see C Laborde, 'Equal Liberty, Non-Establishment and Religious Freedom' (March 2014) 20 (1) *Legal Theory* 52–77.

3 An example of a liberty-based theory of freedom of religion in the European context is R Ahdar and I Leigh, *Religious Freedom in the Liberal State* (OUP 2005). Other examples include D Laycock, 'Religious Liberty as Liberty' (1996) 7 *Journal of Contemporary Legal Issues* 313; A Koppelman, 'Is It Fair to Give Religion Special Treatment?' (2006) *University of Illinois Law Review* 571.

4 Examples of equality-based theories of freedom of religion include C Eisgruber and L Sager, *Religious Freedom and the Constitution* (Harvard University Press 2007); R Dworkin, *Religion without God* (Harvard University Press 2013); J Maclure and C Taylor, *Secularism and Freedom of Conscience* (Harvard University Press 2011).

5 See Laborde (n 2). For a similar distinction, see N Feldman, 'From Liberty to Equality: The Transformation of the Establishment Clause' (2002) 90 (3) *California Law Review* 673–731.

6 For an overview of the issue of freedom of religion in foreign policy, see P Annicchino, *Freedom of Religion or Belief in Foreign Policy: Which One?* (European University Institute 2013), available at <http://cadmus.eui.eu/handle/1814/30059> accessed 26 June 2014.

7 For an in-depth discussion, see Zucca (n 1), especially chapter 4. For another compelling critique of neutrality in the Indian context, see R Bhargava, *The Promise of India's Secular Democracy* (OUP 2010).

8 For an attempt to deny the existence of a conflict in the context of freedom of religion, see Dworkin (n 4).

former attempts to posit a number of values that are superior and antecedent to the practice: one hopes that the State will treat everyone in a neutral and even-handed way.[9] The genealogical approach, by contrast, explains the role of values as being dependent upon the existence of a genuine conflict between religious and non-religious worldviews, which I term the theologico-political conflict (hereinafter TPC). In this picture values are considered to be responsive rather than foundational; as a consequence, the conflict between liberty and equality is put aside. The gist of the genealogical approach is to understand the TPC and the way it evolves, rather than dreaming up an ideal normative framework that will never be achieved in practice. In the end, the TPC will never be avoided or defined away. It will present itself in different guises and will transform itself. Political institutions cannot solve the TPC, but can evolve in order to be more responsive to it. In what follows I will sketch the genealogical approach and contrast it with the normative one. Then I will briefly address the role left to play for supranational and international institutions.[10]

The Genealogical Approach

The modern nation-State is the Westphalian response to the TPC. Religion was the source of bloody wars, and cohabitation of people of different religions was no longer possible in seventeenth-century Europe. To bring peace to a ravaged space, the Treaty of Westphalia (1648) divided Europe into self-contained entities, each with a high degree of religious homogeneity. It was the denial of freedom of religion and the establishment of one country–one religion rule (*cuius regio, eius religio*).

The birth of the modern nation-State is coeval with the denial of both freedom of religion and equality. There was clearly no space for freedom, since every religion was about domination. There was no space for equality between religions because domination admitted only one power and one religion. Officially, the nation-State was the champion of one religion. Religious institutions had to accept this compromise, which put an end to the imperial aspirations of the Catholic Church. The TPC was then transformed into a State–church confrontation, which would take on enormous proportions later in the nineteenth century.

Of course, between zealous idealism and practice there is a big gap. Thus, ideally homogeneous States had to cope with diversity from the word go. In the history of England, for example, there is a definite progression towards official recognition of plurality: a process that goes from the Toleration Act of 1688, which made religion free for dissenting Protestants, to the Catholic Relief Acts of 1791 that extended toleration to Catholics, to the Religious Disabilities Act of 1846, which included Jews. From 1855 onward, all religious denominations were allowed to step forward and have their churches recognised as places of worship.

The evolution of toleration in Britain clearly demonstrates that homogeneity cannot be engineered normatively. It also goes to show that the State is never neutral, but always makes value choices regarding acceptable and non-acceptable religions. Even today, the State has to police the boundary, for not everyone can claim the special status of religious protection. If that were the case, then freedom of religion would not protect anyone in particular.

The TPC transforms but does not disappear: in the seventeenth century it is about supremacy between Christian factions. In the eighteenth century, it is about the relationship between Christian majorities and other religious minorities. In the nineteenth and twentieth centuries it is about State and church, with the eventual victory of the State at the national level. The twenty-first century has witnessed a resurgence of religion at the supranational level.

Part of the problem is that we still think of the State as the relevant frame of reference to deal with the TPC. But in the many historical transformations of the theological–political problems the State is the winner, not the umpire. How can the winner of the contest be neutral and remain fair to the loser? In any case, religion does not want to be treated neutrally. Religion claims to be different from other social phenomena. It wants

9 Ronald Dworkin argues that what unites religious and non-religious people is the faith in shared moral values; in this idiosyncratic sense, religious and non-religious people can both be presented as having a religious attitude. See Dworkin (n 4) 7–9.

10 For a more developed approach, see L Zucca, 'Freedom of Religion in a Secular World' in R Cruft, SM Liao and M Renzo (eds), *Philosophical Foundations of Human Rights* (OUP 2014).

for itself special treatment. In fact, it claims for itself freedom – and it means by that, freedom from the State. Religion wants to be free to impose a certain number of obligations that may be at odds with ordinary laws. Religion wants to be able to discriminate between its people and others. And within its community religion often wants to be able to treat men and women differently.

In the twenty-first century, however, it is clear that religion does not want to engage in yet another battle with the State. Partly this is because the State is not the sole locus of norm production. There are other sources of rules, including supranational and international organisations. Partly it is because religion is happy to collaborate with the State. To this extent, the authors of the RELIGARE report are absolutely correct that the metaphor of separation is unhelpful and can only obfuscate rather than illuminate.

So the point is to know who defines the terms of collaboration. Can it be the State? We have seen that the State is part of the game, not a neutral umpire. I submit that the umpire should be beyond the State.[11] The reason is that the genealogical approach should be distinguished from the normative approach. The genealogical approach points to the fact that there is no such thing as value neutrality on the part of the State. In fact, the State needs to be helped to establish a greater degree of pluralism. The umpire of the contest will by necessity be at the European level.

The European Role

The role of European institutions is precisely that of correcting the original sin: the forced imposition of religious and cultural homogeneity that came about with the creation of the modern European State. Supranational and international institutions should help to foster the natural state of any community that is intrinsically pluralistic.

For example, the ECtHR can help correct the State bias towards protection of a single religion. *Kokkinakis*,[12] the first case to reach Strasbourg, was precisely about the added protection that the Greek Orthodox Church drew from the prohibition against proselytism. The ECtHR is asking the State to remove the barriers to an open marketplace of religions. In this light *Lautsi*,[13] the crucifix in the classroom case, was a mistake, not because it left a margin of appreciation for the State, but because it did not hold the Italian State responsible for its own commitment to secularism. How can a State be constitutionally secular and still single out one religious symbol to be displayed in classrooms? The ECtHR can help the State create a free marketplace of religions where the guiding principle is pluralism.

The EU can also help the State run the marketplace of religions. The EU is good at removing barriers to access to the religious marketplace. It has developed serious policies against discrimination of all sorts, which can usefully be extended to religious discrimination. It can ask the Member States to refrain from creating such barriers.

Both the EU and the ECtHR can help put in place correctives, but it is clear that the main site of action remains the State. The main frame of reference is local, and the definition of religion would have to be left to domestic institutions that have to mirror their own constitutional histories. France will have to start from its own commitment to *laïcité*: perhaps it would have to reinterpret it in a context that is new and profoundly different from 1905.[14] It is not about seeing religion as the nemesis of the State; religion could well be the ally of the State in many ways, including in trying to better integrate people.

The UK will have to deal with a constitutional trajectory of toleration and pluralism. Its boundaries will be tested. If there is too much pluralism and too much autonomy, then religion re-creates isolated archipelagos that are difficult to integrate into mainstream society. The right balance between engagement and distance should be struck. The State can do this easily, simply by treating religions as partners. As partners, what they will need to do is collaborate on a fair and open basis. Economic benefits will have to be distributed according to that criterion.

11 Zucca (n 1) chapter 5 passim.

12 *Kokkinakis v Greece* (14307/88) [1993] ECHR 20 (25 May 1993).

13 *Lautsi v Italy* (30814/06) [2011] ECHR 33 (18 March 2011). For a comment about *Lautsi*, see Zucca, *Lautsi: A Commentary on a Decision by the ECtHR Grand Chamber*, I-Con (2013), vol 11, no 1, 218–29.

14 For an important discussion of *laïcité*, see O Roy, *Secularism and Islam* (Columbia University Press 2009).

Can We Rely on Experts?

I think experts can provide useful insights. To be sure, they cannot help solve the theological–political problem, but they can be helpful when it comes to understanding the deep complexity of the dilemma.

Religion is a slippery object. It cannot be easily defined, and it escapes most efforts to contain it. There is no legal definition capable of dealing with all the issues revolving around religion. Religion has social, legal, moral and cultural dimensions, not to mention its transcendental dimension. It cannot be easily boxed in, and no expert can elucidate all those aspects without obscuring others. Religion is very much a cubist concept – when you shed light on one dimension, you cast shadows on others.

For these reasons, it is not easy to pin down exactly what the contribution of permanent experts could be. RELIGARE proposes that the EU should constitute such a committee of experts, but this does not take into account the simple fact that, at the end of the day, someone will have to make a decision. So the burning question is: What would the power of such a committee be? Would it be consultative or would it be more straightforwardly decisional? The latter role is difficult to back, as there is little chance that a committee of experts could command the necessary legitimacy and authority because it would not have the democratic seal. It is easier to imagine that it would have a consultative role; but then again, to what extent can an EU-level committee make recommendations on the resolution of domestic problems?

We have come full circle to the necessity of understanding the European role as a corrective role at best. The point is to steer domestic approaches to freedom of religion towards greater pluralism and away from orthodox understandings of religion centred on Judeo-Christian assumptions.

Conclusion

The RELIGARE project is a very timely effort to bring together and analyse all the relevant European trends dealing with the central dilemma generated by the clash between religious freedom and anti-discrimination norms. At the descriptive level, one cannot but celebrate a very valuable effort to bring together and compare different national solutions and then analyse the overarching European perspective.

Where I part company is at the normative level: I am not sure that we can single out a list of values that can meaningfully guide the actions of institutions in a neutral way. The theological–political contest sees the State as a player rather than as an umpire. It cannot evaluate religion from a detached perspective, because the State will inevitably want to constrain religion. I have suggested here that it is more productive to embrace a genealogical perspective that reconstrues the contemporary relationship between State and church as one of collaboration rather than as one of conflict and separation.

Once we start afresh with this perspective, we will be in a position to ask what religion can offer to the State rather than what the State can offer to religion. When religion offers valuable services, it can clearly be assisted and promoted. If, to the contrary, it entrenches inequalities and discrimination, religion needs to be brought back into the fold like a wayward sheep. Religion's main service is to protect the most vulnerable in the society. It should not create new vulnerabilities. Finally, religions only benefit from a secular State that embraces pluralism. It is high time for religions themselves to become more pluralistic within their own ranks.

Chapter 25
Critical Remarks on the Pro-Religion Apriority of the RELIGARE Project

Patrick Loobuyck

Introduction

The protection of the right of freedom of religion and belief plays a central role in the normative assumptions of the RELIGARE project. When this right is linked to the application or further expansion of non-discrimination norms, questions arise at two levels: collective and individual. At the collective level, it raises questions regarding the extent to which the right of association and the freedom of religion of firms, associations or groups also grants them the right to 'discriminate' according to religion in their policies for recruitment, employment, enrolment or admissions. At the individual level, two types of questions arise. The first type of question concerns whether existing, historical rules (for example, dress codes or the observance of holidays) might be unnecessarily discriminatory (whether directly or indirectly) towards existing or new religious minorities. The second type of question concerns the extent to which an employer or a government should respond to specific requests for special treatment from religious minorities (for example, by exempting them from certain rules or by providing access to a prayer space).

The RELIGARE project consistently adopts a position that favours maximising religious freedom. At the collective level, the RELIGARE perspective requires that religious employers and organisations be granted exemptions from anti-discrimination laws and labour laws (*Report*, 21). At the individual level, the RELIGARE team advocate reasonable accommodation, not as a favour, but as a 'legally enshrined' duty (*Report*, 19).

In this chapter, I make several critical comments regarding the weight that the RELIGARE team assign to religious freedom, which must be compromised as little as possible at both the individual and the collective level. The apriority from which the project proceeds is clearly pro-religion, with other freedoms and basic rights almost automatically being overruled by the freedom of religion. It is less clear, however, why religious freedom should always weigh so heavily and why there should not be more space for balancing the freedom of religion with other collective and individual rights, freedoms and interests.

Like the RELIGARE project, my reflections proceed from the normative political philosophical framework that is part of the foundation of liberal democracy. This framework is based on the notion that the government should treat all citizens as free and equal individuals. People are bearers of rights, which the government must ensure and protect.[1] All individuals must have equal freedom to live according to the convictions that seem most meaningful to them at any given time. Will Kymlicka summarises the liberal approach as follows: 'My life only goes better if I am leading it from the inside, according to my beliefs about value.'[2] By definition, therefore, the liberal government must be ideologically neutral, and both the government and religions must respect the separation of church and State.[3]

Given that no one is simply born free, the government should ensure that its citizens are able to develop into free people. In this regard, Joseph Raz refers to the 'autonomy-based duties' of the liberal government: in addition to avoiding coercion, the government should guarantee education and training, provide citizens with

1 J Rawls, *Political Liberalism* (Columbia University Press 1993); R Dworkin, *Taking Rights Seriously* (Harvard University Press 1978); R Dworkin, *Justice for Hedgehogs* (Belknap Press of Harvard University Press 2011) ch 17, 'Liberty'.

2 W Kymlicka, *Contemporary Political Philosophy: An Introduction* (OUP 2002) 216; W Kymlicka, *Liberalism, Community and Culture* (OUP 1989) 12.

3 A Stepan, 'Religion, Democracy, and the "Twin Tolerations"' (2000) 11 (4) *Journal of Democracy* 37–57.

proper information and offer a sufficient and realistic range of options.[4] For the agent to be able to lead an autonomous life, three 'conditions of autonomy' must be fulfilled: independence, appropriate mental abilities and an adequate range of options.

Discrimination as a Collective Right for all Religious Groups and Employers?

The right of association obviously implies that people must be allowed to organise themselves according to religion. This applies not only to self-organisation for purposes of institutionalising their religion or facilitating the collective experience of their faith and worship (for example, church communities). It also applies to organising and offering other activities based on their faith (for example, religiously inspired schools, hospitals, care facilities, labour unions, youth movements and other civil society organisations).

Private associations and organisations that do not claim any public resources enjoy a large degree of autonomy. People are free to establish private associations that are accessible only to certain people with certain beliefs or certain characteristics. In this regard, such associations or organisations may operate in a selective (discriminatory) manner: those who do not possess the desired characteristics or subscribe to the proper views cannot participate. The rules that such organisations or associations apply internally should not be subject to the secular liberal principles of freedom and equality. They may operate according to non-democratic rules, adopt a certain hierarchy, reserve particular functions only for men and restrict the freedom of their members in a variety of ways.

The Conditional Freedom of Private Organisations (Religious or Otherwise)

A liberal society offers space for non-liberal and non-democratically organised private associations, as long as they comply with certain conditions. First, membership should always be voluntary, and no coercion or intimidation should be exercised on current or prospective members. Both before and during the membership, people should be free to consider alternatives, and they should be aware of the customs, practices and expectations of the associations in which they are (or would like to become) members. This voluntary character also implies a permanent and realistic possibility for members to change their minds: groups may operate in a non-liberal manner internally, but they must always leave open a realistic exit possibility.

Furthermore, political liberalism does not allow non-liberal organisations to call for discrimination against people outside their own association. There is greater leeway with regard to internal members than there is with regard to external parties. For example, although women may be excluded from certain internal functions, the organisation may not call for discrimination against women and for treating them as inferior in other sectors of society. An association may restrict the freedom of its members, but it may not call for compromising the freedom and equality of non-members. Individuals, organisations, associations, ideologies and religions that do not comply should be legally prosecuted and punished. Anti-discrimination and anti-racism legislation should be applied in this regard. The philosophy of liberal neutrality does not imply a *laissez-faire* policy. The neutrality of the government is not an end in itself. It serves a higher ethical end: as free and equal individuals, citizens should be allowed to be themselves. When radical (or other) associations and organisations jeopardise this ethical goal, the government should intervene.[5] As stated by John Rawls, government neutrality should not be understood as 'neutrality of opportunity'.[6] Not every way of life and not every religion, moral doctrine or ideology should receive equal opportunity. Liberalism must not allow the existence of Nazism, racism and religious extremism. This would be contrary to the very ethical foundations of liberalism.

4 J Raz, *The Morality of Freedom* (OUP 1986) 369–429. Raz defends a liberal-perfectionist government according to these three duties. I do not subscribe to this view: a non-perfectionist, neutral government could also fulfil these requirements. cf W Kymlicka, 'Liberal Individualism and Liberal Neutrality' (1989) 99 (4) *Ethics* 883–905.

5 For further discussion on this point, see P Loobuyck, 'Back to Basics. Politiek Filosofische Overwegingen over Democratie en Radicalisme' ('Back to Basics. Political Philosophical Reflections on Democracy and Radicalism') (2013) 62 *Orde van de Dag* 17–25.

6 J Rawls, *Political Liberalism* (Columbia University Press 1993 (1996)) 192–93.

If these conditions are met, a church or religious organisation should be allowed to discriminate in matters of admission or employment. The latter is particularly applicable for jobs that are directly related to the preservation and dissemination of the ideological identity. The European Anti-Discrimination Directive therefore stipulates that 'churches and other public or private organisations the ethos of which is based on religion or belief' should be allowed to discriminate according to 'a person's religion or belief' when 'by reason of the nature of these activities or of the context in which they are carried out, a person's religion or belief constitute[s] a genuine, legitimate and justified occupational requirement, having regard to the organisation's ethos'.[7] It is evident that faith communities, religions and churches should be free to make their own decisions regarding who may become a member and who may lead worship services, as well as regarding the conditions that they must meet. The separation of church and State renders government intervention in such matters illegitimate, even in systems involving State financial support for churches.

It is less clear whether churches and ideological organisations should also be allowed to discriminate with regard to jobs that are not directly related to their ideological identities. In this context, the Council Directive mentioned above stipulates that employees may be required to express some form of loyalty to the ideological principles of the association or organisation.[8] The possibility of a group, association or employer to discriminate is thus limited. With reference to the British Equality Act of 2010, Peter Jones writes, 'there is no problem in a church's discriminating on religious grounds in its appointment of a priest or in a mosque's doing so in its appointment of an imam, although there may well be a problem if either takes account of an applicant's faith when it appoints a gardener or a cleaner or an accountant'.[9]

Religious Organisations with State Aid

The situation becomes even more complicated when the associations or organisations also receive financial support from the government. The RELIGARE team are apparently not averse to the practice of governments providing financial support for ideologies, religions and their organisations and activities (*Report*, 33–41), although they ignore the question of whether this practice should alter in some way the right of these organisations to discriminate (for example, in recruiting). Organisations that do not receive public funds can be freer on that point than can those that receive subsidies or funding from the State. A privately funded Catholic hospital or a privately funded Jewish school can discriminate in its policies regarding admission and employment,[10] but one might wonder whether this would also apply for Catholic hospitals and Jewish schools that receive full or partial funding from the government. This is less obvious. One could reason that institutions that provide general social services for which everyone pays through taxes should also be accessible to everyone – in terms of patients or students as well as physicians or teachers. It would be difficult to defend the argument that publicly funded hospitals and schools should be permitted to refuse patients or students for ideological reasons. All patients and students have a right to care and education in these institutions, given that everyone contributes to their funding and education. Religiously inspired schools with strictly private financing can be selective in their enrolment policies, but private religiously inspired schools that are funded through general resources should be open to students with different ideologies, in addition to having to conform to curriculum requirements.

With regard to staff as well, discrimination according to religion should be kept to a minimum. If a Catholic institution or hospital is fully funded by the government, it is hardly tenable to argue that it should be allowed to require its staff to demonstrate a commitment to Catholic ideology for jobs falling outside of the strictly religious realm. Questions concerning religious or ecclesiastical involvement during job interviews

7 Article 4.2 of the Council Directive 2000/78/EC of 27 November 2000, establishing a general framework for equal treatment in employment and occupation. See also Article 13 of the Belgian anti-discrimination law of 2007.

8 ibid: 'This Directive shall thus not prejudice the right of churches and other public or private organisations, the ethos of which is based on religion or belief, acting in conformity with national constitutions and laws, to require individuals working for them to act in good faith and with loyalty to the organisation's ethos.' For European Court rulings in which this is applied, see *Obst v Germany*, App no 425/03 (ECtHR 2010); *Siebenhaar v Germany* (ECtHR 2011).

9 P Jones, 'Toleration, Religion and Accommodation' (2012) *European Journal of Philosophy*, 12–13, available at <http://onlinelibrary.wiley.com/doi/10.1111/j.1468–0378.2012.00549.x/pdf> accessed 27 June 2014.

10 cf *Siebenhaar v Germany* (n 8).

with physicians or nursing staff are therefore inappropriate. The case *Rommelfanger v Germany* (1986), in which the European Court permitted a Catholic hospital in Germany to discharge a physician who had expressed public disagreement with the Church's stand on abortion, is problematic in this regard – particularly if the physician was loyal to the directives of the employer in performing his job.

In the case of a publicly funded Catholic school, it should be possible to restrict discrimination to teachers of Catholic religion, given that the requirement to be Catholic stems from the nature of the job itself.[11] This does not automatically apply for other teachers and instructors.[12] This is because there is no Catholic or Jewish system of mathematics, geography, biology or physics. From the perspective of the Catholic school, it is understandable that they would prefer to have a Catholic mathematics teacher (because this could contribute to the school's ideological identity, even outside class). From the perspective of non-Catholic mathematics teachers, however, it would be unfair to deny them employment in schools that are funded by everyone. This problem becomes even more important when Catholic schools or hospitals have a large share of the market. If Catholic schools have a market share of 70 per cent (as is the case in Dutch-speaking Belgium), a non-Catholic teacher would have access to only one-third of the labour market. This is not in keeping with the principle that everyone should be treated as equal, and that they should therefore have equal employment opportunities. In this respect, it is not surprising that the European Court of Human Rights takes the employment opportunities of the individual into account. When someone is discharged for religious reasons, the Court considers the employee's likelihood of finding a new job in its ruling.

In the Court's opinion, the fact that an employee who has been dismissed by a church has limited opportunities of finding another job is of particular importance. This is especially true where the employer has a predominant position in a given sector of activity and enjoys certain derogations from the ordinary law, as is the case of the two big churches in certain regions of Germany, notably in the field of social activities (for example kindergartens and hospitals).[13]

It remains a difficult exercise to balance the collective religious freedom of the company, organisation or association with the individual's religious freedom and right to employment. It is difficult to apply general rules in this regard. The US Supreme Court is currently deliberating on the question of whether the 'religious objections' of employers outweigh their obligation to cover contraception, as specified in the new American healthcare legislation ('Obamacare'). Each situation requires a nuanced and contextualised balancing of various elements, interests and freedoms. It is true that the organisation's right to discriminate diminishes in inverse proportion to the government's use of general resources to fund organisations, particularly with regard to functions that fall outside the realm of religion. It is also true that greater State funding increases the ability of the government and the judiciary to focus on the rights of individual citizens, given that all of them contribute to this funding.

Neutrality as an Ideological Identity?

Following the above reasoning, private companies with an ethos based on religion[14] should be allowed to discriminate in their recruitment policies, particularly for positions having to do with their ideological identities. Enterprises and firms that do not operate according to ideological principles, however, have no reason to discriminate, except for proportional considerations.[15] This raises another question that is not addressed by the RELIGARE team: to what extent should companies be able to claim ideological neutrality as a foundation for their identity, and to what extent should they be free to discriminate on this basis?

In Belgium, the Labour Tribunal in Tongeren ruled against the chain-store concern HEMA in early 2013 for having discharged a female employee for wearing a headscarf. The judge ruled that the company's argument

11 cf *Fernández Martínez v Spain*, App no 56030/07 (ECtHR, 2012).

12 cf *Lombardi Vallauri v Italy*, App no 39128/05 (ECtHR, 2009).

13 *Schüth v Germany*, App no 1620/03 (ECtHR, 2010) para 73. The Court also considers employment-related matters in other rulings. If the Court deems that the defendant has sufficient opportunities for employment elsewhere, the employer has more right to be selective and to discriminate according to ideology. cf *Obst v Germany*, App no 425/03 (ECtHR, 2010).

14 In German, *Tendenzbetrieb*; in English, *expressive associations*; in Dutch, *tendensonderneming*.

15 cf *Eweida and Others v the United Kingdom*, App no 48420/10 (ECtHR, 2013).

that customers had expressed a preference not to be served by Muslims did not constitute legitimate grounds for the dismissal. The judge also ruled that, if the company in question did not explicitly operate according to a policy of neutrality, it could not simply discriminate according to ideological characteristics. Extending this case further, one could wonder about the likelihood that the judge would have issued a different ruling if the company had indeed clearly followed a policy of neutrality, promoting it as a basic tenet of operations. Would the company then have been allowed to discriminate against those wishing to wear ideological symbols? If a Muslim businessman who wishes to conduct banking affairs explicitly according to the rules of Islam is allowed to discharge an openly atheistic employee, or if a Catholic enterprise is allowed to give preference to employees who have been baptised, why should companies and institutions that wish to be explicitly neutral with regard to ideology not be allowed to introduce rules with regard to the perception and visibility of religion in the workplace? It is unclear why the pursuit of a neutral identity for the self-organised workplace should provide less justification for discrimination than does the pursuit of a Catholic, liberal, Jewish or Islamic identity. Critics might argue that neutrality is not an ideology. They would be right – neutrality is a stance towards ideologies. Nevertheless, this does not alter the fact that it can serve as the ideological identity of a company. One could question the moral desirability of allowing private companies in our society to strive for neutrality and to use it as justification for discharging people, although denying private companies the right to opt for neutrality is at least equally problematic.

Reasonable Accommodation: Four Comments

The preceding section focuses largely on religious freedom at the collective level, as a right of associations and organisations. In this section, I consider freedom of religion at the individual level. More specifically, I consider the RELIGARE project's recommendations that individuals' religious freedom should not be restricted unnecessarily by historically developed rules, and that we should be as open as possible to exceptions and regulations intended to protect the religious freedom of people belonging to minority religions.

In its publications and conclusions, the RELIGARE project advocates reasonable accommodation – not only as a matter of goodwill, but as an enforceable right. In this stance, the team depart from the European tradition, which is more reserved with regard to the practice of reasonable accommodation in response to minority claims. This restraint is manifested in the case law of the European Court of Human Rights, which appeals to the margin of appreciation to grant Member States considerable freedom to implement religious freedom without requiring them to adopt some form of reasonable accommodation. On the contrary, the RELIGARE team advocate the American tradition, as defended and contrasted to the European way of thinking by Martha Nussbaum.[16] On this point, Nussbaum contrasts the views of John Locke with those of the seventeenth-century Protestant theologian and philosopher Roger Williams. According to Nussbaum, Locke is positioned at the foundation of the European tradition, which tends to be blind to differences and which places particular emphasis on the notion that everyone should be equal before the law. Actions that are generally permitted should also be permitted in a religious context, and that which is prohibited for everyone by law cannot be permitted for religious reasons. Laws must thus always apply equally to everyone. In contrast, Williams allows for exceptions to general rules in some cases, based on the principle of freedom of conscience for minorities. This is because majority laws can sometimes be unfair to minorities, even if they are not intended as such. If such laws jeopardise the free exercise of the freedom of conscience, exceptions can be made and a form of reasonable accommodation applied.

Even George Washington expressed a favourable opinion regarding such a policy of accommodation. In 1789, he wrote to the Quakers:

> I assure you very explicitly, that in my opinion the conscientious scruples of all men should be treated with great delicacy and tenderness: and it is my wish and desire, that the laws may always be as extensively accommodated to them, as a due regard for the protection and essential interests of the nation may justify and permit.[17]

16 MC Nussbaum, *Liberty of Conscience: In Defense of America's Tradition of Religious Equality* (Basic Books 2008).

17 Quoted from Nussbaum, ibid 115.

This American tradition is exemplified in the decision of the US Supreme Court in the Sherbert case (1963). Adell Sherbert had worked in a factory for several years until it suddenly introduced the six-day work week, thereby requiring Sherbert to work on Saturdays as well. As a Seventh-Day Adventist, whose religion forbids working on Saturday, she refused. She was unable to find another job, as all employers required Saturday work. She resigned and sought unemployment compensation. The state of South Carolina denied her claim because she had refused 'suitable work'. She took the matter to court, and the court agreed with Sherbert.

Nussbaum notes that accommodation is not always applied in the same way in case law, and that the justices of the Supreme Court are not always on the same wavelength in this regard, even today. For example, Antonin Scalia, one of the nine justices of the US Supreme Court, is a disciple of Locke, who prefers to allow no exceptions.[18] This nevertheless does not alter the fact that the use of accommodation as a way to ensure equal freedom of conscience for minorities continues to be an important and distinctive feature of the American tradition.[19] It is one of the reasons why Nussbaum – and the RELIGARE team, so it seems – place so much stock in the American tradition.[20] According to Nussbaum, the tradition that permits accommodation when no 'compelling state interests' are at stake is 'superior', because 'it reaches subtle forms of discrimination that are ubiquitous in majoritarian democratic life'.[21] This quotation could just as well have come from the RELIGARE report.

Reasonable Accommodation as a Legal Duty?

Like the RELIGARE team, I tend to be more sympathetic to the 'difference-sensitive approach' and the idea of 'open secularism' than I am to the 'difference-blind' approach, which pays little or no attention to the claims of minorities.[22] Nevertheless, I would like to make four comments with regard to the RELIGARE proposal for a legally enshrined duty of reasonable accommodation. First, it seems to me that the legal obligation to provide reasonable accommodation is an excessively strong formulation. From the perspective of political liberalism, the option of searching for solutions for situations in which someone is placed at a disadvantage with regard to the freedom of conscience by an otherwise neutral rule or law should be seen more as a favour than as a generally enforceable law. Indeed, as long as equal services can be guaranteed for all, one option would be to retain the dissenting civil servant (for example, a civil celebrant who refuses to register same-sex marriages or civil partnerships), but a government may not be (legally) required to do so.[23] Employers may also permit Muslims to excuse themselves several times each day to perform their prayer rituals or to request a customised schedule that allows them to have Fridays off. Restaurant owners can respond to requests from Jews or Muslims to adapt the menu in the restaurant. Whether a company will consider such 'favour arrangements' and, if it does, the limits of such arrangements depend upon not only practical capabilities and limitations, but also the context and the extent to which sensitivity to ideological diversity and individual freedom of conscience are allowed to play a role. Each request for accommodation should still be balanced against other interests (for example, the proper functioning of a business or a government). A request for accommodation does not exist in itself; it is usually a quest to find a balance between 'enough accommodation' and 'enough sacrifice for the common good'.[24]

18 This Lockean perspective was dominant in the judgment of the case *Employment Division v Smith* (1990).

19 cf The Religious Freedom Restoration Act, enacted by Congress in 1993.

20 The practice of reasonable accommodation is also characteristic of the way in which Canada addresses minority claims. See G Bouchard and C Taylor, *Building the Future: A Time for Reconciliation* (Gouvernement du Québec 2008); J Maclure and C Taylor, *Secularism and Freedom of Conscience* (Harvard University Press 2011).

21 MC Nussbaum, *The New Religious Intolerance: Overcoming the Politics of Fear in an Anxious Age* (The Belknap Press of Harvard University Press 2013) 87. Eisgruber and Sager also defend reasonable accommodation because our conscience is supposed to be especially vulnerable to discriminatory treatment; see C Eisgruber and L Sager, *Religious Freedom and the Constitution* (Harvard University Press 2007); C Eisgruber and L Sager, 'The Vulnerability of Conscience: The Constitutional Basis for Protecting Religious Conduct' (1994) 61 *U Chi L Rev* 1245.

22 P Loobuyck, *De Seculiere Samenleving. Over Religie, Atheïsme en Democratie* (*The Secular Society: About Religion, Atheism and Democracy*) (Houtekiet 2013); F Levrau and P Loobuyck, 'Is Multiculturalism Bad for Social Cohesion and Redistribution?' (2013) 84 (1) *The Political Quarterly* 101–09; P Loobuyck, 'Liberal Multiculturalism: A Defence of Multicultural Measures without Minority Rights' (2005) 5 (1) *Ethnicities* 108–23.

23 cf *Liliane Ladele v the United Kingdom*, App no 51671/10 (ECtHR, 2013).

24 Eisgruber and Sager (n 21, 2007) 87.

Rule-and-Exemption Approach as a Second-Best Option

My second point concerns the manner in which reasonable accommodation is carried out. In many cases, the rule-and-exemption approach is applied: there is a generally applicable rule, but exceptions are allowed for certain groups. Examples include the use of cannabis and peyote in the US: the substances are prohibited, with the exception of use within religious, ritual contexts.[25] Another example involves the religious exceptions that many countries make with regard to the prohibition on slaughtering animals without anaesthesia.[26]

This way of working is problematic for at least two reasons, neither of which receives sufficient attention from the RELIGARE team. First, a law or rule that does not apply to everybody might not be a good law. Many claims to exceptions could be better resolved by amending or eliminating the law. If it is no longer applicable to everyone, one might question whether there is still a need for that law. In general, I agree with Brian Barry: 'Usually, though, either the case for the law (or some version of it) is strong enough to rule out exemptions, or the case that can be made for exemptions is strong enough to suggest that there should be no law anyway.'[27]

Second, the rule-and-exemption approach is a threat to the principle of equality. Working with exceptions always gives the impression that certain groups of people are simply entitled to more than others. This is disastrous to the base of support for a multicultural society and harmonious coexistence in diversity. For reasons of political practicality as well as for reasons of a more philosophically principled nature, it is better to strive for as much equality under the law as possible.

Within the context of difference-sensitive policy and reasonable accommodation, therefore, I advocate using the rule-and-exemption approach only in extraordinary cases.[28] Whenever possible, efforts should be made to provide reasonable accommodation without recourse to such an *ad hoc* approach. If a rule affects certain minorities unnecessarily, it would be preferable to amend the rule and make it more neutral, rather than permit exceptions to the rule. For example, if Muslims should request an exception to legislation requiring the deceased to be buried in a coffin, one option for reasonable accommodation could be to uphold the law while allowing an exception for Muslims. It would make more sense, however, to start by determining the actual necessity of the law to which an exception has been requested. If such is not the case, the law could be amended in the light of the new situation. For example, Flanders adjusted its legislation, partly in response to requests from Muslims. Burial in a shroud has been an option since 2004. This approach offers a way to respond to requests from minorities without having to provide an exception.

If it is found that the legislation in question is still necessary, it should be applied to everyone in the same manner. For this reason, Flanders (in contrast to the UK in 1976) did not accommodate the request of Sikhs to be permitted to operate a moped or a motorcycle without wearing a helmet. In the interest of legal certainty and general safety, the wearing of the helmet is a legitimate requirement for everyone. Just imagine what would happen if you were to hit a Sikh motorcyclist accidentally, but through your own fault, and the victim were to die because he had not been wearing a helmet. Rules relating to traffic safety exist not only to protect people from themselves, but also to protect third parties. Moreover, the requirement to wear a motorcycle helmet does not contradict the religious freedom of Sikhs. It limits them only in their preferences with regard to operating a motorcycle, and this is obviously not a matter of human rights.

Only in extraordinary cases is it useful to apply the rule-and-exemption approach. This involves situations in which enforcing the generally applicable law is desirable for *pragmatic* reasons and in which granting an exception would enhance the freedom of minorities without placing anyone else at a disadvantage. For example, a school could have pragmatic reasons for enforcing a dress code that prohibits students from wearing head coverings but still permit Sikhs, Muslim girls and Jewish boys to deviate from this rule. The school holidays in many Western European countries provide another example. In most of these countries, school holidays coincide with Christmas, Ash Wednesday, Easter, Ascension, Pentecost and All Saints' Day. While this enhances the religious freedom of Christians, it places religious minorities at a disadvantage. There may be *pragmatic* reasons for not completely re-engineering the existing calendar (which is indeed coloured

25 cf The Religious Freedom Restoration Act of 1993.

26 For example, Article 17 of the European Convention for the Protection of Animals for Slaughter (1979).

27 B Barry, *Culture and Equality: An Egalitarian Critique of Multiculturalism* (Polity 2001) 39.

28 Loobuyck (n 22, 2005) 119–21.

by Christianity) in an attempt to make it more neutral or difference-sensitive, motivated by the philosophy of equality. In this case, the rule-and-exemption approach might offer solace, allowing both religious minorities and Christians to enjoy their religious freedom.[29] For example, in 2002, the Flemish minister of education issued a circular specifying that children could be legitimately absent in order to celebrate holidays that are inherent in their constitutionally recognised ideological belief systems. Muslim children may therefore be absent from school for *Eid al-Fitr* (Feast of Breaking the Fast) and *Eid al-Adha* (Feast of the Sacrifice), and Jewish children may stay home for *Sukkot* (Feast of Tabernacles) and Passover.

Good and Bad Minority Rights

Reasonable accommodation is a subject of dispute and controversy, particularly in Europe. Critics who are more inclined to be sympathetic to a difference-blind approach than they are to liberal multiculturalism often try to use the slippery-slope argument when addressing the question of reasonable accommodation: where will it end, and will it not lead to chaos and anarchy? If we give religious people an inch, they'll take a mile or even a league – so goes their argument – and we would thus do well not to give them anything at all.

Those venturing into the territory of reasonable accommodation should therefore always have a very clear idea of which requests are eligible for accommodation and which are not. Although this distinction is implicitly used by the RELIGARE team, it should have been developed more, if only to circumvent the previously mentioned criticism of those who advocate a difference-blind approach.

In theory, this distinction is not very difficult to draw: minority claims that impinge upon fundamental rights should not be considered. In this regard, the political philosopher Will Kymlicka distinguishes between unacceptable minority rights as internal restrictions and acceptable minority rights as external protections.[30] The latter are aimed at enhancing equality between groups and the individual freedom of people. The circular regarding absence from school on religious holidays is an example. Minority rights should not be taken into consideration, however, if they serve to restrict the freedom of individuals (internal restriction). No minority rights or special exemptions or measures should thus be allowed in order to silence dissident voices, to inflict genital mutilation on young women, to trample women's rights, to deny blood transfusions to children, to allow forced marriages, to keep children out of education, to disrespect the equality between men and women in matters of divorce, to penalise adultery with corporal punishment or for other such purposes. These matters should not be accommodated, but actively contested. Reasonable accommodation and the corresponding minority rights can be considered only if they serve to enhance both the equality between groups and the freedom of individuals within a group.

In practice, such matters are not always clear. Denying children the right to engage in mixed-gender sports or swimming could be seen as an internal restriction, which schools should thus not allow. On the other hand, in certain contexts, the option of opening a swimming pool exclusively to women for a few hours would be worthy of consideration, as it would enhance the freedom of women who would otherwise never swim. Ritual slaughter without anaesthesia is another case in point. In Belgium, the rule-and-exemption approach has been applied. The royal decree of 1998 on the protection of animals at the time of slaughter or killing does not apply to 'animals slaughtered according to special methods required for certain religious rites'. This exception arrangement also exists in other countries, including the Netherlands and the UK. The question of whether this is an acceptable minority right is legitimate and pertinent. The ideological interests of people (religious freedom) must be weighed against the physical welfare of animals. Religious freedom should therefore take a back seat to those for whom the latter is a fundamental ethical value. It would be inconsistent for anyone who slaughters animals without anaesthesia to be subject to criminal penalties, except for Muslims and Jews. If we are truly concerned with animal welfare – which is not reflected in our industrial manner of fattening animals for consumption[31] – the exceptions should be eliminated.[32] This could best be accomplished in consultation

29 This example comes close to the minority rights assigned to ethnic minorities by the liberal political philosopher Will Kymlicka; cf W Kymlicka, *Multicultural Citizenship: A Liberal Theory of Minority Rights* (OUP 1995).

30 ibid 35ff.

31 cf JS Foer, *Eating Animals* (Little, Brown and Co. 2009).

32 cf P Casal, 'Is Multiculturalism Bad for Animals? (2003) 11 (1) *The Journal of Political Philosophy* 1–22.

with the parties involved and with the greatest possible respect for religious freedom: a prohibition against slaughter without anaesthesia is not the same as a prohibition against ritual slaughter.

Reasonable Accommodation: Only for Religions?

The practice of reasonable accommodation has also been criticised by atheists and humanists, who argue that such 'concessions' give the impression that those who adhere to a religion are permitted to do more than other people are. In order to respond to this criticism, proponents of reasonable accommodation must expand their area of application and strive to include other, non-religious considerations. For example, there is no reason why a school should allow an exception to the dress code for a Jewish boy who wishes to wear a yarmulke, but not for someone from a fishing culture who has an earring and a tattoo.

Jocelyn Maclure, Charles Taylor and, to some extent, Martha Nussbaum thus propose that 'all core beliefs that allow individuals to structure their moral identity' should be taken into account in matters of reasonable accommodation.[33] They rightly consider religious freedom a subcategory of the more inclusive freedom of conscience and the right to a sense of personal identity. In this regard, they refer to the fact that both the Canadian and the American Supreme Courts have recognised the existence of non-religious beliefs that can provide moral direction for the lives of individuals and that can provide a foundation upon which they can rely in problems of conscience. For example, people with secular reasons for being pacifists can expect alternatives within the context of military service. If meal services in aircraft and prisons take Muslim and Jewish dietary restrictions into account, in principle, they should also consider vegetarians' restrictions. It does not matter whether a person is vegetarian because he or she is Hindu or because he or she is a fan of the ideas of the utilitarian animal philosopher Peter Singer. If reasonable accommodation is chosen, it must be applied to protect the moral integrity of people, and not solely to respond to religious demands.

This approach to reasonable accommodation presupposes the ability clearly to distinguish ordinary individual preferences, tastes and penchants from meaning-giving beliefs and deep commitments. There is a difference between requiring a morally motivated vegetarian to eat meat and requiring someone who likes to sleep late to be at work at nine in the morning. This distinction is not always clear, however, and it is impossible for a government or employer to arrive at an exceptional arrangement for every request.

In this regard, the proponents of reasonable accommodation must also consider the possibility that, at some point, there might be too many claims. In that case, such a policy would become impossible, and accommodation would fall outside of the boundaries of what people could reasonably expect. A policy of reasonable accommodation thus also calls for common sense. Should at pastafarian wearing a colander on the head to honour the divine spaghetti monster receive special accommodation arrangements based on the freedom of conscience? No. It would be ludicrous for such clowns to foreclose the possibility of reasonable accommodation for people with serious requests.

For the sake of clarity, let me stress that the critical comments expressed above offer insufficient reason to cease the consideration of reasonable accommodation. Reasonable accommodation is intended to be a nuanced manner of taking into account the freedom of conscience of people and, in certain contexts, guaranteeing maximum equality of freedom for all, if it is feasible. A secular society in which reasonable accommodation is applied in a sensible manner is freer, and thus more liberal, than is a society in which all forms of reasonable accommodation are excluded in advance.

Conclusion: Do We Really Need Religious Freedom?

The RELIGARE team have produced very interesting work that relates the freedom of religion and belief to the application of non-discrimination norms. They call for the maximisation of religious freedom at both the collective and the individual levels. To this end, religiously oriented organisations should be allowed to preserve their individuality, and individuals should have the right to reasonable accommodation if a certain law or rule would unnecessarily violate their religious freedom.

33 Maclure and Taylor (n 20) 89. See also Nussbaum (n 16) 164–74; Eisgruber and Sager (n 21, 2007).

The comments that I express refer largely to the pro-religion apriority of the RELIGARE team, in which the freedom of religion can be used quasi-automatically as a trump card – at both the individual and the collective level. This apriority creates a situation in which, with regard to the collective level, no questions are asked with regard to whether organisations should also have the right to adopt neutrality as an ideology and to use it as a basis for imposing discriminatory measures (for example, prohibiting all ideological symbols in the workplace). If neutral organisations are not allowed to do this, arguments are needed to explain why religious organisations are allowed to be more discriminating than organisations that would like to be neutral. This does not appear to be an exercise in the obvious. On the other hand, the claim that neutrality could also serve as a basis for discrimination generates difficulties regarding the plea for reasonable accommodation as a legally enforceable right. Providing maximum protection for individual religious freedom through reasonable accommodation implies the restriction of religious freedom for organisations. Conversely, providing maximum protection for the religious freedom of organisations would undermine individual religious freedom. This tension receives insufficient attention in the RELIGARE report.

This touches upon a fundamental point. The apriority of the RELIGARE report is religious freedom as a trump card – but is this the right approach? Nowhere does the report address the question of whether we still have religious freedom as a separate right. Historically, religious freedom has obviously been an important fundamental right, but might freedom of conscience, freedom of expression, freedom of action and freedom of organisation have since come to suffice for the same purposes? Are there discriminatory, degrading, socially disruptive actions or opinions that should be allowed and that are not covered by these freedoms and that can be protected only by religious freedom? As noted by Steven Smith, 'In recent years, theorists have tried to address the question of whether there is any good justification, or at least any good *secular* justification, for treating religion as a special category – and have concluded, often, that there is not.'[34] As long as the freedom of religion continues to exist as a separate category, it is suggested that, under the guise of religion, individuals, groups and organisations might be permitted more latitude than others. This is contrary to the basic principle upon which our democratic rule of law is based: the government should treat its citizens as free and equal individuals, regardless of their ideological background.

Religious freedom ultimately adds nothing to the freedom of expression. If religious leaders claim that homosexuality is an unnatural disease, this claim should not be protected by the freedom of religion, but by the freedom of expression. Those who would protect the expression of an opinion based on religious freedom give the impression that people who adhere to a religion should be permitted to say more than other people. If believers are allowed to say something, regardless of how erroneous, provocative or offensive, non-believers should be allowed to do so as well. Conversely, religions should not be allowed to use religious freedom to censor profane or offensive statements from religious critics. In this case as well, freedom of expression should take precedence over freedom of religion.

From the perspective of the secular government, there is no reason to protect religion as a separate category with its own legal privileges. This does not mean that religious freedom should be deleted from the law books, but it should never be misused to allow things that would be unacceptable without religious freedom. This means that, in a secular society, we should assign a more modest and subordinate place to religious freedom, or we should interpret it more broadly and treat it as freedom of thought and conscience – with religious freedom and its limits being applicable to non-religious practices and beliefs as well.

In a secular rule of law, religious freedom is only one of the many freedoms that conflict with one another and that should be balanced proportionally. In this regard, freedom of religion does not always have the advantage, and it is thus not a trump card that can be used anywhere and at any time. Where fundamental rights are in jeopardy, religious freedom must often yield. Excessive emphasis on the freedom of religion as a separate category could lead to permitting things that should be prohibited.

34 SD Smith, 'Discourse in the Dusk: The Twilight of Religious Freedom?' (2009) 122 (7) *Harvard Law Review* 1884. For discussion, see also R Dworkin, *Religion without God* (Harvard University Press 2013) 128–37; B Leiter, 'Why Tolerate Religion?' (2008) 1 *Const Comment* 1–27; B. Leiter, *Why Tolerate Religion?* (Princeton University Press 2012).

Chapter 26
RELIGARE, Believers and Non-Believers: But Where is the Citizen?

Koen Lemmens[1]

> L'opposé de la 'laïcité' n'est pas la 'religion' … mais le laisser-faire, laisser-passer, la viscosité du coutumier et l'emprise agressive des convictions, exacerbée dans les sectes.
>
> – R. Debray, *Ce que nous voile le voile*

Introduction

The final report of RELIGARE is an interesting piece of academic work on freedom of religion. It was a very ambitious endeavour to integrate not only scholars from different legal orders, but also from various disciplines, in one research project. The result is a dense, original and very thought-provoking paper. However, its strength is sometimes its main weakness. First, the authors deal with many sensitive issues, such as State–religion relations, discrimination, protection of minorities, migration and the like. Although these different topics are in practice often interrelated – this is the complex issue of intersectional discrimination – I wonder whether we do not have to try harder to disentangle the issues at stake, however difficult this may be, and consider them in the first place from the perspective of freedom of religion rather than from an anti-discrimination perspective.[2] By dealing with everything together, we run, of course, the risk of confusing questions of religious discrimination with issues of ethnic or cultural discrimination. I like to reflect on the relationship between State, law and religion *etsi peregrini non daretur* (as if there were no foreigners), to paraphrase the famous Grotian phrase *etsi Deus non daretur* (as if there were no God). In today's world, however, it has become very complicated to criticise certain elements of 'new' or 'foreign' religions, without being at least implicitly accused of racism, ethnocentrism or, as the case may be, 'Islamophobia'. Needless to say, the fear of a bad reputation (the opponent is a 'racist'!) may inhibit some people from voicing their opinions, however reasonable they may be.[3]

Furthermore, to adopt a philosophical, sociological and legal approach to the question of State, law and religion relations is certainly enriching, but entails the danger that some elementary questions are not properly addressed or answered. Fundamental legal and philosophical questions are often countered by policy arguments. A good illustration of this is the report's final sentence:

> What should not happen is that a significant number of persons in the EU *see* themselves as increasingly subject to restrictions that *they* consider unjustified and that, *in their view*, constitute discrimination against them. That would certainly not be a trustworthy blueprint on which to build when rethinking the interface of religion and secularism in the Europe of the future. (*Report*, 50, my emphasis)

As a citizen, I can see what the authors mean and I would, to some extent, consider it indeed a wise attitude for legislators not to *create* the impression that 'a significant number'[4] of persons feel themselves

---

1 I want to thank Toon Agten for his patience and the long discussions on the topic.

2 T Lock, 'Religious Freedom and Belief Discrimination in Germany and the United Kingdom: Towards a Common European Standard?' (2013) 38 *E L Rev* 655–76.

3 See G Haarscher, 'Secularism, the Veil and "Reasonable Interlocutors": Why France is not that Wrong' (2009–2010) 28 *Penn St Int'l L Rev* 368; K Lemmens, '*Larvatus prodeo*? Why Concealing the Face can be Incompatible with a European Conception of Human Rights' (2014 forthcoming) 39 *E L Rev*. See also Elisabeth Badinter in an interview that was published in the Belgian newspaper *De Morgen* at the moment I was writing this contribution (9 November 2013, 'Zeno', p. 8).

4 The adjective 'significant' illustrates quite clearly the pitfall of minority protection through the prism of groups. What about non-significant groups?

subject to unjustified treatment. As a lawyer, however, I find this statement highly questionable. People who are confronted with restrictions on their freedom almost always tend to see themselves as victims of unjustified treatment. However, the truth here is not in the eyes of the beholder: what has to be condemned is discrimination that is acknowledged as such by (constitutional) courts. What the report seems to suggest is that, even if legal rules are in line with the constitutional and international legal framework, they still can be challenged because people *see* or experience the rules as being unjust. Now, of course, any rule can be called into question – *de omnibus disputandum* – but there is a clear difference between a situation in which the law violates fundamental rights and a situation in which the law does not violate fundamental rights, but is nevertheless felt to be unfair. In the latter case, there is no *compelling legal* argument to change the law. The reasons to do so are a matter of mere policymaking. As a lawyer, I can have my opinions, but they are not particularly relevant to policy, since in a democratic debate my arguments should not be given more weight than those of my fellow citizens when it comes to policy choices.

Finally, it should be borne in mind that legislation has as well an *expressive* function.[5] By focusing so much on the practical side of the questions, the project tends to underestimate the fact that legislators sometimes want to underline basic social values by protecting them through law. If, for instance, the French want to stress the fundamental *republican* – and therefore, in the French conception, secular – nature of public schools by banning religious symbols, the (pragmatic) argument that some very religious children may prefer private schools or home education – which is worse from the viewpoint of integration – will not suffice to change the lawmaker's mind.[6] Compare this to the discussion on abortion legislation: whether or not to allow abortion is a complicated moral, ethical and legal question that deserves a fundamental answer. But the argument that women may travel abroad to escape strict legislation in their home country is of course not very helpful in answering the fundamental question. I am not saying that pragmatic arguments should be ignored or should always be set aside when more fundamental questions enter into the debate. I am instead saying that the arguments belong to different spheres and that it may be inadequate to answer fundamental questions by using pragmatic arguments (although it can be a very good way to alleviate tensions and avoid conflicts). This is, by the way, in general the basic attitude of the report, made especially clear when it comes to reasonable accommodations: avoiding conflicts, searching for alternatives, and so on. But it sometimes makes me think of a mother who sees two children fighting over a fancy remote-controlled car and then says to one of them that there is also a beautiful red ball to play with. Now this may end the row, but leaves the fundamental question untouched: who was entitled to play at that very moment with the remote-controlled car?

In this short chapter, I will mainly focus on three aspects of the report. First, I will examine the normative framework. Next, I will highlight that some basic assumptions underlying the research have not been sufficiently made explicit. Finally, I will argue that an overly broad protection of the *forum externum* will create new inequalities.

The Normative Framework

The RELIGARE partners have come up with a normative framework that they call 'inclusive State neutrality' and which they oppose to 'strict separation'. Strict State neutrality could, in their view, too easily be interpreted as 'public hostility towards churches/religious communities and/or secular values'. The question here is, of course, 'Interpreted by whom?' And, once again, whether the truth here is not in the eyes of the beholder. Furthermore, the authors highlight that strict neutrality can become an ideology that 'risks entering into competition with other ideas or systems – including religions – with claims on the public space' (*Report*, 16).

I think this critique is too severe toward 'strict State neutrality' and too benevolent to the very concept of inclusive State neutrality. Of course, the RELIGARE authors are right that 'strict' State neutrality is seldom strict all the way down. In countries such as Belgium, although the terminology of separation is used, mutual

5 R Debray, *Ce que nous voile le voile* (Gallimard 2004) 17.

6 P Scheffer, *Het land van aankomst* (De Bezige Bij 2010) 445 argues that the possibility that parents and children could escape from the application of gender equality rules should not prevent us from upholding them. Therefore, no accommodations in public schools should be considered in this respect.

dependence seems to be a better qualification to describe State–religion relations.[7] Nevertheless, one could wonder whether some incoherence in the model should lead to abandoning the model altogether. Making the existing models more coherent could as well be an option. Admittedly, to prefer the one over the other is a matter of policy and politics.

But before going into the differences between both policy models, it seems useful to stress the similarities between 'strict State neutrality' and 'inclusive State neutrality'. As I understand the concepts, they are both instances of secularism. Although they seem quite critical of the concept of secularism, Ahdar and Leigh give a good account of what secularism stands for. According to these authors, secularism is a philosophy that encompasses the views that

> all religions are equal or at least are worthy of equal respect and may participate in the public sphere; none, not even the oldest, most culturally embedded or numerically larger ones, are to be privileged; the unity of society does not require unity of faith and religion; governments are ill-suited to identify religious truth and error; laws must have a non-religious justification; any form of State coercion of religious practice is wrong; the State is to be concerned with citizens' temporal needs, not their souls; and so on.[8]

Defined in this way, secularism is not substantive, but relational. Indeed, secularism does not uphold any transcendental position. As such, it is not incompatible with religion or belief, that is, people can be both secularist and religious. There is no contradiction in adhering to religious beliefs while at the same time defending a secularist position. Secularism therefore does not imply atheism or agnosticism.[9] As the Italian scholar Sergio Luzzatto has pointed out, *laïcité* – which we can translate here as secularism – 'is not the opposite of faith', nor is it a philosophical system; it is a mere method to distinguish matters of faith from matters of reason.[10]

Now, within secularism, it is possible to distinguish, as the German constitutionalist Böckenförde has proposed, between *distanzierender Neutralität* (he refers to the French model) and *übergreifender offener Neutralität* (he refers to the German model). The difference between the models is essentially the room they leave to individuals to live according to their beliefs and worldviews, without however touching upon the basic rules of the society.[11]

It is my impression that the RELIGARE authors are too severe towards strict separation, but they are considerably less demanding when it comes to inclusive State neutrality. In the first place, I fail to understand why inclusive State neutrality would be any less of an 'ideology' than (strict) separation, which, as the authors themselves point out, is said to take on an ideological dimension. According to the defenders of the new concept, it would be an 'overarching framework for managing competing claims on the public space … while also refusing to favour one over another'. Well, I would disagree with this statement, precisely because the new concept obviously favours itself over strict State neutrality, which is, according to the authors themselves, a claim on the public space. I do not see a problem with authors pretending that their model is 'better' than another – that is precisely the point of developing models – yet I find it problematic that the new model is as much a claim on the public space as all the others models on State and religion. The added value of inclusive State neutrality cannot be that it would be less of an ideological stance. The added value lies, on the contrary, in the fact that citizens will have better protection of their *forum externum*, at least when compared to the protection offered by strict State neutrality. The question remains, however, to what extent claims explicitly related to the *forum externum* can be taken into consideration.

---

7 M Adams, *Recht en democratie ter discussie* (Universitaire Pers Leuven 2006) 202.

8 R Ahdar and I Leigh, *Religious Freedom in the Liberal State* (OUP 2013) 98.

9 A Sajo, 'Preliminaries to a Concept of Constitutional Secularism' [2008] *I-CON* 607.

10 S Luzzatto, *Il crocifisso di Stato* (Einaudi 2011) 83. Jean-Marc Piret clearly states that even in its purest form, the concept of *laïcité* was not meant to eliminate religion from French society. It is not an anti-religious ideology; J-M Piret, 'De verhouding tussen godsdienst en staat (in het onderwijs)' in P De Hert and K Meerschaut (eds), *Scheiding van Kerk en Staat of Actief Pluralisme?* (Intersentia 2007) 131.

11 E-W Böckenförde, 'Wie können die Religionen friedlich und frei beisammen leben? Über den säkularen Staat, seine Neutralität und die Probleme, mit denen er im 21. Jahrhundert konfrontiert ist', *Neue Zürcher Zeitung* (23–24 June 2007) 28.

Furthermore, as I will explain in the next section, inclusive State neutrality can only work if a set of values that are not open to balancing are predefined. If not, it only creates the impression that everything is open to negotiation. Religious, and possibly cultural, claims can then tip the balance in any discussion.

Unanswered Questions

The normative framework of RELIGARE is based on certain assumptions, yet they are either not made very explicit or, if they are, they require more thorough explanation. Obviously, in this short contribution I cannot elaborate on all of them. I will briefly mention three points that may need some further reflection.

The first pertains to the general global context in which the research is done. I will not deny that Europe today is more diverse than it was 30 years ago. A growing number of Europeans have different ethnic and national backgrounds. That is a sociological observation, but it does not explain why existing State–religion relations should necessarily be changed. Reading the report, one might get the impression that this causal link is taken for granted. It is, however, hard to deduce normative conclusions from descriptive observations. I am not convinced that we have to fundamentally rethink our legal approach to religions because a growing number of people from different ethnic and national backgrounds are now living in Europe. This could be so for people coming from a different *religious* background. Yet, here as well, we have to be careful: the State–religion relations in many countries are the result of an attempt to find a suitable compromise between freedom of religion on the one hand and the rights of others and public order on the other. These rules have already been established for a religiously plural context. Take for instance the French law of 1905 on the *laïcité* of the State. It cannot be denied that even in 1905, France was already religiously diverse, even if an overwhelming majority of the population was Roman Catholic. The interests of atheists, Protestants and Jews were duly considered – it is noteworthy that precisely the members of the minority religions welcomed the law most. In other words, the most important transition takes place when a monoreligious society is confronted with at least one other religion. A pluralistic society that sees new religions becoming popular does not necessarily need to reconsider its constitutional framework, but it has to focus on the equality principle. That is, it should apply the existing rules to the new religions, faiths and beliefs – *patere legem quam ipse fecisti* ('abide by your own rules'). Of course, one could object that the dice may be loaded, and that the existing rules are inherently sympathetic to the Abrahamic religions and the atheists. Now, apart from the obvious observation that this should be illustrated with clear examples,[12] this would in fact be a strong argument in favour of strict neutrality. The more a legal system is indeed indifferent to religion, the less it is likely to favour any given religion and the easier it is to remediate certain 'anomalies'.

My main problem with the RELIGARE report is that it fails to see that freedom of religion, belief and conscience is important, but that it is not more important than other fundamental freedoms.[13] I do not read the case law of the ECtHR as privileging Article 9 of the ECHR over any other freedom protected by the Convention. Reading the RELIGARE report, one is tempted to believe that for the authors religion is the *maître mot*. Of course, the authors affirm that freedom of religion is to be balanced against other fundamental rights, but between the lines it is clear that the balance is weighted: religion enjoys a privileged position. One could obviously object that this was the very aim of the project, but that is not a very helpful comment, since similar projects could be conducted on sexual minority rights, freedom of speech and so on; every time a different fundamental freedom would enjoy a preferred position. The question, however, is how the legal system, which has to protect all fundamental rights on an equal footing, can possibly cope with all those claims to preferential treatment.

---

12 An obvious example here is the problem of religious holidays. Elsewhere I have defended the idea that, as a matter of equality, the calendar of religious holidays should be revised. See K Lemmens, 'Interculturaliteit of de ironie van de democratische rechtsstaat: over religieuze feestdagen en staatsneutraliteit' in M-C Foblets and J-P Schreiber (eds), *The Round Tables on Interculturalism* (Larcier 2013) 393–413.

13 In this respect, the author's guidelines provided by the publisher of this volume are remarkable. They state that 'inflammatory language must not be used in relation to religious beliefs'. And how about inflammatory language in relation to non-religious beliefs, political convictions and so forth? This statement illustrates that often, although it is affirmed that religious and non-religious (secular) beliefs should be treated on par, there is considerably more respect for the religious beliefs. Why?

A clear example of this preference for religious freedom is to be found on page 17 of the report. The researchers indicate that the entire project was inspired by 'the search for a balance between the protection of freedom of religion and belief, on the one hand, and the principle of equal treatment and non-discrimination on the other'. However, when reading the report, it becomes clear that the case for equal treatment and non-discrimination is almost exclusively made on behalf of people from 'new' religions or beliefs and minority religions. In this respect, the project's underlying rationale was to a large extent tautological, because what is presented here as an exercise in balancing is, in reality, nothing but a reformulation of the same assertion. This is a logical choice, since non-discrimination appears to be a much stronger way to protect religious claims than freedom of religion.[14] The claims made in the name of new religions are indeed often made by people who, if they have the feeling that their needs are not respected, will argue that they are discriminated against and therefore subject to unequal treatment. Denying, for instance, a Pastafarian[15] the right to wear a colander on his head for a driver's license photograph constitutes not only an interference with his rights of free exercise of religion, but it can be as well a clear case of unequal treatment whenever kippahs, turbans, veils and so on are accepted. I think, therefore, that the balancing exercise concerns, on the one hand, the right to freedom of religion and belief and, on the other hand, the rights of others (including their 'religious rights') and public order.

Finally, coming to public order, I believe that this concept touches on the core of the debate. Yet I only found the term four times in the report. For a good understanding, I use the term here as defined by the Belgian lawyer Henri De Page.[16] In his view, public order should be understood as encompassing the set of rules and principles 'qui touche aux intérêts essentiels de l'Etat ou de la collectivité, ou qui fixe, dans le droit privé, les bases juridiques fondamentales sur lesquelles *repose l'ordre* économique ou *moral* d'une société déterminée ('that touches upon the essential interests of the State or the community, or that sets down, in private law, the fundamental legal bases on which *rests* the economic or *moral order* of a given society'). In other words, by reflecting upon the very concept of public order, we explain what kind of society we want to be. In doing so, we also define the realm of personal autonomy and the limits of the freedom of contracting (cf. Article 6 of the French and Belgian civil codes). In practice, this kind of reflection boils down to affirming that certain values and principles are sacrosanct and cannot be subject to exemptions, exceptions, compromises and the like.

It appears to me that the RELIGARE consortium advocates a multicultural conception of society. Personally, I have serious objections to this conception. It is not the place here, given the limited space, to expose them, but I do think that a society is not just a mere aggregate of individuals (the Thatcherian 'there is no such a thing as society') who can, as the case may be, create almost parallel societies along ethnic, religious, cultural or political lines to create a 'community of communities' (to quote Bhikhu Parekh).[17] *Laïcité*, as Debray has pointed out, is precisely the opposite, since it disconnects the public interest from particularities and it thereby allows the republic to be more than just collected bits and pieces of a society ('l'idée laïque est le nom donné à une déconnexion toujours laborieuse entre intérêt général et intérêts particuliers, qui permet à une République d'être plus qu'une addition en puzzle de fragments de société').[18] Be that as it may, whether we hallow the European device *unitas in diversitate* or the American *e pluribus unum*, there is a link between the 'unity' and the 'diversity'. Differentialism and multiculturalism, at least in some of their interpretations, tend to neglect this aspect of unity by stressing almost exclusively the differences between citizens. I believe that our societies should get rid of this one-sided approach – in Freudian terms, the 'narcissism of small differences' – and focus on the elements that unite citizens, whatever be their origins, religion, sexual orientation and so on.[19] The point is not whether the members of the RELIGARE consortium prefer multiculturalism or not, or whether I subscribe rather to republicanism (in the French sense of the

14 T Lock, 'Religious Freedom and Belief Discrimination in Germany and the United Kingdom: Towards a Common European Standard?' (2013) 38 *E L Rev* 665.

15 Pastafarians 'believe' in the Flying Spaghetti Monster. See C Cusack, *Invented Religions: Imagination, Fiction and Faith* (Ashgate 2010) 113 et seq.

16 H De Page, *Traité élémentaire de droit civil* (vol 1, Bruylant 1962) 111 (emphasis added).

17 <www.runnymedetrust.org/projects-and-publications/projects/past-projects/meb/report/reportIntroduction.html> accessed 27 June 2014.

18 Debray (n 5) 48.

19 A similar point is made by Elisabeth Badinter (n 3). For a similar critique from a British perspective, see T Philips, 'After 7/7: Sleepwalking to Segregation' <www.humanities.manchester.ac.uk/socialchange/research/social-change/summer

term). The only relevant point is that European States are divided themselves. Admittedly, the British model shows much more sympathy for political multiculturalism than the French. In Belgium, however, Parliament explicitly rejected multiculturalism as a model to govern our diverse society. It did so when the bill on the interdiction of concealing the face in public was passed. This so-called *burqa* ban was almost unanimously adopted (with only one vote cast against); its *exposé des motifs* literally rejected multiculturalism.[20] The main lesson here is that there is no European consensus on this very sensitive issue, and the EU should therefore give subsidiarity its full effect. That is also a matter of respecting diversity.

Religion as Indulgence: Toward New Inequalities – *Suum cuique*?

The sympathetic attitude toward religion becomes very clear when the authors apply their model to horizontal relations. Typical here is the debate on reasonable accommodations in the workplace. Although I strongly believe that ideally employers and employees should find, on an informal basis, a compromise between the interests at stake, I am not so sure that the discussion can be easily framed in terms of legally enforceable rights. Yet, according to the authors of the RELIGARE project, the religious claim of the believer is so strong that it can ground considerable 'reasonable accommodations'. The employee should be granted a meaningful right to freedom of religion (*Report*, 20). Nothing is said, however, on the rights of the employers, who can of course refer to their property rights, not to mention their right to freedom of belief or conscience. Supposedly, their rights are implicitly taken into account through the assessment of the reasonableness of the accommodations.

Let us then have a look at the horizontal anti-discrimination directive, that is, the proposed Council Directive on implementing equal treatment between persons irrespective of religion or belief, disability, age or sexual orientation.[21] Since the concern of combatting discrimination is central to the RELIGARE project, one would expect that the proposed directive would be wholeheartedly welcomed. The reaction is, however, much more nuanced. The authors of the report warn against perverse effects of the directive, since non-discrimination obligations (pertaining to sexual orientation) would affect commercial operators with strongly held beliefs, companies with a religious ethos and so on. The example of a hotel owner is given. Although it is not clearly stated, the underlying idea seems to be that hotel owners, should they have outspoken religious beliefs, are allowed to refuse to rent rooms to same-sex couples. Not a word, this time, on the 'meaningful right' of non-discrimination, autonomy and so on of LGBT people, to name just these citizens.

I am not saying that both positions are necessarily in contradiction with each other. Quite on the contrary, if one accepts that the religious interest is overriding, they are perfectly in line with one another. Yet, and this is my point, there is little to balance, little to manage or to mediate when freedom of religion is anyhow the preferred freedom.

Comparing the two sets of claims does give rise to many critiques. I will limit myself to three comments.

First, when it comes to the meaningful freedom of religion in the workplace, I wonder whether the authors have considered the possibility that employers truly believe that 'strict'[22] neutrality, or call it secularism, is the best way to manage religious diversity on the work floor as well as in their relations with customers. It is common knowledge that grocers and their personnel do not talk about party politics or religion with their customers, since their clients are of all allegiances and convictions. With a somewhat negative undertone, the authors depict this attitude as 'European discomfort with public statements of religious commitment'. Relegating discussions on religion (or party politics, to give a less controversial issue) to the private sphere does not need to be a sign of discomfort, however; it may very well be the illustration of a conception of

-workshops/documents/sleepwalking.pdf> accessed 27 June 2014. P. Scheffer drew attention to this speech; see P Scheffer, *Het land van aankomst* (De Bezige Bij 2010) 427.

20 Chambre des représentants, *Proposition de loi visant à interdire le port de tout vêtement cachant totalement ou de manière principale le visage*, 28 September 2010, doc. 53 0219/001, 4 et seq.

21 <http://eur-lex.europa.eu/LexUriServ/LexUriServ.do?uri=COM:2008:0426:FIN:EN:PDF> accessed 27 June 2014.

22 Of course, the term strict is not very helpful here, since employers, if they are not related to public authorities, are private parties who are not bound by the principles of *laïcité* or secularism. Still, they could perfectly believe that, in order to create a harmonious work floor, employees should be modest in affirming their political, religious and syndical beliefs or convictions.

citizenship that is highly inspired by Montesquieu's appraisal of moderation. Under such a conception of citizenship, a strong public/private divide is maintained, and citizens know that they cannot display the same form of authenticity in the public sphere as in the private.[23]

Could such a policy, whereby employers mirror the State's neutrality, possibly be considered a sufficiently strongly held belief as to allow employers to apply it notwithstanding the religious claims of their personnel? If the answer is no, we are in the presence of a discriminatory situation in which one set of values and beliefs is outweighed by another set of beliefs and values, on the sole ground that the set that prevails does so because it is 'believed' to be more deeply held, coherent and serious. But why should this be so? And who decides whether convictions are sufficiently up to standard? Isn't this already a form of bias in favour of established beliefs and religions, to the detriment of especially secular beliefs, which perhaps in postmodern times lack the coherence and comprehensiveness of some more established religions or worldviews? But if the answer is yes, I think the RELIGARE solution will be of little practical use, since many employers will refer to their 'modest secularism' as a strongly developed belief in order to avoid any specific religious claim on the work floor.

Secondly, I am not so sure that the development of our societies can back the model defined by RELIGARE. The emancipation of women and homosexuals, the fight against discrimination and xenophobia, and other such developments have made our societies and legal systems more open, equal and tolerant, and have improved the daily lives of many disempowered groups in society. Often, these struggles for emancipation have been hampered by opposition and resistance from religions. If I look at my own country, Belgium, I can only witness how much the Roman Catholic Church has opposed legislation on the use of contraception, abortion, euthanasia and same-sex marriage. Religious claims have been made against mixed schools, sex education in schools, against single mothers, against divorced people teaching at Catholic schools and so on. Yet what matters is that Belgian Roman Catholics – in accordance with the spirit of the Second Vatican Council[24] – have embraced the pluralist society and accepted it. This secularisation process in Western Europe would have been impossible if the legal system had supported religious exceptionalism. Of course, there have been backlashes. In one French case, Roman Catholic pharmacists argued before the European Court of Human Rights that they should be allowed to refuse to sell contraceptives. Their claim was declared inadmissible. The point is, as confirmed by the Strasbourg Court, that 'Article 9 of the Convention does not always guarantee the right to behave in public in a manner governed by that belief. The word "practice" used in Article 9 § 1 does not denote each and every act or form of behaviour motivated or inspired by a religion or a belief.'[25]

Finally, there is obviously a risk of introducing new inequalities. I find it very hard to defend the idea that, on the one hand, conservative landlords living in a traditional way without, however, being particularly committed to a religion on the basis of which they disapprove of homosexuality, would be in legal trouble if they refused to rent an apartment to a same-sex couple (as is, for example, the case under Belgian anti-discrimination law), while as soon as the homophobic behaviour is based on religious grounds, exceptions should be made. Would it matter to the homosexual whether the discrimination he or she experiences is inspired by strong religious beliefs, by weaker convictions or just by mere homophobia? Would it make a difference to women whether their discrimination resulted from some specific religious beliefs or just from some deep-rooted cultural practices? By the way, the problematic nature of these claims becomes even clearer if one replaces gender or sexual orientation with race. Would we accept someone refusing to shake hands with black people, or refusing to hire Africans, for religious or convictional reasons?

The point is that anti-discrimination laws as they have been developed in the last decades set important limits to the citizens' freedoms in order to promote equality and to emancipate groups who, in (civil) society, have experienced (structural) discrimination. The emblematic white chauvinist male can no longer refuse to rent houses to black people, prohibit the access of sports clubs to Jews, or refuse to hire Muslims or women.

---

23 In recent times, René Foqué has stressed the importance of moderated or 'decent' citizenship. R Foqué, *De democratische rechtsstaat: een onrustig bezit* (Forum 2011); R Foqué, 'Nationaliteit en burgerschap' in M-C Foblets, R Foqué and M Verwilghen (eds), *Devenir belge* (Bruylant 2002) 21–68.

24 See P Loobuyck, 'Ook de islam zal in het reine moeten komen met de vrijheid van meningsuiting', *De Morgen* <www.demorgen.be/dm/nl/2461/Opinie/article/detail/1745931/2013/11/24/Ook-de-islam-zal-in-het-reine-moeten-komen-met-de-vrijheid-van-meningsuiting.dhtml> accessed 27 June 2014.

25 ECtHR, *Pichon and Sajous v France* (admissibility) App no 49853/99, 2 October 2001.

The anti-discrimination laws are surely not 'neutral', if neutrality is to be understood as value free. Yet they embody the core values of our societies, to which the equality principle is central.

I do not think it is wise to exempt people from their legal and civic duties on religious grounds. There are two main reasons for this. First, it creates new inequalities: identical behaviour will be treated differently according to the religious (or cultural/ethnic) background of the persons adopting it. Secondly, precisely because we do not have a precise definition of religion or belief, anything can be a religion. This is judge Scalia's point in *Employment Division v Smith*, where he has written,

> Precisely because we are a cosmopolitan nation made up of people of almost every conceivable religious preference and precisely because we value and protect that religious divergence, we cannot afford the luxury of deeming presumptively invalid, as applied to the religious objector, every regulation of conduct that does not protect an interest of the highest order. The rule respondents favor would open the prospect of constitutionally required religious exemptions from civic obligations of almost every conceivable kind.[26]

Conclusion

I am not quite sure whether the model RELIGARE has developed really offers so much more to society than the existing models. As a particular instance of secularism, the difference between 'inclusive State neutrality' and 'separation' may be rather a matter of degree than of principle. Just to give one example, the Commission Stasi that was set up in France in 2003 to reflect on the application of the principle of *laïcité* called for some reasonable accommodations, notably in the field of religious holidays (while at the same time a ban of visible religious symbols at school was defended). So a strict interpretation of 'inclusive State neutrality' and a liberal approach to strict separation may in practice lead to quite similar results.

In my understanding, the crucial problem is the balancing of rights, interests and values. The RELIGARE partners defend the idea of balancing, but since they did not reflect upon the very notion of *ordre public*, they did not single out fields or domains that are non-negotiable. This, however, is fundamental: religious freedom operates within the boundaries set out by law. It is not up to the religions, beliefs, zealots, preachers, followers and so on to unilaterally decide on the *marge de manoeuvre* they should enjoy. Some clear basic principles should be formulated and upheld: the State is indeed sovereign and regulates religion in the sense that it is up to the 'secular law' to decide how the relationship between religion and law should be conceived.[27] It is, therefore, up to the State to have the last word.

This reflection on the common core of the basic values of our society is all the more necessary as the balancing exercise as proposed by the consortium easily becomes a slippery slope – today we accept that men and women have separate hours in public swimming pools, tomorrow we allow exceptions to biology lessons, but what's next? Polygamy? Female circumcision if the women consent? Moreover, I fear that the kind of *ad hoc* balancing RELIGARE seems to support may as well create a profound feeling of frustration and inequality. Many of the religious claims will be accepted or refused on the mere basis of context. I wonder whether this will not lead to a feeling of injustice: specific contingent and trivial elements decide on fundamental questions pertaining to fundamental concerns regarding religion and belief.

Finally, I feel very uncomfortable with the ambiguous attitude regarding the horizontal application of the non-discrimination principle. Admittedly, as Lock pointed out, non-discrimination may be a more promising way to legally enforce religious claims than freedom of religion.[28] However, it occurs to me that one has to be coherent in the application of the principle: whoever claims that (s)he should benefit from the non-discrimination principle (thereby laying a burden on others) should accept that others claim the application of the same right and be thus willing to bear similar burdens. To the extent that precisely those who make very strong claims with regard to respect from others would try to exempt themselves from the duty to respect others, the approach runs the risk of being one-sided. Double standards do not contribute much to the promotion of equality and inclusiveness.

26 494 US 872 (1990). Footnotes omitted.

27 M Troper, 'Sovereignty and Laïcité' (2008–2009) 30 *Cardozo L Rev* 2561.

28 T Lock, 'Religious Freedom and Belief Discrimination in Germany and the United Kingdom: Towards a Common European Standard?' (2013) 38 *E L Rev* 672–73.

Chapter 27
An Ill-Disguised Defence of Religious Privilege

David Pollock

The RELIGARE project set out four years ago to explore policy responses to the emerging conflicts between equality and non-discrimination laws and freedom of religion or belief against the background of the 'social reality' of widening religious and cultural diversity in Europe.

This ambitious project has produced interesting papers and resources, but its short and low-key final report is fundamentally flawed by a patent bias in favour of religion: at the very beginning, the report states the expectation that the international courts will in future have a 'greater role' in protecting freedom of religion or belief (*Report*, 12), but it offers no balancing message that the courts will also be called on to protect the rights of vulnerable minorities oppressed by religion.

The problem is that the project starts from an unexamined assumption that religion is an unmitigated good.[1] Nowhere is there any examination of the nature of religion or belief, the meaning of secularism, the propositions and policies that religions support, the role that religious institutions play in our communities, or public attitudes towards religion as evinced in surveys and statistics of churchgoing or the like.[2] These omissions are not excused by the project's focus on matters lying within the competence of the EU; they are essential prolegomena to any such broad study as that undertaken by RELIGARE.

Unsurprisingly, therefore, the RELIGARE report's recommendations are a mixed bag: some are useful, others irrelevant and yet others, examined below, risk undermining equality, secularism, democracy and the rights of vulnerable individuals such as women, gays and lesbians.[3]

This is not the place to remedy the gaping deficiencies in the report, but an indication of what it fails to cover is necessary before I review briefly some of RELIGARE's problematic recommendations.[4]

The Nature of Religion or Belief

Religions (and the same is true of explicit non-religious beliefs such as Humanism) invariably make claims about the nature of life and the universe and draw conclusions about how one should behave. It is this intellectual content that makes religion or belief profoundly different from other strands covered by equality law – race, gender, nationality, disability, sexuality and so on. Unlike any of them, religions

- can (though not at will) be chosen, put aside or selectively followed;
- make extensive and mutually incompatible claims about the nature of life and the world, claims that are by their nature rarely capable of being definitively settled;
- deliberately influence their followers' attitudes and behaviour, often condemning the beliefs, attitudes and behaviour of others;

---

1 RELIGARE starts by talking of 'freedom of religion or belief', but usually shortens this prejudicially to 'freedom of religion', and the report's focus is almost always on religion and religious organisations.

2 I believe this is true also of the supporting papers produced by the project, but I cannot be categorical as I have not read them all.

3 See M Malik, 'From Conflict to Cohesion: Competing Interests in Equality Law and Policy', available at <www.edf.org.uk/blog/wp-content/uploads/2009/02/competing-rigts-report_web.pdf> accessed 27 June 2014.

4 The European Humanist Federation's submission to RELIGARE (which I prepared) provides some of the missing considerations. It is available at <http://humanistfederation.eu/ckfinder/userfiles/files/position/religion%20in%20society/160-EHF-submission-to-Religare-project%20(1).pdf> accessed 27 June 2014, and, with some updated references, at <http://david-pollock.org.uk/religion/religion-in-society/> accessed 27 June 2014.

- are in principle and often in practice in competition with each other: evangelists come to our front doors, set up television and radio stations and conduct crusades to make converts;
- sometimes put their followers under an obligation to react strongly to any criticism or insult offered to their deities, prophets or beliefs, however mild or reasonable;
- are expressed through organisations that are often wealthy and that in the name of their faith sometimes exercise power far outside the realm of religion, influencing social attitudes and seeking to change the way others live, sometimes by recruiting the power of the State.

Race, gender, sexuality and other 'strands' in equality law provide (other things being equal) no respectable reason for treating people in other 'strands' differently, and people so grouped ask only to be treated fairly. Rarely if ever do these other characteristics result in clashing demands, save perhaps in priority for action. Religious groups, however, often make judgements about those in other 'strands' and demand special treatment in the form of legal privileges and exemptions. When difficulties arise in reconciling religious freedom with equality for other strands, it is generally religion with its propositions and injunctions that is the cause of the difficulty, not the rest of society with its movement towards non-discrimination. Religion, in other words, is an anomaly in equality law.

Secularisation and Secularism

Most people in Europe continue to adhere in some sense to a religion, fewer by far actively practise one, and fewer still hold or can even describe the essential teachings of their religion (see below). For many people their religion nevertheless plays a part in their identity, in creating meaning in their lives and in shaping their attitudes and behaviour; for a minority it is of paramount importance. Many others ignore religion, some positively reject it, a few are explicitly hostile. A small number adhere to explicit non-religious beliefs, principally Humanism, and large numbers share its attitudes and beliefs without so labelling them.

Learning from the horrors of the religious wars of past centuries, Europe has moved a considerable distance towards institutional secularisation,[5] but the churches still have significant influence, both with governments and in society. This is partly because morality was for centuries tied to religion, so religious doctrines are assumed to embody moral teachings, but it is also partly because during their past dominance the churches became wealthy, gained lasting political influence and established institutions – hospitals, schools, universities – that survive to this day, now almost always supported by public funds.[6]

None of this background is examined by RELIGARE; nor does it examine the principles of secularism and its strong claim to be the best guarantor of freedom of religion or belief. It does not take account of the unresolved disagreement between those secularists who support separation of religion and politics and those who support the neutral but potentially engaged State (as with so-called 'pillar constitutions'). Instead, and extraordinarily, it classifies models of church–State relations entirely from the viewpoint of the churches (see *Report*, § 1.1 and the table on page 13) and fails to acknowledge that separation does not necessarily entail relegation of religion to private life: a secular State can allow religious organisations to engage in politics in the same way that any other NGO does, simply as a body of citizens with a shared interest.

5 However, an early claim in the report (§ 1.1) is highly contestable: is it actually true that 'the majority of national legislatures … have made the historic decision to secularise State law'? Is it not closer to the truth that States have drifted into quasi-secularism as democracy confronted diversity and met demands to end discrimination? In most States (the exceptions are France and Turkey plus – insofar as engaged neutrality is secularism – the Netherlands, Belgium and Bulgaria) there have been serial *ad hoc* changes, not a principled decision to adopt secularism.

6 For example, in an authoritative article in the *Frankfurter Rundschau* (19 December 2010) Carsten Frerk estimated such public funding of religious institutions in Germany at 10 billion euros a year (see 'Die CaritasLegende' <www.fr-online.de/meinung/ gastbeitrag-die-caritas-legende,1472602,5027372.html> accessed 27 June 2014).

Religious Propositions, Policies and Practices

Religion's influence in society is undoubtedly often benign and uncontroversial, as when religious groups provide relief to the poor, help asylum seekers, and plead the cause of the oppressed to politicians. But in other ways the Christian churches – and the other religions – are socially reactionary.[7] Of course, religious claims and teaching have evolved over time. Bible literalism is now confined to a fringe of Christianity, women are rarely now treated as appendages to fathers or husbands, and single parenthood, divorce and abortion – anathema in living memory – have been accepted by a majority of Christians as regrettable necessities or even normal. But significant religious organisations still too often apply the moral codes of the past, shaped hundreds or even thousands of years ago in circumstances utterly unlike ours today. They have fought decriminalisation of homosexuality and still resist gay marriage and try to prevent gay couples from adopting children. They opposed legalisation or liberalisation of divorce, fighting bitterly to the end in Malta only three years ago.[8] They opposed legalisation of abortion, and the Roman Catholic Church still campaigns ceaselessly to keep it illegal or to drive it back underground – regrettably succeeding recently in Spain.[9] The Holy See opposes sexual and reproductive health and rights in the United Nations, preventing inclusion in aid packages of contraception and even condoms as protection against AIDS, though this is noticed mainly outside Europe (within Europe its denunciations are largely ignored). Some religious bodies have tried to maintain criminal sanctions against the religious offence of blasphemy, and they have even succeeded in Ireland. Elsewhere they flirt with laws against insulting or mocking religion. They are still mostly successful in preventing the legalisation, whatever the safeguards, of assisted dying or euthanasia. They maintain universally that they have the right to instruct children, at public expense, in their own religious beliefs, paying scant attention to children's right to freedom of thought, conscience and religion (UN Convention on the Rights of the Child, Article 14).

The right to manifest a religion might well include the right to denounce in inflammatory terms people whose nature or behaviour offends one's religious principles: gays (think Westboro Baptist Church), blacks (think Dutch Reformed Church in apartheid South Africa),[10] abortion doctors (even urging that they be murdered, as has happened too often in the United States), unbelievers and 'infidels' who follow other religions (including apostates for whom in Islam the death sentence is routinely demanded), disabled people (think Calvin and demonic possession) and so on. The question is not whether these examples are typical – they are not – but whether RELIGARE upholds such religious freedoms. This is not clear from the report, but if RELIGARE does *not* uphold such freedoms, then the boundary it draws between these and other manifestations that it (and almost everyone) does uphold (for example, the right to wear a religious badge in public) remains undefined. This is a difficult frontier, and RELIGARE has ducked the challenge of trying to demarcate it.

---

7 Brevity demands broad generalisations; there are, of course, honourable exceptions, more or less numerous, to all the points cited in this and the following paragraph.

8 In the campaign leading to the divorce referendum on 28 May 2011, the Roman Catholic Church spent hugely under the banner 'Christ Yes, Divorce No'.

9 Pressure from the Catholic Church, which organised large street demonstrations, led the conservative government to reverse reforms made by the previous socialist government that allowed terminations without restrictions until the fourteenth week of pregnancy – reforms that did not lead to a significant rise in the number of abortions (in fact, in some regions, such as Madrid, the total actually fell). Spain is the first country within the European Union to reverse legalisation of abortion; see *Daily Telegraph* (London, 20 December 2013) <www.telegraph.co.uk/news/worldnews/europe/spain/10531811/Spainapproves-new-restrictive-abortion-law.html> accessed 27 June 2014.

10 In volume 5 of its final report, the Truth and Reconciliation Commission found that 'Christianity, as the dominant religion in South Africa, promoted the ideology of Apartheid in a range of different ways that included Biblical and theological teaching in support of Apartheid; ecclesiastical Apartheid by appointing ministers to congregations based on race, and the payment of unequal stipends; a failure to support dissident clergy who found themselves in confrontation with the State; and a failure to provide economic support to those most severely affected by Apartheid'; see <www.justice.gov.za/trc/report/finalreport/Volume5.pdf> accessed 27 June 2014.

Public Attitudes towards Religion

Finally, in this rapid survey of what RELIGARE leaves unexamined, there is the fact that religion is of ever decreasing significance in Europe, as witnessed by the EU's large *Eurobarometer* surveys across all EU States. *Eurobarometer* found in 2005 that only 52 per cent of people believed in God, while 18 per cent rejected outright even the idea of 'some sort of spirit or life force'.[11] In 2012, 23 per cent called themselves atheist or agnostic.[12] When asked to pick up to three from a list of 12 'values', people in Europe twice placed religion last: only 5 per cent chose it as important to them personally, and only 3 per cent saw it as a value representative of the EU.[13] Surveys also show the abysmal ignorance of self-proclaimed Christians about the basic propositions of their religion.[14] Plainly, although the majority when asked still identify with Christianity, that affiliation means little to most of them, making it quite misguided to put significant emphasis on it. Meanwhile, popular morality is secular and highlights instead the need for fairness and equality.

The problems that arise from this progression from an authoritarian age of religious privilege in near mono-credal societies to a democratic age of human rights in distinctly multi-credal societies form the focus of the RELIGARE project. Our old laws and traditional attitudes, shaped around a Judeo-Christian culture, are being asked to adapt not only to an unprecedented rise in disbelief and disenchantment with religion, but also to the arrival of (mainly immigrant) followers of other world religions who, on average, are probably more devout than most Christians. Not only that, but with more moderate believers relatively indifferent, Christianity's more fervent and uncompromising followers gain in influence. Sometimes they find themselves making common cause with the ardent believers of non-Christian religions. Under the banner of conscientious objection we see militant attempts to use politics and the law to preserve privileges, establish exemptions to accommodate beliefs and practices, and restrict the liberty of others to live as they wish.[15]

None of this, however, finds a place in the thinking of the RELIGARE team. In their report minorities are almost always religious minorities and rights (except for general references to human rights) are almost always those of religious believers or institutions; the rights of groups liable to suffer at the hands of religion go unexamined, and homosexuality (never named) is seen only as a problem for religion. There are formidable religious campaigns everywhere against abortion, gay marriage and assisted dying – but no one is being forced to have an abortion, to marry someone of the same sex or to be assisted to die.[16] Instead, religious

11 Special *Eurobarometer* 225, 'Social Values, Science and Technology' (*European Commission*, June 2005), see <http://ec.europa.eu/public_opinion/archives/ebs/ebs_225_report_en.pdf> accessed 27 June 2014.

12 Special *Eurobarometer* 393, 'Discrimination in the EU in 2012' (*European Commission*, November 2012); see <http://ec.europa.eu/public_opinion/archives/ebs/ebs_393_en.pdf> accessed 27 June 2014.

13 *Eurobarometer* 79, 'Public Opinion in the European Union' (*European Commission*, Spring 2013); see <http://ec.europa.eu/public_opinion/archives/eb/eb79/eb79_anx_en.pdf> accessed 27 June 2014.

14 For example, see the Ipsos MORI poll for the Richard Dawkins Foundation for Reason and Science (UK), February 2012; see <www.ipsos-mori.com/Assets/Docs/Polls/ipsos-mori-religious-and-social-attitudes-topline-2012.pdf> accessed 27 June 2014.

15 On this see my articles 'The Limits to Legal Accommodation of Conscientious Objection', at <http://david-pollock.org.uk/religion/the-limits-to-legal-accommodation-of-conscientious-objection/> accessed 27 June 2014, and 'Is Conscientious Objection an Absolute Right?' in A Haworth (ed), *Right to Object? Conscientious Objection and Religious Conviction* (British Humanist Association 2011).

16 For example, the 'One of Us' movement is a fundamentally religious campaign across Europe to outlaw not only abortion but also research using human embryonic stem cells; see <www.oneofus.eu/initiative-explanation/> accessed 27 June 2014. Its president, Grégor Puppinck, is Director General of the European Centre for Law and Justice, an offshoot of US evangelist Pat Robertson's US campaigns for conservative Christian values. The European Centre for Law and Justice collaborates with the Roman Catholic Church and works with some success in the Council of Europe and the European Court of Human Rights. Puppinck was central to the successful campaign by the churches to overturn the unanimous chamber judgment against Italy's law compelling the display of a crucifix in every classroom in all State schools; see P Annicchino, 'Winning the Battle by Losing the War: The Lautsi Case and the Holy Alliance between American Conservative Evangelicals, the Russian Orthodox Church and the Vatican to Reshape European Identity' (2011) 6 *Religion and Human Rights* 213–19. Puppinck sees moves towards gay rights as an attempt to 'impose acceptance of homosexuality'; see <www.aleteia.org/en/politics/documents/manif-pour-tous-lgbt-rights-and-gender-in-the-council-of-europe-2092006> accessed 27 June 2014. The campaign in France against gay marriage was spearheaded by the Roman Catholic Church; there were violent protests despite the general public support for the change; see <www.catholicherald.co.uk/news/2013/06/10/french-

zealots are trying to prevent others from having such freedoms. These attempts to curtail the liberty of others are seen as virtuous because they are based on religion, yet any interference with the right to wear a cross or to refuse hotel rooms to LGBT couples is roundly denounced.

Nor in its one-sided approach does RELIGARE acknowledge that courts of law, since they are not competent to examine the plausibility of religious beliefs or, unless *in extremis*, their effects, but only whether they are being treated even-handedly by the State and the law, must give equal consideration (including, in RELIGARE's view, financial support and broadcasting platforms) to Scientology with its extortionate hard sell of its hierarchy of auditing, Christian Science with its ban on blood transfusions, and beliefs from the even wilder fringes of religiosity. Here the assumption that religion is benign hits the buffers. Is the law not only to avoid taking paternalistic steps to safeguard believers from their own folly (which is arguable), but actually to *support* such religions? Is not equal treatment best delivered by equal indifference rather than equal support?

RELIGARE's Two Principles

So what, after ignoring all this background, does RELIGARE propose?

It bases its recommendations on two 'principles' – 'inclusive State neutrality' and 'justice as even-handedness' – but these are never defined, scarcely illustrated, only invoked. Perhaps the need to win agreement from its large team, drawn from 13 universities across Europe, frustrated anything more explicit, but the result is that they are reduced almost to slogans. One can recognise their well-intentioned aims while doubting if such unfocused feel-good terms can sustain the weight placed on them. What about justice as justice? Even-handedness is valuable as between parties in the same circumstances, but otherwise it risks decisions being based on splitting the difference.[17]

'Inclusive State neutrality' is similarly undefined but is said to reject any form of separation or State neutrality that 'could be interpreted as public hostility towards churches/religious communities and/or secular values', which reveals a strange notion of neutrality. After rejecting 'hostile' neutrality, RELIGARE immediately adds that 'experience shows that it is impossible to rigidly uphold a strict separation between and a strict neutrality towards religion and belief'. This is an extraordinary assertion to make without argument on a matter central to the report. Not only is it far from clear that experience shows any such thing, but RELIGARE leaves unexamined the possibility that aiming at neutrality, even with occasional lapses,[18] may be preferable to settling for a deliberate rejection of separation.

Of course, RELIGARE produces some sensible suggestions. The proposal to base any controls over the wearing of religious clothing or symbols in the public space on a distinction between different types of space (common, political, institutional) and the different functions (as private citizens or as State representatives) of people in those spaces is welcome, if not original. Strangely, however, these distinctions make no appearance in their recommendations. The recommendations on family issues appear to make good sense to this novice in the tangled field of private international law, with the exception of the broad endorsement of alternative dispute resolution as an option without a single mention of the need to uphold the best interests of any children involved.

---

catholic-leader-calls-for-continued-opposition-to-same-sex-marriage/> accessed 27 June 2014. Opposition to euthanasia is largely religious, again despite public support. Well-financed groups with strong religious backing such as European Dignity Watch and Care are skilled lobbyists in the European institutions, and the Catholic bishops were central to the successful opposition to EU funding of medical research using human embryonic stem cells; see <www.comece.eu/site/en/press/pressreleases/newsletter.content/1483.html?SWS=9c10870f2d9549bcec86fc1e5660118a> accessed 27 June 2014. A massive and at root religious lobbying campaign was successful in persuading MEPs to turn down by the narrowest margin a resolution supporting sexual reproductive health and rights; see <www.aleteia.org/en/politics/article/the-estrela-draft-resolution-remains-morally-unacceptable-5894733628964864> accessed 27 June 2014. There are endless other examples of attempts by religious groups to curtail the freedoms of others who do not share their beliefs.

17 See also below on reasonable accommodation.

18 It is a distortion – in fact, a denial – of secularism, which as a political principle is neutral by definition, to use it to prevent religious groups from taking part in public life or (worse) to curtail the rights of vulnerable, often immigrant, minorities, and it is regrettable that something like this has happened from time to time in small parts of Europe.

But elsewhere its recommendations are open to criticism, sometimes severe. I shall confine my detailed comments to two questions about employment – 'reasonable accommodation' and the 'collective dimension' – and to the matter of State support and the role of the European Union.

Employment: 'Reasonable Accommodation'

RELIGARE's bias in favour of religion comes out starkly in its treatment of issues that may arise in employment. These, it says, may include demands for exemption from duties or customary practice:

> issues such as workers refusing to perform certain job functions (registering same-sex partnerships, handling alcohol or pork), refusing to adhere to dominant socialising customs (for example shaking hands with people of the opposite sex), challenging the position of women in managerial positions in the workplace, and seeking to be excused from parties at work, among others. (Report, § 2.1.1)

The report offers no criteria by which such claims are to be judged, proceeding instead on the assumption that wherever possible they should be met. But this should not be taken for granted. Are we to accept refusal to recognise 'women in managerial positions'? Apparently so, for the report supports its position by quoting an article on reasonable accommodation: 'Instead of requiring … people to conform to existing norms, the aim is to develop a concept of equality which requires (mutual) adaptation and change.'[19] So employers must, if possible, accede to objections to women managers. But RELIGARE's justificatory quote is about disability, a very different context – unless of course we are being invited to see religious belief as a disability!

The report jumps from two examples in which the EU law on indirect discrimination appears not to have been properly applied to proposing a legal presumptive right to 'reasonable accommodation'. A footnote says that there are 'important differences' between reasonable accommodation and indirect discrimination: to discover what RELIGARE has in mind, one must refer to an earlier paper which identifies that reasonable accommodation 'concentrates on the situation of the individual employee' rather than on his or her position as a member of a religious group.[20] In other words, any demand counts if it is labelled religious by the employee.

RELIGARE does not define what is reasonable and offers an employer no defence against unpredictable personal and intransigent demands. This is unlike indirect discrimination, which looks objectively at whether a practice bears more heavily on a particular religious group than on the generality of employees. By contrast, reasonable accommodation is essentially a process of compromise, of splitting the difference. There are circumstances where this may in practice be sensible, but it is an unprincipled process: the more excessive the demands made, the more the concessions needed to reach accommodation.

RELIGARE argues fairly that it is not just the employer whose costs are relevant – religious employees also pay a cost in adapting to the work environment. But the report, in asking 'What is a fair distribution of burdens?', is so focussed on the religious employee that it does not recognise the impact of accommodating religious demands on such third parties as other employees, clients and users of services. Reasonable accommodation for the believer may ride roughshod over other people's human rights.

As the earlier paper says, 'Accepting the idea of reasonable accommodations … entails a mentality switch'.[21] Indeed, a switch to a mentality where religion carries all before it. But in the face of some demands, it is proper to say 'no'. Religion should not necessarily be a free ride. Priests accept some limitations on their freedom as a result of their occupation – why should devout believers not do the same? Conscientious objectors in wartime do not get off scot-free; they have to do alternative war work or else go to jail. And in

19 See, for example, LB Waddington, 'Reasonable Accommodation: Time to Extend the Duty to Accommodate beyond Disability?' (2011) 38 (2) *NJCM Bulletin: Nederlands Tijdschrift voor de Mensenrechten* 186–98.

20 K Alidadi, 'A Comparative Legal Study Addressing Religious or Belief Discrimination in Employment and Reasonable Accommodations for Employees' Religious or Philosophical Beliefs or Practice' (May 2012), see <www.religareproject.eu/content/comparative-legal-study-addressing-religious-or-belief-discrimination-employment-and> accessed 27 June 2014.

21 ibid.

any case why should we indulge religion-based requests for special treatment above others? If I need to leave work early on Friday afternoons because my childminder has to leave at four o'clock every Friday, why should my Jewish colleague have a legal right to time off to observe the Sabbath but I no right to time off to look after my child? If I have a secular belief that alcohol is baneful, why should my conscience be ignored but a colleague whose shunning of alcohol is based on religion be indulged?

Employment: The 'Collective Dimension'

RELIGARE often refers to the 'collective dimension', which it defines as 'the human rights position of religious and non-religious communities of conviction', but its treatment both in the report and elsewhere[22] is seriously wanting.

There can be no dispute (despite the obstacles imposed in some European States) that freedom of religion or belief includes the right to set up religious organisations such as churches which, like any other voluntary organisation, can have 'legal personality', so as to be able to own property, enter into contracts and so on. Further, it is plainly right that some religious organisations must have some exemptions from some laws: employment equality laws must allow for only Roman Catholics to be cardinals, or only Anglicans to be eligible to become the Archbishop of Canterbury.

But RELIGARE's brief treatment of 'religiously oriented' employers is either naive or disingenuous. For example, it recommends that '[e]nforcement of human rights and equality legislation ... may require that religious employers/organisations be granted exemptions from anti-discrimination laws and labour laws', without any recognition of either the fact that wide exemptions already exist under the Employment Directive or that arguably they have been implemented more generously than the Directive envisaged.[23]

Moreover, the RELIGARE report fails to distinguish between types of religious employer. Not only are there churches, mosques and other institutions with the specific goal of advancing a religion or belief, but there are hospitals, children's and retirement homes, schools and other public services that are run – usually at public expense – by institutions with a religious connection. There are also private commercial undertakings run along religious lines. When RELIGARE fails to distinguish between these categories or to recognise that there is a persistent, highly controversial campaign to treat such organisations as if they had human rights as such,[24] by default it takes the side of the religious zealots who, in a small way, are trying to re-create the autonomous church of mediaeval times, standing apart from the State as a rival authority. This is scarcely an exaggerated comparison: consider the United States, where hospitals and schools run by the churches – largely at public expense – are at the time of this writing winning exemptions from providing health insurance for certain procedures for their employees,[25] where even 'religious' commercial concerns are claiming the same exemptions,[26] and where religious bodies can effectively circumvent employment laws by classifying their employees as ministers.[27]

And, once again, RELIGARE fails to recognise that the cost falls on third parties when, for example, pharmacists refuse to dispense contraceptives, when hospitals refuse to perform abortions, when hotels turn away gay couples or retirement homes assign them separate rooms, and when non-religious employees of any such institution find their careers blighted because they do not have the right religion or belief.

---

22 In particular in K Alidadi, 'State of the Art Report: Religion and the Workplace' (September 2010) <www.religareproject.eu/content/state-art-report-religion-and-workplace> accessed 27 June 2014.

23 For example, EU Commission rulings are pending on a number of formal complaints that assert that the United Kingdom's exemptions for religious schools go well beyond what the Employment Directive allows.

24 See, for example, resolution 1763(2010) of the Parliamentary Assembly of the Council of Europe, crudely amended in a last minute ambush; <assembly.coe.int/main.asp?Link=/documents/adoptedtext/ta10/eres1763.htm>.

25 *Roman Catholic Archdiocese of New York v Sebelius*, 12cv2542, US District Court, Eastern District of New York (Brooklyn), in which the religious objection was extended even to facilitating third-party contraceptive health coverage for employees. The archdiocese was helped in the case by the Becket Fund, an intensely conservative law firm that has involved itself in European litigation, including *Lautsi v Italy and Others*.

26 *Sebelius v Hobby Lobby Stores Inc*.

27 *Hosanna–Tabor Evangelical Lutheran Church and School v Equal Employment Opportunity Commission*.

State Support

RELIGARE recognises that typical current patterns of State support for one or a few churches are increasingly seen as discriminatory and unfair as the number of religions or beliefs becomes greater, beliefs more personal and society more secular. According to the RELIGARE report, the jurisprudence of the European Court of Human Rights suggests the need to offer 'equivalent benefits to *all*' – fitting RELIGARE's slogans of 'inclusive State neutrality' and 'justice as even-handedness'. The report therefore suggests that tax relief should (subject to minimal conditions) be provided to all belief groups on the basis of their public benefit (which goes undefined but raises huge questions, as is demonstrated by the problems it creates in UK charity law); that (controversially) the State should finance the training of religious leaders; that (uncontroversially) subsidies be paid to protect ancient buildings as part of our historical heritage; and that access to public service broadcasting and perhaps support for it be more fairly allocated.

But despite devoting *nine pages* to State support, RELIGARE does not even mention the most egregious and objectionable form of support for religion from public funds – namely, direct subsidies. Examples are not hard to find: Denmark's established church receives grants that meet about one-eighth of its budget – worth an estimated 100 million euros a year. The Evangelical-Lutheran Church of Finland gets 1.94 per cent of the proceeds of corporation tax, worth a similar sum. Belgium hands out taxpayers' money to a variety of churches and other religious and non-religious belief organisations, totalling approximately 240 million euros in 2008, of which the Roman Catholic Church received about 90 per cent. Greece pays for the training, salaries and pensions of Greek Orthodox clergy and for their church buildings, and France maintains all pre-1905 Roman Catholic churches free of charge.[28]

Now, the huge variety of arrangements – traditions, constitutions, laws – across Europe makes for intractable complexity, and imposing any single solution is effectively impossible. But was it impossible to point in a direction of travel in the shape of general principles, and to identify if not an end-state at least a wayfaring point in the middle distance, with a recommendation that, from our several current positions, we should travel towards it? Why not propose that State support be phased out over a sufficient period of years to allow the churches to build up voluntary giving by their followers? This is something the Church of England, with no public subsidy, has successfully done in recent years.[29] Doing so would acknowledge the increasing secularisation of the population of Europe and avoid the problem (under RELIGARE's policy of enthusiastic and impartially dispensed support) of more and more small religious groups – verging on sects – being encouraged and aided with public resources.

These are not wholly benign, uncontroversial organisations. Any case for State support has to be made at a meta level that argues that any belief is better than none and that, despite the failure to deal with sexual assaults on children by clergy, despite Vatican opposition to contraception and abortion in the face of overwhelming public support, despite the proliferation of fundamentalist sects, on balance religious bodies do more good than harm and the 'social capital' of communal life they promote is worth subsidising. Support for such propositions requires strong evidence, but RELIGARE produces none.

The European Union

Finally, RELIGARE calls for stronger and pro-active coordination by the European Union of national policy on religion in society, thereby not just calling into question Article 17(1) of the Treaty on the Functioning of the European Union (TFEU), with its abjuration of EU interference with 'the status under national law of churches and religious associations', but also running counter to the spirit of the times, which increasingly questions the ambition of 'ever closer union'. In so doing, RELIGARE compounds its bias in favour of the

28 See F Cranmer, 'Notes on Church and State in the European Economic Area 2011' <www.law.cf.ac.uk/clr/networks/Frank%20Cranmer_%20Church%20&%20State%20in%20W%20Europe.pdf> accessed 27 June 2014.

29 The average member of the Church of England gives almost 400 euros a year to the Church, which in total raises about 550 million euros a year in voluntary donations from its congregations; see <www.churchofengland.org/media/1791665/2011financestatistics.pdf> accessed 27 June 2014.

churches by recommending a 'permanent consultative mechanism' or 'inter-service group on religion and belief' for 'internal and external networking'. The role for this group appears in part to be to prevent equality legislation from impinging on freedom of religion. Here again RELIGARE shows its support for the religious agenda over equality for gays and women and the non-religious, who too often have to rely on public services channelled through religious organisations. If the proposed unit were created, it would without doubt rapidly become the 'small "liaison office" within the services of the European Commission' that COMECE and CEC (the two conferences of European bishops) jointly sought for the sake of 'pre-legislative consultation' in their secret memorandum to the EU Commission of June 2002.[30]

RELIGARE also recommends that the EU enhance the dialogue with religions and non-religious belief organisations under Article 17(3) TFEU. It takes no note of the strong and principled opposition of European non-religious organisations, led by the European Humanist Federation, to a dialogue that privileges religion and belief organisations over other NGOs by providing them with routine access to the highest levels of the EU.[31] It does not recognise that in practice the dialogue offers disproportionate gains to the main Christian churches (owing to their funding, itself partly from public sources, and their history of involvement in diplomacy and State affairs) over non-Christian and non-religious organisations – the latter in particular since, although they in some sense represent between a third and a half of all European citizens, they are of their nature not mass membership organisations (why join an organisation defined by what you are not?).[32] If the Article 17 dialogue were to be given more weight as RELIGARE recommends, it would give the churches, with their undemocratic agendas, far more influence in the government of Europe.

That indeed is the principal likely effect of RELIGARE's proposals, flying in the face of European public opinion. In 2007, *Eurobarometer* found that 46 per cent of people across the EU already thought religion had too important a place in society.[33] Is it sensible to strengthen its position even further?

---

30 See <http://humanistfederation.eu/ckfinder/userfiles/files/our-work/Campaign%20opposing%20special%20rights%20for%20churches%20in%20the%20EU/The%20Churches%20submission%202002.pdf> accessed 27 June 2014.

31 See <http://humanistfederation.eu/our-work.php?page=no-to-special-rights-for-churches-in-the-EU> accessed 27 June 2014.

32 Footnote 104 of the RELIGARE report reveals the inaccuracy of the report's authors' understanding, making the extraordinary claim that the European Humanist Federation, like the conferences of European bishops COMECE and CEC, is 'represented (by their own "diplomats") in Brussels'. COMECE, which is concerned solely with the Roman Catholic Church's relations with the European Union, names on its website 12 staff in its secretariat and has large offices in Brussels. CEC has offices in Brussels, Strasbourg and Geneva, and names 10 staff on its website just for its Church and Society Commission. By contrast, the EHF has no staff and a total budget of about 25,000 euros, operating only through volunteers and with some assistance from one of its member organisations.

33 *Eurobarometer* 66, 'Public Opinion in the European Union' (*European Commission*, September 2007), see <http://ec.europa.eu/public_opinion/archives/eb/eb66/eb66_en.pdf> accessed 27 June 2014.

Section 5
Recent Developments

Chapter 28

Coherence (and Consistency) or Organised Hypocrisy? Religious Freedom in the Law of the European Union

Pasquale Annicchino[1]

Introduction

In recent years, many research projects have investigated the relationship between law and religion, especially in the United States and Europe.[2] Among them, the RELIGARE project has deliberately chosen to focus on a number of definite issues representing the core of these relationships: the labour market, public space, the family, and State support to religious groups. The RELIGARE final report has highlighted the importance of two key principles: 'inclusive State neutrality' and 'justice as even-handedness'. According to the RELIGARE description, the notion of 'inclusive State neutrality' 'rejects a strict separation and "strict neutrality" between the State and any religions or secular beliefs insofar as those positions could be interpreted as public hostility towards churches/religious communities and/or secular values' (*Report*, 16), while that of 'justice as even-handedness' 'further builds on this concept and recognises the legitimacy of active policies towards religion and belief, as long as they are applied in an inclusive way' (*Report*, 16). These developments are to be understood within the wider framework of the advancement of the protection of human rights within the European Union, which is characterised by the 'deep diversity' in European societies.[3] The purpose of this chapter is to investigate and

---

1 The author acknowledges travel and research funding from the ReligioWest project based at the Robert Schuman Centre and financed by the European Research Council.

2 Among others, see Religion in the West: The (Re)construction and Formatting through Courts, Social Practices, Public Discourse and Transnational Institutions (RELIGIOWEST) (2011–2015), European University Institute <www.eui.eu> accessed 27 June 2014; Religious Diversity and Secular Models in Europe. Innovative Approaches to Law and Policy (RELIGARE) (2010–2013), Catholic University Leuven, Belgium <www.religareproject.eu> accessed 27 June 2014; Religion and Society Research Programme (2007–2013), Lancaster University, United Kingdom <www.religionandsociety.org.uk> accessed 27 June 2014; The Impact of Religion – Challenges for Society, Law and Democracy (IMPACT) (2008–2018), a Linnaeus Research Programme, Uppsala University, Sweden <www.impactofreligion.uu.se> accessed 27 June 2014; Religion in Pluralistic Societies (PluRel) (2008–), University of Oslo, Norway <www.uio.no/english/research/interfaculty-research-areas/plurel/> accessed 27 June 2014; The Role of Religion in the Public Sphere. A Comparative Study of Five Nordic Countries (NOREL) (2009–2013), Church Research Centre, KIFO, Oslo, Norway <www.kifo.no/index.cfm?id=266149> accessed 27 June 2014; Religion and Diversity Project (2010–2017), Department of Classic and Religious Studies, University of Ottawa, Canada <www.religionanddiversity.ca> accessed 27 June 2014; International Law, Religion and Empire, Erik Castrén Institute of International Law and Human Rights, University of Helsinki, Finland <www.helsinki.fi/intlawhistory/> accessed 27 June 2014; Post-Secular Culture and Changing Religious Landscape (PCCR) (2010–2014), Abo Akademi University, Finland <http://web.abo.fi/fak/hf/relvet/pccr/> accessed 27 June 2014; Religion and the Public Sphere. Advancing and Mobilizing New Knowledge about Religion, Secularism and Public Life, Social Science Research Council, USA <www.ssrc.org/programs/religion-and-public-sphere/> accessed June 2014; The Politics of Religious Freedom. Contested Norms and Local Practices (2011–2014), Henry R. Luce Initiative on Religion in International Affairs <www.hluce.org/hrlucerelintaff.aspx> accessed 27 June 2014; Religion and Human Rights, An International Empirical Research Program (2013–2017), University of Wuerzburg, Germany <www.rp.theologie.uni-wuerzburg.de/research/religion_and_human_rights_2012_2017/> accessed 27 June 2014.

3 According to K Alidadi and M-C Foblets, 'deep diversity' is defined by 'an open-ended engagement with the already-there factual heterogeneity in beliefs, practices and values on the ground in Europe, which is not a priori limited by conceptions and categories motivated by more common or majoritarian values in society. Under such an approach, individual interests (of minorities) are "taken seriously" and not easily trumped by considerations derived from "social cohesion" or "common values", which are the marks of a more "utilitarian" approach'; K Alidadi and M-C Foblets,

assess the coherence (and consistency) of EU action in the field by comparing the action of EU institutions internally with their external relations, taking into consideration the findings of the RELIGARE report. The coherence between the EU's internal and external actions is not a new topic, but can serve to illuminate particular aspects of the interaction of law and religion within the EU legal order.[4]

Coherence in the Law and Policy of Religious Freedom within the European Union

In legal theory, the argument for coherence is of particular significance. Coherence represents an appeal to rationality and intelligibility. As Stefano Bertea argues, 'Coherence relates to the idea that the system has to make sense as a whole. And making sense as a whole is a precondition of intelligibility, which in turn is a requirement essential to law, at least to the extent that law is understood as an institution purposing to guide action.'[5] At least at a general level, coherence can be defined as a 'lack of inconsistencies'. This definition does not take into account the 'positive' side of coherence which, on the other hand, would entail 'consistency, comprehensiveness and completeness (at least to some degree), support (of varying scope and force), and cross-connection and mutual justification between the parts as a whole'.[6] Therefore, we should always link a parallel appeal to consistency to the appeal to coherence. Marise Cremona identifies three possible levels of analysis for coherence within the EU legal order:

> A first level requirement of coherence would be consistency, encompassing rules for conflict avoidance between potentially conflicting norms and for resolving conflicts when they arise: *rules of hierarchy* .... A second level of coherence is the effective allocation of tasks between actors (and instruments), avoiding both duplication and gaps: *rules of delimitation*. ... A third level of coherence implies synergy between norms, actors and instruments: principles of *cooperation and complementarity*.[7]

The description of these three levels is useful in assessing how policies dealing with law and religion have been implemented at the EU level. The examination of coherence (and consistency) may represent an important yardstick with which to evaluate EU policies on the regulation of religion, both internally and in its external relations, while also taking into consideration the fact that the principle of coherence can be assumed to be 'one of the main constitutional values of the EU'.[8] According to the new Article 7 of the Treaty of Lisbon, 'The Union shall ensure consistency between its policies and activities, taking all of its objectives into account and in accordance with the principle of conferral of powers'. In the case of the EU, the search for coherence (and consistency) is further complicated by the very nature of the EU legal order, which constitutes a polycentric union where different sovereign States coexist and share fields of competencies. Competence, in fact, tends to be the first issue raised when the regulation of religion is at stake at the EU level. Does the EU have an explicit competence to regulate issues pertaining to religion and religious freedom? Which EU

'Framing Multicultural Challenges in Freedom of Religion Terms: Limitations of Minimal Human Rights for Managing Religious Diversity in Europe' (2012) 30 (4) *Netherlands Quarterly of Human Rights* 389.

4 See S Stetter, *EU Foreign and Interior Policies: Cross-Pillar Politics and the Social Construction of Sovereignty* (Routledge 2007); RA Wessel, 'The Dynamics of the European Union Legal Order: An Increasingly Coherent Framework of Action and Interpretation' (2009) 5 (1) *European Constitutional Law Review* 117–42.

5 S Bertea, 'The Argument from Coherence' (2009) *IVR Encyclopedia of Jurisprudence, Legal Theory and Philosophy of Law*, available at <http://ivr-enc.info/index.php?title=The_Argument_from_Coherence> accessed 27 June 2014.

6 ibid.

7 M Cremona, 'Coherence through Law: What Difference Will the Treaty of Lisbon Make?' (2008) 3 (1) *Hamburg Review of Social Sciences* 14–16. Cremona also adds to her analysis 'vertical' and 'horizontal' coherence: 'Vertical coherence refers to the relationship between Member States and Union action, in particular in contexts where the Member States and the EU (or EC) may act simultaneously in relation to the same policy or subject matter. ... Horizontal coherence is the term used to refer to inter-policy and inter-pillar coherence'; ibid 16, 19. See also S Prechal and B Van Roermund, *The Coherence of EU Law: The Search for Unity in Divergent Concepts* (OUP 2008).

8 See C Tietje, 'The Concept of Coherence in the TEU and the CFSP' (1997) 2 *European Foreign Affairs Review* 211.

institution is competent?[9] Should the EU refrain from action in this sensitive field and leave a large margin of discretion to Member States, taking into consideration the historical and sociological differences between them? Determining these particular aspects would involve an analysis from the point of view of the *rules of delimitation* and the principles of *cooperation* and *complementarity* outlined by Cremona.

These specific aspects are also addressed in the RELIGARE report, where a distinction is made between EU competence and EU relevance in the field (*Report*, 14),[10] but it is in fact in the interplay between competence and relevance that coherence is called into play. While it is true that the EU has no direct explicit competence to regulate religion or religious groups, one cannot neglect the fact that many pieces of EU legislation affect religion and religious groups deeply.[11] For instance, how is it possible to disentangle the debate on religious freedom from the wider debate on citizenship and immigration, given the growing presence of Muslim believers in Europe?[12] How is it possible to separate anti-discrimination policies from their potential relevance to the regulation of the relationships between different States and religious groups? As the RELIGARE report puts it, one problem related to the coherence (and consistency) of EU action on the regulation of religion is the lack of coordination 'internally among the different services that, within the European institutions, are called upon to consider questions of religious discrimination' (*Report*, 44–45). This may be the result of several factors: a perceived lack of competence on a topic (religion) which has thus become difficult to define or identify; the different perceptions of EU officials and the policy options available to them; the lack of an efficient system enabling coordination among the different offices;[13] and, very possibly, deliberate political attempts to prevent the engagement of EU law in the management of the relationship between religions and European States. As the perennial debate on the so-called Horizontal Directive on combating discrimination has also shown, there is also a significant degree of political resistance *vis-à-vis* any expansion of the EU role (*Report*, 14).

Today, issues pertaining to law and religion within the EU legal order are to be dealt with using the new institutional framework provided by the Lisbon Treaty, incorporating the Charter of Fundamental Rights into the primary law of the Union, which entered into force on 1 December 2009. As Emma Svensson suggests, one question worth asking is: 'What changes could be expected when religious freedom now serves as a part of European Union primary law?'[14] Article 10 of the Charter recognises the right to freedom of thought, conscience and religion[15] in a system that holds the deeper harmonisation and convergence of Member States among its fundamental goals, even though, as Svensson remarks, it 'seems that the Court of Justice is

9 See S Carrera and J Parkin, *The Place of Religion in European Union Law and Policy: Competing Approaches and Actors inside the European Commission*, RELIGARE Working Document no 1, September 2010.

10 See also P Annicchino, 'Religion and EU Institutions' (2013) 15 (3) *Ecclesiastical Law Journal* 326–31.

11 See P Annicchino, 'Il Dialogo con i gruppi religiosi e le organizzazioni non confessionali nel diritto dell'Unione europea. A proposito di una recente pronuncia del Mediatore europeo' (2013) 3 *Quaderni di Diritto e Politica Ecclesiastica* 747–56. On the debate on the issue of EU competence in the field, see M Ventura, *Dynamic Law and Religion in Europe: Acknowledging Change. Choosing Change*, EUI working paper RSCAS 2013/91, 17.

12 As Alidadi and Foblets (n 3) 394 highlight, 'The fact that Islam and other less familiar religious traditions are introduced in Europe through immigration complicates and charges the nature of the debate, in particular by entangling the debate on religious pluralism with that concerning assimilation, integration and citizenship'. See also S Morano-Foadi, 'EU Citizenship and Religious Liberty in an Enlarged Europe' (2010) 4 *European Law Journal* 417–38.

13 As highlighted in the RELIGARE report (p. 45), 'A suggestion that thus emerges from the RELIGARE project ... is that a permanent consultative mechanism be put in place among the services in order to enable the teams to listen to each other's views on certain priorities and, as far as possible, to undertake joint actions.'

14 E Svensson, 'The Constitutionalization of Freedom of Religion in the European Union: What Changes Are the Charter of Fundamental Rights Expected to Bring About?' in WC Durham, S Ferrari, D Thayer and C Cianitto (eds), *Law, Religion Constitution: Freedom of Religion, Equal Treatment and the Law* (Ashgate 2013) 268.

15 According to Article 10 of the Charter for Fundamental Rights:

> 1. Everyone has the right to freedom of thought, conscience and religion. This right includes freedom to change religion or belief and freedom, either alone or in community with others and in public or in private, to manifest religion or belief, in worship, teaching, practice and observance.
>
> 2. The right to conscientious objection is recognized, in accordance with the national laws governing the exercise of this right.

increasingly willing to accept national restrictions of Union fundamental freedoms, on the basis of "cardinal constitutional principles" inherent in a particular national constitutional identity'.[16]

The relation between the expansion of the roles of EU institutions and the margin of discretion to be left to Member States in the regulation of this particular domain will be the cornerstone of the debate in defining the policy action of the EU. It goes without saying that the same problem is today faced by the European Court of Human Rights (ECtHR).[17] The problem of coherence (and consistency) in this case is also underlined by the case law of the different Member States, as well as that of the supranational courts. As the RELIGARE report highlights, the analysis of court decisions reveals many inconsistencies, and one of the features, especially of the ECtHR, is the fragmentation of case law.[18] The choices to be made by EU policymakers are increasingly driven by the narrative of identity and willingness to preserve the status quo in the name of the old models, on the one hand, and by the need to find new tools and a new paradigm with which to deal with the increasing pluralisation of European societies on the other.[19] The route to be taken will lie in the balance between the different options, legislative or judicial, that the EU decides to follow. From the legislative point of view, one clear option would be to empower Directive 2000/78/EC.[20] To this end, and in the interests of achieving a coherent (and consistent) approach in the case law of national and supranational courts, it will also be relevant to emphasise a coherent approach in the legislative instruments used by the European Union to intervene in all the different fields that touch upon sensitive religious issues.

Law and Policy of Religious Freedom in the External Action of the European Union

Aside from the roles played by religion and the policies on religious freedom within the European Union's internal order, the EU has recently developed a set of tools with which to deal with fundamental rights and freedom of religion or belief in its external action. This dimension was not at the core of the RELIGARE project, which focused its research on the regulation of religion within the European Union, but it is worth drawing attention to this dimension of the EU institutions' actions. Many religious groups have raised their voices against religious persecution. Within the European Union, Christians have been particularly vocal, linking these concerns to the political developments of the Arab Spring and the rising role of Islamist parties. According to Tom Heneghan, 'The rise of radical Islamist attacks on Christians, first in Iraq and now in Egypt after dictators there were overthrown, has alarmed religious minorities across the Middle East and prompted support efforts from Christian Churches abroad'.[21] Egregious and systematic violations of the religious freedom of Christians have also attracted the gaze of the academic and media communities, which have paid

16 See Svensson (n 14) 278.

17 See M Lugato, 'The "Margin of Appreciation" and Freedom of Religion: Between Treaty Interpretation and Subsidiarity' (2013) 52 (1–2) *Journal of Catholic Legal Studies* 49–70; P Annicchino, 'Tra Margine di Apprezzamento e Neutralità il caso Lautsi e I nuovi equilibri della tutela europea della libertà religiosa' in R Mazzola (ed), *Diritto e Religione in Europa. Rapporto sulla giurisprudenza della Corte Europea dei Diritti dell'Uomo in materia di Libertà Religiosa* (Il Mulino 2012) 179–93.

18 The RELIGARE report (p. 45) highlights how, regarding the 'public space', 'recent (national) court decisions have driven Member States further apart in their views of the place of religious expression in the public space'.

19 The point is underlined by Marco Ventura (n 11) 33: 'European religious pluralism designates both the factual, objective development of Europe as an area in which multiple faiths and convictions coexist and interact and the political project aiming at supporting and enhancing the plurality of beliefs as an essential ingredient for a better Europe.'

20 This is a possibility envisaged in the RELIGARE report (p. 42): 'Building on the EU's existing framework of rights, and more particularly on Directive 2000/78/EC, the EU could decide to *extend* its non-discrimination (and integration) arsenal to issues pertaining to religion and belief *outside the scope of employment* by giving further support to the legislative procedure leading to the adoption of the proposed Council Directive on implementing equal treatment between persons irrespective of religion or belief, disability, age, or sexual orientation.' (Emphasis in original)

21 T Heneghan, 'Russian Orthodox Leader: Protect Mideast Christians' (2 December 2011), available at <www.reuters.com/article/2011/12/02/russia-church-mideast-idAFL5E7N23QQ20111202?sp=true> accessed 27 June 2014.

close attention to the issue.[22] Through a complex political process, in June 2013 the EU's Foreign Affairs Council came to approve the text of the *European Guidelines for the Protection and Promotion of Freedom of Religion or Belief*[23] to be applied to the European Union's external actions. The text provides reasons, options and tools for EU diplomats with which to integrate the promotion and protection of the right to freedom of religion or belief, both in the EU's foreign policy and in relationships with third countries – for instance, through association agreements or general agreements of a commercial nature. It is also worth mentioning the roles that civil society, human rights defenders and NGOs could play in this process. Interestingly, the text of the guidelines offers some fundamental legal notions, such as a broad understanding of what constitutes 'freedom of religion or belief', as well as the possibility of deploying EU financial resources for the protection and promotion of the rights at stake.

Relationships with third countries are also now a concern in the expanding field of asylum law within the EU, which consists of a growing body of instruments and procedures. In the case of *Bundesrepublik Deutschland v Y and Z*, concerning Ahmadi Muslims who moved to Germany from Pakistan and were threatened with deportation, the European Court of Justice issued a decision that could potentially have important consequences as regards the protection of the right to freedom of religion or belief. As is widely known, Ahmadi Muslims suffer from persecution in Pakistan, and as a result of this persecution, the two applicants decided to enter Germany and apply for asylum.[24] The German courts of first instance decided that they could be deported, as the restriction in Pakistan could not prevent them from holding their beliefs, but merely from practising and manifesting their religion. For the German court, as the Court of Justice of the European Union highlighted in the final judgment, '[T]here could be deemed to be persecution relevant for the purposes of the right of asylum only where there was interference with the "core areas" of religious freedom, but not when there were restrictions on the public practice of the faith'.[25] The Court of Justice of the European Union disagreed with the view of the German Court, stating that, '[I]t may reasonably be thought that, upon his return to his country of origin, [the refugee] will engage in religious practice which will expose him to a real risk of persecution. In assessing an application for refugee status on an individual basis, those authorities cannot reasonably expect the applicant to abstain from those religious practices.'[26] According to paragraph 80 of the decision, it is for the authorities that make the decisions on asylum requests to assess whether the risk of persecution is relevant; however, no clear guidelines are provided as to how to determine this relevance. This decision offers another angle from which to observe

---

22 See, among others, J Allen Jr, *The Global War on Christians: Dispatches from the Front Lines of Anti-Christian Persecution* (Image 2013); P Marshall, L Gilbert, N Shea, *Persecuted: The Global Assault on Christians* (Thomas Nelson 2013). Also, see the papers presented at the conference 'Christianity and Freedom: Historical and Contemporary Perspectives', organised by the Religious Freedom Project (Georgetown University), available at <http://berkleycenter.georgetown.edu/rfp/events/christianity-and-freedom-historical-and-contemporary-perspectives> accessed 27 June 2014.

23 <http://eeas.europa.eu/delegations/fiji/press_corner/all_news/news/2013/eu_guidelines_on_the_promotion_and_protection_of_freedom_of_religion_or_belief_(28june_24_2013_fac)29.pdf> accessed 24 August 2014. See P Annicchino (ed), *Freedom of Religion or Belief in Foreign Policy: Which One?* (EUI University Press 2013); P Annicchino, 'The New Guidelines on Freedom of Religion and LGBTI Rights in the External Action of the European Union' (2013) 6 *European Human Rights Law Review* 624–30.

24 The judgment of the Court acknowledges the rationale behind the application for asylum:

> In support of their respective applications, they claimed that their membership of the Muslim Ahmadiyya community, which is an Islamic reformist movement, had forced them to leave their country of origin. In particular, Y stated that on several occasions he had been beaten in his home village by a group of people and had stones thrown at him at his community's place of prayer. Those people threatened to kill him and reported him to the police for insulting the Prophet Mohammed. Z claimed that he was mistreated and imprisoned as a result of his religious belief.

See CJEU, *Bundesrepublik Deutschland v Y and Z* (C-71/11-C-99/11), 5/09/2012, para 30.

25 ibid para 42.

26 ibid para 80.

how freedom of religion or belief plays a role within an important sector of EU law[27] and to evaluate the coherence of the EU legal order.[28]

What Is Seen and What Is Unseen: Coherence and Religious Freedom between Internal and External Action of the European Union

As in every social sphere, law can have multiple effects. Some of these effects are immediate and visible. Others can only be seen in the long term, when they emerge through the interaction of the letter of the law and the particular social contexts in which it operates. The story of EU law and religion is one which is still to be told. On one side, it is the story of the will that exists to prevent EU law from influencing legal developments regarding protection of the right to freedom of religion or belief, told mainly through a narrative concerning the impossibility of changing the status quo of the different national juridical and political situations. This is the picture that Article 17 of the Lisbon Treaty is assumed to have created, bringing to an end the process which began with Declaration no. 11, annexed to the Treaty of Amsterdam.[29] But the dynamics of the longer term tell a different story. It is a story of the growing influence of EU law, both in determining the status of religious groups, mainly through the prism of non-discrimination laws,[30] and, as the European Ombudsman's recent decision revealed,[31] in the relations between EU institutions and religious groups. What we see, if we do not want to deepen our analysis, is the static dimension represented by Article 17 of the Lisbon Treaty. What we do not see are the remarkable developments in European societies that policymakers are called upon to address.[32] The challenges go beyond the single issue of the degree of protection of freedom of religion or belief, and in fact, involve the entire European institutional structure.[33] It is the battle to win the hearts and minds of European citizens.[34] How much must be decided by EU institutions? How much is to be left to the Member States? It would be naïve, as well as useless, to think that a uniform relationship model for dealings between States and religious groups could be centrally imposed upon all Member States. On the other side, as Marie Anne Glendon has argued, 'To accept that there are no universal models is not to deny that religious freedom is a universal right. Rather, it is to recognize that there must be room for a degree of pluralism in modes of bringing religious freedom and other fundamental human rights to life under diverse cultural

27 Similar cases have been decided by the European Court of Human Rights; see N Hervieu, 'Une progression sans révolution dans l'appréhension européenne des persécution religieuses' (June 2013) *Stato, Chiese e Pluralismo Confessionale*, available at <www.statoechiese.it/images/stories/2013.6/hervieum_une_progression.pdf> accessed 27 June 2014.

28 For a general introduction to the role of 'coherence' within EU External Relations, see L den Hertog and S Strob, 'Coherence in EU External Relations: Concepts and Legal Rooting of an Ambiguous Term' (2013) 18 (3) *European Foreign Affairs Review* 373–88.

29 According to Article 17: '1. The Union respects and does not prejudice the status under national law of churches and religious associations or communities in the Member States. 2. The Union equally respects the status under national law of philosophical and non-confessional organizations. 3. Recognizing their identity and their specific contribution, the Union shall maintain an open, transparent and regular dialogue with these churches and organizations.'

30 See M Ventura, 'Libertà religiosa e divieto di discriminazione nel diritto dell'Unione Europea' (2010) 3–4 *Il Diritto Ecclesiastico* 482–90.

31 See P Annicchino, 'Religion and EU Institutions' (2013) 15 (3) *Ecclesiastical Law Journal* 326–31, commenting on the decision of the European Ombudsman in his inquiry into complaint 2097/2011/RA against the European Commission dealing with the implementation of Art. 17 of the Lisbon Treaty.

32 As Marco Ventura (n 11) 27 points out, 'Since 2007, the principle of a domestic priority over the European initiative and competence in religious affairs has been the key element in the approach to law and religion in Europe, widely shared by governmental and religious actors, EU officers and experts. The gap has widened between the socio-legal reality and such illusionary domestic priority, coming with the ancillary illusion of keeping religion out of the market.'

33 In general, see JHH Weiler, 'The Political and Legal Culture of European Integration: An Exploratory Essay' (2011) 9 (3–4) *International Journal of Constitutional Law* 678–94. As far as the protection of human rights is concerned, see R White, 'A New Era for Human Rights in the European Union?' (2011) 30 (1) *Yearbook of European Law* 100–130.

34 See M Dougan, 'The Treaty of Lisbon 2007: Winning Minds not Hearts' (2008) 45 *Common Market Law Review* 617–703.

circumstances.'[35] Those elements, if any, that European societies seek to agree upon as common may at least serve as minimum standards for the protection of freedom of religion or belief. To this extent, a minimum degree of coherence (and consistency) is required. It would otherwise be impossible to include the protection of freedom of religion or belief as one of the pillars of EU external human rights action. As highlighted by Marco Ventura,

> The prospect of Europe playing a worldwide role for the promotion of freedom of religion or belief, depends on the constant effort to assess problematic situations within Europe and redress violations of fundamental rights. Without a European consistency in religious laws and policies, Europe lacks the credibility and authority to denounce and counter violations in other parts of the world.[36]

The same religious groups are called to play an active role in this process. Otherwise, it would be impossible to ask the EU to remain silent with regard to internal policies on religious freedoms while simultaneously asking the same institutions to protect freedom of religion or belief abroad. In the end, it will be an easy choice: one between an attempt to achieve a minimum degree of coherence (and consistency) and the temptation to find an easy route in an organised hypocrisy.[37] It is up to policymakers and religious groups to decide. *Tertium non datur.*

---

35 MA Glendon, 'Religious Freedom in the 21st Century: Old Biases, Fresh Challenges, New Frontiers' in MA Glendon and HF Zacher (eds) *Universal Rights in a World of Diversity: The Case of Religious Freedom* (Pontifical Academy of Social Sciences, 2012) 659 <http://www.pass.va/content/dam/scienzesociali/pdf/actapass17.pdf> accessed 24 August 2014.

36 Ventura (n 11) 35.

37 On this point, see Marco Ventura (n 11) 34: 'While the suppression of cultural, religious, national and regional diversity in Europe is highly undesirable, and deeply contradictory with European history and the European project, a European consistency is a compelling necessity.'

Chapter 29
Improving Justice in the 'Burqa Ban' Debates: Group Vulnerability and Procedural Justice

Eva Brems, Saïla Ouald Chaib and Lourdes Peroni

This chapter focuses on one of the four areas of participation in social life examined in the RELIGARE report: access to and use of public space (*Report*, § 2.3; especially § 2.3.1.1). In particular, it suggests two ways of advancing the greater inclusiveness and fuller equality of women wearing the full veil in public spaces.[1] We argue that a more equal and inclusive access to public places may be furthered by focusing on the vulnerability of this group of women to negative social attitudes (the 'group vulnerability' approach). Fuller inclusiveness and equality may be additionally advanced by taking due account of their perspectives and human rights in the decision-making processes (the 'procedural justice' approach).

These two proposed ways of addressing the issue of access to and use of public spaces should be viewed as lanes in the non-discrimination and freedom of religion routes followed in the RELIGARE report. Indeed, the group vulnerability approach allows for closer scrutiny of measures directly or indirectly restricting the access to public spaces of particularly vulnerable groups such as women wearing the face veil. In turn, the procedural justice approach ensures, inter alia, that these restrictive measures are not taken without due consideration of the impact on the freedom of religion of face-veiled women. Moreover, the procedural justice approach may be instrumental in furthering the 'justice as even-handedness' standard developed by RELIGARE for assessing non-discrimination and freedom of religion. This is because procedural justice seeks to ensure that the interests at stake of all those affected are equally considered in the decision-making process.

The suggested approaches of group vulnerability and procedural justice may ultimately prove instrumentally valuable in achieving two of RELIGARE's stated aims with regard to wearing religious dress in public spaces: to combat discrimination and to avoid unnecessary prohibitions.

A Group Vulnerability Approach to Face Veil Bans: Enhancing Non-Discrimination in the Access to Public Space

Drawing on the case law of the European Court of Human Rights (ECtHR, 'the Court' or 'the Strasbourg Court') and building on the work of two of our team members,[2] this section proposes to enhance the non-discrimination assessment of measures excluding women wearing the full veil from public places by suggesting a 'group vulnerability' perspective.

Introducing Group Vulnerability as an ECtHR Concept

Over the past decade, the Strasbourg Court has increasingly used the concept of 'vulnerable groups' to refer to groups as varied as Roma, people with mental disabilities and asylum seekers.[3] Though the Court has not

1 Our arguments build on research carried out within the framework of the research project Strengthening the European Court of Human Rights: More Accountability through Better Legal Reasoning, funded by the European Research Council. More specifically, we build on the works of S Ouald Chaib and E Brems, 'Doing Minority Justice through Procedural Fairness: Face Veil Bans in Europe' (2013) 2 *Journal of Muslims in Europe* 1–26; L Peroni and A Timmer, 'Vulnerable Groups: The Promise of an Emerging Concept in European Human Rights Convention Law' (2013) 11 *International Journal of Constitutional Law I-CON* 1056–85.

2 Peroni and Timmer (n 1).

3 ibid.

yet fully developed a clear set of criteria to determine whether a certain group is particularly vulnerable, a number of factors seem to be emerging in its legal reasoning.[4] One of them is (historical) prejudice, stereotyping and stigmatisation.[5] For example, in *Alajos Kiss v Hungary* – a case concerning the blanket disenfranchisement of people with mental disabilities – the Court regarded this group as 'particularly vulnerable' given that they have been 'historically subject to prejudice with lasting consequences, resulting in their social exclusion'.[6] 'Such prejudice', the Court explains, 'may entail legislative stereotyping which prohibits the individualised evaluation of their capacities and needs.'[7] In a similar vein, in *Kiyutin v Russia* – a case dealing with the refusal of a residence permit to a person living with HIV – the Court held that 'people living with HIV are a vulnerable group with a history of prejudice and stigmatisation'.[8] The Strasbourg Court's understanding of 'group vulnerability' thus makes clear that the members of some groups are particularly vulnerable in society as a result of prejudice, stigma and stereotypes rather than as something inherent in their nature.[9]

In a critical assessment of the Court's use of the concept of 'vulnerable groups', Alexandra Timmer and Lourdes Peroni argue that its insertion is, overall, a positive development given its capacity to advance substantive equality.[10] In elaborating this argument, these authors show how the use of the concept has enabled the Court to examine more closely the negative societal attitudes that (re)produce the vulnerabilities of these groups and to assess more thoroughly the harm of 'misrecognition'[11] they suffer as a consequence.[12] One way in which this type of analysis has manifested itself in the Court's case law is through the narrowing of the margin of appreciation.[13] Indeed, the Court has applied stricter scrutiny to the reasons advanced by States to justify restrictions on vulnerable group members' rights.[14] It held for instance in *Kiyutin*: 'If a restriction on fundamental rights applies to a particularly vulnerable group in society that has suffered considerable discrimination in the past, then the State's margin of appreciation is substantially narrower and it must have very weighty reasons for the restrictions in question.'[15]

Our argument is that this type of group vulnerability analysis holds great potential to turn the analytical gaze towards the societal circumstances and attitudes that heighten the vulnerability of certain groups to religious discrimination. In particular, an analysis based on group vulnerability could serve to identify and bring under closer scrutiny prejudices and negative stereotypes underlying reasons to justify restrictions on religious people's access to public spaces. Women wearing the full veil – a minority within a religious minority in Europe – are certainly a particularly vulnerable group in the sense established by the Strasbourg Court in its jurisprudence.[16] As a number of Council of Europe documents show, they are the frequent target of prejudice and stereotyping in many European countries.[17] Their situation, recent empirical studies further

4 ibid 1064–65.

5 ibid 1065.

6 ECtHR, *Alajos Kiss v Hungary*, App no 38832/06 (20 May 2010) para 42.

7 ibid.

8 ECtHR, *Kiyutin v Russia*, App no 2700/10 (10 March 2011) para 64.

9 The Strasbourg Court's concept implicitly incorporates a crucial insight from theorists of difference: it avoids locating the problem 'in the identity group' and locates it instead 'in the social relations that produce identity groupings'; see M Minow, *Not Only for Myself: Identity, Politics and the Law* (The New York Press 1997) 56.

10 Peroni and Timmer (n 1).

11 Misrecognition takes place when 'institutionalised patterns of cultural value … constitute some actors as inferior, excluded, wholly other, or simply invisible'; N Fraser, 'Rethinking Recognition' (2000) 3 *New Left Review* 113.

12 Peroni and Timmer (n 1) 1080–82.

13 ibid.

14 ibid.

15 *Kiyutin v Russia* (n 8) para 63. Timmer and Peroni (n 1) 1082 argue that '[b]y narrowing the margin of appreciation, the Court more carefully scrutinizes the possible misrecognition harms of prejudice, stigma, and stereotyping, therein advancing … substantive equality'.

16 This approach has been advocated in the Written Comments of the Human Rights Centre of Ghent University, submitted on 9 July 2012 in its capacity as third-party intervener in the case of *S.A.S. v France* (App no 43835/11). The case is currently pending before the Court's Grand Chamber. Thus far, however, the Strasbourg Court has not applied group vulnerability analysis in the context of freedom of religion or religious discrimination claims.

17 These documents highlight the vulnerability of Muslims in Europe – and of Muslim women wearing religious apparel in particular – to widespread prejudice and stereotyping. See T Hammarberg, *Human Rights in Europe: No Grounds*

indicate, is characterised by aggression and discrimination on the part of the society at large in various parts of Europe.[18] One of the negative stereotypes at the root of such discriminatory attitudes is the assumption that Muslim women wearing the (full) veil are oppressed.[19] The stereotype of 'the imperilled Muslim women' waiting to be 'saved' from 'the dangerous Muslim man' by 'the civilised European', though not new, has come to dominate broader public discourses in the aftermath of the events of 11 September 2001.[20]

We therefore propose that, once the vulnerability of women wearing the full veil to stereotyping, stigmatisation and discrimination is established on the basis of these documents and studies, courts will become more sceptical – and, as a result, more rigorous in their scrutiny – of the justifications offered in support of excluding such women from the public space.

Group Vulnerability and Face Covering Bans

A group vulnerability approach may come in particularly handy in cases where the neutrality of the norm is in fact misleading – that is to say, when in reality the norm is either conceived with the idea of restricting certain groups' religious practices or applied in a discriminatory fashion while remaining neutral on its face.[21] A good example of this kind of deceptive neutrality is precisely the face-covering bans passed in some European countries, such as France and Belgium. As Brems, Vrielink and Ouald Chaib argue, 'the background of the bans as well as the reasons advanced to support them … unambiguously indicate that in both states the legislators were concerned primarily with the Islamic face veil, the neutral formulation being chosen mainly to avoid claims of direct discrimination'.[22] Group vulnerability analysis may thus serve to bring to light any legislative stereotyping underlying blanket restrictions that do not allow for an individualised evaluation of the capacities and needs of those concerned.[23] As we will discuss in the next section,[24] stereotypical constructions of Muslim women as helpless and victimised, and therefore in need of paternalistic protection, have been at the heart of the legislative debates surrounding the face covering bans.[25]

for Complacency (Council of Europe 2011) 36–39 and 47–48; Group of Eminent Persons of the Council of Europe, 'Living Together: Combining Diversity and Freedom in 21st-Century Europe' (Council of Europe 2011) 15–16; Parliamentary Assembly of the Council of Europe (PACE), Resolution 1743 'Islam, Islamism and Islamophobia in Europe' (Council of Europe 2010) 1; European Commission against Racism and Intolerance (ECRI), General Policy Recommendation No. 5 'On Combating Intolerance and Discrimination against Muslims', 16 March 2000.

18 See E Brems, Y Janssens, K Lecoyer, S Ouald Chaib and V Vandersteen, 'Wearing the Face Veil in Belgium: Views and Experiences of 27 Women Living in Belgium concerning the Islamic Full Face Veil and the Belgian Ban on Face Covering' (2012), 4.5, available at <www.ugent.be/re/publiekrecht/en/research/human-rights/faceveil.pdf> accessed 27 June 2014; Open Society Foundations, 'Unveiling the Truth: Why 32 Muslim Women Wear the Full-Face Veil in France' (2011) 55–61, available at <www.opensocietyfoundations.org/sites/default/files/a-unveiling-the-truth-20100510_0.pdf> accessed 27 June 2014. Other studies similarly highlight the hostility experienced by Muslim women wearing either the veil or the full-face veil in several European countries. See Amnesty International, 'Choice and Prejudice: Discrimination against Muslims in Europe' (2012), available at <www.amnesty.eu/content/assets/REPORT.pdf> accessed 27 June 2014.

19 On this stereotypical depiction of Muslim women in historical and contemporary discourses, see generally L Abu-Lughod, *Do Muslim Women Need Saving?* (Harvard University Press 2013); S Fernandez, 'The Crusade over the Bodies of Women' in M Malik (ed), *Anti-Muslim Prejudice: Past and Present* (Routledge 2012) 61–78.

20 SH Razack, *Casting Out: The Eviction of Muslims from Western Law and Politics* (University of Toronto Press 2007) 5. See also Abu-Lughod (n 19) 6–7.

21 See C Evans, *Freedom of Religion under the European Convention on Human Rights* (OUP 2001) 169 (making the point that neutral and general laws may sometimes be deceptive and merely create an impression of generality and neutrality when they are in fact applied in a discriminatory manner).

22 E Brems, J Vrielink and S Ouald Chaib, 'Uncovering French and Belgian Face Covering Bans' (2013) 2 *Journal of Law, Religion and State* 74. See also Open Society Foundations (n 18).

23 See *Alajos Kiss v Hungary* (n 6).

24 See the subsection 'Procedural Justice and Face Covering Bans' (below), in particular, the headings 'Accuracy' and 'Respect'.

25 Indeed, one of the most influential justifications of these bans includes the view of this item of clothing as a 'symbol of patriarchal authority and of female subservience to men'; R Grillo and P Shah, 'Reasons to Ban? The Anti-Burqa Movement in Western Europe' (2012) Max Planck Institute for the Study of Religious and Ethnic Diversity, Working Paper 12–05, 27.

Group vulnerability analysis, however, should be deployed reflectively.[26] An uncritical application of the concept – that is to say, an application that does not attend to the risks of stereotyping, stigmatising and paternalising inherent in the concept – may end up reinforcing the very discriminatory attitudes and misplaced paternalism it seeks to remedy.[27] If the concept is to retain its ability to remedy such wrongs, it is first of all crucial to avoid conceiving of vulnerability as inherently located in the group rather than in the social context. The focus of the analysis should be 'on the various circumstances that *render* certain groups vulnerable'.[28] In other words, the inquiry should revolve around the institutional, historical and social contexts that originate and reinforce certain groups' vulnerabilities.

What does all this mean for the case of face covering bans? It means that the analysis should focus on the dominant frameworks and assumptions that render women wearing the full veil 'visible' or 'different' in the first place and, moreover, on the ensuing social hostility towards such 'visibility' or 'difference'. Put another way, the emphasis should be on how such 'visibility' and 'difference' are produced and on how this makes the women concerned more likely to experience (or be more vulnerable to) discrimination and other human rights violations.

A reflective group vulnerability approach should also make sure that vulnerability does not take on what is known as 'master status': vulnerability should not eclipse all other aspects of the particular individuals (for example capabilities, agency).[29] Portraying certain groups as *purely* vulnerable may be deeply stigmatising and disempowering for its members. Group vulnerability reasoning should therefore go hand in hand with an analysis of the individual's particular circumstances and capacities.[30] Put differently, it 'should not trivialise the abilities of persons who belong to an otherwise vulnerable group'.[31] In the context of face-covering bans, an uncritical application of group vulnerability – that is, an application that overshadows the agency and other particular circumstances of the women concerned – runs the risk of further victimising them and justifying misplaced paternalism rather than tackling social prejudice towards them. In the next part, we thus insist and elaborate on the importance of ensuring the *inclusion* of the voices of women wearing the full veil in the decision-making processes that affect them. We furthermore insist on the need to rely on *evidence* rather than on stereotypical constructions that, in homogenising certain experiences (for example oppression, powerlessness) as representative of the whole group, allow for 'the silencing of the voices of Muslim women while simultaneously proclaiming a desire to free them from such silencing'.[32]

In short, a reflective use of group vulnerability in the analysis of face-covering bans in public spaces may enable national authorities in EU Member States – in particular courts – to more closely scrutinise such bans. In turn, this closer scrutiny may allow national authorities to distinguish more effectively discriminatory restrictions from those objectively and reasonably justified in certain contexts. This kind of analysis may therefore prove valuable in implementing one of RELIGARE's recommendations with regard to religious dress codes: combating discrimination.

A Procedural Justice Approach to Face Veil Bans: Taking the Interests at Stake Equally Seriously

In this section, we look at the legislative processes resulting in the banning of face veils from public spaces in two countries covered by the RELIGARE research: France and Belgium. We assess these processes through the lens of procedural justice. Moreover, we show that this approach – in particular the aspects requiring consideration of the interests of *all* those concerned – may prove valuable in assessing the competing interests in an even-handed way, as proposed by RELIGARE.

26 Peroni and Timmer (n 1).

27 ibid 1070–73. This is because 'for many people [the term "vulnerable"] carries solely negative associations such as harm and injury'; ibid 1072.

28 ibid 1073.

29 ibid 1072 (drawing on the work of RA Lenhardt, 'Understanding the Mark: Race, Stigma, and Equality in Context' (2004) 79 *New York University Law Review* 819).

30 ibid 1073–74.

31 ibid 1074.

32 Fernandez (n 19) 61.

The French and Belgian bans are extreme examples of legislative processes taking place above the heads of the people concerned. Not only were the voices of the women concerned missing from the debates, even more striking was the fact that a discussion of the ban's human rights impact – including the impact on freedom of religion – was nearly non-existent. Therefore, in addition to our substantive analysis of face veil bans[33] and our empirical research among women wearing the face veil in Belgium,[34] we have analysed the face veil debate from a procedural justice angle.

Introducing Procedural Justice

Procedural fairness or procedural justice refers to the fairness of the procedures by which a decision is taken or by which an outcome is arrived at in a case. Social psychology research has shown that in their fairness assessment of authorities and the law, people tend to accord more importance to procedural fairness than to distributive justice.[35] In other words, the way people are treated by judges and authorities is more relevant to them than the particular outcome in their case or the policy decision taken. This does not mean, however, that the outcome is considered irrelevant.[36] Procedural fairness and distributive justice should be seen as mutually strengthening approaches rather than substitutes.[37]

Initially, procedural justice research focused on the question of compliance with the law. Tyler and his associates found that the *legitimacy* of an authority shapes compliance and that legitimacy is rooted in procedural fairness judgments.[38] As a consequence, procedural fairness also enhances *cooperation* with authorities.[39] Moreover, it promotes *social cohesion and individual well-being*. Research has consistently shown that '[p]eople ... value fair treatment by legal authorities because it communicates a message about their identities – that they are respected and valued members of society'[40] and that they can count on the authorities for protection, benevolence and consideration when needed.[41]

Although it follows from Tyler's research that procedural fairness is equally important to majority populations as it is to minorities,[42] there are several reasons to believe that procedural fairness is particularly crucial for *minority justice*. First, overcoming minority members' above-average distrust of authorities[43] may require particular vigilance regarding procedural fairness.[44] Second, perceptions of social standing in the society have a special significance for minority members. When certain people, for example youth, minorities

33 See, inter alia, Brems, Vrielink and Ouald Chaib (n 22).

34 Brems, Janssens, Lecoyer, Ouald Chaib and Vandersteen (n 18). The findings of the empirical research are discussed in E Brems, Y Janssens, K Lecoyer, S Ouald Chaib, V Vandersteen and J Vrielink, 'The Belgian "Burqa Ban" Confronted with Insider Realities' in E Brems (ed), *The Face Veil in Europe Inside and Out* (forthcoming 2014).

35 TR Tyler, 'Procedural Justice and the Courts' (2008) 44 (1/2) *Court Review* 26; TR Tyler, 'What is Procedural Justice?: Criteria Used by Citizens to Assess the Fairness of Legal Procedures' (1988) 22 *Law and Society Review* 121; A Gangl, 'Procedural Justice Theory and Evaluations of the Lawmaking Process' (2003) 25 (2) *Political Behavior* 120 (with reference to JR Hibbing and E Theiss-Morse, 'Process Preferences and American Politics: What the People Want Government to Be' (2001) 95 (1) *The American Political Science Review* 145–53).

36 TR Tyler, 'Governing Amid Diversity: Can Fair Decision-Making Procedures Bridge Competing Public Interests and Values?' (1994) 28 *Law and Society Review* 820–21.

37 E Brems and L Lavrysen, 'Procedural Justice in Human Rights Adjudication: The European Court of Human Rights' (2013) 35 *Human Rights Quarterly* 176–200.

38 TR Tyler, *Why People Obey the Law* (Princeton University Press 2006) 270.

39 ibid 271.

40 TR Tyler and Y Huo, *Trust in the Law* (Russell Sage Foundation 2002) 167.

41 Tyler (n 38) 175–76.

42 Tyler and Huo (n 40) 152; K Burke and S Leben, 'Procedural Fairness: A Key Ingredient in Public Satisfaction', White paper for the American Judges Association (2007) 18; TR Tyler, 'Public Trust and Confidence in Legal Authorities: What Do Majority and Minority Group Members Want from the Law and Legal Institutions?' (2001) 19 (2) *Behavioral Sciences and the Law* 217 (with references).

43 Tyler (n 38) 270; Tyler and Huo (n 40) 142–46; Tyler (n 42) 217; M Levi, A Sacks and TR Tyler, 'Conceptualizing Legitimacy, Measuring Legitimating Beliefs' (2009) 53 (3) *American Behavioral Scientist* 369.

44 See also S Ouald Chaib, '*Suku Phull v France* Rewritten from a Procedural Justice Perspective: Taking Religious Minorities Seriously' in E Brems (ed), *Diversity and European Human Rights: Rewriting Judgments of the ECHR* (CUP 2012) 221.

or people with disabilities, are treated unfairly, authorities might be sending the signal that these groups are marginal in society.[45] In contrast, by treating minority individuals fairly, the authorities convey a message of inclusion among the valued members of society. Tyler and others highlight four criteria according to which people evaluate procedural fairness: participation, trustworthiness, neutrality and respect.[46]

Participation, frequently called 'voice', represents the need of people to be able to express their own perspective, regardless of whether or not their voice will have an impact.[47] Valuing participation requires moreover that people feel that their views are genuinely considered.[48]

Trustworthiness refers to authorities' intentions. The question at hand is whether authorities are making an effort to be fair;[49] people will evaluate whether they 'are being honest and open about the basis for their actions; are trying to do what is right for everyone involved, and are acting … not out of personal prejudices'.[50]

Neutrality requires, among other features, transparency about the way decisions are taken and how the rules are applied,[51] as well as consistency across people, over time and across cases.[52] All views should be considered, and no one view should be granted an obvious advantage.[53] Neutrality also requires *accuracy*: informed decisions based on accurate information.[54]

The final criterion, *respect*, means that people's human dignity is not infringed and that authorities treat people in a polite and respectful way.[55]

Procedural Justice and Face Covering Bans

Both in France and Belgium, the processes leading up to the nationwide face veil bans reveal serious shortcomings with respect to several procedural fairness requirements.

Accuracy

First of all, there is the issue of *accuracy*, an aspect of the neutrality of the law.[56] This means simply that the law has to be based on information that is correct. In this respect, both the Belgian and French '*burqa* ban' laws are seriously flawed. Several commentators have noted that, in the legislative process, no evidence was adduced that would allow identification of the exact problem the law would remedy, nor to support the claim that the specific remedy – that is the ban – would be effective with respect to that problem.[57] The Belgian and French legislatures were rather well tuned in with majority sentiments *vis-à-vis* the face veil, yet they were working on erroneous assumptions concerning the profiles and experiences of women wearing the face veil.[58] The central error is the assumption that all – or nearly all – women who wear the face veil are forced

45 Tyler (n 38) 176.

46 See, for example, Tyler (n 35, 2008) 30.

47 ibid and Burke and Leben (n 42) 11–12.

48 Tyler (n 38) 149 and 276.

49 Tyler (n 35, 1988) 129 and Tyler (n 38) 164.

50 Tyler (n 35, 2008) 30.

51 ibid 30 and Burke and Leben (n 42) 6.

52 Tyler (n 35, 2008) 30 and Ouald Chaib (n 44) 223.

53 Gangl (n 35) 121.

54 Tyler (n 36) 824.

55 Burke and Leben (n 42) 7; Tyler (n 38) 152; see also M Nussbaum, *The New Religious Intolerance* (Harvard University Press 2012) 65.

56 Tyler (n 38) 119, referring to the criteria developed by GS Leventhal, 'What Should Be Done with Equity Theory?' in KJ Gergen, MS Greenberg and RH Weiss (eds), *Social Exchange: Advances in Theory and Research* (Plenum 1980) 27–55.

57 GWG Leane, 'Rights of Ethnic Minorities in Liberal Democracies: Has France Gone too far in Banning Muslim Women from Wearing the Burka?' (2011) 33 *Human Rights Quarterly* 1053; M. Hunter-Henin, 'Why the French Don't Like the *Burqa*: *Laïcité*, National Identity and Religious Freedom' (2012) 61 (3) *International and Comparative Law Quarterly* 613; S Nanwani, 'The Burqa Ban: An Unreasonable Limitation on Religious Freedom or a Justifiable Restriction?' (2011) 25 *Emory International Law Review* 1464. cf on the Netherlands, P van Sasse van Ysselt, 'Over het verbod op. het dragen van een gezichtssluier en van andere gelaatsbedekkende kleding' (2010) 1 *Tijdschrift voor Religie, Recht en Beleid* 7.

58 For an extensive discussion of the erroneous assumptions of the Belgian legislature as confronted with empirical reality, see Brems, Janssens, Lecoyer, Ouald Chaib, Vandersteen and Vrielink (n 34).

or pressured to do so. Since the adoption of the bans, empirical research based on interviews with face veil wearers in France[59] and Belgium[60] has shown that in fact the main profile is that of women choosing to wear the veil as a matter of their individual spiritual journey, generally despite the objections of their families and in many cases of their partners as well.

Disregarding essential evidence in the course of lawmaking is highly problematic; it is even more so when it concerns legislation restricting fundamental rights. In Belgium, the disregard seems deliberate, as Parliament insisted on moving fast, and in that spirit rejected both a request for the hearing of experts who could have advanced evidence and requests for an advice of the Council of State, who could have checked whether the proponents of the ban advanced sufficient evidence to support their arguments. In France, however, a parliamentary commission (the Gerin Commission) heard 211 people and produced a 658-page report,[61] and the French Council of State examined the legality of a potential ban and offered negative advice.[62] Nevertheless, the French Parliament voted for the ban and the same flaws occurred.

Neutrality

Then there is the requirement of *neutrality*, which for lawmakers comes close to those of *sincerity* and *transparency*. It is about being clear on the purpose of the legislation, and seriously striving to best achieve that purpose. In the case of conflicting interests between different categories of people affected by the law, it is also about taking the interests of all categories equally seriously. Both the French and Belgian laws ban face covering in general, even though the legal history and the accompanying discourse make clear that they target the Islamic face veil specifically. The neutral wording is intended chiefly to avoid legal challenges of discrimination on grounds of religion. Yet it goes at the expense of *sincerity* and *transparency*. Furthermore, commentators of the French Gerin Commission and the ensuing legislative process have alleged bias in the selection of the persons to be heard,[63] as well as in the interpretation of the information from the hearings by the Commission. It was noted that the final report erased the plurality of reasons for the practice of wearing the face veil that were advanced at the Commission's hearings.[64] Moreover, it can be argued that parliamentarians interpreted the Gerin report in a selective and biased manner, as in addition to a ban, the report also proposed a number of positive measures related to sensitisation, mediation, respect for diversity and the rejection of discrimination, none of which were taken up in the political work that followed the report.[65]

Participation

In the process of lawmaking, individuals cannot expect to be heard in person.[66] Yet individuals belonging to a group that is directly affected or targeted by a law have a legitimate expectation that their side of the story is somehow on the table. Moreover, substantive participation requires some evidence that these people's views have been considered by the decision maker. This is yet another procedural fairness component that has been seriously neglected by the French and Belgian lawmakers who banned the face veil. Empirical research in Belgium has shown that women wearing the face veil experience intense frustration at the fact

59 Open Society Foundations (n 18).

60 Brems, Janssens, Lecoyer, Ouald Chaib and Vandersteen (n 18).

61 A Gerin, 'Rapport d'information fait en application de l'article 145 du reglement au nom de la mission d'information sur la pratique du port du voile integral sur le territoire national', 26 January 2010, 469. cf also S Amghar, 'Le "niqâb" pour s'affirmer?' 2 January 2010, at <www.ceras-projet.org/index.php?id=4196> accessed 27 June 2014.

62 'Etude relative aux possibilites juridiques d'interdiction du port du voile integral', *Rapport Assemblée Générale Plénière du Conseil d'Etat*, 25 March 2010.

63 E Yahyaoui Krivenko, 'The Islamic Veil and its Discontents: How Do They Undermine Gender Equality' (2012) 7 *Religion and Human Rights* 20–21.

64 S Mullally, 'Civic Integration, Migrant Women and the Veil: At the Limits of Rights?' (2011) 74 (1) *The Modern Law Review* 34.

65 X Delgrange, 'Quand la burqa passe a l'Ouest, la Belgique per-elle le Nord?' in O Roy and D Koussens (eds), *Quand la burqa passé à l'Ouest. Enjeux éthiques, politiques et juridiques* (Presses Universitaires de Rennes 2014) 24.

66 However, the small numbers, in particular in Belgium, would have made that possible. See (on the Netherlands) W Witteveen, 'Montesquieu en het boerkaverbod', 20 May 2010, at <www.recht.nl/proxycache.html?cid=94079> accessed 27 June 2014. On the local level, where bans had been enacted in Belgium before the nationwide ban, individual contact seems a logical approach, as the localities concerned usually counted only a handful of face veils.

that this political intervention in their lives took place without consulting them or researching their situation.[67] Indeed, the lawmakers apparently were not really interested in information from the perspective of the face veil wearers. During the massive information gathering effort undertaken by the French Gerin Commission, the idea of talking to a woman who wears the face veil came as an afterthought. Kenza Drider, the only face veil wearer who was heard by the Commission, states that she had written several letters to Mr Gerin asking to appear before the Commission, and that she had to mobilise her media contacts in order to succeed. During her hearing, summarised in 10 lines in the 658-page report, she had to unveil her face.[68] The bypassing of the legislation's target group is all the more remarkable given the fact that both Belgium and France have strong traditions of consulting with stakeholders in the run-up to law making.[69]

Respect

Under this heading, at least three issues are of concern in the face veil banning process. The first has been called 'a neo-colonial form of paternalism'.[70] Throughout their discourse, the legislators picture face veil wearers as subjugated, dependent creatures. Being denied autonomy and voice, the women behind the veil lose their humanity. In the second place, the legislators do not take seriously the infringement they are creating on a fundamental right, that is, the freedom to express one's religion. They consistently downplay the religious factor, despite the fact that for most women who wear the face veil, the central reason for doing so is a deep religious commitment. Even more importantly, they take tampering with a fundamental right lightly. This is evidenced most clearly in the blatant ignoring of the negative advice of the French Council of State, and in the refusal to consult the Belgian Council of State.

Third, the discourse surrounding the introduction of the bans shows a strong tendency towards 'othering'.[71] Women who wear a face veil are not portrayed as members of the same society as those who encounter them on the street and those who decide to ban the veil. Nicolas Sarkozy set the tone when he announced that 'the *burqa* will not be welcome on French territory'. Sarkozy's 'colonial gaze' at the face veil mobilises the French around self-proclaimed French values while excluding the face veil wearers from both those values and the idea of Frenchness.[72]

Trust/caring

The criterion of trust relates to the feeling among those affected by the law that those who are making the law sincerely strive for justice.[73] It is about the lawmakers showing the people that they care. To the extent that the lawmakers in the face veil banning process show caring, it is caring about the majority population, for whom the face veil may engender feelings of insecurity, who dislike the sight of a face veil on the street, and who see the face veil as a symbol of the denial of women's rights. The arguments advanced by both parliaments to ban the veil – women's rights, security and social cohesion – make sense only from the (subjective) perspective of those who do not wear the face veil. As empirical research shows, for the face veil wearers the bans have reduced women's rights, social integration and security.[74] This lack of caring for the women concerned is most flagrant in the Belgian law,[75] as – different from the French law[76] – it does not include a stipulation against forcing a person to cover her face. While the authors of the ban were assuming that women wearing the face veil are coerced to do so, they apparently did not care enough about these women to punish the perpetrators.

---

67 Brems, Janssens, Lecoyer, Ouald Chaib and Vandersteen (n 18).

68 Open Society Foundations (n 18) 20.

69 cf (on the Netherlands) Witteveen (n 66).

70 S Hennette-Vauchez, 'La burqa, la femme et l'Etat' (*Raison Publique*, 12 May 2010), at <www.raison-publique.fr/article317.html> accessed 27 June 2014.

71 On the 'otherisation' of the face veil, see N Chakraborti and I Zempi, 'The Veil under Attack: Gendered Dimensions of Islamophobic Victimization' (2012) 18 (3) *International Review of Victimology* 8.

72 ibid 21.

73 Tyler (n 35, 1988) 129.

74 Brems, Janssens, Lecoyer, Ouald Chaib, Vandersteen and Vrielink (n 34).

75 Loi visant à interdire le port de tout vêtement cachant totalement ou de manière principale le visage, 11 June 2011.

76 Loi n° 2010–1192 du 11 octobre 2010 interdisant la dissimulation du visage dans l'espace public.

In sum, the lawmaking processes leading to the French and Belgian face veil bans show flagrant procedural justice flaws. This is a serious problem in and of itself. Yet in this case, there appears to be in addition a direct link between the failure of procedural justice and the denial of substantive justice. Processes based on inaccurate assumptions lead to bad laws that do not achieve their stated purposes. They also lead to stigmatisation and dehumanisation of the women concerned. A procedural justice approach involves taking women wearing a face veil seriously by genuinely considering their perspective and their human rights and by treating them in a respectful and unbiased way. This approach would not only further the quality of the legislation, but would also ensure the inclusion of the women concerned.

The procedural justice approach may thus be viewed as one way of putting into practice RELIGARE's standard of 'justice as even-handedness'. The approach ensures the application of this standard by insisting that decision-making processes take the interests of all those concerned equally seriously in cases of conflicting interests between different groups. Moreover, the procedural justice approach may prove valuable in the implementation of one of RELIGARE's recommendations on religious dress: avoiding unnecessary prohibitions. Indeed, in demanding an evidence-based identification of the problem that the restriction in question purports to remedy, procedural justice may encourage more proportionate responses. Wearing the full-face veil will thus be prohibited only when there is evidence showing that the prohibition will be effective in addressing a problem accurately identified beforehand.

To Conclude

Numerous human rights reports leave no room for doubt: European Muslim women wearing religious garments are particularly vulnerable to prejudice and discrimination in many countries across Europe.[77] Being a minority within a minority, women wearing a face veil are in a particularly vulnerable position. Legislation such as the French and Belgian blanket bans on the wearing of the face veil in the public space is not only discriminatory against the women concerned, but also further marginalises and stigmatises them. Instead of redressing the vulnerable position of face-veiled women, the French and Belgian authorities actually reinforce it. Indeed, this legislation was enacted over their heads, without taking their perspective into account. As such, women wearing a face veil were considered by the lawmakers to be voiceless and incapable of making autonomous decisions, 'the other' in need of saving. The laws are therefore based on stereotypical assumptions rather than on accurate facts. Moreover, the women's fundamental rights, including their freedom of religion, were deliberately not taken into consideration in the parliamentary discussions. As a consequence, the ban not only (literally) excludes face-veiled women from the public space, but also conveys to them a message of exclusion from the society at large.

A more egalitarian and inclusive access to and use of public space necessitates an acknowledgment of the position of face-veiled women as a particularly vulnerable group and requires authorities to be procedurally fair towards them. All this simply means treating these women and their rights with respect and in a neutral way, something every member of our society should be entitled to, even if she wears a face veil.

77 See Hammarberg (n 17) 36–39 and 47–48; Group of Eminent Persons of the Council of Europe (n 17) 15–16; Parliamentary Assembly of the Council of Europe (PACE) (n 17) 1; and European Commission against Racism and Intolerance (ECRI) (n 17).

Chapter 30
Recent Developments in Relation to the RELIGARE Project Report

Eric Roux

It is not an easy task to write a comment on such a carefully written and well-presented report as that written to summarise the findings of the RELIGARE project. Criticising is not an option when you have nothing to criticise, and paraphrasing would be useless.

So the only remaining option is to see if some areas of concern could benefit from additional perspectives, and see whether in those areas of concern that are evolving every day – this being evidence that these topics are living topics – some new developments may be analysed in order to supplement the analysis and recommendations of the project.

Indeed, I think that in relation to the four areas of recommendation of the project, and within the scope of the two major concepts developed as the normative framework, 'inclusive State neutrality' and 'justice as even-handedness', some recent developments at the national, European and international levels shed new light on the way these topics should be dealt with.

In analysing these new developments, I decided not to limit myself to a national or European level, as it appears that all the countries studied within the framework of the project are subject to the international law contained in the United Nations' International Covenant on Civil and Political Rights (ICCPR), particularly Article 18 on Freedom of Thought, Conscience and Religion.

The conclusion of the report states that the 'right of minorities – whether religious or other – to religious freedom comes under pressure if the majority in a diverse society puts the imprint of its own conception of the "good life" upon legislation. Freedom of religion and belief is also and should remain, if not primarily, a fundamental right of minorities' (*Report*, 49–50). In my comments I will take this injunction seriously and focus on the rights of minorities, as this is always the most crucial concern when human rights are involved, specifically when religious freedom is at stake.

First of all, I will discuss the new *EU Guidelines on the Promotion and Protection of Freedom of Religion or Belief*,[1] which were adopted by the European Council on 24 June 2013. These guidelines take a very strong position on behalf of the EU institutions on this subject, even if they were initially intended for application to EU external actions and are not legally binding for European Union members. I will then cover some recent decisions by the European Court of Human Rights (ECtHR), the United Nations Human Rights Committee, and national jurisprudence in relation to the four areas of research of the project.

EU Guidelines on the Promotion and Protection of Freedom of Religion or Belief

On 24 June 2013, the Foreign Affairs Council of the Council of the European Union adopted the *EU Guidelines on the Promotion and Protection of Freedom of Religion or Belief*, with the stated purpose of reaffirming the EU's 'determination to promote, in its external human rights policy, freedom of religion or belief as a right to be exercised by everyone everywhere, based on the principles of equality, non-discrimination and universality'.[2] While it is clear that the Foreign Affairs Council passed these guidelines so they now form the external policy of the EU on matters of religious freedom, they obviously should have force inside the

1 Available at <http://consilium.europa.eu/uedocs/cms_data/docs/pressdata/EN/foraff/137585.pdf> accessed 16 June 2014.

2 ibid para 6.

EU too, as they articulate the principles of religious freedom and non-discrimination the EU is committed to upholding throughout the world. Furthermore, paragraph 5 states that the EU and its Member States are, in essence, committed to these principles 'within their borders'.

Based on this, and on the fact that these guidelines refer explicitly to a non-exhaustive list of international norms, standards and principles, including the ICCPR and the European Convention on Human Rights and Fundamental Freedoms, which are legally binding within the EU Member States, there would be no contradiction if European Union institutions would base their future legislation on these international instruments.

This is not the first time the Council of the European Union has spoken on religious freedom – in November 2009 the Council recognised 'the strategic importance of freedom of religion or belief and of countering religious intolerance, and reaffirms its intention to continue to give priority to the issues as part of the European Union's human rights policy'.[3] These *EU Guidelines*, however, go much further than anything that had already been adopted by the EU institutions, formally recognising international principles and standards as part of the EU commitments in a practical document that develops the principles recognised by the Charter of Fundamental Rights of the European Union.

The guidelines contain a strong and unequivocal commitment to respect – and to ensure respect of – a whole range of international standards on freedom of religion or belief. Regarding religious minorities and the RELIGARE report's central concepts of 'inclusive State neutrality' and 'justice as even-handedness', the guidelines stress some very important points, especially in paragraphs 14, 21, 22, 35, 37 and 42(f), which refer to the UN Human Rights Committee's General Comment 22 on Article 18 of the ICCPR.[4] These paragraphs stress that States should avoid any limitation on the freedom to manifest one's religion or belief that is not prescribed by law and necessary to protect public safety, order, health or morals, or the fundamental rights and freedoms of others, applying a strict interpretation by the States of Article 18. Moreover, States must make sure that any limitations are 'not imposed for discriminatory purposes or applied in a discriminatory manner'. In addition, it states that any 'such restrictions must be based on principles not deriving exclusively from a single tradition, as the concept of morals derives from many social, philosophical and religious traditions'. This admonition is particularly aligned with the recommendations of the RELIGARE report. Paragraph 10 of the *Guidelines* recalls that 'freedom of thought, conscience, religion or belief, applies equally to all persons. It is a fundamental freedom that includes all religions or beliefs, including those that have not been traditionally practised in a particular country, the beliefs of persons belonging to religious minorities, as well as non-theistic and atheistic beliefs.'

Moreover, these guidelines are in accord with long-standing commitments of the Organisation for Security and Cooperation in Europe (OSCE) as laid out in various documents by the Office for Democratic Institutions and Human Rights (ODIHR) of the OSCE, such as the *ODIHR Background Paper 1999/4*,[5] published for the OSCE Review Conference of September 1999, and the *Guidelines for Review of Legislation Pertaining to Religion or Belief*,[6] prepared by ODIHR and the Venice Commission, endorsed in June 2004 by the Venice Commission and welcomed in July 2004 by the OSCE Parliamentary Assembly.

So without being a legally binding document, these guidelines are 'soft law' that should be a great inspiration for future legally binding policies and laws that will come from EU institutions. They should likewise inspire Member States to develop their own internal policies and guidelines, as they contain almost all the important concepts and standards that should govern freedom of religion or belief anywhere in the world and which underpin the approach of the RELIGARE project and complement it. As suggested in the RELIGARE report, EU guidelines for national governments should be drafted to provide appropriate protection to individuals and communities claiming their freedom of religion and belief; such guidelines could

3 Council of the European Union, Council Conclusions on Freedom of Religion or Belief, 2973rd General Affairs Council Meeting, Brussels, 16 November 2009, 2, available at <www.consilium.europa.eu/uedocs/cmsUpload/111190.pdf> accessed 16 June 2014.

4 See <http://docstore.ohchr.org/SelfServices/FilesHandler.ashx?enc=6QkG1d%2fPPRiCAqhKb7yhsjYoiCfMKoIRv2FVaVzRkMjTnjRO%2bfud3cPVrcM9YR0iUh4IvOtM7YUcKE6R1aBpKmYAstxgdf4vXLMslHe1LcOio8z%2f9pGJsac2JNOOTO4jAaVkCo02vVbw65HVERDHhA%3d%3d> accessed 21 June 2014.

5 See <www.osce.org/odihr/16698#p4> accessed 16 June 2014.

6 See <www.osce.org/odihr/13993> accessed 16 June 2014.

draw their inspiration from the *EU Guidelines on the Promotion and Protection of Freedom of Religion or Belief* already adopted for external action.

Recent Decisions by the European Court of Human Rights

Recently, the European Court of Human Rights (ECtHR) issued some very important decisions regarding freedom of religion or belief on violations of Article 9 of the European Convention on Human Rights. One of them is the landmark decision of 10 June 2010 in favour of religious freedom in the case *Jehovah's Witnesses of Moscow v Russia*,[7] which has direct application to issues relating to religious minorities. In this decision, the ECtHR strongly reaffirmed rights, which flow from the Convention, that encompass the freedom of religion or belief in both its individual and collective form:

- the right to conduct one's life in a manner of one's own choosing following one's religious beliefs
- the right to freedom of association and of self-dedication to religious matters
- the right to engage in voluntary work or missionary activities and
- the right of parents to ensure education and teaching in conformity with their own religious convictions

The ECtHR delineated in that decision the State's duty of neutrality and impartiality and its implications:

> 119. The Court further reiterates that the State's duty of neutrality and impartiality prohibits it from assessing the legitimacy of religious beliefs or the ways in which those beliefs are expressed or manifested (see *Leyla Şahin*, cited above, § 107, and *Hasan and Chaush*, cited above, § 78). Accordingly, the State has a narrow margin of appreciation and must advance serious and compelling reasons for an interference with the choices that people may make in pursuance of the religious standard of behaviour within the sphere of their personal autonomy.

The ECtHR thereby reaffirmed the right to one's own choice in religious matters and the prohibition against States' assessing the legitimacy of beliefs. This is of an utmost importance for religious minorities and 'non-traditional religions', as they are usually the ones that are challenged on their religious beliefs and doctrines.

Regarding the sphere of family law, in Section 111 of the *Jehovah's Witnesses of Moscow v Russia* decision the ECtHR also noted that confrontational situations might arise when parents have different convictions, and that these situations should not be treated differently for a non-traditional religion than for a traditional one:

> It is true that friction often exists in marriages where the spouses belong to different religious denominations or one of the spouses is a non-believer. However, this situation is common to all mixed-belief marriages and Jehovah's Witnesses are no exception.

And in Section 125 the Court confirmed that in cases of conflict both parents have an equal right to raise their children in accordance with their beliefs:

> Both parents, even in a situation where they adhere to differing doctrines or beliefs, have the same right to raise their children in accordance with their religious or non-religious convictions and any disagreements between them in relation to the necessity and extent of the children's participation in religious practices and education are private disputes that are to be resolved according to the procedure established in domestic family law.

This decision clearly opposes policies of intolerance towards non-traditional and new religious movements such as those that exist in certain European countries. France, for example, has chosen to deal with religious minorities through a governmental agency called MIVILUDES,[8] which is in charge of fighting against what the

7 App no 302/02.

8 Mission Interministérielle de Vigilance et de Lutte contre les Dérives Sectaires (Interministerial Mission of Vigilance and Fight Against Sectarian Drifts).

agency calls 'sectarian abuses'. As regards family law and the rights of parents, MIVILUDES recommends an infringement of the rights of minority believers, contrary to the principles developed in *Jehovah's Witnesses of Moscow v Russia*.

In MIVILUDES Annual Report 2009, under the heading 'Assimilation only of the beliefs of the movement', it is explained that children brought up in a context of 'sectarian subjection' are ideologically isolated because they are subjected to a unique and exclusive discourse, for example by the daily repetition of a credo of allegiance to a superior entity or the substitution of a mythical discourse to rational explanations. According to this report, such education – which could apply to the raising of children in any religion – enslaves the child and diminishes his or her possibilities.[9] It concluded with this question:

> If such a [psychological] risk is established, is not the solution, as is often the case, to protect the young, especially the teenager, from a univocal vision of the world, to arrange for him, by giving the greatest possible prominence to the non-follower parent, views of other realities, even if, while in the exclusive sphere of his follower parent, he seems fulfilled and is working well at school and does not complain of anything?[10]

Since the above-quoted *Jehovah's Witnesses* decision, another decision from the ECtHR, *Vojnity v Hungary* of 12 February 2013, has tackled this very issue. In that judgment the Court concluded that there was no reasonable relationship of proportionality between the total denial of the applicant's right to access his child and the aim pursued, namely the protection of the best interests of the child. The ECtHR found that the applicant had been discriminated against on the basis of his religious convictions (as a member of a new Pentecostal evangelical movement) in the exercise of his right to respect for family life, as he had been denied his access rights on the basis of an expert opinion upheld by a domestic court according to which the applicant's 'irrational worldview made him incapable of bringing up his child'. The expert opinion furthermore asserted that he 'did not exercise his right of access in accordance with its purpose ... but to impose his religious convictions on the child'.

In another judgement issued on 30 June 2011, *Association Les Temoins de Jehovah v France*,[11] the ECtHR, after having analysed the impact of taxation on the association's main source of funding and on its ability to assure its members the free exercise of religion, and after criticising the lack of precision of the law on which the taxation was based, concluded there was indeed a violation of Article 9. In that decision, the Court determined that Jehovah's Witnesses had been subject to a series of special measures against so-called 'cults':

> 10. During the debate on the report of the commission on cults in the National Assembly, 8 February 1996 (Official Journal of 9 February 1996), the Minister of Budget expressed himself as follows:
>
> '... First, I thank the rapporteur for having, in his excellent report, paid tribute to the tax authorities whose action allowed, on several occasions, some suppression of the activity of cults. ... Beyond fiscal control, the consequences can be even more serious. Indeed, the control can lead to judicial settlement procedures or criminal actions against the leaders of the cult, actions that are likely to destabilise the functioning of the association, or to put it in the obligation to cease operations in our territory. Fiscal control may therefore be the first step in a process that profoundly disrupts the cult or leads to its dissolution ....'[12]

The Court reiterated that the free exercise of the Jehovah's Witnesses' right to freedom of religion is protected under Article 9 of the ECHR. It added that, according to the strict requirements of Article 9, paragraph 2, any denial of recognition of a religious association, dissolution, or use of derogatory terms against it are all examples of interference with this right, in its external and collective dimension, towards the community and its members. In this case, the Court found that the interference of the French authorities could not be justified.

---

9 See Report to Prime Minister 2009, 128–29 <www.derives-sectes.gouv.fr/sites/default/files/publications/francais/rapport2009_mise_en_ligne.pdf> accessed 21 June 2014 (translation by the author).

10 ibid 214 (translation by the author).

11 See <http://hudoc.echr.coe.int/sites/eng-press/pages/search.aspx?i=001-105386#{"itemid":["001-105386"]}> accessed 21 June 2014.

12 ibid (translation by the author).

This decision is particularly relevant to the topic of State support mechanisms, which the RELIGARE report asserts should be handled in accordance with 'inclusive State neutrality' and 'justice as even-handedness'. In fact, The ECtHR has consistently reaffirmed 'inclusive State neutrality' and 'justice as even-handedness', albeit not expressed in exactly those terms, as basic requirements in dealing with religious minorities at the national level.

The Sikhs versus France regarding Religious Dress

Three decisions particularly relevant to *the access to and use of public spaces*, one of the RELIGARE report's four key areas, are those rendered by the UN Human Rights Committee against France in cases involving the Sikh community and the difficulties they encounter in their practice due to French limitations to the exercise of freedom of religion regarding religious dress codes.

On 27 September 2011, the Committee issued a decision[13] about a Sikh having been denied the right to renew his residence permit because he provided two photographs showing him wearing a turban. The Sikh explained that wearing a turban was 'a religious obligation and an integral part of Sikhism, his religion'. The Committee said that France had failed to explain how the Sikh turban hindered identification since the wearer's face would be visible and he would be wearing the turban at all times, and that the regulation therefore constituted a violation of Article 18 of the ICCPR, which entered into force for France on 4 February 1981. As regards *religious dress codes*, the Committee declared:

> 8.3 The Committee refers to its general comment No. 22 concerning Article 18 of the Covenant and considers that the freedom to manifest a religion encompasses the wearing of distinctive clothing or head coverings.[14] The fact that the Sikh religion requires its members to wear a turban in public is not contested. The wearing of a turban is regarded as a religious duty and is also tied in with a person's identity.

A similar case was heard by the UN Human Rights Committee on 26 September 2013,[15] where the Committee concluded that France had violated the religious freedom of 57-year-old Shingara Mann Singh when he was asked to remove his turban for his passport photograph. Shingara Singh, a French national since 1989, was unable to renew his passport in 2005 because the French authorities insisted that he remove his turban for his ID photograph, which he refused to do. The Court found that this limitation was unnecessary and disproportionate:

> 9.5 Consequently, the Committee is of the view that the State party has not demonstrated that the limitation placed on the author is necessary within the meaning of Article 18, paragraph 3, of the Covenant. It also observes that, even if the obligation to remove the turban for the identity photograph might be described as a one-time requirement, it would potentially interfere with the author's freedom of religion on a continuing basis because he would always appear without his religious head covering in the identity photograph and could thus be compelled to remove his turban during identity checks. The Committee therefore concludes that the regulation requiring persons to appear bareheaded in their passport photographs is a disproportionate limitation that infringes the author's freedom of religion and constitutes a violation of Article 18 of the Covenant.

Between these two decisions, the UN Human Rights Committee issued another communication on 4 December 2012,[16] following facts related to Act No. 2004–228 of 15 March 2004, which, in conformity with the principle of secularism, covers the wearing of symbols and clothing manifesting a religious affiliation in public primary schools, secondary schools and *lycées*. This Act had led to the introduction of Article L.141–5-1 in the Education Code, which states, 'In public primary schools, secondary schools and *lycées*, the

13 See <www.ccprcentre.org/doc/OP1/Decisions/102/1876%202009%20France_en.pdf> accessed 21 June 2014.
14 See General Comment No 22, CCPR/C/21/Rev.1/Add.4 (1993) (n 4), para 4.
15 See <http://daccess-dds-ny.un.org/doc/UNDOC/GEN/G13/471/24/PDF/G1347124.pdf>.
16 See <http://unitedsikhs.org/rtt/doc/BikramjitSinghDecision.pdf> accessed 17 June 2014.

wearing of symbols or clothing by which pupils manifest their religious affiliation in a conspicuous manner is forbidden'. The author of the complaint, a French Sikh student, had alleged a violation of Article 18 on the grounds that he had been subject to discriminatory treatment on account of his religion and/or ethnic origin, after having been expelled from his school for wearing the *keski*.[17]

The Committee agreed that France was entitled to uphold the principle of secularism as 'a means by which a State Party may seek to protect the religious freedom of all its population' and recognised that the adoption of the 2004 Act had responded to actual incidents of interference with the religious freedom of pupils and sometimes even threats to their physical safety. However, it also ruled that the wearing of a turban is regarded as a religious duty for a Sikh and is tied in with his identity, and that France had not justified the prohibition on the wearing of the turban:

> 8.7 [T]he State party imposed this harmful sanction on the author, not because his personal conduct created any concrete risk, but solely because of his inclusion in a broad category of persons defined by their religious conduct. In this regard, the Committee notes the State party's assertion that the broad extension of the category of persons forbidden to comply with their religious duties simplifies the administration of the restrictive policy. However, in the Committee's view, the State party has not shown how the sacrifice of those persons' rights is either necessary or proportionate to the benefits achieved. For all these reasons the Committee concludes that the expulsion of the author from his *lycée* was not necessary under Article 18, paragraph 3, it infringed his right to manifest his religion and constitutes a violation of Article 18 of the Covenant.

This decision is clearly in line with the recommendation put forward in the RELIGARE report that 'authorities should limit the prohibition against students wearing symbols and clothing expressing their religious or philosophical convictions to situations where such restriction is strictly required to guarantee the carrying out of school activities and no reasonable accommodation of the religious needs of the student seems negotiable' (*Report*, 33).

It is to be noted that in these three decisions, the UN Human Rights Committee recalled:

> By becoming a party to the Optional Protocol, the State party has recognized the competence of the Committee to determine whether or not there has been a violation of the Covenant and that, pursuant to Article 2 of the Covenant, the State party has undertaken to ensure to all individuals within its territory or subject to its jurisdiction the rights recognized in the Covenant and to provide an effective and enforceable remedy when a violation has been established.[18]

No remedy has been proposed yet to the Sikh students who were deprived of the possibility to attend French public schools.

United Kingdom Supreme Court Landmark Decision on Scientology

On 11 December 2013, the United Kingdom Supreme Court issued a landmark decision[19] regarding the exercise of freedom of religion or belief that should have a resounding influence on the implementation of 'inclusive State neutrality' and 'justice as even-handedness' throughout Europe. In that case, Louisa Hodkin (the first appellant) and her fiancé, Alessandro Calcioli, wanted to be married in the chapel of the Church of Scientology of London, but the Registrar General of births, deaths and marriages refused to register the chapel to conduct marriages because it was not recognised as a place of 'religious worship'. This decision stemmed from a 1970 court case[20] which excluded chapels of the Church of Scientology because they did not fit within

---

17 The *keski* is a small light piece of material of a dark colour, often used as a mini-turban, covering the long uncut hair considered sacred in the Sikh religion.

18 Bikramjit Singh Decision (n 16) 16.

19 See <www.supremecourt.uk/decided-cases/docs/UKSC_2013_0030_Judgment.pdf> accessed 21 June 2014.

20 *R v Registrar General*, Ex p Segerdal [1970] 2 QB 697.

the terms of the 1855 Places of Worship Registration Act, which counts only groups that revere a 'deity' as true religions.

The Supreme Court considered several pieces of evidence, including the fact that Scientology scriptures refer to God, albeit not in a way that shows reverence for God as a specific being, and ruled that excluding Scientology chapels as places of worship would constitute unacceptable discrimination in today's society. It also ruled that the criteria of believing in a 'supreme deity' and revering God are not – in this day and age – relevant criteria:

> 52. Further, to confine religion to a religion which involves belief in a 'supreme deity' leads into difficult theological territory. On the evidence of Mrs Wilks, Scientologists do believe in a supreme deity of a kind, but of an abstract and impersonal nature. Ideas about the nature of God are the stuff of theological debate.

Beside these considerations, the Court also noted that refusing to register the Scientology chapel as a place of worship would lead to a double disability:

> 64. There is a further significant point. If, as I have held, Scientology comes within the meaning of a religion, but its chapel cannot be registered under PWRA because its services do not involve the kind of veneration which the Court of Appeal in Segerdal considered essential, the result would be to prevent Scientologists from being married anywhere in a form which involved use of their marriage service. They could have a service in their chapel, but it would not be a legal marriage, and they could have a civil marriage on other 'approved premises' under Section 26(1)(bb) of the Marriage Act, but they could not incorporate any form of religious service because of the prohibition in Section 46B(4). They would therefore be under a double disability, not shared by atheists, agnostics or most religious groups. This would be illogical, discriminatory and unjust.

This decision has paved the way for many European countries to take measures in order to ensure that all religious minorities, including non-traditional religions, are treated equally in regard to the actual diversity that is now the common ground throughout Europe. This decision is also a concrete application of the principles contained in point 2 of the OSCE's and Venice Commission's *Guidelines for Review of Legislation Pertaining to Religion or Belief*:[21]

> 2. The definition of 'religion'. Legislation often includes the understandable attempt to define 'religion' or related terms ('sects', 'cults', 'traditional religion', and so on). There is no generally accepted definition for such terms in international law, and many States have had difficulty defining these terms. It has been argued that such terms cannot be defined in a legal sense because of the inherent ambiguity of the concept of religion. A common definitional mistake is to require that a belief in God be necessary for something to be considered a religion. The most obvious counterexamples are classical Buddhism, which is not theistic, and Hinduism, which is polytheistic.

'Inclusive State Neutrality' and 'Justice as Even-Handedness' under General Comment 22 of the UN Human Rights Committee

To conclude, I think that the documents and decisions that I have mentioned above are all relevant to the focus of the RELIGARE project, as well as to the two principal concepts of its chosen normative framework, 'inclusive State neutrality' and 'justice as even-handedness'. These new developments in the field of freedom of religion or belief show that there is increasing willingness to deal with religious freedom in accordance with basic human rights standards. However, as developed in the RELIGARE report, this is not only a question of 'case law'. As the report has adopted a comparative and interdisciplinary approach, it has been able to recommend the implementation of many measures to enhance the awareness of governments as well as the media and civil society. These measures are perhaps the most important ones, as they come

21 See <www.osce.org/odihr/13993> accessed 21 June 2014.

before the case law, which is often negatively influenced by hostile political views on various religious or philosophical movements.

It is important to note that General Comment 22 on Article 18 of the ICCPR by the UN Human Rights Committee, issued on 30 July 1993, established the way to address these problems in accordance with a correct interpretation of Article 18 of the ICPPR, specifically with regard to religious or belief minorities:

> 2. Article 18 protects theistic, non-theistic and atheistic beliefs, as well as the right not to profess any religion or belief. The terms 'belief' and 'religion' are to be broadly construed. Article 18 is not limited in its application to traditional religions or to religions and beliefs with institutional characteristics or practices analogous to those of traditional religions. The Committee therefore views with concern any tendency to discriminate against any religion or belief for any reason, including the fact that they are newly established, or represent religious minorities that may be the subject of hostility on the part of a predominant religious community.

General Comment 22 pinpoints the most critical stumbling blocks that may arise in the European Union as a result of increasing social, cultural, religious and philosophical diversity. Any effort to implement these recommendations in the actual practice of the Member States will be rewarded by an increasing awareness and a better application of the human rights standards that govern our modern world, which are often not evenly applied from country to country, or from one religion to another, by courts, governmental authorities or the media.

Index